NATIONS IN
TRANSIT 2008

Nations in Transit 2008

Democratization from
Central Europe to Eurasia

Edited by Jeannette Goehring

Freedom House
New York ▪ Washington, D.C. ▪ Budapest

FREEDOM HOUSE
Published in the United States of America.

Freedom House, Inc.
120 Wall Street, New York, NY 10005 USA
1301 Connecticut Avenue, NW, Washington, D.C., 20036 USA
http://www.freedomhouse.org

Freedom House Europe Kht.
Falk Miksa u. 30, H–1055 Budapest, Hungary
http://www.freedomhouse.hu

Published 2008
Printed in the United States and Hungary
11 10 09 08 07   1 2 3 4 5

ISBN–10: 0 932088 63 5
ISBN–13: 978 0 932088 63 5 (paperback)

Freedom House gratefully acknowledges the U.S. Agency for International Development whose generous
support made the production of this volume possible.

Library of Congress Cataloging-in-Publication Data Available

Typography: Judit Kovács · Createch Ltd.

The paper used in this publication meets the minimum requirements of American National Standard for
Information Sciences—Permanence of Paper for Printed Library Materials, ANSI/NISO Z39.48-1992.

Contents

Acknowledgements

ations in Transit 2008 could not have been completed without the contributions of numerous Freedom House staff and consultants. This study was also made possible by the generous support of the U.S. Agency for International Development.

Freedom House is grateful to the country authors for their painstaking efforts to provide clear, concise, and informed analysis of the dramatic changes occurring in the countries under study. They are: Annette Bohr, Ditmir Bushati, Bhavna Dave, Ilir Deda, Petar Dorić, Rashko Dorosiev, Juris Dreifelds, Jeremy Druker, George Dura, Georgy Ganev, Christian Ghinea, Jasna Jelisić, Miroslav Kollár, Balázs Kovács, Andrzej Krajewski, Damjan Lajh, Lisa McLean, Erica Marat, Slobodan Markovich, Grigorij Mesežnikov, Vladimir Misev, Bálint Molnár, Raissa Muhutdinova, Alina Mungiu-Pippidi, H. Kann Nazli, Ghia Nodia, Robert Orttung, Bruce Pannier, Aneta Piasecka, Olena Prystayko, Sabrina P. Ramet, Vitali Silitski, Oleksandr Sushko, Michal Vašečka, Liliana Vitu, and Anna Walker.

A number of distinguished scholars and regional experts served on this year's academic oversight committees and ratings board. They are: Audrey Altstadt of the University of Massachusetts, Amherst (United States), Zamira Eshanova of Radio Free Europe/Radio Liberty, Prague (Czech Republic), Kristie D. Evenson of the University of Bristol, Split (Croatia), Charles Gati of Johns Hopkins University, Washington, D.C. (United States), Rajan Menon of Lehigh University (United States), Sergiu Mişcoiu of Babes Bolyai University, Cluj-Napoca (Romania), Alexander Motyl of Rutgers University, Newark (United States), and Susan Woodward of the Graduate Center, City University of New York (United States).

Freedom House also thanks: Anton Bebler of the University of Ljubljana (Slovenia), Zhidas Daskalovski of the Center for Research and Policy Making, Skopje (Macedonia), Krzysztof Filcek of the Poland-America-Ukraine Cooperation Initiative Warsaw, (Poland), Paul A. Goble of Windows on Eurasia, Vienna, Virginia (United States), Juhani Grossman of Management Systems International, Kyiv (Ukraine), Flóra Hevesi of Magyar Televízió Budapest (Hungary), Valts

Kalniņš of the Centre for Public Policy Providus, Riga (Latvia), Charles Kovacs of Híd Radio, Budapest (Hungary), Alexander Kurylev of the European University at St. Petersburg, Nottingham (United Kingdom), Tomila Lankina of De Montfort University, Leicester (United Kingdom), Tamás Meszerics of Central European University, Budapest (Hungary), Elena Parfenova of STASIA s.r.o., Prague (Czech Republic), Vello Pettai of the University of Tartu (Estonia), Egdūnas Račius of the Institute of International Relations and Political Science, Vilnius (Lithuania), Jiří Pehe of New York University, Prague (Czech Republic), Sanja Pesek of Central European University, Budapest (Hungary), Jan Pieklo of the Poland-America-Ukraine Cooperation Initiative Warsaw, (Poland), Ivan Presniakov of the International Centre for Policy Studies, Kyiv (Ukraine), Sabrina P. Ramet of the Norwegian University of Science and Technology, Trondheim (Norway), Bashkim Rrahmani of the Foundation for Democratic Initiatives, Gjakova (Kosovo), Yervand Shirinyan of the Open Society Institute, Budapest (Hungary), David J. Smith of the University of Glasgow, (United Kingdom), Kathryn Stoner-Weiss of Stanford University, Stanford, California (United States), Lenka Surotchak of Pontis Foundation, Bratislava (Slovakia), Andraž Teršek of the University of Ljubljana (Slovenia), Eno Trimçev of the London School of Economics (United Kingdom), and Aziz Umarov of the American Bar Association/Rule of Law Initiative, Arlington, Virginia (United States) for their comments on specific reports.

Several members of the Freedom House staff took time out of their schedules to read and provide valuable feedback on the country reports. They are: Lazar Nikolić of the Belgrade office; Roland Kováts of the Europe office; Stuart Kahn of the Bishkek office; Matthew Briggs, Jeffrey Goldstein, Damian Murphy, and Bakhtiyor Nishanov of the Washington, D.C. office.

Freedom House staff devoted extensive time and energy to develop this project. Jeannette Goehring was the project manager and editor-in-chief of the study. Christopher Walker, director of studies, Roland Kováts, director of the Europe office, Thomas O. Melia, deputy executive director, and Jennifer Windsor, executive director of Freedom House provided overall guidance and support for the project. Editorial assistant Lisa Mootz provided important editorial, research, and administrative support, as did Orsolya Richter, Katrina Neubauer, Lauren Abel, and Sarah Cook.

Judit Kovács of Createch Ltd. was responsible for the design and layout of the book. Sona Vogel served as copy editor; John Ewing as line editor; and Victoria Hill as proofreader. Freedom House extends gratitude to everyone who assisted with *Nations in Transit 2008.*

Methodology

Nations in Transit 2008 measures progress and setbacks in democratization in 29 countries and administrative areas from Central Europe to the Eurasian region of the Former Soviet Union. This volume, which covers events from January 1 through December 31, 2007, is an updated edition of surveys published in 2007, 2006, 2005, 2004, 2003, 2002, 2001, 2000, 1998, 1997, and 1995.

Country Reports

The country reports in *Nations in Transit 2008* follow an essay format that allowed the report authors to provide a broad analysis of the progress of democratic change in their country of expertise. Freedom House provided them with guidelines for ratings and a checklist of questions covering seven categories: electoral process; civil society; independent media; national democratic governance; local democratic governance; judicial framework and independence; and corruption. Starting with the 2005 edition Freedom House introduced separate analysis and ratings for national democratic governance and local democratic governance to provide readers with more detailed and nuanced analysis of these two important subjects. Previous editions included only one governance category. The ratings for all categories reflect the consensus of Freedom House, the *Nations in Transit* advisers, and the report authors.

Each country report is organized according to the following outline:

- **National Democratic Governance.** Considers the democratic character and stability of the governmental system; the independence, effectiveness, and accountability of legislative and executive branches; and the democratic oversight of military and security services.

- **Electoral Process.** Examines national executive and legislative elections, electoral processes, the development of multiparty systems, and popular participation in the political process.

▮ **Civil Society.** Assesses the growth of nongovernmental organizations (NGOs), their organizational capacity and financial sustainability, and the legal and political environment in which they function; the development of free trade unions; and interest group participation in the policy process.

▮ **Independent Media.** Addresses the current state of press freedom, including libel laws, harassment of journalists, editorial independence, the emergence of a financially viable private press, and Internet access for private citizens.

▮ **Local Democratic Governance.** Considers the decentralization of power; the responsibilities, election, and capacity of local governmental bodies; and the transparency and accountability of local authorities.

▮ **Judicial Framework and Independence.** Highlights constitutional reform, human rights protections, criminal code reform, judicial independence, the status of ethnic minority rights, guarantees of equality before the law, treatment of suspects and prisoners, and compliance with judicial decisions.

▮ **Corruption.** Looks at public perceptions of corruption, the business interests of top policy makers, laws on financial disclosure and conflict of interest, and the efficacy of anticorruption initiatives.

Ratings and Scores

For all 29 countries and administrative areas in *Nations in Transit 2008*, Freedom House, in consultation with the report authors and a panel of academic advisers, has provided numerical ratings in the seven categories listed above. The ratings are based on a scale of 1 to 7, with 1 representing the highest and 7 the lowest level of democratic progress.

The ratings follow a quarter-point scale. Minor to moderate developments typically warrant a positive or negative change of a quarter (0.25) to a half (0.50) point. Significant developments typically warrant a positive or negative change of three-quarters (0.75) to a full (1.00) point. It is rare that the rating in any category will fluctuate by more than a full point (1.00) in a single year.

As with *Freedom in the World,* Freedom House's global annual survey of political rights and civil liberties, *Nations in Transit* does not rate governments per se. Nor does it rate countries based on governmental intentions or legislation alone. Rather, a country's ratings are determined by considering the practical effect of the state and nongovernmental actors on an individual's rights and freedoms.

The *Nations in Transit* ratings, which should not be taken as absolute indicators of the situation in a given country, are valuable for making general assessments of how democratic or authoritarian a country is. They also allow for comparative analysis of reforms among the countries surveyed and for analysis of long-term developments in a particular country.

The ratings process for *Nations in Transit 2008* involved four steps:

1. Authors of individual country reports suggested preliminary ratings in all seven categories covered by the study.

2. The U.S. and Central Europe & Eurasia academic advisers evaluated the ratings and made revisions.

3. Report authors were given the opportunity to dispute any revised rating that differed from the original by more than 0.50 point.

4. Freedom House refereed any disputed ratings and, if the evidence warranted, considered further adjustments. Final editorial authority for the ratings rested with Freedom House.

Nations in Transit 2008 Checklist of Questions

National Democratic Governance

1. Is the country's governmental system democratic?

    ♦ Does the Constitution or other national legislation enshrine the principles of democratic government?

    ♦ Is the government open to meaningful citizen participation in political processes and decision-making in practice?

    ♦ Is there an effective system of checks and balances among legislative, executive, and judicial authority?

    ♦ Does a freedom of information act or similar legislation ensure access to government information by citizens and the media?

    ♦ Is the economy free of government domination?

2. Is the country's governmental system stable?

    ♦ Is there consensus among political groups and citizens on democracy as the basis of the country's political system?

    ♦ Is stability of the governmental system achieved without coercion, violence, or other abuses of basic rights and civil liberties by state or non-state actors?

    ♦ Do citizens recognize the legitimacy of national authorities and the laws and policies that govern them?

    ♦ Does the government's authority extend over the full territory of the country?

    ♦ Is the governmental system free of threats to stability such as war, insurgencies, and domination by the military, foreign powers, or other powerful groups?

3. Is the legislature independent, effective, and accountable to the public?
   - Does the legislature have autonomy from the executive branch?
   - Does the legislature have the resources and capacity it needs to fulfill its law-making and investigative responsibilities? (consider financial resources, professional staffs, democratic management structures, etc)
   - Do citizens and the media have regular access to legislators and the legislative process through public hearings, town meetings, published congressional records, etc?
   - Do legislative bodies operate under effective audit and investigative rules that are free of political influence?
   - Does the legislature provide leadership and reflect societal preferences by providing a forum for the peaceful and democratic resolution of differences?

4. Is the executive branch independent, effective, and accountable to the public?
   - Is the executive branch's role in policy making clearly defined vis-à-vis other branches of government?
   - Does the executive branch have the resources and capacity it needs to formulate and implement policies?
   - Do citizens and the media have regular access to the executive branch to comment on the formulation and implementation of policies?
   - Does a competent and professional civil service function according to democratic standards and practices?
   - Do executive bodies operate under effective audit and investigative rules that are free of political influence?
   - Does the executive branch provide leadership and reflect societal preferences in resolving conflicts and supporting democratic development?

5. Are the military and security services subject to democratic oversight?
   - Does the Constitution or other legislation provide for democratic oversight and civilian authority over the military and security services?
   - Is there sufficient judicial oversight of the military and security services to prevent impunity?
   - Does the legislature have transparent oversight of military and security budgets and spending?
   - Do legislators, the media, and civil society groups have sufficient information on military and security matters to provide oversight of the military and security services?
   - Does the government provide the public with accurate and timely information about the military, the security services, and their roles?

Electoral Process

1. Is the authority of government based upon universal and equal suffrage and the will of the people as expressed by regular, free, and fair elections conducted by secret ballot?

2. Are there fair electoral laws, equal campaigning opportunities, fair polling, and honest tabulation of ballots?

3. Is the electoral system free of significant barriers to political organization and registration?

4. Is the electoral system multiparty based, with viable political parties, including an opposition party, functioning at all levels of government?

5. Is the public engaged in the political life of the country, as evidenced by membership in political parties, voter turnout for elections, or other factors?

6. Do ethnic and other minority groups have sufficient openings to participate in the political process?

7. Is there opportunity for the effective rotation of power among a range of different political parties representing competing interests and policy options?

8. Are the people's choices free from domination by the specific interests of power groups (the military, foreign powers, totalitarian parties, regional hierarchies, and/or economic oligarchies)?

9. Were the most recent national legislative elections judged free and fair by domestic and international election-monitoring organizations?

10. Were the most recent presidential elections judged free and fair by domestic and international election-monitoring organizations?

Civil Society

1. Does the state protect the rights of the independent civic sector?

2. Is the civil society vibrant? (Consider growth in the number of charitable, nonprofit, and nongovernmental organizations; improvements in the quality of performance of civil society groups; locally led efforts to increase philanthropy and volunteerism; the public's active participation in private voluntary activity; the presence of effective civic and cultural organizations for women and ethnic groups; the participation of religious groups in charitable activity; or other factors.)

3. Is society free of excessive influence from extremist and intolerant nongovernmental institutions and organizations? (Consider racists, groups advocating violence or terrorism, xenophobes, private militias and vigilante groups, or other groups whose actions threaten political and social stability and the transition to democracy.)

4. Is the legal and regulatory environment for civil society groups free of excessive state pressures and bureaucracy? (Consider ease of registration, legal rights, government regulation, fund-raising, taxation, procurement, and access-to-information issues.)

5. Do civil society groups have sufficient organizational capacity to sustain their work? (Consider management structures with clearly delineated authority and responsibility; a core of experienced practitioners, trainers, and the like; access to information on NGO management issues in the native language; and so forth.)

6. Are civil society groups financially viable, with adequate conditions and opportunities for raising funds that sustain their work? (Consider sufficient organizational capacity to raise funds; option of nonprofit tax status; freedom to raise funds from domestic or foreign sources; legal or tax environment that encourages private sector support; ability to compete for government procurement opportunities; ability to earn income or collect cost recovery fees.)

7. Is the government receptive to policy advocacy by interest groups, public policy research groups, and other nonprofit organizations? Do government officials engage civil society groups by inviting them to testify, comment on, and influence pending policies or legislation?

8. Are the media receptive to civil society groups as independent and reliable sources of information and commentary? Are they positive contributors to the country's civic life?

9. Does the state respect the right to form and join free trade unions?

10. Is the education system free of political influence and propaganda?

Independent Media

1. Are there legal protections for press freedom?

2. Are journalists, especially investigative reporters, protected from victimization by powerful state or nonstate actors?

3. Does the state oppose onerous libel laws and other excessive legal penalties for "irresponsible" journalism?

4. Are the media's editorial independence and news-gathering functions free of interference from the government or private owners?

5. Does the public enjoy a diverse selection of print and electronic sources of information, at both the national and local level, that represent a range of political viewpoints?

6. Are the majority of print and electronic media privately owned and free of excessive ownership concentration?

7. Is the private media's financial viability subject only to market forces (that is, is it free of political or other influences)?

8. Is the distribution of newspapers privately controlled?

9. Are journalists and media outlets able to form their own viable professional associations?

10. Does society enjoy free access to and use of-; is there diversity of opinions available on-; and does government attempt to control the Internet?

Local Democratic Governance

1. Are the principles of local democratic government enshrined in law and respected in practice?

    ♦ Does the Constitution or other national legislation provide a framework for democratic local self-government?

    ♦ Have substantial government powers and responsibilities been decentralized in practice?

    ♦ Are local authorities free to design and adopt institutions and processes of governance that reflect local needs and conditions?

    ♦ Do central authorities consult local governments in planning and decision-making processes that directly affect the local level?

2. Are citizens able to choose their local leaders in free and fair elections?

    ♦ Does the Constitution or other national legislation provide for local elections held on the basis of universal, equal, and direct suffrage by secret ballot?

    ♦ Do local governments derive their power on the basis of regular, free, and fair local elections (either through direct election or through election by local assemblies or councils)?

    ♦ Are free and fair local elections held at regular intervals and subject to independent monitoring and oversight?

    ♦ Do multiple candidates representing a range of views participate in local elections and in local government bodies?

    ♦ Are voters' choices in local elections free from domination by power groups such as national political parties, central authorities, economic oligarchies, and the like?

    ♦ Are citizens engaged in local electoral processes, as evidenced by party membership, voter turnout, or other factors?

3. Are citizens ensured meaningful participation in local government decision making?

    ♦ Do local governments invite input from civil society, business, trade unions, and other groups on important policy issues before decisions are made and implemented?

♦ Do local governments initiate committees, focus groups, or other partnerships with civil society to address common concerns and needs?

♦ Are individuals and civil society groups free to submit petitions, organize demonstrations, or initiate other activities that influence local decision making?

♦ Do women, ethnic groups, and other minorities participate in local government?

♦ Do the media regularly report the views of local civic groups, the private business sector, and other nongovernmental entities about local government policy and performance?

4. Do democratically elected local authorities exercise their powers freely and autonomously?

♦ Do central authorities respect local decision-making authority and independence?

♦ Are local governments free to pass and enforce laws needed to fulfill their responsibilities?

♦ Do local authorities have the right to judicial remedy to protect their powers?

♦ Do local governments have the right to form associations at domestic and international levels for protecting and promoting their interests?

5. Do democratically elected local authorities have the resources and capacity needed to fulfill their responsibilities?

♦ Are local governments free to collect taxes, fees, and other revenues commensurate with their responsibilities?

♦ Do local governments automatically and regularly receive resources that are due from central authorities?

♦ Do local governments set budgets and allocate resources free of excessive political influences and central controls?

♦ Are local authorities empowered to set staff salaries, staff size, and staffing patterns, and is recruitment based on merit and experience?

♦ Do local governments have the resources (material, financial, and human) to provide quality services, ensure a safe local environment, and implement sound policies in practice?

6. Do democratically elected local authorities operate with transparency and accountability to citizens?

♦ Are local authorities subject to clear and consistent standards of disclosure, oversight, and accountability?

◆ Are local authorities free from domination by power groups (economic oligarchies, organized crime, and so forth) that prevent them from representing the views and needs of the citizens who elected them?

◆ Are public meetings mandated by law and held at regular intervals?

◆ Do citizens and the media have regular access to public records and information?

◆ Are media free to investigate and report on local politics and government without fear of victimization?

Judicial Framework and Independence

1. Does the constitutional or other national legislation provide protections for fundamental political, civil, and human rights? (Includes freedom of expression, freedom of conscience and religion, freedom of association, and business and property rights.)

2. Do the state and nongovernmental actors respect fundamental political, civil, and human rights in practice?

3. Is there independence and impartiality in the interpretation and enforcement of the constitution?

4. Is there equality before the law?

5. Has there been effective reform of the criminal code/criminal law? (Consider presumption of innocence until proven guilty, access to a fair and public hearing, introduction of jury trials, access to independent counsel/public defender, independence of prosecutors, and so forth.)

6. Are suspects and prisoners protected in practice against arbitrary arrest, detention without trial, searches without warrants, torture and abuse, and excessive delays in the criminal justice system?

7. Are judges appointed in a fair and unbiased manner, and do they have adequate legal training before assuming the bench?

8. Do judges rule fairly and impartially, and are courts free of political control and influence?

9. Do legislative, executive, and other governmental authorities comply with judicial decisions, and are judicial decisions effectively enforced?

Corruption

1. Has the government implemented effective anticorruption initiatives?

2. Is the country's economy free of excessive state involvement?

3. Is the government free from excessive bureaucratic regulations, registration requirements, and other controls that increase opportunities for corruption?

4. Are there significant limitations on the participation of government officials in economic life?

5. Are there adequate laws requiring financial disclosure and disallowing conflict of interest?

6. Does the government advertise jobs and contracts?

7. Does the state enforce an effective legislative or administrative process—particularly one that is free of prejudice against one's political opponents—to prevent, investigate, and prosecute the corruption of government officials and civil servants?

8. Do whistle-blowers, anticorruption activists, investigators, and journalists enjoy legal protections that make them feel secure about reporting cases of bribery and corruption?

9. Are allegations of corruption given wide and extensive airing in the media?

10. Does the public display a high intolerance for official corruption?

Democracy Score

Freedom House introduced a Democracy Score—a straight average of the ratings for all categories covered by *Nations in Transit*—beginning with the 2004 edition. Freedom House provided this aggregate for comparative and interpretive purposes of evaluating progress and setbacks in the countries under study.

> *Background Note:* In years before the 2004 edition, Freedom House used two aggregate scores to assist in the analysis of reform in the 27 countries covered by the *Nations in Transit* study. These were *Democratization* (average of electoral process, civil society, independent media, and governance) and *Rule of Law* (average of corruption and constitutional, legislative, and judicial framework). Analysis showed a high level of correlation between the previous scoring categories and the Democracy Score.

For *Nations in Transit 2008*, Freedom House once again uses the Democracy Score. Based on the Democracy Score and its scale of 1 to 7, Freedom House defined the following regime types:

Democracy Score	Regime Type
1–2	Consolidated Democracy
3	Semiconsolidated Democracy
4	Transitional Government or Hybrid Regime
5	Semiconsolidated Authoritarian Regime
6–7	Consolidated Authoritarian Regime

Ratings and Democracy Score Guidelines

Beginning with the 2006 edition, the following guidelines were used to assist Freedom House staff and consultants in determining the ratings for electoral process; civil society; independent media; governance; constitutional, legislative, and judicial framework; and corruption. Based on the aggregate Democracy Scores, the descriptions are intended to explain generally the conditions of democratic institutions in the different regime classifications.

1.00–2.99 Consolidated Democracies

1.00–1.99 Countries receiving a Democracy Score of 1.00–1.99 closely embody the best policies and practices of liberal democracy.

∎ The authority of government is based on universal and equal suffrage as expressed in regular, free, and fair elections conducted by secret ballot. Elections are competitive, and power rotates among a range of different political parties.

∎ Civil society is independent, vibrant, and sustainable. Rights of assembly and association are protected and free of excessive state pressures and bureaucracy.

∎ Media are independent, diverse, and sustainable. Freedom of expression is protected, and journalists are free from excessive interference by powerful political and economic interests.

∎ National and local governmental systems are stable, democratic, and accountable to the public. Central branches of government are independent, and an effective system of checks and balances exists. Local authorities exercise their powers freely and autonomously of the central government.

∎ The judiciary is independent, impartial, timely, and able to defend fundamental political, civil, and human rights. There is equality before the law, and judicial decisions are enforced.

∎ Government, the economy, and society are free of excessive corruption. Legislative framework, including strong conflict-of-interest protection, is in place so that journalists and other citizens feel secure to investigate, provide media coverage of, and prosecute allegations of corruption.

2.00–2.99 Countries receiving a Democracy Score of 2.00–2.99 closely embody the best policies and practices of liberal democracy. However, challenges largely associated with corruption contribute to a slightly lower score.

∎ The authority of government is based on universal and equal suffrage as expressed in regular, free, and fair elections conducted by secret ballot. Elections are competitive, and power rotates among a range of different political parties.

- Civil society is independent, vibrant, and sustainable. Rights of assembly and association are protected and free of excessive state pressures and bureaucracy.

- Media are independent, diverse, and sustainable. Freedom of expression is protected, and journalists are free from excessive interference by powerful political or economic interests.

- National and local governmental systems are stable, democratic, and accountable to the public. Central branches of government are independent, and an effective system of checks and balances exists. Local authorities exercise their powers freely and autonomously of the central government.

- The judiciary is independent, impartial, and able to defend fundamental political, civil, and human rights. There is equality before the law, and judicial decisions are enforced, though timeliness remains an area of concern.

- While government, the economy, and society are increasingly free of corruption, implementation of effective anticorruption programs may be slow and revelations of high-level corruption may be frequent.

3.00–3.99 Semi-Consolidated Democracies

Countries receiving a Democracy Score of 3.00–3.99 are electoral democracies that meet relatively high standards for the selection of national leaders but exhibit some weaknesses in their defense of political rights and civil liberties.

- The authority of government is based on universal and equal suffrage as expressed in regular elections conducted by secret ballot. While elections are typically free, fair, and competitive, irregularities may occur. Power rotates among a range of different political parties.

- Civil society is independent and active. Rights of assembly and association are protected. However, the organizational capacity of groups remains limited and dependence on foreign funding is a barrier to long-term sustainability. Groups may be susceptible to some political or economic pressure.

- Media are generally independent and diverse, and freedom of expression is largely protected in legislative framework and in practice. However, special interests—both political and economic—do exert influence on reporting and editorial independence and may lead to self-censorship. While print media are largely free of government influence and control, electronic media are not.

- National and local systems of government are stable and democratic. While laws and structures are in place to promote government transparency and accountability, implementation is lacking. The system of checks and balances may be weak, and decentralization of powers and resources to local self-governments incomplete.

▪ The framework for an independent judiciary is in place. However, judicial independence and the protection of basic rights, especially those of ethnic and religious minorities, are weak. Judicial processes are slow, inconsistent, and open to abuse.

▪ Corruption is widespread and state capacities to investigate and prosecute corruption are weak. Efforts to combat the problem produce limited results.

4.00–4.99 Transitional or Hybrid Regimes

Countries receiving a Democracy Score of 4.00–4.99 are typically electoral democracies that meet only minimum standards for the selection of national leaders. Democratic institutions are fragile and substantial challenges to the protection of political rights and civil liberties exist. The potential for sustainable, liberal democracy is unclear.

▪ National elections are regular and competitive, but substantial irregularities may prevent them from being free and fair. Government pressure on opposition parties and candidates may be common.

▪ Civil society is independent and growing, and rights of assembly and association are generally protected. However, philanthropy and volunteerism are weak, and dependence on foreign funding is a barrier to long-term sustainability. Democratically oriented NGOs are the most visible and active groups, especially during election seasons, and may be subject to government pressure.

▪ Media are generally independent and diverse. Legislative framework to protect media may be in place but is not matched by practice. Special interests—both political and economic—exert influence on reporting and editorial independence, and may lead to self-censorship. Harassment of and pressure on journalists may occur.

▪ National and local systems of government are weak and lacking in transparency. While the balance of power is fragile, a vocal yet fractionalized opposition may be present in parliament. Governance may remain highly centralized. Local self-government is not fully in place, with some local or regional authorities owing allegiance to the central authorities who appointed them.

▪ The judiciary struggles to maintain its independence from the government. Respect for basic political, civil, and human rights is selective, and equality before the law is not guaranteed. In addition to the judiciary being slow, abuses occur. Use of torture in prisons may be a problem.

∎ Corruption is widespread and presents a major impediment to political and economic development. Anticorruption efforts are inconsistent.

5.00–5.99 Semi-Consolidated Authoritarian Regimes

Countries receiving a Democracy Score of 5.00–5.99 attempt to mask authoritarianism with limited respect for the institutions and practices of democracy. They typically fail to meet even the minimum standards of electoral democracy.

∎ While national elections may be held at regular intervals and contested by opposition parties and candidates, they are marred by irregularities and deemed undemocratic by international observers. Public resources and state employees are used to guarantee incumbent victories. Political power may change hands, yet turnovers in the executive are well orchestrated and may fail to reflect voter preferences.

∎ Power is highly centralized, and national and local levels of government are neither democratic nor accountable to citizens. Meaningful checks on executive power do not exist, and stability is achieved by undemocratic means.

∎ Space for independent civil society is narrow. While governments encourage nongovernmental organizations that perform important social functions, they are hostile to groups that challenge state policy. Institutional weaknesses and insufficient funding, save international support, also contribute to the limited impact of politically oriented groups.

∎ While independent media exist, they operate under government pressure and risk harassment for reporting that is critical of the regime. Investigative reporting on corruption and organized crime is especially risky. Harsh libel laws sustain a culture of self-censorship. Most media, particularly radio and television, are controlled or co-opted by the state.

∎ The judiciary is restrained in its ability to act independently of the executive, and equality before the law is not guaranteed. The judiciary is frequently co-opted as a tool to silence opposition figures and has limited ability to protect the basic rights and liberties of citizens.

∎ State involvement in the economic sector is sizable and corruption is widespread. Efforts to combat corruption are usually politically motivated.

6.00–7.00 Consolidated Authoritarian Regimes

Countries receiving a Democracy Score of 6.00–7.00 are closed societies in which dictators prevent political competition and pluralism and are responsible for widespread violations of basic political, civil, and human rights.

▮ Elections serve to reinforce the rule of dictators who enjoy unlimited authority for prolonged periods of time. Pro-governmental parties and candidates dominate elections, while an independent opposition is typically barred from seeking office. Rotations of executive power are unlikely absent death or revolution.

▮ Power is highly centralized, and the country's national and local governmental systems are neither democratic nor accountable to the public.

▮ Civil society faces excessive government restrictions and repression. A formal state ideology, or cult of personality, may dominate society and serve to justify the regime.

▮ Freedom of expression is stifled, and independent media are virtually nonexistent. Media are typically state-owned or controlled by individuals connected to the regime. Censorship is pervasive, and repression for independent reporting or criticism of the government is severe.

▮ The rule of law is subordinate to the regime, and violations of basic political, civil, and human rights are widespread. Courts are used to harass members of the opposition.

▮ Corruption and state involvement in the economy are excessive. Allegations of corruption are usually intended to silence political opponents of the regime.

Research Team and Data Sources

Freedom House developed the initial survey and subsequent editions after consultations with the U.S. Agency for International Development. Freedom House staff members and consultants researched and wrote the country reports. Consultants are regional or country specialists recommended by recognized authorities. The research team used a wide variety of sources in writing the reports, including information from nongovernmental organizations, multilateral lending institutions and other international organizations, local newspapers and magazines, and select government data.

The economic and social data contained in the country header pages of the 2008 edition were taken from the following sources:

▊ **GNI/capita**
World Development Indicators 2008 (Washington, D.C.: World Bank, 2008)

▊ **Population**
Transition Report 2007: People in Transition (London, U.K.: European Bank for Reconstruction and Development, 2007)

Exceptions

▊ *Kosovo/UNMIK-Administered*
GDP/capita & Population: *UNMIK Factsheet 2007* (UNMIK, 2007).

▊ *Turkmenistan*
GDP/capita & Population: *Transition Report 2006: Finance in Transition* (London, UK: European Bank for Reconstruction and Development, 2006).

Nations in Transit 2008:
Petro-Authoritarianism and Eurasia's New Divides

Christopher Walker and Jeannette Goehring

Nearly two decades after the fall of the Berlin Wall, the vision of a wider Europe, "whole and free," remains unrealized. A massive swath of Eurasia is still unfree, its peoples denied the democratic aspirations that are the foundations of the European community of states. Within the expanse of what was the Soviet Union, its satellite states, and the countries of the former Yugoslavia—the regions analyzed in *Nations in Transit*—there is a distinct and growing divergence in democratic performance. This is among the principal findings of *Nations in Transit 2008*, Freedom House's annual study of democratic development from Central Europe to Eurasia.

A second central point is that energy needs are increasingly distorting relationships between democracies that consume hydrocarbons and the authoritarian states that produce them. Euro-Atlantic democracies have yet to agree on a common strategy that advances both energy-security needs and basic democratic values. Energy dependence is promoting an uncoordinated and short-term approach to relations with authoritarian governments, the hardening core of which is located in the non-Baltic former Soviet Union. These democratically unaccountable countries are moving farther from the Euro-Atlantic neighborhood and creating alliances and networks outside of the Western community. As energy wealth has emboldened authoritarian rulers, the Euro-Atlantic democracies have seemingly lost their resolve and sense of common purpose in advancing democratic practices.

A third major finding is that the new democracies of Central Europe are making progress in entrenching democratic change, but still face serious domestic challenges and an uncertain geopolitical situation that could hinder the further consolidation of political reforms.

Today's map of Europe, while dramatically different than that of the Cold War era, suggests a period in which obstacles to the development of democratic standards and institutions in many countries have increased, at the same time that interstate tensions have worsened as authoritarian regimes seek to suppress local pressures for change and fend off external ones. The growing geopolitical division is explained in part by the emergence of a distinct set of authoritarian states, boosted in several key cases by extraordinary energy riches, which are playing an influential role in subverting democratic governance.

> Energy needs are increasingly distorting relationships between democracies that consume hydrocarbons and the authoritarian states that produce them. Euro-Atlantic democracies have yet to agree on a common strategy that advances both energy-security needs and basic democratic values.

The post-Soviet authoritarian bloc represents part of a larger, global phenomenon of oil-fueled authoritarian influence. Propelled by a surge of hydrocarbon wealth, Russia in particular has become the leading antidemocratic force in its region. Russia's leaders promote what they call "sovereign democracy" as an alternative model for political development, which has been adopted in spirit and practice by other authoritarian regimes.

Striking Decline in Petro-States: Azerbaijan, Kazakhstan, and Russia

The durability of the sovereign democracy model is uncertain, but one thing is clear: as the price of oil has risen over the past 10 years, *Nations in Transit* findings have registered a concurrent and striking decline in the openness and independence of institutions that could be paving the way for more transparent and accountable governance. The extent of this correlation is evident in three key post-Soviet states that have enjoyed economic growth on the basis of oil and gas exports—Azerbaijan, Kazakhstan, and Russia. Remarkably, from 1999 to 2008 these three countries moved backward on every *NIT* indicator, the only exception being Russia's still very low score on corruption, which is slightly better in 2008 than a decade earlier. The marked regression in Azerbaijan, Kazakhstan, and Russia has occurred systematically and across different sectors, affecting the spheres of electoral process, civil society, independent media, and judicial independence.

The data do not suggest that abundant energy resources transformed these countries into authoritarian polities. Instead, where transparency and accountability were already weak, the new wealth has functioned as an "authoritarian propellant," allowing dominant elites to further muzzle independent voices and assert control over crucial institutions. At the same time, the abundance of the hydrocarbon resources has masked negative practices, like pervasive rent-seeking behavior and widespread corruption, which are preventing meaningful institutional reform in these systems.

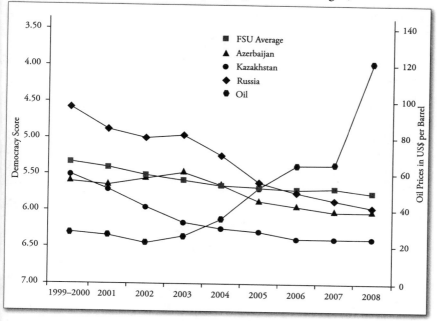

Figure 1.
Average Democracy Score in the Former Soviet Union (FSU)
Compared to Price of Oil
(7 the weakest democratic progress, 1 the strongest)

Challenges in the New Democracies

The picture in the wider *Nations in Transit* region is not entirely grim. Central and Southeastern Europe, along with the Baltic countries, are pressing forward with their reform agendas. The new democracies of Central Europe have secured fundamental political changes, and through European Union (EU) and NATO membership, they are achieving their ambition to join the European community of democratic states. However, these countries continue to navigate the complex and sometimes messy realities of establishing democratic systems. The temptation of political elites in a number of the new EU member states to pursue narrow, private interests rather than the broader public good remains a serious problem in settings where many ordinary citizens feel alienated from those who govern. Equally worrying is the emergence of "political reform fatigue." Several governments in Central Europe, for instance, have made only half-hearted attempts to tackle entrenched corruption and have at times appeared to be acting at cross-purposes with anticorruption bodies. News media in the new democracies have also come under greater pressure from governmental and other powerful elites. Public cynicism and frustration has fed populist impulses in these societies and a growing distrust of state officials and institutions.

The Balkans

The diverse countries of the Balkans have incrementally advanced democratic reforms in recent years. Especially noteworthy is the resilience of civil society, which is on average the region's best performing indicator. Residual postconflict issues and weak institutions, however, pose ongoing challenges to the deepening of democratic roots. *NIT* findings nevertheless suggest progress and promise in the region, where the attraction of the European idea and the prospect of EU membership remain powerful positive forces. The countries of the western Balkans in particular have their eyes on the EU prize. To the east, Bulgaria and Romania have already joined both the EU and NATO, which offer a solid framework for further democratic development. The southern Balkans represent the most significant reform challenge. Kosovo performs well below the regional average on every *NIT* indicator and faces a host of serious obstacles in its pursuit of difficult reforms. Kosovo's government must undertake these critical measures—improvement of the judiciary and tackling corruption, for example—while simultaneously building a viable state and seeking a peaceful resolution of simmering tensions with its Serb minority.

Figure 2.
Average Democracy Score, Balkans *versus* Kosovo
(7 the weakest democratic progress, 1 the strongest)

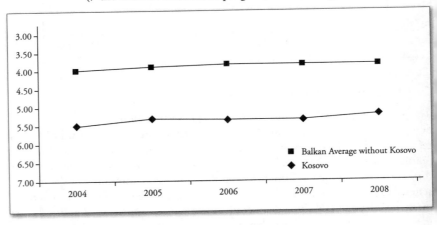

Deepening Authoritarianism in the Former Soviet Union

In distinct contrast to the trajectory of the other regions, the former Soviet Union has moved toward a more deeply anchored authoritarianism. Democratic accountability is an ever-scarcer commodity in these countries, whose regimes put a premium on their own security and use increasingly coercive and predatory means to govern. The latest *NIT* findings show that on average, the region is drifting in a less democratic direction. On the *NIT* scale, with a score of 7.00 representing the weakest democratic performance and 1.00 the strongest, the former Soviet Union achieves an average democracy score of nearly 6.00. Of the non-Baltic former Soviet countries, only Georgia (4.79) and Ukraine (4.25) manage to score better than 5.00. Kyrgyzstan, which experienced a political opening in 2005, has slid backward since that time. In 2007, the country saw declines in a number of areas, including electoral process, independent media, corruption, and local and national governance. The only clearly positive news among the former Soviet republics is in post–Orange Revolution Ukraine, where authoritarian control has given way to politics that are messy but vibrant and competitive. Despite the many problems it faces in its new period of democratic development, Ukraine has safeguarded civil society and the news media, two indispensable tools for advancing deeper political reform.

Among the **major developments** in the *NIT* region in 2007:

- *Resurgent Russia*: In a year in which *Time* magazine named Vladimir Putin its "Person of the Year" and presidential succession became the authorities' point of focus, Russia saw a further shrinking of public space as the Kremlin exerted even greater control over the country's political life and strategic parts of the economy. It became clear in 2007 that the new elite ushered in by the Putin era has swiftly arrogated power to itself and jealously guards its political and economic prerogatives. The confluence of political power with the commanding heights of industry—along with the security services—has forged a deeply entrenched "Iron Triangle" of interests in Russia. These interests have worked to ensure a succession scenario that will not alter the status quo. Using elaborate political choreography made possible by the dominance of state institutions and state-owned companies, Putin set the stage for a new and enduring role for himself at the pinnacle of the Russian system. The regime's argument that Putin has become an indispensable figure for the country's governance entails a tacit recognition that Russia's vital institutions have been atrophied and shunted to superficial status, serving principally as instruments of the incumbent authorities. In the absence of a sound institutional basis for development, it is unclear how the still-evolving Russian experiment in authoritarian capitalism will fare in the future. This suggests that the Russian system is now at a point of fragile stability. In 2007, the negative trajectory of Russia's democratic indicators continued, with steps backward for electoral process, civil society, and national governance.

- *Authoritarians' Growing International Assertiveness*: As leaders in activist authoritarian countries have increased control over political opposition, civil society, and news media, independent voices of consequence have been muzzled and are unable to challenge or mitigate the leadership's whims and excesses. Events in 2007 suggest that the growing authoritarianism of Russia's domestic politics, for example, is shaping the contours of its foreign policy. The country has adopted a more assertive and often belligerent posture toward its neighbors, with aspiring democracies on its periphery absorbing the brunt of the Kremlin's increasingly hard-edged approach. Russia continued its effort to undercut Georgia's reform progress through the implementation of a travel and trade embargo and other attempts at intimidation. In August 2007, for instance, an aircraft entering from Russian airspace dropped a Russian-made guided missile on Georgian territory, not far from the frontier with South Ossetia. The overwhelming suspicion is that the Russian authorities were behind this provocative act. The Kremlin also countenanced an unprecedented cyber-attack launched from Russia against its neighbor Estonia, an EU and NATO member state.

- *Assault on Rules-Based Institutions*: As part of the broader antidemocratic trend across the region, authoritarian governments within the Organization for Security and Cooperation in Europe (OSCE) successfully concluded a campaign to deliver that body's chairmanship to Kazakhstan, the first nondemocratic country to take the post (Kazakhstan will serve its one-year term in 2010). Concurrent with the OSCE chairmanship effort was a parallel initiative, led by Russia and supported by a number of other former Soviet countries, to gut the capacity of the OSCE's Office of Democratic Institutions and Human Rights (ODIHR), including its well-regarded election-monitoring function. As the *NIT* report on Kazakhstan describes, the country was selected for the OSCE chairmanship in a year when President Nursultan Nazarbaev, already in power for 17 years, secured "a package of constitutional amendments, swiftly passed by a pliant Parliament before announcing elections two years ahead of schedule, that removed the president's two-term limit." The August 2007 parliamentary elections "resulted in Nur Otan, [the party] headed by the president, capturing all seats in the Parliament." In the process, the country's beleaguered opposition lost its sole seat in that body. The OSCE's final observation report on the election cited a host of irregularities and indicated that Kazakhstan did not meet a number of critical OSCE commitments.

- *Reform Fatigue in New EU States*: Countries that traditionally have been the strongest *NIT* performers have recently revealed themselves to be increasingly allergic to further reforms. For instance, a number of new EU member states have engaged in decidedly un-EU-like behavior by attacking independent anticorruption bodies. Slovenia's Commission for the Prevention of Corruption, led by Drago Kos, was the target of a campaign to close its doors. In Romania, Monica Macovei, a justice minister who took the lead combating that country's pervasive corruption, was pushed from her post in an unprecedented no-confidence motion. In Latvia, then prime minister Aigars Kalvitis sought to remove Aleksejs Loskutovs, the head of the country's highly effective anticorruption agency.

known as KNAB. Thousands of Latvians took to the streets in October and November 2007 to voice their support for Loskutovs, who had been looking into alleged irregularities involving campaign contributions to Kalvitis's People's Party, among other high-level investigations.

> From 1999 to 2008 Azerbaijan, Kazakhstan, and Russia moved backward on virtually every NIT indicator. The regression in these countries has occurred systematically and across different sectors, affecting the electoral process, civil society, independent media, and judicial independence.

- *Georgia's Reform Knocked Off Course*: Georgia's reform ambitions came under extreme duress in 2007. Thousands of people took to the streets to oppose President Mikheil Saakashvili in October and November, in the largest demonstrations since the 2003 Rose Revolution. The Georgian authorities, who violently dispersed the demonstrators, closed an opposition television station and declared a state of emergency on November 7. The upheaval illuminated deeper fissures in the Georgian political landscape that have no easy solutions. The state of emergency, which remained in effect until November 16, restricted public assembly and banned news broadcasts except by state-controlled television. Despite their stated interest in joining NATO, the Georgian authorities have yet to demonstrate that dissenting voices can be heard and can play a meaningful role in the country's policy debate. At the same time, the country's political opposition has yet to show that it can buck the norm in the former Soviet Union by offering a mature and responsible alternative to the incumbents.

The Last Five Years: Key Developments

Over the past half-decade, a number of specific trends and issues stand out in *NIT* findings. The consolidated authoritarian regimes of the former Soviet Union have tilted an already dramatically uneven playing field more sharply by refocusing state power to restrict critical voices and institutions. Newest EU member states Bulgaria and Romania have improved over the last five years as they moved to meet accession obligations, although they are still well below the average democracy score for the larger crop of new EU members. Now that the two countries have achieved accession and are no longer driven by accession-related inducements and deadlines, the pace and quality of reforms in Romania and Bulgaria will be tested.

A number of noteworthy developments are highlighted by *NIT* findings over the last five years:

A Troubling Picture for Independent Media: The *NIT* region has suffered broad declines during this period, with a total of 15 countries slipping backward. Only one country, Ukraine, has experienced improvement. For new EU members, the average independent media score has fallen, influenced by the downward trajectory in Hungary, Latvia, Poland, Slovenia, and Slovakia. There was also a slight negative drift in the Balkans. No country in that region improved its media performance, and Serbia and Montenegro slipped backward, with violence against journalists a driving factor. In the former Soviet Union, a markedly bleaker picture has emerged. In environments that were already inhospitable to independent media, authoritarian governments have focused intensely on controlling and manipulating media infrastructure and content. The internet, the freest medium and principal challenger to media hegemony in the region, is receiving new and negative attention from the authorities. Over the past five years, media scores worsened in 8 of the 12 non-Baltic former Soviet republics. Armenia, Azerbaijan, Moldova, and Russia underwent the steepest declines, as powerful elites exerted greater influence over news outlets. Other countries, including Georgia, Kazakhstan, Tajikistan, and Uzbekistan, experienced somewhat smaller declines. Standing in direct contrast, Ukraine, which received the strongest media score in the region (3.50), also enjoyed the most positive upward trajectory during this period.

Figure 3.
Average Independent Media Ratings in the Former Soviet Union (FSU)
(7 the weakest democratic progress, 1 the strongest)

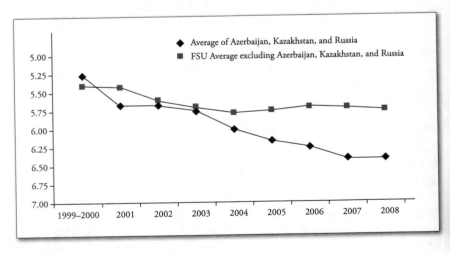

Emerging Petro-States: The model of pursuing economic growth while eroding the independence of critical institutions has been adopted by three oil-rich states in the former Soviet Union: Azerbaijan, Kazakhstan, and Russia. Over the past five years, despite the opportunities for political reform offered by bulging state coffers, all three of these countries have experienced declines in overall democracy scores. Electoral process and independent media worsened as the regimes worked more intensively to control political succession and the information that shapes citizens' views. Russia and Azerbaijan also saw sharp declines for civil society, as legal controls and political intimidation mounted.

A Growing Civil Society Divide: The divergence in civil society performance between the countries of the former Soviet Union and the two other groupings of countries in *NIT* has come into sharper relief. In this year's findings, civil society on average performed at a very poor 5.02 in the former Soviet Union, slipping over the past five years. A crackdown on freedom of association, including a number of new laws and other restrictions, has contributed to the weakening of this sector. In contrast, civil society in the new EU states and the Balkans was rated 1.75 and 3.14, respectively, improving in each case. Ukraine's civil society has distinguished itself over this period, improving its performance by a full point to 2.75.

Figure 4.
Average Regional Civil Society Ratings
(7 the weakest democratic progress, 1 the strongest)

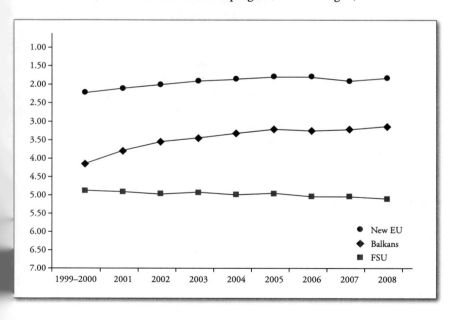

A Commonwealth of Free Nations?

When President George H.W. Bush delivered his "A Europe Whole and Free" speech in Germany in May 1989, the assumptions of the time suggested a clear path for creating what he called a "commonwealth of free nations" in Europe and Eurasia that would be open and democratic. But despite extraordinary progress in significant portions of post-Soviet Europe, the inevitability of that vision is now in doubt.

Today it is evident that the new democracies of Central Europe and the authoritarian states of the former Soviet Union inhabit entirely different political spaces. Despite efforts to engage them, the governments of Russia and many of its neighbors are slipping away from the Euro-Atlantic community. With the proportion of EU energy imports coming from Russia expected to grow from 50 percent to 70 percent over the next decade and a half, realizing the vision of a generation ago will become even more challenging.

> The confluence of political power with the commanding heights of industry —along with the security services— has forged a deeply entrenched "Iron Triangle" of interests in Russia.

States such as Russia, Kazakhstan, and Azerbaijan have ambitions to be more deeply integrated into the global economy, to expand business with the EU and the Western community, and to be accepted as "normal" countries. They seek the prestige and benefits of membership in rules-based Western organizations, while blatantly failing to uphold their commitments. All three countries belong to the OSCE, which Kazakhstan will chair in 2010. Russia and Azerbaijan are members of the Council of Europe. Both Russia and Kazakhstan hope to join the World Trade Organization in the near future. At a minimum, these countries should be required to respect the pledges they have made to such institutions and adhere to their accepted standards both at home and internationally.

Overview of Ratings Changes

Electoral Process
↑ Three ratings improvements in electoral process: Albania, Kosovo, and Montenegro.
↓ Five declines in electoral process: Georgia, Kazakhstan, Kyrgyzstan, Russia, and Uzbekistan.

Civil Society
↑ Six gains in civil society: Czech Republic, Estonia, Kazakhstan, Kosovo, Montenegro, and Poland.
↓ Two setbacks in civil society: Russia and Tajikistan.

Independent Media

↑ Three improvements in independent media: Croatia, Tajikistan, and Ukraine.

↓ Nine declines in independent media: Bosnia, Georgia, Kyrgyzstan, Latvia, Moldova, Montenegro, Serbia, Slovakia, and Slovenia.

National Democratic Governance

↑ Four improvements in national democratic governance: Czech Republic, Croatia, Kosovo, and Montenegro.

↓ Nine declines in national democratic governance: Bosnia, Georgia, Kyrgyzstan, Macedonia, Poland, Romania, Russia, Serbia, and Slovakia.

Local Democratic Governance

↑ Two improvements in local democratic governance: Latvia and Turkmenistan.

↓ Four declines in local democratic governance: Belarus, Kyrgyzstan, Slovakia, and Tajikistan.

Judicial Framework and Independence

↑ One, Montenegro, had a ratings improvement in this category.

↓ Nine setbacks in ratings for this category: Armenia, Kyrgyzstan, Macedonia, Poland, Romania, Serbia, Slovakia, Tajikistan, and Ukraine.

Corruption

↑ Seven improvements in ratings for corruption: Bulgaria, Croatia, Czech Republic, Kosovo, Lithuania, Macedonia, and Montenegro.

↓ One, Kyrgyzstan, regressed in corruption.

Christopher Walker is director of studies at Freedom House. Jeannette Goehring is editor of Nations in Transit. *Lisa Mootz assisted with this report.*

Tables

Table 1. Nations in Transit 2008
Ratings and Democracy Score Summary

Country, Territory	EP	CS	IM	NGOV	LGOV	JFI	CO	DS
Albania	4.00	3.00	3.75	4.25	2.75	4.00	5.00	3.82
Armenia	5.50	3.50	5.75	5.25	5.50	5.25	5.75	5.21
Azerbaijan	6.50	5.25	6.25	6.00	6.00	5.75	6.25	6.00
Belarus	7.00	6.50	6.75	7.00	6.75	6.75	6.25	6.71
Bosnia	3.00	3.50	4.25	5.00	4.75	4.00	4.25	4.11
Bulgaria	1.75	2.50	3.50	3.00	3.00	2.75	3.50	2.86
Croatia	3.25	2.75	3.75	3.25	3.75	4.25	4.50	3.64
Czech Republic	1.75	1.25	2.25	2.75	1.75	2.00	3.25	2.14
Estonia	1.50	1.75	1.50	2.25	2.50	1.50	2.50	1.93
Georgia	4.75	3.50	4.25	5.75	5.50	4.75	5.00	4.79
Hungary	1.75	1.50	2.50	2.25	2.25	1.75	3.00	2.14
Kazakhstan	6.75	5.50	6.75	6.75	6.25	6.25	6.50	6.39
Kosovo	4.50	4.00	5.50	5.50	5.50	5.75	5.75	5.21
Kyrgyzstan	6.00	4.50	6.00	6.25	6.50	6.00	6.25	5.93
Latvia	2.00	1.75	1.75	2.00	2.25	1.75	3.00	2.07
Lithuania	1.75	1.75	1.75	2.50	2.50	1.75	3.75	2.25
Macedonia	3.25	3.25	4.25	4.00	3.75	4.00	4.50	3.86
Moldova	3.75	3.75	5.50	5.75	5.75	4.50	6.00	5.00
Montenegro	3.25	2.75	3.75	4.25	3.25	4.00	5.25	3.79
Poland	2.00	1.25	2.25	3.50	2.25	2.50	3.00	2.39
Romania	2.75	2.25	3.75	3.75	3.00	4.00	4.00	3.36
Russia	6.75	5.50	6.25	6.25	5.75	5.25	6.00	5.96
Serbia	3.25	2.75	3.75	4.00	3.75	4.50	4.50	3.79
Slovakia	1.50	1.50	2.50	2.50	2.25	2.50	3.25	2.29
Slovenia	1.50	2.00	2.25	2.00	1.50	1.50	2.25	1.86
Tajikistan	6.50	5.50	6.00	6.25	6.00	6.00	6.25	6.07
Turkmenistan	7.00	7.00	7.00	7.00	6.75	7.00	6.75	6.93
Ukraine	3.00	2.75	3.50	4.75	5.25	4.75	5.75	4.25
Uzbekistan	7.00	7.00	7.00	7.00	6.75	6.75	6.50	6.86
Average	3.91	3.44	4.28	4.51	4.26	4.19	4.78	4.19
Median	3.25	3.00	3.75	4.25	3.75	4.25	5.00	3.86

NOTES: The ratings are based on a scale of 1 to 7, with 1 representing the highest level of democratic progress and 7 the lowest. The 2008 ratings reflect the period January 1 through December 31, 2007.

The Democracy Score is an average of ratings for Electoral Process (EP); Civil Society (CS); Independent Media (IM); National Democratic Governance (NGOV); Local Democratic Governance (LGOV); Judicial Framework and Independence (JFI); and Corruption (CO).

Table 2. Electoral Process

Ratings History and Regional Breakdown

	1999–2000	2001	2002	2003	2004	2005	2006	2007	2008
New EU Members									
Bulgaria	2.25	2.00	2.00	2.00	1.75	1.75	1.75	1.75	1.75
Czech Republic	1.75	1.75	2.00	2.00	2.00	2.00	2.00	1.75	1.75
Estonia	1.75	1.75	1.75	1.75	1.50	1.50	1.50	1.50	1.50
Hungary	1.25	1.25	1.25	1.25	1.25	1.25	1.25	1.75	1.75
Latvia	1.75	1.75	1.75	1.75	1.75	1.75	1.75	2.00	2.00
Lithuania	1.75	1.75	1.75	1.75	1.75	1.75	1.75	1.75	1.75
Poland	1.25	1.25	1.25	1.50	1.50	1.75	1.75	2.00	2.00
Romania	2.75	3.00	3.00	2.75	2.75	2.75	2.75	2.75	2.75
Slovakia	2.50	2.25	1.75	1.50	1.50	1.25	1.25	1.50	1.50
Slovenia	2.00	1.75	1.75	1.50	1.50	1.50	1.50	1.50	1.50
Average	1.90	1.85	1.83	1.78	1.73	1.73	1.73	1.83	1.83
Median	1.75	1.75	1.75	1.75	1.63	1.75	1.75	1.75	1.75
The Balkans									
Albania	4.25	4.00	3.75	3.75	3.75	3.75	3.50	4.00	4.00
Bosnia	5.00	4.75	4.25	3.75	3.50	3.25	3.00	3.00	3.00
Croatia	4.25	3.25	3.25	3.25	3.25	3.00	3.25	3.25	3.25
Macedonia	3.50	3.75	4.50	3.50	3.50	3.00	3.25	3.25	3.25
Yugoslavia	5.50	4.75	3.75	3.75	n/a	n/a	n/a	n/a	n/a
Serbia	n/a	n/a	n/a	n/a	3.50	3.25	3.25	3.25	3.25
Montenegro	n/a	n/a	n/a	n/a	3.50	3.25	3.50	3.50	3.25
Kosovo	n/a	n/a	n/a	n/a	5.25	4.75	4.75	4.75	4.50
Average	4.50	4.10	3.90	3.60	3.75	3.46	3.50	3.57	3.50
Median	4.25	4.00	3.75	3.75	3.50	3.25	3.25	3.25	3.25
Non-Baltic Former Soviet States									
Armenia	5.25	5.50	5.50	5.50	5.75	5.75	5.75	5.75	5.50
Azerbaijan	5.50	5.75	5.75	5.75	6.00	6.25	6.50	6.50	6.50
Belarus	6.75	6.75	6.75	6.75	6.75	7.00	7.00	7.00	7.00
Georgia	4.00	4.50	5.00	5.25	5.25	4.75	4.75	4.50	4.75
Kazakhstan	6.00	6.25	6.25	6.50	6.50	6.50	6.50	6.50	6.75
Kyrgyzstan	5.00	5.75	5.75	6.00	6.00	6.00	5.75	5.75	6.00
Moldova	3.25	3.25	3.50	3.75	4.00	4.00	3.75	3.75	3.75
Russia	4.00	4.25	4.50	4.75	5.50	6.00	6.25	6.50	6.75
Tajikistan	5.50	5.25	5.25	5.25	5.75	6.00	6.25	6.50	6.50
Turkmenistan	7.00	7.00	7.00	7.00	7.00	7.00	7.00	7.00	7.00
Ukraine	3.50	4.00	4.50	4.00	4.25	3.50	3.25	3.00	3.00
Uzbekistan	6.50	6.75	6.75	6.75	6.75	6.75	6.75	6.75	6.75
Average	5.19	5.42	5.54	5.60	5.79	5.79	5.79	5.79	5.88
Median	5.38	5.63	5.63	5.63	5.88	6.00	6.25	6.50	6.50

NOTES: The ratings are based on a scale of 1 to 7, with 1 representing the highest level of democratic progress and 7 the lowest. The 2008 ratings reflect the period January 1 through December 31, 2007.

In *Nations in Transit 2008*, Freedom House provides separate ratings for Serbia and Kosovo in order to provide a clearer picture of processes and conditions in the different administrative areas. Doing so does not indicate a position on the part of Freedom House regarding Kosovo's status during the study year.

Table 3. Civil Society

Ratings History and Regional Breakdown

	1999–2000	2001	2002	2003	2004	2005	2006	2007	2008
New EU Members									
Bulgaria	3.75	3.50	3.25	3.25	3.00	2.75	2.75	2.50	2.50
Czech Republic	1.50	1.50	1.75	1.50	1.50	1.50	1.50	1.50	1.25
Estonia	2.50	2.25	2.00	2.00	2.00	2.00	2.00	2.00	1.75
Hungary	1.25	1.25	1.25	1.25	1.25	1.25	1.25	1.50	1.50
Latvia	2.25	2.00	2.00	2.00	2.00	1.75	1.75	1.75	1.75
Lithuania	2.00	1.75	1.50	1.50	1.50	1.50	1.50	1.75	1.75
Poland	1.25	1.25	1.25	1.25	1.25	1.25	1.25	1.50	1.25
Romania	3.00	3.00	3.00	2.75	2.50	2.25	2.25	2.25	2.25
Slovakia	2.25	2.00	1.75	1.50	1.25	1.25	1.25	1.50	1.50
Slovenia	1.75	1.75	1.50	1.50	1.50	1.75	1.75	2.00	2.00
Average	**2.15**	**2.03**	**1.93**	**1.85**	**1.78**	**1.73**	**1.73**	**1.83**	**1.75**
Median	**2.13**	**1.88**	**1.75**	**1.50**	**1.50**	**1.63**	**1.63**	**1.75**	**1.75**
The Balkans									
Albania	4.00	4.00	3.75	3.75	3.50	3.25	3.00	3.00	3.00
Bosnia	4.50	4.50	4.25	4.00	3.75	3.75	3.75	3.50	3.50
Croatia	3.50	2.75	2.75	3.00	3.00	3.00	2.75	2.75	2.75
Macedonia	3.50	3.75	4.00	3.75	3.25	3.25	3.25	3.25	3.25
Yugoslavia	5.25	4.00	3.00	2.75	n/a	n/a	n/a	n/a	n/a
Serbia	n/a	n/a	n/a	n/a	2.75	2.75	2.75	2.75	2.75
Montenegro	n/a	n/a	n/a	n/a	2.75	2.50	3.00	3.00	2.75
Kosovo	n/a	n/a	n/a	n/a	4.25	4.00	4.25	4.25	4.00
Average	**4.15**	**3.80**	**3.55**	**3.45**	**3.32**	**3.21**	**3.25**	**3.21**	**3.14**
Median	**4.00**	**4.00**	**3.75**	**3.75**	**3.25**	**3.25**	**3.00**	**3.00**	**3.00**
Non-Baltic Former Soviet States									
Armenia	3.50	3.50	3.50	3.50	3.50	3.50	3.50	3.50	3.50
Azerbaijan	4.75	4.50	4.50	4.25	4.50	4.75	5.00	5.25	5.25
Belarus	6.00	6.50	6.25	6.50	6.75	6.75	6.75	6.50	6.50
Georgia	3.75	4.00	4.00	4.00	3.50	3.50	3.50	3.50	3.50
Kazakhstan	5.00	5.00	5.50	5.50	5.50	5.50	5.75	5.75	5.50
Kyrgyzstan	4.50	4.50	4.50	4.50	4.50	4.50	4.50	4.50	4.50
Moldova	3.75	3.75	4.00	3.75	4.00	4.00	4.00	3.75	3.75
Russia	3.75	4.00	4.00	4.25	4.50	4.75	5.00	5.25	5.50
Tajikistan	5.25	5.00	5.00	5.00	5.00	4.75	5.00	5.00	5.50
Turkmenistan	7.00	7.00	7.00	7.00	7.00	7.00	7.00	7.00	7.00
Ukraine	4.00	3.75	3.75	3.50	3.75	3.00	2.75	2.75	2.75
Uzbekistan	6.50	6.50	6.75	6.50	6.50	6.50	7.00	7.00	7.00
Average	**4.81**	**4.83**	**4.90**	**4.85**	**4.92**	**4.88**	**4.98**	**4.98**	**5.02**
Median	**4.63**	**4.50**	**4.50**	**4.38**	**4.50**	**4.75**	**5.00**	**5.13**	**5.38**

NOTES: The ratings are based on a scale of 1 to 7, with 1 representing the highest level of democratic progress and 7 the lowest. The 2008 ratings reflect the period January 1 through December 31, 2007.

In *Nations in Transit 2008*, Freedom House provides separate ratings for Serbia and Kosovo in order to provide a clearer picture of processes and conditions in the different administrative areas. Doing so does not indicate position on the part of Freedom House regarding Kosovo's status during the study year.

Table 4. Independent Media
Ratings History and Regional Breakdown

	1999–2000	2001	2002	2003	2004	2005	2006	2007	2008
New EU Members									
Bulgaria	3.50	3.25	3.25	3.50	3.50	3.50	3.25	3.50	3.50
Czech Republic	1.75	2.00	2.50	2.25	2.25	2.00	2.00	2.25	2.25
Estonia	1.75	1.75	1.75	1.75	1.50	1.50	1.50	1.50	1.50
Hungary	2.00	2.25	2.25	2.25	2.25	2.50	2.50	2.50	2.50
Latvia	1.75	1.75	1.75	1.75	1.50	1.50	1.50	1.50	1.75
Lithuania	1.75	1.75	1.75	1.75	1.75	1.75	1.75	1.75	1.75
Poland	1.50	1.50	1.50	1.75	1.75	1.50	1.75	2.25	2.25
Romania	3.50	3.50	3.50	3.75	3.75	4.00	4.00	3.75	3.75
Slovakia	2.25	2.00	2.00	2.00	2.25	2.25	2.25	2.25	2.50
Slovenia	1.75	1.75	1.75	1.75	1.75	1.50	1.75	2.00	2.25
Average	**2.15**	**2.15**	**2.20**	**2.25**	**2.23**	**2.20**	**2.23**	**2.33**	**2.40**
Median	**1.75**	**1.88**	**1.88**	**1.88**	**2.00**	**1.88**	**1.88**	**2.25**	**2.25**
The Balkans									
Albania	4.50	4.25	4.00	4.00	3.75	4.00	3.75	3.75	3.75
Bosnia	5.00	4.50	4.25	4.25	4.25	4.00	4.00	4.00	4.25
Croatia	5.00	3.50	3.50	3.75	3.75	3.75	3.75	4.00	3.75
Macedonia	3.75	3.75	3.75	4.00	4.25	4.25	4.25	4.25	4.25
Yugoslavia	5.75	4.50	3.50	3.25	n/a	n/a	n/a	n/a	n/a
Serbia	n/a	n/a	n/a	n/a	3.50	3.25	3.25	3.50	3.75
Montenegro	n/a	n/a	n/a	n/a	3.25	3.25	3.25	3.50	3.75
Kosovo	n/a	n/a	n/a	n/a	5.50	5.50	5.50	5.50	5.50
Average	**4.80**	**4.10**	**3.80**	**3.85**	**4.04**	**4.00**	**3.96**	**4.07**	**4.14**
Median	**5.00**	**4.25**	**3.75**	**4.00**	**3.75**	**4.00**	**3.75**	**4.00**	**3.75**
Non-Baltic Former Soviet States									
Armenia	4.75	4.75	4.75	5.00	5.25	5.50	5.50	5.75	5.75
Azerbaijan	5.50	5.75	5.50	5.50	5.75	6.00	6.00	6.25	6.25
Belarus	6.75	6.75	6.75	6.75	6.75	6.75	6.75	6.75	6.75
Georgia	3.75	3.50	3.75	4.00	4.00	4.25	4.25	4.00	4.25
Kazakhstan	5.50	6.00	6.00	6.25	6.50	6.50	6.75	6.75	6.75
Kyrgyzstan	5.00	5.00	5.75	6.00	6.00	5.75	5.75	5.75	6.00
Moldova	4.00	4.25	4.50	4.75	5.00	5.00	5.00	5.25	5.50
Russia	4.75	5.25	5.50	5.50	5.75	6.00	6.00	6.25	6.25
Tajikistan	5.75	5.50	5.75	5.75	5.75	6.00	6.25	6.25	6.00
Turkmenistan	7.00	7.00	7.00	7.00	7.00	7.00	7.00	7.00	7.00
Ukraine	5.00	5.25	5.50	5.50	5.50	4.75	3.75	3.75	3.50
Uzbekistan	6.50	6.75	6.75	6.75	6.75	6.75	7.00	7.00	7.00
Average	**5.35**	**5.48**	**5.63**	**5.73**	**5.83**	**5.85**	**5.83**	**5.90**	**5.92**
Median	**5.25**	**5.38**	**5.63**	**5.63**	**5.75**	**6.00**	**6.00**	**6.25**	**6.13**

NOTES: The ratings are based on a scale of 1 to 7, with 1 representing the highest level of democratic progress and 7 the lowest. The 2008 ratings reflect the period January 1 through December 31, 2007.

In *Nations in Transit 2008*, Freedom House provides separate ratings for Serbia and Kosovo in order to provide a clearer picture of processes and conditions in the different administrative areas. Doing so does not indicate a position on the part of Freedom House regarding Kosovo's status during the study year.

Table 5. National Democratic Governance
Ratings History and Regional Breakdown

	1999–2000 GOV	2001 GOV	2002 GOV	2003 GOV	2004 GOV	2005 NGOV	2006 NGOV	2007 NGOV	2008 NGOV
New EU Members									
Bulgaria	3.75	3.50	3.50	3.75	3.75	3.50	3.00	3.00	3.00
Czech Rep.	2.00	2.00	2.25	2.25	2.25	2.50	2.50	3.00	2.75
Estonia	2.25	2.25	2.25	2.25	2.25	2.25	2.25	2.25	2.25
Hungary	2.50	3.00	3.00	2.50	2.50	2.00	2.00	2.25	2.25
Latvia	2.50	2.25	2.25	2.25	2.25	2.25	2.00	2.00	2.00
Lithuania	2.50	2.50	2.50	2.50	2.50	2.50	2.50	2.50	2.50
Poland	1.75	1.75	2.00	2.00	2.00	2.50	2.75	3.25	3.50
Romania	3.50	3.75	3.75	3.75	3.75	3.50	3.50	3.50	3.75
Slovakia	3.00	2.75	2.25	2.25	2.25	2.00	2.00	2.25	2.50
Slovenia	2.25	2.50	2.25	2.25	2.00	2.00	2.00	2.00	2.00
Average	**2.60**	**2.63**	**2.60**	**2.58**	**2.55**	**2.50**	**2.45**	**2.60**	**2.65**
Median	**2.50**	**2.50**	**2.25**	**2.25**	**2.25**	**2.38**	**2.38**	**2.38**	**2.50**
The Balkans									
Albania	4.75	4.25	4.25	4.25	4.25	4.25	4.00	4.25	4.25
Bosnia	6.00	6.00	5.50	5.25	5.00	4.75	4.75	4.75	5.00
Croatia	4.00	3.50	3.50	3.75	3.75	3.50	3.50	3.50	3.25
Macedonia	3.00	3.75	4.25	4.50	4.00	4.00	3.75	3.75	4.00
Yugoslavia	5.50	5.25	4.25	4.25	n/a	n/a	n/a	n/a	n/a
Serbia	n/a	n/a	n/a	n/a	4.00	4.00	4.00	3.75	4.00
Montenegro	n/a	n/a	n/a	n/a	4.00	4.50	4.50	4.50	4.25
Kosovo	n/a	n/a	n/a	n/a	6.00	5.75	5.75	5.75	5.50
Average	**4.65**	**4.55**	**4.35**	**4.40**	**4.43**	**4.39**	**4.32**	**4.32**	**4.32**
Median	**4.75**	**4.25**	**4.25**	**4.25**	**4.00**	**4.25**	**4.00**	**4.25**	**4.25**
Non-Baltic Former Soviet States									
Armenia	4.50	4.50	4.50	4.75	4.75	5.00	5.00	5.25	5.25
Azerbaijan	6.25	6.25	6.00	5.75	5.75	6.00	6.00	6.00	6.00
Belarus	6.25	6.25	6.50	6.50	6.50	6.75	7.00	7.00	7.00
Georgia	4.50	4.75	5.00	5.50	5.75	5.50	5.50	5.50	5.75
Kazakhstan	5.00	5.00	5.75	6.25	6.25	6.50	6.75	6.75	6.75
Kyrgyzstan	5.00	5.25	5.50	6.00	6.00	6.00	6.00	6.00	6.25
Moldova	4.50	4.50	4.75	5.25	5.50	5.75	5.75	5.75	5.75
Russia	4.50	5.00	5.25	5.00	5.25	5.75	6.00	6.00	6.25
Tajikistan	6.25	6.00	6.00	6.00	5.75	6.00	6.25	6.25	6.25
Turkmenistan	6.75	6.75	6.75	6.75	7.00	7.00	7.00	7.00	7.00
Ukraine	4.75	4.75	5.00	5.00	5.25	5.00	4.50	4.75	4.75
Uzbekistan	6.25	6.00	6.00	6.25	6.25	6.50	7.00	7.00	7.00
Average	**5.38**	**5.42**	**5.58**	**5.75**	**5.83**	**5.98**	**6.06**	**6.10**	**6.17**
Median	**5.00**	**5.13**	**5.63**	**5.88**	**5.75**	**6.00**	**6.00**	**6.00**	**6.25**

NOTES: The ratings are based on a scale of 1 to 7, with 1 representing the highest level of democratic progress and 7 the lowest. The 2008 ratings reflect the period January 1 through December 31, 2007.

Starting with the 2005 edition, Freedom House introduced separate ratings for national democratic governance and local democratic governance. Previous editions included only one governance category.

Table 6. Local Democratic Governance
Ratings History and Regional Breakdown

	1999–2000 GOV	2001 GOV	2002 GOV	2003 GOV	2004 GOV	2005 LGOV	2006 LGOV	2007 LGOV	2008 LGOV
New EU Members									
Bulgaria	3.75	3.50	3.50	3.75	3.75	3.50	3.00	3.00	3.00
Czech Rep.	2.00	2.00	2.25	2.25	2.25	2.00	2.00	1.75	1.75
Estonia	2.25	2.25	2.25	2.25	2.25	2.50	2.50	2.50	2.50
Hungary	2.50	3.00	3.00	2.50	2.50	2.25	2.25	2.25	2.25
Latvia	2.50	2.25	2.25	2.25	2.25	2.50	2.50	2.50	2.25
Lithuania	2.50	2.50	2.50	2.50	2.50	2.50	2.50	2.50	2.50
Poland	1.75	1.75	2.00	2.00	2.00	2.00	2.00	2.25	2.25
Romania	3.50	3.75	3.75	3.75	3.75	3.00	3.00	3.00	3.00
Slovakia	3.00	2.75	2.25	2.25	2.25	2.25	2.00	2.00	2.25
Slovenia	2.25	2.50	2.25	2.25	2.00	1.50	1.50	1.50	1.50
Average	**2.60**	**2.63**	**2.60**	**2.58**	**2.55**	**2.40**	**2.33**	**2.33**	**2.33**
Median	**2.50**	**2.50**	**2.25**	**2.25**	**2.25**	**2.38**	**2.38**	**2.38**	**2.25**
The Balkans									
Albania	4.75	4.25	4.25	4.25	4.25	3.25	2.75	2.75	2.75
Bosnia	6.00	6.00	5.50	5.25	5.00	4.75	4.75	4.75	4.75
Croatia	4.00	3.50	3.50	3.75	3.75	3.75	3.75	3.75	3.75
Macedonia	3.00	3.75	4.25	4.50	4.00	4.00	3.75	3.75	3.75
Yugoslavia	5.50	5.25	4.25	4.25	n/a	n/a	n/a	n/a	n/a
Serbia	n/a	n/a	n/a	n/a	4.00	3.75	3.75	3.75	3.75
Montenegro	n/a	n/a	n/a	n/a	4.00	3.50	3.50	3.25	3.25
Kosovo	n/a	n/a	n/a	n/a	6.00	5.50	5.50	5.50	5.50
Average	**4.65**	**4.55**	**4.35**	**4.40**	**4.43**	**4.07**	**3.96**	**3.93**	**3.93**
Median	**4.75**	**4.25**	**4.25**	**4.25**	**4.00**	**3.75**	**3.75**	**3.75**	**3.75**
Non-Baltic Former Soviet States									
Armenia	4.50	4.50	4.50	4.75	4.75	5.50	5.50	5.50	5.50
Azerbaijan	6.25	6.25	6.00	5.75	5.75	6.00	6.00	6.00	6.00
Belarus	6.25	6.25	6.50	6.50	6.50	6.50	6.50	6.50	6.75
Georgia	4.50	4.75	5.00	5.50	5.75	6.00	5.75	5.50	5.50
Kazakhstan	5.00	5.00	5.75	6.25	6.25	6.25	6.25	6.25	6.25
Kyrgyzstan	5.00	5.25	5.50	6.00	6.00	5.75	6.25	6.25	6.50
Moldova	4.50	4.50	4.75	5.25	5.50	5.75	5.75	5.75	5.75
Russia	4.50	5.00	5.25	5.00	5.25	5.75	5.75	5.75	5.75
Tajikistan	6.25	6.00	6.00	6.00	5.75	5.75	5.75	5.75	6.00
Turkmenistan	6.75	6.75	6.75	6.75	7.00	7.00	7.00	7.00	6.75
Ukraine	4.75	4.75	5.00	5.00	5.25	5.25	5.25	5.25	5.25
Uzbekistan	6.25	6.00	6.00	6.25	6.25	6.25	6.75	6.75	6.75
Average	**5.38**	**5.42**	**5.58**	**5.75**	**5.83**	**5.98**	**6.04**	**6.02**	**6.06**
Median	**5.00**	**5.13**	**5.63**	**5.88**	**5.75**	**5.88**	**5.88**	**5.88**	**6.00**

NOTES: The ratings are based on a scale of 1 to 7, with 1 representing the highest level of democratic progress and 7 the lowest. The 2008 ratings reflect the period January 1 through December 31, 2007.

Starting with the 2005 edition, Freedom House introduced separate ratings for national democratic governance and local democratic governance. Previous editions included only one governance category.

Table 7. Judicial Framework and Independence

Ratings History and Regional Breakdown

	1999–2000	2001	2002	2003	2004	2005	2006	2007	2008
New EU Members									
Bulgaria	3.50	3.50	3.50	3.50	3.25	3.25	3.00	2.75	2.75
Czech Republic	2.25	2.50	2.50	2.50	2.50	2.50	2.25	2.00	2.00
Estonia	2.00	2.00	1.75	1.75	1.75	1.50	1.50	1.50	1.50
Hungary	1.75	2.00	2.00	1.75	1.75	1.75	1.75	1.75	1.75
Latvia	2.00	2.00	2.00	2.25	2.00	1.75	1.75	1.75	1.75
Lithuania	2.00	1.75	2.00	1.75	1.75	1.75	1.50	1.75	1.75
Poland	1.50	1.50	1.50	1.50	1.50	2.00	2.25	2.25	2.50
Romania	4.25	4.25	4.25	4.25	4.25	4.00	4.00	3.75	4.00
Slovakia	2.50	2.25	2.00	2.00	2.00	2.00	2.00	2.25	2.50
Slovenia	1.50	1.50	1.75	1.75	1.75	1.50	1.50	1.50	1.50
Average	**2.33**	**2.33**	**2.33**	**2.30**	**2.25**	**2.20**	**2.15**	**2.13**	**2.20**
Median	**2.00**	**2.00**	**2.00**	**1.88**	**1.88**	**1.88**	**1.88**	**1.88**	**1.88**
The Balkans									
Albania	5.00	4.50	4.50	4.25	4.25	4.50	4.25	4.00	4.00
Bosnia	6.00	5.50	5.25	5.00	4.50	4.25	4.00	4.00	4.00
Croatia	4.75	3.75	3.75	4.25	4.50	4.50	4.25	4.25	4.25
Macedonia	4.25	4.25	4.75	4.50	4.00	3.75	3.75	3.75	4.00
Yugoslavia	5.75	5.50	4.25	4.25	n/a	n/a	n/a	n/a	n/a
Serbia	n/a	n/a	n/a	n/a	4.25	4.25	4.25	4.25	4.50
Montenegro	n/a	n/a	n/a	n/a	4.25	4.25	4.25	4.25	4.00
Kosovo	n/a	n/a	n/a	n/a	6.00	5.75	5.75	5.75	5.75
Average	**5.15**	**4.70**	**4.50**	**4.45**	**4.54**	**4.46**	**4.36**	**4.32**	**4.36**
Median	**5.00**	**4.50**	**4.50**	**4.25**	**4.25**	**4.25**	**4.25**	**4.25**	**4.00**
Non-Baltic Former Soviet States									
Armenia	5.00	5.00	5.00	5.00	5.00	5.25	5.00	5.00	5.25
Azerbaijan	5.50	5.25	5.25	5.25	5.50	5.75	5.75	5.75	5.75
Belarus	6.50	6.75	6.75	6.75	6.75	6.75	6.75	6.75	6.75
Georgia	4.00	4.00	4.25	4.50	4.50	5.00	4.75	4.75	4.75
Kazakhstan	5.50	5.75	6.00	6.25	6.25	6.25	6.25	6.25	6.25
Kyrgyzstan	5.00	5.25	5.25	5.50	5.50	5.50	5.50	5.50	6.00
Moldova	4.00	4.00	4.00	4.50	4.50	4.75	4.50	4.50	4.50
Russia	4.25	4.50	4.75	4.50	4.75	5.25	5.25	5.25	5.25
Tajikistan	5.75	5.75	5.75	5.75	5.75	5.75	5.75	5.75	6.00
Turkmenistan	6.75	7.00	7.00	7.00	7.00	7.00	7.00	7.00	7.00
Ukraine	4.50	4.50	4.75	4.50	4.75	4.25	4.25	4.50	4.75
Uzbekistan	6.50	6.50	6.50	6.50	6.50	6.25	6.75	6.75	6.75
Average	**5.27**	**5.35**	**5.44**	**5.50**	**5.56**	**5.65**	**5.63**	**5.65**	**5.75**
Median	**5.25**	**5.25**	**5.25**	**5.38**	**5.50**	**5.63**	**5.63**	**5.63**	**5.88**

NOTES: The ratings are based on a scale of 1 to 7, with 1 representing the highest level of democratic progress and 7 the lowest. The 2008 ratings reflect the period January 1 through December 31, 2007.

This category was called Constitutional, Legislative, & Judicial Framework in editions before 2005.

In *Nations in Transit 2008*, Freedom House provides separate ratings for Serbia and Kosovo in order to provide a clearer picture of processes and conditions in the different administrative areas. Doing so does not indicate a position on the part of Freedom House regarding Kosovo's status during the study year.

Table 8. Corruption
Ratings History and Regional Breakdown

	1999–2000	2001	2002	2003	2004	2005	2006	2007	2008
New EU Members									
Bulgaria	4.75	4.75	4.50	4.25	4.25	4.00	3.75	3.75	3.50
Czech Republic	3.25	3.75	3.75	3.50	3.50	3.50	3.50	3.50	3.25
Estonia	3.25	2.75	2.50	2.50	2.50	2.50	2.50	2.50	2.50
Hungary	2.50	3.00	3.00	2.75	2.75	2.75	3.00	3.00	3.00
Latvia	3.50	3.50	3.75	3.50	3.50	3.50	3.25	3.00	3.00
Lithuania	3.75	3.75	3.75	3.50	3.50	3.75	4.00	4.00	3.75
Poland	2.25	2.25	2.25	2.50	2.50	3.00	3.25	3.00	3.00
Romania	4.25	4.50	4.75	4.50	4.50	4.25	4.25	4.00	4.00
Slovakia	3.75	3.75	3.25	3.25	3.25	3.00	3.00	3.25	3.25
Slovenia	2.00	2.00	2.00	2.00	2.00	2.00	2.25	2.25	2.25
Average	3.33	3.40	3.35	3.23	3.23	3.23	3.28	3.23	3.15
Median	3.38	3.63	3.50	3.38	3.38	3.25	3.25	3.13	3.13
The Balkans									
Albania	6.00	5.50	5.25	5.00	5.25	5.25	5.25	5.00	5.00
Bosnia	6.00	5.75	5.50	5.00	4.75	4.50	4.25	4.25	4.25
Croatia	5.25	4.50	4.50	4.75	4.75	4.75	4.75	4.75	4.50
Macedonia	5.00	5.00	5.50	5.50	5.00	5.00	4.75	4.75	4.50
Yugoslavia	6.25	6.25	5.25	5.00	n/a	n/a	n/a	n/a	n/a
Serbia	n/a	n/a	n/a	n/a	5.00	5.00	4.75	4.50	4.50
Montenegro	n/a	n/a	n/a	n/a	5.25	5.25	5.25	5.50	5.25
Kosovo	n/a	n/a	n/a	n/a	6.00	6.00	6.00	6.00	5.75
Average	5.70	5.40	5.20	5.05	5.14	5.11	5.00	4.96	4.82
Median	6.00	5.50	5.25	5.00	5.00	5.00	4.75	4.75	4.50
Non-Baltic Former Soviet States									
Armenia	5.75	5.75	5.75	5.75	5.75	5.75	5.75	5.75	5.75
Azerbaijan	6.00	6.25	6.25	6.25	6.25	6.25	6.25	6.25	6.25
Belarus	5.25	5.25	5.25	5.50	5.75	6.00	6.25	6.25	6.25
Georgia	5.00	5.25	5.50	5.75	6.00	5.75	5.50	5.00	5.00
Kazakhstan	6.00	6.25	6.25	6.25	6.50	6.50	6.50	6.50	6.50
Kyrgyzstan	6.00	6.00	6.00	6.00	6.00	6.00	6.00	6.00	6.25
Moldova	6.00	6.00	6.25	6.25	6.25	6.25	6.00	6.00	6.00
Russia	6.25	6.25	6.00	5.75	5.75	5.75	6.00	6.00	6.00
Tajikistan	6.00	6.00	6.00	6.00	6.25	6.25	6.25	6.25	6.25
Turkmenistan	6.00	6.25	6.25	6.25	6.25	6.50	6.75	6.75	6.75
Ukraine	6.00	6.00	6.00	5.75	5.75	5.75	5.75	5.75	5.75
Uzbekistan	6.00	6.00	6.00	6.00	6.00	6.00	6.50	6.50	6.50
Average	5.85	5.94	5.96	5.96	6.04	6.06	6.13	6.08	6.10
Median	6.00	6.00	6.00	6.00	6.00	6.00	6.13	6.13	6.25

NOTES: The ratings are based on a scale of 1 to 7, with 1 representing the highest level of democratic progress and 7 the lowest. The 2008 ratings reflect the period January 1 through December 31, 2007.

In *Nations in Transit 2008*, Freedom House provides separate ratings for Serbia and Kosovo in order to provide a clearer picture of processes and conditions in the different administrative areas. Doing so does not indicate a position on the part of Freedom House regarding Kosovo's status during the study year.

Table 9. Democracy Score
Year-To-Year Summaries by Region

	1999–2000	2001	2002	2003	2004	2005	2006	2007	2008
New EU Members									
Bulgaria	3.58	3.42	3.33	3.38	3.25	3.18	2.93	2.89	2.86
Czech Republic	2.08	2.25	2.46	2.33	2.33	2.29	2.25	2.25	2.14
Estonia	2.25	2.13	2.00	2.00	1.92	1.96	1.96	1.96	1.93
Hungary	1.88	2.13	2.13	1.96	1.96	1.96	2.00	2.14	2.14
Latvia	2.29	2.21	2.25	2.25	2.17	2.14	2.07	2.07	2.07
Lithuania	2.29	2.21	2.21	2.13	2.13	2.21	2.21	2.29	2.25
Poland	1.58	1.58	1.63	1.75	1.75	2.00	2.14	2.36	2.39
Romania	3.54	3.67	3.71	3.63	3.58	3.39	3.39	3.29	3.36
Slovakia	2.71	2.50	2.17	2.08	2.08	2.00	1.96	2.14	2.29
Slovenia	1.88	1.88	1.83	1.79	1.75	1.68	1.75	1.82	1.86
Average	**2.41**	**2.40**	**2.37**	**2.33**	**2.29**	**2.28**	**2.27**	**2.32**	**2.33**
Median	**2.27**	**2.21**	**2.19**	**2.10**	**2.10**	**2.07**	**2.11**	**2.20**	**2.20**
The Balkans									
Albania	4.75	4.42	4.25	4.17	4.13	4.04	3.79	3.82	3.82
Bosnia	5.42	5.17	4.83	4.54	4.29	4.18	4.07	4.04	4.11
Croatia	4.46	3.54	3.54	3.79	3.83	3.75	3.71	3.75	3.64
Macedonia	3.83	4.04	4.46	4.29	4.00	3.89	3.82	3.82	3.86
Yugoslavia	5.67	5.04	4.00	3.88	n/a	n/a	n/a	n/a	n/a
Serbia	n/a	n/a	n/a	n/a	3.83	3.75	3.71	3.68	3.79
Montenegro	n/a	n/a	n/a	n/a	3.83	3.79	3.89	3.93	3.79
Kosovo	n/a	n/a	n/a	n/a	5.50	5.32	5.36	5.36	5.21
Average	**4.83**	**4.44**	**4.22**	**4.13**	**4.20**	**4.10**	**4.05**	**4.06**	**4.03**
Median	**4.75**	**4.42**	**4.25**	**4.17**	**4.00**	**3.89**	**3.82**	**3.82**	**3.82**
Non-Baltic Former Soviet States									
Armenia	4.79	4.83	4.83	4.92	5.00	5.18	5.14	5.21	5.21
Azerbaijan	5.58	5.63	5.54	5.46	5.63	5.86	5.93	6.00	6.00
Belarus	6.25	6.38	6.38	6.46	6.54	6.64	6.71	6.68	6.71
Georgia	4.17	4.33	4.58	4.83	4.83	4.96	4.86	4.68	4.79
Kazakhstan	5.50	5.71	5.96	6.17	6.25	6.29	6.39	6.39	6.39
Kyrgyzstan	5.08	5.29	5.46	5.67	5.67	5.64	5.68	5.68	5.93
Moldova	4.25	4.29	4.50	4.71	4.88	5.07	4.96	4.96	5.00
Russia	4.58	4.88	5.00	4.96	5.25	5.61	5.75	5.86	5.96
Tajikistan	5.75	5.58	5.63	5.63	5.71	5.79	5.93	5.96	6.07
Turkmenistan	6.75	6.83	6.83	6.83	6.88	6.93	6.96	6.96	6.93
Ukraine	4.63	4.71	4.92	4.71	4.88	4.50	4.21	4.25	4.25
Uzbekistan	6.38	6.42	6.46	6.46	6.46	6.43	6.82	6.82	6.86
Average	**5.31**	**5.41**	**5.51**	**5.57**	**5.66**	**5.74**	**5.78**	**5.79**	**5.84**
Median	**5.29**	**5.44**	**5.50**	**5.54**	**5.65**	**5.72**	**5.84**	**5.91**	**5.98**

NOTES: The ratings are based on a scale of 1 to 7, with 1 representing the highest level of democratic progress and 7 the lowest. The 2008 ratings reflect the period January 1 through December 31, 2007.

The Democracy Score is an average of ratings for Electoral Process (EP); Civil Society (CS); Independent Media (IM); National Democratic Governance (NGOV); Local Democratic Governance (LGOV); Judicial Framework and Independence (JFI); and Corruption (CO).

In *Nations in Transit 2008*, Freedom House provides separate ratings for Serbia and Kosovo in order to provide a clearer picture of processes and conditions in the different administrative areas. Doing so does not indicate a position on the part of Freedom House regarding Kosovo's status during the study year.

Table 10. Democracy Score
2008 Rankings by Regime Type

Consolidated Democracies (1.00–2.99)	
Slovenia	1.86
Estonia	1.93
Latvia	2.07
Hungary	2.14
Czech Republic	2.14
Lithuania	2.25
Slovakia	2.29
Poland	2.39
Bulgaria	2.86

Semi-Consolidated Democracies (3.00–3.99)	
Romania	3.36
Croatia	3.64
Serbia	3.79
Montenegro	3.79
Albania	3.82
Macedonia	3.86

Transitional Governments or Hybrid Regimes (4.00–4.99)	
Bosnia	4.11
Ukraine	4.25
Georgia	4.79

Semi-Consolidated Authoritarian Regimes or Internationally-Administered Areas (5.00–5.99)	
Moldova	5.00
Armenia	5.21
Kosovo	5.21
Kyrgyzstan	5.93
Russia	5.96

Consolidated Authoritarian Regimes (6.00–7.00)	
Azerbaijan	6.00
Tajikistan	6.07
Kazakhstan	6.39
Belarus	6.71
Uzbekistan	6.86
Turkmenistan	6.93

NOTES: The ratings are based on a scale of 1 to 7, with 1 representing the highest level of democratic progress and 7 the lowest. The 2008 ratings reflect the period January 1 through December 31, 2007.

The Democracy Score is an average of ratings for Electoral Process (EP); Civil Society (CS); Independent Media (IM); National Democratic Governance (NGOV); Local Democratic Governance (LGOV); Judicial Framework and Independence (JFI); and Corruption (CO).

In *Nations in Transit 2008*, Freedom House provides separate ratings for Serbia and Kosovo in order to provide a clearer picture of processes and conditions in the different administrative areas. Doing so does not indicate a position on the part of Freedom House regarding Kosovo's status during the study year.

Albania

by Ditmir Bushati

Capital: Tirana
Population: 3.2 million
GNI/capita: US$6,000

The social data above was taken from the European Bank for Reconstruction and Development's *Transition Report 2007: People in Transition*, and the economic data from the World Bank's *World Development Indicators 2008*.

Nations in Transit Ratings and Averaged Scores

	1999	2001	2002	2003	2004	2005	2006	2007	2008
Electoral Process	4.25	4.00	3.75	3.75	3.75	3.75	3.50	4.00	4.00
Civil Society	4.00	4.00	3.75	3.75	3.50	3.25	3.00	3.00	3.00
Independent Media	4.50	4.25	4.00	4.00	3.75	4.00	3.75	3.75	3.75
Governance*	4.75	4.25	4.25	4.25	4.25	n/a	n/a	n/a	n/a
National Democratic Governance	n/a	n/a	n/a	n/a	n/a	4.25	4.00	4.25	4.25
Local Democratic Governance	n/a	n/a	n/a	n/a	n/a	3.25	2.75	2.75	2.75
Judicial Framework and Independence	5.00	4.50	4.50	4.25	4.25	4.50	4.25	4.00	4.00
Corruption	6.00	5.50	5.25	5.00	5.25	5.25	5.25	5.00	5.00
Democracy Score	4.75	4.42	4.25	4.17	4.13	4.04	3.79	3.82	3.82

* With the 2005 edition, Freedom House introduced separate analysis and ratings for national democratic governance and local democratic governance to provide readers with more detailed and nuanced analysis of these two important subjects.

NOTE: The ratings reflect the consensus of Freedom House, its academic advisers, and the author(s) of this report. The opinions expressed in this report are those of the author(s). The ratings are based on a scale of 1 to 7, with 1 representing the highest level of democratic progress and 7 the lowest. The Democracy Score is an average of ratings for the categories tracked in a given year.

EXECUTIVE SUMMARY

Since the end of the Communist regime in 1990, Albania has experienced major political, institutional, and socioeconomic changes. Breaking the barriers of a hermetically closed social order that was deeply apprehensive of the outside world was a dramatic achievement. The population at large was profoundly disillusioned by the country's slide into anarchy and crisis in 1997 that accompanied the difficult transition, but Albania has pulled through these challenges.

In 2006, Albania signed the Stabilization and Association Agreement establishing a new contractual relationship with the European Union. The country worked throughout 2007 to qualify for an invitation to join NATO in April 2008. Despite these positive achievements, Albania's transition to democracy and a market economy seems to be a rather long journey. Albania still faces problems organizing elections in accordance with international standards, although shifts in power have been increasingly peaceful. More attention must be paid to reforming the public administration, improving the business climate, reforming the judiciary, and enhancing the fight against corruption and organized crime by embracing a systemic and strategic approach. Above all, stronger efforts are needed to bring the public back to politics to build trust in democratic institutions as tools for transformation.

National Democratic Governance. During 2007, Albania's system of democratic governance suffered from the so-called "governmentalization of society" and a splintered opposition that failed to capitalize on this. The government moved to control independent institutions gradually. The most significant example was the blatant attitude against the Office of the General Prosecutor and the judiciary, both considered by the government to be obstacles in the fight against corruption and organized crime. Instead of proposing a package of measures on how to reform the judiciary, the government decided to remove the prosecutor general from office and create new ties between the ruling party and the Constitutional Court, the High Council of Justice, and the public procurement ombudsman through new appointments to these institutions. The local elections of February 18, 2007 were considered competitive but not fully in line with international commitments and standards. The election of the new President of the Republic took place within the constitutional framework but did not reflect a consensual process, which is lacking in Albanian governance. *The national democratic governance rating remains at 4.25.*

Electoral Process. Although anticipated as the "last year" of the electoral reform saga, which has hindered the democratization process in Albania's transition, 2007 proved to be the contrary. For the first time, elections were rescheduled owing to the failure of the major political parties to agree on amendments to the Constitution and the electoral code. The last-minute amendments, completed only 35 days before the elections, affected the electoral preparations and the process itself. The local elections, which according to the OSCE Office for Democratic Institutions and Human Rights "only partly met OSCE commitments," were followed by protracted litigation, with the final election results declared three months later. *Albania's electoral process remains at 4.00.*

Civil Society. Albania's civil society reflects a dominant culture imported from the donor community and an underdeveloped philanthropic culture domestically. Limited financial resources hamper the development of human capacities within the sector. However, unlike 2006, when many prominent civil society activists joined the governmental sector, 2007 saw civil society increase in vibrancy. Activists were involved in monitoring and communicating the results of the February 2007 local elections in real time via the Internet. This was a successful endeavor that ultimately increased the transparency of the electoral process. Civil society actors participated actively in discussions on important new laws, such as the Law on Gender Equality, the Law on the State Police, and the Law on Higher Education. *Albania's civil society rating remains at 3.00.*

Independent Media. The high number of daily newspapers and low number of sold copies indicate a fragmented market and poor business management among print media in Albania. Distribution infrastructure is also poor throughout the country. Financial resources and ownership structures continue to be a concern for the media market. The current legal framework, including the Law on Digital Broadcasting, is not fully implemented and does not reflect developments in the growing digital broadcasting market in Albania. The human resources and enforcement capabilities of the National Council on Radio and Television remain limited. The biggest media controversy in 2007 involved Top Media, a leading media group critical of the current government, which received a fine of €11 million (US$17.1 million) for tax evasion. Scant information was disclosed about the enforcement of the fine, which puts in question the objectivity of the government's action. Albania's independent media rating remains unchanged at 3.75.

Local Democratic Governance. Since 1998, decentralization has become one of the major irreversible reforms in the country, with important implications for reforms in other areas. The broad consensus achieved to date and the high level of engagement suggests that there is a serious and solid political will to proceed with implementation of the reforms. After a tense relationship between the central and local governments in 2006, the political climate following the February 18, 2007 local elections could be characterized as one of cooperation. Jurisdiction over the inspectorate of the Construction Police was transferred to the local governments, which are responsible for verifying that projects have gone through proper licensing procedures. During 2007, legal and institutional measures were taken to transfer competences for the value added tax, local taxation, water supply, and sanitation from the central government to municipalities. *Albania's rating for local democratic governance remains at 2.75.*

Judicial Framework and Independence. Justice reform is one of the most serious and pressing problems for Albanian society. While the constitutional and legal framework for an independent justice system is in place, its organization and functioning have problems. Judicial proceedings are slow, court infrastructure remains poor, and prosecution is ineffective. The High Council of Justice needs to improve its system of appointing and evaluating judges to increase transparency. During 2007, the pace of reforms was slow, and in lieu of a clear strategy for building an efficient, professional, independent, and accountable judiciary, the government indulged in high rhetoric, blaming the justice system as the chief obstacle in the fight against corruption and organized crime. *The rating for judicial framework and independence remains unchanged at 4.00.*

Corruption. An anticorruption platform dominated the electoral campaigns and promises of the current government. Yet the European Commission's Albania 2007 Progress Report still considers corruption to be widespread and a serious problem in Albania. A series of measures were taken in 2007, including new legislation to simplify business registration and the introduction of the flat tax. However, the business climate is weak, and corruption is perceived as one of the factors that hinders economic development and investment. The most debated issue was the investigation by the Office of the General Prosecutor into the tendering procedures for a massive highway project connecting Durrës, the busiest port city of Albania, with Pristina in Kosovo. The investigation culminated with the prosecutor general's request to Parliament to lift the immunity of the former minister of public works, transport, and telecommunications, currently Albania's minister of foreign affairs, which Parliament agreed to do in the end. *The rating for corruption remains unchanged at 5.00.*

Outlook for 2008. In spring 2008, the NATO Summit in Bucharest will decide whether to invite Albania to join the organization in the near future. This decision is expected to have a crucial impact on the political stability of Albania and to affect the overall status of electoral and justice system reforms in the country.

Main Report

National Democratic Governance

1999	2001	2002	2003	2004	2005	2006	2007	2008
n/a	n/a	n/a	n/a	n/a	4.25	4.00	4.25	4.25

In 2006, Albania successfully concluded negotiations on the Stabilization and Association Agreement (SAA) with the European Union (EU). In Albania's post-SAA phase, 2007 was a crucial year to show political maturity by meeting required international standards for presidential and local elections.

Thanks to the mediation of then president Alfred Moisiu and international community backing, local elections were held on February 18, 2007. The center-left coalition succeeded in urban areas, including the capital. Edi Rama, leader of the Socialist Party, won his third consecutive mandate as mayor of Tirana in a race against former minister of the interior Sokol Olldashi from the ruling coalition. The center-right coalition won in areas that were traditionally considered strongholds of the Left. This showed an increased level of political maturity among the electorate but also a divided center-left opposition in some areas. On March 11, June 17, and September 23, 2007, three parliamentary by-elections were won by the Democratic Party. Although they were held in a polarized environment, they were conducted peacefully, but with irregularities verified by the Central Electoral Commission (CEC).

A three-fifths consensus among members of Parliament (MPs) is required to elect the president of the republic. The ruling party conditioned its participation in the consensus on the 2007 presidential election on the dismissal of the prosecutor general. This proposal led to the boycott of four parliamentary sessions by the opposition. On July 20, in the fourth round, the votes of six Socialist MPs, who acted against their parties' decision not to take part in the election, allowed the ruling coalition candidate, Bamir Topi, to receive 85 votes and become the next president.

Overall, parliamentary life in Albania has been dominated by interparty accusations and an acceleration of investigative commissions, leading to polarization and few tangible results. The most significant example of this is Parliament's failure to achieve progress on electoral and judicial reforms, which constitutionally need a broad political consensus.

In October 2007, the OSCE, together with the nongovernmental organization (NGO) European Movement in Albania, initiated a project to increase the role of Parliament in fulfilling Albania's SAA obligations by organizing policy forums with various stakeholders and constituencies in the country. However, it remains to be seen whether this initiative will strengthen the ties between Parliament and special interest groups or contribute to the improvement of policy making in Albania's EU-integration agenda.

The government has made it a priority to improve the functioning of Albania's market economy through reforms. Modernizing the fiscal system, reducing the informal economy, simplifying business registration through a "one-stop-shop" system, and reducing corruption are stated goals of these reforms. However, new legislation on tax fines was approved in April 2007 without consulting the business community, showing that the constitutional obligation to consult with interested groups prior to undertaking legislative initiatives is still lacking. The new law requires that a business pay a disputed tax figure, along with 15 percent of any penalty, before the business can file a legally allowed court appeal disputing the sum. This law, which was criticized by the business community, is not in line with EU practices.[1] An €11 million (US$17.1 million) fine imposed for tax evasion on Top Media, known for its criticism of the government, caused controversy in the media community, civil society, and opposition, which jointly organized protests against the ruling.

In October 2007, Prosecutor General Theodhori Sollaku asked Parliament to lift the immunity of then Minister of Public Works, Transport, and Telecommunications Lulzim Basha, regarding corruption charges involving the biggest infrastructure project in decades, the building of the Durrës-Morinë highway between Albania and Kosovo. The ruling coalition was reluctant at first,[2] but faced with political and public pressure from the opposition and media, it removed Basha's immunity on December 27, 2007. Simultaneously, Parliament initiated dismissal proceedings on Sollaku by setting up an investigative commission and accusing him of political bias; Sollaku was dismissed by President Topi on December 22.

On November 14, Minister of Justice Ilir Rusmali was forced to resign after his subordinate, General Director of Prisons Sajmir Shehri, disclosed in a press conference a recorded conversation of the brother of the minister asking for favors in a public tender for the renovation of a pre-detention facility in Durrës. Prime Minister Sali Berisha accepted Rusmali's resignation as setting a new positive precedent for Albanian democracy.

On the whole, national democratic governance in Albania in 2007 was characterized by the ruling coalition's tendency to control independent institutions (including the Constitutional Court, the Office of the General Prosecutor, the High Council of Justice, and the Office of the Public Procurement Ombudsman) through the appointment of figures closely linked with the ruling coalition, and the failure of a splintered opposition to capitalize on this trend.

Electoral Process

1999	2001	2002	2003	2004	2005	2006	2007	2008
4.25	4.00	3.75	3.75	3.75	3.75	3.50	4.00	4.00

Albania's transition toward democracy has been accompanied by contested election and accusations of electoral fraud from both sides of the political spectrum. The last parliamentary elections held in 2005, which brought to power the center-right coalition led by the Democratic Party, met international standards and partially paved the way for concluding the SAA with the EU. In November 2005, the OSCE/Office for Democratic Institutions and Human Rights (ODIHR) issued a report on the parliamentary elections, with recommendations concerning voter lists, ID cards for voters, election management without political interference, and the disclosure of political party finances.

To address these issues before the local elections in 2007, an ad hoc parliamentary committee on electoral reform was set up in January 2006, but members failed to reach an agreement on changes to the electoral code. This had a negative impact on the elections. The main issues of disagreement related to the interim civil registry of electors and the use of birth certificates as voter identification. Similarly, Parliament's nomination of a CEC member on a proposal from the right wing provoked the opposition, which claimed that such a proposal should come from the left wing, in accordance with the electoral code.

Delays in amending the electoral code and the failure of political parties to cooperate with the CEC led to practical problems in organizing the local elections. In the absence of a political consensus, the president, honoring his constitutional obligation, set January 20, 2007 as the date for holding the elections. On January 3, upon the president's initiative, the political parties signed an agreement that opened the way for amendments to the electoral code. Following that, the president changed the date for local elections to February 18, 2007.

The electoral changes only partly reflect the OSCE/ODIHR recommendations. The interim civil registry now allows citizens to register to vote in a different constituency from that of their residence using birth certificates. Article 154 of the Constitution was amended to increase the number of CEC members from 7 to 9 and the number of election commissioners of the ballot-counting groups from 7 to 14. The local elections went smoothly without major incidents, although the process of counting the votes did not meet the legal deadlines and the final results were not declared until three months later. According to the final report of the OSCE/ODIHR on June 5, 2007, the local government elections "only partly met OSCE commitments."

As revealed in the elections, voting with birth certificates, accompanied by two other documents, was a complicated procedure that created confusion in some cases. Electors did not have sufficient time to familiarize themselves with the voter lists. Simultaneously, the increased membership of the CEC and counting groups was not sufficiently justified, and political party interference often blocked the electoral process.

Moreover, Albania entered the local elections without a complete and accurate civil registry or identification documents in place. The setting up of a full, accurate, and computerized national civil registry, based on an accurate address system, is needed to avoid the use of birth certificates, which are prone to forgery. According to Minister of the Interior Bujar Nishani, "The preparation of identification documents with the inclusion of biometric data is expected to be realized in 2008."[3]

In May 2007, the Parliament created another ad hoc committee to complete the electoral reform, this time in view of the parliamentary elections due in 2009. The committee discussed how to make election structures apolitical, starting with the CEC and lower-level commissions, as well as how to better handle appeals and complaints.

Civil Society

1999	2001	2002	2003	2004	2005	2006	2007	2008
4.00	4.00	3.75	3.75	3.50	3.25	3.00	3.00	3.00

During the Communist regime, the concept of civil society was nonexistent in Albania. A form of collective association, although formally not under the umbrella of the Communist Party, was used as a political weapon by the regime and created a low regard for associations in public opinion. Seventeen years after the fall of communism, despite some positive achievements, Albania is still struggling to develop a vibrant civil society.

Freedom of assembly and association in Albania are guaranteed by the Constitution. The legal framework for civil society organizations is open and non-restrictive. Consequently, the creation of business associations, trade unions, professional associations, NGOs, and Chambers of Commerce are free of state intervention. However, after a weak year in 2006, when most prominent civil society activists joined the governmental sector, limited improvement was noticed in the third sector in 2007. Civil society activists were involved in discussions on important new laws, such as the Law on Gender Equality, the Law on the State Police, preparation for electoral reform, and the Law on Higher Education.

NGOs were engaged throughout the country in monitoring the February local elections, which featured online reporting of the results. The Open Society Foundation in Albania supported a joint initiative of two NGOs, Elections to Conduct Agency and MJAFT!, to communicate the election results in real time from 12 regions of the country. Activists from these organizations were stationed in the ballot-counting centers and reported periodically. This project increased the transparency of the process and communicated election results to citizens in record time. These were consistent with the final results officially published by the CEC three months after the elections.

In May 2007, a group of civil society representatives drafted a set of moral criteria for 2007 presidential candidates regarding corruption, cooperation with the Communist intelligence service, declaration of assets, and political loyalty. Unfortunately, this initiative was not adopted by political actors in the process of electing the new president in July.

In October, the government started a series of debates with civil society actors and special interest groups in connection with the draft Strategy on Development and Integration, slated for adoption in early 2008. The debate was structured in three pillars: European and Euro-Atlantic integration, good governance, and social and economic development. However, it remains to be seen whether this strategy will be a conduit for civil society input to policy formulation. The government failed, however, to consult civil society actors on amendments to the Law on Nongovernmental Organizations, which were adopted by Parliament in October. According to these amendments, NGOs are not exempt from taxes on profit-making activities.

The civil society agenda in Albania continues to be donor-driven, and limited financial resources hamper the development of human capacities within the sector. The line distinguishing NGOs and consultancy firms is in some cases blurred. Civil society organizations still lack sustainable resources, organizational capacity, and advocacy skills.

The role of the media in promoting civil society organizations remains essential. Some examples of this are media coverage of the Transparency International report for Albania on corruption perceptions and MJAFT! reports monitoring the country's parliamentary life.

For the first time, the 2007–2008 state budget allocated some €1.5 million (US$2 million) for civil society, although by the end of 2007, no funds had yet been made available to civil society. The official procedure for allocating this budget to various initiatives is unclear, and there is a risk that funds will go to organizations closest to the government.

Albanian legislation does not provide any fiscal incentives for NGOs involved in social services. Regarding independent media, a new journalist trade union was established to negotiate a collective contract with media owners. This is considered of paramount importance since the relationship between media owners and journalists is to a large extent not governed by labor law.

Independent Media

1999	2001	2002	2003	2004	2005	2006	2007	2008
4.50	4.25	4.00	4.00	3.75	4.00	3.75	3.75	3.75

Albania's Constitution guarantees freedom of expression and freedom of the press, and no criminal proceedings against journalists were reported in 2007. The government has made a commitment to press freedom, which is reflected in an order by the prime minister that government officials shall not bring defamation charges against journalists.

However, many media outlets are under the influence of political and economic interests. As Remzi Lani, executive director of the Albanian Media Institute, put it: "In the case of Albania, the media equation encompasses a variety of problems related to the market, the relations between media owners and government, media transparency and ownership, the relations between journalists and media owners, lack of investigative journalism, and editorial independence."[4]

The current legal framework does not safeguard journalistic independence from the pressure of media owners. Yet since May 2007, legislation is pending in Parliament to remove prison sentencing for defamation, based on a draft prepared by the Albanian Media Institute and the Justice Initiative. Bringing Albania legislation on defamation in line with European standards has been a continuous recommendation by the EU and is included as a short-term priority in the revised European Partnership for Albania.

The government prepared a draft Law on Digital Broadcasting that was approved on May 28, 2007. Though it was not signed by the president, it became effective after the legal waiting period for action by the president. The law takes into account suggestions from the European Commission and the Council of Europe regarding pluralism and transparency.

The Albanian media market is saturated but fragmented, as evidenced by the high number of daily newspapers and low number of copies sold. There are 27 national dailies with fewer than 100,000 copies sold altogether—an imbalance for a country with 3.5 million people. Newspaper distribution is poor throughout Albania; consequently, print media do not regularly reach areas that are far from the capital.

According to the National Council on Radio and Television (NCRT), Albania has 85 television and 49 radio broadcasters. There are three national public television broadcasters, including Albanian Radio Television, and two national public TV broadcasters, TV Klan and TV Arbëria. In spite of the number of broadcasters, local media continue to be sensational and focused on celebrity news, rather than substantive or political content.

Financial resources and ownership structures in the media market continue to be a concern. None of the media mentioned above has ever declared bankruptcy, although generally speaking, most of them do not generate income. They are used more by their owners to gain influence. A study entitled *Indicator of Public Interest* published in August 2007 by the Media Plan Institute (based in Sarajevo) shows that Albanian Radio Television (the former state television broadcaster) serves the interests of the government, while other broadcasters primarily serve the interests of their owners.[5]

In September 2007, the Parliament adopted new legislation that increased membership of the NCRT and the steering council of Albanian Radio Television with experts suggested by the parliamentary opposition. It remains to be seen whether this amendment will increase the confidence of political actors and operators in the NCRT, which in the past has been accused of bias and licensing media close to the government. The NCRT is a regulatory and monitoring body but it has shown little capacity to fulfill its responsibilities; during past years, three chairpersons have been replaced or forced to resign.

In May 2007, the NCRT began a campaign to close down media outlets broadcasting outside their licensed areas, yet it failed to take action against nationwide broadcasters similarly in breach of license. The operators concerned accused the NCRT of selectively targeting those media that were critical of the government. The fine imposed on Top Media for tax evasion stirred a heated debate in the media community, political circles, and civil society, which considered this action an attack on independent media. The fine had not yet been enforced as of year's end.

Local Democratic Governance

1999	2001	2002	2003	2004	2005	2006	2007	2008
n/a	n/a	n/a	n/a	n/a	3.25	2.75	2.75	2.75

In the Albanian Constitution, Article 13 reflects the requirements of the European Charter of Local Self-Government by stating that "local government in the Republic of Albania is founded upon the basic principle of decentralization of power and is exercised according to the principle of local autonomy." Legislation on the organization and functioning of local government serves as a basic tool in expanding this principle by recognizing the existence of different identities and communities in Albania. Since 1998, decentralization has become one of the major irreversible reforms in the country. The broad consensus achieved to date and the high level of political engagement suggest that there is a serious and solid political willingness to proceed with the implementation of reforms.[6]

Albanian local government consists of 373 local units: 65 municipalities in urban areas and 308 communes in rural areas. The municipalities and communes have representative councils, which are elected by the population through a proportional system and closed lists. The mayors and heads of communes are directly elected by the population through a majority system. There are 12 regional councils, which comprise the mayors and heads of communes of the municipalities and communes within their boundaries, as well as representatives of the municipal and communal councils in proportion to their respective populations.

Additionally, there are a number of state services that conduct their activity at the local or regional level. The central government is represented in regions by the prefects. Their main mission is to guarantee sovereignty, constitutional order, and protection of public health and to manage, supervise, monitor, and coordinate the activity of state institutions at the local level.

The legal framework provides that local governments are financed by revenues collected from local taxes and fees, funds transferred from the central government, and funds derived from shared national taxes. Local government authorities are authorized to borrow funds for public purposes in a manner that is consistent with law. However, no such law had been adopted in Parliament as of the end of 2007.

The state budget for 2006–2007 introduced a new method of transferring unconditional funds, which were usually kept by line institutions at the central level and primarily included infrastructure projects. Investments in educational and social programs do not fall under unconditional transfers, since they are considered to be shared responsibilities between the central and local governments. On the contrary, conditional transfers to fund investments are not transparent or predictable and generate significant regional disparities.[7]

After a tense relationship between the central and local governments in 2006, the political climate that followed the local elections of February 18, 2007, could be characterized as one of cooperation. During 2007, legal measures were taken to transfer competences for the value added tax, local taxation, water supply, and sanitation from the central government to municipalities. However, no implementing measures had been adopted by the government by year's end.

Upon request from the municipality of Tirana, the Constitutional Court[8] found the powers of the Construction Police and the Council for Regulation of Territory of the Republic of Albania (CRTA) to be in conflict with the constitutional and European principles of autonomy and decentralization, and the Parliament adopted a new law in May 2007. According to this law, the Construction Police were transformed into an inspectorate under local government jurisdiction, and the composition of the CRTA was changed in favor of local government representation. Besides the mayor and the representative of the minister of public works, three members of the CRTA will be elected by the majority in the municipal council, three others by the minority, and one member by three-fifths of the municipal council.

However, the process of defining the geographic scope and competences of regional authorities, based on recommendations of the Congress of Local and Regional Authorities of the Council of Europe, had not been finalized by the end of 2007. The allocation of financial resources and tasks between central and local governments as well as among municipalities remains unbalanced. Yet on the whole, 2007 was a year of moderate progress in transferring responsibilities from central to local authorities.

Judicial Framework and Independence

1999	2001	2002	2003	2004	2005	2006	2007	2008
5.00	4.50	4.50	4.25	4.25	4.50	4.25	4.00	4.00

Though reforms in the Albanian justice system are crucial for the country's development, and serve as a guarantee for proper implementation of the SAA, these reforms continue to be quite slow. The main concerns include the independence and accountability of judges, appointment procedures and performance evaluations, unclear division of competences, slow judicial proceedings, and lack of transparency.

Legal reform of the justice system has had mixed results. For instance, the 2006 amendment to the Law on the High Council of Justice aimed to eliminate conflict of interest among members of the High Council of Justice, but it failed to address other important issues facing the institution. The amendment to the Law on Organization and Functioning of the Ministry of Justice in March 2007 simply eliminated the names of departments in the organizational charts of the ministry, leaving substantial issues unaddressed.

The most significant events during 2007 were the reorganization of district courts, the dismissal of Prosecutor General Theodhori Sollaku, and the draft of the Law on Judicial Power, which was still pending in Parliament at year's end. The draft law provides for the creation of administrative courts, transparent assignment of cases, and improvements in the career structure of judges. Contrary to the existing law, the new draft requires that appointed judges be graduates of the School of Magistrates in order to increase professionalism among judges.

The draft law fails to address the division of competences between the two inspectorates of the High Council of Justice and the Ministry of Justice. However, regarding disciplinary proceedings and the discharge of judges, the draft law is considered an improvement over existing legislation. Furthermore, the draft law specifies the criteria and procedures for appointing court chairmen and provides a list of their duties.

One of the most disputed decisions in the judicial system was the reorganization and reduction of district courts from a total of 29 to 21 in an effort to increase court efficiency and transparency. According to the National Strategy for the Development and Integration, reorganization of the courts should increase both efficiency and transparency of trials and provide the necessary space and infrastructure within the courts. However, the reorganization raised serious problems because there is a constitutional guarantee for the continuous employment of judges. In the reorganizations, 24 judges—along with many administrative staff—lost their jobs.

The European Assistance Mission to the Albanian Justice System (EURALIUS) made recommendations concerning a three-step strategy for the organization of courts, but these guidelines were ignored by the Ministry of Justice.[9] The strategy features, as step one, the smooth integration of small courts into branches of bigger courts while preserving full jurisdiction; step two, reducing jurisdictions of court branches to certain criminal cases and small contested civil cases; and step three, closing the court branches at a specified time for each district court.

According to a EURALIUS report in November 2007, in just two months after the implementation of Albania's own reorganization project, workloads increased in central courts, efficiency was reduced, and costs increased owing to the frequent traveling of judges, secretaries, and case files.[10] Judicial infrastructure remains poor, and most courts lack adequate courtrooms, archives, and equipment.

At the beginning of 2007, the High Council of Justice approved a new system for evaluating judges, developed with assistance from the Council of Europe. The system was applied only in Durrës and Elbasan district courts during the year, but will be expanded gradually to all district and appeals courts in Albania.

In October 2007, on the request of 28 MPs from the ruling majority, a second investigation commission was established in connection with the discharge of Prosecutor General Theodhori Sollaku. The first attempt to discharge Sollaku was unsuccessful owing to then President Alfred Moisiu's refusal to sign the discharge decree. President Moisiu maintained there were insufficient constitutional grounds for taking such action. The Constitutional Court, which was asked by the prosecutor general to rule on the constitutionality of the parliamentary investigation, upheld its previous decision, saying that "the Parliament has no competence to check and evaluate the decision of the prosecutors in concrete cases."[11]

However, the July 2007 election of President Bamir Topi, who previously served as leader of the parliamentary group of the Democratic Party, was considered a second chance for the ruling party to discharge the prosecutor general. The opposition boycotted the second committee, considering it biased, but on November 5, Parliament voted for the second time for the prosecutor general's dismissal. According to Spartak Ngjela, an MP who used to be one of the more distinguished leaders of the right-wing coalition and a former close aide of Prime Minister Berisha, "The dismissal of the prosecutor general is an attempt of the prime minister to control independent institutions."[12] On November 22, President Topi discharged Sollaku, and Parliament approved Ina Rama as the new prosecutor general on the president's proposal.

The history of Albanian prosecutors general since the fall of the Communist regime abounds with dismissals, resignations, and judgments by the Constitutional Court that have never been enforced.[13] Yet, overall relations between the government and the High Council of Justice have improved with the election of President Topi and the replacement of High Council of Justice deputy chairman Ilir Panda with Kreshnik Spahiu.

Corruption

1999	2001	2002	2003	2004	2005	2006	2007	2008
6.00	5.50	5.25	5.00	5.25	5.25	5.25	5.00	5.00

An anticorruption platform made up the bulk of the electoral campaign of the current government led by Prime Minister Sali Berisha. Yet more than two and a half years since this coalition came to power, corruption is widespread in Albania and continues to be a serious problem.

The main commitments undertaken to fight corruption are improving the legislative framework; increasing professionalism, transparency, and efficiency in public administration; aligning public procurement legislation and practices with the EU *acquis*; and reducing the list of officials with immunity. The government has implemented the United Nations Convention Against Transnational Organized Crime, and the criminal code is in line with the Council of Europe Criminal Law Convention on Corruption (though civil legislation needs to be brought into line with the Council of Europe Civil Law Convention on Corruption). The High Inspectorate for Declaration and Audit of Assets made some progress on enforcing asset declaration obligations, although there is no proper investigative mechanism within this institution. Out of 3,500 persons who are under legal obligation to declare their assets and private interests, only 87 failed to meet this obligation.

Progress has been made in computerizing business registration with the so-called "one-stop shop" established in September 2007. However, the costs of starting and closing a business in Albania remain relatively high, and corruption is perceived as one of the factors that hinders economic development and investment.

A special corruption and economic crime unit was established within the Office of the Prosecutor General that has led to the arrest of a number of high-level officials. In September 2007, nine officials were arrested on corruption charges, including the deputy minister of public works, transport, and telecommunications and the general director of road construction, in connection with key public tenders for the reconstruction of national roadways.

Both officials came from the ranks of the Christian Democratic Party (CDP), which entered into the governing coalition after the February 2007 local elections. The leader of the CDP, who is now minister of health, considered the arrests to be attacks from segments of the Democratic Party in an effort to damage the reputation of the growing CDP.

In October 2007, Prosecutor General Sollaku asked Parliament to lift the immunity of then minister of public works, transport, and telecommunications Lulzim Basha, accused of corruption involving the Durrës-Morinë highway project between Albania and Kosovo. The government entered into a contract with a construction company without a secured project, as required by Albanian legislation on public procurement. The ruling coalition considered the prosecutor general's request politically motivated and was reluctant to lift Basha's immunity. But faced with political and public pressure from the opposition and the media, Parliament decided to lift Basha's immunity on December 27, 2007 (although Sollaku was already discharged in November).

On November 7, 2007—the day after the release of the Albania Progress Report by the European Commission, which considered Albania to have widespread corruption[14]—the anticorruption unit within the Office of the General Prosecutor arrested the secretary general of the Ministry of Labor and Social Affairs on corruption charges involving a public tender for the reconstruction of the ministry building.

According to Transparency International's Corruption Perceptions Index, Albania continues to be perceived as the most corrupt country in the Western Balkans region, but there are improvements in terms of worldwide ratings: Albania's score improved from 2.6 in 2006 to 2.9 in 2007 (on a scale of 1 to 10 where 10 indicates the lowest levels of perceived corruption.)

The financial transparency of political parties remains an issue. According to the Constitution, political parties are under an obligation to declare their financial sources. Although the electoral code empowers the CEC to collect political party financial declarations, the CEC lacks the proper mechanisms to investigate them.

In January 2007, the government approved rules of public procurement that complement the newly approved Law on Public Procurement. The Public Procurement Agency also approved bid standard documents, complying with the new legislation. These new procedures are steps toward full alignment of Albanian legislation and practice with the EU *acquis*. However, the current system does not guarantee impartiality on review procedures, marking a clear deviation from SAA obligations. The Public Procurement Agency remains responsible for decisions on complaints. The establishment of the public procurement ombudsman, elected by the Parliament on a proposal from the government, has not yielded the desired results owing to insufficient independence and lack of executive powers.

On the whole, 2007 showed that even the current government, which came to power on an anticorruption platform, is not immune to corruption. A more systematic and strategic approach is needed in fighting corruption by putting in place systems of accountability in the administration and judiciary and by increasing transparency.

▌ AUTHOR: DITMIR BUSHATI

Ditmir Bushati is executive director of European Movement in Albania, a nonprofit think tank based in Tirana. He was assisted in the preparation of this report by Elvana Thaci.

---

[1] *Albania 2007 Progress Report*, Commission of the European Communities, Brussels, November 6, 2007, p. 29.

[2] On November 8, 2007, the Committee on Mandates and Immunities asked further clarifications from the prosecutor general—in essence, considering his request as unacceptable.

[3] Report submitted by Minister of Interior Bujar Nishani to the Parliament, on November 1, 2007.

[4] Interview with Remzi Lani, executive director of Albanian Media Institute, November 8, 2007.

[5] See, Ilda Londo, "Reporting in line with specific interests of TV Stations" pp. 41–42 in "Indicator of Public Interest" available in the magazine on media developments in South East Europe at www.mediaonline.ba and South East European Network for Professionalization of Media at at www.seenpm.org.

[6] Francis Conway and Sabina Ymeri, *Albania Decentralization Status Report, Local Government and Decentralization in Albania Program*, USAID, Washington, D.C., 2007, p. 1.

[7] Ibid., p. 8.

[8] See Judgment of the Constitutional Court No. 29, dated December 21, 2006.

[9] See EURALIUS recommendations on different models of reorganization of district courts available at www.euralius.org.

[10] See EURALIUS Report on the impact on reorganization of district courts available at www.euralius.org.

[11] See Judgment of the Constitutional Court No. 26/2006 available in English language at: www.gjk.gov.al.

[12] Statement made by Member of Parliament Spartak Ngjela, November 5, 2007, plenary session on dismissal of the prosecutor general, Albanian Parliament; also Interview with Spartak Ngjela, TV Vizion Plus, November 5, 2007.

[13] See, Judgments of the Constitutional Court No. 75/2002, No. 76/2002, No. 18/2003, No. 26/2006.

[14] *Albania 2007 Progress Report*, Commission of the European Communities, Brussels, November 6, 2007, p. 10.

Armenia

by Anna Walker

Capital: Yerevan
Population: 3.2 million
GNI/capita: US$4,950

The social data above was taken from the European Bank for Reconstruction and Development's *Transition Report 2007: People in Transition*, and the economic data from the World Bank's *World Development Indicators 2008*.

Nations in Transit Ratings and Averaged Scores

	1999	2001	2002	2003	2004	2005	2006	2007	2008
Electoral Process	5.25	5.50	5.50	5.50	5.75	5.75	5.75	5.75	5.50
Civil Society	3.50	3.50	3.50	3.50	3.50	3.50	3.50	3.50	3.50
Independent Media	4.75	4.75	4.75	5.00	5.25	5.50	5.50	5.75	5.75
Governance*	4.50	4.50	4.50	4.75	4.75	n/a	n/a	n/a	n/a
National Democratic Governance	n/a	n/a	n/a	n/a	n/a	5.00	5.00	5.25	5.25
Local Democratic Governance	n/a	n/a	n/a	n/a	n/a	5.50	5.50	5.50	5.50
Judicial Framework and Independence	5.00	5.00	5.00	5.00	5.00	5.25	5.00	5.00	5.25
Corruption	5.75	5.75	5.75	5.75	5.75	5.75	5.75	5.75	5.75
Democracy Score	4.79	4.83	4.83	4.92	5.00	5.18	5.14	5.21	5.21

With the 2005 edition, Freedom House introduced separate analysis and ratings for national democratic governance and local democratic governance to provide readers with more detailed and nuanced analysis of these two important subjects.

NOTE: The ratings reflect the consensus of Freedom House, its academic advisers, and the author(s) of this report. The opinions expressed in this report are those of the author(s). The ratings are based on a scale of 1 to 7, with 1 representing the highest level of democratic progress and 7 the lowest. The Democracy Score is an average of ratings for the categories tracked in a given year.

EXECUTIVE SUMMARY

Since Armenia gained independence in 1991, its democratic development has been hampered by the absence of an effective system of checks and balances, concentration of power in the presidency, and a centralized system of government, which together have fostered weak governance and widespread corruption. Close links between the country's political and business elites have impeded the development of transparent, democratic state institutions. Flawed elections have contributed to public cynicism toward the authorities and skepticism about the value of participating in political and civic activities. The unresolved conflict with Azerbaijan over the territory of Nagorno-Karabakh has deterred foreign investors and hampered trade diversification and regional cooperation. However, Armenia's progress in macroeconomic stabilization has been relatively successful, with annual average real growth in gross domestic product reaching over 13 percent in 2003–2007. Although poverty rates are declining, there remains a popular perception that many Armenians have yet to benefit from these macroeconomic successes. This has contributed to disillusionment in Armenia's political and economic transition.

Parliamentary elections, held on May 12, were the focus of political activity in 2007. Observers judged that the conduct of the elections improved compared with earlier ones, but concerns remained over issues such as vote counting and tabulation. A consolidation of power among the business and political elites was also evident. The authorities made some progress in approving the legislation necessary to enable constitutional reforms enacted in 2005 to come into effect, including the passage of a new judicial code, but the impact of these reforms will not be fully realized until 2008. Treatment of witnesses in police custody continued to cause concern, as did a number of attacks on journalists. Delays in the approval of a new anticorruption strategy strengthened doubts as to the authorities' commitment to addressing corrupt practices.

National Democratic Governance. Although progress was made in harmonizing Armenia's legislation with the revised Constitution (amended in 2005), in actuality the balance of power continued to lie with the presidency and the government in 2007. Moreover, the May parliamentary elections further entrenched the close links between business and politics. The weak rule of law remained a concern, highlighted by several attacks on businessmen and public figures. *Although the legislative framework for improved governance is being strengthened, concrete steps toward a more accountable political system and more even distribution of the balance of power were lacking in 2007. Thus, Armenia's rating for national democratic governance remains at 5.25.*

Electoral Process. Observers judged Armenia's parliamentary elections, held on May 12, 2007, to have demonstrated improvement compared with earlier elections, although there were still significant shortcomings. Amendments to the electoral code allowed for a fairer electoral process, and training of election officials ensured that they were better able to fulfill their roles. However, some parties exploited unclear legislation related to campaign financing to their advantage, and the counting and tabulation of votes remained problematic. *Ongoing concerns for the close connections between business and politics, which hinder the rotation of power, and flawed vote tabulation, mitigate the comparatively positive assessments of the election; thus, Armenia's rating for electoral process improves only slightly from 5.75 to 5.50.*

Civil Society. Nongovernmental organizations are becoming more active in public life but remain hampered by financial constraints and a reliance on external funding. Progress in developing legislation to improve the financial sustainability of civic groups stalled in 2007. The government is engaging more with civil society, but increased state funding for such groups raises fears that their independence will be compromised. The mobilization of civil society groups to protest proposed new legislation that would have restricted the retransmission of foreign programs by public broadcast media was a positive development in 2007. *Armenia's rating for civil society remains at 3.50.*

Independent Media. Observers judged media coverage of the parliamentary elections to have improved compared with previous years, although bias toward pro-establishment parties was still evident, and opposition parties reported that the high cost of advertisements was prohibitive. Moreover, government attempts to restrict the retransmission of foreign broadcasts heightened concerns over the lack of pluralism in the broadcast media in 2007 and raised fears that media objectivity in the run-up to the 2008 presidential election would suffer. Amendments to broadcast media legislation provide for a more balanced composition of the regulatory body, reducing the number of presidential appointees. But, these changes will come into effect only in 2011, and media organizations were unable to influence the drafting process. *Although media coverage of the elections improved in 2007, the government's attempts to limit foreign broadcasts raise fears that pluralism will be further eroded, keeping Armenia's rating for independent media at 5.75.*

Local Democratic Governance. Some progress was made toward drafting legislation that would enable the decentralization of authority to local bodies in 2007. More controversially, in October 2007 the authorities presented proposals for the election of the mayor of Yerevan by a municipal council. Although the new system removes the president from the appointment process, it does not allow for the direct election of the mayor by residents, nor does it allow independent candidates to stand. Furthermore, the new mayor would have the power to appoint the heads of Yerevan's districts; these are currently chosen by direct election. Reliance on transfers from the state budget for around 60 percent of revenues continued to impede local governments' autonomy in 2007, as did their absence of powers to set local tax rates. *As new legislation to decentralize government authority has yet to be enacted and the proposed system for electing Yerevan's mayor is of concern, Armenia's rating for local democratic governance remains unchanged at 5.50.*

Judicial Framework and Independence. In 2007 the Parliament approved a new judicial code aimed at enhancing judicial independence and transparency, but this will come into effect only in 2008. Concerns remained at the influence of the executive over the judiciary in 2007, following the dismissal by the president of a judge who had earlier acquitted two businessmen charged with fraud and tax evasion. The authorities attributed his dismissal to charges that he had violated Armenian law when presiding over several cases; critics contended that he had been sacked for his acquittal of the businessmen. Prosecutors have lost the right to conduct pre-trial investigations; this prerogative passes to the police and the national security service. The death of a witness in police custody in May highlighted ongoing concerns at the mistreatment of witnesses and prisoners, and the passage of new legislation allows the police to conduct surveillance without first seeking judicial approval. *The newly passed judicial code is commendable and when it comes into effect will likely yield improvements. However, given continued concerns about the current influence of the executive over the judiciary and the mistreatment of witnesses, Armenia's rating for judicial framework and independence worsens slightly from 5.00 to 5.25.*

Corruption. Corruption remains a substantial obstacle to Armenia's political and economic development. The close links between the political and economic elite were reinforced by the May parliamentary elections, which saw many wealthy businessmen returned to Parliament. The authorities began work on a new anticorruption strategy only toward the end of the year; it had been due to be approved at the end of 2006. In a July survey commissioned by the International Republican Institute, 97 percent of respondents considered the wrongdoing and corruption of political leaders or authorities to be a "rather serious" or "very serious" problem in Armenia. *The authorities' failure to produce a new anticorruption strategy reinforces existing doubts about their lack of political will to make genuine inroads into reducing corruption; thus, Armenia's rating for corruption remains at 5.75.*

Outlook for 2008. Attention has already turned to the presidential election, scheduled for early 2008, in which the current prime minister, Serzh Sarkisian, has long been considered the front-runner candidate. The reemergence of former president Levon Ter-Petrossian could nevertheless render Sarkisian's passage to the presidency more problematic, if Ter-Petrossian is able to rally broad-based support behind his candidacy. In these circumstances, opposition supporters and the independent media are likely to face greater restrictions on their activities, either overtly or through administrative pressure such as the use of tax investigations. Implementation of the new judicial code and of anticorruption measures will demonstrate the extent of the authorities' commitment to a more democratic and accountable political system.

MAIN REPORT

National Democratic Governance

1999	2001	2002	2003	2004	2005	2006	2007	2008
n/a	n/a	n/a	n/a	n/a	5.00	5.00	5.25	5.25

The Constitution enshrines the principle that Armenia "is a sovereign, democratic, social state governed by rule of law" and provides for the separation of powers. However, it has so far failed to ensure an effective system of checks and balances among the branches of government.

In 2007, although progress was made in harmonizing Armenia's legislation with the revised Constitution (amended in 2005), the balance of power continued to lie with the presidency and the government. Moreover, the outcome of the May 2007 parliamentary elections, in which pro-government forces won an overwhelming majority of seats, reinforced the government's influence over the legislative agenda. As a result, the Parliament generally continues to act as a rubber stamp for government initiatives. A further negative development in 2007 was the entrenchment of the close links between business and politics that have become a defining feature of Armenia's political scene.

Weak financial resources continued to hamper the effectiveness of the government and the Parliament in 2007; central government tax revenue was equivalent to just 15.4 percent of gross domestic product in 2007, according to the National Statistical Service.[1] In May, the government announced a new three-year program to combat tax evasion, including the abolition of privileges for businesses and strengthened tax administration. However, previous initiatives to improve tax collection have had little success, seemingly owing to an absence of political will to address the issue. Moreover, many of Armenia's largest businesses—including some owned by parliamentarians—continue to make tax payments that appear inconsistent with their commercial success.

Public confidence in the Parliament and government is low, reflecting the fact that even though Armenia has adopted a progressive legislative framework in some areas, implementation remains weak. A survey of 1,200 households (the Armenia National Voter Study) conducted for the International Republican Institute (IRI) in July 2007, found 65 percent expressed an "unfavorable" opinion toward the Parliament and 61 percent held a similar attitude toward the government.[2]

Public access to information about the activities of government and other public service bodies is enshrined in the 2003 Law on Freedom of Information. Imperfect enforcement of the legislation and a lack of awareness among officials of the requirements of the law have hampered its effectiveness. Nevertheless, the Freedom of Information Center, a nongovernmental organization (NGO) that— among other activities—monitors use of the law, has reported that journalists and

NGOs are increasingly making use of the legislation to challenge official refusals to release information.

The Parliament has a Web site, debates are usually open to the public and reported in the media, draft legislation is generally made publicly available, and all legislation approved by the Parliament is published in an official bulletin. The Ministry of Justice's Web site contains a database of legislation, government decisions, and Constitutional Court rulings. A negative development in 2007 was a ruling by the Constitutional Court that public television should no longer be legally obliged to broadcast parliamentary sessions, a decision that has reduced Parliament's accountability to the public. The speed with which controversial legislation can be approved with minimal or no public consultation also remained a concern.

In 2007, public procurement procedures were being reviewed to increase transparency. In addition, a new audit body, the Control Chamber, was established as provided in the revised Constitution. The new body replaces one that operated under the Parliament as a public accounts watchdog but lacked powers to act effectively. The new organization brings together several other audit and investigative bodies within ministries and is intended to be independent of parliamentary or government structures. However, the fact that appointing the chairman is a presidential prerogative—subject to parliamentary approval—raises the risk that this independence could be jeopardized.

As in 2006, several physical attacks against public figures in 2007 reinforced concerns of the "criminalization" of Armenian society and demonstrated that the rule of law is not yet well entrenched. In April, the mayor of Gyumri, Armenia's second largest city, survived an assassination attempt (which killed three of his bodyguards), while in August, the chief prosecutor of Lori region was shot dead. Relatives of people taken in for questioning by the police in connection with the latter incident asserted that violence had been used during the interrogations. Business disputes also escalated into gunfights on several occasions, and there were a few violent incidents among supporters of rival parties close to the election. A global survey of governance released by the World Bank in July 2007 concluded that Armenia had regressed in terms of rule of law compared with its 2002 report, although the Bank judged that it had improved its legal framework and developed a more stable political situation.[3]

The ongoing dispute with Azerbaijan over Nagorno-Karabakh remained a potential source of instability in 2007, particularly as there were increased clashes along the cease-fire line. The conflict has had wide-ranging economic repercussions, preventing intra-regional development projects; notably, in 2007 Armenia was excluded from a new railway project that will link Azerbaijan with Turkey via Georgia. The dispute has led to substantial expenditures for defense (the military received the largest share of state budget spending in 2007, at 16.9 percent) to the detriment of other sectors (such as health care and education).[4] A new National Security Strategy, approved by President Kocharian in February 2007, identifies Azerbaijan's growing threats to resolve the conflict by force as a specific threat to Armenia's security.

One legacy of the 1988–1994 war with Azerbaijan over the area of Nagorno-Karabakh has been that the armed forces and security services have played a large role in the country's political development, including the election to Parliament of several veterans in 2007. The Yerkrapah parliamentary faction of Nagorno-Karabakh veterans was instrumental in forcing the resignation of President Levon Ter-Petrossian in 1998, having rejected his apparent willingness to negotiate a stage-by-stage resolution of the conflict with Azerbaijan. This issue had particular resonance in 2007, when Ter-Petrossian broke a near decade-long silence to return to politics. Criticizing Armenia's current leadership and accusing it of presiding over a corrupt regime, Ter-Petrossian announced that he intended to stand for the presidency in the 2008 election and stated that Armenia's sustainable development depended on a resolution of the Nagorno-Karabakh conflict.

Electoral Process

1999	2001	2002	2003	2004	2005	2006	2007	2008
5.25	5.50	5.50	5.50	5.75	5.75	5.75	5.75	5.50

Armenia's constitutional and electoral framework enshrines the principle of universal and equal suffrage by secret ballot and provides for regular, free, and fair elections. In most elections since independence, observers have concluded that the authorities failed to ensure free and fair elections. Observers' conclusions about the most recent national legislative election (held on May 12, 2007) were generally more positive, although they noted that there were still significant shortcomings.

A total of 22 political parties and 1 bloc contested the proportional part of the election, under which 90 of the 131 seats in the National Assembly were allocated. (The share of mandates elected by party list was raised from 75 to reduce opportunities for vote buying.) A further 119 candidates stood for election in the 41 majoritarian constituencies. Few candidates reported difficulties registering, and the large number of parties participating indicates that the registration process was inclusive. Voter turnout was 59.4 percent, up from 52 percent in the 2003 parliamentary election, suggesting greater voter confidence in the electoral process.

Amendments to the electoral code made since the 2003 election were generally held to have paved the way for a fairer process. Steps were taken to rectify inaccuracies in the voter register by establishing a central computerized list, which enabled voters to check in advance whether they were registered. The inclusion of names of non-residents nevertheless opened up opportunities for abuse. Moreover, the removal of the right of citizens to vote abroad, which resulted from changes to the citizenship legislation in 2007, in effect disenfranchised many Armenians working abroad.

The Central Election Commission (CEC) increased the transparency of its operations in the 2007 election, holding regular press conferences. Training for members of election commissions at all levels ensured that they were better able to fulfill their roles. However, even though the composition of election commissions was broadened from being just presidential nominees to include representatives from parliamentary factions, the fact that the president still has the right to appoint one commission member remained an issue of concern.

The Republican Party of Armenia (RPA), the leading party of the outgoing government, secured the largest number of seats (63), followed by Prosperous Armenia (25). The two parties formed a coalition government led by Serzh Sarkisian, the former defense minister who was first appointed prime minister in March, following the sudden death of Andranik Markarian from a heart attack. The coalition government was also supported by the Armenian Revolutionary Federation (ARF) on an issue-by-issue basis.

Prosperous Armenia had been founded by a wealthy businessman, Gagik Tsarukian, in 2006. Although Tsarukian claimed that his party offered an alternative to Armenia's longer-standing political groupings, its close connections to the existing political elite were apparent. Pre-election opinion polls suggested that the party would perform much more strongly than it did and that it might even rival the RPA for a parliamentary majority. However, despite its financial largesse in the run-up to the election, Prosperous Armenia failed to win over as many voters as it had expected. The result of the election nevertheless demonstrated the consolidation of power among Armenia's business and political elites that has occurred in recent years. Inadequate legislation regarding party funding has left parties reliant on private financial sources and therefore susceptible to donor influence. The immunity from prosecution enjoyed by parliamentary deputies has also encouraged business monopolists to seek election.

Opposition parties performed poorly in the election, having failed to present a united front—a reflection of the fact that parties tend to be driven more by personality than by policy. Only Orinats Yerkir (Country of Law), led by Artur Baghdasarian, and Heritage, led by Raffi Hovannisian, won seats, taking 10 and 7, respectively. (Two members of Orinats Yerkir have since defected.) The Alliance Party, led by a former Nagorno-Karabakh veteran, Samvel Babayan, also won 1 seat; nonpartisan (in practice pro-government) candidates secured the remaining 9 mandates.

The amendments to the electoral code required that at least 15 percent of candidates on every party or bloc list be women, but only 5 of the 119 majoritarian candidates were women. A total of 12 women won seats, up from 7 in the outgoing Parliament; none of these were in single-mandate constituencies.

According to observers from the OSCE/ODIHR, the conduct of voting was good or very good in 94 percent of polling stations observed. The largest domestic observer, the It's Your Choice NGO, reported that the voting and vote counting proceeded in a comparably peaceful and balanced environment.

However, observation reports from both missions noted that there were still shortcomings in the conduct of the election, in particular questions surrounding campaign finances and problems with the counting and tabulation of votes. Even though the formal campaign started only a month before the election, in practice parties used a combination of administrative resources and private funds to begin campaigning much earlier. Moreover, 19 civil society groups issued a joint statement criticizing both the pre-election period and the election campaign, noting in their press release that the methods used had created "an atmosphere of fear, suspicion, and personal insecurity."[5]

The OSCE/ODIHR noted that the separation between the state and the governing party, the RPA, appeared to be blurred in the run-up to the election (one example being high-profile celebrations marking the fifteenth anniversary of Armenia's army). Moreover, in addition to Prosperous Armenia, Gagik Tsarukian established a charity that distributed financial and other assistance to rural inhabitants in the year prior to the election, apparently contravening legislation prohibiting political parties from offering financial aid to the public.

Vote counting and tabulation procedures were bad or very bad in 34 percent of polling stations observed, according to the OSCE/ODIHR, and It's Your Choice also reported shortcomings in the summarization and announcement of the election results. Three opposition parties and the Impeachment Bloc (a coalition of opposition groups formed to push for the impeachment of Kocharian) tried unsuccessfully to appeal the results in the Constitutional Court. Although the Court upheld the CEC's decision, it did acknowledge deficiencies with regard to campaign and party financing.

A failure to investigate electoral fraud and bring perpetrators to justice has been one of the main factors behind public disillusionment with the electoral process. In a positive move, three criminal cases were prosecuted successfully in conjunction with violations in the 2007 election, including charges of bribery and falsification.

The most recent presidential election was won by the incumbent, Robert Kocharian, beating Stepan Demirchian in a second-round runoff in 2003 with winning 67.5 percent of the vote (according to the CEC). However, international and domestic observers did not judge the election to be free and fair.

Civil Society

1999	2001	2002	2003	2004	2005	2006	2007	2008
3.50	3.50	3.50	3.50	3.50	3.50	3.50	3.50	3.50

Public participation in civil society activities in Armenia remains limited. Several developments in 2007 indicate that civil society groups are becoming more effective and better able to engage with the government and the public. However, the increased activity of so-called GONGOs (government-operated nongovernmental organizations), particularly in election observation, was of concern because of the negative implications for the independence of civil society.

A total of 52 domestic groups monitored the May 2007 parliamentary elections; the largest, It's Your Choice, had around 4,000 volunteers. The fact that some of these groups had no prior involvement in election-related or democracy-building activities but had amended their charters shortly before the elections to include election observation among their missions raised doubts about their effectiveness or impartiality.

Most NGOs are still concentrated in the capital, Yerevan, and in the northern regions, where they tend to have better-developed organizational and management capacity than those in other regions. One noteworthy development is an increasing interest in the formation of umbrella organizations, to provide the manpower for grassroots activities in the case of election-related activities or to strengthen advocacy and lobbying skills. For example, the nonprofit Foundation for Small and Medium Business has formed a Business Advocacy Network to improve business operating conditions.

Civil society groups are generally able to carry out their work without interference either from the government or from extremist organizations. The registration process for organizations is relatively straightforward, although because it is centralized, it is more difficult for regional organizations to complete the process. The International Center for Not-for-Profit Law has judged the legislation governing charities and NGOs to be in compliance with international good practices of NGO regulation, although implementation of the legislation is at times patchy.

Nonprofit organizations are subject to taxation on property, vehicles, and employee wages, and NGOs must disclose their revenue sources in order to establish their tax liability. Nonprofit organizations are prohibited from direct income generation and are not permitted to participate in government tenders. This has serious implications for their financial sustainability. The establishment of limited liability companies is one way in which they can generate income, but these are subject to taxation in the same way as businesses. Progress on enacting a Law on Volunteers, which would have eased the tax burden and improved access to donor funding that requires in-kind contributions, stalled in 2007.

Most civil society groups remained dependent on foreign financing in 2007, for example from diasporic organizations, leading to continued concern that this practice weakens the civic sector's incentive to establish strong links with Armenian society. It has also led to public perceptions of civil society groups as businesses sponsored by foreign donors rather than civic organizations. Of concern to some civil society groups is the fact that government funding of NGOs is increasing, leading to fears that this will negatively affect the sector's independence. In addition, foreign governments are decreasing their direct financing of NGOs, preferring to distribute resources to the government that are then allocated to civic initiatives.

Armenia's legislative framework has not kept pace with the complexity of civil society, and changes in ministerial personnel have slowed progress in developing policy. For example, the development of new mental health legislation, pushed for by the Mental Health Foundation, stalled in 2007 following personnel changes in the Ministry of Health. Moreover, NGOs have complained that even though they are able to participate in the drafting of government initiatives, this is merely to satisfy international pressure for NGO inclusion in policy making and that their opinions are not taken into consideration in final documents.

More positively, state bodies such as the Public Services Regulatory Commission and the Ministry of Agriculture continued to cooperate with the Consumer Rights Association (a local NGO), which in 2007 pushed successfully for the establishment of a working group to monitor food security issues. In addition, a number of independent civil society groups participate in the monitoring of the U.S.-funded Millennium Challenge Corporation's five-year (US$236 million) rural development program, which began to distribute funds in 2007.

Media coverage of civil society activity is increasing, possibly because this provides less controversial material than, for example, political issues. Media groups and civil society united in mid-2007 to protest proposed new legislation that would have imposed restrictions on the transmission of foreign programs on public radio; the vote subsequently failed in the Parliament for lack of a quorum, indicating that the protest had played a part in influencing deputies. However, a less successful campaign was one by environmental groups, which failed in their attempts to persuade the government to reject the award of a license to a mining company, Armenian Copper Program, to develop mines in a forested region in northern Armenia. In addition, media organizations failed to influence the content of amendments to Armenia's broadcasting legislation, approved in February, that appear to allow for continued political influence over regulatory and licensing decisions.

Armenia's Constitution guarantees the right to establish and join trade unions, although this right can be restricted for those serving in the armed forces and law enforcement agencies. Issues such as wage increases and the payment of back wages have in the past led to strikes, but these are rare. The Union of Industrialists and Entrepreneurs represents the interests of Armenia's largest businesses.

Political influence over universities remained an issue of concern in 2007, when a lecturer at Yerevan State University was dismissed after students presented a petition to the rector stating that he had used his lectures to discredit the government. Although the court of appeals ruled that the dismissal was unsubstantiated, it also judged that he could not return to work because of his poor relations with the university's management. Anecdotal reports of teachers being encouraged to vote for the RPA in the May 2007 parliamentary election raised further concerns about the politicization of the education system.

Independent Media

1999	2001	2002	2003	2004	2005	2006	2007	2008
4.75	4.75	4.75	5.00	5.25	5.50	5.50	5.75	5.75

Press freedoms are guaranteed in Article 27 of the Constitution. In practice, these freedoms have come under threat in recent years, and 2007 was no exception, witnessing government attempts to restrict the retransmission of foreign broadcasts and several instances of violence against journalists. Although media coverage of the parliamentary elections improved compared with previous years (notwithstanding continued bias in favor of pro-government parties), coverage of political parties throughout the rest of the year lacked objectivity.

Election observers reported that the public broadcast media met their legal obligations concerning free airtime to political parties during the campaign. However, in their pre-election reporting most private national broadcast media focused on the activities of the government and three pro-government parties, offering virtually no critical coverage. Positive developments were the broadcasting of pre-election debates and of video information for voters about the election code. The public television channel H1 offered the most coverage of opposition activities. Radio coverage of the election was more comprehensive, including more critical viewpoints. Print media provided more diverse, if not necessarily more balanced or analytical, viewpoints, reflecting their ownership; the majority of Armenia's more than 100 print publications are privately owned but have limited circulation and hence are less influential than the broadcast media.

Opposition parties and observers expressed concern at the rates charged by broadcast media for pre-election political advertisements. These tended to be higher than the commercial fees normally charged, rendering the cost of access prohibitive for many of the parties. Some local television stations opted not to accept any party advertisements at all. Given the lack of objectivity in election-related coverage by the national broadcast media, both these measures put opposition parties at a disadvantage.

Contrary to fears of media associations, violence against journalists did not increase in the run-up to the parliamentary election, as had happened before in previous polls. However, unrelated to the election there were several assaults against journalists in 2007, including, in September, an attack on Hovhannes Galajian, editor of *Iskakan Iravunk*—the second time that he had been assaulted in a year. He again attributed the attack to his reporting. Two other editors, Suren Baghdasarian and Ara Saghatelian, reported arson attacks on their cars, which they also attributed to their work.

Several journalists also faced court cases. In June, a freelance journalist, Gagik Shamshian, was given a 30-month suspended prison sentence following his conviction on charges including fraud; protesting his innocence, he linked his arrest to his reporting. In November, two editors of opposition newspapers faced charges including assault, following their arrest in the run-up to an opposition rally organized by Levon Ter-Petrossian.

Although advertising revenue is growing, most broadcast media remain dependent on private financing, and their reporting tends to be supportive of the authorities, reflecting the close connections between business and political circles. Those media outlets that do try to report alternative viewpoints have experienced difficulties. For example, media outlets that attempted to report on Ter-Petrossian's political activities faced pressure that appeared to be connected to their coverage. In

October, tax officials inspected Gala television company in Gyumri shortly after it had broadcast a speech made by Ter-Petrossian, one of only two regional outlets to do so. The company subsequently faced accusations of tax evasion and had some of its assets and bank accounts frozen.

In 2007, libel remained a criminal offense, although no journalists were prosecuted; critics argue that the independent media use self-censorship, preferring to offer noncontroversial programs to avoid attracting libel charges or antagonizing the authorities. In October, the Yerevan Press Club (YPC) expressed concern that television channels had ceased to cover events such as news conferences. The fear is that this will further limit opposition access to the media in the run-up to the presidential election. In December, the YPC reported that the broadcast media were openly promoting Serzh Sarkisian's campaign and displaying obvious bias against Ter-Petrossian. The broadcasters responded that they were reporting on Sarkisian in his capacity as prime minister, not as a presidential candidate.

Government attempts to restrict the retransmission of foreign broadcasts heightened concerns over the lack of pluralism in the broadcast media in 2007. In June, the government put forward legislative proposals that would have made it illegal for state outlets to retransmit foreign programs and would have raised substantially the tax paid by private companies to do this. These changes would have affected in particular radio broadcasts by the U.S.-funded Radio Free Europe/Radio Liberty (RFE/RL). Although there is a legitimate business case for public media not to be obliged to broadcast foreign programs, the proposed restrictions had negative implications for media pluralism; observers judged RFE/RL's election coverage to have been among the most objective.

The bill unexpectedly failed to pass in the second reading, owing to the absence of a parliamentary quorum. Protests by NGOs and media associations were believed to have been instrumental in persuading some deputies not to attend. However, shortly afterward Armenian Public Television and Radio refused to renew its contract with RFE/RL, citing legal, technical, and contractual issues. RFE/RL is now broadcast only by a Yerevan-based private company, Ar Radio Intercontinental, whose coverage is not nationwide.

Changes enacted to broadcasting legislation in February 2007 to bring it in line with the constitutional amendments approved in 2005 should eventually ensure a more diverse composition of the National Commission for Television and Radio, responsible for regulating the broadcast media and granting licenses. Parliament will appoint four of the council's eight members, with the remaining four appointed by the president (who currently appoints all the members). However, the amendments will come into effect only in 2011, ensuring continued presidential influence. Media organizations criticized the government for not allowing them to participate in the drafting of the amendments.

The Internet continued to offer a diversity of opinions, and there were no instances of government attempts to control access to or to censor Web sites in 2007. The high cost of connecting nevertheless remained a barrier, but the removal of all monopoly services from the telecom service provider Armentel (including that of connecting to international services) and cuts to duties imposed on Internet service providers should eventually reduce costs by increasing competition. About 6 percent of the population used the Internet in August 2007, according to the International Telecommunication Union.

Local Democratic Governance

1999	2001	2002	2003	2004	2005	2006	2007	2008
n/a	n/a	n/a	n/a	n/a	5.50	5.50	5.50	5.50

Chapter 7 of the Constitution and national legislation provide a framework for local self-government, but in practice weak financial resources and extensive central government control circumscribe the authority and activities of local administrations. In 2007, the focus on the parliamentary election and subsequent preparations for the presidential election resulted in little progress being made in decentralizing authority to local governments.

For administrative purposes, Armenia is divided into 10 regions, subdivided into around 930 communities. Governors appointed by the central government, and approved by the president, administer the 10 regions and in turn appoint their own staff. Regional governors are responsible for administering policy in a wide range of fields (including finances, public utilities, and urban development), coordinating the activities of regional agencies of state administration, mediating between the central and local governments, and regulating intercommunity issues. The Ministry of Territorial Administration exercises control over the regional governors.

Constitutional amendments approved in 2005 provide for the election of the mayor of Yerevan (which is designated a community), who is currently appointed by the president. In October 2007, the authorities revealed proposals to set up a new municipal council, elected by proportional representation, that would in turn elect the mayor. Although this removes the president from the appointment process, it does not allow for independent candidates to stand for mayor; nor does it allow for the mayor to be directly elected by residents. Moreover, the new mayor would have the right to appoint the heads of Yerevan's administrative districts; these are currently chosen by direct election.

Councils of Aldermen (the representative body for communities) ranging from 5 to 15 members are responsible for approving community budgets and supervising their implementation. However, the central government has authority over budgetary loans, credits, and guarantees and establishes procedures for the collection and distribution of local taxes. Local governments are given little opportunity to participate in the drafting of legislation; once laws have been approved, implementation programs are often lacking.

Land and property taxes and revenue from state duties are the main sources of local tax revenue. Even these must be collected by regional branches of the state treasury. Local authorities have no powers to set tax rates and are therefore heavily dependent on financial transfers from the state budget, which provided around 60 percent of total local budget revenue in 2007. Disbursement delays are common, limiting the capacity of local governments to meet their spending requirements, draft long-term development programs, or ensure the timely payment of staff salaries. The distribution of financial resources from central to local government is uneven and poorly targeted, but discussions over how to better distribute these resources were ongoing in 2007. In addition, legislation on intercommunity unions, under discussion in 2007, should enable communities to better provide services.

Community heads (equivalent to a mayor) are accountable to the Council of Aldermen; they are elected for three-year terms on the basis of universal, equal, and direct suffrage by secret ballot. They can be dismissed by the regional governor only following a court decision. Regional governors nevertheless have often used administrative resources as a means of influencing local authorities. In theory, local authorities have the courts to protect their powers and defend the rights of the local community, but because of the judiciary's dependence on the executive, its impartiality in such cases is questionable.

Local governments have the right to form associations to protect and promote their interests. Such associations include the Communities Union of Armenia and the Communities Finance Officers Association of Armenia. International organizations are working with local government associations to strengthen the capacity of local government (for example, through more effective budget mechanisms and increased decentralization). One such project is the Armenia Local Government Program, funded by USAID.

Although citizens are allowed to participate in local decision making, interaction between local governments and their constituents is generally limited. Citizens are entitled to submit draft resolutions to local governments, and most meetings of the Council of Aldermen are open to the media and the public. The public is entitled to full access to information concerning the activities and decisions of regional and local governments. However, many local officials are unaware of their obligation to inform the public; in addition, a lack of funds restricts their capacity to publicize the information.

Political parties do not play a major role in local elections, although they are entitled to nominate candidates. More commonly, citizens are nominated as independent candidates through civil initiatives; party affiliation can be stated on the ballot. The most recent local elections were held in September–October 2005. As in previous years, the opposition largely boycotted the elections, regarding the process as deeply flawed. Although the elections were to a certain extent competitive—in that multiple candidates took part—these tended to be rival pro-government figures vying for influence over local resources. Reports of vote buying and indirect bribery of voters by candidates with promises to repair local infrastructure remained a defining feature of the 2005 local elections.

Assessments of the elections varied. A local election-monitoring group, It's Your Choice, reported that candidates had been hindered during the campaign and that voter lists remained inaccurate. A small observation mission sent by the Council of Europe judged that the electoral process and voter lists had improved compared with previous elections.

Judicial Framework and Independence

1999	2001	2002	2003	2004	2005	2006	2007	2008
5.00	5.00	5.00	5.00	5.00	5.25	5.00	5.00	5.25

Chapter 2 of Armenia's Constitution provides for fundamental political, civil, and human rights, but there are substantial barriers to protecting them effectively. These stem largely from the weak judiciary, which lacks independence. This has led to low public confidence in the capacity of the judicial system to protect the population from unjust treatment by the state.

In February 2007, the Parliament approved a new judicial code aimed at enhancing the independence and effectiveness of the judiciary. International experts have described the new code as progressive. However, as it is scheduled to enter into force on January 1, 2008, its effectiveness remains to be seen. Throughout 2007 the influence that the executive enjoys over the judiciary remained a concern. This was highlighted by the dismissal in October of Parven Ohanian, a judge of a court of the first instance. In July, Ohanian had acquitted two senior executives from a coffee-importing company, Royal Armenia, on a range of charges (including tax evasion and fraud) in a rare example of a judgment going against the prosecution. Shortly afterward, the Justice Department requested that the Council of Justice investigate apparent violations of Armenian law presided over by Ohanian. Having found him guilty, the council requested that President Kocharian remove Ohanian from office. Ohanian stated publicly that his dismissal was linked to his acquittal of the businessmen, but the Council of Justice stated that the two events were unrelated.

Mistreatment of prisoners and witnesses by the authorities remained a concern in 2007. In May, Levon Gulyan, a restaurant owner who had witnessed a shooting, died after falling out of a window while being questioned at the Ministry of Internal Affairs. The police claimed that he jumped out of the window, either trying to escape or committing suicide; Gulyan's family and human rights organizations affirm that he was killed by his interrogators. A medical report by foreign independent experts concluded there was some evidence that he had been beaten prior to the fall.

According to *Monitoring of Democratic Reforms*, a report compiled by the YPC in conjunction with members of the Partnership for Open Society Initiative and released in June 2007, 80 percent of defendants deny the testimony they gave during pre-trial investigations, on the grounds that it was extracted under torture. Victims of abuse are often reluctant to press charges for fear of the consequences. In 2007, three former soldiers who had spent three years in prison for killing two colleagues continued to assert that their confessions had been extracted under torture. A court annulled the verdict against them in December 2006 on the grounds that the trial was flawed, but in 2007 military prosecutors continued to press for their retrial.

In 2007, some local human rights groups supported claims by several people that they had been imprisoned on political grounds. In July, Vartan Malkhasian was sentenced to two years' imprisonment following his conviction on charges of plotting to overthrow the government, while a fellow member of the Alliance of Armenian Volunteers (which opposes any territorial concessions by Armenia to Azerbaijan), Zhirayr Sefilian, received an 18-month sentence for possession of illegal weapons. The case against them was built on the basis of statements they had made during a meeting of the alliance in December 2006. The men denied the charges and claimed that they had been imprisoned to prevent them from organizing post-election protests.

A high-profile detainee in 2007 was Aleksandr Arzumanian, a former minister of foreign affairs, who was arrested in May on charges of money laundering. Arzumanian was eventually released in September, but the charges against him were not dropped. Arzumanian asserts that the charges were politically motivated and stem from the authorities' fear that he would help coordinate demonstrations after the parliamentary election.

Armenia's judicial system provides for the presumption of innocence, the right of persons not to incriminate themselves, and access to a public hearing by a fair and impartial court. However, prosecutors' requests for arrests are seldom refused, bail is infrequently granted, and acquittals are rare. One development in 2007 was the ending in December of prosecutors' rights to conduct pre-trial investigations, aimed at reducing the substantial influence prosecutors have had over the investigative process; this authority passes to the police and national security service. Although in theory a positive step, continued reports of torture of witnesses and suspects during police interrogations raise concerns that this authority could be misused. Also of concern was new legislation approved in October that grants more powers to the police to conduct surveillance operations (for example, phone tapping) without the need to secure court approval.

Although Armenia's procedural justice code sets a one-year maximum for criminal inquiries, delays in the criminal justice system are common, owing in part to a shortage of qualified judges. The April 2003 criminal code stipulates a maximum sentence of life imprisonment; prisoners are entitled to apply for parole after 20 years. In 2007, the maximum sentence other than life remained 15 years.

The Armenian Constitution and laws guarantee freedom of religion. However, the Armenian Apostolic Church enjoys privileges that are not accorded to other religions. A total of 63 religious groups were reported as registered with the Office of the State Registrar in 2007. There were no reports of any being refused registration, but societal discrimination against groups such as Jehovah's Witnesses remained a concern.

Since 2006, evasion of either military or civilian service has been deemed a criminal offense. Those choosing the civilian option must serve for 42 months—almost twice as long as those carrying out military service. As of September 2007, 69 Jehovah's Witnesses were in prison for refusing to carry out the alternative service on the grounds that it was overseen by the military.

Chapter 2 of the Constitution guarantees intellectual property rights and the right to own and inherit property; it states that no one can arbitrarily deprive a citizen of his or her property. However, in 2006 Parliament approved legislation that enables the government to confiscate private real estate for use by property developers where this is deemed to be in the public or state interest. In 2007, the eviction of residents from central Yerevan to make way for the development of new commercial and residential property and streets remained an issue of concern among local lawyers, NGOs, and opposition politicians, who argued that people's property rights were not being respected. Citizens were unsuccessful in challenging the evictions in court. With respect to business rights, a lack of training for judges in commercial issues has left many investors disillusioned with the court system as a viable legal recourse.

Although the Constitution enshrines freedom of assembly, the authorities have discretionary powers to restrict demonstrations. In the run-up to the 2007 parliamentary election, several opposition parties—including Heritage and Country of Law—reported that they had faced difficulties in holding public meetings because of governmental pressure on authorities who refused to allow them to rent out meeting rooms.

Several Web sites offer information and advice to citizens on judicial issues. The World Bank is funding judicial reform projects with a view to increasing the efficiency of judicial services and to broadening public access to information about the system. Armenia is also receiving support for judicial reforms from the European Union under an Action Plan concluded in November 2006.

Corruption

1999	2001	2002	2003	2004	2005	2006	2007	2008
5.75	5.75	5.75	5.75	5.75	5.75	5.75	5.75	5.75

Corruption at all levels of government continues to impede Armenia's political and economic development. Not only has this fostered public cynicism toward the authorities, it has inhibited the development of a competitive business environment.

The government made little progress in implementing anticorruption initiatives in 2007. Its three-year anticorruption strategy ended in 2006, but the drafting of a new program for 2008–2012 began only toward the end of the year.

A total of 157 corruption-related crimes were registered in January–August 2007; in 2007, no high-ranking officials were prosecuted for corruption-related crimes. In 2006, the Council of Europe's Group of States Against Corruption highlighted concerns over the wide scope of people enjoying immunity from prosecution and the lack of protection for witnesses, victims of corruption, and whistle-blowers. Armenia was due to present a report on fulfilling the body's recommendations at a plenary session of the organization in December 2007.

A survey of 1,500 households conducted in August 2006 by the Center for Regional Development/Transparency International (TI) Armenia, with the support of the United Nations Development Program, found that 89 percent of respondents believed that corruption was a problem, up from 80 percent in the 2002 survey.[6] In findings that were published in January 2007, 33.5 percent of respondents to the survey believed that corruption had increased significantly over the previous three years. Among the services and sectors considered most corrupt were the health care and education systems, the electoral system, and the traffic police; the president, prime minister, and ministers were judged the most corrupt institutions. In addition, 18.3 percent of respondents believed absence of political will to be the main cause of corruption. Dominance of clan interests over state interests and poor law enforcement were also considered important factors.

The TI survey found that 87.8 percent of respondents judged public tolerance to be a cause of corruption in Armenia, suggesting that the majority of people perceive corruption to be too deeply entrenched to be eradicated. In the Armenia National Voter Study conducted in July 2007 for the IRI, 97 percent of those questioned judged the wrongdoing and corruption of political leaders and authorities to be a "rather serious" or "very serious" problem. However, only 11 percent of respondents said that corruption was one of the most important issues facing Armenia.

Armenia's score in the Transparency International 2007 Corruption Perceptions Index was 3.0 (with 10 being the least corrupt). Although this was a slight improvement compared with 2006 (2.9), the failure to register greater progress adds justification to the skepticism among observers that the government's anticorruption initiatives have had little impact.

The state's formal involvement in the economy is low in comparison with that in other transition countries. However, despite constitutional provisions explicitly banning parliamentary deputies and government members from engaging in business interests, public officials in practice encounter few limitations to economic participation and have extensive business interests. The 2007 election returned many wealthy businessmen to Parliament.

Armenia's financial disclosure laws are insufficient to combat corruption. All government officials and civil servants are required by law to annually declare revenue and property belonging to them and their families. However, the tax authorities are not required to verify financial statements, and gaps in the legislation enable government officials to register property in the names of relatives. The authorities have limited powers of investigation and can impose only relatively lenient fines for reporting false information. Moreover, weak implementation of generally sound business-related legislation and the complexity of the tax and customs system increase the opportunities for official corruption. There is a perception that it is difficult to run a successful business without personal connections to public officials.

The Civil Service Council advertises employment vacancies on its Web site, but opportunities for discretionary decision making with respect to employment are still broad. Despite progressive salary raises since 2003, average monthly civil service wages, at 98,610 dram (US$324) in November 2007,[7] are still insufficient to attract and retain high-caliber staff or deter them from seeking bribes. A focus on inspections and audits as the main tools of legislation enforcement increases the opportunity for bribe taking.

Attempts to expose official corruption carry risks. Following allegations of corruption against the customs system, two senior officials from a coffee importer, Royal Armenia, were arrested in 2005 on charges of fraud. Released in July 2007 after being cleared of all charges, the men were subsequently rearrested, and in November the court of appeals sentenced them to prison terms of six and two years on charges including fraud and tax evasion.

▮ Author: Anna Walker

Anna Walker is a senior editor specializing in the South Caucasus and Central Asia at the Economist Intelligence Unit in London.

---

[1] National Statistical Service of the Republic of Armenia, Tax and Budget Sector, Statistics of the State Budget on Finances for period January–December 2007. http://www.armstat.am/file/article/sv_12_07r_211.pdf.

[2] Armenia National Voter Study July 2007, International Republican Institute, et al., July 2007. http://www.iri.org/eurasia/armenia/pdfs/2007%20September%2017%20Survey%20of%20Armenian%20Public%20Opinion%20July%205-12%202007.pdf.

[3] *Worldwide Governance Indicators,* World Bank, 2007. http://www.worldbank.org/governance/wgi2007.

[4] National Statistical Service of the Republic of Armenia, Tax and Budget Sector, Statistics of the State Budget on Finances for period January–December 2007. http://www.armstat.am/file/article/sv_12_07r_211.pdf.

[5] Social Policy and Development Center, *Public Statement,* May 14, 2007. http://www.cspda.org/articles/Statement.htm.

[6] *2006 Corruption Perception in Armenia,* Center for Regional Development/Transparency International Armenia and the United Nations Development Program, 2006. http://www.transparency.am/dbdata/UNDPbook_eng_web_2.pdf.

[7] National Statistical Service of the Republic of Armenia. Real Sector, Income and Expenses of Population, Salary and Other Expenses for period January–December 2007. http://www.armstat.am/file/article/sv_12_07r_142.pdf.

Azerbaijan

by H. Kaan Nazli

Capital:	Baku
Population:	8.4 million
GNI/capita:	US$5,430

The social data above was taken from the European Bank for Reconstruction and Development's *Transition Report 2007: People in Transition*, and the economic data from the World Bank's *World Development Indicators 2008*.

Nations in Transit Ratings and Averaged Scores

	1999	2001	2002	2003	2004	2005	2006	2007	2008
Electoral Process	5.50	5.75	5.75	5.75	6.00	6.25	6.50	6.50	6.50
Civil Society	4.75	4.50	4.50	4.25	4.50	4.75	5.00	5.25	5.25
Independent Media	5.50	5.75	5.50	5.50	5.75	6.00	6.00	6.25	6.25
Governance*	6.25	6.25	6.00	5.75	5.75	n/a	n/a	n/a	n/a
National Democratic Governance	n/a	n/a	n/a	n/a	n/a	6.00	6.00	6.00	6.00
Local Democratic Governance	n/a	n/a	n/a	n/a	n/a	6.00	6.00	6.00	6.00
Judicial Framework and Independence	5.50	5.25	5.25	5.25	5.50	5.75	5.75	5.75	5.75
Corruption	6.00	6.25	6.25	6.25	6.25	6.25	6.25	6.25	6.25
Democracy Score	5.58	5.63	5.54	5.46	5.63	5.86	5.93	6.00	6.00

* With the 2005 edition, Freedom House introduced separate analysis and ratings for national democratic governance and local democratic governance to provide readers with more detailed and nuanced analysis of these two important subjects.

NOTE: The ratings reflect the consensus of Freedom House, its academic advisers, and the author(s) of this report. The opinions expressed in this report are those of the author(s). The ratings are based on a scale of 1 to 7, with 1 representing the highest level of democratic progress and 7 the lowest. The Democracy Score is an average of ratings for the categories tracked in a given year.

EXECUTIVE SUMMARY

zerbaijan had a brief period of independence between 1918 and 1920 and regained independence when the Soviet Union collapsed in 1991. The transition was complicated by the war with Armenia and separatist Armenians over the Nagorno-Karabakh enclave. The conflict resulted in massive social problems and more than one million internally displaced persons. The sides signed a cease-fire agreement in May 1994, shortly after President Heydar Aliyev (Heydər Əliyev) came to power. During his 10-year term in office, Aliyev strengthened his hold on the country through an enormous concentration of power in the presidency. In October 2003, the presidency changed hands when former prime minister Ilham Aliyev (İlham Əliyev), son of Heydar Aliyev, gained the office following controversial elections that were deemed not free and fair by the OSCE. The 2005 parliamentary elections, including the reruns in May 2006, registered improvement in some areas, mostly on the campaigning period, but did not meet a number of international standards. The lack of comprehensive election reform and continued governmental pressure on the political opposition in 2007 weakened hopes further that the Ilham Aliyev administration would push forward a genuine democratization program.

National Democratic Governance. President Aliyev continued to enjoy significant authority in Azerbaijan's governmental system in 2007 and was able to sustain political and economic stability thanks to a high level of economic growth. The National Assembly, Azerbaijan's legislative branch, maintained a low profile. Opposition participation in parliamentary proceedings has been low, owing to a continued boycott of the Parliament by some opposition parties. *Owing to a lack of significant changes in the balance of power between the president and the legislature in 2007, Azerbaijan's rating for national democratic governance remains at 6.00.*

Electoral Process. There was little discussion during 2007 about electoral processes as there were no by-elections or reruns and the presidential elections will be held no earlier than late 2008. Both the government and the ruling party signaled that they would coalesce behind President Aliyev in the coming elections, while the authorities continued talks with the Council of Europe Venice Commission on reforming election commissions to increase opposition representation, with no obvious sign of progress in 2007. Governmental pressure on local opposition representatives continued. *The lack of any significant changes on the legislative or policy environment leaves Azerbaijan's rating for electoral process unchanged at 6.50.*

Civil Society. Little progress was made in 2007 in Azerbaijan's civil society sector, with nongovernmental organizations (NGOs) still facing registration, tax, and funding problems. The trend of increasing governmental pressure on NGOs and religious communities continued. *Owing to little change in the legislative or policy environment for organizations, Azerbaijan's rating for civil society remains at 5.25.*

Independent Media. The media continued to operate under governmental and legal pressure, with Azerbaijan criticized by the international community for having the highest number of imprisoned journalists among all members of the OSCE. President Aliyev did not respond to local and international demands raised throughout the year to pardon seven journalists currently in prison, and there was no progress in changing press laws to expand freedom of speech. *Azerbaijan's rating for independent media remains at 6.25.*

Local Democratic Governance. Local governance in Azerbaijan is not democratic, as the government continues its practice of directly appointing local administrators. The national government continued to dominate local governance in 2007. *Reflecting the central government's continued authority in local governance, Azerbaijan's rating for local democratic governance remains at 6.00.*

Judicial Framework and Independence. The government maintained substantial authority over the judiciary in 2007. The trials of Farhad Aliyev (Farhəd Əliyev) and former health minister Ali Insanov (Əli İnsanov) on corruption charges were concluded nearly two years after the arrests of the former government ministers. *Owing to the judiciary's continued restrictions on the access of media to high-profile trials (such as Ali Insanov and Farhad Aliyev) and capricious implementation of the rule of law, Azerbaijan's rating for judicial framework and independence remains 5.75.*

Corruption. Corruption continued to be a pervasive and problematic issue for Azerbaijan in 2007, as the auditing capacity of the legislative branch remained weak and government investigations of former officials and civil servants appeared to be politically driven. More time is needed to assess whether certain improvements regarding the transparency of the State Oil Fund of Azerbaijan Republic (SOFAZ) represent a long-term trend that is sustainable in the absence of international pressure. The government maintains a strong presence in anticorruption commissions. *Azerbaijan's rating for corruption remains 6.25.*

Outlook for 2008. President Ilham Aliyev is expected to maintain his position in the presidential elections in October 2008 thanks to Azerbaijan's impressive level of economic growth from substantial oil revenues, which will increase even further as the Baku-Tbilisi-Ceyhan oil and South Caspian natural gas pipelines step up exports. Rising inflation and the overwhelming share of oil exports in the national economy will continue to pose challenges to the authorities. There appears to be little chance of progressing toward a resolution of the Nagorno-Karabakh conflict in 2008, as both Armenia and Azerbaijan face presidential elections in which the Karabakh issue is expected to feature prominently.

MAIN REPORT

National Democratic Governance

1999	2001	2002	2003	2004	2005	2006	2007	2008
n/a	n/a	n/a	n/a	n/a	6.00	6.00	6.00	6.00

Azerbaijan has a centralized presidential system, with an executive branch made up of the president, the Office of the President, the prime minister, and the Cabinet of Ministers. The president enjoys significant authority over the executive, legislative, and judicial branches and is elected directly by the people for a five-year term. The president appoints all cabinet-level government administrators.

President Ilham Aliyev (İlham Əliyev) maintained his strong position throughout 2007 as his authority went uncontested, and an impressive level of economic growth continued to fuel the administration's popular support. Economic growth in 2007 was 25 percent, as exports from the Baku-Tbilisi-Ceyhan oil pipeline increased and the Baku-Tbilisi-Erzurum natural gas export pipeline began operations. Aliyev stated in April that his administration had created 535,000 jobs, an impressive achievement, if confirmed—most of them permanent and outside of Baku.[1] The president had pledged in 2003 to create as many as 600,000 jobs. Inflation also surged in the same period: 20 percent in 2007.

The administration undertook an ambitious infrastructure upgrade campaign in 2007, spending 87 percent of the government's US$2.2 billion investment program for the year for this purpose.[2] Under this plan, Azerbaijan will upgrade existing airports and build new ones. At the same time, the government plans to spend US$500 million (an increase of 80 percent over last year's expenditures) on construction and repair of highways.

The president serves as commander in chief of the Azerbaijani armed forces. In this capacity, he oversees defense and security efforts undertaken by the prime minister and the ministers of defense, internal affairs, and security. The Defense Council, created prior to Azerbaijan's independence in 1991, reports to and advises the president on defense matters. There is no civilian oversight of the Defense Council.

Azerbaijan's first National Security Concept, signed by Aliyev on May 24, emphasizes a need to improve the country's defensive capabilities in order to better respond to separatism and regional conflicts.[3] The document highlights the alignment of the Azerbaijani military more closely with NATO standards.[4] Annual military spending was reported to have reached US$1 billion in 2007 and is expected to go up to US$1.2–1.3 billion in 2008.[5] The government's priority remains that Azerbaijan start manufacturing its own military *materiel* in 2008, when a defense review focused on the 2009 to 2015 timeframe is scheduled to be finalized by the administration.

A June 10 meeting between President Aliyev and his Armenian counterpart, Robert Kocharian, did not make any visible progress on the resolution of the conflict over Nagorno-Karabakh,[6] and the work toward resolution appeared to be almost frozen through the year.[7] President Kocharian himself acknowledged in October that chances of a settlement are low before the 2008 presidential elections in both countries.[8]

The legislative branch consists of the 125-member National Assembly (Milli Mejlis). Members are elected for five-year terms from single-mandate constituencies —a rule that was established by a constitutional referendum in August 2002. The third National Assembly since independence was chosen in the November 2005 parliamentary elections, which gave the ruling New Azerbaijan Party (YAP) the largest number of seats—58 out of 125. The opposition parties won 10 seats, with the Azadliq (Azadlıq—meaning Freedom) bloc getting 6, while the mostly pro-government independents won the remaining 42 seats. YAP gained 5 additional seats in the rerun elections in May 2006, bringing its total to 63.

While the president cannot dissolve the Parliament, he enjoys a high level of authority over the legislature through YAP. Parliamentary sessions in 2007 were boycotted by the mainstream opposition parties except for the Musavat (Müsavat— meaning Equality) party of former parliamentary Speaker Isa Gambar (İsa Qəmbər), which won four of the six seats awarded to the Azadliq bloc that joined Musavat with the Popular Front of Azerbaijan (AXCP) and the Democratic Party of Azerbaijan in the run-up to the November 2005 elections.

President Ilham Aliyev maintained his strong support from within YAP in 2007, with high-level YAP officials announcing already that Aliyev will be the party's nominee for the 2008 presidential elections.[9] The party itself, however, did not seem fully cohesive owing to tensions among different factions. Sirus Tabrizli (Təbrizli), a founding member of YAP and its deputy chairman, was expelled in an emergency session of the party on March 27 after accusing a group allegedly led by Ramiz Mehdiyev (Məhdiyev), head of the Office of the President, of providing the president with false information about the situation in Azerbaijan.[10] YAP deputy and high-profile businessman Husein (Hüsein) Abdullayev was arrested and stripped of his parliamentary immunity in March after denouncing the government's performance in a heated session at the National Assembly.

Parliamentary sessions are generally open to the media, but the public and media have little direct access to the financial operations of the government. It is difficult for the public or nongovernmental organizations (NGOs) to obtain copies of draft laws and deputies' voting records, since these are not published in a consistent or timely fashion. The prime minister and the Cabinet of Ministers are required to present an annual report to the National Assembly at the beginning of the year, and this is made available to the public according to amendments approved by the 2002 constitutional referendum.

Electoral Process

1999	2001	2002	2003	2004	2005	2006	2007	2008
5.50	5.75	5.75	5.75	6.00	6.25	6.50	6.50	6.50

Elections in Azerbaijan have been characterized by significant irregularities and government interference in nearly all elections since independence. The October 2003 elections that brought then prime minister Ilham Aliyev (İlham Əliyev) to power with 77 percent of the vote and the November 2005 parliamentary elections were deemed fraudulent by monitors, although the latter showed some improvements in election legislation and campaigning.

Limited discussion related to electoral processes occurred in 2007, since no reruns or by-elections were held and Azerbaijan's next presidential election is not scheduled until October 2008. All indications are that President Aliyev would seek re-election, with YAP executive secretary, Ali Ahmadov (Əli Əhmədov), stating that the party had no doubts about the president's overwhelming victory in the polls.[11]

There were also indications that YAP's tendency to present loyalty to the regime as a guarantee for public employment would continue in the election year. In September, Education Minister Misir Merdanov (Mərdanov) called on teachers in Baku to promote the successes achieved under Aliyev's presidency, particularly during the 2008 election year.

Meanwhile, the political opposition has given mixed signals about its level of engagement, ranging from a potential boycott of the polls to the possibility of a candidate from a unified opposition.[12] Ali Kerimli (Kərimli), leader of the reformist wing of the AXCP, argued that shortcomings on rule of law and media freedom made it difficult for the party, as well as the Azadliq bloc—now comprising the Liberal and the Citizen and Development parties—to participate in the election. Signaling intentions to contest the elections,[13] Musavat chairman Isa Gambar (Qəmbər) continued to call for changes in the election code that would ensure parity between pro-government and opposition parties in district electoral commissions.

The OSCE Office for Democratic Institutions and Human Rights confirmed on December 19 that it will monitor the presidential elections in October 2008. Central Election Commission (CEC) Chairman Mazahir Panahov (Məzahir Pənahov) assured the international organization that the election process would be smooth, citing the construction of new buildings for election commissions and training courses for members of district election commissions and staff at polling stations.[14]

The election code divides the 18-member CEC equally among candidates put forward by the ruling party, opposition parties represented in the Parliament, and independent deputies. But the code continues to favor the ruling party in elections since most independents are pro-government and there were only six opposition deputies in the Parliament in 2007.

The Venice Commission of the Council of Europe continued consultations in 2007 with the authorities on election code modifications to overcome the dominance of YAP, whose representatives currently hold chairmanships in both constituency and precinct commissions. Panahov announced in November that a document including amendments and suggestions to the election code was being developed and would be submitted to the legislature;[15] the document was not finalized by the end of 2007.

Both AXCP and Musavat signaled their openness to presenting a single opposition candidate despite differences between the parties that led to Musavat's departure from the Azadliq bloc shortly after the November 2005 elections. Having garnered four of the six deputies won by Azadliq in the elections, Musavat chose its representatives to be involved in the new National Assembly, differing from other Azadliq allies who then pushed for a boycott of the legislature in protest of election irregularities.

Meanwhile, governmental pressure on political opposition continued. The office of the local branch of the AXCP in the exclave of Nakhichevan (Naxçıvan)—the Nakhichevani Autonomous Republic—was closed down in 2007. Prominent AXCP member Alesker Ismaylov (İsmaylov) was arrested on September 20 and, after interrogation, taken to a local psychiatric institution,[16] an unfortunate yet common way of dealing with political opponents in post-Soviet republics. His detention followed an incident in which he formally filed complaints about his neighbor, Farid Mammadov (Fərid Məmmədov), the local police chief in the Sadarak region. The U.S. embassy in Baku sent two representatives to Nakhichevan to discuss Ismaylov's case, but there had been no change in his status by the end of 2007.

Civil Society

1999	2001	2002	2003	2004	2005	2006	2007	2008
4.75	4.50	4.50	4.25	4.50	4.75	5.00	5.25	5.25

In Azerbaijan, freedom of association is recognized and protected by Article 58 of the Constitution and the European Convention on Human Rights, which came into force in the country in 2002. While grassroots activity continues to flourish, the Aliyev administration exerts a dominating influence on civil society organizations, particularly those critical of the government's democratic shortcomings, and the National Assembly has shown little willingness to engage NGOs in the legislative process or invite their input on draft legislation.

There are approximately 2,100 NGOs in Azerbaijan. The strongest and most active are concerned with internally displaced persons (IDPs) of the Nagorno-Karabakh region, health and children's issues, human rights, women's rights, and environmental and ecology issues. There are also 74 international aid organizations active in the country, mainly assisting the roughly one million IDPs who have been expelled as a result of the Nagorno-Karabakh conflict. NGO representatives continue to complain about government restrictions, in particular how the government keeps many groups in legal limbo by not registering them officially.

Local financial support to NGOs is limited, as the tax code does not allow tax-deductible contributions. The code does provide tax exemption to charitable organizations, unless they engage in entrepreneurial activities. Therefore, most NGOs rely primarily on foreign grants to continue their activities. The Law on NGOs prohibits civil society organizations from providing political parties with financial and other kinds of assistance, although they can conduct advocacy activities to improve laws and regulations.

The breakup of public protests by the use of force is common. Mahammad (Məhəmməd) Rzayev, head of the Civic Union for a Healthy Future, a local NGO in the Nakhichevani Autonomous Republic, has claimed to have been kidnapped by police and beaten in August.[17] In a separate event, on August 20–22, police forcefully broke up a demonstration by opposition Azerbaijan National Independence Party in Baku. The demonstration was a protest to what the party views as violations of the rights of the (sizeable) population of ethnic Azerbaijanis in Iran and was organized in response to Iranian president Mahmoud Ahmadinejad's visit to the Azeri capital.[18]

Azerbaijan's educational system includes approximately 4,600 primary and secondary schools, 180 technical high schools, 90 colleges, and 27 institutions of higher education (including 8 universities and 5 academies). Education is compulsory for at least eight years according to the Constitution; the state guarantees to cover educational costs. The Ministry of Education develops state education policy and manages the educational system.

Nearly 96 percent of Azerbaijanis are Muslim. There are 1,300 officially certified mosques in the country, although no more than 500 offer regular religious services. The government founded the State Committee for Work with Religious Associations (SCWRA) in 2001 to re-register religious groups, giving its chairman sweeping powers that included control over religious literature. The SCWRA reported 392 registered religious communities in the country.

The U.S. State Department Bureau of Democracy, Human Rights, and Labor issued a report in October 2007 that criticized the SCWRA for not registering the Christian-Baptist communities in the Aliabad and Neftcala districts. The report also claimed that there is a negative attitude toward Azerbaijanis who have adopted Christianity and that difficulties are created for those with Christian names to obtain birth certificates. The SCWRA said that it had not received an application from the community of Aliabad and the application from Neftcala was lacking documents.[19] The committee confirmed that it registered 48 new groups from May 2006 through June 2007, all of which were Muslim communities, but said it did not reject any completed applications.

Muslim religious groups must receive a letter of approval prior to registration with the SCWRA from the state-dominated Caucasus Muslim Board (DUMK), a body that appoints Muslim clerics to mosques and monitors sermons. The DUMK has been subject to interference by the SCWRA, which has attempted to share control over the appointment and certification of clerics and internal financial control of the country's mosques. The DUMK, headed by Sheikh Allahsukur Pasazade (Allahşükür Paşazade), also organizes annual pilgrimages to Mecca for the Muslim Hajj.

Azerbaijan has a long secular tradition during which religion has not played a central role in political or social life. Post-independence government policies have aimed at developing a "national Islam" and diminishing Sunni-Shiite cleavages while strengthening the national identity. There are signs, however, that more radical strains of Islam have been developing in Azerbaijan. Many young Azerbaijanis are turning to the Salafi strain of Sunni Islam, a trend that has been attributed partly to the corruption and poor image of the local Shiite clergy,[20] although a more radical version of Shiite Islam promoted by missionaries from Iran is also on the rise.

The Ministry of National Security announced on October 29 that it had arrested several individuals linked to Islamic radical groups that planned to undertake a terrorist attack in Baku.[21] A first lieutenant in the Azerbaijani Armed Forces, identified as Kamran Asadov (Əsədov), was suspected to have supplied the group with arms, including 4 machine guns, a mortar, and 20 hand grenades. The ministry associated the suspects with Wahhabism, a puritanical form of Islam with roots in Saudi Arabia. The announcement was seemingly taken very seriously by the U.S. and U.K. embassies in Baku, and several foreign oil companies such as the United Kingdom's British Petroleum (BP) and Norway's Statoil chose to close their offices that day. The alleged conspiracy was reported to have targeted a number of Azerbaijani government buildings and the U.S. embassy. Media reports suggested that roughly 10 officers and cadets at Azerbaijan's Higher Military School were being questioned in connection with the incident, although no formal linkage was made by the end of the year. Since the initial October 27 raid, Azerbaijani authorities have been carrying out a security sweep in and around Baku, resulting in the detention of at least 17 individuals.

The Court for Serious Crimes began the trial of 16 men involved in a group named Nima in a closed session on October 8.[22] The Ministry of National Security claims that the group—allegedly led by Said Dadashbayli (Səid Dadaşbəyli), an Azerbaijani citizen—worked with radical Islamic organizations and Iranian intelligence agents to set up a religious fundamentalist regime[23] and has gathered intelligence about U.S. and Israeli embassies in Baku. Dadashbeyli is a well-educated cleric who is considered to have a rising influence in Azerbaijan. The group, which claims to have been involved in charity work only,[24] is charged with high treason, illegal arms possession, illegal contact with foreign intelligence services, robbery, and other crimes.[25]

A more moderate strain of Islam (yet characterized by the authorities as radical) is promoted by Ilgar Ibrahimoglu (İbrahimoğlu), a young Islamic scholar who received religious education in Iran and studied human rights in Poland. His open criticism of the corruption and democratic shortcomings of the ruling regime has attracted many followers. Ibrahimoglu was given a five-year suspended sentence in

April 2004 for charges of involvement in the mass clashes between the police and opposition supporters after the October 2003 presidential elections.[26] The police forced his congregation (never registered formally with the DUMK) to vacate the Juma mosque in Baku that it had used since 1992. Ibrahimoglu complained in October that the Center to Protect Freedom of Conscience and Faith, a rights group he heads, had received several female students who were being forced to endure disciplinary interviews by school administrations for wearing the Islamic head scarf.[27]

Independent Media

1999	2001	2002	2003	2004	2005	2006	2007	2008
5.50	5.75	5.50	5.50	5.75	6.00	6.00	6.25	6.25

The National Assembly adopted Azerbaijan's Law on Mass Media in 2000. It guarantees freedom of speech, support for media, access to information, and protection of journalists' rights. In practice, though, Azerbaijan's media sector encounters numerous obstacles to conducting its work and maintaining independence; this is especially true of media that are critical of official corruption and the government's democratic shortcomings. Azerbaijani authorities resist demands by the OSCE and the Council of Europe to abolish Articles 147 and 148 of the criminal code, which make a journalist criminally responsible for defamation.

Television serves as the chief media source in Azerbaijan. There are 7 channels that broadcast to a national audience (state-owned AzTV, ANS, Space TV, ATV, Lider TV, ITV [the state-owned public TV], and Xazar, in order of date of establishment) and 12 regional TV channels. A November 2006 opinion poll conducted by the Democratic League of Journalists among 1,000 people in Baku and Sumqayit (Sumqayıt) found ATV (Azad Azerbaycan TV) to be the most popular television station with 44 percent of the viewers surveyed, followed by independent TV channel ANS and the state-owned ITV (opened in 2005 by the authorities to meet a Council of Europe demand to establish a public broadcaster). ANS and ITV were watched regularly by 32 percent of the viewers. Meanwhile, 72 percent said they prefer ANS for news, while 73 percent said they preferred ITV for entertainment programs. AzTV was considered the most biased broadcaster, leading 69 percent to report they preferred to keep up with current news developments by watching ANS.

Ending months of uncertainty, the authorities decided to grant a broadcast license to private television and radio broadcaster ANS on April 27.[28] The National Television and Radio Council (NTRC), the state media watchdog, had suspended ANS broadcasting in November 2006, only to restore it a month later under public and international pressure but leaving the future of the channel in a legal limbo until the license was renewed in April.[29]

The NTRC initially dragged its feet regarding the issuance, claiming that the law required the council to receive applications from alternative bidders before approving any tender, and granted it only after tenders for ANS's frequency did not attract any other bidders. This approach contradicted a fall 2006 decision by the NTRC to issue licenses in Alibayramli (Alibayramlı) and Yevlakh districts to two new regional television companies that were also the only bidders for their broadcast frequencies.

A monitoring study by the independent Najaf Najafov (Nəcəf Nəcəfov) Foundation into the activities of ITV between June and November 2006 found an increase over the previous period in broadcasting in foreign languages, particularly Russian and English, with the share of Azerbaijani-language programs reduced to 76 percent from 90.8 percent. Entertainment programs made up 56 percent of the broadcasts. Some 79 percent of ITV's programming was deemed impartial, although this did not include news programs that, according to the study, maintained a one-sided coverage of events. Results for August found that there had been an improved level of impartiality since the 2005 parliamentary election and that ITV allotted most of its airtime to local developments (62.8 percent), while foreign news was broadcast 37.2 percent of the time. In total 37.8 percent of the news was about social issues, 37 percent about politics, 10 percent about sports, 8 percent about the weather, 5.2 percent about economics, and 2 percent about culture.

Since the formal banning of censorship in 1998, the print media in Azerbaijan have remained freer than television and radio outlets, although they too are generally biased in their coverage. Of the 2,470 newspapers and journals published in Azerbaijan, the most popular are *Yeni Musavat* (*Müsavat;* 7 percent of readers surveyed), *Zerkalo* (7 percent), *Azarbaycan* (*Azərbaycan;* 5 percent), *Xalq Gazeti* (*Gəzeti;* 5 percent), *Azadliq* (4 percent), *Ekho* (4 percent), and *Azarbaycan Muallimi* (*Azərbaycan Müəllimi;* 4 percent). The Russian dailies *Ekho* and *Zerkalo* are generally considered to be nonpartisan. Newspapers such as *Yeni Musavat* and *Azadliq* serve as the political mouthpieces of certain opposition parties and are generally faulted for unprofessional reporting. The pro-government, state-funded newspapers *Xalq Gəzeti* and *Azarbaycan* cover only the ruling party's position on issues.

Opposition journalists continued to face legal and other troubles throughout 2007. OSCE Representative on Freedom of the Media Miklós Haraszti told President Aliyev in April that the country has the highest number of arrested journalists among all 56 members of the OSCE.[30] Since then, the number of imprisoned journalists has risen from five to seven with the May 16 sentencing of opposition newspaper *Muxalifat* editor Rovshan Kebirli (Rovşan Kəbirli) and correspondent Yashar Agazada (Yaşar Ağazadə). Each received prison sentences of two years and six months for allegedly slandering Jalal Aliyev (Əliyev) the president's uncle. Agazada had described Jalal Aliyev as "the most corrupt person in Azerbaijan."[31] Aliyev demanded evidence of the charges, which the newspaper did not provide. In May, a Parliamentary amnesty for prisoners was granted at the suggestion of Mehriban Aliyeva (Əliyeva), the president's wife and a YAP parliamentarian—however, imprisoned journalists were excluded.

The highest-profile journalist case in 2007 involved Eylnulla Fatullayev (Fatüllayev), editor of the now defunct *Realny Azerbaijan* and Azeri-language *Gundalik Azarbaycan* (*Gündalik Azarbaycan*) newspapers, who was sentenced to 30 months in prison in April for slander and insulting the Azerbaijani people after *Realny Azerbaijan* published a statement by an Armenian army officer who said that Armenian forces kept open an exit corridor for civilians during the 1992 Khojali massacres in Nagorno-Karabakh. His replacement at *Gundalik Azarbaycan*, Uzeir Jafarov (Üzeyir Cəfərov), was beaten brutally the day of Fatullayev's sentencing. He claimed that a police officer who attended Fatullayev's trial was among his assailants. The charge had not been investigated by the close of the year.[32]

The Ministry of National Security pressed further charges against Fatullayev in July for inciting ethnic and religious hatred and promoting "terrorism."[33] Fatullayev faced a third charge in September that he concealed 242,522 manats (roughly US$279,000) from *Realny Azerbaijan*'s accounts.[34] The Court for Serious Crimes sentenced Fatullayev to eight-and-a-half years in prison on both charges in October. He was fined more than 200,000 manats (approximately US$235,000) on the charge of tax evasion. [35]

Sanat newspaper editor Samir Sadagtogulu (Sadagtoğulu) and reporter Rafiq Taghi (Rafiq Tağı) received three- and four-year prison sentences, respectively, on May 4 for the publication of a 2006 article that described Christian values as more progressive than Islamic values. The Office of the Prosecutor General had brought charges against the journalists for "inflaming religious conflict". A Baku court sentenced Faramaz Novruzoglu (Novruzoğlu), a reporter with the weekly *Nota Bene* newspaper, to two years in prison for allegedly slandering Interior Minister Ramil Usubov and State Committee for Diaspora Affairs chairman Nazim Ibrahimov. The newspaper's editor in chief, Sardar Alibeyli (Sərdar Əlibəyli), received a suspended one-and-a-half-year sentence.

Hakimeldostu Mehdiyav (Mehdiyəv), the *Yeni Musavat* correspondent for Nakhichevan, was arrested after giving an interview to Radio Free Europe/Radio Liberty about conditions in the autonomous republic.[36] He was sentenced by a court to 15 days in prison on a charge of resisting arrest yet was released after three days in custody.

In September, Council of Europe Commissioner for Human Rights Thomas Hammarberg discussed with government officials the imprisonment of seven Azerbaijani journalists, all on charges of defamation or incitement and formerly working for non-government-controlled or pro-opposition media outlets. In a June 2007 report to the OSCE Permanent Council, Freedom of the Media Representative Miklós Haraszti also urged that the seven journalists be released and that the persecution of the remaining independent media be stopped.

The OSCE has also pushed for changes that would make libel, defamation, and verbal insults civil rather than criminal code violations. A draft law on the topic has been under consideration in the National Assembly since late 2006, but President Aliyev's approach has generally been to issue presidential pardons for imprisoned journalists occasionally rather than facilitating legislative changes that would loosen government restrictions on independent media.

Internet access remains free of governmental control and influence, but a small percent of the country is actually connected to the Internet. According to the International Telecommunications Union, in 2007 there were 23 Internet subscribers per 1,000 people in Azerbaijan. The number of Internet cafés around the country has increased rapidly, but there were a few instances where owners were harassed by the authorities.

Local Democratic Governance

1999	2001	2002	2003	2004	2005	2006	2007	2008
n/a	n/a	n/a	n/a	n/a	6.00	6.00	6.00	6.00

Azerbaijan is divided into 59 districts, 11 cities, and 1 autonomous region (Nakhichevani Autonomous Republic, which itself is subdivided into 7 districts and 1 city). Local executive committees (excoms) and municipal councils share power at the local governmental level. Although the Constitution defines municipalities as bodies for local self-government, the municipal councils lack a complete legal framework and proper funding and are subordinate to the excoms. The president appoints the members and heads of the excoms, as required by the Constitution, whereas seats on municipal councils are filled through municipal elections held every five years. The government set up municipal councils for the first time in 1999, but the municipal elections held that same year and in December 2004 were characterized by the OSCE as falling short of international standards.

According to a 2006 decree issued by Vasif Talibov (Talıbov), chairman of the local legislature in the Nakhichevani Autonomous Republic, all staff members of publicly funded agencies are required to do weekly volunteer work, such as cleaning streets, working in the fields, and collecting rubbish.[37] Nakhichevan state television has referred to such unpaid weekend work and those taking part as "subbotniks," making a thinly veiled comparison to similar practices during the Soviet period when people were called to work in the fields on Saturdays. The scheme has been criticized as a means of allowing forced free labor.

The World Bank estimates that a third of Azerbaijan's 8.4 million population lived below the poverty line in 2007. Some 80 percent of rural households receive remittances from friends and relatives abroad to help make ends meet, according to the government's 2005 Household Survey Data. The United Nations World Food Programme has estimated that food supplies are uncertain for between 400,000 and 600,000 residents of the country's rural regions, which contain just over 48 percent of the population.

The Baku-Tbilisi-Ceyhan (BTC) Pipeline Company, comprising Azerbaijani and international companies and responsible for oil exports from the BTC Pipeline, paid over US$14.7 million to Azerbaijani landowners during the pipeline's three-year construction period for use of their land, according to BP, the project's largest investor. The single largest compensation (US$300,000) was paid to a farmer in the region of Tovuz, while the smallest (US$150) went to a family in the region of Hajigabul, about 20 kilometers from Baku. A group of 14 families in the village of Hajali, located in western Azerbaijan accused local authorities of illegally registering the land under the names of their own relatives to gain compensation.[38] When the Azerbaijani Supreme Court rejected the families' claims, they appealed to the European Court of Human Rights. In 2007 the Court had not yet issued a ruling.

The Azerbaijani government continued to have no administrative control over the self-proclaimed Nagorno-Karabakh Republic and the seven surrounding regions (Kelbajar [Kəlbəcər], Gubatli [Qubadlı], Djabrail [Cəbrayıl], Fizuli, Zengilan [Zengilan], Lachin [Laçın], and Agdam [Ağdam]) that are de facto controlled by Armenia. This area constitutes about 17 percent of the territory of Azerbaijan. The self-declared regime in Nagorno-Karabakh held presidential elections on July 19. Bako Saakian (Bako Saakyan) formerly the territory's security chief, backed by outgoing de facto president Arkady Ghukassian (Arkadi Qukasyan), won more than 85 percent of the vote, in contrast with the 12 percent won by de facto deputy foreign minister Masis Mailian (Masis Mailyan).[39] The region also held local elections on October 14.[40] The international community did not pass judgment on the legitimacy of either of the ballots because the entity is not internationally recognized.

Azerbaijani ambassador to Russia, Polad Bulbuloglu (Bülbüloğlu), along with the Armenian ambassador to Russia, Armen Smbatian, led a cultural delegation to Nagorno-Karabakh on June 30 to meet with Ghukassian. This was the first meeting of official delegations from Azerbaijan and Armenia since the 1994 cease-fire. The trip included a visit to the town of Shusha, which holds strong cultural symbolism for Azerbaijan, and a meeting with Armenian president Robert Kocharian in Yerevan. The meetings produced no concrete progress in the peace talks, however.

Judicial Framework and Independence

1999	2001	2002	2003	2004	2005	2006	2007	2008
5.50	5.25	5.25	5.25	5.50	5.75	5.75	5.75	5.75

The Azerbaijani Constitution, adopted in 1995, provides a wide range of human rights protections, yet these rights are often violated in practice. Judicial power is implemented through the Constitutional Court, Supreme Court, Economic Court, and the ordinary and specialized courts. Judges of the high courts are appointed by the National Assembly on the recommendation of the president and remain heavily dependent on the executive branch. The president appoints and dismisses the prosecutor general of the Azerbaijan Republic.

The Law on the Judicial Legal Council, as well as the law amending and completing the 1997 Law on Courts and Judges, entered into force in January 2005. In a positive move, the National Assembly made changes to the Law on Advocacy that went into effect in August 2005, simplifying the requirements for over 200 formerly licensed lawyers to join the Collegium of Advocates (the bar) and practice law whether or not they have passed a separate bar exam. Other legislation established a new selection process for judges, which has set a more professional standard according to international observers.

The trial of former economic development minister Farhad Aliyev (Farhəd Əliyev) was concluded on October 31, 2007. In October 2005—just prior to the parliamentary elections in November—Farhad Aliyev and his brother Rafiq Aliyev (Əliyev), former head of Azpetrol International Holdings, the country's then largest private oil services firm, were arrested. The two men were initially charged with attempting to stage a coup—a charge that was later dropped. Farhad Aliyev was instead tried on charges of corruption, abuse of power, and other "economic crimes."[41] An earlier allegation that he had ordered the 2005 murder of journalist Elmar Huseynov (Hüseynov) was not considered.

A Baku criminal court handed the former minister a 10-year sentence, along with the confiscation of his property, after a trial of some five months, while Rafiq Aliyev received a 9-year term for alleged smuggling and tax evasion.[42] Four former high-ranking ministry officials also were sentenced to jail terms of varying length. Another 13 defendants—all former ministry officials and businessmen—were released, but with restrictions on their movements and activities.

The ability of journalists and international observers to attend the trial was restricted,[43] while defense attorneys complained that they were not permitted to fully review the evidence against their clients. One attorney for Farhad Aliyev was not allowed to attend the trial, while another one was removed by the Azerbaijani Bar Association for alleged violation of procedural rules. Isakhan Ashurov (İsaxan Aşurov), another of the attorneys, asserted that the judge denied defense requests for "more than 30" individuals to testify at the trial.[44]

The trial of former health minister Ali Insanov (Əli İnsanov), a YAP founder who was arrested at the same time as the Aliyev brothers, was concluded in July. Initial charges against him of planning to overthrow the government were transformed similarly into corruption charges during his arrest. Facing charges that he misappropriated US$3.5 billion from health care privatizations, public displays of support for Insanov, have been muted as his 12-year term in charge of the country's health care system was seen to be highly corrupt. Insanov argued that his arrest was politically driven and due mainly to his criticism of government policies in YAP meetings. He did not deny that his relatives enjoyed privileges during privatization tenders but said that all government members had conceivably acted in a similar manner.[45] A number of opposition media and international correspondents were blocked from several of Insanov's trial sessions, although the ban was later lifted.

Azerbaijan's prison conditions remained harsh in 2007. Even after a number of renovations and the construction of five new prisons in 2004, the majority of prisoners still depended on their families for basic needs, such as food and medicine, with tuberculosis the primary cause of death in prisons. Some pretrial detainees were kept in solitary confinement, where interrogators reportedly deprived them of food and sleep to secure confessions (without physical evidence of abuse). Detained poet and journalist Sakit Zahidov (popularly known as Mirza Sakit) went on a hunger strike to protest his transfer on October 20 back to N14 prison, which is notorious for its poor hygiene.[46] Zahidov, who has heart and stomach problems, had been receiving treatment at a Ministry of Justice medical center.

The Military Court for Serious Crimes sentenced Lieutenant Colonel Rasim Muradov to eight years in prison for bribery on October 22.[47] His lawyer was not allowed to attend the trial, as "he was late." The trial was closed to the media. Muradov disputed the charge, saying that he was prosecuted for revealing violations in Azerbaijan's peacekeeping battalion, which is serving in Kosovo, Afghanistan, and Iraq.

Corruption

1999	2001	2002	2003	2004	2005	2006	2007	2008
6.00	6.25	6.25	6.25	6.25	6.25	6.25	6.25	6.25

Corruption remains one of the most problematic issues in Azerbaijan. Despite some improvements in recent years, the government's strong presence in anticorruption commissions makes any independent inquiry difficult.

Azerbaijan's rating in Transparency International's 2007 Corruption Perceptions Index worsened to 2.1 from 2.4 from the year before, and the country was ranked 150 among the 163 surveyed (near the bottom of the scale, which signifies the highest level of corruption perception).

The criminal code does not define penalties for most corrupt activities, other than bribery. It does, however, forbid a government official from receiving gifts valued at more than US$55, holding other jobs (other than in education or the arts), and being engaged in business activity (whether directly indirectly or through proxies).

The collapse of a nearly finished apartment building in downtown Baku that killed 20 construction workers in August fueled debate about corruption in the construction sector. The Ministry of Emergency Situations has attributed the cause of the implosion of the building to uneven foundations and low-quality construction work.[48] It was later revealed that Mutefekkir Company, the firm responsible for the building, did not have a construction permit or approval for the final design, which had added three stories to the original plan. A court order in 2002 banning work on the site was later overturned by a Baku appeals court, raising questions that the firm enjoyed support from certain officials in the Baku city government.

In response, President Aliyev issued a decree later in the month giving additional authority to the Ministry of Emergency Situations to intervene in construction projects to ensure quality standards. The government decided to allocate 10,000 manats (about US$11,700) to the families of workers killed in the incident, and 3,000 manats (about US$3,500) to families of injured workers.

The authorities also arrested the director and three managers of Mutefekkir, as well as the head of the Baku city government's Department for Apartments and Cooperative Buildings. The authorities announced in September that they confirmed the existence of an additional 74 new buildings in Baku that have been inhabited without authorization. Since the start of the year, eight buildings under construction (seven in Baku, one in Ganja) have entirely or partially collapsed, killing 40 people. A total of 1,200 new buildings were approved for construction since January. Despite these changes, the sector is generally non-transparent, with many construction companies unregistered and operating without paying taxes.

A new Law on Combating Corruption, which defines corruption and outlines official responsibilities, and a State Program on Fighting Corruption came into force in January 2005. In addition, the statute for an Anticorruption Commission set up in April 2004 was approved in May 2005. The commission is led by Ramiz Mehdiyev (Məhdiyev), head of the Office of the President, and is composed equally of presidential, parliamentary, and Constitutional Court appointees, but it lacks the participation of civil society and media representatives. The commission created an ad hoc Anticorruption Legislative Working Group, which has had several meetings but has yet to have a direct effect on any cases. The group is staffed with 13 government officials, 3 NGO representatives, and 2 foreign experts from the American Bar Association's Central European and Eurasian Law Initiative and the OSCE. NGO and international organization representatives do not have voting rights.

In a significant step toward increased transparency, the National Assembly approved a new Law on Access to Information in December 2005, although a number of important provisions have yet to be enforced. The administration has not appointed a media ombudsman, which according to the law should have occurred within six months.

The transparency of operations of the State Oil Fund of Azerbaijan Republic (SOFAZ) improved with the government's 2002 decision to join the Extractive Industries Transparency Initiative, which requires oil companies to publicly report payments to SOFAZ but does not require the government to specifically disclose where money has been spent other than general budget classifications. Set up in 1999, SOFAZ has assets over US$2 billion and is accountable only to the president, who appoints its chairman and advisory council.

In the IFES 2005 Public Opinion Survey, 49 percent of Azerbaijanis report they have paid bribes to public officials (up from 33 percent in 2004). And 26 percent say they have not been asked for bribes (a decline from 33 percent in 2004). In addition, many more Azerbaijanis reported paying bribes for passports and other official documents.[49]

The National Assembly's Audit Chamber remains weak and inefficient, and NGOs and media lack access to information about its activities or statistics regarding government revenues and expenditures. So far, the state has failed to enforce an effective legislative or administrative process—and one free of prejudice against political opponents—to investigate the corruption of government officials and civil servants. The law does allow anonymous tip-offs to report on corrupt activities, bь as yet there are no effective legal protections for witnesses.

▌ AUTHOR: H. KAAN NAZLI

H. Kaan Nazli covers Central and Eastern Europe and the Caspian region f *Medley Global Advisors, a policy research and consulting firm with offices in Ne* *York City, Washington, D.C., London, and Tokyo. Formerly a research analyst f* *Eurasia Group, he has written for the* Financial Times, National Interest, Turkis Policy Quarterly, Insight Turkey, Caspian Investor, Russia/Eurasia Executiv Guide, *and EurasiaNet.*

1   BBC Monitoring (Turan News Agency), "Azeri Leader's 'Neo-Soviet' Speeches Aim ɪ Mislead People, Think Tank Says," October 24, 2007.
2   Khazri Bakinsky and Mina Muradova, "Azerbaijan: Building Bridges for President Aliyeᵥ Re-Election?," EurasiaNet, May 30, 2007.
3   BBC Monitoring (Ayna), "Paper Notes Positive Changes in Azeri Army," October 1ː 2007.
4   Khazri Bakinsky and Mina Muradova, "Azerbaijan Pursues NATO Integration," EurasiaNɛ March 16, 2007.
5   BBC Monitoring (Day.az), "Azeri Leader Vows to Increase Military Spending Furtheɪ October 22, 2007.
6   Rovshan Ismayilov, "Experts: Azerbaijan Military Build-Up for Diplomatic, Domest Advantage," EurasiaNet, July 3, 2007.
7   BBC Monitoring (Turan News Agency), "Azeri, Armenian Talks on Karabakh Stalled– Ministry Official," October 26, 2007.
8   BBC Monitoring (ANS TV), "Azeri Official Says No Progress in Karabakh Talks Due ɪ Armenia's Position," October 11, 2007.
9   Rovshan Ismayilov, "Azerbaijan: Politicians Gear Up for Next Year's Presidential Election EurasiaNet, October 3, 2007.
10 Rovshan Ismayilov, "Azerbaijan: President Presses Generational Change Within Governir Party," EurasiaNet, April 10, 2007.
11 ———, "Azerbaijan: Politicians Gear Up for Next Year's Presidential Election," EurasiaNɛ October 3, 2007.
12 Ibid.
13 BBC Monitoring (Ayna), "Azeri Opposition Camp Faces Dilemma Ahead of 200 Presidential Poll—Daily," October 27, 2007.
14 Azer-Press, "OSCE to Monitor Presidential Elections in Azerbaijan," December 19, 2007.
15 Trend News Agency, "Suggestions on Amendments and Changes to Azerbaijani Electio Code Being Developed—Chairman of Central Election Committee," November 27, 2007

16 Babek Bakir, "Azerbaijan: Teachers, Doctors in Naxcivan Tend the Fields to Keep Their Jobs," EurasiaNet, October 6, 2007.

17 Ibid.

18 Rovshan Ismayilov, "Iran-Azerbaijan Summit: 'Brotherly' Feelings, Without Results," EurasiaNet, August 24, 2007.

19 BBC Monitoring (Trend News Agency), "Azeri Regulator Critical of US Report on Religious Freedom," October 16, 2007.

20 BBC Monitoring (Zerkalo), "Azeri Daily Urges Caution in Dealing with Religious Groups," October 12, 2007.

21 Rovshan Ismayilov, "Azerbaijan: Terror Attack Foiled in Baku," EurasiaNet, October 29, 2007.

22 BBC Monitoring (Turan News Agency), "Azeri Group Goes on Trial for Alleged Links to Iran's Revolutionary Guards," October 8, 2007.

23 Rovshan Ismayilov, "Azerbaijan: Is Iran the Reason for the CIA Director's Recent Visit to Baku?," EurasiaNet, October 4, 2007.

24 BBC Monitoring (APA News Agency), "Main Defendant Pleads Not Guilty in Azeri Treason Trial," October 8, 2007.

25 ———, "Azerbaijan: Is Iran the Reason for the CIA Director's Recent Visit to Baku?," EurasiaNet, October 4, 2007.

26 Babek Bakir and Liz Fuller, "Azerbaijan: 'Alternative Islam' Takes Several Forms," EurasiaNet, August 16, 2007.

27 BBC Monitoring (Day.az), Azeri Rights Campaigner Reports Crackdown on Students Wearing Headscarves," October 23, 2007.

28 Rovshan Ismayilov, "Azerbaijan Tops the Charts for Number of Imprisoned Journalists," EurasiaNet, May 22, 2007.

29 ———, "Azerbaijan: Fate of Independent Broadcaster Still in Limbo," EurasiaNet, February 12, 2007.

30 ———, "Azerbaijan Tops the Charts for Number of Imprisoned Journalists," EurasiaNet, May 22, 2007.

31 Rovshan Ismayilov, "Azerbaijan Tops the Charts for Number of Imprisoned Journalists," EurasiaNet, May 22, 2007.

32 Ibid.

33 It is common in Azerbaijan for state officials to equate the continued Armenian occupation of Azerbaijani territories with "state terrorism" owing to lack of access for ethnic Azerbaijanis who were originally residents of the occupied regions to those territories. In this case, the ministry argued that Fatullayev's actions were encouraging Armenia to maintain this policy.

34 BBC Monitoring (Gun Sahar), "Azeri Ministry Fines Jailed Editor 200,000 Dollars for Alleged Tax Evasion," October 9, 2007.

35 BBC Monitoring (Turan News Agency), "Azeri Opposition Journalist Jailed for 8.5 Years for 'Terror Threats,'" October 30, 2007.

36 Babek Bakir, "Azerbaijan: Teachers, Doctors in Naxcivan Tend the Fields to Keep Their Jobs," EurasiaNet, October 6, 2007.

37 Ibid.

38 Rovshan Ismayilov, "Life Along the Pipeline: BTC's Impact on Azerbaijan," EurasiaNet, March 15, 2007.

39 Elizabeth Owen, "Karabakh Territory Undergoes Political Transition," EurasiaNet, July 23, 2007.

40 BBC Monitoring (Arminfo), "Business Executive Wins Mayoral Election in Breakaway Karabakh," October 15, 2007.

41 BBC Monitoring (Turan News Agency), "Azeri Ex-Minister on Trial Claims Innocence in Last Statement," October 4, 2007.

42 Rovshan Ismayilov, "Azerbaijan: Former Minister of Economic Development Receives 10-Year Term," EurasiaNet, November 1, 2007.

43 BBC Monitoring, "Backgrounder: Azeri Ex-Minister Sentenced to 10 Years for Embezzlement," October 25, 2007.

44 Rovshan Ismayilov, "Azerbaijan: Former Minister of Economic Development Receives 10-Year Term," EurasiaNet, November 1, 2007.

45 Rovshan Ismayilov, "Azerbaijan: Ex-Minister's Trial Creates Political Sensation," EurasiaNet, March 6, 2007.

46 Reporters Without Borders press release, October 23, 2007.

47 BBC Monitoring (APA News Agency), "Azeri Army Officer Gets Eight Years in Prison for Bribery," October 22, 2007.

48 Rovshan Ismayilov, "Azerbaijan: Building Collapse Exposes 'Chaos' in Baku's Urban Planning," EurasiaNet, September 6, 2007.

49 *Public Opinion in Azerbaijan 2005: Findings from a Public Opinion Survey*, IFES (Washington D.C.: 2006), http://www.ifes.org/publication/72475dd9a26b472c52a1d08306c12ac4/public%20opinion%20in%20Azerbaijan_2005-IFES.pdf.

Belarus

by Vitali Silitski

Capital:	Minsk
Population:	9.7 million
GNI/capita:	US$9,700

The social data above was taken from the European Bank for Reconstruction and Development's *Transition Report 2007: People in Transition*, and the economic data from the World Bank's *World Development Indicators 2008*.

Nations in Transit Ratings and Averaged Scores

	1999	2001	2002	2003	2004	2005	2006	2007	2008
Electoral Process	6.75	6.75	6.75	6.75	6.75	7.00	7.00	7.00	7.00
Civil Society	6.00	6.50	6.25	6.50	6.75	6.75	6.75	6.50	6.50
Independent Media	6.75	6.75	6.75	6.75	6.75	6.75	6.75	6.75	6.75
Governance*	6.25	6.25	6.50	6.50	6.50	n/a	n/a	n/a	n/a
National Democratic Governance	n/a	n/a	n/a	n/a	n/a	6.75	7.00	7.00	7.00
Local Democratic Governance	n/a	n/a	n/a	n/a	n/a	6.50	6.50	6.50	6.75
Judicial Framework and Independence	6.50	6.757	6.75	6.75	6.75	6.75	6.75	6.75	6.75
Corruption	5.25	5.25	5.25	5.50	5.75	6.00	6.25	6.25	6.25
Democracy Score	6.25	6.38	6.38	6.46	6.54	6.64	6.71	6.68	6.71

* With the 2005 edition, Freedom House introduced separate analysis and ratings for national democratic governance and local democratic governance to provide readers with more detailed and nuanced analysis of these two important subjects.

NOTE: The ratings reflect the consensus of Freedom House, its academic advisers, and the author(s) of this report. The opinions expressed in this report are those of the author(s). The ratings are based on a scale of 1 to 7, with 1 representing the highest level of democratic progress and 7 the lowest. The Democracy Score is an average of ratings for the categories tracked in a given year.

EXECUTIVE SUMMARY

Belarus earned the dubious reputation of "the last dictatorship of Europe," although the country's first democratically elected president, Alexande Lukashenka, won Belarus' first presidential elections in 1994 on promises to halt market reforms, fight corruption, and reestablish Soviet-era social guarantees. He has remained president since then and has instituted direct presidential powe over all institutions, controlled the electoral process, marginalized the opposition reduced the independent press to a bare minimum, and created pervasive mechanism for controlling the economy and society. The country's unreformed and extensively bureaucratized economy performed strongly for most of the last decade owing to an economic upturn in countries traditionally importing Belarusian goods, and generous discounts on energy prices provided by Russia. In 2007, Russia's decision to raise energy prices and develop market-based relations with Belarus shook th prospect of long-term stability for Lukashenka's political and economic system. Th price hikes reflected the Kremlin's irritation with Lukashenka's persistent failure to honor his commitments to federate Belarus with Russia and led to an "energy war" between the two countries throughout the winter of 2006–2007. The adjustmen to new economic realities underscored the domestic political dynamics in Belaru in 2007.

In the economic sphere, the government reversed its long-standing policy and began a period of reform by revamping the social benefits system and privatizing some state-owned assets. Even more radically, in an attempt to secure alternative sources of investment beyond Russia, the government eased political repressio in the first half of 2007 and expressed interest in cooperation with the Europea Union (EU) on such issues as energy security. Lukashenka himself, however declared that these overtures to the West did not presage impending change to domestic policy. As a result, the attempt to normalize relations with the EU quickly dissolved, and political repression was in full swing by the end of summe 2007. Overall, the "energy war" ended with a deal allowing Russian gas monopol Gazprom to purchase a 50 percent stake in the key Belarusian gas distribution and transportation network, Beltransgaz, in exchange for a five-year-long transition to European-level energy prices for Belarus.

National Democratic Governance. The institutions securing the absolut presidential control over state, society, and the electoral process remain fully in place although conflicts among security agencies in the summer of 2007 demonstrated signs of internal power struggles. A more lenient treatment of the opposition in 200 offered a temporary break in the regime's widespread practice of repressing politica opponents and civil society. *Belarus' rating for national democratic governance stands unchanged at 7.00.*

Electoral Process. Local elections carried out on January 14, 2007 reduced opposition representation in local councils to a minimum, thus eliminating the last islands of institutionalized political pluralism in Belarus. Infighting for leadership widened the gap between the opposition and society and further promoted public apathy and disinterest in politics. *Owing to the continued absence of meaningful electoral competition and the inability of democratic forces to deliver a credible political alternative, Belarus' rating for electoral process remains unchanged at 7.00.*

Civil Society. Several long-term prisoners remained incarcerated during 2007 for creating unregistered nongovernmental organizations (NGOs), while civil society activists put on trial under anti-NGO laws avoided long prison sentences. At the same time, despite official attempts, a few key NGOs avoided liquidation. Disillusionment and overall lack of direction within civil society led to a sharp decline in the activities of informal groups that arose during the 2006 presidential election. *The balance of negative and positive tendencies in the independent civic sector keeps Belarus' rating for civil society unchanged at 6.50.*

Independent Media. Discriminatory practices against the independent press and harassment of independent journalists continued in 2007. The government hindered access to information by restricting state officials from speaking to the press. In 2007, the trial against Andrej Klimau set a new precedent for attacking freedom of speech online. *Belarus' rating for independent media remains unchanged at 6.75.*

Local Democratic Governance. Local democratic government remains nonexistent in Belarus, and the top-down system of appointing local bureaucrats remains fully in place. Local elections in 2007 resulted in the near total disappearance of opposition representation in local councils. *Owing to the removal of political pluralism at the local level, Belarus' rating for local democratic governance deteriorated from 6.50 to 6.75.*

Judicial Framework and Independence. De facto subordination of the judiciary to the executive makes it an instrument of political reprisal. Imprisoned opposition activists report mistreatment, and several faced new criminal charges in an apparent attempt to prevent their release. *Belarus' rating for judicial framework and independence remains unchanged at 6.75 owing to a lack of progress in ensuring fairness and impartiality of the courts.*

Corruption. Modest improvements in the Belarusian business climate were made in 2007 with the activation of previous presidential directives aimed at reducing the bureaucracy. Yet, public perception of corruption continued to grow as government operations and budgetary policies remained non-transparent. Authorities bypassed legal requirements for open tenders when authorizing key privatization deals in 2007, a source of concern for future privatization of state-owned enterprises *Belarus' rating for corruption remains unchanged at 6.25.*

Outlook for 2008. Emerging challenges to the stability of Lukashenka's political and economic model will not likely push the government toward conscious reform or political liberalization. Rather, it is likely to continue the stop-start approac taken in 2007. Parliamentary elections scheduled for September 2008 will not ope a space for genuine political competition. Furthermore, Lukashenka will continu to consolidate his grasp on power with an eye on the next presidential election in 2011.

Main Report

National Democratic Governance

1999	2001	2002	2003	2004	2005	2006	2007	2008
n/a	n/a	n/a	n/a	n/a	6.75	7.00	7.00	7.00

The government in Belarus is based on unlimited presidential authority, without presidential term limits. The Constitution severely restricts the legislative powers of the Parliament, the National Assembly, giving priority to decrees and orders signed by the president.

Parliament is entrusted with nominal control over the cabinet and must gain the consent of the president or government to adopt any law concerning government spending. The president appoints head regional administrators and members of the Council of Ministers. Only the prime minister is subject to parliamentary approval. However, the House of Representatives faces dissolution should it fail twice to approve the president's candidate.

The assembly's bicameral composition enforces its subordination to the president. While 110 members of the House of Representatives are elected on a single-member constituency basis, the upper Council of the Republic is appointed by regional assemblies of local councils, with the president selecting 8 of its 64 members. Most key appointments, including half of the Constitutional Court and the chairman of Supreme Court, are carried by the unelected upper house.

Texts of major legislation are available to the public in printed and free Internet versions. However, an extensive range of data on government activities, including international treaties, military and defense spending, and state-sponsored research and development programs, remains classified. The Parliament is not obliged by law to make public either its records or the voting records of deputies. Members of the government and civil servants are required to gain permission from superior officers before speaking with the press. Civil servants must also pass ideology tests before entering a position in the state administration to ensure their political loyalty to the regime.

The absolute authority of the president over all institutions of power, and marginalization of the opposition by means of repression and an information blockade, promotes a sense of government stability to the extent it provides Lukashenka's regime immunity from internal and external pressures. Yet the energy conflict with Russia that erupted December 2006–January 2007 challenged the government's ability to provide acceptable living standards for the population. In May 2007, the government began to abolish the wide-scale system of social privileges and subsidies, such as free public transport for students and medical subsidies for pensioners. These measures, although not critical to public welfare, contributed to the steady decline of the president's popularity, according to independent polls throughout the year.

Furthermore, as the government opened the economy to privatization, top-level struggles for assets and influence intensified. The summer of 2007 saw the authorities shaken by a series of high-profile conflicts among security agencies. These conflicts began in May 2007 with the KGB arrest of the management of petrochemical giant Belneftekhim, one of the country's top hard-currency earners, whose privatization was debated throughout the year.[1] Later, the KGB and the Ministry of the Interior exchanged attacks and arrested scores of officers on both sides on corruption charges.[2] The "war of *siloviki*" (security-service personnel) reached a peak when Zianon Lomat, head of the State Control Committee (an agency traditionally competing for influence with the KGB), was beaten on July 1, 2007, by plainclothes KGB and Security Council agents.[3] Following the incident President Lukashenka fired KGB head Sciapan Sukharenka and his deputy Vasil Dziemianciej. The president replaced Sukharenka with former head of the presidential bodyguard service, Jury Zhadobin, whom Lukashenka openly admitted lacked competence as the new head of the KGB but would "put the KGB in order." At the same time, Lukashenka accused former KGB leadership of providing illegal protection (in Russian, *kryshevaniye*: literally "roof") to corrupt business groups. The slang meaning of "roof" refers to the criminal protection racket.

Lukashenka's promise to rid the KGB of corruption and to promote a young generation of more energetic officers reflected the tendency toward generation change inside the regime. This was confirmed throughout the year with the removal of: the Speaker of the House of Representatives, Uladzimir Kanapleu, in September 2007; a powerful governor in a Minsk province, Mikalaj Damashkevich, in July 2007; and the July 2007 replacement of top management of Beltransgaz and Belarusian Oil Company, two giants within the petrochemical complex.

The energy conflict also undermined established government spending patterns and as a result, the government began to consider its 'Westward options,' including the European Union (EU). However, in December 2006, in response to violations of civil and trade union rights, the EU authorized the exclusion of Belarus from its generalized system of trade preferences (GSP). Despite taking some liberalizing measures in the first half of 2007 to regain trade preference status, Lukashenka emphasized that the government acted in the interest of the economy first and that while wooing the EU required relaxation of some political controls, no real political change was on the table. Once the EU made it clear that without a full stop to political repression no compromise on GSP was possible, the government fully resumed its previous practices.[6]

In 2007, the United States government authorized new sanctions against Belarusian officials, extending visa bans to medium-level representatives of the regime, local officials, and members of electoral commissions.[7] And in November 2007, the assets of the state-run energy conglomerate Belneftekhim were frozen in the United States.[8] These sanctions, however, proved largely ceremonial, as they did not create serious obstacles for officials save for minor personal disturbances.

Street demonstrations remain the key method for the opposition to publicize its message. As the government attempted to mend its relations with the EU, the repression of opposition street rallies declined in 2007, and several demonstrations, such as the opposition marches of March 25, April 26, October 14, and November 4, were allowed to assemble peacefully. At the same time, the government employed somewhat more subtle tactics through preventive arrests of potential crowd leaders to weaken authorized rallies before they convened. For example, authorities detained 40 activists prior to the Freedom Day celebrations on March 25 and again before the European March on October 14.[9]

The largest opposition demonstration attracted barely 10,000 participants for the Chernobyl commemorative march on April 26. Attempts to refocus the protest on social rather than political issues by staging the Social March on November 4 attracted just over 1,000 participants. Nevertheless, authorities noted the opposition's change in street strategy; in December 2007, local authorities authorized only 2 of more than 400 pickets protesting the withdrawal of social privileges.

Following the government's failure to prevent Belarus' exclusion from EU trade preferences, police crackdowns on unauthorized rallies grew. For example, 11 participants of the July 27 demonstration to commemorate the outlawed Sovereignty Day (marking proclamation of sovereignty from the Soviet Union in 1990) were beaten and arrested.[10] On December 12, 2007, a small rally to protest Russian president Vladimir Putin's visit to Minsk was also dispersed brutally, with one participant delivered unconscious to an emergency clinic.[11]

Electoral Process

1999	2001	2002	2003	2004	2005	2006	2007	2008
6.75	6.75	6.75	6.75	6.75	7.00	7.00	7.00	7.00

Consolidation of absolute presidential rule in Belarus eliminates the possibility for meaningful electoral contestation. The country's electoral legislation, the electoral code, does not guarantee election commissions with multiparty representation and independence and fails to provide sufficient transparency of the vote count or uniform appeals for the decisions of election commissions. The president and the Council of the Republic appoint the Central Election Commission (CEC) for five years. Rather than serve as impartial observer of the law, the CEC actively ensures the interpretation of the electoral legislation to the advantage of lower-level commissions and candidates nominated by the government. The CEC head, Lidzia Yarmoshyna, openly described pro-presidential parties in the press as "constructive" and "patriotic" while labeling opposition parties as "subversive" and issued charges against independent election-observing nongovernmental organizations (NGOs) as "puppets" of Western financiers.[12]

The most recent parliamentary elections took place in October 2004. Accordir to the CEC, all of the declared winners were pro-government and supported th president. International organizations, as well as the opposition, challenged th election results.[13] Elections to the upper house of Parliament, the Council of th Republic, took place in November 2004, with the assemblies of local counci voting to fill 56 seats, or 8 per region, with an additional 8 members appointed b the president. All members of the upper house support the president.

Presidential elections held on March 19, 2006, were accompanied by widesprea violence, intimidation, and government repression. Official election results grante an overwhelming victory (83 percent) to Lukashenka, compared with 6 percent fo United Democratic Forces (UDF) leader Alyaksandr Milinkevich, 4 percent fo pro-presidential leader Siarhej Hajdukevich, and 2 percent for Belarusian Soci Democratic Party leader Alyaksandr Kazulin.[14] While independent observe accused the government of fraud, Lukashenka declared that the government ha indeed tampered with results to decrease his margin of victory and to please Wester countries. The wave of protests following the election represented the largest-sca opposition activities against the government in years. Hundreds of activists stage a protest tent camp in the central square of Minsk. Alyaksandr Kazulin, form presidential candidate for the opposition who launched scathing media attacl against Lukashenka, was arrested and sentenced to five and a half years in jail fo organizing mass disorder.

Local elections held on January 14, 2007, took place without meaningf competition or genuine choice. Opposition candidates faced obstacles in registerir their candidacy and authorities warned some that electoral participation put the jobs in danger.[15] The opposition Belarusian Party of Communists could register on 32 candidates out of the 245 it intended to place, whereas the Belarusian Popul Front secured 40 registered candidates out of 148 who attempted to run.[16] In tota 609 candidates were denied registration, most representing opposition parties an NGOs. Furthermore, the state-run press actively discredited the opposition, issuir charges that opposition parties received Western support, and local authoriti on several occasions refused to offer independent candidates meeting plac for campaigning and impeded the distribution of campaign materials.[17] Mar opposition candidates were also denied the right to publish their platforms in th local press despite guarantees issued by the electoral code.[18]

Elections were carried out in 22,661 single-member constituencies, wit 23,791 registered candidates. Some semblance of competitiveness was present in th Minsk City Council elections (168 candidates for 55 constituencies) and region councils (729 candidates for 460 constituencies); however, all but 200 of the 16,60 constituencies in village council elections went uncontested.[19] According to CE data, 79 percent of voters took part in the elections, including 24.6 percent who ca their ballots ahead of time,[20] a procedure criticized by the opposition for its lack guarantees to prevent voting fraud. According to independent observers, monito could be present only in the vote tabulation room and could not see the vote cou *per se*. Out of the 22,639 deputies elected, only 20 represented opposition parti according to CEC data,[21] down from 227 in 2003. These opposition deputies come from the Belarusian Party of Communists (17), Belarusian Social Democratic Party (2), and the United Civic Party (1).[22]

Apart from an uneven and discriminatory playing field, the election outcomes also reflected the failure of the Belarusian opposition to put aside infighting and develop an adequate campaign message for voters. Instead, the campaign caught the opposition in a brewing conflict between former presidential candidate Alyaksandr Milinkevich and leaders of major opposition parties. The conflict focused on the process of nominating candidates for the upcoming Congress of Democratic Forces (CDF), the umbrella body of the UDF electing the new leadership of the opposition. The UDF coordinating council declared that any candidate securing 300 signatures supporting his or her candidacy for local elections would become a CDF delegate. Consequently, several prospective candidates lost interest in the elections once the necessary signatures were collected. Some opposition leaders, while actively arguing against a boycott, eventually withdrew their own candidacies.

The CDF convened on May 27–28, 2007, was dominated by representatives of political parties with minimal representation of the NGO activists who secured Milinkevich's nomination in October 2005. The 2007 CDF replaced Milinkevich with the collective leadership of four major opposition party leaders, who accused Milinkevich of attempting to monopolize control of the opposition. Milinkevich was offered the seat of co-chairman of the UDF, but he refused, having formed his own movement (For Freedom) instead.

The struggle to develop a meaningful political agenda after the eventful presidential election campaign of 2006 deepened the general lack of direction among Lukashenka's opponents. The opposition focused on political issues and regime change to the detriment of creating a new message for society. As a result, Lukashenka's opponents consistently failed to address pressing issues for the majority of citizens. For example, the opposition largely ignored the Belarus-Russia energy conflict and did little to present its position on issues such as energy security or economic policy, even while the public became increasingly concerned. As a result, Lukashenka scored propaganda points with his pro-independence and anti-Russian rhetoric.

As of 2007, a total of 14 political parties had registered in Belarus: 7 pro-president, one neutral and 6 opposition. Several parties, such as the Belarusian Social Democratic Party and Party of Freedom and Progress, lack official registration. A new party, Belarusian Christian Democracy, was created in 2007. At the same time, the foundation of the pro-presidential movement Belaya Rus (White Rus`) gave rise to speculations that authorities may eventually transform it into a political party and introduce a proportional electoral system to the Parliament, although such a change seems highly unlikely.

Recently, the government moved to further restrict the activities of political parties by closing down regional party branches and de-registering several parties. In 2007, authorities closed down two small parties, the Belarusian Environmental Party BEZ and a women's party, Nadzeya (Hope), both for failure to comply

with registration requirements—that is, insufficient membership and lack of th
required number of regional branches.[23] The Belarusian Party of Communists,
major opposition party, was suspended for six months in August 2007 for simila
reasons.[24]

Civil Society

1999	2001	2002	2003	2004	2005	2006	2007	2008
6.00	6.50	6.25	6.50	6.75	6.75	6.75	6.50	6.50

Belarusian NGOs operate in a hostile legal environment aimed at de-legitimizin
and even criminalizing most forms of independent civic activity. According to th
Ministry of Justice of the Republic, as of July 1, there were 2,223 NGOs in existenc
in Belarus (230 international, 715 national, and 1,278 local organizations), 1
NGO unions, 63 foundations, and 37 trade unions.[25] Most of these organization
represented non-politicized NGOs loyal to the regime. Meanwhile, civic group
that defined themselves in opposition to the government or operated withou
official approval, were pushed underground.

The campaign to liquidate NGOs began in 2003, spurred by government fear
of the role played by the independent civic sector in the democratic so-called colo
revolutions in Georgia (2003) and Ukraine (2004). During this period, accordin
to the Assembly of Democratic Nongovernmental Organizations, the courts close
at least 200 NGOs, and official pressure forced more than 100 to self-liquidate.[2]
The most widespread reason for liquidations was the failure to obtain a lega
address, a requirement demanded by law and nearly impossible to fulfill owing t
prohibitively high rents or the outright denial of a lease.

The wave of liquidations subsided somewhat in 2007, as few active oppositio
NGOs remained. NGOs closed in 2007 included Old Town and the Belarusia
Literary Foundation. Several NGOs, either starting out or trying to renew thei
registration, were denied registration in 2007, including the new civic movement
For Freedom and the Young Front, the human rights center Viasna, and the Unio
of Chernobyl Workers (also known as Liquidators[27]). On a more positive not
several NGOs, including the Supolnasc (Community) Center in Minsk and th
Belarusian Helsinki Committee, avoided liquidation in 2007 even though th
motions for their closure were presented by the Ministry of Justice.

In December 2005, prior to the March 2006 presidential elections, th
National Assembly of the Republic of Belarus adopted a series of amendment
to the criminal code, including provisions that made establishing, running, o
participating in a liquidized or unregistered organization punishable by up t
three years in prison (Article 193-1). The new provision took immediate effec
and primarily targeted groups the government most suspected would attempt
so-called color revolution—such as election monitors and youth NGOs wit
a clearly defined anti-regime agenda. During 2007, repression of activists c

unregistered organizations subsided somewhat, as courts were reluctant to sentence activists under Article 193-1. Most of the accused, primarily seven members of the Young Front, received lenient fines—up to 10 times lower than the prosecution's demanded sum.[28] Mikhail Yakovchuk of Russian National Unity from the city of Homel was the only person jailed in 2007 on anti-NGO legislation. He received a six-month jail sentence.[29] By the end of the year, however, NGO crackdowns returned in full swing, as exemplified by the retrial of Artur Finkevich, a Young Front activist sentenced to two years of forced labor in 2006 for anti-presidential graffiti. In November 2007, near the end of his sentence, Finkevich was tried again and received an additional one and a half years in prison for violating the internal rules of the labor camp. Many analysts considered this harsh sentence a sign of the regime's lack of interest in normalizing relations with the EU after the Kremlin agreed to support the Belarusian economy with a generous stabilization loan.[30]

Members of several unregistered NGOs received warnings about possible prosecution if they continued to work for illegal NGOs. At the end of 2007, three members of the Young Front remained under criminal investigation according to Article 193-1. Criminal proceedings also began against the unregistered civil initiative Bunt (Riot) but were later quietly dropped by the authorities.

Many civil society events, owing to legal restrictions and consistent practices of refusing to rent conference premises or concert halls, were carried out abroad. Participants of such events are routinely searched and detained at the border. In August 2007, authorities arrested actors, directors, and the audience of a private performance in Minsk by the clandestine Free Theater.[31] Belarusian-language rock groups Krama, NRM, and Neiro Dubel, who are suspected of being sympathetic to the opposition, could not gain permission to perform at concert venues beyond small rock bars. At the same time, the authorities attempted to engage part of the dissident cultural underground. Deputy head of the presidential administration Aleh Praliaskouski met Krama, NRM, and Neiro Dubel in November 2007 and offered to restore their ability to perform at larger venues provided they sever their ties with the opposition. The groups accepted the deal, sparking harsh public debate as many opposition activists felt betrayed by this act of conformism. Others believed that the groups' presence onstage was worth the compromise. The debate, which turned many supporters against the groups, played to the advantage of the authorities.

Government-organized NGOs (GONGOs) are actively promoted and generously supported by the government. They are excluded from many repressive regulations applied to independent organizations. The Belarusian Republican Youth Union (BRSM), a replica of the Soviet-era Komsomol, imitates its predecessor in structure and ideology and serves as a tool to instill loyalty among the younger generation. BRSM tries to attract members with privileged university admission and various discounts, but many have been coerced to join.[32] The official trade unions, while avoiding direct confrontation with authorities and management of state enterprises, also attract members with benefits such as longer vacation leave and extra salary bonuses. As a result, membership in the independent trade union of the Hrodna Azot chemical enterprise fell in two year (2006–2007) from 580 to 200. [33]

The government also controls special interest organizations, such as women unions, veterans' organizations, and various creative associations, which are traditio nal hotbeds of intellectual dissidence. In 2007, Mikalaj Charhiniec, a member of th Council of the Republic and head of the Union of Writers of Belarus, a governmer organization mirroring the independent Union of Belarusian Writers, endorse government policies, including the expulsion from school programs of works c writers advocating national revival and criticizing Russification. [34] Furthermore the development of Belaya Rus, a public association to rally support beyon regime policies created in 2007, raised questions regarding the overlap among pro government civil movements, NGOs, and political parties as it first formed region. branches that later converged into the countrywide congress.

The government rarely consults independent NGOs, and cooperatio occurs only when civil society groups find ways to effectively exert pressure o authorities (mostly by persistent acts of civil disobedience). In one rare example nongovernmental civil society groups participated in public hearings in the Hous of Representatives on the new Law on Protection of Information, which resulte in the removal from the draft law of the most outrageous proposals to regulate an control the electronic press. [35]

The outburst of independent civic activism during and following the 200 presidential elections receded in 2007 to an atmosphere of apathy and disillusionmer among both the political opposition and the NGO sector. Attempts to reorganiz the opposition have not yielded any results. Despite having won a moral victor by organizing the camp city and large groups of people who appeared sudden in public places (known as flash mobs) after the presidential elections, it did nc manage to unite its program and win the support of current opposition leader Youth groups suffered from the wave of emigration of students expelled from the universities for taking part in the 2006 mass protests. Moreover, according t independent studies, only 10 percent of Belarusian students are oriented towar any kind of civic activism, and only 2 percent are seriously interested in politics c concerned about things such as the future of the country. [36]

The spirit of the 2006 protests did appear throughout the year in solidarit actions led by civil society groups. Young Front actions attracted, on certai occasions, hundreds of participants and exerted pressure on the courts to abstai from harsh measures against detained activists. The campaign in defense of Unite Civic Party activist Dzianis Dzianisau arrested for participation in street protest proved another remarkable act of solidarity when, through private donatior solicited largely online, Dzianisau was released on bail.

Independent Media

1999	2001	2002	2003	2004	2005	2006	2007	2008
6.75	6.75	6.75	6.75	6.75	6.75	6.75	6.75	6.75

Article 33 of the Constitution guarantees freedom of speech. The government, however, regards this article in practice as dissenting voices, and media outlets are silenced by repressive media laws and licensing rules, libel suits, arbitrary closure of nongovernmental media outlets, discriminatory pricing for print and distribution, and systematic harassment of journalists.

As of July 1, there were 1,247 printed media in Belarus, including 701 newspapers and 508 magazines.[37] While more than two-thirds of periodicals are private, the state-owned press heavily dominates the information field in terms of copies distributed. The largest independent newspaper, *Narodnaya Volya*, has just over 20,000 copies per print, compared with 500,000 for the top state publication, *SB-Belarus Segodnya*. Only the Belarusian edition of Moscow-based *Komsomolskaya Pravda* (with up to 300,000 copies for the weekend edition) competes with *SB-Belarus Segodnya* and offers uncensored views of government policies.

The Ministry of Information crackdown in 2002–2007 greatly damaged the independent press with the closure of dozens of nongovernment publications, including most regional newspapers critical of the government. In 2007, the Ministry of Information continued to issue official warnings to independent media, with two warnings a year often leading to a publication's closure. *ARCHE* magazine, suspended for three months in 2006, received two official warnings in February 2007 for printing back issues blocked by a previous suspension.[38]

The government generously supports state-owned press. The independent press faces discriminatory pricing at printing houses, while publications overtly critical of the regime's policies do not appear in subscription catalogs or in the distribution of the state-run retail network, Belsajuzdruk. Newspapers denied distribution in 2007 included Babruisk-based *Bobruiskiy Kuryer, Niasvizhski Chas* from Niasvizh, and *Miascovy Chas,* a newspaper based in the city of Pinsk.[39] Several newspapers, such as Viciebsk-based *Viciebski Chas-M* and *Viciebski Kuryer,* lost their leases suddenly without explanation.[40] State printing houses may flatly refuse to publish independent media, and many nonstate newspapers must be printed abroad or, in the case of opposition publication, in *samizdat* form. Police routinely confiscate print runs at the border, particularly on the eve of key opposition events, and return them days or even weeks after their date of issue.[41] The independent press depends on private sellers required to register as private entrepreneurs. Even in these cases, they distribute without any guarantee against detainment and confiscation of newspapers performing their work without licenses.

The government routinely denies independent journalists access to official events and information, suggesting that their activities "destabilize the situation in the country."[42] Prime Minister Siarhej Sidorski issued an order to government agencies to "control" information distributed to the independent press and "take steps" against "unobjective" data and commentaries.[43] On June 28, 2007, the Hous of Representatives approved a law requiring all state officials to receive approva from higher authorities before speaking to the press.[44] Independent journalist continued to face arrest and physical harassment in 2007.[45] On a positive note citizens won two libel suits against the official press in 2007, and state newspaper were ordered to publish apologies. One case involved a democratic activist fron the city of Homel whom a state newspaper charged with financial wrongdoing: In the other case, the Catholic Church brought charges against the state press fo accusations that the church was "staging a crusade" against Belarus.[46]

Independent journalists have faced arbitrary lawsuits under criminal cod Article 367 (slander against the president), Article 368 (insulting the president), an Article 369 (insulting government officials). These articles stipulate large fines an prison sentences for those found guilty. The largest libel suit (27 million Belarusia rubles [US$12,000], awarded in 2007) was brought against *Narodnaya Volya* b the regime's chief ideologist, Deputy Head of the Presidential Administratio Aleh Praliaskouski. *Narodnaya Volya,* in coverage of the arrest of Praliaskouski deputy Uladzimir Cholad, asserted that Cholad "did not collect bribes for himself. Praliaskouski considered the statement a personal insult, even though he faile to prove the publication implicated him personally.[47] In 2007, Senator Mikal: Charhiniec, notorious for routinely bringing libel suits against the independen media, pressed charges against the newspaper *Novy Chas* for over 50 millio Belarusian rubles (US$23,000). Charhiniec considered it offensive, for exampl that the newspaper called his union "a righteous Union of Writers."[48] Journali: Alexander Sdvizhkov from the newspaper *Zhoda* was arrested upon his arriv from Russia to visit his parents' grave and went on trial for fomenting religiou hatred in November 2007, having previously been banned (in February 2006) fo republishing the infamous Muhammad cartoons from the Danish newspapers.[49]

Independent journalists working without official accreditation for foreig media may officially be accused of performing illegal activities. For example, i 2007, journalist Anatol Hatouchyc received a fine for "illegal activity on behalf c the foreign media outlets."[50] These charges resulted from the capricious accreditatio practices of the Belarusian Foreign Ministry, which deny accreditation to certai media outlets. The Belarusian Association of Journalists appealed the decision t the Constitutional Court, but the Court confirmed the decision as "correspondin to international standards."[51]

The state dominates electronic media in Belarus. Currently, the country has fou national television channels—Channel 1 (formerly BT-1), All-National Televisio (ONT), Capital TV, and Lad—all of which report on domestic and internation: affairs in a manner acceptable to the government without alternative political view: In 2007, attacks on the opposition and the West were toned down in electroni media but did not add fairness and impartiality in official media broadcasts; rathe they reflected the changing focus toward entertainment and popular cultur The public received little information regarding the independent BelSat satellit channel that began broadcasting in December 2007 with financial support fror the Polish government. Moreover, in May–June 2007, local authorities attempted to remove "unauthorized" satellite dishes from residential apartment houses in cities across Belarus.[52]

The Internet remains the only available source of alternative information in Belarus. According to the Vilnius-based Independent Institute for Socioeconomic and Political Studies, 25 percent of the adult population used the Internet at least once a month in 2007.[53] At the same time, 180,000 people (2 percent of the adult population) used the Internet daily, a 29 percent increase since 2006.[54] Internet access is restricted by heavy costs and lack of high-speed Internet services or 'open access' (such as wireless hot spots). State providers restrict access to opposition Web sites during key political events such as elections or demonstrations. Nevertheless, there is an obvious upward trend in the use of the Internet as an alternative source of expression (for example, the Belarusian livejournal.com segment has over 18,000 registered Web logs). Many opposition newspapers closed by the government or forced to cease publication for financial reasons, continue as online editions.

The Internet also allows a space for investigative journalism silenced by libel suits and self-censorship in printed media. In 2007, the Web portal of the Agency of Financial News attracted attention for investigating and disclosing details of several privatization and investment deals announced by the government. The Agency provided evidence connecting purchasers of state assets and investors with shadow offshore companies.

The Internet poses a concern for the government as a competitor in the information field. Veteran opposition politician Andrej Klimau received the first sentence in 2007 on libel charges. In a closed trial in August, Klimau was given a two-year prison sentence for calls to overthrow the government in an article published on the Web site of the United Civic Party.[55] The sentence established an important precedent to silence independent opinion online. On September 19, Anatol Liabedzka, leader of the United Civic Party, received a warning from the Office of the Prosecutor General for posting an opinion critical of the government on the same Web site.[56]

President Lukashenka, in his August 2007 speech to the editorial board of *SB-Belarus Segodnya*, warned that the Internet, as an information resource, equaled the entire media network controlled by the government and demanded an "end to the anarchy online."[57] In 2007, the National Assembly debated a draft Law on Protection of Information, which if adopted would require all Internet editions to go through procedures similar to those of the printed press, including obtaining official registration. Experts point to the unenforceability of such a regulation, as Web sites can easily be re-registered with foreign hosts. Nevertheless, by creating a "shadow" legal territory (that is, by failing to clearly define legal limits for online editions), the law would create the grounds to prosecute online journalists and bloggers or to permanently block independent Web sites from operating without registration. "The obvious aim of the law is to exclude from the free area entire segments of information resources, to restrict or even rule out altogether their distribution," declared former justice of the Constitutional Court Michail Pastuchou.[58]

Local Democratic Governance

1999	2001	2002	2003	2004	2005	2006	2007	2008
n/a	n/a	n/a	n/a	n/a	6.50	6.50	6.50	6.75

Since 1994, all levels of local government have been united into a single system of state authority. By law, heads of regional administrations are appointed by, and subordinate to, the president. Local councils are popularly elected but have no control over the executive bodies. Nearly 1,700 local governments exist, subdivided into three levels: regional (*voblasc*), district (*raion*), and village or (in urban areas) township.

The Constitution establishes that local councils have the exclusive right to adopt regional programs in social and economic development, establish local taxes and adopt budgets, manage communal property within limits proclaimed by the law, and call local referendums. Notwithstanding these prerogatives, local governments have little control over their finances, as the central budget absorbs nearly 70 percent of the consolidated national budget and local authorities are heavily dependent on transfers and subsidies.

Local elections carried out on January 14, 2007, reduced to a bare minimum the already minuscule representation of the opposition in local councils. Out of 23,000 elected parliamentarians, only 20 opposition representatives won seats in the councils at all levels. In spite of a high turnout, the elections raised little public discussion about pressing local issues. The opposition failed to attract much attention to the electoral process by campaigning, and their overall failure in the elections led to the closure of the opposition-dominated Assembly of the Deputies of Local Councils.

Local governments implement many of the repressive policies of the central government, including harassment of democratic activists and local free press. In theory, state bodies are obliged to present nonclassified information, but local authorities may deny access to information to independent journalists, NGOs, or opposition-minded local deputies. Several local governments actively carried out the campaign of the satellite dish removal on the grounds of what was explained to be "beautification" of the cities. During the period of May–June 2007 local authorities removed "unauthorized" satellite dishes from facades of residential apartment houses in cities across Belarus. Local authorities usually avoid cooperation with local civil society groups, except organizations sponsored by the government. However, civil society groups in Minsk, through a series of protests (some of which were dispersed by the police), managed to postpone the destruction of the historic St. Joseph Monastery in the city center to build a hotel and entertainment complex approved by local authorities.

Judicial Framework and Independence

1999	2001	2002	2003	2004	2005	2006	2007	2008
6.50	6.75	6.75	6.75	6.75	6.75	6.75	6.75	6.75

Judiciary power in Belarus is de facto subordinated to the presidency. In the first half of 2007, the government authorized the early release of the former leader of the Belarusian Social Democratic Party, Mikalaj Statkevich, and the former leader of the Young Front youth movement, Pavel Seviaryniec, both sentenced to hard labor for staging protests against the constitutional referendum of 2004. Kaciaryna Sadouskaja, sentenced in 2006 to two years for insulting the president, was also released. Statkevich declared his release an attempt to "trade" him to prevent the loss of EU trade preferences. Meanwhile, authorities failed to release other high-profile prisoners, such as former presidential candidate Alyaksandr Kazulin.

The authorities extensively use fines and prison sentences to threaten the activities of young democratic activists, whom they single out as the most credible threat to the regime. Seviaryniec has been arrested several times and has spent a total of two months in jail on various charges since May. An imprisoned leader of the organization Young Front, Zmitser Dashkevich, was charged, while in prison, for failing to testify against friends who faced prosecution for the same offense. He eventually received a large fine.[59] Another young activist, Artur Finkevich, who served two years of hard labor for political graffiti, was charged with insubordination and curfew violation in the detention. He received an additional sentence of one and a half years.

Police crackdowns on opposition rallies, pickets, and flash mobs continued in 2007. The police arrested activists on the standard charges of swearing in public, insubordination, and drunkenness, for which the accused received sentencing or a heavy fine. The courts frivolously applied regulations on mass rallies and pickets, even issuing sentences for participation in indoor meetings, for which the law does not require an official permit. According to their relatives, youths arrested on October 31, 2007, for an unauthorized flash mob celebrating Halloween in a shopping center in Minsk were detained for two days without food.[60] An activist from Minsk was acquitted on charges of organizing an unauthorized picket but was immediately sentenced for insubordination to the police officer who demanded he stop conducting an unauthorized picket.[61]

Closed trials continued in 2007 with the prosecution of Andrei Klimau, charged with insulting the president in an online publication. Kazulin, arrested in April 2007, was sentenced to two years in jail in August. Information about the sentence reached the public through Klimau's wife weeks after the trial. Kazulin notified the public that prison authorities kept him "in a complete information vacuum,"[62] as the administration denied him access to information and reportedly withheld letters from relatives and friends. The court declined Kazulin's appeal in 2007, despite evidence confirming his innocence of fomenting mass disorder and attacking the police during the demonstrations of March 25, 2007.[63] Furthermore, in July 2007, Kazulin's daughter lost her job without explanation.[64]

The presidential decree of December 17 ended a practice requiring special permission stamps validating foreign passports for travel.[65] This decree came four years after the Constitutional Court declared such stamps illegal. Exit stamp refusal was often used in the past to prevent opposition activists from traveling abroad. The new regulation technically removed restrictions on foreign travel for many Belarusian citizens. At the same time, the authorities prepared a list of as many as 100,000 citizens banned from traveling abroad. According to officials, the list mostly includes those with outstanding debt, alimony, and tax liabilities or those facing criminal charges. Since this list has not been publicized, opposition members may not know whether they are blacklisted until they attempt to cross the border. At the same time, authorities refused to compensate the exit stamp fees for the years 2008–2011.[66] The end to the Soviet-era system of *propiska*, or registering each citizen to a location according to his or her permanent residence, and its replacement with much more lenient registration rules proved another window-dressing measure passed off as liberalization in 2007.

Corruption

1999	2001	2002	2003	2004	2005	2006	2007	2008
5.25	5.25	5.25	5.50	5.75	6.00	6.25	6.25	6.25

Belarusian law, although abundant with anticorruption legislation, blurs the line between corrupt and clean practices, as some activities generally considered corrupt are legal in Belarus. For example, the controversial constitutional referendum of 1996 eliminated requirements for government programs to gain financing from official budgets and to make public spending transparent. Part of the public sector is operated under the auspices of the Presidential Business Office, a business empire directly subordinated to the presidency whose revenues bypass the official budget and reportedly go to unpublicized presidential funds. The official budget is debated and adopted by the Parliament, fully controlled by the executive.

The predominance of the state sector (controlling 80 percent of all assets) creates ubiquitous opportunities for officials to reap administrative rents, take advantage of uncontrolled financial flows, and offer privileges to companies to which they have connections at the expense of destroying competition. Indeed, Transparency International's Corruption Perceptions Index in 2007 assigned Belarus the rating of 2.1 on a scale of 0 to 10, where 0 denotes highly corrupt. One example of these practices within powerful institutions was the July 2007 arrest of Uladzimir Cholad, first deputy head of the Main Ideological Department within the Presidential Administration, who was charged with extorting a bribe and fraud, although his agency is not officially authorized to control financial flows or property management.[67] Nonetheless, top Belarusian officials enjoy a measure of protection from prosecution; they cannot be charged unless the president approves the prosecution's request.

Contrary to the president's claim that all privatizations in Belarus would proceed on the basis of open tenders, sales in 2007 were conducted in an atmosphere of secrecy, and details reached the public only through the efforts of independent online whistle-blowers. The most surprising deal of the year was the sale in August 2007 of the cellular network operator Velcom. Initially, the Cyprus-based SB Telecom company (a Velcom minority shareholder), whose head meets frequently with Lukashenka, appeared as the interested purchaser. In September, SB Telecom resold 70 percent of its shares in Velcom to Telecom Austria. While it appeared that the sale of Velcom was necessary to pay back debt secured by the Belarusian government from Austrian banks at the high point of the Belarus-Russia "energy war" in the winter of 2007, SB Telecom was used as an intermediary to bypass Belarusian legal requirements that demand an open tender for sale of public enterprises but excludes shareholders aiming to increase their stake in the company. Although no direct implications of corruption arose in the Velcom sale, the non-transparent nature of the transactions raised questions about further privatization deals.

On a positive note, the World Bank marked a modest improvement in the business climate in Belarus in its *Doing Business 2008* survey. Belarus rose in ease of doing business, to 110th from 119th place in the 2007 survey.[68] The improvement resulted from shortening the period necessary to start a new business, reducing the number of necessary procedures to start a new business, and reducing the costs of starting a business. These modest improvements sprang from the government's campaign to reduce bureaucracy, particularly Directive No. 2 issued by President Lukashenka in 2006 to reduce bureaucratic procedures for citizens and businesses.

At the same time, in 2007 the president backtracked on promises made to private entrepreneurs during the 2006 re-election campaign to keep regulations stable for private business. Decree No. 360, signed on December 29, 2006, and enacted in January 2007, severely restricted conditions for individual entrepreneurs who work without a legal entity. The decree allowed individual entrepreneurs (predominantly petty market traders) to hire close relatives and mandated them to form small, private companies if additional employees were necessary. Compared with private entrepreneurs, small private companies are subject to much heavier taxation and regulations. The authorities explained the decree would level the competitive playing field, even though, opponents claimed, they could have chosen to liberalize the tax regime for small companies instead. The new regulations are likely to force many petty traders into corrupt dealings with the authorities, such as the registration of phony companies, in order to stay in business.[69]

In spite of the modest improvement in the business climate, Belarus continues to be the worst country in the world for taxes (in terms of complexity of the tax code, number of taxes paid, and time necessary to deal with the procedures). If all taxes were paid legally, a typical Belarusian company would have to pay 144 percent of its profits, down from 161 percent in 2006.[70] These unenforceable regulations create ubiquitous opportunities for bribery among tax authorities. One of the most publicized corruption cases in 2007 was the regional tax inspection in Minsk, as seven officials were brought under criminal investigation at one time.[71]

▌ Author: Vitali Silitski

Vitali Silitski is a director of the Vilnius-based Belarusian Institute for Strategic Studies. In 2006–2007, he was a visiting scholar at the Center on Democracy, Development, and the Rule of Law at Stanford University.

1   "Yury Chizh: I See No Grounds for My Arrest," Belorusskiy partisan Web site, May 30, 2007, http://www.belaruspartisan.org/bp-forte/?page=100&backPage=13&news=13185&news Page=0.

2   "Sukhorenko and Naumov Exchanged Strikes," Belorusskiy partisan Web site, June 8, 2007, http://www.belaruspartisan.org/bp-forte/?page=100&news=13498.

3   "How Lomat Got Himself in Trouble," Belorusskiy partisan Web site, July 19, 2007, http://www.belaruspartisan.org/bp-forte/?page=100&backPage=52&news=14881&newsPage=0.

4   Ibid.

5   "Lukashenka Explained Why KGB Failed to Satisfy Him." UNIAN news service, July 19, 2007, http://unian.net/rus/news/news-204118.html.

6   "Belarus Exclusion from GSP: Possible Repercussions," Analysis of the Belarusian Institute for Strategic Studies, April 13, 2007, http://www.belinstitute.eu/images/stories/documents/biss_gsp_eng.pdf.

7   "Belarus Dismisses New U.S. Sanctions," *Washington Post*, March 1, 2007, http://www.washingtonpost.com/wp-dyn/content/article/2007/03/01/AR2007030101445.html.

8   "Freezing of Belnaftakhim Assets: To Be Continued?," *BISS Blitz*, December 19, 2007, Belarusian Institute for Strategic Studies. Available online at http://www.belinstitute.eu/images/stories/documents/blitz20071217belneftekhimen.pdf.

9   "What Conclusions Can Be Drawn from the March?," Charter-97 news service, October 21, 2007, http://www.charter97.org/ru/news/2007/10/21/863.

10 "European Commissions Condemned Arrests on 27 July," Charter-97 news service, July 30, 2007, http://www.charter97.org/bel/news/2007/07/30/aktiv.

11 "Zmicier Chviedaruk Experiences Vision Problem," Charter-97 news service, December 17, 2007, http://www.charter97.org/ru/news/2007/12/17/2460.

12 *Local Elections in Belarus,* a report by the Belarusian Helsinki Committee, p. 29, http://www.belhelcom.org/files/HulakMON.doc.

13 Official information of the Central Election Commission, http://rec.gov.by/elect/ppns3/ppns3name.html.

14 Information of the Central Election Commission, March 23, 2007. Available online at the Central Election Commission Web site, http://rec.gov.by/elect/prrb2006/mess13.html.

15 *Local Elections in Belarus,* a report by the Belarusian Helsinki Committee, p. 43, http://www.belhelcom.org/files/HulakMON.doc.

16   Ibid., p. 84.

17   Ibid., p. 53.

18   "State Radio Once Again Failed to Broadcast a Candidate's Address Due to 'Technical Problems,'" Internet service of the Belarusian Association of Journalists, January 4, 2007, http://www.baj.by/news/?id=590; "State Regional Newspaper Refused to Print the Material of the Candidate from the Belarusian Popular Front," Internet service of the Belarusian Association of Journalists, January 8, 2007, http://www.baj.by/news/?id=594.

19   Information of the Central Election Commission, December 21, 2006. Available online at the Central Election Commission Web site, http://rec.gov.by/elect/ms25/mess009.html.

20   Information of the Central Election Commission, available online at the Central Election Commission Web site, http://rec.gov.by/elect/ms25/mess011.html.

21   Ibid.

22   Local Elections in Belarus, p. 83.

23   "Belarusian Women's Party Nadzeja Liquidated by Supreme Court," Tut.by information portal, October 11, 2007, http://news.tut.by/96036.html.

24   Communist Party Suspended for Six Months in Belarus," News.ru news service, August 2, 2007, http://www.newsru.com/world/02aug2007/kom.html.

25   Official information of the Ministry of Justice, available online at http://www.minjust.by/struct/ua.htm.

26   Viktor Chernov, "Third Sector in Belarus," Nashe Mneniye Internet journal, February 18, 2008, http://www.nmnby.org/pub/0802/18m.html.

27   Liquidator is the name given to the people who were in charge of the removal of the consequences of the exploded nuclear reactor at Chernobyl.

28   "Nasta Plazhanka: Heta velmi miakkaje pakarannie na jakoje my nie razlichyvali." [Nasta Palazhanka—It is a Very Small Punishment That We Did Not Expect] Nash Niva 29 May 2007, http://www.nn.by/index.php?c=ar&i=9170

29   "Belarusian Helsinki Committee Calls for Trial of the RNE Activists for Fomenting Racial Hatred," Telegraf.by Web site, July 27, 2007, http://telegraf.by/belarus/2007/07/27/rne.

30   Jury Drakakhrust, "Artur Finkevich and Russian Loan," Radio Liberty Belarusian Service, December 23, 2007, http://by.slobodka.org/Article.aspx?id=868726.

31   Nikolay Khalezin, "Main Enemies of the State are Writers, Actors, Bards." Charter-97 internet service, September 12, 2007, http://www.charter97.org/bel/news/2007/09/12/marsh.

32   "Youth Protests the Compulsory BRSM Membership," Charter-97 internet service, September 21, 2007, http://www.charter97.org/bel/news/2007/09/21/protiv.

33   "The Regime Change(s) Survey of Current Trends and Development in Belarus Summer 2007," Pontis Foundation Belarus Brief, p. 9, http://www.nadaciapontis.sk/tmp/asset_cache/link/0000017223/Pontis%20Survey%20The%20Regime%20Change(s).pdf.

34   "School Program Will Get Rid of 'Tutejsyja'?," Belarusian News information service, March 17, 2007, http://naviny.by/rubrics/culture/2007/03/18/ic_articles_117_150136.

35   "International Expertise of the Belarusian Draft Law On Information," Belarusian Institute for Strategic Studies, October 8, 2007, http://www.belinstitute.eu/index.php?option=com_content&task=view&id=113&Itemid=75; http://www.e-belarus.org/docs/expertise_eng.pdf.

36   Taciana Belashova and Aleksandryna Funt, "Value Orientations and Civil Activism of Belarusian Students," available online at http://www.belinstitute.eu/images/stories/documents/values_students_ru.pdf.

37   Official information of the Ministry of Information, http://www.mininform.gov.by/main/massmedia/publishing/condition.

38   "ARCHE Magazine Received Two Warnings from the Ministry of Information," Internet service of the Belarusian Association of Journalists, February 12, 2007, http://www.baj.by/news/?id=655.

39   "Non-State Newspaper *Niasvizhski Chas* Is Kicked Out of Belsajuzdruk," Internet service of the Belarusian Association of Journalists, January 25, 2007, http://www.baj.by/news/?id=617; "Mahileusajuzdruk Refuses to Distribute Non-State Newspaper *Bobruiskiy Kuryer*," Internet service of the Belarusian Association of Journalists, January 31, 2007, http://www.baj.by/news/?id=629.

40   "Viciebski Kuryer-M Files Appeal," January 25, 2007, http://www.baj.by/news/?id=618; "Contract with Independent Newspaper *Viciebski Kuryer M* Cancelled," Information service of the Belarusian Association of Journalists, March 23, 2007, http://www.baj.by/news/?id=689; http://www.baj.by/news/?id=724; "Non-State Weekly 'Miascovy Chas' Was Not Allowed to Be Sold in Pinsk," Information service of the Belarusian Association of Journalists, April 2, 2007, http://baj.by/m-p-viewpub-tid-1-pid-716.html.

41   "Print of Narodnaja Volja and Tovarishch Arrested," Internet service of the Belarusian Association of Journalists, April 26, 2007, http://www.baj.by/news/?id=761.

42   "Management of the Zhabinka Sugar Plant Consider that Journalists 'Destabilize the Situation' in the Region," Internet service of the Belarusian Association of Journalists, February 1, 2007, http://www.baj.by/news/?id=631.

43   "Authors of the Prime Minister's Directive: No Lapses and Wrong Numbers in the Media," Internet service of the Belarusian Association of Journalists, March 1, 2007, http://www.baj.by/news/?id=664.

44   "Statement by the Belarusian Association of Journalists," Internet service of the Belarusian Association of Journalists, June 28, 2007, http://www.baj.by/news/?id=864.

45   "Journalists Arrested in Baranavichy," Internet service of the Belarusian Association of Journalists, September 10, 2007, http://www.baj.by/news/?id=980.

46   "Homelskaja Prauda Apologized to the United Civic Party Activist," Internet service of the Belarusian Association of Journalists, March 16, 2007, http://www.baj.by/news/?id=681; "Hazeta Respublika Apologized," Internet service of the Belarusian Association of Journalists, June 21, 2007, http://www.baj.by/news/?id=852.

47   "Warning for Opinion Online," Internet service of the Belarusian Association of Journalists, September 18, 2007, http://www.baj.by/news/?id=995.

48   "Deputy Nikolay Charhiniec Presses Libel Suit Against 'Novy Chas' Newspaper." *Belorusskiye Novosti* Internet Newspaper, November 23, 2007, http://naviny.by/rubrics/society/2007/11/23/ic_news_116_281012.

49   "Freedom Remains Elusive for Journalist from Belarus Jailed for Printing Islamic Cartoons," Fox News online service, February 18, 2008, http://www.foxnews.com/story/0,2933,331188,00.html.

50   "Journalist Anatol Hatouchyc Fined for Illegal Activities in the Interests of Foreign Media," Internet service of the Belarusian Association of Journalists, March 27, 2007, http://www.baj.by/news/?id=716.

51   "Mikhail Pastukhou: It Is a Pity That the Constitutional Court Failed to Mention Obvious Violations of the Legislation," Internet service of the Belarusian Association of Journalists, August 3, 2007, http://www.baj.by/news/?id=915.

52   "Mikhail Pastukhou: Fight with Dishes Can Turn Nationwide," Internet service of the Belarusian Association of Journalists, May 16, 2007, http://www.baj.by/news/?id=790.

53   Information available at http://www.iiseps.org/data07-02-12.html.

54   "Belarusians Go Online," http://news.bsb.by/rubrics/comments/0426914.

55   "Andrej Klimau, a Political Prisoner," Charter-97 news service, available online at http://www.charter97.org/index.phtml?sid=3&did=aklimov.

56   "BAJ Statement Concerning the Criminal Prosecutions for Publications Online," Internet service of the Belarusian Association of Journalists, April 11, 2007, http://www.baj.by/news/?id=995; and "Warnings for Opinions Online," Internet service of the Belarusian Association of Journalists, September 18, 2007, http://www.baj.by/news/?id=910.

57 "Lukashenka: End Anarchy Online," Internet service of the Belarusian Association of Journalists, August 2, 2007, http://www.baj.by/news/?id=741.

58 "Mikhail Pastukhou: This Law Is an Attempt to Limit the Citizens' Access to Information," Internet service of the Belarusian Association of Journalists, April 12, 2007, http://www.baj.by/news/?id=741.

59 "Political Prisoner Zmicier Dashkievich Will Be Jailed (Right in Prison) on 6 November," Charter-97 internet service, October 30, 2007, http://www.charter97.org/be/news/2007/10/30/1141.

60 "Arrested Halloween Celebrator Placed in the Hospital," Charter-97 Internet service, November 4, 2007, http://www.charter97.org/be/news/2007/11/4/1273.

61 "Judges Give Stupid Sentences," Charter-97 Internet service, June 2007, http://www.charter97.org/bel/news/2007/06/12/sud.

62 "Full Isolation of Political Prisoners Klimau and Kazulin," July 8, 2007, http://www.charter97.org/bel/news/2007/07/08/polit.

63 "Kazulin's Case Is Falling Apart," Charter-97 Internet service, June 1, 2007, http://www.charter97.org/bel/news/2007/06/01/delo.

64 Ibid.

65 "Lukashenka Signed a Decree Canceling Exit Stamps," Telegraf.by Internet service, December 17, 2007, http://www.telegraf.by/belarus/2007/12/17/stamp.

66 "Belarusian Citizens Will Not Get Back Money Paid for Permission Stamp," Tut.by online service, December 20, 2007, http://news.tut.by/society/100159.html.

67 "Distrust Grows," Charter-97 Internet service, July 11, 2007, http://www.charter97.org/bel/news/2007/07/11/nedoverie.

68 *Doing Business 2008*, Belarus: World Bank, 2007, http://www.doingbusiness.org/Documents/CountryProfiles/BLR.pdf.

69 Text of the decree can be found at http://www.lawbelarus.com/repub/sub01/texa0161.htm.

70 Ibid.

71 "Massive Purges in Tax Inspections," Charter-97 Internet service, July 16, 2007, http://www.charter97.org/bel/news/2007/07/16/inspect.

Bosnia-Herzegovina

by Jasna Jelisić

Capital:	Sarajevo
Population:	3.8 million
GNI/capita:	US$6,780

The social data above was taken from the European Bank for Reconstruction and Development's *Transition Report 2007: People in Transition*, and the economic data from the World Bank's *World Development Indicators 2008*.

Nations in Transit Ratings and Averaged Scores

	1999	2001	2002	2003	2004	2005	2006	2007	2008
Electoral Process	5.00	4.75	4.25	3.75	3.50	3.25	3.00	3.00	3.00
Civil Society	4.50	4.50	4.25	4.00	3.75	3.75	3.75	3.50	3.50
Independent Media	5.00	4.50	4.25	4.25	4.25	4.00	4.00	4.00	4.25
Governance*	6.00	6.00	5.50	5.25	5.00	n/a	n/a	n/a	n/a
National Democratic Governance	n/a	n/a	n/a	n/a	n/a	4.75	4.75	4.75	5.00
Local Democratic Governance	n/a	n/a	n/a	n/a	n/a	4.75	4.75	4.75	4.75
Judicial Framework and Independence	6.00	5.50	5.25	5.00	4.50	4.25	4.00	4.00	4.00
Corruption	6.00	5.75	5.50	5.00	4.75	4.50	4.25	4.25	4.25
Democracy Score	5.42	5.17	4.83	4.54	4.29	4.18	4.07	4.04	4.11

* *With the 2005 edition, Freedom House introduced separate analysis and ratings for national democratic governance and local democratic governance to provide readers with more detailed and nuanced analysis of these two important subjects.*

NOTE: The ratings reflect the consensus of Freedom House, its academic advisers, and the author(s) of this report. The opinions expressed in this report are those of the author(s). The ratings are based on a scale of 1 to 7, with 1 representing the highest level of democratic progress and 7 the lowest. The Democracy Score is an average of ratings for the categories tracked in a given year.

EXECUTIVE SUMMARY

During a year of near constant political crisis, Bosnia-Herzegovina (BiH) in 2007 continued trends begun in October 2006 when coalition parties with opposite views on the future of BiH won the general elections. The international community and European Union (EU) enthusiasts in BiH believed that the incentive to join the EU would be irresistible to the local political elites and would push them to make difficult compromises. That did not happen during 2007, and the country remained the only one (together with Serbia) at the end of the western Balkans "regatta" without even the first contractual relationship with the EU—a Stabilization and Association Agreement (SAA).

The previous High Representative (HR), Christian Schwartz-Schilling[1], sought to increase the focus on local ownership. However, he did not succeed in making domestic institutions function without international intervention. Instead the local political leaders assumed ownership by engaging in harsh nationalistic rhetoric and stalled the reform agenda. Yet there were no serious attempts by the international community to unblock the process or confront local actors who jeopardized all the major peace- and state-building achievements made since 1995. The situation was unstable and looked more like the beginning of the 1990s, when local elites first tried to "take ownership" in BiH, and the war started.

Politicians from the two Bosnian entities—the Federation of Bosnia-Herzegovina (FBiH) and the Republika Srpska (RS)—sensed that the international community had grown tired of keeping BiH together, so they returned to the rhetoric of the 1990s, reinforcing opposing views on the future of BiH. On the FBiH side, they insisted on preservation of BiH and a diminishment of the RS; and on the RS side, politicians advocated strengthening the RS and weakening the state. The international community was indeed looking for an exit strategy and an opportunity to finally close the Office of the High Representative (OHR). However, the announcement of the possible secession of the RS after the decision on the final status of Kosovo was crucial in delaying this decision. Linking Kosovo independence with RS independence as a follow-up remained an excellent negotiating chip for Serbia's prime minister, Vojislav Koštunica, throughout 2007. This devastated the functioning of state institutions, despite frequent statements by international officials that the status of Kosovo and the status of the RS were not connected.

The new RS prime minister, Milorad Dodik—elected in October 2006, who firmly kept power in the RS in 2007—halted the strengthening of the state in 2007 and announced the return of the competences that had been previously transferred to the state.[2] On several occasions, he even threatened a referendum on RS independence while in the presence of international community representatives in

BiH. This rhetoric radicalized the political atmosphere, amplified by Haris Silajdžić's equally radicalizing rhetoric as the Bosniak member of the BiH presidency.

The new HR, ambassador Miroslav Lajčák[3] arrived in July, promising that he would use all his powers to fully implement the Dayton Peace Accords and bring Bosnia closer to the EU under his second hat as the EU Special Representative (EUSR) in BiH.

The new HR/EUSR decided to focus on negotiations for police reform, since that was one of the most important preconditions for initialing an SAA with BiH. This reform needed to be accomplished before the European Commission finished its annual report on the country's progress, which would lead to either a recommendation or a decline by the EU to initial the SAA.

Despite the HR/EUSR's focused efforts, local political leaders failed to agree on police reform, and the SAA initialing was postponed. By the end of October, the ruling political leaders had only signed yet another agreement to, in effect, agree later. In the declaration, they promised to implement police reform in accordance with the three EU principles after they agreed on constitutional reform,[4] yet they failed to follow up on these promises during 2007.

With the EU agenda off the table for the time being, the HR focused on Dayton implementation and announced a set of state-building measures to improve the decision-making system in BiH. These measures met a fierce confrontation in the RS, whose prime minister openly threatened to remove all RS officials from the state structures and possibly hold a referendum on secession.[5] The Council of Ministers chair, Nikola Špirić, resigned on November 1 in protest of the measures. The country's tripartite presidency attempted to choose a new state-level prime minister and future government, which ended up with the same nominee, Nikola Špirić, who became Council of Ministers chair designate on December 27. The Špirić government remained in an interim mandate at the end of the year, bringing cabinet work largely to a standstill.

After a series of meetings between international community officials and the country's politicians, a deep institutional crisis was temporarily calmed by the end of the year. The BiH Parliament adopted the HR's altered measures, which was enough for the EU to give a green light to initial the SAA without the agreement on police reform. EU enlargement commissioner Olli Rehn traveled to Sarajevo and initialed an SAA with BiH on December 4 on the promise from domestic politicians to agree on police reform by mid-February 2008. Yet this seemed unlikely.

In general, the ruling coalition could not agree on any substantial solution that would lead to stability, sustainability, and the economic and democratic development of BiH. Their actions and public disagreements worsened the political situation in the country. Serbia's and Russia's opposition to the HR state-strengthening measures caused additional cautiousness in international community circles, which made the planned closure of the OHR in mid-2008 less likely, especially with the Kosovo status negotiations and the unilateral proclamation of independence by Kosovo Albanians foreseen on the horizon.

National Democratic Governance. In 2007, democratic governance in BiH had one of its worst years since the beginning of the Dayton Peace Accords implementation in 1995 and proved the fragility of the country's democratic institutions. The ruling coalition kept BiH in a constant political crisis, demonstrating a significant lack of progress on key reforms necessary for the final stabilization of the country and its Euro-Atlantic integration. The deteriorated political atmosphere, which the ruling coalition produced by not agreeing on any substantial reform and putting into question many state-building achievements in the post-Dayton period, posed substantial challenges to the stability of the country. The negative developments in 2007 proved that under the current constitutional setup, the potential for a sustainable, liberal democracy in BiH is very weak. *Owing to constant disagreements in the BiH presidency, a difficult and often stalled decision-making process in the BiH Council of Ministers, and very slow legislative activity in the BiH Parliamentary Assembly, in addition to RS government attempts to weaken the state authority and block the decision-making process, causing a serious institutional crisis at the end of the year, BiH's national democratic governance rating deteriorated from 4.75 to 5.00.*

Electoral Process. Elections in BiH are usually characterized as free and fair by international monitors, but the Law on Elections based on the Constitution continues to disregard the political rights of all citizens, especially minorities. There was no government pressure on opposition parties since they did not represent any serious threat to the ruling coalition. The opposition was too weak to confront BiH's ethno-nationalist political parties, which have a strong advantage provided by the electoral system. These parties dominated the political scene during 2007, determining the tone of public discussion and narrowing it to hard security issues. *Owing to a lack of improvement in the electoral dynamic in the country, BiH's electoral process rating remains at 3.00.*

Civil Society. Civil society is independent in BiH, and the rights of assembly and association are generally protected. There were no improvements in philanthropy and volunteerism during 2007. Dependence on foreign funding and low fund-raising capabilities remain a barrier to the long-term sustainability of nongovernmental organizations (NGOs) and the country's civic sector on the whole. Civil society organizations have not made any serious effort to pressure politicians to agree on reforms that would bring BiH closer to the EU, which according to polls is what more than 70 percent of the population wishes. The most visibly active civil society groups were those under the influence of politicians or religious groups, often serving the political agenda of elected politicians. Ethnic divisions, which still exist in education in BiH, continue to seriously hinder the reconciliation process. The framework Law on Higher Education was finally adopted; this could be recorded as an improvement if the government showed strong indications that it means to implement it swiftly, which was not noticed by the end of the year. *BiH's civil society rating remains at 3.50.*

Independent Media. BiH law provides for diversity and independence of the media. However, there are indications of strong alliances between political circles, business interests and media. Additionally, the media mostly represent the three dominant ethnic groups and are ethno-territorially defined. Special interests, both political and economic, exert influence on reporting and editorial independence and often lead to self-censorship. *These negative developments, combined with the still unresolved status of the broadcasting system and physical threats to journalists in 2007, have led to a worsening of the independent media rating from 4.00 to 4.25.*

Local Democratic Governance. Local self-government is not fully in place in BiH, since there was no significant improvement in the implementation of the entity legislation on local self-governance in accordance with the European Charter on Local Self-Governance. The RS authorities worked on producing amendments to the entity Constitution that would provide constitutional status for local self-governance, but these were not adopted in 2007, nor were there any practical steps toward real decentralization. The FBiH continued to ignore its obligations toward the European Charter on Local Self-Governance and the implementation of the FBiH Law on Local Self-Governance. As a consequence, the majority of local authorities continued to pay allegiance to the entity and cantonal authorities throughout BiH or face the threat of being overthrown. *Owing to a lack of improvement, the rating for local democratic governance remains at 4.75.*

Judicial Framework and Independence. The judiciary struggles to maintain its independence from the government, which tried to exert pressure on judges and courts. Respect for basic political, civil, and human rights is selective. The judiciary is slow, and abuses occur. Among the rare encouraging signs is the continuing good work by the Court of BiH, which so far has professionally handled cases of terrorism, war crimes, and organized crime offenses. The country still has no Supreme Court, which would harmonize legal systems throughout the country. *Owing to a lack of improvement and the political will to approach constitutional reform that would improve many aspects of the judiciary in BiH, the rating for judicial framework and independence remains at 4.00.*

Corruption. Corruption is widespread in BiH and combined with the country's constitutional setup presents a major impediment to political and economic development. The government's anticorruption efforts are inconsistent. Alliances between business and political circles seem stronger than ever. The high-profile corruption cases in 2007 and their outcomes have not improved corruption perceptions in BiH. *Owing to a lack of improvement in fighting corruption, BiH's rating for corruption remains at 4.25.*

Outlook for 2008. Substantial changes to the current government structure (based on the Dayton Peace Accords) are needed to create the conditions for sustainable peace, efficient functioning, and the stability of state institutions before the international community can leave BiH without risking the loss of positive results that have been achieved since the peace implementation started in 1995. A year ago, it was a common argument in BiH that the country could not negotiate efficiently with the EU on its membership as long as it had such complex and uncoordinated government structures. Negative developments in 2007 demonstrated that the country not only lacks mechanisms for implementing the *acquis*, but struggles with basic functionality and stability.

There is a broad consensus among BiH parties and civil society that the Constitution of BiH provides neither functional and efficient state institutions nor a system capable of satisfying the demands of Euro-Atlantic integration.[6] Constitutional reform remains an imperative for BiH's functionality, stability, and capacity to seriously approach an EU integration agenda. The rhetoric of local political elites that questions the survival of the entities or the state is likely to intensify in the coming year due to local elections (scheduled for October 2008). It was widely recognized that this would leave little chance for any constructive discussion on constitutional changes or improvement in democratic governance.

Throughout 2007, it was obvious that the ruling authorities strongly (and rightly) believed that the international community was focused on Kosovo, which they saw as an opportunity to test how far they could push their opposing demands without suffering serious consequences. As a result, the capability of the BiH government to create a calmer political environment in 2008 and deliver required reforms is questionable. The developments in Serbia and Kosovo also have a potential to raise tensions in BiH, which would prolong the life of the OHR and Bonn powers and likely prevent any faster progress toward the EU.

By the end of 2007, some actors in the international community seemed more decisive in their efforts to protect the political and financial investments in the survival of BiH. However, it did not appear that all major capitals understood the seriousness of the crisis in the country's functioning and stability. As developments in BiH always require careful treatment, the international community, and the EU in particular, would need to carefully design its future role, as well as policies in BiH that would contribute to BiH's long-term stability and country's capacity to acquire full membership in the EU.

Main Report

National Democratic Governance

1999	2001	2002	2003	2004	2005	2006	2007	2008
n/a	n/a	n/a	n/a	n/a	4.75	4.75	4.75	5.00

The political dynamic in Bosnia-Herzegovina (BiH) started to worsen in April 2006, when the first package of reforms to the Dayton Constitution failed to pass in the Bosnia-Herzegovina (BiH) Parliamentary Assembly. From that point, the political climate continued to deteriorate, followed by a prolonged process of government formation at all levels, with the exception of the Republika Srpska (RS) government, which formed immediately after the October 2006 elections owing to the sweeping victory of the Serb Union of Independent Social Democrats (SNSD).

This deteriorating trend continued in 2007 and the state-ruling coalition of intransigent parties put a halt to the Dayton Accords implementation and European Union (EU) reforms. In this setup, only one new law related to EU integration was adopted in the state Parliament in the first 12 months of its functioning.[7]

The new government of BiH was formed in February 2007. The SNSD and the Party of Democratic Progress (PDP), the Bosniak Party of Democratic Action (SDA) and Party for BiH (SBiH), the Croatian Democratic Union (HDZ) of BiH, and HDZ 1990 formed the ruling coalition. The Council of Ministers of BiH comprises parties with opposing stances on almost every substantial issue in Bosnia. Especially confrontational have been parties with influential leaders—namely, Haris Silajdžić and Milorad Dodik, on the Bosniak and Serb sides, respectively.

On several occasions during the year, RS prime minister Dodik announced the possibility of a referendum on the secession of the RS. Such a referendum would be unconstitutional and was opposed by the international community, but Dodik's rhetoric served to radicalize the political atmosphere. The same was happening on the Bosniak side, especially after the International Court of Justice (ICJ) announced the verdict in the *Bosnia and Herzegovina v. Serbia and Montenegro* case on application of the Convention on the Prevention and Punishment of the Crime of Genocide.[8] After the verdict, BiH president Silajdžić made equally radical statements about abolishing the RS police inflaming the grievances of all who had suffered from the Srebrenica genocide and had personal knowledge of Serbia's involvement in the war in BiH.[9]

SNSD's Nikola Špirić became Council of Ministers chairman and promised to accelerate BiH's Euro-Atlantic integration process, stating that the securing of a Stabilization and Association Agreement (SAA) with the EU would be his top priority.

Expectations were low for the new government and sank further. The SNSD remained the strongest Serb political party in the RS, firmly determining developments in the RS as well as at the state level. Among the major Croat political parties, the post-2006 election division of power between HDZ BiH and HDZ 1990 left bitterness that prevented the two parties from merging, despite several announcements. The major dynamic among the Bosniak parties was the competition between SDA and SBiH leaders to be "first among the Bosniaks" and their occasional alliances with the head of the Islamic community in BiH, Mustafa Cerić, and influential media outlets.

The first strong indications of nonfunctional governance strongly affected the decision of the Peace Implementation Council in February to prolong the Office of the High Representative (OHR) mandate until mid-2008. The other important factor in the decision was the delay in the Kosovo status settlement process—this negatively affected the political situation in BiH, since Kosovo independence was used by politicians in the RS and Serbia as a precedent for independence of the RS and dissolution of BiH.

RS prime minister Dodik projected an image of a proactive and economy-oriented government at the entity level, while stalling the majority of reforms at the state level and even questioning those that had already been adopted. The FBiH government performed even more poorly at the entity level since it took nine months to be formed. Even after it started working, it did not produce tangible results or deal in any substantive manner with reform in BiH (such as canceling the segregated and discriminatory education system, unifying Mostar, or agreeing on a law to regulate the federal broadcasting system). Political activity in the FBiH was focused on dividing control over the entity's biggest economic assets among the political parties. In addition, the FBiH government could not devise any practical or strategic plan to respond to policy initiatives coming from Dodik and finally blamed the international community for not confronting the state-threatening initiatives of the RS prime minister.

Leaders from both entities demonstrated great inflexibility in reaching compromises on necessary reforms. The EU insisted on a reform that would place competences for police legislation and budget at the state level, design regional police areas on the basis of functional policing criteria, and free police from political interference. After months of nerve-wracking negotiations on police reform, the Bosniak position came down to the name of the RS police, while the Serb side argued continually over the first two EU principles, wanting to preserve a separate police force that would be financed through the consolidated state budget. Ruling coalition leaders failed to reach an agreement on police reform, thus stalling the EU initialing of an SAA with BiH. This unwillingness to make compromises demonstrated the local elites' greater interest in narrow political goals than in BiH's future in the EU.

Trying to secure BiH's progress, High Representative (HR)/EU Special Representative (EUSR) Miroslav Lajčák put forward his own proposal for police reform reflecting the parties' major concerns, but both sides—Serb and Bosniak—refused it.[10] The Croat parties were fully cooperative in the process, basically accepting any kind of police reform that would secure an SAA for BiH. By mid-October even the Bosniak parties softened, but Prime Minister Dodik continued with the argument that the preservation of the RS police means the preservation of RS and rejected the HR/EUSR's proposal.

Disappointed with BiH's stalemate, the HR/EUSR turned his attention to the full implementation of the Dayton Peace Accords and put forward a set of state-strengthening decisions on October 19. The HR's measures aimed at healing the "ailing" state system in BiH and strengthening the functionality of its institutions,[11] were fiercely opposed by RS politicians as well as the public. The RS threatened to withdraw its representatives from the state institutions, attacked the authority of the HR, and even threatened a referendum on secession from BiH. The PDP threatened to take the HR to the European Court of Human Rights (ECHR) in Strasbourg and tried to push the Peace Implementation Council to rescind the Bonn powers.[12] On the other side, the majority in the FBiH saw the HR's measures as a means of restoring the authority of the HR office and as a long overdue effort to unblock the BiH decision-making system.

Escalation of the political crisis was prevented momentarily by a meeting on October 28 of the ruling political party leaders; at that time, in the presence of the HR, they agreed to implement police reform in accordance with the future constitutional arrangement respecting the three EU principles (democratic equality, representative democracy, and participatory democracy). However, police reform still was not implemented by the end of the year.

While stalling reforms at the state level, the RS authorities intensified implementation of the Agreement on Special and Parallel Relations Between RS and Serbia, what many in the FBiH part of the country read as the RS turning away from BiH.[13] The RS-Serbia Cooperation Council established a joint food reserves and electrical energy system in 2007, which parties in the FBiH saw as "the most flagrant violation of the sovereignty and territorial integrity of BiH."[14]

Even in the case of Bosnian obligations to the Central European Free Trade Agreement, which the BiH Parliament ratified in September, the coalition partners almost completely stalled the progress of reform. Also, the Indirect Taxation Authority Governing Board had problems in its functioning, failing again to agree on a lasting formula for dividing value-added tax revenues among the two entities and Brčko District.

Local authorities made no progress in transferring property from the entities to the state as required by the Law on Defense. The process of property transfer has been going on for three years. However, an agreement apportioning the ownership and use of state property had not been reached in 2007. In order to preserve state property, the HR used Bonn powers and announced decisions amending the laws on the temporary prohibition of disposal of state property in the RS and FBiH and on the transfer of social property into state property.[15] The ruling coalition attempted to make a political charade even out of the selection of the state human rights ombudsmen, nominating candidates who were directly linked with major political parties.[16]

The ruling coalition also remained divided on building new highways. Corridor 5c,[17] part of a 210-mile superhighway linking Budapest to the Adriatic Sea, was supposed to be Bosnia's fast track to Europe. The Bosniak and Croat officials in the Council of Ministers of BiH believed that the corridor—the country's largest public works project ever—should be coordinated from the capital. But the Serb representatives, in fighting almost all forms of state authority in 2007, claimed that building the road should be the entity responsibility and the RS government should be responsible for the part on its territory. There was no agreement on this issue. The struggle finished with the state institution funding the preparation of the project, while not having any competences to prevent the entities from undertaking uncoordinated activities in this regard.

Throughout the year, RS prime minister Dodik openly challenged the state sovereignty, directly linking the issues of Kosovo and RS independence. Facing a serious deterioration of the political situation, analysts speculated on whether the 2,500 EU peacekeepers currently deployed in BiH were sufficient.

Electoral Process

1999	2001	2002	2003	2004	2005	2006	2007	2008
5.00	4.75	4.25	3.75	3.50	3.25	3.00	3.00	3.00

During 2007, the Intergovernmental Working Group drafted amendments to the Law on Elections in BiH, Law on Conflict of Interest in the Governmental Institutions of BiH, and Law on Political Party Financing. The group also considered technical, constitutional, and political amendments to these laws. None of these was adopted by the end of the year.

There were improvements in the Central Election Commission (CEC) application of the Law on Political Party Financing, which strengthened the credibility of the CEC.[18] Yet the commission faced problems with two successive appeal cases returned by the Social Democrat Party of BiH (SDP) and SDA. This new area for the Court of BiH caused difficulties and prevented the CEC from fully applying this law. There was no agreement on constitutional reform in 2007; hence the Law on Elections in BiH remained tied to the current constitutional setup, which utterly disregards the European Convention for Human Rights, especially its social and political protocols.

There were no regular elections in 2007. The parties' finances continued to depend on their attachment to strong financial circles. Likewise, their political influence depended on the support of religious leaders, especially among Bosniaks and Croats. The RS-ruling SNSD for the first time turned to the Serbian Orthodox Church to gain support in areas that were not SNSD strongholds.

BiH authorities organize elections, and the OSCE has usually qualified them as free and fair and did so again after the early presidential elections in the RS. The electoral system in BiH is multiparty based, but political parties are still mainly national movements with a low level of expertise among top members. The exception is SNSD, which throughout 2007 was open to experts formulating its public stances and policies.

After the sweeping victory of SNSD in October 2006, the opposition in the RS has been effectively nonexistent, while in the FBiH, the strongest opposition party, SDP, has failed to stimulate any sophisticated and progressive debates that would draw public attention to serious social issues or put any significant pressure on the ruling parties.

There was no progress in increasing public engagement in political life in 2007. During the year, the population mostly continued to claim that "there is nobody to vote for." Even when voters go to the polls, they do so on the basis of security and border issues stressed by ethnic leaders. The need for new faces and ideas in politics remained, as did the need to improve the democratic conditions of the election system.

Citizens have sufficient chances to participate in public life, while ethnic minorities and others remain discriminated against on the basis of the BiH Constitution and resulting laws. Jews, for example, cannot run for the BiH presidency, nor can any Bosnian who does not declare to be a Croat, Bosniak, or Serb. The head of the Jewish community in BiH, Jakob Finci, appealed to the ECHR in January 2007, alleging a breach by a participating state of the European Convention for Human Rights—namely, the right to run for public office. The electoral system is tailored to favor ethno-nationalist groups, and there is no real rotation of power within a range of political parties representing competing interests and policy options.

The RS president, Milan Jelić, suffered a heart attack and died in September. Early elections for his replacement were held on December 9, according to the decision of the CEC.[19] The SNSD candidate, Rajko Kuzmanović, won with 41.33 percent of votes. The leading opposition party candidate, Ognjen Tadić (Serb Democratic Party, SDS), scored surprisingly high, winning 34.77 percent. The elections were deemed free and fair by the OSCE.

Civil Society

1999	2001	2002	2003	2004	2005	2006	2007	2008
4.50	4.50	4.25	4.00	3.75	3.75	3.75	3.50	3.50

It is difficult to assess the state's role in the independent civic sector, as the state of BiH hardly exercised its powers during the year and the country's institutions did not provide a positive environment for any sector, let alone civil society, while the lower levels of government showed no responsiveness to civil society demands. It was clear that civil society advocacy was not on their agenda unless the organizations were of a religious origin or a type that could be manipulated for political purposes or economic gain. This refers mainly to all three major religious communities in BiH, which tried to influence politicians or serve them in cases of a common agenda, or to veteran and union organizations, which often served political goals.

There was no significant growth in the number of charitable, nonprofit, and nongovernmental organizations (NGOs), nor were there significant improvements in the quality of performance of civil society groups or active public participation. The three primary religious organizations and their leaders (Islamic, Catholic, and Orthodox) were very active, never missing an opportunity to give their view on any major political issue (from future constitutional reform to the design of local police areas) or to support the claim of a particular political party.

There is little evidence that the government responded to civil society pressure since there were no well-organized advocacy actions connected to real issues in 2007. No NGO attempted to articulate the public demand for EU integration during the year. In a country where all polls show that more than 70 percent of the population wants BiH to join the EU, the NGO sector basically slept while politicians moved the country into isolation and blocked its progress toward EU membership in 2007.

The educational system remains divided. There were no improvements in this area during the year, and education remains one of the most devastating factors for the future of BiH because of the segregation that promulgates and deepens the country's nationalist divisions.

The RS and Serbian officials signed a protocol on building a school named "Serbia" in Pale, while Bosniak and Croat pupils in Croat-dominated cantons in the FBiH continued to be separated in schools. In some of them, Bosniak children enter through the back door and Croat children through the front. Pupils also remained physically separated during classes as a result of school scheduling; classes are organized in shifts which have breaks in-between that are long enough so the children from different ethnic groups cannot meet in school lobbies. The head of the OSCE mission in BiH, American ambassador Douglas Davidson, stated several times during 2007 that the current educational methods threaten BiH long-term stability.[20] Through the teaching of different histories, geographies, and languages, schools remained a means to separate the country's three constitutive peoples from one another.

There are arguments that segregated schools aim to secure self-protection of ethnic communities and their identities. However, the pre- and postwar empirical evidence shows that attending mixed schools has not diminished the ethnic identity of pupils. In addition, some media reports showed that pupils who go to mixed schools like them and oppose being separated,[21] which suggests that ethnic political parties want to use the educational system to produce party "soldiers" who fear neighbors of different ethnic backgrounds. The educational needs of others (minorities, children from mixed marriages, and all who refuse to declare themselves as Serb, Croat, or Bosniak) continued to be ignored, since they effectively have no political representation.

Yet adoption of the long overdue state framework Law on Higher Education in BiH represented a step forward. The law was published in the *Official Gazette* on August 7, 2007, and was a result of a political compromise.[22] Though imperfect, it provided a basis for further improvements in this area and a potential to bring

BiH's higher education toward European standards as envisioned by the Bologna process.[23] However, there were no strong indications in 2007 that the Council of Ministers would adopt all decisions necessary for the full implementation of this law.

Independent Media

1999	2001	2002	2003	2004	2005	2006	2007	2008
5.00	4.50	4.25	4.25	4.25	4.00	4.00	4.00	4.25

BiH media laws provide freedoms to broadcasters, but alliances between political groups and media and the resulting biased coverage are taken as a fact and considered normal. Developments in BiH in 2007 indicated that the public broadcasters were dedicated to more professional reporting and less willing to comply with demands of political power holders, while print media were much more open to biased reporting. In fact, it was sometimes difficult to identify who was controlling whom—did politicians control major print outlets by co-opting them in pushing their political agendas, or did the outlet owners have even greater influence over politicians, using these "alliances" to support their private interests?

There is a diversity of print and electronic sources of information, but the range of political viewpoints varies around the major political options in the country, which are now dominated by ethno-territorial biases. The use of the Internet is limited since the infrastructure is underdeveloped and still expensive, and a narrow interpretation of the regulatory laws so far has protected the dominant position of the three major telecom operators, which correspond to ethnically-defined territories.[24]

No concrete progress has been made to adopt the long overdue Law on Public Radio and Television Service in FBiH. The law was adopted in two houses in different texts, and the Croat caucus in the House of Peoples invoked the vital national interest to which the texts must be harmonized.[25] This has not been done, and the proposed law was sent to the FBiH Constitutional Court for consideration.

Journalists and reporters are generally protected, but incidents occur, as in the case of Vitomir Popović, the Serb representative in the Office of the State Ombudsman for Human Rights. In the middle of his attempt to be reelected in October 2007, while responding to a journalist's question in his Banja Luka office, Popović openly threatened Federal Television (FTV) journalist Damir Kaletović, stating that the reporter and his editor in chief, Bakir Hadžiomerović, "deserve a bullet in their foreheads."[26] This statement was broadcast on the Federal Television. The Society of BiH Journalists strongly condemned the threat and asked that the responsible organs, in accordance with their official duty, start a criminal investigation against Popović (who also served in a wartime government led by Radovan Karadžić).

Bosniak representatives in the FBiH Parliament on several occasions tried to exercise pressure on the Federal television, in response to criticism from this public broadcaster. RS prime minister Dodik also tried to exercise pressure on the national

BHT 1 by publicly criticizing its editorial policy. In the first half of the year, RS officials boycotted BHT 1 by not giving statements to its reporters.

Local Democratic Governance

1999	2001	2002	2003	2004	2005	2006	2007	2008
n/a	n/a	n/a	n/a	n/a	4.75	4.75	4.75	4.75

The entity governments made no serious progress in 2007 toward implementing the Laws on Local Self-Governance, which are in accordance with the European Charter on Local Self-Governance. Therefore, local communities continued to surrender competences and revenues that belong to municipalities to the (higher) entity and cantonal levels of government. The most vocal figure on this issue was the mayor of Foča, Zdravko Krsmanović. He claimed that 90 percent of public needs in the RS are solved by municipalities, while they enjoy only 10 percent of responsibilities and revenues and no budget to function effectively, which makes municipalities dependent on entity government. He stated publicly on several occasions that municipalities have no chance to run capital investment projects and day-to-day operations free from political and fiscal intrusion and pointed to "parasitism by the cantons and entities."[27]

According to current laws, municipalities may collect taxes, fees, and other revenues commensurate with their responsibilities, but their responsibilities are quite limited. The state and entity constitutions in BiH still do not provide for local self-governance. The RS government made an effort to prepare the local self-governance amendments to the RS Constitution, but they had not been adopted by the end of the year.

The RS diminished this positive development with attempts to overthrow local mayors who did not belong to the ruling SNSD, which seriously overshadowed efforts to strengthen local self-governance. The most famous case was the failed recall referendum against Mayor Krsmanović in Foča. This move was seen as politically orchestrated in Banja Luka as part of a strategy to remove mayors deemed "disloyal" or difficult to control.

Local communities in BiH want to be free to design and adopt programs that reflect local needs and conditions, but they have no resources to do so since higher levels of authority exhaust local resources without sending back proceeds. Mayors claim that they can make better use of their resources and collect revenues for the services they provide, which would cancel their dependency on top political figures in Sarajevo, Banja Luka, and Mostar and strongly contribute to increasing development of grassroots democracy.

Local authorities still widely fail to implement a constitutional obligation to employ municipality staff according to the 1991 census (the latest in BiH). The report of the FBiH Office of the Ombudsman from June 2007 identified grave violations of citizens' basic rights established by amendments to the FBiH Constitution, implementation of the BiH Constitutional Court decision on constitutive people equality in BiH, and laws regulating their proportional representation in FBiH civil service on the basis of the 1991 census. Municipality offices across BiH are reported as almost or totally monoethnic,[28] and violations of these rights are significant in both parts of the country.

There was little progress toward the unification of Mostar during 2007 as the two ethno-political elites' divergent interests prevent the potential unification of the city.[29] The HR openly warned that no one in BiH should expect his support for any project that is ethnically selective and reassured that he will support everything that emphasizes the multiethnic character of BiH. These kinds of statements did not affect the practices of Mostar political leaders in 2007.

Brčko District is still a BiH oasis where ethnic politics did not play a major role and where the administration scored far better in terms of economic development and employment. Privatization in the district has been considered the most successful in BiH. In 2007, the Brčko District administration implemented an employment program supporting companies with business development plans. Compared with the entities, the Brčko administration achieved far more in improving the business environment, investment climate, and economic development. As a result, the gross domestic product per capita, as well as average net salaries, have been higher in the Brčko District than in the entities, and unemployment decreased in 2007.[30]

The BiH Parliament adopted a Law on Amendments on the Law on the Council of Ministers in September, which established in law the Brčko District Coordinator's Office as a permanent body in the Council of Ministers. Brčko District still has no access to the BiH Constitutional Court since it has not been recognized in the BiH Constitution. The implementation of the Brčko Final Award is still pending, as is the adoption of amendments that would secure constitutional status for the district.

Judicial Framework and Independence

1999	2001	2002	2003	2004	2005	2006	2007	2008
6.00	5.50	5.25	5.00	4.50	4.25	4.00	4.00	4.00

Local political elites and the international community fully agree that changes to the Bosnian Constitution defined in Dayton are necessary. However, no progress was made in 2007 toward opening constitutional talks that would have any serious chance of succeeding. Progress on the EU membership path, a crucial issue for the future of BiH, was focused in 2007 on police reform as the key condition for initialing and later signing an SAA. The initiative of former HR Christian Schwartz-Schilling to open the constitutional reform process before he ended his mandate in

BiH was unsuccessful and was hurriedly dismissed by SDA president Sulejman Tihić in June.

A series of public discussions was organized throughout BiH in 2007, in which all participants agreed that constitutional reform was of critical importance for the future of BiH, but parties from FBiH and the RS remained utterly divided on the country's constitutional redesign. While most parties generally agree on protections for human rights in accordance with the European Convention for Human Rights, state institutions necessary for Euro-Atlantic integration, and the importance of constitutional recognition for local self-governance, the ruling ethno-nationalist parties are still divided on how to organize the middle level of government.

Prime Minister Dodik and his SNSD repeatedly proposed that Bosnia be organized as a federation, in which the RS, within its current entity borders, would be one federal unit while the other constitutive ethnic groups—Croats and Bosniaks—would get their own federal units, all with the possible right to self-determination through a referendum. The major Bosniak parties continued to argue for a decentralized country of multiethnic regions based on functional, economic, historical, geographic, and ethnic criteria.

The five Croat parties, which claim that constitutional reform is the most urgent issue for the Croat people in BiH (and want it before the end of the mandate of the current HR),[31] signed a joint Declaration on Principles of the BiH Constitution in late September. They implied that their constitutional position in BiH and the FBiH leads to their disappearance as a people, while the position of Serbs and Bosniaks is far better secured in the Dayton framework. The Croat parties argued for the elimination of the current two-entity structure and the creation of a decentralized state organized on a consociation model and envisioned the possibility for a "territorially discontinuous" Croat federal unit, which would—at the middle level of government—link the separate Croat majority areas of Herzegovina and Posavina. This was the first time that the Croat parties verbally articulated the third-entity claim after the international community action in 2001, when this political project was demolished for the time being.

After the police reform failure and before the last session of the Peace Implementation Council of 2007 held in Sarajevo on October 30, the ruling parties signed a declaration in which they promised to start dealing with the issue of constitutional changes and implement long overdue police reform (on the basis of European principles, in accordance with the changed Constitution), but no progress on constitutional reform happened in 2007. The lack of international community guidance on what kind of constitutional setup would secure long-lasting stability and remove the obstacles on BiH's road toward Euro-Atlantic integration resulted in the development of three irreconcilable constitutional proposals by the three major ethnic political camps in 2007. This diminished the chances for any meaningful discussion on constitutional reform in 2008 among the major domestic political figures.

Excessive delays in the criminal justice system are still present, and some elected officials try to exercise pressure on the judiciary. The head of the High Judicial and Prosecutorial Council, Branko Perić, rejected the accusations of Prime Minister Dodik, which were viewed as a direct attempt to pressure the judiciary.[32] On several occasions during the year, Dodik accused the Court of BiH of bias against Serbs; the court argued that its record of indictments related to war crimes and organized crime refuted Dodik's claims.[33]

There has been insufficient cooperation among regional judicial bodies related to war crimes proceedings, and the impunity gap for war crimes suspects is still wide. The gap in BiH widened even further when Serbia announced it would award Serbian citizenship to those who claim Serbia as their motherland, which could be misused in the future. This was the case for former Croat member of the BiH presidency Ante Jelavić, who escaped from Bosnia in 2005 after being sentenced to 10 years' imprisonment by the Court of BiH for abuse of office, embezzlement of office, and lack of commitment in office[34] and who has been hiding in Croatia protected by his Croatian citizenship and the Croatian law that forbids extradition of nationals.

During 2007, there were discussions on a comprehensive domestic strategy that would prepare the BiH judicial system and its state court to cope with more than 10,000 potential war crimes cases. Soon after he took office in July, HR Lajčák used his Bonn powers to issue a series of orders that make the work of BiH's prosecutors and police easier to investigate, prosecute persons suspected of war crimes and those who help them evade justice, and make it harder for war criminals convicted by the Court of BiH to evade prison.[35] The practice in postwar BiH has been to send Bosnian Serb convicts to prisons in the RS, Croat convicts to prisons in Herzegovina, and Bosniaks to prisons in central Bosnia; such a practice is considered a serious deficiency.

Bosnia still has no state prison and needs to deal with the inadequacy of its detention system, as well as devise a strategy for dealing with youth delinquency and providing general correctional facilities. Some of these problems became obvious especially after the escape of former Bosnian Serb soldier, Radovan Stanković, from a prison in Foča in May (where he was serving a 20-year sentence for the enslavement, torture, imprisonment, and rape of non-Serb civilians during the 1992–1995 conflict in BiH).[36] Stanković was the first war criminal indicted by the UN tribunal to be transferred to BiH for trial. He escaped while being taken for a dental treatment. The nine prison guards who were escorting him did not shoot at him or at the car in which he fled, which was later found near the Serbian border with Montenegro. The escape highlighted the inadequacies of the overstretched and underfunded prison system in BiH and the urgent need for proper coordination among the country's law enforcement and judicial agencies.

Corruption

1999	2001	2002	2003	2004	2005	2006	2007	2008
6.00	5.75	5.50	5.00	4.75	4.50	4.25	4.25	4.25

During 2007, there was no significant improvement in the government's implementation of efficient anticorruption initiatives. The BiH economy is still not free of government involvement, mainly because of delays in privatization of state-owned capital, especially in the FBiH, where the government has delayed privatization of BH Telecom. On the other side, RS Telecom was sold to Telecom of Serbia above the market price, which was seen as more of a political than economic transaction, providing the RS prime minister with additional funds during an election year. The political and economic oligarchies remained intertwined in both entities, which provided favorable ground for corruption.

Some improvement was recorded in the RS, where the government adopted measures to speed up registration of businesses, while the FBiH was overwhelmed with its government formation and riddled with bureaucratic obstacles, among which business registration remained a nightmare and provided significant opportunities for corruption.

Additional improvement has been recorded at the state level in terms of enforcing the Law on Conflict of Interest and the Law on Political Party Financing thanks to the activities of the CEC. Sanctions and fines for political parties that break the law are still limited, but the process is moving in a positive direction.

The government regularly advertises jobs and contracts, but implementation of the Law on Civil Service still privileges ethnicity over professional capabilities, which became a discriminatory hiring tool in state, entity, and cantonal institutions.

According to Transparency International's Corruption Perceptions Index of 2007, BiH scored 3.3 and shares the 84–93 ranking with Macedonia, Montenegro, and several underdeveloped African and Asian economies. BiH lags well behind EU member states and accession candidates, and within the Western Balkans, only Albania stands behind BiH.

The auditor's offices at state and entity levels improved in producing well-founded reports on the financial dealings of the government, detecting major flaws in this area. However, follow-up on these reports by the prosecutor's offices and investigation agencies is not yet perceived as a matter of utmost importance. Corruption at all levels was present to such an extent that the public almost perceives it as normal. There were several prominent corruption cases in 2007, but the public remained silent and maintained the opinion that the crimes would likely go unpunished.

The BiH public did not react to corruption-related verdicts handed down to prominent officials and for the most part anticipated that the charges would be dropped under political pressure. HDZ BiH leader Dragan Čović, who was dismissed from the BiH presidency when the proceedings started, was sentenced to five years in prison for misuse of office. The BiH Office of the Prosecuto appealed the verdict, demanding a 15-year prison sentence for Čović, while his defense insisted on dropping all charges. In September, the state court revoked the trial panel's verdict and ordered a retrial before the appellate panel. The decision stated that the appeals were upheld on the basis of essential violations of criminal procedure provisions.[37] The commencement of the trial before the appellate panel of the Court of BiH in this case was scheduled for November, and it was not over by the end of 2007.

Josip Merdžo, secretary of HDZ 1990, appealed a guilty verdict in an abuse of office case for which he was sentenced to one year in prison. The BiH Constitutional Court rejected his appeal and concluded that there were no violations of the criminal code since the verdicts of the FBiH Supreme Court and Mostar Cantonal Court included explanations with precise and justified reasons for applying the laws.

The Court of BiH also indicted the deputy Speaker of the BiH House of Peoples[38] and the president of the PDP, former BiH foreign minister and former RS prime minister Mladen Ivanić, for "abuse of office, criminal association, incitement to abuse of office, and giving gifts to a state prosecutor."[39]

One more warning sign of corruption was a plot against Banja Luka regional prosecutor Milan Tegeltija, made public by the RS police. The police cautioned Tegeltija that criminal circles in RS and Serbia were planning an attempt on his life. Reportedly, the threat was connected to several organized crime, drugs, and arms-trafficking cases that Tegeltija had been handling.[40]

Transparency International's 2007 Global Corruption Barometer showed the overwhelming influence of politics on the work of BiH police and a significant level of corruption in police, greater than in traditionally corrupt areas like health care and education. The Global Corruption Barometer distinguished administrative corruption (that happens between police and citizens) from high-level corruption, which includes political pressure and influence on police and security agencies.

▌ AUTHOR: JASNA JELISIĆ

Jasna Jelisić has worked in BiH since 1997 as a journalist, political advisor and analyst.

Christian Schwartz-Schilling was High Representative and EU Special Representative in BiH from January 2006 to June 2007.

Political directors of the Peace Implementation Council (PIC) Steering Board expressed concern over suggestions that certain reforms could be reversed unilaterally by entity decisions to retrieve competences previously transferred to the state. They stressed that an entity cannot withdraw unilaterally from a previously-agreed reform and firmly stated that the consolidation of state-level institutions must continue. See Declaration by the Steering Board of the Peace Implementation Council, October 30 and 31, 2007.

[3] Ambassador Miroslav Lajčák is a high-ranking Slovak diplomat with extensive experience i the western Balkans.

[4] "Deklaracija o preuzimanju obaveza za sprovođenje reforme policije s ciljem parafiranja potpisivanja Sporazuma o stabilizaciji i pridruživanju" [Declaration On Taking the Obligatic to Implement Police Reform with the Goal of Initialing and Signing a Stabilization ar Association Agreement], signed by six leaders of the ruling coalition in Mostar, October 2 2007.

[5] The HR's approach and the measures he announced were firmly supported by the politic directors of the PIC Steering Board during the session held in Sarajevo on October 30 ar 31. The Russian Federation had a separate opinion expressing its "deepest concern by tl consequences of the measures taken by the High Representative that change the procedur of the adoption of decisions by the Council of Ministers and the Parliamentary Assemb of BiH." See more in the Declaration by the Steering Board of the Peace Implementatic Council, Sarajevo, October 30 and 31.

[6] See details in the *Thirty-Second Report of the High Representative for Implementation of t Peace Agreement on Bosnia and Herzegovina to the Secretary-General of the United Nation April 1–September 30, 2007*, OHR, November 15, 2007, http://www.ohr.int/other-doc/h reports/default.asp?content_id=40835.

[7] It was the framework Law on Higher Education, which was finally adopted and gazette in August 2007. See more in the *Report on Monitoring the Performance of the Parliamenta Assembly BiH*, produced by the Center for Civil Initiatives, available at http://www.ccib org/dataf/PBiHsummary.pdf.

[8] See the judgment, Application of the Convention on the Prevention and Punishment of tl Crime of Genocide (*Bosnia and Herzegovina v. Serbia and Montenegro*), February 26, 200' available at http://www.icj-cij.org/docket/files/91/13685.pdf#view=FitH&pagemode=nor &search=%22judgement Bosnia%22.

[9] The verdict stated that the RS army and police committed genocide in Srebrenica, ar found Serbia not directly responsible for, but having played a role in, the genocide. The IC stated that Serbia violated the Genocide Convention for "not using its influence on the R leaders to prevent genocide from happening in BiH". On public perception of the verdic see "Justice Unseen as Bosnians Awaits Translation of ICJ Verdict," Balkan Investigativ Reporting Network, April 25, 2007, available at http://www.birn.eu.com/en/79/15/2682.

[10] The absurdity surrounding the protocol refusal is clear, considering the fact that the two mo prominent Bosniak leaders, Haris Silajdzic and Sulejman Tihic, refused it on the basis the argument that "it preserves the RS police," while the major Serb leader, Milorad Dodi refused it claiming that it "abolished the RS police." Even after the refusal, the HR insiste on so-called technical negotiations, which continued with no results.

[11] See Office of the High Representative statement of October 18, 2007. Despite hars criticism coming from RS political leaders, Lajčák was clear that BiH does not functic as a healthy, normal state and the goal of the international community is to change that– since the international community cannot complete its mission until changes are made i the direction of establishing a stable, European, democratic, multiethnic society in Bosn and Herzegovina. See press conference statement by High Representative Miroslav Lajčá Sarajevo, October 19, 2007, available at http://www.ohr.int/ohr-dept/presso/pressb/defau asp?content_id=40693.

[12] The international media reported that the Russians promised not to block the HR's decisior when they were announced, but when they were put forward the Russian government allie with Dodik, as the Russians allied similarly with Vojislav Kostunica, Serbian prime ministe over Kosovo. See "Bosnian Politics: Cracking Up," *The Economist*, October 25, 2007.

[13] Croat presidency member Zeljko Komsic, for example, was talking about "worrying politic events," referring to the meeting of RS and Serbian officials in Banja Luka in September, whe the RS-Serbia Cooperation Council was formed, and questioned if agreements on speci and parallel relations could be concluded without the approval of the BiH Parliament.

14   The RS and Serbia Ministries of Energy and Trade signed the first protocol on September 11, 2007. The protocol foresees construction of the school named "Srbija" (Serbia) in Pale and the Buk-Bijela Hydropower Plant in Foča municipality, which marked the beginning of the implementation of the Agreement of Special Parallel Relations between the RS and Serbia.

15   See more at the Office of the High Representative (OHR) Official Decisions web archive, http://www.ohr.int/decisions/archive.asp.

16   The case that took most media attention was the nomination of Vitomir Popović, one of the most influential figures in the Serb Democratic Party, as wartime minister in the government controlled by Radovan Karadzic.

17   Corridor 5c is a branch of the fifth Pan-European corridor. The longest part of this corridor goes through BiH.

18   In May, the CEC decided to fine the SDA on the basis of the Law on Political Party Financing with 34,000 convertible marks (US$26,840) for receiving free services from Holiday Inn Hotel in an amount that exceeds the limit of contributions established in the Law on Political Party Financing. The SDA appealed to the Court of BiH. The CEC also fined the SDP in the amount of 555,000 convertible marks (US$438,000) for the party's violations of the Law on Political Party Financing.

19   The CEC verified the following candidates: Rajko Kuzmanović (SNSD), Mladen Ivanić (PDP), Ognjen Tadić (SDS), Slobodan Popović (SDP), Nedžad Delić (Democratic Party of Invalids BiH), Anton Josipović (NSRzB), Krsto Jandrić (NDS), Nikola Lazarević (European Ecological Party E-5), Mirko Blagojević (SRS 'Dr. Vojislav Šešelj').

20   "Education belongs to a 'soft area' of security and over the long term may pose just as great a threat to a country's stability as people with guns," stressed Ambassador Davidson. See "The Current Educational Methods Threaten BiH Stability in the Future," interview of Ambassador Douglas Davidson, FENA, Sarajevo, September 4, 2007.

21   "Zajednička jezgra na promaji" [Common Curricula on Draft], Radio Free Europe, TV Liberty, available at http://www.slobodnaevropa.org/content/Article/870280.html.

22   The current law in its original form was submitted by the Bosnian Council of Ministers to the Parliament for urgent adoption in June 2006, but it took over a year of further arguments before it was finally passed. The local politicians appeared ready to sacrifice this important EU accession–related reform in order to preserve their political and financial control over education, holding BiH's higher education reform a hostage for almost three years.

23   The Bologna process aims to create a European Higher Education Area by 2010, in which students can choose from a wide and transparent range of high-quality courses and benefit from smooth recognition procedures. See the Bologna declaration at http://www.crue.org/eurec/bolognaexplanation.htm.

24   All three major telecom operators in BiH are under some form of control of the three ethnically-determined political elites.

25   "Vital national interest" is a constitutional instrument for the protection of the national interests of the three constituent peoples in BiH.

26   See the official statement of the Society of BiH Journalists (Drustvo novinara BiH) from October 3, 2007. Web link with the footage is available on You Tube http://www.youtube.com/watch?v=ajhhy68IEIE.

27   Krsmanović publicly claimed that the RS government has been exploiting Foča's highly profitable natural resources such as timber and hydroelectric power, yet it has returned none of the revenue to the municipality through capital investment. See Kurt Bassuener and Vanja Filipović, "Bosnia: Mayor with a Plan," Transitions Online, July 3, 2007.

28   The Serbs have been dominantly employed in the RS municipalities and other institutions, while, according to the ombudsmen reports, they have been discriminated against when searching for employment in FBiH municipalities' institutions. For more details, see *FBiH Ombudsman Report on FBiH Institutions Violating Constitutional Provisions Related to Proportional Representation in the Executive Bodies*, June 2007.

[29] See more in Chapter 12 of the *Thirty-Second Report of the High Representative f[ ]Implementation of the Peace Agreement on Bosnia and Herzegovina to the Secretary-General the United Nations, April 1–September 30, 2007,* OHR, November 15, 2007, http://ww[ ]ohr.int/other-doc/hr-reports/default.asp?content_id=40835.

[30] For specific data, go to BiH Directorate for Economic Planning: http://www.dep.gov.ba/b[ ]index.php.

[31] The current HR has a mandate until June 2008, and it can be extended by decision of th[ ]Peace Implementation Council.

[32] The HJPC complained about Dodik's "continuing negative and undermining publ[ ]statements with the exclusive aim to discredit the judiciary, and systematically diminish th[ ]successes of the judiciary reform." See HJPC's open letter: "VSTV otvoreno pismo Milorad[ ]Dodiku, premijeru RS: Reagovanje VTVS-a BiH na Vase istupe u javnosti" [HJPC open lett[ ]to Milorad Dodik, prime minister of the RS: HJPC Reaction to Your Public Statements[ ]BCTC-08-1750-24082007, August 24, 2007.

[33] "Dodik pritiska sud " [Dodik Is Pressuring the Court], *Glas Javnosti,* Beograd, August 1[ ]2007, and official page of the Court of BiH, http://www.sudbih.gov.ba/.

[34] See the verdict in the case against Ante Jelavić, Court of Bosnia and Herzegovina, Sarajev[ ]November 4, 2005. http://www.sudbih.gov.ba/files/docs/presude/2005/Jelavic_ENG_KPV[ ]10_04.pdf.

[35] The HR ordered the seizure of passports and travel documents of 93 persons being investigate[ ]for war crimes and for being a part of the network to help fugitives from the ICTY to eva[ ]justice, and who were the subjects of investigations that were already opened by the Bi[ ]prosecutor. The investigations involved mostly people who were on the so-called Srebreni[ ]List. Of the 93 individuals, 35 were serving members of the RS police and were suspende[ ]by his decision until the indictment or closure of their files. Dragomir Andan was remove[ ]from his position as deputy head of administration for police education of the Minist[ ]of the Interior of the RS; see more at http://www.ohr.int/decisions/removalssdec/defaul[ ]asp?content_id=40172.

[36] See the verdict in the case against Radovan Stanković, Court of Bosnia and Herzegovin[ ]Sarajevo, March 28, 2007. http://www.sudbih.gov.ba/files/docs/presude/2007/Radovar[ ]Stankovic_-_Final_Verdict_-_ENG.pdf

[37] "Bosnian State Court: Verdict in Case of Former Bosnian Resident Dragan Čović and Othe[ ]Revoked," Sarajevo, *Bosnia News,* September 28, 2007, available at http://bosnianew[ ]blogspot.com/2007/09/bosnian-state-court-verdict-in-case-of.html.

[38] Bosnia-Herzegovina has a bicameral parliament comprising the House of Representativ[ ](42 members) and the House of Peoples (15 members). The House of Peoples consists [ ]5 Bosniaks, 5 Croats, and 5 Serbs elected by entity-level institutions. Two-thirds of th[ ]members of the House of Representatives are elected from the FBiH and one-third fro[ ]the RS.

[39] During his mandate as prime minister in 2001 and 2002, Ivanić allegedly allowed a compan[ ]Srpske Sume (Serb Woods), to cut wood in a forest of the northwestern municipality [ ]Ribnik without proper authorization. The damage was estimated at some 263,000 eur[ ](US$407,000). Four other PDP members were also accused of collecting at least 51,00[ ]euros (US$79,000) from the company, Srpske Sume, for campaigning in 2002. In 200[ ]Ivanić and two other people tried to offer 50,000 euros (US$77,000) to an international[ ]appointed prosecutor working with the Bosnian State Court in exchange for droppin[ ]charges against them, according to the indictment. "The State Court Indicts Ivanić," FOCU[ ]News Agency, October 26, 2007.

[40] "Banja Luka Regional Prosecutor Allegedly Targeted for Assassination," *Nezavisne Novin[ ]*Banja Luka, January 4, 2007.

Bulgaria

by Rashko Dorosiev and Georgy Ganev

Capital:	Sofia
Population:	7.7 million
GNI/capita:	US$10.270

The social data above was taken from the European Bank for Reconstruction and Development's *Transition Report 2007: People in Transition,* and the economic data from the World Bank's *World Development Indicators 2008.*

Nations in Transit Ratings and Averaged Scores

	1999	2001	2002	2003	2004	2005	2006	2007	2008
Electoral Process	2.25	2.00	2.00	2.00	1.75	1.75	1.75	1.75	1.75
Civil Society	3.75	3.50	3.25	3.25	3.00	2.75	2.75	2.50	2.50
Independent Media	3.50	3.25	3.25	3.50	3.50	3.50	3.25	3.50	3.50
Governance*	3.75	3.50	3.50	3.75	3.75	n/a	n/a	n/a	n/a
National Democratic Governance	n/a	n/a	n/a	n/a	n/a	3.50	3.00	3.00	3.00
Local Democratic Governance	n/a	n/a	n/a	n/a	n/a	3.50	3.00	3.00	3.00
Judicial Framework and Independence	3.50	3.50	3.50	3.50	3.25	3.25	3.00	2.75	2.75
Corruption	4.75	4.75	4.50	4.25	4.25	4.00	3.75	3.75	3.50
Democracy Score	3.58	3.42	3.33	3.38	3.25	3.18	2.93	2.89	2.86

* *With the 2005 edition, Freedom House introduced separate analysis and ratings for national democratic governance and local democratic governance to provide readers with more detailed and nuanced analysis of these two important subjects.*

NOTE: The ratings reflect the consensus of Freedom House, its academic advisers, and the author(s) of this report. The opinions expressed in this report are those of the author(s). The ratings are based on a scale of 1 to 7, with 1 representing the highest level of democratic progress and 7 the lowest. The Democracy Score is an average of ratings for the categories tracked in a given year.

EXECUTIVE SUMMARY

In the 17 years since the collapse of communism, Bulgaria has managed to consolidate its democratic governance system with a stable Parliament, sound government structures, an active civil society, and a free media. Over this period, a number of general, presidential, and local elections have been held freely, fairly, and without disturbance. Power has changed hands peacefully. Bulgaria has made significant progress in establishing the rule of law, yet further efforts are needed. After a period of poor performance, the economy has recorded 10 years of robust growth. Economic reforms have advanced considerably, with more work needed to improve the business environment. In 2004, the country officially became a NATO member. On January 1, 2007, Bulgaria became a full member of the European Union (EU), completing its integrationist agenda, which dominated political discourse within the country over the period of transition. Despite these positive achievements, more attention must be paid to reforming the judiciary and to fighting corruption and organized crime.

National Democratic Governance. The national system of democratic governance in Bulgaria continued to function well in 2007. The three-party coalition government continued its term in office without serious threats to its stability and demonstrated a good capacity to negotiate issues, displaying the ideological and policy differences among its members. The pace of reforms slowed following Bulgaria's accession to the EU on January 1, 2007, but a full-scale national teachers strike brought the problem of reforming the secondary education sector to the forefront. The strike was resolved peacefully, and a comprehensive reform package for 2008 was adopted. *In 2007, the pace of many EU-related reforms slowed down, while at the same time the government remained stable and took the opportunity offered by the national teachers strike to promote reforms in the secondary education sector, which leaves the rating for national democratic governance unchanged at 3.00.*

Electoral Process. In May 2007, Bulgarians for the first time exercised their right to vote for members of the European Parliament. Voter turnout was 29 percent. Regular municipal elections were held in October; voter turnout was 42 percent in the first round and 29 percent in the second. Local elections were marked by the intrusion of business interests into politics and suspicions of vote buying. With low public interest, the elections featured no real engagement of political ideas and the races were reduced to a competition of personalities. At the same time, there was a strong popular perception that corruption is widespread among politicians. The local level also saw growing attention among business interests to gain control over local authorities and local decision-making processes, which perhaps contributes to the phenomenon of vote buying, a potentially serious challenge to the Bulgarian democratic system. *There are no considerable changes to indicate either an improvement or a decline in the electoral process rating for Bulgaria, which remains unchanged at 1.75.*

Civil Society. Over the last 17 years, Bulgaria has managed to develop a vibrant civil society. However, the nongovernmental organization (NGO) sector has still not developed sustainable fund-raising mechanisms. Bulgarian civil society was formed with a top-down approach, led by donor demands and not by Bulgarian citizens. A significant number of large foreign NGOs and their donors withdrew from Bulgaria in 2007, which was likely to have caused funding problems for some organizations. On the other hand, Bulgaria's EU accession opens new funding possibilities. There are, however, some negative effects as a result of this process. Often, EU financial assistance is distributed by the state, and this might have a negative influence over NGO independence. There were positive developments in 2007, too. Some environmental organizations managed to engage young people in protest campaigns against unregulated construction projects on the Black Sea and at mountain ski resorts. *Owing to no considerable changes that indicate an improvement or decline, the civil society rating for Bulgaria remains unchanged at 2.50.*

Independent Media. The structures for media freedoms in Bulgaria remained largely unchanged in 2007. Print media are generally independent from state interference. Libel is still a criminal offense in the penal code, but in most cases the courts interpreted the law in favor of journalistic expression. According to several international organizations monitoring media development and performance, Bulgarian media are not fully independent from direct economic and indirect political interests. The economic interests of media owners can be inconsistent with their news functions. Editors and reporters respond to this environment through self-censorship. Another problem with the Bulgarian media is the inadequate transparency of media ownership, which fails to fully guarantee economic or political independence. In addition, the content of most print and electronic media is largely commercial, contributing to the general public's low interest in politics. *There were no considerable changes in the Bulgarian media sector in 2007, and the country's independent media rating remains unchanged at 3.50.*

Local Democratic Governance. Two major opportunities for better local governance opened in Bulgaria in 2007. First, the Constitution was amended to allow municipalities to set their own local tax rates. Second, EU structural funds contain large allotments that can significantly benefit municipalities and districts. At the same time, the quality of local governance in Bulgaria may be diverging between municipalities with improving practices and others falling into the hands of local business interests. The local elections in late 2007 indicated a worrisome trend in vote buying by some candidates, which may decrease the level of democratic control over the local authorities. The resource base of many local governments to fulfill policies is still limited, and decentralization is advancing slowly. *Improved access to funding for the formulation and implementation of policies by local governments in Bulgaria was counterbalanced by vote buying and other negative practices during the 2007 local elections, which leaves the local democratic governance rating for Bulgaria unchanged at 3.00.*

Judicial Framework and Independence. The performance of the Bulgarian judiciary has been a problem area throughout the period of transition. While the judicial system is independent and basic human, civil, and political rights are in place, the implementation of justice is criticized by both public and external observers. The Law on the Judicial System was changed to make the Supreme Judicial Council a permanent body and to create an inspectorate for monitoring the integrity of the judicial process. The first public accounts on the activities of the two supreme courts and the prosecution were made in front of Parliament in 2007. Transparency in the activities of the prosecution has improved, with many regional offices allowing Internet access to information about individual cases. A specific strategy for the development of the prosecution was undertaken at the request of the prosecutor general. *While improvements continue to be made in Bulgaria's judicial sector, more are needed, and the rating for judicial framework and independence remains at 2.75.*

Corruption. In 2007, Bulgaria demonstrated weaknesses in the institutional setup for fighting high-level corruption. At the same time, the mechanisms for reporting, monitoring, investigating, and prosecuting public officials with respect to their property status were significantly enhanced and more actively used by the National Audit Office. Fighting corruption at lower levels, especially in customs, has improved visibly. Also, the general public and businesses reported the lowest levels of bribery since such measures started. This evidence is supported by studies of improvements in the business environment and Bulgaria's ratings for economic freedom. *While the fight against high-level corruption is stagnating, there are visible improvements at lower levels, with corruption reported by the public and businesses and an increasing level of economic freedom; thus Bulgaria's corruption rating is improved from 3.75 to 3.50.*

Outlook for 2008. In 2008, Bulgaria will begin receiving EU structural funds, which will be a major challenge at both national and local levels of governance. Municipalities will have the opportunity for the first time to set local tax rates within certain limits. In 2008, a package of reforms is envisaged for the secondary education sector. With respect to the judiciary and security branches, monitoring by the European Commission on progress in the judiciary and in fighting corruption and organized crime will continue, while the new National Security Agency may become operational.

MAIN REPORT

National Democratic Governance

1999	2001	2002	2003	2004	2005	2006	2007	2008
n/a	n/a	n/a	n/a	n/a	3.50	3.00	3.00	3.00

The current Constitution of Bulgaria has been in place since 1991; it provides for a system of governance featuring a parliamentary regime and checks and balances guaranteed by the legislative, executive, and judicial branches. Citizens are involved in the political process through elections, via consultations during the legislative process, and through civil society organizations and the media. Bulgaria's political system is stable, with two consecutive governments having served their full constitutional terms without any major political disturbances and a third government well under way. Democracy has firmly taken root in society, and even though the public voices its dissatisfaction with the performance of Bulgarian democracy, no alternative non-democratic projects exist or seem viable. The anti-democratic messages of the xenophobic Attack party, which entered Parliament in 2005 and whose leader placed second in the 2006 presidential elections, tempered considerably in 2007 during the campaigns for the European Parliament elections in May and local elections in October.

Among the three branches of government, the judiciary is highly independent and creates an imbalance in democratic accountability. This problem was addressed in 2007 by introducing annual reports from the three highest figures in the judicial branch to Parliament on the state of the judiciary, as well as by changing the Law on the Judicial System to make the Supreme Judicial Council a permanent body whose members are no longer engaged in everyday work as judges, prosecutors, or investigators. The functioning of the Bulgarian judicial system is under review by the European Commission, which in its May 2007 evaluation marked progress but noted further needed improvements.

Bulgarian citizens and media have access to government information under the Law on Access to Public Information, in force since 2000. The law includes a mechanism to initiate proceedings when these rights are violated. In recent years, citizens and civil society organizations have actively exercised their right to information, and the nongovernmental organization (NGO) Access to Information Program reports a correllation between the decrease in government impediments to providing information and increasing public awareness and skills in using the law. In spring 2007, the State Commission for Information Technologies and Telecommunications attempted to introduce amendments to the Law on Access to Public Information, which some feared would severely worsen the performance of the law and decrease public access. After public outcry and petitions to Parliament with assistance from opposition parliamentarians (MPs), the amendments actually were much more positive, but the fact that a state agency tried to change the law, to the detriment of citizens, is worrisome.

After Bulgaria became a member of the European Union (EU) on January 1, 2007, the pace of reforms decreased. The government is a coalition between the leftist Bulgarian Socialist Party, the centrist Simeon II National Movement, and the largely Turkish, Movement for Rights and Freedoms. The three parties have differing ideologies, and, having achieved EU membership, made negotiations on reforms very difficult. Thus, even though the European Commission reported in June 2007 that considerable progress had been made, implementation was still lagging and the pace of reforms needed to increase.

Similar developments can be observed in other spheres of public policy, especially in education and health care. In 2007, reforms in health care were completely stalled in negotiations within the ruling coalition. The same was true for reforms in education until a national teachers strike in late September over salaries brought the problems of the secondary education system to the forefront. The government seized this opportunity to not only offer teachers salary increases of close to 50 percent, but also moved neglected reform steps to the fast-track to be implemented in 2008.

The Bulgarian military and security services went through reforms during the country's NATO candidacy. Insufficient progress in combating corruption and organized crime, however, has caused the government and Parliament to begin discussing changes to the internal security system. More specifically, a draft law was introduced in Parliament for the creation of a National Security Agency as a separate state agency accountable to the prime minister and the Council of Ministers. The process of drafting this law is in an early stage, and it will be one of the major developments in 2008.

Electoral Process

1999	2001	2002	2003	2004	2005	2006	2007	2008
2.25	2.00	2.00	2.00	1.75	1.75	1.75	1.75	1.75

Bulgaria has developed a stable electoral system that ensures free and fair legislative, presidential, and municipal elections. Some recent problems aside, elections since 1991 have been free, fair, and in compliance with electoral law. The last parliamentary elections in 2005, presidential elections in 2006, and European Parliament elections in May 2007 were also generally assessed as free and fair by all political parties and observers. However, the last local elections, held in October 2007, demonstrated some negative effects of the increasing commercialization of politics. There were suspicions among political parties, the media, and the general public that numerous candidates for mayoral positions and municipal councils had attempted to buy votes.

According to the Bulgarian Constitution, all citizens over 18 have the right to vote by secret ballot. Bulgaria has a proportional electoral system for parliamentary elections, which ensures fair polling and honest tabulation of ballots. Up to 2005, legislation for parliamentary elections provided all political parties, coalitions, and candidates with equal campaigning opportunities. However, amendments to the electoral law in 2005 required a monetary deposit in order to register MP candidates. The rationale for the amendments was to reduce the number of parties participating in elections, since many represent niche interests. As a result, the number of registered parties and coalitions decreased from 65 in 2001 to 22 in 2005.

In the elections for members to the European Parliament in May 2007, the system of preferential voting was introduced. Many analysts insisted that this would increase public participation in politics, but there was no real impact on the final results. The law provided that changes in the order of candidates on the ballot would be made only in cases where one or more of the party candidates received more than 15 percent of the votes. The 2007 Law on Elections introduced certain voting limitations for Bulgarian citizens in the European Parliament elections that indirectly aimed to prevent many Bulgarian-Turks—who live permanently in Turkey—from voting. According to some observers, this was a positive step since these voters have significant influence over election outcomes without really being residents of the country. According to others, this is a dangerous precedent that violates political rights not only of Bulgarian-Turks, but of all Bulgarians living outside the EU, which could impact the overall functioning of democracy in the country.

In May 2007, when Bulgarian citizens voted for members of the European Parliament for the first time since Bulgaria joined the EU, the Bulgarian Socialist Party (BSP) and newly established Citizens for European Development of Bulgaria (GERB) won five seats each. The movement for Rights and Freedoms (MRF) followed with four seats, the antidemocratic and xenophobic Attack party gained three seats, and Simeon II National Movement (SIINM) got one seat. Surprisingly, both center-right parties, Union of Democratic Forces (UDF) and Democrats for Strong Bulgaria (DSB), failed to make the threshold of 5.6 percent.

Regular local elections were held in October 2007. BSP and GERB won most of the mayoral positions and municipal council seats in regional cities with almost equal electoral results. They were followed by MRF, which managed to keep and even broaden its influence at the local level, and by UDF and DSB. The 2007 local elections were marked by suspicions of vote buying, and there is growing interest within the private sector to gain control of local authorities. Businesses are interested in gaining access to EU structural funds, which will be administrated by municipalities starting in 2008. Another factor is the recent real estate boom, where having representation in local governance enables business interests to wield influence over construction permits and regulations.

The last general elections in 2005 were won by the left-wing BSP, successor to the Bulgarian Communist Party, with 34 percent of the votes and 82 seats. After failing

to elect a minority government in coalition with the ethnic Turkish MRF, the BS
agreed to a government coalition with the previously ruling SIINM. Since 1996
the party has tried to move away from its Communist legacy and build a moder
leftist organization. In 2003, it was accepted for full membership in the Sociali
International, indicating international recognition of the party's reformation. Serge
Stanishev, a former BSP international affairs secretary, is the current party leade
and was appointed prime minister after the 2005 elections. BSP has lost some of i
public support since it has been in power, but the results from the 2007 Europea
Parliament and local elections showed that the party still remains one of the mo
popular among voters. For the first time in recent history, the presidential electior
in 2006 reelected the incumbent, former BSP leader Georgi Parvanov, who wo
with an impressive 75 percent of the votes in the runoff.

Electoral support for the Attack coalition, a political formation benefiting fro
the traditional protest vote in Bulgaria, is an effect of deeper public perceptio
about the unfairness of the country's transition process. Although Attack does n
question the current democratic system, the ease with which its xenophobic messag
won popularity and a position in the Parliament is worrisome.

In December 2006, a new party formation, Citizens for European Developme
of Bulgaria (GERB), was established by the incumbent mayor of Sofia, Boyk
Borissov. GERB managed to create a stable local organization and achieved goo
results at the 2007 European Parliament and local elections. Public opinion po
from the end of 2007 indicated that GERB is the first political party in Bulgar
with 22 percent of public support.

The Bulgarian Constitution guarantees all citizens the right to organize politic
parties, movements, or other political entities. It bans the establishment of politic
organizations that act against national integrity and state sovereignty; that ca
for ethnic, national, or religious hostility; or that create secret military structure
Additionally, the Constitution prohibits the establishment of organizations th
achieve their goals through violence. Until 2005, no substantial organizatio
"played the ethnic card" in their political rhetoric or practice. The Attack coalitio
was the first to use anti-minority statements in a campaign, which led a broa
alliance of NGOs to initiate a court case still under consideration in 2007.

Political party registration is transparent and uncomplicated and requir
a threshold of 5,000 members. The large number of parties participating i
local elections indicates that local interests usually work through independe
participation, a strategy that is less likely to succeed at the national level. Vot
turnout in the October 2007 local elections was 42 percent in the first rour
and 29 percent in the second round. Voter turnout in the European Parliamer
elections held in May 2007 was 29 percent. According to the Alpha Resear
agency, approximately 6 percent of the population is currently affiliated wi
political parties. This low number reflects a growing distance between voters ar
politicians, based on public disappointment with government reforms from bo
the Left and the Right.

The general legislative framework in Bulgaria provides all minority groups with essential political rights and participation in the political process. Although MRF bylaws state that members are welcome regardless of their ethnicity or religion, the party essentially represents the interests of Bulgarian Turks. As part of the current governing coalition, MRF is well represented at all levels. However, there are problems that have become clearly visible over the last several years. The MRF has created a monopolistic, strict, and hierarchical clientelistic structure that controls the lives of Bulgarian-Turks not only politically but economically. In practice, few political options exist for Bulgarian-Turks, since the MRF is the only party that guarantees economic protection and development in return for votes.

By contrast, the Roma minority is still poorly represented in government structures, with some exceptions at the municipal level. Observers agree that the political system discriminates against the Roma minority and impedes its political expression. Equally important, however, is the fact that a political party consolidating and representing Roma interests at the national level still does not exist, despite attempts to create one.

Civil Society

1999	2001	2002	2003	2004	2005	2006	2007	2008
3.75	3.50	3.25	3.25	3.00	2.75	2.75	2.50	2.50

The Bulgarian Constitution guarantees citizens the right to organize freely in associations, movements, societies, or other civil society organizations. There have been no administrative or other barriers to NGOs over the last 17 years, nor do they experience significant state or other influence on their activities, which are regulated by the Law on Non–Economic Purpose Legal Entities.

The 2005 Bulgarian Statistics Register indicates that there are 22,366 registered nonprofit organizations in the country. Of these, 4,010 are foundations, 18,305 are societies, and 51 are local branches of international nonprofits. The number of active groups is not known, but according to the Central Register for Nonprofit Legal Entities, in 2007 there were 4,592 registered nonprofit organizations acting for public benefit. Both private and public benefit NGOs are involved in human rights, minority issues, health care, education, women's issues, charity work, public policy, the environment, culture, science, social services, information technology, religion, sports, and business development. There are no clear statistics on volunteerism in Bulgaria.

The growth of civil society in Bulgaria after 1989 goes hand in hand with the emergence of programs and grants for NGO development. The sector was formed with a top-down approach led by donors. A positive result of the donor-driven emergence of Bulgarian NGOs is their well-developed instructional framework, human resources, and networking capacity. One of the major shortcomings is their inability to involve the community in decision making. NGOs expect resource from the central and local governments but are doing little to empower their ow target groups within the community. Thus, citizen participation in civil societ primarily takes the role of passive beneficiary.

Most ethnic and religious groups, including Turks, Roma, Muslims, Armenian and Jews, have their own NGOs engaged in a variety of civic activities. Althoug the Roma ethnic minority is not represented in government, some Roma NGC function as political discussion clubs and proto-parties. There are around 15 functioning Roma NGOs throughout the country, and the number of registere Roma groups is at least three times greater. Churches engage in charitable activitie by distributing aid and creating local networks that assist the elderly and childrer Organizations of Muslim, Catholic, and Protestant communities are among th most dynamic in the country. Although the Orthodox Church remains the mo influential in Bulgaria, only a small percentage of the population attends service regularly. Anti-liberal nonprofit institutions are constitutionally banned, and non are officially registered. Several informal organizations could be considered ant liberal, but they have weak public influence.

NGO registration is inexpensive and takes approximately one month t complete. Public NGOs are not obliged to pay taxes on their funding resource but they must be listed and report their activities annually in the register. NGC are allowed to carry out for-profit activities, provided the work does not clas with their stated organizational aims and is registered separately. Groups must pa normal taxes on all such for-profit work, and they must invest all net profits in the main activities.

A significant number of large foreign NGOs and their donors withdrew fror Bulgaria in 2007, which is likely to cause funding problems for some organization On the other hand, the accession of Bulgaria into the EU opens new fundin possibilities, with EU financial assistance often distributed by the state. This migh have a negative influence over NGO independence, favoring those NGOs that ar supportive of government policies and programs.

Despite these issues, there are some positive recent developments in Bulgaria civil society. Environmental organizations managed to engage a large number (young people in protest campaigns against unregulated construction projects o the Black Sea and at mountain ski resorts. In 2001, a permanent parliamentar Committee on the Problems of Civil Society was created to serve as a bridg between civil society and the Parliament, reflecting the government's changin attitudes toward the NGO sector. The committee's public council includes 2 members representing 28 NGOs. Other parliamentary committees recruit NGC experts as advisers for public hearings on issues of national importance. Despit this positive practice, no formal mechanism exists for civil society to consult in th development of legislation.

The partnership between the media and NGOs has become reliable and stabl Additionally, NGOs have been involved in preparing projects and monitoring th spending of financial assistance received through EU pre-accession and accessio programs. However, partnerships between civil society and the government continue to work primarily on a project-based approach. As noted by Balkan Assist, interaction between the government and civil society is most often built on the "opportunistic" goal of securing financial resources from international or domestic government funders.

The activities of interest groups are largely unregulated. Bulgarian think tanks have advocated for increased transparency and decreased clientelism and have repeatedly urged the Parliament to legalize and regulate lobbying. As a result, the Committee on the Problems of Civil Society launched a bill in 2002 calling for the registration of lobbyists, but there were still no developments on this legislation at year's end.

Bulgaria has three major independent trade unions, and the rights of workers to engage in collective bargaining and strike are protected by law. Trade unions take part along with the government and employers in the Tripartite Commission for Negotiations on various issues. There is also a growing number of farmers groups and small-business associations. The activity of trade unions is focused mostly on bargaining with the government for common social policies rather than protecting the labor rights of employees in private companies.

Bulgaria's education system is largely free of political influence and propaganda. Low wages and poor funding for secondary education led to a teachers strike in September–October 2007. The government agreed to raise teacher salaries in exchange for an agreement on a package of reforms. According to data from the National Statistical Institute for 2005–2006, there are 5,838 educational institutions in Bulgaria, including 2,470 child care centers, 2,654 primary and secondary schools, 661 professional schools, and 53 colleges and universities. Of these, 303 are privately owned, including 32 child care centers; 255 primary, secondary, and professional schools; and 16 colleges and universities.

Independent Media

1999	2001	2002	2003	2004	2005	2006	2007	2008
3.50	3.25	3.25	3.50	3.50	3.50	3.25	3.50	3.50

The Bulgarian Constitution proclaims that media are free and shall not be subject to censorship, and the country's media freedoms are further developed in legislation. A court decision is required for an injunction or confiscation of printed matter or other media. The right of citizens to seek, obtain, and disseminate information is also guaranteed by the Constitution and the Law on Access to Public Information.

There is still no specific legislation protecting journalists from victimization by state or nonstate actors. Libel, which can include criticizing government officials, is a criminal offense in the penal code. Both prosecutors and individual citizens can bring libel charges, with penalties running as high as US$6,400. Since the penal code was amended in 2000, a number of cases have been brought, but in most the courts interpreted the law in a manner that favored journalistic expression, with only a few convictions. The previous prosecutor general filed several charges against reporters for illegal use of surveillance devices investigating corruption. However, the policy of the new prosecutor general (appointed in March 2006) is leaning in favor of journalistic expression. Shortly after taking office, the prosecutor general canceled a preliminary investigation of BBC journalists who created the film *Buying the Games*. The film accused former Bulgarian International Olympic Committee member Ivan Slavkov of corruption.

In general, there is free competition among media outlets and differing viewpoints. Print and electronic media have successfully emancipated themselves from governmental control, while the state-owned National Radio and National Television are still not sufficiently independent from the state. They are governed directly by the Council for Electronic Media (CEM), whose nine members are appointed by the National Assembly and the president. Although the CEM is not under government orders, the parliamentary majority approves its budget. Throughout its existence, the council has had a reputation of political dependence. The licensing of private electronic media was a CEM task until 2001, when it was placed under parliamentary control. In 2005, the Parliament adopted a strategy for developing broadcast media, but licensing has not yet started, which has led to insecurity in Bulgaria's electronic media sector.

While media in Bulgaria are generally free from direct government interference, it is not certain whether they are independent of special interests, either political or economic. According to the 2007 Media Sustainability Index, prepared by the International Research & Exchanges Board, the economic interests of media owners are not always consistent with the news function of the media. Editors and reporters respond to this environment through self-censorship. Another problem is the lack of ownership transparency, which hinders full economic or political independence. Reporters Without Borders reports that Bulgarian media were more dependent on political and economic interests in 2007 than in 2006. Bulgaria was ranked 35 in the 2007 Worldwide Press Freedom Index of 168 countries published by the organization.

With the exception of a few local newspapers and the official *State Gazette*, all print media in Bulgaria are privately owned. Overall, there are more than 500 newspapers and magazines. At the end of 2006, the nation's largest newspapers were *Troud*, *24 Hours*, *Standard*, *Monitor*, *Sega*, *Novinar*, *Douma*, *Dnevnik*, and the weeklies *Democracia Dnes* and *Capital*. *Troud* and *24 Hours*, which enjoy the highest circulation, are owned by the German publishing group Westdeutsche Allgemeine Zeitung. The newspaper market includes many other dailies, guaranteeing that readers have a broad selection of information sources and points of view.

As of 2003, there were 89 radio stations in Bulgaria. Of these, 11 provide national coverage and 1 is state owned. There are also 77 local radio stations. As for television, there are 98 stations in the country: 3 reach national audiences through wireless broadcasting, 1 is state owned, and the rest are cable networks.

The public's interest in politics has declined over the last few years, which has resulted in a decrease in circulation at the top newspapers, especially those with ties to political parties. Only the BSP-affiliated *Douma* maintains wide public significance. Low public interest in newspapers has led to their increased commercialization. It is often suspected that newspapers are used by different economic players to pursue financial or political interests. The largest private newspapers are printed by IPK Rodina, the state-owned print house. In some cases, this permits a degree of government interference. However, during the last few years this has not resulted in any direct political pressure. There are a number of private distribution networks, as well.

Among Bulgaria's most important journalistic associations are the Media Coalition and the Free Speech Civil Forum Association; another, the Journalists Union, is a holdover from the Communist era currently attempting to reform its image. More than half of the journalists in Bulgaria are women. The publishers of the biggest newspapers are united in their own organizations, such as the Union of Newspaper Publishers. Of the few NGOs that work on media issues, the most important is the Media Development Center, which provides journalists with training and legal advice.

The Bulgarian media code of ethics, signed in 2004 by 160 national and regional outlets, includes standards for the use of information by unidentified sources, preliminary nondisclosure of a source's identity, respect of personal information, and nonpublication of children's personal pictures (unless of public interest). Adopting the code of ethics demonstrated that Bulgarian media have matured enough to assume self-regulation. As a next step, two commissions on ethics in all media started in 2006 to collect and deal with complaints and infringements of the code. The major functions of the commissions include promoting adherence to the code, resolving arguments between media outlets and audiences, and encouraging public debate on journalistic ethics.

The Internet in Bulgaria is free of any regulation and restrictions, and access is easy and inexpensive. Over the last few years, the number of Bulgarian Web sites has grown significantly. According to data reported by the Alpha Research polling agency in July 2007, the percentage of adult Bulgarians who have access to the Internet has expanded to 30.5 percent over the last year.

Local Democratic Governance

1999	2001	2002	2003	2004	2005	2006	2007	2008
n/a	n/a	n/a	n/a	n/a	3.50	3.00	3.00	3.00

The municipality, with an elected municipal council and mayor, is the basic unit of local governance in Bulgaria. Municipalities can formulate, implement, and regulate policies, own property, make budgets, and conduct financial transactions. The public's right to hold local referendums and general assemblies is also envisaged by the Constitution.

In February 2007, a major constitutional impediment to fiscal decentralization and bringing policy decision making closer to the local public was removed. An act of Parliament amended the Constitution to allow municipalities to set local tax rates according to their discretion, within certain limits specified by Parliament. This development was combined with an increased opportunity for municipalities to participate in the absorption of EU structural funds beginning in 2008. Additionally, municipalities are deriving greater revenues from managing their properties, owing to the continued rise in property values and improvements in the collection of local taxes, which was transferred to the municipalities.

The usually hotly-contested local elections in Bulgaria were especially so in 2007. They marked the real entrance to positions of power by GERB, a new and popular political party. In some of the larger cities, GERB managed not only to win the mayoral position, but also to secure majorities in the municipal council. In other municipalities, however, the tendency to have councils without clear leading parties (requiring complex coalitions) was preserved. For the next four years, Bulgarian municipalities will be split between ones with clear one-party power and ones with complicated coalition politics.

The result of these developments may be both a risk and an opportunity. Municipalities may start to diverge in their performance along the dimensions of administrative and managerial capacity, access to resources, and clarity of political responsibility. Such a divergence may create redistributive pressures, which could divert public energy away from improving governance. On the other hand, an opportunity exists for some municipalities to start leading others in good governance practices and thus to enhance the overall performance of local governments in Bulgaria.

Judicial Framework and Independence

1999	2001	2002	2003	2004	2005	2006	2007	2008
3.50	3.50	3.50	3.50	3.25	3.25	3.00	2.75	2.75

Basic rights such as freedom of expression, association, and religious beliefs, as well as the rights to privacy, property and inheritance, and economic initiative and enterprise, are enshrined in the Bulgarian Constitution and generally protected in practice. Major problem areas are discrimination against the Roma minority and against certain religious beliefs, cases of abuse of the rights of suspects, and significant delays in judicial decisions.

The European Commission report in June 2007 on judicial reforms in Bulgaria indicates that progress has been made but challenges remain. Progress areas include the introduction of new legislation, such as amendments to the Constitution allowing an independent inspectorate to monitor the judicial system, and the adoption of a new Law on the Judicial System to balance the independence and accountability of the judiciary, relative to the public and other branches of power.

This is done in three ways. First, the amendments provide Parliament with the right to public hearing of accounts by the prosecutor general, the chairperson of the Supreme Administrative Court, and the chairperson of the Supreme Court of Cassation about court activities, as well as prosecution and investigation in applying the law. The first such accounts were publicly made in front of the Parliament in 2007.

Second, the right of the minister of justice to propose personnel decisions to the Supreme Judicial Council was made operative through the new Law on the Judicial System and the creation of an inspectorate under the Supreme Judicial Council. The inspectorate is envisaged to be an independent body, elected by Parliament, that will monitor the performance of magistrates and propose sanctions to the Supreme Judicial Council.

Third, the new Law on the Judicial System has made the Supreme Judicial Council a permanent body, which takes its members out of everyday judicial work for the duration of its mandate. In this manner, the governance of the judiciary is functionally separated from jurisprudence activities, clarifying the roles and incentives of the different members of the branch.

Another new development in the judicial system in 2007 was the Action Plan for Reforms in the Prosecution. This plan is based on the American Bar Association's 2006 Prosecutorial Reform Index for Bulgaria, which assessed weaknesses in Bulgaria's justice system and was prepared on an initiative of the prosecutor general. Reforms include programs for qualifying and training prosecutors, the creation of ethics commissions at all levels of the prosecution, improved communication with other members of the judicial system, and active and transparent relations with the media and public. These reforms still require implementation, an aspect of Bulgarian governance criticized by the European Commission throughout 2007.

In reality, the Bulgarian judiciary provides an effective check on both the legislature and the executive. The Supreme Judicial Council, which has five-year mandates, consists of 25 members appointed in a manner preventing complete political control over the council. The Bulgarian Constitution is applied directly by the Constitutional Court, consisting of 12 justices appointed in equal quotas by Parliament, the president, and the Supreme Judicial Council, with rotating nine-year mandates. Both bodies have successfully opposed government decisions and acts of Parliament. The two supreme courts have also made decisions in favor of citizens against government bodies on numerous occasions.

Judges in Bulgaria are appointed and dismissed by the Supreme Judicial Council, with all new appointments in the system during 2007 following the legally-envisaged competitive procedures. Also in 2007, the Supreme Judicial Council continued its activities in sanctioning judges whose performance was unsatisfactory. The authority of the courts is recognized, and judicial decisions are enforced effectively. New legislation adopted in 2005 allows private firms and court clerks to enforce court decisions, which has since led to significant improvements in both the number and the value of enforced decisions.

Corruption

1999	2001	2002	2003	2004	2005	2006	2007	2008
4.75	4.75	4.50	4.25	4.25	4.00	3.75	3.75	3.50

By 2007, each branch of power in Bulgaria had an established body with the specific task of fighting corruption, including a parliamentary commission and committee within the Council of Ministers and Supreme Judicial Council. In 2006, a coordinating council consisting of representatives from these three bodies was created. Various inspectorates also exist in the executive branch. In this setup, no one government unit is responsible for the fight against corruption, and the results are relatively weak.

An important innovation in addressing high-level corruption is the change in the Law on Publicity of the Property Owned by Persons Occupying High State Positions, wherein Bulgarian officials must declare property information or suffer penal prosecution, and political parties risk losing state subsidies and registration for national and local elections if not in compliance. The National Audit Office has the right to cross-check the declarations with documentation provided to other public bodies, to publicize the information, and to address the National Revenue Agency and the prosecution regarding possible corrupt practices. At present, while the National Audit Office has actively used its new rights, it is too early to tell whether this will lead to the prosecution of high-level corruption.

The 2007 European Commission report on Bulgaria's post-accession judiciary indicates substantial progress in curbing corruption at the borders and at the local level of government. This evidence is corroborated by the finding of a leading Bulgarian NGO that perceptions of corruption have dropped significantly by businesspersons interacting with customs officers.[1] Among a test sample of businesspersons, one study showed a drop in reported corrupt practices, such as bribery, by almost 50 percent between the end of 2005 and the beginning of 2007. Evidence that corruption in Bulgarian business has decreased significantly over recent years is also reported by the World Bank's measurement of the frequency of bribe payments, which between 2002 and 2005 dropped by half. The Bulgarian branch of Transparency International indicates a slight improvement in perception of corruption, with Bulgaria's score in 2007 improving to 4.1 from 4.0 in 2006.

The Bulgarian economy is free from excessive state involvement. The private sector produces more than 80 percent of the gross value added and provides about 75 percent of the country's employment. Above 90 percent of all state assets subject to privatization, have been privatized. The budget has been in surpluses since 2004 and another surplus is envisaged for 2008. The ratio of state budget expenditures to gross domestic product was less than 39 percent in 2007, but the projected budget for 2008 plans an increase in the level of state redistribution.

Over the past two years, the most burdensome direct tax—the social security contribution—has dropped by about one-third, with the economy responding with rapid growth in reported wages in the private sector, indicating a decrease in hidden salaries and the shadow economy. In 2007, Bulgaria registered a significant improvement in the Fraser Institute's ranking of economic freedom, moving from 6.3 to 6.9. The data for 2007 from the Heritage Foundation's Index of Economic Freedom is more difficult to interpret, because there were major changes in data sources and in the classification of countries. However, the index for Bulgaria registers a slight drop from 64.3 to 62.2.

Administrative pressure on economic activity in Bulgaria has continued to slowly decrease, owing mainly to the lower share of government expenditures in proportion to total economic activity, and with the private enforcement of court decisions. However, many other opportunities for corruption remain, especially in licensing, registration of firms, and safety and other regulations, as well as in public procurement tenders. The reform of the public register of legal entities, which envisages taking this activity out of the courts and computerizing it, was delayed at the end of 2007.

All state bodies are obliged under the Law on Administration, the Law on Public Servants, and the Law on Public Procurement to publicize job openings and procurement contracts and to use objective criteria for selection. State bodies regularly announce job openings in the media and on their Web sites. Public procurement announcements are also publicized in the media and on the Internet, with many procedures becoming more competitive after Bulgaria's EU accession. However, there are still reports of cronyism and preferential treatment in the appointment of officials and public procurements.

Bulgarian media feel free to report corruption, and numerous stories appear every month. Yet there are still problems regarding the media's heavy spin and lack of consistent investigation and follow-up of these allegations. As a result, while media are indeed instrumental in exposing cases of corruption, they may also be nurturing the public's perception of the widespread nature of the problem. During the local elections in October 2007, the media exposed and created public intolerance against the practice of purchasing votes by some candidates, which caused the police to raid several campaign centers and the prosecution to investigate a number of alleged vote buyers. In general, the Bulgarian public is highly sensitive to the issue of corruption, and there's a significant level of intolerance for it. Corruption is regularly among the top concerns in national polls and surveys.

▌ AUTHORS: Rashko Dorosiev and Georgy Ganev

Rashko Dorosiev, project director and political analyst, and Georgy Ganev, program director for economic research at the Center for Liberal Strategies, a nonprofit think tank based in Sofia, Bulgaria.

---

[1]   Center for the Study of Democracy, Anticorruption Reforms in Bulgaria, Key Results and Risks, Sofia, 2007, p. 17, table 3, http://www.csd.bg/fileSrc.php?id=2152.

[2]   Ibid., p. 13, figure 3.

Croatia

by Petar Dorić

Capital: Zagreb
Population: 4.4 million
GNI/capita: US$13,850

The social data above was taken from the European Bank for Reconstruction and Development's *Transition Report 2007: People in Transition*, and the economic data from the World Bank's *World Development Indicators 2008*.

Nations in Transit Ratings and Averaged Scores

	1999	2001	2002	2003	2004	2005	2006	2007	2008
Electoral Process	4.25	3.25	3.25	3.25	3.25	3.00	3.25	3.25	3.25
Civil Society	3.50	2.75	2.75	3.00	3.00	3.00	2.75	2.75	2.75
Independent Media	5.00	3.50	3.50	3.75	3.75	3.75	3.75	4.00	3.75
Governance*	4.00	3.50	3.50	3.75	3.75	n/a	n/a	n/a	n/a
National Democratic Governance	n/a	n/a	n/a	n/a	n/a	3.50	3.50	3.50	3.25
Local Democratic Governance	n/a	n/a	n/a	n/a	n/a	3.75	3.75	3.75	3.75
Judicial Framework and Independence	4.75	3.75	3.75	4.25	4.50	4.50	4.25	4.25	4.25
Corruption	5.25	4.50	4.50	4.75	4.75	4.75	4.75	4.75	4.50
Democracy Score	4.46	3.54	3.54	3.79	3.83	3.75	3.71	3.75	3.64

* *With the 2005 edition, Freedom House introduced separate analysis and ratings for national democratic governance and local democratic governance to provide readers with more detailed and nuanced analysis of these two important subjects.*

NOTE: The ratings reflect the consensus of Freedom House, its academic advisers, and the author(s) of this report. The opinions expressed in this report are those of the author(s). The ratings are based on a scale of 1 to 7, with 1 representing the highest level of democratic progress and 7 the lowest. The Democracy Score is an average of ratings for the categories tracked in a given year.

EXECUTIVE SUMMARY

Croatia made some gains in institutionalizing reform during 2007 even a more entrenched problems, such as improving the judiciary, will require longer and more diligent government efforts. The moderate-nationalis government led by Prime Minister Ivo Sanader ended its first four-year mandat with few radical moves but displayed rather stable (if slow) governmental attempt to further reform. Perhaps most significant in Sanader's administration has been the mainstreaming of a pro-Europe reform agenda, one that few politicians or citizen would now dispute.

A narrow victory in the November parliamentary elections gave the Croatia Democratic Union (HDZ) another four-year mandate, but only after a mont of negotiations that allowed HDZ to gain a majority through coalitions wit several centrist parties and minority representatives. The election and subsequen negotiations between HDZ and its potential allies and the opposition Socia Democrats (SDP) and its coalition partners demonstrated, despite electoral rhetoric that all major parties are in general agreement on strategic areas of reform and th objective of Euro-Atlantic integration.

Croatia's election as a non-permanent UN Security Council member in th autumn of 2007 clearly marked a high point for foreign policy and domesti democratization; in 17 years, Croatia has transitioned from a war zone to Securit Council member. The closing of the Organization for Security and Cooperation i Europe (OSCE) mission in Croatia at the end of 2007 also signaled that Croati has reached some level of democratic maturity, despite few signs that efforts to assis Serbian returnees and their reintegration improved during 2007.

Croatia continues its process of European Union (EU) accession as an EU candidate country, but progress reports from Brussels have been mixed. Of particula concern remain the independence and professionalism of judicial institution minority treatment, and the prevalence of corruption. Partially in response to EU and increasing citizen concern, a high-profile investigation of corruption withi the state privatization fund took place in 2007. Cooperation with the Internation Criminal Tribunal for the Former Yugoslavia (ICTY) and dealing with the legac of the homeland war proceeded without particular social or political turbulenc owing partly to the slow proceedings of several high-profile cases.

National Democratic Governance. The HDZ-led government with its particula brand of moderate nationalism continued its slow consolidation of reform acros government institutions in 2007. While no spectacular achievements were note the government demonstrated that it could balance at least moderate reform domestic institutions without significant social or political turbulence. Politic consensus on Euro-Atlantic integration is broad, and the trend toward resolvi conflicts through—rather than outside of—institutions intensified in 2007. *As recognition of this trend, the rating for national democratic governance improves from 3.50 to 3.25.*

Electoral Process. Croatia held parliamentary elections on November 25 in what was declared by domestic nongovernmental monitors as a generally democratic environment with no significant procedural transgressions except ongoing problems with some election registers. However, given the tight race between incumbent HDZ and opposition SDP, additional attention was paid to the issue of the diaspora vote and its potential influence on deciding the new government. SDP refused to be on the diaspora list and strongly suggested that electoral regulations regarding the diaspora need to be changed. Although the diaspora issue has not been resolved and some procedural problems with transparent registration continue to cause concern, neither is likely to have significantly altered the outcomes. *Croatia's electoral process rating remains at 3.25.*

Civil Society. The position of civil society in Croatia is strong but constantly challenged by the country's most influential nongovernmental organizations (NGOs), which are fed by a populism that contradicts the usual perception of civil society. NGOs associated with the Catholic Church and war veterans are often on the side of rigid nationalism and ethnic exclusivity and demand state independence from international mechanisms, whether it be the EU or ICTY. At the same time, the most influential pro-Western NGOs like GONG (Citizens Organized for Observing Voting) and Transparency International, followed by numerous ecological and animal rights organizations, continue to build a following while working to engage with and monitor government activities. *Croatia's civil society rating remains at 2.75.*

Independent Media. Croatia is under the strong influence of corporate journalism (particularly in print media) that tends to minimize professional standards in order to maintain market positions among advertising companies. The most influential media remains the national television HTV, which continues to exist under political patronage despite efforts to evolve into a public television. This was evidenced by the 2007 appointment of a Tudjman-era figure as HTV's new head. *The media sector remains among several areas of transition that have developed more slowly than expected, however, owing to some self-regulatory actions noticeable in 2007 the rating improved from 4.00 to 3.75*

Local Democratic Governance. The wide gap between decentralizing responsibilities, local-level capacities, and accountability continues to be a challenge to local democratic governance. In 2007, this was demonstrated most clearly in the town of Dubrovnik, where the illogical separation of powers and coordination among local, prefect, and state levels made fighting particularly severe. Also, in Osijek a political stalemate left the town without a mayor and paralyzed the local government for months. A newly passed election law on local government will allow direct election of mayors and county prefects and should improve accountability when it goes into effect in 2009. *There are overall positive trends in establishing a more decentralized system in Croatia, while at the ground level confusion remains in practice; thus, the rating for local democratic governance stays the same at 3.75.*

Judicial Framework and Independence. Croatia's weak domestic judicial tradition, combined with the transition and conflict turbulence of the 1990s, has produced very fragile judicial institutions. Despite efforts at reform, many local courts are much lower than the national standard and continue to produce questionable results; erratic rulings from the Split and Lika regions in 2007 illustrate this ongoing challenge. At the same time, politicians continue to advocate the use of domestic courts for war crimes cases that are currently under ICTY jurisdiction. But, it is questionable just how realistic this idea is given the state of the domestic war crimes trial process. A number of practical reforms to help efficiency were enacted in 2007, but their effects are yet marginal. *Judicial framework and independence remains a weak point in Croatia while current attempts at improvements do not yet show significant progress; thus, the rating remains at 4.25.*

Corruption. Corruption remains one of the key challenges facing Croatia as it attempts to fulfill EU accession criteria. Corruption is considered pervasive throughout public institutions, particularly health and judicial institutions. Government efforts to combat higher-level corruption were taken up a notch in 2007 with Operation Maestro, an investigation and prosecution of officials related to the Croatian Privatization Fund (Hrvatski Privatizacijski Fond). Despite the fact that Maestro targeted obvious institutional corruption, the operation has so far led to the prosecution and imprisonment of only three low-level officials. However, owing partly to this and other government efforts, the public now perceives corruption as one of the country's central problems and is demanding a more serious anticorruption policy as evidenced by the campaign platforms of all major political parties during the November elections. *Owing to improvements in public and political will in Croatia, as well as actions taken by the government, the rating for corruption improves from 4.75 to 4.50.*

Outlook. Political agreement on Euro-Atlantic integration will go only so far in satisfying an electorate increasingly worried about the domestic economic situation. The November 2007 election results confirmed the dominance of the two major parties but did little to distinguish their specific reform and economic programs. It is likely that 2008 will witness a NATO membership invitation as well as further progress on EU accession. However, less than serious attempts to address EU concerns on judicial reform, corruption, and economic reform, or further political disputes with Slovenia (head of the EU presidency at the beginning of 2008) over sea borders and fishing rights, could further slow Croatia's progress toward EU integration and further fuel citizen distrust of the government and its institutions

Main Report

National Democratic Governance

1999	2001	2002	2003	2004	2005	2006	2007	2008
n/a	n/a	n/a	n/a	n/a	3.50	3.50	3.50	3.25

Croatia's internal stability and modest economic growth in 2007 strengthened the country's democratic framework and continued its transitional progress toward full European Union (EU) membership. Prime Minister Ivo Sanader completed his first four-year mandate, and after a narrow election victory at the end of November, he began a second mandate using his brand of moderate nationalism to continue governmental reforms. Four years ago, there were few outside of the Croatian Democratic Union (HDZ) who claimed that Ivo Sanader would maintain a pro-EU path. Yet, overall, his government has managed to make enough accession-related reforms to keep sight of EU standards and to prevent a backward slide into the more authoritarian institutional tendencies of the Tudjman era.

At the same time, investigating and cleaning up the non-democratic actions and crimes of the Tudjman era has been less rigorous than many in the opposition and independent observers would like. At the top of the list, war crimes committed against Croatian Serb civilians and soldiers until now have been poorly investigated and prosecuted. The Lora prison trials in Split still linger without much end or purpose in sight. Also, hidden or shadow government institutions that existed during the war years have not been fully disclosed. For example, while Sanader has not engaged in near the level of institutional manipulation as Tudjman, the scandal that erupted in 2007 with Slovenia in the ongoing dispute over the Croatian/Slovenian sea border illustrated two areas of enduring institutional weakness: Sanader—like his Slovenian counterpart—showed that he is not above using his government to encourage nationalist radicals to instigate tensions against Slovenian nationalists. Second, the fact that such an incident was "coincidentally" captured on tape by security services and later released to the media points to the still somewhat messy management of the security services.

On a more institutional level, the numerous suspicious privatizations of large national companies to close Tudjman associates have yet to be thoroughly investigated. Despite the complexity of untangling all the government institutions involved, a properly reformed judicial system would go a long way toward making the privatization process more transparent, as well as achieving EU standards on war crimes prosecution.

However, it should be noted that while many weaknesses in Croatian democratic governance remain, fear that these will spill outside of the institutional framework has lessened significantly. All mainstream political parties now reflect the general popular consensus that Croatia should engage and aspire to Euro-

Atlantic integration and democratic standards. No main political party aims to stop negotiations with the EU, but also no main political party necessarily supports radical changes toward eliminating corruption.

In mid-2007, Ivica Račan, long-term leader of the Social Democratic Party (SDP), died of cancer, leaving the largest opposition party without a chairman. At the same time, Račan was a symbol of the SDP's softening of its ideological position toward liberalism.

The subsequent party convention brought the young face of Zoran Milanović to the head of SDP, but election platforms and the pre-election decision to propose economist Ljubo Jurčić as the potential prime minister all suggested that SDP was shifting its more traditional left social democratic message to appeal to a more centrist one. This in effect blurred the differences between the two main political parties; SDP's edging from left to right was simultaneous with similar moves inside HDZ, where the elite have become much more in favor of Euro-Atlantic integration and much less nationalist than their own base of voters.

Public frustration with the Parliament's failure to clean up government institutions can be attributed partly to what is perceived as a growing gulf between the lives of parliamentarians and those of average citizens. As the so-called political elite, each member of Parliament (MP) has a salary of roughly four times the monthly national average (4,000 kuna, or approximately US$800) and enjoy perks such as a generous lifetime pension. The transparency of officials' finances has improved, yet the perception remains that although Parliament performs well enough to pass the EU-related reform legislation, it is slow to address key domestic issues. For most, Croatia's high unemployment rate, corruption, and economic conditions are top concerns. The World Bank[1] ranked Croatia slightly higher in terms of economic development, but many concerns remain regarding the country's growing foreign debt.[2]

The security services provoked several public scandals in 2007 but fewer than usual for Croatia, so this sector can be understood as continuing its reform toward professionalization and transparent oversight. In January, the Central Intelligence Agency (Središnja Obavještajna Agencija) began checking the background of several nongovernmental organization (NGO) activists who, while cooperating with state institutions, could come in contact with top-secret materials. The background checks were not conducted in the proper manner or through proper channels and consequently, were considered a breach of individual privacy rights. An investigation concluded that the government, not the secret services, was primarily responsible.

Another incident involved three women MPs who publicly stated[3] that they suspected the secret services of following them and offering details of their personal lives to the media. Finally, an internal conflict or lack of coordination between the secret services and the Ministry of the Interior resulted in the arrest of blog journalist Željko Peratović for republishing already released security services–related documents on his website, indicating the need for further improvement in the professionalization and oversight of the security services.

Since the establishment of the International Criminal Tribunal for the Former Yugoslavia (ICTY), Croatia has been closely observed in its cooperation with the prosecution of war criminals. From the arrest of General Ante Gotovina at the end of 2005, Croatia's cooperation has been considered positive. But distrust of the process still scores high domestic political points. There are many public statements from both social and political arenas that depict the ICTY as an enemy of Croatia's sovereignty. Yet in terms of the official cooperation between the government and the tribunal, 2007 passed without many negative incidents.

However, at the end of the year a scandal broke out when General Mladen Markac, indicted and under house arrest in Croatia while on trial at the ICTY, was caught boar hunting with the minister of the interior, Ivica Kirin, a clear violation of tribunal regulations. General government disrespect for Hague institutions likely played a part, but it is also likely that the parties involved sought public sympathy for Markac to offset attention on the actual sensitivities discussed at the trial. Markac is one of three Croats (along with Gotovina and General Ivan Čermak) facing ICTY charges for planning, organizing, and carrying out ethnic cleansing of Croatian Serb villages in North Dalmatia (the former Krajina region). For Croatia, this is the most important ICTY trial to date, since the possibility of a negative ruling would challenge the official line (and general public understanding) that Croatia was only defending itself and did not have a plan to cleanse the territory of ethnic Serbs.

Ethnic tensions remain a concern, especially in the Lika region as well as the area north of the city of Zadar. During 2007, there were fewer incidents than in previous years, but the situation is far from stabilized and includes night vandalism on property of Serbian returnees. And while authorities are now properly reporting on such criminal acts, actual integration of the minority populations is very low. According to political representatives of the local Croatian Serb population, there are still significant problems with ownership of agricultural land as well as other property issues.[4] Also, there are still many areas where no Serb is employed in the police force or any other state or national institutions, such as post offices, hospitals, schools, and electric or water companies.[5] While the Organization for Security and Cooperation in Europe (OSCE) nearly ended its mandate in Croatia at the end of 2007, declaring that it had met its objectives in assisting democratic transition and minority integration, the situation on the ground in these regions looks significantly less optimistic.

At the national level, Croatian Serb minority parliamentary representatives, together with other ethnic minority representatives, helped the HDZ piece together enough seats to form a new-old government. Slobodan Uzelac from Milorad Pupovac's leading Independent Democratic Serbian Party (Samostalna Demokratska Srpska Stranka; SDSS) was appointed vice president of government for economic development, reconstruction, and return of displaced people. This symbolic gesture represents governmental orientation toward further normalization of ethnic relations within the country. The real impact will be seen during the coming year.

Electoral Process

1999	2001	2002	2003	2004	2005	2006	2007	2008
4.25	3.25	3.25	3.25	3.25	3.00	3.25	3.25	3.25

The 2007 parliamentary elections[6] were held on November 25 in a generally democratic and transparent process. However, the close race further highlighted key areas for election reform relating to the diaspora vote, voter lists, and campaign financing.

Results showed that the HDZ received the largest number of votes; however no one party or coalition of parties secured a parliamentary majority. A relatively narrow win by HDZ with 66 parliamentary representatives over SDP's 56 seats and its coalition partners—Croatian Peoples Party (Hrvatska Narodna Stranka; HNS) with 7 seats and Istrian Democratic Party (Istarska Demokratska Stranka; IDS) with 3 seats—forced both major parties to seek additional coalition partners to form a government.

This political horse trading took three tense weeks,[7] but the HDZ finally convinced the centrist Croatian Peasant Party (Hrvatska Seljačka Stranka; HSS) and Croatian Social-Liberal Party (Hrvatska Socijalno-Liberalna Stranka; HSLS)—which in coalition (HSS-HSLS) comprised eight representatives—to come over to its camp. These seats, combined with deals made with all of the ethnic minority representatives, allowed the HDZ to form a government.

At one point when it looked as though the stalemate would not be resolved, President Stipe Mesić invoked constitutional Article 97, which defined 77 representatives as a majority to be given a mandate for government. This in turn opened the question of possible changes to current regulations in order to provide clear guidelines for such situations. However, right after this debate began, the HDZ managed to finalize its deal with the HSS-HSLS; thus the issue lost attention and is likely to be forgotten.

Other election controversies are more likely to linger in the public's attention. The question of the diaspora's right to vote remains a hot political issue, with the two main political parties taking opposite positions. HDZ supports current regulation where Croatian citizens living abroad have the right to vote and have one separate list that carries eight MPs. On the other side, SDP supports the idea of changing this regulation in order to dismiss the right of Croatian citizens (primarily) living in Bosnia and Herzegovina (BiH) to vote in elections in Croatia. There are a large number of BiH citizens living in BiH who obtained double citizenship as Croat, as all BiH ethnic Croats have the right to apply for a Croatian passport.[8] These BiH citizens vote regularly in Croatian elections. The votes traditionally go to HDZ; thus, it is understandable why HDZ has pushed to keep the current electoral regulations.

To demonstrate its disagreement, SDP refused to be on the election list for the diaspora in the 2007 parliamentary elections. Given the close race, SDP could argue that the diaspora helped tip the balance in HDZ's favor. While again opposition, it is likely that SDP will continue to push for regulations closer to those in other European countries.[10]

The diaspora issue also affects how elections are conducted. For example, during 2007 there were several court rulings on diaspora cases from the 2005 presidential elections. In the case where the NGO GONG (Citizens Organized for Observing Voting) sued members of one of the diaspora voting commissions, Split's local prosecution office confirmed irregularities but dropped all charges against the commission members.[11] GONG also complained repeatedly about confusion in the voter registries that allows manipulation and listing of the deceased as regular voters. GONG posted monitors at diaspora sites in BiH during the elections, but diaspora voting is generally more difficult to regulate given the multiple voter sites.

The elections also highlighted the fact that registration lists are still not completely accurate. According to official data, 4,073,294 voters were registered in 2007, 105,000 more than in 2003. This information is even more questionable given the fact that there are at least 900,000 underage citizens out of a total population of 4.5 million, not 5 million as voter registration data would suggest. Elections were repeated in a few places, such as Negoslavci, Mursko Središće, and Batina, owing to irregularities resulting from a larger number of ballots than voters.

Election financing also continues to be a concern. GONG has been the key organization to raise attention on this issue,[12] and although other organizations and political actors have also raised concerns, the will to tackle this issue will likely not be high on the agendas of either of the two largest parties until forced by public opinion.

On the same day as the parliamentary elections, the city of Osijek[13] held local elections to fill the seat of a dismissed mayor. GONG[14] protested this idea, claiming that different regulations for parliamentary and local elections would cause additional confusion, cost, and possible mistakes. Elections were held without major irregularities. However, the poll simply repeated earlier results: No single party received enough votes to form a government, and no combination of parties could agree on forming a government. Re-elections are likely in early 2008.

In addition to elections, Croatia finalized changes to some electoral regulations during 2007, with the most significant change related to local elections: Voters will now directly choose mayors and *župans* (county prefects). These changes will be tested for the first time in 2009, when the next local elections are scheduled. Overall, these changes should improve the representation quality of the local government, even as a number of concerns have emerged (see "Local Democratic Governance").

The new law also proposes some changes relating to mayoral and *župan* candidates, including a provision that all candidates must have at least six months of residency in the area where they are running. The law also stipulates that both mayors and *župans* could be elected during the first round if they collect more than 50 percent of the votes. Otherwise the two main candidates would go on to a second round.

According to the new regulations, candidates must file their candidacy with a certain number of signatures. For instance, the threshold is 50 signatures in smaller rural areas, while 5,000 signatures are necessary for Zagreb mayoral candidates. A referendum to dismiss the elected mayor or *župan* can be called by 33 percent of registered voters or by the local Parliament or council. Finally, the new law obligates the local ruling party to offer at least one vice presidential position to representatives of national minorities if they have 15 percent of voters.

Civil Society

1999	2001	2002	2003	2004	2005	2006	2007	2008
3.50	2.75	2.75	3.00	3.00	3.00	2.75	2.75	2.75

The development of Croatian civil society remains high in most of the relevant statistics and is understood to be more developed than many other transitional areas of Croatian society. Unlike other sectors, Croatia's civil society developed significantly during the decade of the late president Tudjman's authoritarian government. The NGO scene of strong human rights groups and their opposition to Tudjman policies, as well as generally strong public acceptance of trade unions, became much less influential as both the Račan and Sanader governments proceeded to adopt almost all of the basic standards that civil society groups demanded during the 1990s.

The state protects the rights of the civic sector according to accepted standards of a democratic society. While legislative controversies periodically occur—for example, over the taxing of civil society organizations—the basic legislative framework has been set to allow the growth and development of a vibrant civil society in Croatia. This has also included the state's establishment (like that of many countries in the Central Europe region) of the National Fund for Civil Society Development, which provides some level of funding to groups applying for grants.

However, while this formula meets the approval of most donors, it should be noted that the state continues to provide significant support to civil society organizations that do not necessarily conform to the envisioned Western liberal civil society model. In this way, the state makes some civil society organizations stronger than others and makes it challenging for those not under "state patronage" to be sustainable. The most influential civil society institutions remain those organized around the Croatian Catholic Church and the former soldiers of the homeland war, neither of which arena is known for exhibiting liberal and tolerant attitudes. The social and political roles of this powerful religious institution permeate government decisions regarding civil society groups. During 2007, the most influential church activities were connected with strong pressure on the state education system to use church teachings on sexual abstinence, abortion, and homosexuality as the main basis for the Croatian education system.

Today, human rights–oriented civil society organizations are generally far less focused on basic human rights issues than during the 1990s. This is because there are fewer human rights abuses, but also because many human rights protections (and their donors) have moved on to other issues of reform. The Croatian Citizens Committee (Hrvatska Helsinški Odbor; HHO) remains the largest national human rights–oriented NGO. However, like many others, it has refocused much of its effort on monitoring government transparency and so forth. While international organizations such as Human Rights Watch[15] point out that essential human rights problems in Croatia are still connected with Serbian returnees, few domestic NGOs focus attention on these issues apart from those groups established by Serbian returnees.[16]

Donor funds for basic human rights work have for the most part shifted to the issues of governance and transparency, which many of the large domestic organizations are tackling. However, even this concentration of efforts on such necessary activities has done little for the overall sustainability of the more politically focused civil society organizations in Croatia. A 2007 report by the American Academy for Education Development concludes that civil society in Croatia is among the most vibrant in the region,[17] but its long-term sustainability (notwithstanding external donor efforts and institutional grants) remains a question. For example, at the end of October, even the previously well-financed HHO publicly announced that it was having financial problems and requested citizens to make donations.

Women's rights organizations, such B.a.B.e (Be Active Be Emancipated) and the gender issues–oriented Iskorak and Kontra, are among the most active civil society organizations and are campaigning continuously on issues such as domestic violence. For example, these groups heavily criticized HDZ MP Ivana Sučec-Trakoštanec, who stated in Parliament that each woman is valuable in relation to the number of babies she produces.[18]

Trade unions continue to have a strong social role and political influence, particularly as an increasing number of investigations into suspicious privatizations remind workers that few other actors are willing to protect their interests. The most influential union remains the Union of Independent Trade Unions of Croatia (Savez Samostalnih Sindikata Hrvatske; SSSH), followed by the Union of Workers Trade Unions of Croatia (Udruga Radničkih Sindikata Hrvatske; URS), Croatian Union of Trade Unions (Hrvatska Udruga Sindikata; HUS), Independent Trade Union (Nezavisni Sindikat; NS), and many other combinations of professional and regional unions. Overall, trade unions are seen as being relevant and fairly independent political actors.

In 2007, one of the most prominent national union leaders, Boris Kunst from URS, announced to little fanfare his departure from the union to join HDZ. This was not understood as a scandal, given the general independence of Croatian trade unions from political parties. By contrast, a local union leader from HUS, Jozo Marić, was publicly criticized when he was pictured dining with the owner of a company in dispute with its own workers.[19]

Along with being a tourist destination, Croatia is becoming internationally known for its sports hooliganism.[20] The football (soccer) national division is understood as such an important social issue that every Croatian government (including Socialist) has supported the sport and its fans, both transparently and non-transparently. Football hooligans, who provoke massive public violence at sports events and in the streets, are usually organized in groups financed by the sports clubs, which give privileges like free tickets and organized trips to members.

Football supporters have been instrumental in delivering political messages that "respectable officials" can no longer make, such as support for The Hague-indicted generals, Ante Gotovina and Mirko Norac. This combination can be dangerous, especially in a clash with similar elements from Serbia or BiH, or even with domestic youngsters from Zagreb, Split, and Rijeka. When profiling these youths, studies suggest that the church has some influence on football supporters since many usually claim religion as important among their system of values. Many also tend to share far-right attitudes, with elements of racism and strong nationalism or regionalism. Overall, sports hooliganism has served as a mechanism to release societal pressure, as well as a mirror on extremist values, as the country attempts to deal with its wartime past.

Independent Media

1999	2001	2002	2003	2004	2005	2006	2007	2008
5.00	3.50	3.50	3.75	3.75	3.75	3.75	4.00	3.75

Croatia has few high-quality media outlets offering consumers more than tabloid news or bureaucratic statements from governmental officials and their opposition rebuttals—all of which are packed with advertisements. Professionally driven and publicly responsible media are rare in Croatia, and the quality among each of the 10 most important printing and broadcasting companies has been weak during the past few years. Journalism as a profession deteriorated during the 1990s, thanks to the strong arm of the late president Tudjman's regime, when daily papers and national or local televisions were competing to serve the ruling HDZ.

Subjects such as war crimes committed by domestic soldiers, as well as numerous irregularities in the privatization process and economic transition in general, have not been covered professionally or presented to the public, and still suffer from political and economic influences, as well as self-censorship. This decade of low professional standards gave way to the transitional winds that emerged in the early 2000s, when the first liberal reform government came to power. Media did improve, but not far enough to reach their self-proclaimed professional standards.

Changes at the top of Croatian TV (Hrvatska Televizija; HTV) were the most important media happenings in 2007, given that national television is more influential than all other electronic and printed media combined. HTV's public board includes the requisite civil society representation, but the newly appointed editor in chief, Hloverka Novak-Srzić, has raised questions about the professed aims of HTV to transform from a state TV into a public outlet. Novak-Srzić is an experienced television journalist who, until her appointment, was one of the most influential editors at Nova TV. More significantly, she gained her credentials serving HTV during the Tudjman regime, a troubled era for journalistic standards.

A comparative survey taken in 10 countries of southern Europe[21] on the quality of television broadcasting estimated that HTV's half-hour evening news was watched by 16–21 percent of consumers during April 2007, while Nova TV in comparison drew 7–10 percent of viewers for its news program. None of the smaller national media outlets, including Nova TV and RTV, can seriously compete with the publicly influential HTV.

Croatia has numerous radio stations; most are mainstream oriented, with very few specialized for a specific audience. Besides the HRT network of radio stations, the most influential station is Radio 101 from the capital city, Zagreb, which stands above all others in terms of quality and influence. However, Radio 101 cannot be heard in other regions, such as Dalmatia.

Print media continue to struggle between advertisements and tabloid-style investigations. The main printing house remains Europa Press Holdings (EPH), owned by Ninoslav Pavic. EPH holds the number two best-selling national daily, *Jutarnji List*, the biggest regional daily, *Slobodna Dalmacija*, the best-selling weekly, *Globus*, and the leading women's magazine, *Gloria*. In 2007, EPH acquired the internationally-awarded Croatian political weekly *Feral Tribune*. This magazine had suffered several years of financial crises owing to low advertising,[22] as well as the previous government's policies against independent voices in print, especially the satirical tone that made *Feral Tribune* famous. Rijeka's daily *Novi List* also displays higher than average standards of professionalism. The continuation of both independent papers during 2007 helped to keep the field diversified and held to some professional standards. The Catholic Church's chief news organ remains the weekly *Glas Koncila*.

Overall, there is very low overt government pressure or harassment of the media. The October 2007 arrest of journalist Zeljko Peratović, who runs a conspiracy theory Internet blog, apparently surprised even Prime Minister Sanader. While Peratović spent a day and a night in jail for publishing confidential state materials on his blog, Sanader publicly denied any involvement in the case, criticizing those who produced the scandal. A month after the arrest, it was still unclear why Peratović had been arrested since the allegedly confidential material had already been published several years earlier.

Blog journalism and general Internet usage became trendier and more widespread in 2007. For the first time, parliamentary campaigns used the Internet to communicate with voters outside of the traditional news websites. Many politicians, such as Vesna Pusic, Zoran Milanović, and Vesna Škare Ožbolt, are active bloggers. And on the other side, the minister of the interior, Ivica Kirin, became infamous in the autumn for obscene videos posted on YouTube presenting him as a ridiculous politician ("Kiro Prosviro" [Kiro Went Crazy]). The situation became less funny when Kirin was caught by local media commenting that he knew SDP members were behind the posting of the videos because he recognized the posters' IP addresses. Kirin quickly denied this statement and the scandal was forgotten, but concerns and questions about Internet activities in Croatia lingered for months thereafter.

Local Democratic Governance

1999	2001	2002	2003	2004	2005	2006	2007	2008
n/a	n/a	n/a	n/a	n/a	3.75	3.75	3.75	3.75

Changes adopted in Croatia's Law on Elections in 2007 now allow direct voting for local mayors and *župans* (county prefects) and also make it easier for voters to call referendums to change a mayor or *župan*. Some opposition parties registered concerns about these changes, suggesting that in the case of a referendum, it would be up to the government to install its representative as a part-time mayor or *župan* until the next elections, giving far too much power to the central government at the local level.

Similar to many transitional countries of the post-Soviet world, Croatia is in a constant struggle between state centralism and demands for local governance. Every political party claims that it is attempting to decentralize, each using a different agenda, but with few noticeable results. The main problem in developing high standards in local governance still lies in the fact that no serious attempt has been made to reinvent the administrative regions called *županija* (county). Croatia is divided into 20 counties that represent an executive power between national and city (or municipal) levels. This territorial and bureaucratic division was instituted during the Tudjman years and has been heavily criticized both domestically and internationally. It is true that Croatia has an unusual geographic shape (resembling a boomerang), but the *županija* borders are even less logical when looking at the historical and administrative regions.

Many analysts suggest that this system was designed to allow full control over the whole territory, and the *županija*-level executives were just one of the tools to do so. However, despite the mass production of bureaucratic regulations, the power structures between the national (state) level and *županija* and city levels are highly improvised and easy to manipulate, depending on who is prime minister in Zagreb. Accordingly, any serious attempt to improve local governance must take on the political 'hot potato' of questioning the actual structure of local government administration. Few parties, unless specifically demanded by Brussels to do so, are likely to take this up as a policy priority.

But public scrutiny of the poor performance of local governments increased during the summer of 2007, when unusually strong wildfires threatened local communities. In the historic UNESCO city of Dubrovnik, the local government was stretched to the limit when several large fires burned out of control on the BiH border, only kilometers away. It was clear that the local government did not have the internal communications or necessary connections with the Bosnian firefighting units to properly manage the crisis. This resulted in significant devastation of forest and property on both sides of the border, including outlying areas of Dubrovnik.

Osijek, the largest city in Slavonia, was the other regional city in the spotlight in 2007. For the better part of two years, Osijek has been paralyzed in its attempts to agree on a new mayor after former mayor and war commander Branimir Glavaš soured relations with HDZ president and prime minister Ivo Sanader and formed an independent regional opposition party. After going into opposition, Glavaš was accused of war crimes, which was probably the chief reason he quit (or was ousted from) HDZ.

The wide gap between capabilities and responsibilities of local governments saw little improvement during 2007. A large number of construction sites in the coastal area are mushrooming with no legally issued permits. Despite increased attention to this "wild building" and attempts to match urban plans with national standards, the local executive branches still have no capacity or legal power to deal with this problem and depend on action from Zagreb.

Many local governments, even those close to the national ruling party, accordingly found themselves caught between local demands and national regulations. A number of high-profile demolitions carried out by the National Ministry put local governments in the tough position of carrying out orders for destruction without the necessary capacities. For example, a number of home owners refused to leave their dwellings, causing forcible evictions by the local police.[23] The crackdown on illegal building at the national level has been a positive development in implementing the rule of law, but in general it has still proven to be too tough an issue for Croatian local governments to implement and a constant threat to public order.

Judicial Framework and Independence

1999	2001	2002	2003	2004	2005	2006	2007	2008
4.75	3.75	3.75	4.25	4.50	4.50	4.25	4.25	4.25

Croatian negotiations with the EU are much slower than expected owing to poor results in developing a democratic and professional judicial system, a problem rooted in the 1990s. Like journalism, the judicial system was one of the basic instruments of the authoritative governments run by President Tudjman. A large majority of local and national judges were selected by party loyalty, not by professional standards, and were incapable of dealing with serious legal issues such as war crimes or privatization.

The results are obvious: In 2007, each Croatian court still sits on numerous hidden sentences and non-legal decisions that were made in earlier years in order to hide either traces of state involvement in war crimes or the secret deals of privatization. It is not surprising, then, that President Mesić has stated that the whole process of privatization was one large crime committed by a small minority to take national resources away from citizens.[24]

Owing to significant pressure from the European Commission as well as public demands, Prime Minister Sanader's team did produce some positive results in the judicial sector in 2007. Official data claim a 120 percent increase in court decisions connected with corruption. And the government claims that a group of regulatory changes introduced in 2007 to allow more power to the investigator should significantly decrease corruption.[25]

During 2007, a number of programs continued or were launched to increase the level of judicial functioning, but results are still modest. The government, for example, consolidated similar local courts into one larger court for better efficiency and to reduce case backlogs. A Code of Conduct was adopted for judges, a highly symbolic action that received media attention but did not impress the EU or local citizens. And it should be noted that there have been some improvements in making free legal aid more accessible to those who cannot pay.

But in terms of substance, the courts continued to be challenged. The most important and internationally observed case involves war crimes committed in the Lika region during the conflict years.[26] Here, General Mirko Norac (already sentenced for war crimes in a different case) and General Rahim Ademi are standing trial for crimes in the Gospić area. During the trial, the generals shifted responsibility between each other, reopening the issue of double or parallel systems of command carrying out different duties. As a practical matter, many believe that General Ademi was the official commander while General Norac was the real commander of the infamous liberation action taken by the Croatian army during 1993, when many civilians of Serbian ethnicity were found dead. The main judge in these proceedings, Marin Mrčela, is one of the rare highly respected domestic judges. However, there were many legal gaps during the trial, including several announced protected witnesses who did not show up in court and were likely threatened from doing so. In another instance, one of the infamous local judges from the Lika region, Branko Milanović, made national headlines in August when he agreed to temporarily release a prisoner charged with the high-profile murder of a person of Serbian ethnicity.[27]

The local court system still suffers from significant abuse of office and political influence from Zagreb, often spotlighted whenever there are new appointments. For example, in Split Županijski Sud (county level) in 2007, the brother of the current state minister of education positioned himself to be president of the court and used state connections heavily to disparage his opponents.[28] Several print media were used for these lobbying campaigns, publishing one-sided opinions in favor of the state minister's brother.

Municipal courts in Split offered another symbolic case. Amara Trgo, a local judge, refused to rule in a courtroom where a Christian cross was hung near the state symbol. According to the media, the cross was hung by her colleague Judge Zoran Kežić with the explanation that the law does not forbid the display of Christian religious symbols.[29] However, Trgo's opinion was that the cross should not be displayed in the courtroom since it can be understood to mean the court is following church laws, not state civic laws. The regional paper published a photo of Trgo dressed in Roman costume to suggest the ancient Roman treatment of Christians.[30] There has been no final decision in the matter.

Croatia's domestic judicial system has many deficiencies, including constant pressure from government officials to divert some cases from the ICTY to the Croatian justice system. Pressure to hand over the General Gotovina case to domestic courts is perhaps the most high-profile of these efforts, attracting the support of President Mesić, Prime Minister Sanader, and the main SDP opposition.[31] It is highly questionable how realistic this idea is, keeping in mind the low standards of the system as well as the public denial of war crimes committed by domestic soldiers.

The forgotten war crimes case of Lora prison in Split progressed little during 2007, presumably waiting for the new government to come into power to take on the heavy political work of dealing with the complicated and historically botched legal process. With trial delays of more than a year,[32] this matter provides little confidence that the country can take on additional sensitive war crimes cases from the ICTY without more judicial capacity and greater will.

Corruption

1999	2001	2002	2003	2004	2005	2006	2007	2008
5.25	4.50	4.50	4.75	4.75	4.75	4.75	4.75	4.50

Widespread corruption remains one of the central problems of Croatia's transition toward full democracy. State institutions (especially regional bodies that are part of national systems) are understood to be among the most corrupt. Local courts, public health institutions, county administration, and state companies are not trusted to work transparently nor fully follow legal regulations.

During 2007, Croatia managed to achieve some results in its anticorruption actions. Namely, the adoption of the national anticorruption program, as well as increased penalties and strengthening of the independence and capacities of the special unit USKOK (Office for Fighting Corruption and Organized Crime), resulted in several successful investigations and a somewhat changed public perception regarding corruption.

Perhaps the most high-profile of these efforts was the arrest of several highly ranked officials from the Croatian Privatization Fund in an action called Operation Maestro.[33] The fund functions as the central institution representing the government in the privatization of companies owned by the state. The arrested officials are now awaiting trial for taking bribes to facilitate privatizations. However, political opponents were not satisfied with this action, suggesting that a proper investigation should produce higher-level figures than merely three vice presidents (Ivan Gotovac, Josip Matanović, and Robert Pesa) of the Croatian Privatization Fund.

Months before the parliamentary elections, the political parties unveiled competing anticorruption platforms and promises to modify their party images. These small advances did not improve specific institutional capacities to fight corruption but rather indicated a change in political will to take corruption more seriously.

After Slovenia, Croatia is often cited as the most democratically and economically developed among the former Yugoslavian countries, although Croatia has lagged in terms of fighting corruption. However, in 2007 Transparency International Croatia (TIC) noted improvements in Croatia's attempts to fight corruption.[34] The survey cites similar ratings from other relevant institutions, such as the World Bank, and points out that the largest step forward has been made in the public recognition of corruption as the main cause of Croatia's low living standards.

Prime Minister Sanader has suggested that a number of anticorruption measures carried out by his government are primarily responsible for stopping the further worsening of corruption ratings. However, TIC cautioned that such successful anticorruption measures have been undertaken more to satisfy EU demands than to develop domestic anticorruption forces. Regardless, it should be noted that politicians are now competing to produce better anticorruption ratings, even though these gains are more public image than reality.

Still, Croatia continues with its "double loyalty" system of values, where hidden political agendas are more important than cash payments as basic sources of corruption. For example, analysts suggest that large national companies, both state-owned and semiprivate—such as major construction, telecommunications, oil, and electric companies—are hiding parallel internal networks that are either closely connected or even equal to the government. The result is access to the largest portion of the state budget through guaranteed sources and a system of connected companies in support of development programs. In other words, the general system of public tenders remains nontransparent, noncompetitive, and awarded mostly through pre-established arrangements and political connections.

Many ongoing expensive, nontransparent projects are financed through the Croatian budget. For example, the building of the controversial bridge to the peninsula of Peljesac to bypass BiH territory is a colossal undertaking and of questionable priority as part of the Split-Dubrovnik motorway construction. Some suggest that the group behind the project would not hesitate to provoke an international dispute with BiH in order to secure its own economic gains. Perhaps less dramatic but still lucrative, new scandals emerged in 2007 connected with the disputed building of several handball arenas for the European Handball Championships. Whatever the outcome of these investigations, corruption issues are likely to remain a significant political and institutional challenge for Croatia in the years to come.

▋ AUTHOR: PETAR DORIĆ

Petar Dorić works as a journalist in Croatia and is a political analyst on southeast Europe. He holds an MA in international relations from the City College of New York.

1   World Bank: http://siteresources.worldbank.org/INTCROATIA/Resources/301144-11576
     31699840/croatia_fact_sheet_sept_5_cro.pdf.

2   Wagstyl, Stefan, "Financial Crisis Risks Seen in SE Europe," *Financial Times* online (FT.com),
     October 22, 2007. http://www.ft.com/cms/s/0/f29fad32-802a-11dc-b075-0000779fd2ac.
     html?nclick_check=1.

3   Milanka Opačić (SDP), Vesna Škare-Ožbolt (DC), and Djurdja Adlešić (HSLS).

4   Dorić, Petar, "Žele Nas Getoizirati" [They Want To Put Us in a Ghetto], *Feral Tribune* online
     (Feral.hr) October 3, 2007. http://feral.mediaturtle.com/look/weekly1/article.tpl?IdLangua
     ge=7&IdPublication=1&NrArticle=16638&NrIssue=1148&NrSection=15.

5   "Otvorena Pitanja U Povratku Srba" [Open Questions Regarding the Return of the Serbs],
     Srpski Demokratski Forum Hrvatska (Serbian Democratic Forum Croatia). June 2007.
     http://www.sdf.hr/korisni_sadrzaj/otvr_pitanja.doc.

6   "The Final Report on Election of Representatives to the Croatian Parliament," GONG,
     November 25, 2007, http://www.gong.hr/news.aspx?newsID=1354&pageID=1.

7   Tomac, Zdravko, "Trijumvirat MPM usprkos poraza želi vlast" [Trio MPM Despite the Lost
     Elections Wants to Come to Power], Fokus, November 30, 2007, http://www.fokus-tjednik.
     hr/vijest_arhiva.asp?vijest=2859&izdanje=119.

8   The right to a Croatian passport was offered to ethnic Croats starting with the Tudjman
     government as part of its understanding of Croatia's role as one of the guarantors of the
     Dayton Peace Accords for BiH.

9   Paradoxically, HDZ in BiH split into two political parties in the past years and as a result
     BiH Croatian voters voting in BiH elections in fall 2006 failed to come together to elect a
     HDZ candidate as their ethnic presidential representative in BiH.

10   The regulation of diaspora populations and their rights to vote vary throughout Europe, but
     only Croatia accords its diaspora—here primarily people who are also citizens of Bosnia and
     Herzegovina—the amount of voting influence as written in the current regulations.

11   "Izborna prijevara u Bosni i Hercegovini počinjena—krivci se ne mogu pronaći", [Electoral
     Swindle Has Been Done in BiH—the Guilty Ones Cannot Be Found], GONG, http://www.
     gong.hr/news.aspx?newsID=440&pageID=1.

12   Munjin, Bojan, "Apatijski Festival: Kako Se Nevladine Organizacije u Hrvatskoj Pripremaju
     za Predstojeće Parlamentarne Izbore? [Apathy Festival: How Are Croatian NGOs Preparing
     Themselves for the Upcoming Parliamentary Elections?], August 29, 2007, http://feral.
     mediaturtle.com/look/weekly1/article_tisak.tpl?IdLanguage=7&IdPublication=1&Nr
     Article=16476&NrIssue=1143&NrSection=1&search.x=9&search.y=9&ST1=text&ST_
     T1=teme&ST_AS1=1&ST_max=1.

13   "Izvanredni lokalni izbori", [Extraordinary Local Elections], Hina, October 25, 2007, http://
     www.javno.com/hr/hrvatska/clanak.php?id=92862.

14   "GONG protiv paralelnih izbora u Osijeku" [GONG Against Double Elections in Osijek],
     Halter, October 25, 2007, http://www.h-alter.org/tekst/gong-protiv-paralelnih-izbora-u-
     osijeku/6956.

15   Human Rights Watch, World Report 2007, Croatia. Of the estimated 300,000 to 350,000
     Croatian Serbs who left their homes during the 1991–1995 war, mainly for Serbia,
     Montenegro, and Bosnia-Herzegovina, over 120,000 had registered their return to Croatia
     by August 2006. International and local organizations estimate that only 60 to 65 percent
     remain permanently in Croatia—with many leaving after a short stay. http://hrw.org/
     englishwr2k7/docs/2007/01/11/croati14774.htm.

16   Srpski demokratski forum Hrvatska [Serbian Democratic Forum Croatia], 2007, http://
     www.sdf.hr.

17   "Civil Society: Work in Progress", Conference Report, Zagreb, June 13–15, 2007, Academy
     for Education Development, http://www.aed.hr/en/conf_civilno_drustvo.asp.

[18] "Skandal u Saboru: Žena vrijedi onoliko koliko ima djece," [Scandal in Parliament: A Women is Worth As Many Children As She Has], Index, October, 11, 2007, http://www.index.hr/vijesti/clanak.aspx?id=361306.

[19] "Radnici gladuju, a Marić se gosti s braćom Ladini. Slobodna Dalmacija," [Workers Hungry While Union Leader Eats With Landini Brothers], September 12, 2007, http://arhiv.slobodnadalmacija.hr/20070912/novosti02.asp.

[20] "Hrvatski navijači formirali slovo 'U'?" [Croatian Hooligans Formed Letter 'U'], *Jutarnji List*, August, 24, 2007, http://www.jutarnji.hr/clanak/art-2007,8,24,,87308.jl; http://www.fildzan.info.

[21] "U Dneviku HTV-a previše Zagreba, a na Novoj TV crne kronike," [HTV News Has Too Much on Zagreb, While Nova TV Focuses Too Much on Police Reports], Novi List, September 28, 2007, http://www.novilist.hr/Default.asp?WCI=Pretrazivac&WCU=285A2 860286328612863285A28582858285F28632895289728A228632863285A2861285E28 5E2860285E28632863286328592863S.

[22] Nikolić, Leo Nikolic, "Mentalna carina," [Mental Customs], *Feral Tribune*, June 27, 2007.

[23] For example, during the summer one home owner in the coastal area refused to leave his soon to be destroyed home and threatened that he would "blow himself and his home up" if the police entered. Eventually a solution was found, but such dramas illustrate the tense situation that local governments dealing with national housing issues must enforce.

[24] "Stjepan Mesić o akciji Maestro: Melodija se zna i uštimava, a i partitura je zadana," [Stjepan Mesic Regarding Maestro Action: Melody Is Known and Being Put Into Tune, While Notes Are Already Ordered], *Jutarnji List*, June 21, 2007, http://www.jutarnji.hr/clanak/art-2007,6,21,mesic_maestro,79366.jl.

[25] Obad Orlanda, "Smijenili smo pet loših šefova sudova," [We Have Fired Five Bad Court Chiefs], *Jutarnji List*, September 23, 2007, http://www.jutarnji.hr/dogadjaji_dana/clanak/art-2007,9,23,Lovrin_smjenjivanje,91353.jl.

[26] "Događaji dana Osuđenima za ratni zločin osam dana gratis ako dođu svjedočiti," [Daily News: Those Sentenced for War Crimes Have 8 Days 'Free' If They Come to Testify], *Jutarnji List*, Hrvatska, October 2, 2007, http://www.jutarnji.hr/dogadjaji_dana/clanak/art-2007,10,2,medacki_dzep,92507.jl

[27] "Pravosudna sramota: Svi grijesi gospićkog suca Branka Milanovića," [Judicial Shame: All of the Sins of Gospic's Judge], *Nacional*, August 28, 2007, http://www.nacional.hr/articles/view/37193.

[28] Jurković, Hrvoje, "Sovjetskim metodama protiv struke," [Soviet Methods Against Professionalism], Focus, April 20, 2007, http://www.fokus-tjednik.hr/vijest_arhiva.asp?vijest=1958&izdanje=87.

[29] "Splitska sutkinja odbila suditi pod križem," [Split's Female Judge Refused to Work Under the Cross] September 9, 2007, http://www.split-online.com/fokus/splitska_sutkinja_odbila_suditi_pod_krizem.html.

[30] "Odbila suditi pod križem," [Refused to Work As a Judge Under a Cross], Slobodna Dalmacija, Split, Croatia, September 19, 2007, http://arhiv.slobodnadalmacija.hr/20070919/novosti04.asp.

[31] "Stjepan Mesić: Gotovini, Čermaku i Markaču treba suditi u Hrvatskoj," [Stjepan Mesic: Gotovina, Cermak and Markac Should Be Prosecuted in Croatia] HINA, October 5, 2007.

[32] The Lora trials are divided into several legal processes. The first was focused on war crimes against local civilians, the second against war prisoners, and the third is probably going to be against foreign civilians. The second process has yet to start despite the fact that it was scheduled to begin several years ago. And the third one has not yet even been planned.

[33] "Zbog korupcije uhićena tri potpredsjednika Fonda za privatizaciju," [Three Vice-Presidents from the Privatization Fund Have Been Arrested for Corruption Charges], Nova TV, June, 6, 2007, http://dnevnik.hr/bin/article.php?article_id=19313&show_media=54387.

Czech Republic

by Jeremy Druker

Capital: Prague
Population: 10.3 million
GNI/capita: US$20,920

The social data above was taken from the European Bank for Reconstruction and Development's *Transition Report 2007: People in Transition*, and the economic data from the World Bank's *World Development Indicators 2008*.

Nations in Transit Ratings and Averaged Scores

	1999	2001	2002	2003	2004	2005	2006	2007	2008
Electoral Process	1.75	1.75	2.00	2.00	2.00	2.00	2.00	1.75	1.75
Civil Society	1.50	1.50	1.75	1.50	1.50	1.50	1.50	1.50	1.25
Independent Media	1.75	2.00	2.50	2.25	2.25	2.00	2.00	2.25	2.25
Governance*	2.00	2.00	2.25	2.25	2.25	n/a	n/a	n/a	n/a
National Democratic Governance	n/a	n/a	n/a	n/a	n/a	2.50	2.50	3.00	2.75
Local Democratic Governance	n/a	n/a	n/a	n/a	n/a	2.00	2.00	1.75	1.75
Judicial Framework and Independence	2.25	2.50	2.50	2.50	2.50	2.50	2.25	2.00	2.00
Corruption	3.25	3.75	3.75	3.50	3.50	3.50	3.50	3.50	3.25
Democracy Score	2.08	2.25	2.46	2.33	2.33	2.29	2.25	2.25	2.14

* *With the 2005 edition, Freedom House introduced separate analysis and ratings for national democratic governance and local democratic governance to provide readers with more detailed and nuanced analysis of these two important subjects.*

NOTE: The ratings reflect the consensus of Freedom House, its academic advisers, and the author(s) of this report. The opinions expressed in this report are those of the author(s). The ratings are based on a scale of 1 to 7, with 1 representing the highest level of democratic progress and 7 the lowest. The Democracy Score is an average of ratings for the categories tracked in a given year.

EXECUTIVE SUMMARY

The year 2007 may one day be looked back upon as a period of lost opportunity. After a debilitating political crisis in 2006 that left the country almost entirely without a government for over six months, a center-right coalition finally took over in January 2007. The ruling Civic Democratic Party (ODS) promised radical reform, greater transparency, and a new style of governance. With the economy still booming and the standard of living continuing to rise for much of the population, many felt the government had a window of opportunity— a chance to pass sweeping changes that would overhaul the tax, health, and pension systems with the power to withstand the likely backlash.

In the end, some reforms did sneak through Parliament in the autumn and did represent real change—including a flat tax, mandatory health payments, and new social benefit regulations—but most analysts judged them too conservative and too little to make a real dent in the country's massive deficit. The coalition's dependency on two independent parliamentary deputies to pass any legislation had something to do with that, but so did the absolute inability of the leading political actors to seek consensus toward advancing the Czech Republic to the next stage of development. A string of both major and minor scandals also continually distracted the government from both convincingly selling the reforms to the public and living up to campaign promises of more ethical behavior. Reforms in the judicial system and new initiatives in the fight against corruption, however, look promising, but it is still too early to evaluate their success.

National Democratic Governance. Unlike in 2006, the country spent almost the whole year with a functional government—a dramatic improvement over the impasse that stalled any progress in key areas the previous year. The ruling coalition even managed to push through major reforms, though many complained that the changes did not go nearly far enough. *The Czech Republic often resembles a fully functioning democracy—stable and secure, with checks and balances in place—but the failure to seek any consensus with the opposition and an unabated string of improprieties among politicians highlighted the depths of the country's political immaturity. Still, some reform was better than inaction, leading to an upgrade in the national democratic governance rating from 3.00 to 2.75.*

Electoral Process. No elections took place in 2007, but parliamentary, Senate, and local elections the previous year all took place without any serious violations or complaints. However, the Czech system still allows too little room for new faces in politics, and civic participation remains stunted. *There was little to no progress in political party development or inclusion of the Roma minority, but the country's* *reputation for competitive, well-run elections leaves the rating for electoral process at 1.75.*

Civil Society. The reputation of nongovernmental organizations (NGOs) continues to grow, as has the level of funding from individuals and companies. Grassroots movements around certain issues also appear to be on the upswing. On the other hand, many politicians consider the more advocacy-oriented organizations, especially those attempting to change public policy, as unnecessarily interfering in and complicating their work. *Continued growth in the reputation and activities of NGOs is offset by little happening on the legislative side; the rating for civil society improves slightly from 1.50 to 1.25.*

Independent Media. Czech media are independent and diverse, but critics continue to speculate about behind-the-scenes political and financial interference. The prime minister launched a tirade against the media, calling for new regulations to press freedom, partly in reaction to the growing power of the country's tabloids. *Recovery from the biased election coverage of 2006, combined with the long delayed licensing of digital television, holds the rating for independent media at 2.25.*

Local Democratic Governance. While more control systems need to be put in place to rid local officialdom of clientelism and improve efficiency, true decentralization gained momentum in 2007. For probably the first time, local municipalities teamed up to pressure the central government into a change in policy: allocating more tax revenues to local budgets. *With vibrant political competition intact and the power of local officials growing, the rating remains at 1.75.*

Judicial Framework and Independence. The Justice Ministry announced a series of far-ranging reforms, including the full digitalization of the judicial system and changes in procedural regulations, designed to speed up the notoriously slow settlement of cases. A high-profile dispute between the president and the chairwoman of the Supreme Court once again reaffirmed judicial independence and the Constitutional Court's autonomy. *Those positive developments were dampened somewhat by the ministry's intention to increase the executive's power over the judiciary, keeping the country's ranking for judicial framework and independence at 2.00.*

Corruption. While much of Czech society believes that graft is still widespread at both national and local levels of public administration, progress finally seems a reality. New conflict-of-interest legislation took effect in January 2007, the country's rating in the Transparency International Corruption Perceptions Index again improved, and the government adopted the most far-ranging anticorruption strategy until now. *Still, a pervading lack of transparency and the early stages of the government plans mandate only a slight increase in the corruption rating from 3.50 to 3.25.*

Outlook for 2008. The shaky coalition could be hard-pressed to withstand public pressure if widespread complications occur during the implementation of the reforms, which include a flat tax and mandatory medical payments. Many prices, including utilities, will also increase sharply in the new year. The ruling ODS will, however, likely get a shot in the arm with the expected reelection in February of President Václav Klaus, the party's founding father. A truer indication of the coalition's popularity will come later in the year with regional elections.

Main Report

National Democratic Governance

1999	2001	2002	2003	2004	2005	2006	2007	2008
n/a	n/a	n/a	n/a	n/a	2.50	2.50	3.00	2.75

The institutions of governance in the Czech Republic are stable and democratic. No single party dominates the political scene, and regular rotations of power occur at national and local levels. Political parties generally agree on the nature and direction of democratic change, with one major exception—the largely unreformed Communist Party (KSČM), which has not served in a post-1989 government and continues to attract those nostalgic for the old regime. The KSČM holds 26 of the 200 seats in the powerful lower house of Parliament, but the refusal of other political parties to include it in coalitions has greatly complicated the process of forming stable governments among the remaining, often conflicting parties. That was again the case in 2006, as parliamentary elections in June of that year ended in a tie between the two main left- and right-wing camps.

The months following those elections were full of aggravating false starts and bitter exchanges among the various political actors, which was to be expected given the animosity between the country's two major parties and their heads: the Civic Democrats (ODS), led by Mirek Topolánek, and the Social Democrats (ČSSD), led by Jiří Paroubek. Over the second half of 2006, Topolánek's efforts included a failed early attempt to gain support for a coalition of the ODS, the Christian Democrats (KDU-ČSL), and the Green Party (SZ); a minority government; and short-lived discussions with the ČSSD. Finally, after many had given up hope of avoiding another round of elections, the same ODS–KDU-ČSL–SZ coalition survived a vote of confidence on January 19, 2007—but only after two ČSSD rebels-turned-independents agreed to abstain.

The failure to seek consensus among the political elite was painfully evident throughout the rest of 2007. Topolánek and his coalition partners drafted major reforms in the tax, health, and social systems, with hardly any consultation with the opposition. While the reforms eventually received support in both houses of Parliament, their passage again depended on the two independents (as well as on Topolánek's success at putting down a rebellious faction within his own party). However, the government still has a long way to go toward convincing citizens—even many of its own supporters—that the reforms will bear fruit. A September poll conducted by the Center for Empirical Research showed that only 30 percent of Czechs backed the reforms and that a majority of the voters of the two junior coalition parties— KDU-ČSL and SZ—remained opposed. [1] Another poll by Factum Invenio indicated that most Czechs anticipate that the reforms will negatively impact their lives and fail to improve the deficit-laden financial situation.[2] Changes will commence in 2008, with the full program in place by 2009.

In trying to convince the public of the necessity of reform, coalition leaders found themselves continually distracted by a series of scandals that dogged KDU-ČSL chairman and Deputy Prime Minister Jiří Čunek. In February, the police accused Čunek of corruption after his former secretary claimed that in 2002, when he was mayor of the north Moravian city of Vsetín, he had accepted a bribe from a real estate company of 500,000 crowns (US$30,700). Although he managed to ride out the bribery charges—the case was definitively closed in November for lack of evidence—another scandal finally drove Čunek from office. An October broadcast on Czech TV showed that he had been collecting welfare payments in the late 1990s at the same time he was depositing millions of crowns into various bank accounts—if not illegal, then at least unethical behavior according to most observers. Commentators debated whether Čunek's resignation indicated a maturation of the Czech political scene or a step backward because it took so long.

In general, lobbying the executive and the Parliament remains largely unrestricted, and the public continues to believe that special interests play a major role in determining the political agenda—one poll placed special interests and lobbying behind only corruption in that regard.[3] Evidence of that worrying intersection of political and economic interests surfaced during the police investigation into the 2006 murder of businessman František Mrázek, the reputed king of the Czech underworld. A series of articles published by the daily *Mladá Fronta Dnes* (which relied on leaked transcripts from phones tapped by the police) revealed a web of contacts that Mrazek had cultivated in the police, the Interior Ministry, the Office of the Prime Minister, and the secret services.[4]

Some of those connections reflected badly on the ČSSD, hardly the only time in 2007 that information leaks from high-profile investigations suggested that one part of the Czech police serves the government and the other favors the opposition. In the same vein, compromising information on well-known people's supposed or real collaboration with the Communist secret police appears periodically in the media, often for apparently political purposes. The newly established Institute for the Study of Totalitarian Regimes should at least partly rectify that situation, but some political analysts have expressed doubts that it can remain independent with a supervisory board chosen by politicians.

Although the legislature is independent from the executive branch, critics charge that such autonomy has not prevented the Parliament from passing an excessive number of its own poorly prepared laws. The legislative process is further complicated by the ability of parliamentary deputies to make an unrestricted number of proposed amendments during the second reading of bills. As the weekly *Respekt* has pointed out, this tradition often disorients even the most attentive parliamentarians and serves as a calculated strategy to derail long needed legislation and sneak in calculated additions that have little to nothing in common with the debated bill. As a result of these deficiencies, the Parliament sometimes passes error-ridden laws requiring repeated revisions as well as numerous amendments that serve only to complicate the interpretation of laws.[5]

Some analysts believe that the Constitution creates an overlap of executive power between the government and the president. Actual confrontations depend largely on the personality of the president, since the position is chiefly ceremonial yet retains some important powers, such as forming a government. Over the years, for example, President Václav Klaus, in office since 2003, sought out candidates closely tied to his political philosophy when appointing new governors to the central bank and new justices to the Constitutional Court. In addition, despite government criticism of his activities, he espoused his views at various international forums, clashing with the official government line on issues such as the European Constitution, global warming, and the introduction of the euro.

Electoral Process

1999	2001	2002	2003	2004	2005	2006	2007	2008
1.75	1.75	2.00	2.00	2.00	2.00	2.00	1.75	1.75

The Czech Republic is far beyond the fundamental electoral challenges facing parts of Eastern Europe and the former Soviet Union. No one doubts the fairness of the electoral process, and there are no reports of intimidation, fraud, or any other type of manipulation on the part of the authorities, although the deadlock following the 2006 parliamentary elections led to increased calls for changes to electoral legislation. Political organizations have no problems either registering or campaigning. Although shaky coalition governments have been the norm in recent years, the system itself is solidly multiparty, with a strong opposition and diversity at all levels of government.

The Czech Republic uses a parliamentary system with two houses. Real political power resides in the Chamber of Deputies, the 200-seat lower house, with deputies elected by proportional vote on party ballots. The 81-seat Senate is elected on the basis of single-mandate districts. The Senate can return approved bills to the lower house, but the Chamber of Deputies can override the Senate by a simple majority. Though serving as a check on the Chamber of Deputies, the upper house is weaker and traditionally held in lower regard by the general public, though that reputation has improved in recent years.

No elections were held in 2007 after a busy 2006, when the Czech Republic conducted parliamentary, Senate, and local elections, with the ODS triumphing each time. Since the ODS finally managed to cobble together a coalition in early 2007—albeit a shaky one still dependent on ČSSD outcasts—the party effectively controls both houses. That has raised fears that ODS senators, who have sometimes acted more autonomously than their counterparts in the lower chamber, will be forced to fall in line to ensure their majority. Under that scenario, the Senate would become little more than a meaningless extension of the lower house, simply rubber-stamping legislation.[6] The victory of the ODS also increased the expectation that President Klaus will win reelection in 2008. In a joint session, both houses elect the president for a five-year term by a simple majority.

Low membership in political parties remains the norm. The KSČM is the largest party (nearly 77,100 members), followed by the KDU-ČSL (39,450), the ODS (27,800), the ČSSD (18,100), and the SZ (2,500). In a poll conducted in October by the Center for Public Opinion, only 12 percent of respondents said that they had even considered joining a political party in the last 10 years—not surprising when people have such a low regard for the motivations of those who do join. The same poll found 88 percent saying the main motivation for joining a party was to acquire contacts, 83 percent also citing the acquisition of positions and functions, and 76 percent mentioning financial advantages.[7] Low membership figures persist despite generous state funding—to qualify, parties need receive only 1.5 percent of the vote (well under the 5 percent threshold in the Parliament). The parties' low membership base has clear repercussions for the political elite: With relatively few members to choose from, parties often recycle the same personalities and reward loyalty rather than expertise, handing out ministries to individuals whose primary qualification seems to be their long service to the party.

In addition to these problems, the country's largest minority, the Roma, are effectively shut out of national politics. Although the number of Roma is estimated at between 200,000 and 250,000, there are currently no Roma parliamentarians. Prospective Roma politicians find themselves in a Catch-22: Mainstream parties believe that placing Roma candidates on their lists may do them more harm than good among average voters, while Czech Roma are not organized politically to compete effectively for votes. There are, however, a handful of Roma who are active at the local level.

Civil Society

1999	2001	2002	2003	2004	2005	2006	2007	2008
1.50	1.50	1.75	1.50	1.50	1.50	1.50	1.50	1.25

The reputation of nongovernmental organizations (NGOs) has fully recovered from several scandals that tarnished their early post-Communist existence, and most Czechs now see NGOs as valuable instruments for creating and preserving social cohesion. Roughly half the population characterizes NGOs as influential organizations that help solve social problems and are essential to a well-functioning democracy. In a 2005 survey commissioned by the Donors Forum, almost 81 percent of respondents felt foundations were important and performed work the state did not; 83 percent found that foundations highlighted neglected issues in society. Consequently, there has been an increase in donations to nonprofits from individuals and the business sector.

Over 98,000 NGOs exist in the Czech Republic, falling into four types: civic associations, public benefit organizations, foundations, and foundation funds. The civic association—a legal entity comprising groups of individuals in pursuit of a common interest—is the most common. By December 2007, the Czech Statistical Office had reported 61,802 civic associations, ranging from political think tanks to hobby groups and sports clubs—a growth of over 4,000 from the past year. The office also reported 8 new foundations, bringing the total to 390 foundations.

The relationship of the political elite to the nonprofit sector varies. The state is the largest funder of NGOs, providing extensive financial support through grants and coordinating nonprofit activities through the Council for NGOs. However, the NGO community generally does not look highly upon the council, which it views as unrepresentative, bureaucratic, and ineffective, without any clearly outlined goals and activities. NGO representatives also sit on advisory bodies of various ministries. On the other hand, many politicians—most prominently President Klaus—consider NGOs attempting to influence public policy as interfering unnecessarily in their work. The political elite is wary of more "aggressive" forms of action, such as demonstrations and petition drives, and is quick to label the initiators as politically motivated. Many officials prefer NGOs to serve strictly as service providers, filling in where the state does not or cannot.

NGO experts generally view the legal framework as adequate in terms of easy registration and independent operation, though the inability to clarify the term *nonprofit organization* in Czech legislation has created problems since the 2004 passage of a new Law on Value-Added Tax. The law lowered the limit above which organizations must pay a value-added tax to 1 million crowns (US$43,000) and made no distinction between for-profit and nonprofit organizations—disadvantageous to NGOs also earning funds through their activities. On the positive side, amendments to the law in early 2006 removed the tax from donations made through mobile phone text messages, a popular form of giving in the Czech Republic. Any legal deficiencies appear to be the result of the state's insensitivity to the plight of NGOs rather than a concerted effort to apply financial pressure on their activities and limit their impact.

As foreign funding has become much more difficult to obtain, rising donations from locally based individuals and companies have relieved some of the burden. The Czech Donors Forum reported in 2007 on the growing importance of the concept of corporate responsibility in the business sphere, with leading companies now donating 2 percent of their gross profit—on a par with donors in Western Europe and far ahead of Slovakia and Hungary. According to a survey conducted by Factum Invenio for the Donors Forum, 8 of 10 respondents believed that corporate responsibility should be an inherent part of any business, with 59 percent saying if they knew a company behaved in a socially responsible way, their overall confidence in the company would increase.[8]

Although Czech civil society is certainly more vibrant now, grassroots initiatives are still not commonplace, with the exception of several high-profile causes. For example, groups both big and small formed in protest of the United States' plan to station a radar base on Czech territory, part of a missile defense system that would offer protection from attacks from countries such as Iran and North Korea. Such public movements usually remain dependent on a core group of activists. A 2007 survey by the Center for Research of Public Opinion showed that around 40 percent of respondents were dissatisfied with the possibilities for citizens to participate in public life.[9]

In general, Czech experts on extreme right movements see them in decline, without public support or a unifying leader, and increasingly marginalized, as evidenced by the victory of only seven candidates from right-wing extremist parties in the 2006 local elections.[10] Violent attacks on foreigners and the Roma minority have declined since the 1990s and remain largely out of the headlines. In its 2006 annual report (released in November 2007), the Security Information Service —the domestic intelligence agency—stated that right-wing extremists had adopted a new approach: They are no longer actively provoking confrontation but are playing the role of "orderly" young people.[11] However, this strategy contrasted with the decision of one neo-Nazi group to call for an unsanctioned march through Prague's historic Jewish quarter on November 10, the Kristallnacht anniversary. Met by a massive police presence and impressive counterdemonstrations, the march fizzled out.

Independent Media

1999	2001	2002	2003	2004	2005	2006	2007	2008
1.75	2.00	2.50	2.25	2.25	2.00	2.00	2.25	2.25

For the most part, Czech media display sufficient independence and practice a decent, if unremarkable, level of journalism. Press freedom has long been secure in the Czech Republic, and no major media are state owned. Media are generally free of political or economic bias, though allegations still surface of pressure from both business and political interests. Rarely do newspapers publish comprehensive analyses getting to the heart of policy issues. Instead they prefer shorter, sensational articles, with true investigative journalism at a premium. Still, they do provide the population with an adequate overview of the main events and issues facing society.

The national print media offer a diverse selection of daily newspapers, weeklies, and magazines. Foreign corporations own many of these publications, including nearly all Czech dailies. Media-related legislation includes minimal ownership restrictions and none on foreign ownership. The "serious" press has now matured to a point where it offers more balanced political coverage and opinions; however, some analysts believe that the 2006 elections prompted a relapse, with the press returning to the political polarization of the 1990s both before and after the elections.

Some media critics have charged that certain publications and commercial television stations practice self-censorship by shying away from stories that portray top advertisers in a poor light. Others have reported that public relations agencies continue to insist that they "authorize" stories about their clients before publication, and journalists willingly agree. In general, few journalists rock the boat when confronted with such ethical dilemmas, fearing dismissal and the competitive state of the media job market.[12]

Furthermore, some foreign media owners have been criticized for not adhering to the same employment standards followed in their home countries. The lack of a collective bargaining agreement at the national level between publishers and the Czech Syndicate of Journalists means employers are bound only by normal labor law. The syndicate, a voluntary association of journalists rather than a true labor union, counts few influential members and has played a largely insignificant role in the post-1989 era. It does, however, work in the field of media ethics, which includes setting standards, still not high enough according to many politicians. In September 2007, Prime Minister Mirek Topolánek lambasted the state of Czech journalism, claiming widespread corruption and ethical failings, and called for a new law to regulate press freedom.[13]

With improved news and current affairs coverage over the past few years, the public television and radio stations, Czech TV and Czech Radio, serve as largely effective counterweights to the more biased press. In an opinion poll released by the Center for Research of Public Opinion in June 2007, 86 percent of respondents said Czech TV's main news program broadcast "true" information, while only 3 percent said "untrue."[14] In the past, however, Czech TV's financial difficulties have made it particularly vulnerable to political and business interests.

The Chamber of Deputies appoints Czech TV's supervisory board and controls viewer fees—the station's lifeblood. In 2005, parliamentarians passed legislation phasing in higher fees and banning advertising except during key cultural or sporting events. In 2007, the law mandated only 0.5 percent of airtime for ads, a figure that will drop to zero as of 2008 for Czech TV, to the multimillion-dollar benefit of the commercial stations. It has long been assumed that the private stations' powerful lobbying has had an undue influence on parliamentary deputies, resulting in laws favoring commercial stations over public broadcasters. Such speculation resurfaced in February 2007 when the lower house rejected a proposal that would have restored advertising to 1 percent of airtime.

The licensing of digital television, which should eventually help level the market and provide more plurality in broadcasting, finally moved forward in late 2007. The process has long been delayed by political haggling over license regulation, alleged attempts by politicians to increase their control, and lawsuits filed by failed license bidders.[15] In November 2007, the Senate passed a compromise bill that granted licenses to six stations originally awarded the licenses a year and a half earlier, paving the way for a digital revolution in 2008.

Local Democratic Governance

1999	2001	2002	2003	2004	2005	2006	2007	2008
n/a	n/a	n/a	n/a	n/a	2.00	2.00	1.75	1.75

After long delays, the development of local government structures and authority has become one of the Czech Republic's bright spots in recent years. Landmark legislation passed in 1997 led to the creation of 14 regions, which began functioning in 2001. The central government handed over significant powers to these regions in the fields of education, health care, and road maintenance, among others. Additionally, 205 newly created municipalities replaced 73 district offices, which ceased all activities by the end of 2002.

Self-governed regions and municipalities own property and manage separate budgets. Voters directly elect regional assemblies, which then choose regional councils and regional governors. The regional councils may pass legal resolutions and levy fines. Directly elected municipal assemblies elect municipal councils and mayors. Municipalities wield considerable power over areas such as welfare, building permits, forest and waste management, and motor vehicle registration.

Some analysts consider the creation of the regions to be one of the most important steps in the country's recent history. The regions have made considerable progress in tackling problems neglected by the central government (such as education). Some regions shuttered underpopulated schools and tied funding more strictly to the number of students. Overall, the success in regional management and greater autonomy has made a strong case for allowing regional governments to manage a larger share of the tax money they help collect. The government has assisted occasionally—approving, for example, a transfer of billions of crowns to help impoverished hospitals—but that support has been insufficient. For the large bulk of their budgets, regions essentially act as middlemen for the state, sending money to predetermined recipients.

The failure of funds flowing from the center to keep pace with these newly added responsibilities has proven vexing for officials from smaller towns (where the state returns up to six and a half times less money per capita than Prague).[16] Local politicians complain regularly that the central government has transferred major tasks without also allocating the money necessary to do the jobs well. The funds they do receive, they say, should be based on their communities' relative wealth rather than sheer size.

That growing anger finally led to action in 2007. Within a short period of time, almost 1,400 mayors from across the country signed on to an initiative entitled "A Contract of Municipalities and Cities Against Tax Discrimination."[17] Under pressure from these local officials (including a threat to file a suit at the European Court of Human Rights [ECHR]), the cabinet caved in, allocating around 1 percent more of tax income for 2008 to local municipalities—in total around 4.5 billion crowns (US$250 million). That change did not come at the expense of the big cities (as reformers had hoped), where the ruling ODS has its strongholds. However, it was one of the first times that the municipalities—usually overshadowed by the big cities—teamed up to make their combined strength felt. The current system likely awaits more radical change to coincide with the national tax reform approved in 2007, if the newfound strength of local officials persists.[18]

While the record interest in running for local government seats in the October 2006 elections and the high voter turnout might indicate a healthy flowering of local democracy, the weekly *Týden*, for one, has taken a more sober view, explaining the rough-and-tumble world of local politics as a fight over who gains access to local riches.[19] Greater transparency and corruption-fighting instruments at the national level have not kept up with the transfer of responsibilities and finances to local governments, and endemic cronyism remains a critical problem. Experts believe that most corruption now takes place at the local level—since the pickings are slimmer on the national stage, where almost all of the economy has been privatized and where wrongdoing is more visible. A lack of control across the board over such dealings is a major part of the problem. The Supreme Audit Office (NKÚ) currently has no legal right to examine the financial management of regional governments or municipalities.

Judicial Framework and Independence

1999	2001	2002	2003	2004	2005	2006	2007	2008
2.25	2.50	2.50	2.50	2.50	2.50	2.25	2.00	2.00

The Czech Republic's four-tiered judicial system consists of district courts (86), regional courts (8), high courts (2), and the Supreme Court. The Czech Constitutional Court is a well-respected institution that may be addressed directly by citizens who believe their fundamental rights have been violated. Although the Czech judiciary is constitutionally independent, the minister of justice appoints and dismisses the chairmen and deputy chairmen of the courts. Since the country's founding in 1993, reform attempts have preserved the Ministry of Justice's central role in overseeing the judiciary, drawing criticism that the executive could compromise the true independence of the courts. Still, cases of overt meddling remain rare.

A high-profile case concerning the relationship between the executive and the courts, however, continued to make headlines in 2007. The previous year, President Klaus was foiled in his attempts to fire Iva Brožová, chairwoman of the Supreme Court, when the Constitutional Court ruled the move unconstitutional. An infuriated Klaus labeled the decision as a dangerous move "away from parliamentary democracy toward completely unrestricted judicial autonomy"—a reaction some viewed as interference in the decision of an independent court. In September 2007, the Constitutional Court again defied Klaus, ruling against the president's earlier move to appoint a rival to Brožová as her deputy chairperson.

The Constitutional Court's stance restored some of its luster of independence in 2007. Some respected constitutional experts had felt the Court's independence was compromised after Klaus became president. During a drawn-out dispute with the Senate, Klaus set about appointing new Constitutional Court justices reportedly close to his political philosophy. The improved reputation may be at risk, however, as Justice Minister Jiří Pospíšil of the ruling ODS has promised to change the law to allow the justice minister to remove chief judges and the president to dismiss members of the Court's council. Incidents also still occur at other courts with the executive refusing to recognize Constitutional Court decisions (such as rent control and pension payments for Czech citizens who worked for Slovak companies).[20]

The Czech Republic continues to pay a high price for its slow judicial system, losing numerous cases over the past decade at the ECHR over the length of Czech court proceedings. According to Radio Praha, Czech courts take an average of between two and three years to resolve a business dispute, and around 35 percent of commercial cases currently in court have been heard for more than five years.[21] In general, while some areas continue to have significant backlogs, partly a result of unresolved cases from the turbulent 1990s, the overall situation appears to be improving slowly. The lack of reform, however, has meant that judges continue to perform many other chores, including administrative work.

Justice Minister Pospíšil unveiled an ambitious agenda in November, including full automation of the justice system, whereby citizens can file some documents and view the progress of their cases via the Internet.[22] The government is also encouraging citizens to file comments on and propose changes to various drafts of bills before they are submitted to the cabinet. The government has already received comments on a draft of the new criminal code and even incorporated some of the comments into its new draft.[23]

The country has dragged its heels in passing antidiscrimination legislation in line with the UN Convention and European Union (EU) standards. The Chamber of Deputies finally sent an antidiscrimination bill to the committee level in September 2007 and should take a final vote in early 2008. While the opposition ČSSD believes the bill does not go far enough, the ruling ODS has suggested that the party had only pushed forward the legislation, which it feels is unnecessary, to avoid EU sanctions.[24]

Although an amendment to the labor code in 2001 mandated equal treatment for all employees, implementation lags as women remain under-represented in senior positions and are paid less than men for similar jobs. Overall, few women hold seats in the Parliament or attain other positions of political power. Only 2 of 18 ministers in the previous government were women. Mirek Topolánek doubled that to 4 in 2007 when he finally formed a government in January; however, one minister resigned two weeks later and another in October. There are no female regional governors, and only 15 percent of the representatives in both houses of Parliament are women.[25] No significant government measures have been undertaken to remedy these problems, and the bodies that do exist to combat discrimination remain powerless to do more than simply report it, according to a 2005 Open Society Institute report on equal opportunity.[26]

Discrimination against the Roma in employment and housing is also a serious problem. A 2006 government report estimated that 80,000 Roma—roughly a third of the country's Roma population—live in ghettos, with between 95 and 100 percent unemployment.[51] According to the Open Society Justice Initiative, even though fewer Roma children are automatically being sent to schools for the mentally handicapped, and many more are entering higher education, segregation in education remains widespread. In a landmark decision in November 2007, the ECHR ruled that segregating Roma students into special schools is a form of unlawful discrimination in breach of Article 14 of the European Convention (prohibiting discrimination), taken together with Article 2 of Protocol No. 1 (securing the right to education).[27]

Corruption

1999	2001	2002	2003	2004	2005	2006	2007	2008
3.25	3.75	3.75	3.50	3.50	3.50	3.50	3.50	3.25

Corruption is another area where gradual improvements are more a testament to the country's overall maturation than the result of concrete actions taken by the governing elite or the population at large. Ordinary people still complain about paying bribes or "giving gifts" in exchange for expediting services, as excessive regulation continues to plague parts of the public administration. Yet these are exceptions rather than the rule, and most people are able to conduct their daily lives without engaging in corrupt behavior.

Although few people encounter corruption directly, the perception of illegal activity, especially among the political elite, is widespread. Many view existing anticorruption measures as insufficient to dismantle the intricate web of connections between political and business elites. According to the Transparency International Global Corruption Barometer, a survey that assesses general public attitudes toward and experience of corruption in dozens of countries around the world, 44 percent of Czechs believe the level of corruption will continue to rise and another 29 percent believe it will stay the same. The results, released in December 2007, also indicate that 60 percent do not believe in the effectiveness of government anticorruption measures.[28]

A lack of transparency in major business deals involving the state remains a serious problem at both national and local levels. While the country's highest control body, the NKÚ, has uncovered massive irregularities and overspending on various government contracts, politicians generally ignore its findings, calling the agency incompetent and toothless. Current law does not allow the NKÚ to impose sanctions. Although a Law on Freedom of Information is on the books, journalists often do not invoke their rights and officials frequently refuse to provide the requested information.

Despite those challenges, the Transparency International (TI) Corruption Perceptions Index (CPI), which measures the perceived level of corruption among politicians and public officials, offered positive news. In the 2007 survey, the Czech Republic tied with Italy for 41st place (out of 180 countries), with a rating of 5.2 (10 indicates a country without corruption). That was a significant improvement over the 2006 rating of 4.8 (and a big jump from the 4.3 of 2005). In a press release announcing the new CPI, the Czech branch of TI cited several positive developments in recent times—including the more active approach of the Office for the Protection of Competition in the area of public tenders, the appointment of a strong personality at the head of the NKÚ (František Dohnal, a former deputy regional governor in the area of finance), the passage of conflict-of-interest legislation (which took effect in January 2007, with the first results due in the first half of 2008), and the gradual professionalization of public administration at all levels. On the downside, TIC cited nontransparent public budgets, corruption in the business sector and in the media, insufficient investigation of white-collar crime, and, not surprisingly, ineffectively controlled public tenders.[29]

The decline in perceived corruption will likely continue if the government comes anywhere close to implementing its strategy for 2006–2011—the most wide-ranging plan for fighting corruption to date and one that TIC has praised. Among other items, the plan includes a new hotline for people to report corrupt acts (already launched); the creation of special court chambers that would deal only with corruption cases; a blacklist that would bar certain companies from participating in public tenders; and special secret agents who will collect evidence of corruption. Czech media have, however, reported that the government has backtracked on some of its promises, such as the creation of a special team of prosecutors dealing with the most serious cases of corruption and the writing of a law that would delineate the differences between lobbying and corruption.[30] In addition, the daily *Mladá Fronta Dnes* wrote that the ministries have continued to behave just as opaquely as their predecessors, refusing to supply information because of supposed business or state secrets—despite pledges of greater openness and transparency.[31]

▌ AUTHOR: JEREMY DRUKER

Jeremy Druker is executive director and editor in chief of Transitions Online *(TOL), an Internet newsmagazine covering Central and Eastern Europe, the Balkans, and the former Soviet Union. Kristy Ironside, a TOL assistant editor, and Alice Drukerová, a freelance journalist, assisted in the research for this report.*

1 Czech News Agency, "STEM: One-Third of Czechs in Favor of Reform," September 21, 2007.

2 Czech News Agency, "Poll: Czechs Afraid of Negative Impact of Reform," September 21, 2007.

3 Czech News Agency, "CVVM: People Believe Bribes and Lobbying Most Influence Politicians," September 9, 2005.

4 See, for example, Jaroslav Kmenta, "Kmotr Mrázek 2. díl" [Godfather Mrázek: Part Two], *Mladá Fronta Dnes*, November 10, 2007.

5 Hana Čápová, "Anarchie v parlamentu" [Anarchy in Parliament], *Respekt*, September 19–25, 2005.

6 Tomáš Pavlíček, "Konec starých senátních časů" [The End of the Old Senate Times], *Respekt*, October 16–22, 2006.

7 Czech News Agency, "CVVM: People Enter Parties Mainly to Acquire Influence and Money," November 2, 2007.

8 "Czech People Are Interested in Corporate Responsibility," Czech Donors Forum, October 27, 2007, http://www.donorsforum.cz/en/news?id=594.

9 Naděžda Čadová-Horáková, "Hodnocení stavu některých oblastí a očekávaný vývoj v roce 2007" [Evaluation of the Situation in Some Areas and Expected Development in the Year 2007], February 14, 2007, http://www.cvvm.cas.cz/upl/zpravy/100651s_ps70214.pdf.

10 Czech News Agency, "Extreme Right Marginalized in Czech Republic-Cakl," October 30, 2006.

11 Jan Vaca, Václav Koblenc, "Holohlavá 'spořádaná mládež'" [Skinhead "Orderly Youngsters"], *Mladá Fronta Dnes*, November 23, 2007.

12 Marius Dragomir, "PR's Twist to Independent Reporting," *Czech Business Weekly*, May 21, 2007.

13 Daniela Lazarová, "Czech Prime Minister Takes a Swipe at the Media," Radio Praha, September 25, 2007.

14 Markéta Škodová, "Hodnocení informací v médiích" [Evaluating Information in the Media], Center for Research of Public Opinion, June 20, 2007, http://www.cvvm.cas.cz/upl/zpravy/100699s_om70620.pdf.

15 Marius Dragomir, "Politicians Start to Get Into the Picture over Allocation of Digital Television Licenses," *Czech Business Weekly*, February 21, 2005.

16 Vladimír Ševela, "Vzpoura venkova" [The Rebellion of the Countryside], *Respekt,* October 8–14, 2007.

17 Ibid.

18 Petr Fischer, "Na cestě k decentralizaci" [On the Path Toward Decentralization], *Respekt*, October 8–14, 2007.

19 Tomáš Menschik, "Za demokratičtější komunál" [For More Democratic Local Elections], *Týden*, October 16, 2006.

20 Mark Gillis, "A Delicate Balance," *Prague Post*, September 19, 2007; and Markéta Hulpachová, "Out of Balance," *Prague Post*, September 5, 2007.

21 Rob Cameron, "Government Unveils Ambitious Reform of Justice System," Radio Praha, September 20, 2007.

22 Ibid.

23 František Bouc, "Law Online," *Prague Post*, August 29, 2007.

24 Czech News Agency, "Antidiscrimination Bill Passes First Reading," September 26, 2007.

25 Pavla Horáková, "Polls Suggest Czechs Want More Women in Politics," Radio Praha, January 10, 2007.

26 "Executive Summary for the Czech Republic," pp. 61–66, *Equal Opportunities for Women and Men*, Open Society Institute Network Women's Program, 2005.

27 "Major Conclusions from the D.H. and Others v. Czech Republic's Judgment," OSI Justice Initiative, November 14, 2007, http://www.justiceinitiative.org/db/resource2?res_id=103941.

28 "Czechs Don't Believe the Government Will Fight Successfully With Corruption," Czech News Agency, December 6, 2007.

29 "Index CPI 2007: In Perception of Corruption, Czech Republic Rebounds from the Bottom and Gradually Begins to Improve," Transparency International–Czech Republic press statement, October 26, 2007.

30 Vojtěch Blažek, "Z protikorupčních plánů vláda slevila, zrušila některé sliby" [Government Cuts Back on Anticorruption Plans, Cancels Some Promises], *Hospodářské Noviny*, October 30, 2007.

31 Lucie Tvarůžková, "Komu dáme vaše peníze? To je tajné" [To Whom Do We Give Your Money? It's Secret], *Mladá Fronta Dnes*, November 26, 2007.

Estonia

Capital:	Tallinn
Population:	1.3 million
GNI/capita:	US$18,090

The social data above was taken from the European Bank for Reconstruction and Development's *Transition Report 2007: People in Transition*, and the economic data from the World Bank's *World Development Indicators 2008*.

Nations in Transit Ratings and Averaged Scores

	1999	2001	2002	2003	2004	2005	2006	2007	2008
Electoral Process	1.75	1.75	1.75	1.75	1.50	1.50	1.50	1.50	1.50
Civil Society	2.50	2.25	2.00	2.00	2.00	2.00	2.00	2.00	1.75
Independent Media	1.75	1.75	1.75	1.75	1.50	1.50	1.50	1.50	1.50
Governance*	2.25	2.25	2.25	2.25	2.25	n/a	n/a	n/a	n/a
National Democratic Governance	n/a	n/a	n/a	n/a	n/a	2.25	2.25	2.25	2.25
Local Democratic Governance	n/a	n/a	n/a	n/a	n/a	2.50	2.50	2.50	2.50
Judicial Framework and Independence	2.00	2.00	1.75	1.75	1.75	1.50	1.50	1.50	1.50
Corruption	3.25	2.75	2.50	2.50	2.50	2.50	2.50	2.50	2.50
Democracy Score	2.25	2.13	2.00	2.00	1.92	1.96	1.96	1.96	1.93

* *With the 2005 edition, Freedom House introduced separate analysis and ratings for national democratic governance and local democratic governance to provide readers with more detailed and nuanced analysis of these two important subjects.*

NOTE: The ratings reflect the consensus of Freedom House, its academic advisers, and the author(s) of this report. The opinions expressed in this report are those of the author(s). The ratings are based on a scale of 1 to 7, with 1 representing the highest level of democratic progress and 7 the lowest. The Democracy Score is an average of ratings for the categories tracked in a given year.

EXECUTIVE SUMMARY

As Estonia began to observe the twentieth anniversary of the first demonstrations that eventually led to its re-independence from the Soviet Union, its democratic development exhibited much the same kind of generational problems that young adults often have in their lives. While Estonia's constitutional institutions were stable and strong, politicians continued to suffer from occasionally rash decision-making or party squabbles. The scope of economic transformation had been impressive, but now the country needed to find a new growth model to move beyond simply recovering from communism. Integration of Estonia's Russian-speaking minority had improved noticeably during the last ten years, but experienced a considerable setback with the Bronze Soldier controversy. This incident left Estonia's relations with Russia at perhaps their lowest level ever, although the country's standing in the EU and NATO continued to be good.

Almost every aspect of Estonian societal life was affected in 2007 by the controversy over whether to relocate a Soviet-era World War II monument in Tallinn known as the Bronze Soldier. The dispute, which had begun simmering in 2006, played a role in Prime Minister Andrus Ansip's electoral victory in March 2007. At the same time, two days of rioting in Tallinn by mostly Russian youths after the monument was moved in late April seriously upset interethnic relations. Shortly thereafter Russia threw itself into the crisis, harassing Estonian diplomats in Moscow and sending pro-Kremlin activists into Estonia to stage additional protests. Lastly, in economic terms the episode led to a steep decline in Estonia's transit trade with Russia.

National Democratic Governance. Parliamentary elections in March returned Prime Minister Andrus Ansip to office, the first time since re-independence that such a re-election took place. Although the new governing coalition was different from Ansip's previous cabinet, it was more cohesive since it was made up solely of center-right parties. The coalition remained firm during the Bronze Soldier crisis, although the imbroglio also took away energy from other policy-making. The only major governance issue that divided the coalition concerned whether members of parliament could be appointed by ministers to serve on the oversight boards of state companies. This had been criticized by Estonia's outspoken Legal Chancellor Allar Jõks as a breach of separation of powers, but Ansip personally stood by the practice. At the end of the year, Ansip's Reform Party led a drive to deny Jõks a second term in office, a move largely seen as retribution. *Owing to the increasing politicization of constitutional institutions, which offset the increase in cabinet stability following the March elections, Estonia's rating for national democratic governance remains at 2.25.*

Electoral Process. The March parliamentary elections, in addition to being free and fair, were the first in the world to include voting via the Internet. The victory of Prime Minister Ansip's pro-market Reform Party with 28 percent was a setback for Estonia's previously most successful party, the left-leaning Center Party, which polled 26 percent. Part of this success was stoked by Ansip's strong declarations before the election in favor of moving the Bronze Soldier. At the same time, most of the campaign was focused on economic issues and promises to improve social welfare. The election also saw the emergence of a new Green Party, while ethnic Russian parties received very few votes. *While Estonia advanced in terms of innovative electoral procedures, concerns remained about a certain vacuousness in its political debates, thus the electoral process rating remains unchanged at 1.50.*

Civil Society. Civil society and ethnic relations were affected the most as a result of the Bronze Soldier affair. Among non-Estonians, the statue crisis was seen as a refusal by the Estonian government to take their historical identity seriously, and trust among them toward the Estonian state fell sharply. At the same time, Russia's behavior during the incident strengthened many Estonians' views that the Russian minority was simply an extension of Moscow's foreign policy. While both of these developments caused worry that Estonia was regressing in terms of its efforts at minority integration, preparations did continue in terms of drafting a new seven-year cycle for the policy program. This indicated a continued commitment by the government to work on ethnic relations and social harmony. Moreover, civic activism as such got a boost after the Tallinn city government convened a special 'civic peace forum' following the crisis, which brought together hundreds of community representatives and organizations. *Owing to this increased vibrancy of civil society as well as the renewed dedication to an integration policy Estonia's civil society rating improves slightly from 2.00 to 1.75.*

Independent Media. Estonia's media continued to be vibrant and free, both among Estonian- and Russian-language outlets. Still, the Bronze Soldier crisis aggravated tensions on both sides, often leading to emotional reporting and subjective analysis. The crisis did lead to a discussion about possibly creating a second state TV channel in Russian, but this was soon dropped because of its high cost. Oliver Kruuda, the owner of a large food conglomerate with close ties to the Center Party, launched a new media group, raising some concerns about partisan broadcasting. *Estonia's independent media rating remains at 1.50.*

Local Democratic Governance. Local democratic governance did not change much during 2007. While local governments do enjoy a range of autonomous rights and obligations, their independent revenue bases are narrow. The new Ansip government tasked its Regional Affairs Minister with working out a broad reform of the public administration system. By the end of the year, however, the minister came under criticism for not moving fast enough. *Estonia's rating for local democratic governance remains at 2.50.*

Judicial Framework and Independence. Estonia's legal system remained relatively stable in 2007. Instead, the spotlight was focused on a number of high-profile court cases, which tested the impartiality of the courts and of judges. In September, a court on the island of Hiiumaa began hearing the trial of Arnold Meri, a cousin of former president Lennart Meri. Arnold Meri who was charged with having participated in the deportation of some 250 people during Stalinist terror in 1949. The proceedings were seen as a sign of how far Estonia was intending to go with the issue of retrospective justice. Meanwhile, in another courtroom the trial of Ardi Šuvalov, a former judge accused of taking bribes for fixing verdicts, continued. In this case, Šuvalov's eventual conviction in early 2008 indicated that the judicial system was also ready to hold one of its own to account where necessary. *Estonia's judicial framework and independence rating remains at 1.50.*

Corruption. The scandal over some questionable land-exchange deals that had forced the resignation of Environment Minister Villu Reiljan in October 2006 expanded in 2007 to include other members of his People's Union party and the head of a major development company, Merko Ehitus. In addition to raising questions about how cozy Estonian politicians were with big businessmen, the affair also revealed loopholes in the country's party financing laws. On the whole, however, Estonia continued to have a relatively low level of corruption, as evidenced by international indices and a new government survey released in 2007. *Estonia's corruption rating remains at 2.50.*

MAIN REPORT

National Democratic Governance

1999	2001	2002	2003	2004	2005	2006	2007	2008
n/a	n/a	n/a	n/a	n/a	2.25	2.25	2.25	2.25

In March 2007 Estonia became one of the few countries in the post-Communist area to return its prime minister to office after a free and fair general election. Prime Minister Andrus Ansip led his pro-market, liberal Reform Party to victory at the polls on March 7, giving him the prerogative to form a second government in succession. The election in this respect improved Estonia's governance, since it yielded a clear center-right government made up of Ansip's Reform Party (RP), the conservative Pro Patria and Res Publica Union (PPRPU) and the centrist Social Democratic Party (SDP). The match-up augured well for the future, since the same three parties had been in power from 1999 to early 2002, when Estonia tackled some major economic difficulties and carried out a number of key European Union accession reforms. The outcome also ended the stop-gap government that Ansip had maintained since May 2005 with the leftist Center Party (CP), which had lacked direction. Estonia was now on much more solid governing ground than before.

The strength of this coalition was also important for the first major crisis the government would face: the decision to relocate the Bronze Soldier war memorial in downtown Tallinn. For years this monument of a Soviet soldier lowering his head in front of a small square where 12 unknown Soviet soldiers had been buried had not caused major controversy. Every May 9, World War II veterans (mostly Russians) would gather peacefully at the site to commemorate Soviet Victory Day. In May 2006, however, a scuffle took place between the veterans and a small group of Estonian nationalists, which prompted the Ansip government to block off the complex for three months. When the site was re-opened, Prime Minister Ansip claimed (citing Estonian security service reports) that the monument was likely to become a perpetual source of potential conflict and therefore it had to be re-located.

Ansip's initial plans, however, were thwarted by the Tallinn city government, which used its legal jurisdiction over the monument to argue that more discussions with veterans groups were needed before relocation could take place. The city's stance appeared high-minded, but it was also deeply political, since the government was controlled by the Center Party, and the party relied heavily on ethnic Russian votes to remain in power. It could not afford to alienate such a large constituency.

Ansip therefore turned to parliament in order to pass special legislation transferring control over the monument to the national government. Although this move strained relations within Ansip's cabinet (since at the time the coalition was still made up of Ansip's Reform Party and the Center Party), the government did not fall and parliament passed the amendments with votes from the PPRPU and the SDP.

During the parliamentary election campaign in early 2007, the memorial did not become a major issue. The PPRPU briefly used images of the monument during one television ad and Prime Minister Ansip continued to stress that if he were re-elected he would re-locate the memorial complex as soon as possible. But Russian parties did not make the monument a rallying cry, nor did any groups attempt to rally at the site.

Still, the issue remained an emotional one. Although over the last 10 years the monument had been altered by the removal of some large red Soviet stars and an eternal flame, it was still a painful reminder for many Estonians of their re-occupation by the Soviet Union in 1944. Moreover, many objected to its location at a prominent intersection in the capital and opposite the national library. Yet, for Russian groups the monument was an important part of their historical identity, and they were indignant at the way the Estonian government appeared determined to disregard their feelings. While the memorialization of World War II has always been strong among Russians, the ascendance of Vladimir Putin in Russia and the re-emergence of many old Soviet traditions in that country have also served to accentuate such sentiments among Russians in Estonia.

The government finally decided to act on April 26, erecting a tent over the monument site in order to begin exhuming the bodies of the unknown Soviet soldiers. By evening, a crowd of over 1000 (mostly Russian) protestors had gathered around the complex and were taunting police. When Estonian police began disbursing the demonstrators, several hundred of them entered neighboring streets and Tallinn's famed old town. They soon began smashing shop windows and looting, in some cases while recorded by television cameras. The Estonian security services spent the better part of the night restoring order, arresting hundreds and treating dozens for injuries. One protestor, a 19-year-old Russian Federation citizen resident in Estonia, was killed when he was among a group that attacked a bar, which Estonian patrons inside attempted to defend. In the midst of the mayhem, the government decided to speed up its work and indeed removed the Bronze Soldier statue immediately for reinstallation in a military cemetery outside the downtown area.

While the shock of violence was great, Prime Minister Ansip insisted the next day that the government had acted appropriately. He decried the vandalism and said this was no way to honor the memory of those fallen in the war. Still, rioting flared again on the night of April 27, while some acts of public disobedience (for example, driving cars slowly through the streets of Tallinn) were also attempted.

By the third day, the situation in Tallinn calmed, but thereafter tensions shifted to Moscow, where activists from the pro-Kremlin Nashi youth organization attempted to blockade the Estonia embassy and harass diplomatic personnel. This led the European Union to rebuke the Russian government harshly for not living up to international conventions protecting diplomats. After two weeks, the bluster from Moscow also died down, although in sum Estonian-Russian relations had reached their lowest point ever. While President Putin denounced the Estonian government's actions, Tallinn accused Russia of having been behind a number of cyberattacks against Estonian government websites.

In the aftermath of the entire crisis, the Estonian government, if anything, was more united. The popularity rating for Prime Minister Ansip's Reform Party (RP) spiked to more than 40 percent, an unprecedented level for any Estonian party, ever. This emboldened the party to be especially tough during the second half of the year, among other things, standing against its coalition partners in a disagreement over whether members of parliament should be allowed to sit on the executive boards of state-owned companies. Estonia's Legal Chancellor, Allar Jõks, had ruled that if MPs are appointed by cabinet ministers to sit on the boards, this was a violation of the separation of powers. The Reform Party disputed this interpretation and continued to allow its cabinet ministers to appoint MPs from the RP to various boards.

For some time, both the Reform Party and the Center Party—Estonia's two largest—had tussled with the legal chancellor over several issues, including party financing laws and local election rules. In another temporary shift of allegiances, the RP decided in December to ally with the CP in opposing President Toomas Hendrik Ilves's nomination of Jõks to a second seven-year term. The popular ombudsman was thus scuttled by an RP–CP majority vote in parliament in what many saw as revenge. A new legal chancellor was appointed later in 2008.

Electoral Process

1999	2001	2002	2003	2004	2005	2006	2007	2008
1.75	1.75	1.75	1.75	1.50	1.50	1.50	1.50	1.50

The parliamentary election that Estonia held on March 7 was its fifth since re-independence in 1991. As with all of Estonia's previous electoral contests, the poll passed off without any major problems. Indeed, Estonia actually achieved a milestone by becoming the first country in the world to allow voting for the national parliament via the Internet as part of its already wide range of e-government services. The procedure was made possible and secure thanks to the existence of microchips implanted in every Estonian's ID card. The chips can be read by an inexpensive reader and are complemented by a set of numerical codes known only to the card holder. Estonia first tested the system successfully during local elections in 2005. In 2007, the number of "e-votes" cast tripled to over 30,000. As a result, analysts began to speculate whether voting during Estonia's next elections (to the European Parliament in 2009) might even be made possible via mobile phones.

Technological advances aside, however, the main political battle during the election involved the two major parties in government at the time, the Reform Party and the Center Party. For years, the two have occupied almost opposite ideological poles. While the Center Party has championed a progressive income tax for Estonia, the Reform Party has called for lowering even further the current flat-rate tax of 22 percent. While the Center Party has called for more social spending, the Reform Party has warned against building a welfare state. The fact that the two parties were together in a coalition was merely an arrangement of convenience following the collapse of a previous center-right government in 2005. At the time, there was no other way to make the parliamentary math work.

For this election, the question therefore quickly became which of the two parties would come out on top. Opinion polls placed the Center Party slightly ahead. Both parties also avoided direct attacks against each other, preferring instead to project positive images. The RP promised to make Estonia "one of the five richest countries" in the European Union, while the CP promised to double average salaries in the public sector. Both of these promises soon brought charges in the media of vacuousness. But on the whole the parties successfully avoided tackling any major issues, including how Estonia would deal with a slowdown in its spectacular 8–10 percent economic growth rates if a world recession occurred. Somewhat from the margins, the other major parties (the Pro Patria and Res Publica Union, the Social Democratic Party, and the agrarian People's Union) tried to bring in other themes. But these proved less effective.

On election night, the Reform Party topped the Center Party by nearly two percentage points. A strong showing also by the PPRPU (18 percent) and the SDP (10.6 percent) meant that a center-right majority coalition was once again possible. Andrus Ansip immediately began consultations, and even tried to include the Green Party, a newcomer which was formed in 2006 and picked up 7 percent of the vote. But since this would have created an oversized coalition, Ansip eventually dropped the Greens and the new cabinet took office on April 5.

The elections were another big disappointment for Estonia's Russian parties, two of which took part in the poll, but received very small vote margins. The Constitution Party scored just 1 percent and the Russian Party of Estonia returned 0.2 percent. The explanation behind this result was two-fold. First, fewer than half of all ethnic Russians in Estonia have Estonian citizenship allowing them to participate in national elections. This has been a legacy of Estonia's 1991–1992 citizenship legislation, which denied automatic citizenship to all those people who settled in Estonia during Soviet rule as well as their descendants. Since this principle overlapped with the vast majority of Russians in Estonia, Russian political participation has always remained far below the minority's actual 35 percent share of the population.

Second, many ethnic Russian voters preferred Estonian parties, in part because these parties have often succeeded in attracting to their ranks a number of prominent Russian community leaders. Thus, according to different post-electoral polls conducted by the Department of Political Science at the University of Tartu, some 50 percent of ethnic Russians in Estonia generally vote for the Center Party. In 2007, the party did particularly well in the heavily Russian towns of Narva, Sillamäe, and Kohtla-Järve, winning up to two-thirds of the vote.

Civil Society

1999	2001	2002	2003	2004	2005	2006	2007	2008
2.50	2.25	2.00	2.00	2.00	2.00	2.00	2.00	1.75

The events surrounding the Bronze soldier also affected civil society in Estonia by heightening ethnic anxieties and laying bare some of the longer-term issues of minority integration that Estonia still faces. The sight of Russian youths rioting in Estonia's capital city was a shock for most Estonians. Moreover, the degree to which Russia got involved in the crisis reinforced the impression among many ethnic Estonians that the Russian minority remains a potential foreign policy tool of Moscow instead of being a dedicated part of Estonian society. Meanwhile, many Russians felt dismayed at the Estonian government's unilateral approach to relocating the monument. Following the crisis, satisfaction among non-Estonians with leadership in Estonia fell to less than 20 percent.[1] One well-known expert, Marju Lauristin, a professor of communications at the University of Tartu, commented that Estonia risked going back to the days of simplified stereotypes and misgivings, which previously Estonia seemed to have outgrown.[2]

Still, the crisis also generated some positive effects. Barely ten days after the riots, the Tallinn city government launched a "civic peace forum" to restore interethnic and societal dialogue in the capital. The forum's first meeting attracted some 300 people and encompassed over 40 civic organizations. Although some commentators dismissed the event as an attempt by Tallinn mayor and Center Party chairman Edgar Savisaar to cast himself as peacemaker following Prime Minister Ansip's imbroglio, the forum continued to meet throughout the rest of the year and eventually drew up a set of special reconciliation projects to be financed by the city. Within the framework of the forum there was a clear mobilization of varied civil society groups, which hopefully will continue into the future.

Likewise, surveys conducted during the summer showed that both Estonians and Russians continued to trust one another by significant majorities. Some 56 percent of Estonians trusted non-Estonians, while 66 percent of non-Estonians trusted Estonians. The share of people not trusting the other group was just 22 percent.[3] Moreover, among young Russians (under 29 years of age) 70 percent reported being able to speak Estonian either well or adequately as opposed to just 22 percent among Russians aged 60 to 74.[4] This fact indicated that by generation the levels of minority integration were improving.

Part of this success was due to Estonia's official integration program, which since 2000 has sponsored a wide range of projects at both the national and local levels fostering Estonian language training, cultural awareness, mutual tolerance and minority political participation. While many Russian community leaders have complained that the measures actually risk assimilating Russians, and surveys have shown that in general Russians have not yet perceived much help from the integration programs, the policy has changed attitudes among Estonians and convinced them of the need to address Russian minority problems.[5]

In this respect, Estonia's Minister for Population Affairs, Urve Palo, had her work cut out for her when she began in 2007 to draft a new seven-year cycle for the program. During the year, Palo held a number of expert meetings and public forums to discuss both new principles and activities for the policy. The former included a commitment to strengthening national unity, increasing minority participation in societal affairs and ensuring equal opportunities for all. New activities were aimed at advancing the teaching of Estonian in Russian-language schools, reducing ethnic segmentation in the economy and labor market, and expanding information sources for minorities. Although the final policy paper was set for adoption in 2008, the events of 2007 clearly showed that integration was a policy that needed to be continued.

Independent Media

1999	2001	2002	2003	2004	2005	2006	2007	2008
1.75	1.75	1.75	1.75	1.50	1.50	1.50	1.50	1.50

During any national crisis, the independent media play a central role in providing objective information as well as keeping coverage balanced and responsible. Amidst the Bronze Soldier crisis (and throughout the year), the Estonian media were generally free, fair, and reliable. The Estonian government did not interfere with media coverage of the events, allowing both state and private media to operate freely. At the same time, the government did attempt to control its own information flows. For example, during the height of the rioting, only key cabinet officials were allowed to speak to the press. Later the government repeatedly cited special reports from the Estonian Security Police Board (SPB), which it said proved how necessary it was for them to act and avoid additional provocations. No independent verification or analysis of these reports, however, was made possible.

In reporting the crisis itself, some of the coverage became subjective or polemical. The main Estonian-language dailies published large photographs of enraged protestors damaging property and looting shops. On the editorial pages, columnists and readers vented their anger both at the rioters and at Russia, often linking the two together. The Russian-language media, meanwhile, were generally more neutral, criticizing (as they had before the crisis) the relocation of the war monument, but not inciting readers to stage additional protest actions or disturbances.

The crisis did spawn a discussion over whether Estonia should invest in the creation of a second state-run television station, which would be run in Russian language. The argument was that such a station would provide more direct information to viewers about Estonia in the Russian language. This would help also to explain better Estonian government decisions to minority residents, not only about issues such as the Bronze Soldier, but also more practical questions such as naturalization requirements, education reform, Estonian language courses, etc. Such a program also could help offset the degree to which many Russian-speaking residents of Estonia rely exclusively on Russian Federation television channels for their daily information. At the same time, a number of government officials soon pointed to the high price of such an undertaking, citing not only extensive start-up costs, but also recurring production expenditures needed to maintain high quality programming. By the end of the year, the idea had been dropped.

Instead, Estonia's state television and radio underwent a different kind of structural reform, when on January 18, 2007, the Estonian parliament approved a long debated law merging as of June 1 the two services into one unit, to be called Estonian Public Broadcasting (EPB). While some journalists opposed the move, seeing it as an unwise centralization of state broadcasting power, the management on both sides as well as a number of key parliamentarians favored the union so that the two divisions could pool their news-gathering operations, production facilities and Internet resources. Moreover, in August 2007 the EPB unveiled the architectural design for a new headquarters of the joint service to be built by 2010.

Still, a second controversy surrounding the EPB concerned the appointment of members to a new supervisory board. A number of parliamentarians had maintained that only MPs should be appointed to the board in order to ensure parliamentary and political control over the EPB. Others insisted, however, that the board should include independent media experts in order to keep the politicians from colluding and manipulating the EPB in their own interest. After a public outcry against the dangers of politicizing the EPB, parliament finally agreed to name three outside experts to the board alongside six MPs.

Beyond the realm of state broadcasting, it was worth noting that more and more of Estonia's public debate also moved into the Internet during 2007, with newspapers running on-line news portals, readers posting real-time commentaries and politicians blogging. Indeed, often these different forms became inter-linked, with the claims of one politician or another in a blog becoming news in the electronic versions of newspapers or on other websites. Estonia media portals competed to offer readers (especially young people) a wide range of supplementary services to make their sites attractive.

It was in this way that a brand new media concern was launched in September by Oliver Kruuda, the owner of a large food conglomerate called Kalev. Kruuda announced the creation of a new 24-hour news portal, Kalev.ee, that would seek to compete with other outlets by concentrating mainly on local Estonian news. Kruuda decided to sell large parts of his existing business empire in order to finance the venture, which would include a cable sports channel and the ownership of a major sports magazine. At the same time, Kruuda was known to have strong ties with the Center Party and its leader Edgar Savisaar, having helped to fund a number of controversial political advertisements for the party during local elections in 2005. At the end of 2007, it was announced that the new Kalev television station had also won a contract with the Tallinn city government (controlled by the Center Party) to broadcast sessions of the city council as well as produce monthly programs about life in the capital city. These aspects raised questions about how objective the new conglomerate was going to be.

Local Democratic Governance

1999	2001	2002	2003	2004	2005	2006	2007	2008
n/a	n/a	n/a	n/a	n/a	2.50	2.50	2.50	2.50

Estonia's local governments are relatively autonomous in terms of managing their own affairs, but their degree of actual governance has been limited because of a large number of municipalities, which has in turn fragmented their ability to carry out more large-scale projects or combine resources. Although local governments have independent revenue sources thanks to property taxes and a guaranteed share of income tax proceeds, these means are often not enough to go beyond the provision of essential services. Infrastructure projects, and in particular those that might qualify for EU financing, often require much larger co-funding or administrative capacity than the existing capabilities of single municipalities.

To this end, the Estonian government (under different prime ministers) ha long sought to promote a consolidation of the approximate 250 local governments which existed in the 1990s. By 2007, this number had been reduced to 227 thanks to some voluntary mergers between local governments. In the new Ansip government, however, Minister for Regional Affairs Vallo Reimaa was specially requested to develop a new reform of the public administration, including change in local government. Reimaa convened a number of roundtables and was in the process of putting forward some proposals. Yet, at the end of the year he cam under criticism from within his own party (the Pro Patria and Res Publica Union and in particular the party chairman, Mart Laar, who complained that Reimaa wa moving too slowly, risking losing the momentum behind a new effort at publi administration reform.

Judicial Framework and Independence

1999	2001	2002	2003	2004	2005	2006	2007	2008
2.00	2.00	1.75	1.75	1.75	1.50	1.50	1.50	1.50

Estonia's judicial framework and independence were in the spotlight during 200 thanks to a number of high-profile court cases involving both the Bronze Soldi issue as well as more distant issues from the past dating back to 1949. In la February, the Tallinn City Government appealed to Estonia's constitutional cou regarding the special legislation parliament had just passed allowing the nation government to relocate war memorials when necessitated by the public intere The city argued that this was a violation of the Estonian Constitution's guarant of autonomy for local governments, since in general such monuments were und local jurisdiction. The court announced its final ruling only in early June, thus ov a month after the Tallinn riots. Still, the court issued a fairly balanced decision agreeing with the city that the new law was an infringement on local government autonomy, but that in this case such infringement was permissible, since given the international nature of war any monuments erected to commemorate them were automatically of national importance, and the state should have the right to regulate them.

A second court case that raised political eyebrows opened in September on the Estonian island of Hiiumaa, where a decorated Soviet war veteran, Arnold Meri, was accused of having supervised the deportation to Siberia of 251 people during the mass collectivization of agriculture in Estonia after World War II. According to the state prosecutor, Meri was the chief political officer sent to Hiiumaa to carry out the deportations and was as such responsible for the repression of dozens of innocent people. At the same time, the case raised questions about the usefulness of trying such 80-year-old men when so much time had already passed. Press reports in the Russian Federation also questioned whether this wasn't just another attempt to blacken the name of a Soviet military hero. Still, the court case revealed that even the cousin of former president Lennart Meri was not immune from investigation into deeds carried out nearly six decades earlier. The proceedings themselves were expected to last several months.

Lastly, the Estonian court system itself was held accountable during 2007 via the continued trial of Ardi Šuvalov, a former county judge accused of taking bribes to issue favorable verdicts. In April 2006, Šuvalov was arrested by agents of the Security Police Board after he accepted a bribe of 200,000 Estonian kroons ($16,500) from an undercover officer. Overall, Šuvalov was charged with trying to take over a million kroons in bribes in order to end a criminal case against a businessman. Yet, as a former judge, Šuvalov also knew how to drag out a court proceeding, and thus during 2007 Šuvalov himself brought a suit against the state prosecutor's office for having issued a press-release about his case, which he claimed leaked sensitive information about him. In December the Tallinn administrative court threw out the case, and Šuvalov was left to struggle with his own trial. In January 2008, Šuvalov was convicted of taking bribes and sentenced to three and a half years in prison.

Corruption

1999	2001	2002	2003	2004	2005	2006	2007	2008
3.25	2.75	2.50	2.50	2.50	2.50	2.50	2.50	2.50

In 2007 Estonia saw its ranking in Transparency International's Corruption Perception Index slip by 0.2 points to 6.5 on the scale of 1–10 where 10 is the best score (least corrupt), mostly because of an apparent slowdown in the government's efforts to combat corruption.[6] Estonia also ceded its 2006 title of least corrupt country in Central and Eastern Europe to Slovenia, which climbed to 6.6. On the one hand, these developments seemed to run counter to a number of unprecedented corruption investigations which were either launched or continued during 2007. At the same time, part of Transparency International's criticism stemmed from a delay in the adoption of an official government program to fight corruption, which did not come until 2008. Moreover, a survey of corruption released by the Estonian Ministry of Justice in 2007 reported that just 3 percent of individual Estonians and only 12 percent of businesses said they had paid a bribe to a civil servant over the last year. Fully 81 percent of respondents said that neither they nor anyone they knew had come into contact with having to pay bribes.[7]

The scandal, which continued to grab the most headlines during 2007 involved Villu Reiljan, a former Minister of Environment and leader of the agrarian People's Union party. In October 2006, Reiljan had been forced to resign as both minister and party chairman after officials from the Security Police Board accused him of negligence in having failed to prevent some shady deals carried out by officials at Estonia's Land Board. The officials had organized a scheme whereby a number of key businessmen were allowed to exchange privately held rural tracts of land for state-owned properties in major cities as part of a government program to expand national conservation areas. The problem was that in many cases the value of the rural lands was greatly inflated in order to allow the businessmen to receive the desired city properties. Having signed off on the deals as Environment Minister, Reiljan was being investigated to see whether he or his party had received any kickbacks.

During 2007, the SPB's investigation expanded to include Reiljan's party colleague and former Agriculture Minister, Ester Tuiksoo, together with Tooma Annus, the chief executive officer of Merko Ehitus, a prominent construction company and real estate developer. In particular, the Security Police wanted to know whether Tuiksoo had not tried to engineer a move of her ministry to a major new office building completed by Merko Ehitus in exchange for a possible bribe. Moreover, additional inquires soon revealed that the general secretary of the People's Union had been driving around in a sport-utility vehicle provided to her free-of-charge by a major automobile dealer, while other party leaders lived in apartments rented out far below the market price.

All these suspected improprieties brought once again into the spotlight the issue of party financing, since even though Estonia banned corporate contributions to political parties in 2003, single businessmen have still channeled huge sums of money to parties and prominent party leaders have continued to accept small favors such as reduced-price goods. At one point, members of the People's Union (PU) wondered whether they would actually survive all of their scandals politically. During the March parliamentary elections, the PU saw its support drop by half to just 7 percent. Still, the party's new leader, Jaanus Marrandi, vowed to continue fighting all of the charges and to rebuild the Union's image.

Estonian corruption in this sense appeared to take place most of all in the form of never actually violating the letter of the law, but certainly going against its spirit. Indeed, in 2005 Prime Minister Ansip inadvertently coined a phrase to capture this phenomenon by noting how in many such cases "Legally everything is abo board." ("Juriidiliselt on kõik korrektne.") Soon afterwards the abbreviation of this Estonian-language phrase, "Jokk", became a frequently used expression of political sarcasm. During the March 2007 elections the Social Democratic Party even tried to capitalize on the phrase by making it a campaign slogan, promising to end all "Jokk". Thus, even in the midst mounting cynicism about politics and frustration over corruption, Estonian still had a knack for turning a clever phrase.

1   Ivi Proos and Iris Pettai, "Rahvussuhted ja integratsiooni perspektiivid Eestis: sotsioloogilise uurimuse materjalid" [Ethnic Relations and the Prospects for Integration in Estonia: Materials from a Sociological Study], Tallinn: Eesti Avatud Ühiskonna Instituut, 2007, p. 21.

2   Sandra Maasalu, "Uuring: eestlaste eelarvamused venelaste kohta on suurenenud" [Study: Estonian Prejudices Toward Russians Have Grown], Postimees.ee, August 9, 2007, http://www.postimees.ee/090807/esileht/siseuudised/276187.php.

3   Proos and Pettai, p. 18.

4   Ibid, p. 25

5   Ibid, pp. 10, 12, 20.

6   Tarmu Tammerk, "Laisk riik ja kõlavad afäärid kukutasid Eestit korruptsioonitabelis" [A Lazy State and Loud Scandals Tumble Estonia in Corruption Index], Eesti Päevaleht Online, October 15, 2007, http://www.epl.ee/artikkel/403977.

7   Mari-Liis Liiv and Kadri Aas, "Korruptsioon Eestis: kolme sihtrühma uuring 2006" [Corruption in Estonia: A study of Three Target Groups, 2006], Tallinn: Justiitsministeerium ja Tartu Ülikool, 2007, p. 22–3.

Georgia

by Ghia Nodia

Capital: Tbilisi
Population: 4.5 million
GNI/capita: US$3,880

The social data above was taken from the European Bank for Reconstruction and Development's *Transition Report 2007: People in Transition*, and the economic data from the World Bank's *World Development Indicators 2008*.

Nations in Transit Ratings and Averaged Scores

	1999	2001	2002	2003	2004	2005	2006	2007	2008
Electoral Process	4.00	4.50	5.00	5.25	5.25	4.75	4.75	4.50	4.75
Civil Society	3.75	4.00	4.00	4.00	3.50	3.50	3.50	3.50	3.50
Independent Media	3.75	3.50	3.75	4.00	4.00	4.25	4.25	4.00	4.25
Governance*	4.50	4.75	5.00	5.50	5.75	n/a	n/a	n/a	n/a
National Democratic Governance	n/a	n/a	n/a	n/a	n/a	5.50	5.50	5.50	5.75
Local Democratic Governance	n/a	n/a	n/a	n/a	n/a	6.00	5.75	5.50	5.50
Judicial Framework and Independence	4.00	4.00	4.25	4.50	4.50	5.00	4.75	4.75	4.75
Corruption	5.00	5.25	5.50	5.75	6.00	5.75	5.50	5.00	5.00
Democracy Score	4.17	4.33	4.58	4.83	4.83	4.96	4.86	4.68	4.79

* *With the 2005 edition, Freedom House introduced separate analysis and ratings for national democratic governance and local democratic governance to provide readers with more detailed and nuanced analysis of these two important subjects.*

NOTE: The ratings reflect the consensus of Freedom House, its academic advisers, and the author(s) of this report. The opinions expressed in this report are those of the author(s). The ratings are based on a scale of 1 to 7, with 1 representing the highest level of democratic progress and 7 the lowest. The Democracy Score is an average of ratings for the categories tracked in a given year.

EXECUTIVE SUMMARY

Since Georgia's independence, the country's hybrid system has caused widespread internal instability. For most of this period, the opposition and independent media have enjoyed a high level of independence, but there has been a lack of fair competition for political power, causing unconstitutional changes of power in 1992 and 2003. The wars for secession in Abkhazia and South Ossetia from 1991 to 1993 brought some 15 percent of Georgia's territory under the control of unrecognized governments. These unresolved conflicts as well as tense relations with Russia, the major protector of secessionist regimes in these areas, continue to challenge the stability of the country.

The November 2003 events known as the "Rose Revolution," when President Eduard Shevardnadze resigned following mass protests over rigged parliamentary elections, brought to power a group of pro-Western reformers led by the charismatic president Mikheil Saakashvili. Subsequent years were marked by success in rooting out mass corruption, strengthening public institutions, and promoting robust economic growth. As the Monitoring Committee of the Parliamentary Assembly of the Council of Europe remarked in September 2007, "In a remarkably short time Georgia has made stunning progress in carrying out substantial economic, judicial and state reforms. It has laid the foundations that should allow Georgia to become a prosperous liberal market economy and a fully fledged democracy governed by human rights and the rule of law."[1]

However, the crisis at the end of 2007 signified an important setback for Georgia democratic development. On September 27, the arrest on corruption charges of Irakli Okruashvili, a former minister of defense turned opposition politician, led to a series of protest rallies that reached a climax on November 2, when an estimated 50,000–75,000 people called for early parliamentary elections and amendment to election legislation. As the rallies continued, the demands radicalized into calls for the immediate resignation of the president. On November 7, the government dispersed the rallies, closed down two major opposition-oriented TV stations, and introduced a state of emergency that lasted nine days. These actions were justified by the imminent danger of a coup. On November 8, the president unveiled his plan to resign, with a call for snap presidential elections on January 5, 2008, well as a plebiscite on the date of the parliamentary elections. Imedi TV, the major opposition channel, was accused of conspiring to overthrow the government, and its broadcasting was temporarily suspended.

National Democratic Governance. Georgia's mixed political system protects major civil and political rights and provides for political pluralism and meaningful expression of the public will. However, the unbalanced character of the system where the executive branch dominates other state agencies, combined with a weak opposition prevent Georgia from becoming a consolidated democracy. The effectiveness of the government has increased considerably since the Rose Revolution, especially in attracting public revenue and providing public goods. However, the fact that opposition protests led to a political crisis ending in a nine-day state of emergency exposed the vulnerability of Georgia's democratic institutions. The government's lack of full territorial control also constitutes a continuing source of instability. *Reflecting the political crisis caused by mass rallies and the resulting setback to Georgia's unbalanced system of governance, the rating for national democratic governance is downgraded from 5.50 to 5.75.*

Electoral Process. Elections since the Rose Revolution have been generally free and fair, overcoming widespread fraud hitherto endemic to the system. The 2006 legislation on public financing for political parties and free TV airtime for electoral campaigning has created a more even playing field for the government and opposition parties. The dramatic events in November 2007 showed that the opposition is gaining strength, which led to demands for extra-constitutional changes of power as well as disturbing occurrences of violence against opposition figures, though the crisis was resolved by calling for early elections. *Although the crisis was returned to the electoral track, owing to occurrences of violent and unconstitutional means in the political competition the rating for electoral process worsened from 4.50 to 4.75.*

Civil Society. The legislation regulating nongovernmental organizations (NGOs) is quite liberal, and there are no impediments to their activities. Nonprofit organizations are easy to register, and the registration process was made even simpler in 2007. A majority of the public appreciate the role of civil society in advancing democracy. However, after the Rose Revolution, the sector's visibility has diminished. NGO cooperation with the government is productive in some areas, but there is no stable mechanism for interaction between the government and civil society. There are organizations with illiberal, extreme-right agendas, but government has been successful in curbing their activities so the groups are free to express their opinions but violence has largely stopped and their influence is marginal. The social base for NGOs is rather narrow, and organizations in most regions outside the capital are less developed. They are dependent primarily on foreign funding. Trade unions exist but have little influence. *The rating for civil society remains unchanged at 3.50.*

Independent Media. Georgia's Constitution and legislation ensure a liberal environment for the development of independent media. The 2004 Law on Freedom of Speech and Expression took libel off the criminal code and relieved journalists of legal responsibility for revealing state secrets. However, Georgian media demonstrate weak editorial independence and low professional standards and are often used to promote the political interests of their owners. Still, pluralism of voices is guaranteed by the diversity of media ownership. Temporary suspension of Imedi, the major opposition-oriented TV and radio, questioned the government's commitment to media freedom and exposed the fragility of media pluralism. *Owing to the setback in media freedoms caused by the nine-day state of emergency and temporary closing of Imedi TV and radio, the rating for independent media is downgraded from 4.00 to 4.25.*

Local Democratic Governance. The Constitution does not define Georgia's territorial arrangement or the competences of subnational institutions of state power. In December 2005, the Parliament adopted legislation that lays the groundwork to create new local government institutions. In 2007, following the October 2006 local elections, a new system of municipal government was instituted with the potential to create meaningful and effective municipal bodies. However, it has not yet demonstrated the necessary level of competence and independence. *Owing to insufficient data to evaluate the performance of the new system of municipal government, the rating for local democratic governance remains unchanged at 5.50.*

Judicial Framework and Independence. Georgia's Constitution provides important safeguards for the protection of human rights and the independence of the judiciary. However, since the Rose Revolution, the judiciary still finds it difficult to withstand political pressure. There has been a decrease in abuse by law enforcement officers, but the problem is still acute in some parts of the country. In 2007, there was an alarming trend of tampering with the property rights of citizens and businesses. A set of reforms carried out in 2006–2007 will help strengthen the independence of the judiciary. *Positive reforms in the judiciary and penitentiary system and reductions in police abuse were offset by problems in the area of property rights and excessive force used to disperse political demonstration; thus, the rating for judicial framework and independence remains unchanged at 4.75.*

Corruption. Although corruption remains an important concern, resolute measures by the government started to bear fruit, as reflected in considerably lower perceptions of corruption among experts and the general public. While in the aftermath of the Rose Revolution anticorruption efforts consisted of strong but somewhat erratic punitive measures with insufficient respect for due process, later anticorruption policies have become more comprehensive and orderly. Lack of transparency in a number of public institutions contributes to continuing concerns about corruption. *Georgia's corruption rating remains at 5.00.*

Outlook for 2008. The quality of snap presidential and regular parliamentary elections in 2008 will be an important test for measuring the development, direction, and effectiveness of Georgia's democratic institutions. In addition to gauging Georgia's electoral procedures, the polls will test the maturity of opposition parties, as well as the genuine freedom of the media and their ability to facilitate meaningful policy dialogue. The expected recognition of Kosovo's independence may directly affect Russia's attitude toward the self-proclaimed entities of Abkhazia and South Ossetia, thus increasing tensions between Russia and Georgia and destabilizing the zones of conflict.

MAIN REPORT

National Democratic Governance

1999	2001	2002	2003	2004	2005	2006	2007	2008
n/a	n/a	n/a	n/a	n/a	5.50	5.50	5.50	5.75

Georgia's hybrid system of democratic governance represents a mixed picture, which became even less certain following the dramatic events of September–November 2007. The activities of President Mikheil Saakashvili's government since 2004 have led to a general strengthening of public institutions, yet their stability and democratic character remained challenged. While the general development and conspicuous successes of the new government gave grounds for optimistic assessments until the autumn of 2007, the subsequent political crisis in September–November exposed structural weaknesses of the political system.

The Georgian political system is based on democratic principles, and for most of the year it provided for meaningful guarantees of political pluralism and freedom of expression. The declared policy of the government to pursue democratic reforms with an aim to join NATO and the European Union is not openly contested by any significant political group and has broad public support. The rights to join and create political parties, take part in elections, and create and engage in public associations or demonstrations are generally respected. Government agencies have public boards/councils and other formats for dialogue with civil society. The 1999 administrative code includes the equivalent of the U.S. Freedom of Information Act, which makes all public information accessible.

Georgia has had important successes in creating a liberal business climate and was ranked 35th in a 2007 economic freedom index by the Heritage Foundation and *The Wall Street Journal*, moving up from 68th place the previous year. According to the World Bank report *Doing Business 2008*, which analyzes countries' ease of doing business, Georgia was ranked 18th among 178 economies surveyed. Georgia was 37th last year and 132nd the year before.

Until 2004, the design of the central government generally followed the model of the U.S. Constitution. The president could not dissolve the Parliament and needed to secure parliamentary approval when appointing ministers and adopting the budget. On February 6, 2004, the Parliament introduced changes into the Constitution that unraveled the republican balance of power in favor of the president. The positions of prime minister and cabinet ministers were established. The president must secure approval from the Parliament to appoint the prime minister but can dismiss him at will. Most important, the president has acquired powers to dismiss the Parliament in specific circumstances, such as in the event of three consecutive no-confidence votes delivered to the cabinet by the

Parliament. This decreases the independence of the Parliament. The assembly passes an enormous amount of new legislation without sufficient deliberation, though it offers resistance to some draft legislation coming from the executive branch.

In December 2006, the Parliament adopted a new package of constitutional amendments (signed by the president in January 2007). Some were intended to strengthen the independence of the judiciary from the executive; the most controversial of them, however, extended the term of the standing Parliament from April to October–December 2008, anticipating security challenges that might stem from coinciding elections in Russia and Georgia in April 2008. This drew strong criticism from the opposition, and revoking this change became one of the main demands during the mass rallies in November 2007.

In January 2007, President Saakashvili stated that the existing Georgian "Constitution requires fundamental improvements in terms of democratization" and expressed an intention "to create a new constitutional commission to write a new Georgian Constitution in the coming years."[2] He amended himself the following day, saying, "The adoption of a new Constitution will be possible only after total restoration of the country's territorial integrity."[3] Many opposition parties and analysts consider Saakashvili's strong presidentialism as an autocratic trend in Georgia's political system. During protest rallies in September–November 2007, the opposition used the slogan "Georgia Without a President," which implied that in the event of winning parliamentary elections, the opposition would introduce a European-style parliamentary system in Georgia.

Georgian legislation provides for democratic oversight of the military and security services. The military budget has become more detailed and transparent, and the ministers of defense and internal affairs take part in parliamentary hearings. There is a "group of trust" in the Parliament that has access to classified information and is in closer contact with military and security services. However, no opposition member is represented in the group: The parliamentary majority has rejected the candidacy of David Gamkrelidze, leader of the New Rights Party and favored by the opposition, without giving specific reasons.

The unresolved conflicts in Abkhazia and South Ossetia, as well as tensions with Russia linked to these areas, created an unstable background for internal political processes in Georgia proper. In June and November 2007, the two remaining Russian military bases in Akhalkalaki and Batumi were handed over to Georgia without any complications, thus bringing to an end Russian military presence on all of its territory in 2007, save for zones of separatist conflict. This removed an important contentious issue in relations between Russia and Georgia, but still did not ease bilateral tensions. Declarations of Russian leaders, including President Vladimir Putin, that Kosovo's future status should set a universal precedent applicable to the resolution of conflicts in the post-Soviet sphere led to expectations that possible international recognition of Kosovo's independence could lead to Abkhazia and South Ossetia being recognized by Russia, thus causing new tensions in these regions.

In March 2007, Georgian villages in Kodori Gorge, or Upper Abkhazia (part of Abkhazia under Georgian control), were bombed, while in July there was a missile attack in the part of South Ossetia also controlled by Georgia. In both cases, Georgia and independent observers accused Russia, though the latter denied involvement. In a military encounter in Abkhazia in August, two Russian servicemen were killed by Georgian police forces, with Georgia and Russia trading blame for the incident. In November, four Russian diplomats in Tbilisi were expelled for spying.

In May 2007, the Georgian president created an interim administrative unit in the part of South Ossetia headed by Dmitriy Sanakoev, an erstwhile separatist rebel who was elected "president" of South Ossetia in an alternative poll supported by the Georgian government. Sanakoev has advocated for an autonomous South Ossetia within Georgia. In July, the president created a state commission on determination of the autonomous status of South Ossetia under the prime minister, which includes Ossetian representatives from Sanakoev's administration but was boycotted by the separatist administration in Tskhinvali. In the second half of the year, the commission worked to prepare a specific model of South Ossetian autonomy within Georgia.

A series of opposition rallies in September–November 2007 that initially called for early elections and amendments to the election legislation but later developed into demands for government resignation ended in violent dispersal of the opposition rallies, the closing of two opposition-oriented independent TV stations, and declaration of emergency rule on November 7. Officials alleged a conspiracy to overthrow the Georgian government masterminded by Badri Patarkatsishvili, a Georgian-Russian business tycoon and owner of Imedi, a major media company. On November 7, Patarkatsishvili publicly announced his readiness to spend "all to the last penny" to get rid of Saakashvili's "Fascist" government. A number of opposition figures reportedly cooperated with Russian special services with the same goal in mind.

However, the excessive use of force in dispersing the demonstrations and subsequent nine-day emergency rule with a ban on broadcast news constituted a serious setback in Georgia's democratic development. To improve the situation, President Saakashvili called for snap presidential elections on January 5, 2008, as well as a plebiscite on the date of parliamentary elections. This and certain other concessions achieved through dialogue with opposition leaders (such as changing the composition of electoral commissions) defused tensions in the short run. On November 25, the president resigned in order to make room for snap presidential elections, and his position was taken over by parliamentary Speaker Nino Burjanadze.

Electoral Process

1999	2001	2002	2003	2004	2005	2006	2007	2008
4.00	4.50	5.00	5.25	5.25	4.75	4.75	4.50	4.75

Georgia's Constitution and electoral code guarantee universal suffrage, equal electoral rights, and the right to direct and secret ballot. However, standards declined steadily until November 2003, when blatant electoral fraud during parliamentary elections triggered mass protests culminating in the resignation of the president. Several elections have taken place since the "Rose Revolution": extraordinary presidential elections in January 2004, repeat parliamentary elections (party lists only) in March 2004, regional elections in Achara in June 2004, and municipal elections in October 2006. Electoral standards improved in all of them, confirmed by local and international observers. The October 2006 municipal elections continued the trend but were still not competitive enough.

A low level of political competition has been the main trait of post–Rose Revolution elections. Mikheil Saakashvili won extraordinary presidential elections with 96.27 percent of the vote; this could be ascribed to the euphoria after the Rose Revolution, when no major politician stood up to him and those citizens who did not support him chose not to vote. Saakashvili's bloc of the National Movement and United Democrats carried the March 2004 partial repeat parliamentary elections with 66.24 percent of the vote (later, the two parties formally merged into the United National Movement [UNM]). Only one other bloc, the New Rights–Industrialists, overcame the 7 percent threshold, with 7.96 percent. In by-elections on October 1, 2005, all five parliamentary seats in single-mandate districts were taken by UNM, and the 2006 local elections brought a resounding victory to UNM.

These results cannot be explained by fraud or repression against opposition parties. In general parties can operate freely, although there have been allegations of pressure against opposition figures. The most fundamental problem noted by local and international observers was misuse of "administrative resources" or "blurred distinction between the authorities and the governing party"[4] that advantaged the incumbents. Additionally, opposition parties failed to articulate distinct alternative platforms and restricted their campaigning to competition for protest votes.

There are no obstacles to creating and joining political parties. Georgia has about 180 registered parties, with 5 represented in the Parliament. The only important restriction prohibits the creation of regionally-based parties. (This provision was used by the Ministry of Justice to deny registration to Virk, a political party based in the ethnic Armenian–populated province of Samtskhe-Javakheti.) The main challenge is the lack of strong, stable parties that can articulate distinct platforms. Most influential parties are machines for ensuring support for their individual leaders. Moreover, the current party in power continues a tradition of dominant parties that can hardly be distinguished from the state—the Round Table from 1990 to 1991, the Citizens Union of Georgia from 1995 to 2001, and the Union of Revival of Georgia in Achara from 1992 to 2004. During 2007, several members of Parliament (MPs) from the ruling party migrated to the opposition, and a new opposition faction was created. However, the total number of opposition MPs still does not exceed 50 out of 235 MPs.

Although there were no elections in 2007, electoral issues were at the center of political life. In February, after negotiations supervised by the Council of Europe, the ruling UNM and six opposition parties reached an agreement on party financing as well as stricter rules for ensuring transparency of private donations. These amendments significantly increased public financing for political parties. Likewise, amendments to the election code in June 2006 mandated TV stations to provide free airtime for election campaign messages, providing even more public support for parties. In mid-October 2007, President Saakashvili proposed lowering the threshold for party lists in proportional elections from 7 to 5 percent (as demanded by the opposition and recommended by the Council of Europe and most civil society organizations).

Electoral issues constituted three out of the four initial demands made by the opposition during the November rallies (the fourth required the release of "political prisoners"). The government agreed to one of the four demands—amendments enacted in November 2007 added representatives of seven "qualified" parties (six of them opposition) into the electoral administration, thus restoring the practice that had existed before 2005.

The fall protest rallies showed a disturbing trend of street violence. On October 29, two opposition MPs, Bezhan Gunava and Bidzina Gujabidze, were assaulted by unidentified people at a rally in Zugdidi (several perpetrators were charged with hooliganism). On November 3 and 7, respectively, two opposition figures, Rati Maisuradze of the Labor Party and Koba Davitashvili of the People's Party, were severely beaten by the police. Earlier, Gia Tsagareishvili, another opposition MP, was beaten by several MPs from the ruling party for insulting members of UNM.

In the context of the November protests, several prominent opposition figures were accused of spying for Russia. Audio- and videotapes were shown on television depicting their meetings with alleged members of Russian special services (Russian diplomats later extradited from Georgia). Criminal charges were filed (and later dropped) against one of them, Shalva Natelashvili, leader of the Georgian Labor Party, and also against Badri Patarkatsishvili. Both were registered as presidential candidates.

Irakli Okruashvili, former minister of defense, was arrested on charges of corruption and abuse of power in September after launching a new opposition party and accusing President Saakashvili of corruption and commissioning political murders. Okruashvili made a retraction and was released on bail but reconfirmed the allegations from Germany, where he was allowed to travel. The timing of Okruashvili's arrest was widely perceived as political persecution and contributed to the tide of antigovernment rallies in November. However, the government claimed that the criminal investigation against Okruashvili had started as early as

March, and that it was based on findings from the Chamber of Controls from when Okruashvili held his position in the ministry.

Civil Society

1999	2001	2002	2003	2004	2005	2006	2007	2008
3.75	4.00	4.00	4.00	3.50	3.50	3.50	3.50	3.50

Georgian legislation allows civil society groups to register easily (or not at all) and to operate freely. According to the 1997 civil code, nonprofit organizations may be registered as unions (associations) or foundations. Amendments to the civil code in 2007 introduced an even simpler, more uniform registration system based on the U.S. model, and the function of registration was moved from the Ministry of Justice to the Taxation Office.

Nongovernmental organizations (NGOs) enjoy considerable tax benefits. The Law on Grants exempts grants from most taxes. The 2004 tax code instituted tax exemptions to encourage charitable giving. Businesses can now spend up to 8 percent of their gains on charitable activities to avoid taxes on that amount. NGOs can participate in tenders and compete for government contracts at local and national levels. Changes in tax legislation introducing a flat income tax of 25 percent and an employee-paid social security tax of 20 percent bring tax relief for businesses but may imply a higher tax burden for NGO employees, as the Law on Grants had previously exempted nonprofit organizations from social security taxes. However, there's a three-year moratorium on applying the new legislation to nonprofits.

According to a September 2006 estimate, about 10,000 civil society organizations were registered in Georgia. Most exist on paper only or were created for one or two projects. Overall, the NGO community is independent and increasingly professional, with the ability to influence policy decisions in specific areas. Georgian NGOs are diverse: A number are involved in human rights and environmental advocacy, women and minority issues, training and consultancy in various fields, public policy development, and so forth. At the same time, there is a decreasing number of active organizations and lessened overall influence, which reflects the political environment as well as downward trends in donor support.

Most NGOs represent professional groups whose main sources of support are grants from foreign donors. Organizations are much more developed in Tbilisi than in other regions, with large discrepancies across Georgia. NGOs are defined by their capacity, professional record, public platforms, and the personalities of their leaders rather than their constituencies. The number of membership-based organizations is small. Therefore, while negotiating their positions with political actors, many cannot claim to be speaking on behalf of large social groups.

The influence of civil society organizations peaked prior to the 2003 Rose Revolution, when the sector had considerable impact on public opinion and formulating the agenda of reformist groups in the government and the opposition. After the Rose Revolution, most "public faces" in the NGO community moved to the government or (a smaller number) to the opposition. "Graduates" of civil society organizations continue to play leading roles in defining the agenda of the government. This has contributed to a significant decrease in the public visibility of civil society organizations over the last few years.

Some public agencies have more or less continuous cooperation with specific civil society organizations. In the last two years, for instance, cooperative efforts between the Office of the Prosecutor and Open Society–Georgia Foundation have introduced "community prosecution" in the work of the Office of the Prosecutor. Georgian Young Lawyers Association (GYLA) and the Liberty Institute took an active part in finalizing the draft of the new criminal proceedings code (passed by the Parliament in the first reading). GYLA helped the Ministry of Environment set up a new environmental police. A network of watchdog organizations funded by the Open Society–Georgia Foundation helped spur the replacement of leadership at Millennium Corporation–Georgia owing to its lack of transparency.

NGOs have grown more politicized since the Rose Revolution. While some organizations (especially think tanks or service organizations) uphold an image of neutrality, more activist-style groups support specific political actors. During the presidential campaign at the end of 2007, some NGOs openly endorsed certain candidates, usually among the opposition. Some NGOs like the Egalitarian Institute were actively involved in opposition demonstration activities.

Changes in priorities in donor funding also influence the development of the NGO community. In the 1990s, donors gave priority to general programs supporting the proliferation of activist NGOs. In recent years, donors have been focused on a more results-oriented approach. This has led to a deepening gap between the top tier of developed organizations and most other NGOs that struggle from one project to another or stop their activities altogether. Still, there are fairly large networks of NGOs vying for support.

Local philanthropy is gradually developing, and some major businesses declare their commitment to philanthropy. However, funding from Georgian businesses goes more often to the traditional spheres of charity (that is, to humanitarian and cultural projects, student fellowships, and so on) rather than civic activism. Volunteerism is weakly developed, and successful community-based organizations are few.

Georgia has a number of public associations that pursue illiberal causes. These claim mainly to protect Eastern Orthodox values from the "pernicious influence" of Western liberalism. In the past, some groups have been involved in violent attacks against religious minorities, civil society, the media, and the political opposition. The new government has been successful in curbing the activities of such groups, so that violence on behalf of "uncivil society" has largely stopped. These groups are free to express their opinions but do not have much political influence or the ability to seriously disrupt public order.

Georgians are free to organize and join trade unions, but so far only a few viable independent trade unions have been created, mainly in health care and education. However, these have not been significant players in the public sphere.

The government hopes to encourage more grassroots civil society organizations by supporting school boards (in effect, parent-teacher associations) and neighborhood associations. In 2006, within the framework of general education reform, school boards composed of parents and teachers were created with extensive rights to run public schools. The municipalities of Tbilisi and Batumi developed matching funds programs for neighborhood initiatives in large apartment buildings to fix common problems.

In January 2007, the two-year transitional period in the reform of Georgian universities ended. This implied the reestablishment of university autonomy. As a result of the reform, universities receive public funding through student tuitions distributed on the basis of national exams conducted by the Ministry of Education.

Independent Media

1999	2001	2002	2003	2004	2005	2006	2007	2008
3.75	3.50	3.75	4.00	4.00	4.25	4.25	4.00	4.25

After the Rose Revolution, Georgia's media legislation was advanced to the level of best international standards, and the current legal system guarantees media freedoms. The Constitution states that "the mass media are free; censorship is impermissible" and that "citizens of the Republic of Georgia have the right to express, distribute, and defend their opinions via any media, and to receive information on questions of social and state life. Censorship of the press and other media is not permitted."

The June 2004 bill on freedom of speech and expression decriminalized libel, moving litigation from criminal to civil law competences. To file a case, a defendant must prove that the media acted with prior knowledge of a statement's false nature or with reckless disregard for the truth. Journalists can no longer be held responsible for revealing state secrets, which is an important protection for whistle-blowers; only relevant public servants can be charged for failing to guard state secrets properly (no such cases were reported). Courts cannot require journalists to disclose sources of confidential information. Before this law was enacted, litigation against journalists for defamation or other charges was common practice, but it has since become rare.

In June 2007, the Parliament introduced amendments to the Law on Common Courts banning photo, video, and audio recording in the courtroom and court building, although journalists were free to attend court proceedings and take notes. This was widely criticized, but the government claimed that TV cameras had been used as psychological pressure on judges. Although this does restrict media, it does not constitute any substantive breach of media freedom. At the end of 2006, the profit and property tax exemptions for print media expired, and the Parliament refused to renew them despite some opposition protests. As yet, this has had no obvious impact on the cost of newspapers.

Media outlets are licensed by the Broadcasting Commission, an independent body whose five members are appointed by the Parliament. Licenses are issued for 10 years and extended automatically for another term unless the broadcaster violates specific requirements defined by law. In terms of legislation, there are no special procedures for arrests and searches of media property. Currently, media follow the same procedures that apply to any other business, but perceived violations can disrupt their functioning with lengthy court proceedings.

Almost no state-supported media remain in Georgia. The State TV and Radio Corporation was transformed into Georgian Public Broadcasting in summer 2005. It is supervised by a nine-member board of governors appointed by the Parliament, with two candidates for each slot pre-selected by the president. Experts agree that news and political talk shows are fairly balanced, but the overall rating of public TV channels is still low. Achara TV in the Autonomous Republic of Achara is directly dependent on Acharan authorities. In May 2007, the Ministry of Defense rented a TV frequency for its own Sakartvelo channel to provide wider information on army reforms, though the channel also broadcasts entertainment programming. The only remaining state-funded print media are several newspapers published in ethnic minority languages.

During 2007, at least until the November protests that led to the state of emergency declaration, the general trend in media freedom was positive. Media pluralism was ensured through diverse ownership: Among national TV stations, the highest-rated Imedi TV (owned by Badri Patarkatsishvili, a business tycoon turned opposition politician) leaned toward the opposition, while Rustavi-2 (a close second in ratings) had a bias in favor of the government. There was a similar balance among less important TV companies, such as the pro-government Mze and antigovernment Kavkasia. The majority of print media had a strong antigovernment bias. A number of programs on TV and radio were dedicated to policy debates. However, many of these programs were one-sided: The government boycotted live debates on Imedi TV (claiming the program encouraged "cockfights"),[5] while the opposition boycotted Rustavi-2 and Mze. Public TV remained a venue for debates between the government and the opposition.

From January through October, there were almost no reports of physical abuse of journalists, unlike in previous years. However, there were frequent complaints from Trialeti TV, a regional company based in Gori, of pressure aimed at forcing its owner to sell; still, the outlet managed to continue broadcasting its highly critical coverage of the regional authorities. In early September, Mikheil Kareli, the state commissioner in Shida Kartli who was mainly responsible for this pressure, was arrested on corruption charges.

The media situation changed in the wake of the public protests (during November 2–7). Imedi TV was charged with organizing a conspiracy against the government and using its power to incite unlawful actions by the public. Imedi TV was raided on November 7 and its broadcasting license suspended (Imedi returned to the air in mid-December).

In late December, Imedi journalists made their own decision to take programming off the air after tapes released by the government suggested owner Badri Patarkatsishvili had been involved in a coup aimed at overthrowing the government. The Imedi journalists demanded that Patarkatsishvili give up ownership of the channel. After emergency rule was announced, all information and political programming was suspended on all non-print media save for the public broadcaster (no such restrictions were instituted for print media). Broadcasting of Kavkasia TV was also stopped during the emergency rule. Most internal and international observers considered the allegations against Imedi insufficient grounds for taking the channel off the air. During this period, the overall balance in news programming shifted in favor of the pro-government position. The case of Imedi, while being extreme, demonstrated that private media owners tend to use outlets to advance their political agendas without respect for journalists' editorial independence.

There are several journalist and media associations in Georgia, but none has become strong enough to unite the media community around issues of journalistic freedom or professional standards. In 2005, the Media Council was created for monitoring and enforcing the Professional Standards of Media, to which participating media organizations subscribed in 2002. The process was joined by major TV companies but boycotted by a large number of print media. The council's activities have been suspended since 2006 owing to a lack of funding and disagreements among members.

Access to the Internet is unrestricted, and the number of consumers is increasing rapidly: In 2006, the total income of Internet providers increased by 56 percent; in the same period, the number of DSL consumers doubled to reach 30,000. However, the 2006 merger of Caucasus Online, Georgia Online, and Sanet—Georgia's three main Internet providers—has given the new company an almost 90 percent share of the market, leading to increased prices and a decline in service quality. In the 2007 Press Freedom Index by Reporters Without Borders, Georgia was ranked 66 among 169 countries (up from 89th place in 2006 and 99th in 2005).

Local Democratic Governance

1999	2001	2002	2003	2004	2005	2006	2007	2008
n/a	n/a	n/a	n/a	n/a	6.00	5.75	5.50	5.50

Since independence, Georgia's political system has been highly centralized, with rather weak democratic institutions at the subnational level. Paradoxically, at the same time, weak state capacity has made government control in some regions rather precarious, and effective governance often relies on deals between the central government and local elites. The 1995 Constitution did not define the structure of subnational government, postponing this move until after the resolution of conflicts in Abkhazia and South Ossetia.

A new legislative package is creating opportunities for a more independent and effective subnational government at the municipal level and includes a new Law on Local Self-Government and amendments to the Law on Tbilisi, the capital of Georgia, both adopted in 2005. Other legislation regulates taxation and property rights of the municipal government, supervision by the national government over the activities of the municipal government, and so on. In 2007, the new system of municipal government actually started to function.

The new legislation introduces a one-level system based on the *rayon* (district), which used to be the main administrative unit in the Soviet system. There are also several self-governing towns, while the capital, Tbilisi, has a special self-governing status. One of the main traits of the reform is that self-governing units have become much larger. Before 2006, there were 500 smaller municipal units. The new law creates 75 bodies of local government (including the capital), plus several small communities in parts of Abkhazia and South Ossetia where the Georgian government organized elections.

Before the reform, administrators in *rayons* and big cities were centrally appointed and supervised by locally elected councils. Enlarging local government units drew criticism for making local government more distant from citizens. Yet the rationale is that larger units are economically more viable and can carry greater political weight to balance the power of the national government. Exclusive competences of the local government are focused mainly on managing local property, taking care of local roads and other infrastructure, issuing construction licenses, and so forth. There are also competences from the national government, for instance, in education. Local government budgets consist of locally collected taxes and payments as well as moneys transferred from the national government on the basis of precalculated formulas. According to the 2007 Law on the Supervision of Municipal Government, the national government supervises some municipal activities, such as drafting local budgets, implementing delegated competences, and making locally adopted regulations compliant with national legislation. The *rayon* council (*sakrebulo*) elects its chairperson and appoints the mayor (*gamgebeli*), an unelected public servant of local self-government who heads the municipal administration.

Local government elections on October 5, 2006, led to the strong victory of the ruling UNM, which received 77.08 percent of the vote nationally and won in all electoral districts. The bloc of Conservative and Republican parties came second with 8.56 percent, and the Labor Party received 6.42 percent nationally, with slightly better results in the capital. The turnout was 48.04 percent. International observers from the OSCE/Office for Democratic Institutions and Human Rights and the Congress of Local and Regional Authorities of the Council of Europe noted "significant progress"[6] in the conduct of the elections. The main criticism noted the misuse of so-called administrative resources.

The fact that all municipalities are now controlled by a single political party under the new system of local governance created a potential for strong influence by the national government on municipalities. The mayor of Kutaisi was forced to resign after President Saakashvili publicly criticized him for buying an expensive car. Another challenge is the lack of local competence in setting budgets, and as a result, the national Ministry of Finance has taken an active part in drafting local budgets. While there is legal ground for separation of national and municipal properties, in effect the process is very slow, and property that is slated to become municipal is still under the control of the Ministry of Economy.

The Autonomous Republic of Achara has a special status defined by the Constitution and 2004 constitutional Law on the Status of the Autonomous Republic of Achara. It outlines the competences of the republic regarding education, culture, local infrastructure, and so forth but at the same time provides extensive rights to the Georgian president, who appoints the prime minister of Achara. The president can also dismiss Achara's Supreme Council if its activities endanger the sovereignty and territorial integrity of Georgia or if it twice consecutively fails to approve the candidacy of the Achara government's chairman. This law was criticized by some observers as restricting autonomy but did not cause any protests locally. On June 20, 2004, extraordinary elections to the Supreme Council of Achara following the forced resignation of its leadership in May brought a strong victory of 72.1 percent to UNM, with only the Republican Party able to overcome the 7 percent threshold.

Judicial Framework and Independence

1999	2001	2002	2003	2004	2005	2006	2007	2008
4.00	4.00	4.25	4.50	4.50	5.00	4.75	4.75	4.75

Georgia's Constitution guarantees all fundamental human rights and freedoms, using the European Convention on Human Rights as a model. The Constitution also provides for a public defender, who is nominated by the president and elected by the Parliament for a five-year term yet is not accountable to either the president or the Parliament. Since 2004, the public defender has been strongly critical of a variety of government actions and has intervened productively in some instances.

In practice, there are violations of human rights in some areas. Abuse of suspects and prisoners in the law enforcement system has been the most challenging human rights problem in Georgia since independence, with some improvement since the Rose Revolution. This includes the dramatically reduced occurrence of torture in pre-trial detention facilities. However, there are several regions—such as Gori, Zugdidi, and Kvemo Kartli—with continuing reports of physical abuse by law enforcement officers, mainly during arrests.

There was excessive police violence used in dispersing protests on November 7, including the beating of public defender Sozar Subari and a staff member. There were also reports of pressure against drivers bringing participants to the November rallies, though eventually a column of buses brought a large number to Tbilisi. On several occasions, protesters were given administrative penalties (imprisonment of about 25 days), which were contested by the Office of the Public Defender.

Property rights were another concern in 2007. In several cases, private property was destroyed without due process, based on allegations that it had been acquired illegally or did not comply with the architectural image of the respective city. Courts failed to sufficiently protect citizens' interests in these matters. In March, a new law was adopted that established firm ownership rights for all property, and in November, the Parliament ceased all legal contestations of private property by administrative agencies, thus implicitly recognizing the state's earlier, erroneous policy.

Concerns continued over the poor conditions in the Georgian penitentiary system. Strong anticrime measures by the government and slow courts have led to a sharp increase in the prison population, from about 6,500 in 2005 to almost 20,000 in the second half of 2007 (this number dropped by nearly 2,000 after amnesty was given at the end of 2007). With prison conditions often described as "unbearable,"[7] the government has tried to address the problem by building more facilities, including several new penitentiaries meeting modern standards built to house approximately 7,000 inmates. A UN Human Rights Committee report published on October 20, 2007, noted "significant reduction in allegations of [torture and other ill-treatment] of persons in custody."[8]

The Constitution provides for the independence of the judiciary, and new legislation and other measures adopted in the past few years have aimed at increasing its independence and competence. However, there are persistent concerns, and the judiciary is one of the least trusted institutions in Georgia: According to a poll by the International Republican Institute in September 2007, only 22 percent had a favorable view of the Georgian courts, as compared with 86 percent for the army and 65 percent for the police.

As other surveys show, citizens do not consider courts to be corrupt; rather, they allege that courts consistently follow the demands of the prosecution. The rate of acquittals is extremely low: In the first nine months of 2007, only 10 people were acquitted out of 13,952 cases (126 more cases were dropped). On the positive side, there is a growing trend in using bail instead of pre-trial detention: In the first nine months of 2007, bail was used in 54.1 percent of cases, as compared with 35.7 percent the previous year. There has also been an increase in the use of plea bargaining to about half of all court sentences, which has increased the efficiency of courts in reaching decisions. In 2007, private citizens had a good chance against the state: 43.6 percent of claims were won by administrative agencies and 55.1 percent by private (individual and corporate) persons.[9]

As a result of amendments to the Constitution and the Law on Common Courts passed in 2006, judges are now appointed by the High Council of Justice; this politically independent body is led by the chairman of the Supreme Court, with 9 out of 15 members being acting judges elected by the Conference of Judges of Georgia (other members are appointed by the president and the Parliament). The president, prosecutor general, and minister of justice are no longer members of the High Council of Justice. Judges are appointed on the basis of tests and interviews. The disciplinary panel within the High Council of Justice is the only body that can dismiss judges for violations of professional ethics or "manifest infringement of law." The panel consists of three judges and three non-judge members.

The criminal proceedings code was passed by the Parliament in 2007 in the first reading and introduces the jury trial. The limit on pre-trial detentions was reduced from 9 to 4 months, and the limit on trial detention reduced from 24 to 12 months. Ex parte communication with judges is also now regulated: Any pre-trial communication with judges to influence their decisions may lead to fines or (for public servants) administrative penalties.

In 2007, the salaries of district and appeal judges were nearly tripled to approximately US$960 and US$1,080, respectively, while Supreme Court judges receive 3,000 lari, or about US$1,850 monthly (considerably higher than MPs and equal to the salary of government ministers). These increases are expected to decrease the propensity for corruption.

A lack of competent staff is still one of the challenges facing the Georgian judiciary. By the end of 2007, there were more than 100 vacancies in courts due to a lack of competent applicants. In October 2007, the High School of Justice started a new program for training judges. Graduates may be considered for lifetime appointments, which is another measure for increasing the independence of the judiciary.

Corruption

1999	2001	2002	2003	2004	2005	2006	2007	2008
5.00	5.25	5.50	5.75	6.00	5.75	5.50	5.00	5.00

Fighting corruption has been one of the most successful elements of the Georgian government since the Rose Revolution. After independence, corruption was considered a major obstacle to state building and democracy in Georgia. But since 2004, there has been a conspicuous decline in corruption involving the police, public registry, university admissions, and other public functions. In 2007, Georgia's Corruption Perceptions Index, as measured by Transparency International, improved to 3.4, with Georgia ranked 79 among 179 countries. Georgia had rankings of 2.3 in 2005 and 2.8 in 2006. In 2007, the BEEPS (*Doing Business*) study of the World Bank and International Financial Corporation ranked Georgia 18 out of 178 economies for ease of doing business,[10] up from the rankings of 112 and 37 in the previous two years. While the research did not specifically measure corruption, this progress could not have been achieved without a significant reduction in corruption.

In 2006, Georgia ratified the Council of Europe Criminal Law Convention on Corruption (the Civil Law Convention on Corruption has been in force in Georgia since November 2003). In June 2005, the National Anticorruption Strategy and Action Plan were signed by the president. The next step was for different public agencies to draft anticorruption strategies and submit them to the minister of state for implementation. However, government agencies do not give great priority to work in this area, as they no longer consider fighting corruption a major priority for the country.

Successes in anticorruption activities have been achieved through both institutional reforms and punitive measures. Since the Rose Revolution, there have been myriad arrests of high-ranking officials in both the previous government and the current administration: The latter included 1 minister, 2 deputy ministers, 33 *gamgebelis* (heads of local administration, including 17 members of the ruling UNM), 376 policemen, 124 tax and customs officers, and 5 judges.

All public servants are obliged to submit income declarations. In spring 2007, the Georgian Parliament debated a new version of the Law on Corruption and the Incompatibility of Interests in the Public Service, which revamped the mechanisms for reviewing income declarations submitted to the Monitoring Bureau. However, the draft was shelved as too costly to implement.

While successes in fighting corruption are widely acknowledged, there are persistent allegations of elite corruption. Concerns were expressed when the government announced a decision to award the right to manage Georgian railways for 89 years to an obscure British company selected without a public tender. Later, it was reported that the deal had unraveled.

The issue of elite corruption was reopened with the arrest of Irakli Okruashvili, former minister of defense, on corruption charges in September 2007. President Saakashvili spoke about the necessity to strengthen the fight against corruption in the top echelons of power by creating an anticorruption group that would respond directly to the president and monitor the highest officials. The cabinet was expected to come up with specific recommendations for such a group.[11] This episode briefly returned anticorruption efforts to the top of the political agenda, at least until the November political crisis.

The media freely air and discuss allegations of corruption, yet there has been a marked decline in investigative reporting since the Rose Revolution. The Georgian public generally supports the government's anticorruption initiatives, though many are still ready to resort to corrupt practices as an easy solution to problems. The unwillingness of many citizens to serve as court witnesses on corruption cases or to cooperate with law enforcement also decreases the effectiveness of law enforcement. Many Georgians consider cooperation with law enforcement to be an immoral act of "denunciation."

▌ AUTHOR: GHIA NODIA

During the period covered in this study and during its authorship, Ghia Nodia led the Caucasus Institute for Peace, Democracy and Development (Tbilisi, Georgia) He also taught politics at Ilya Chavchavadze State University and published regularly on democracy theory and political development in Georgia. In 2008 he accepted a position with the Georgian government and became Minister of Education and Science.

---

1   See "Stunning Progress achieved in Georgia is an example for the whole region and beyond," Parliamentary Assembly of the Council of Europe (PACE), September 19, 2007, http://assembly.coe.int/ASP/NewsManager/EMB_NewsManagerView.asp?ID=3177; also Ministry of Foreign Affairs of Georgia, http://www.mfa.gov.ge/index.php?lang_id=ENG&sec_id=496&info_id=5086.

2   "Georgian Leader Hails Constitutional Changes, Calls for New Constitution," transcript of Rustavi-2 TV broadcast, January 10, 2007.

3   "Saakashvili: New Constitution Possible After Restoration of Territorial Integrity," Civil Georgia (civil.ge) online news, January 11, 2007, http://www.civilgeorgia.ge/eng/article.php?id=14433&search=Saakashvili:%20New%20Constitution%20Possible%20After%20Restoration%20of%20Territorial%20Integrity

4   OSCE/Office for Democratic Institutions and Human Rights, Congress of Local and Regional Authorities of the Council of Europe, press release, October 6, 2006, http://www.osce.org/documents/pdf_documents/2006/10/21165-1.pdf, accessed November 7, 2006.

5   Interview with Giga Bokeria, Member of Parliament, *Kviris Palitra* newspaper, February 26 2007.

6   OSCE/Office for Democratic Institutions and Human Rights, Congress of Local and Regional Authorities of the Council of Europe, press release, October 6, 2006, http://www.osce.org/documents/pdf_documents/2006/10/21165-1.pdf, accessed November 7, 2006.

7   "CoE Human Rights Commissioner Calls Conditions in Georgian Prisons Unbearable," *Caucasus Press,* February 19, 2007. See also "Report to the Georgian Government on the visit to Georgia Carried out by the European Committee for the Prevention of Torture and Inhuman or Degrading Treatment or Punishment (CPT) from March 21–April 2, 2007, Council of Europe, Strasbourg, October 25, 2007, http://www.cpt.coe.int/documents/geo/2007-42-inf-eng.pdf, accessed November 22, 2007.

8   "Georgia: The government should implement recommendations of the UN Human Rights Committee as a matter of priority," public statement of Amnesty International, October 30, 2007, http://www.amnesty.org/en/library/info/EUR56/009/2007/en

9   *Information on Basic Statistical Data of Common Courts of Georgia for Nine Months,* 2007, compiled by the Supreme Court of Georgia, (Tbilisi: 2007).

10   *Doing Business 2008 Georgia: Comparing Regulation in 178 Economies,* International Bank for Reconstruction and Development/World Bank (Washington, D.C.: 2007), http://www.doingbusiness.org/Documents/CountryProfiles/GEO.pdf, [accessed November 24, 2007].

11   "Georgian President Sets Up Special Anti-Corruption Commission," BBC Monitoring Caucasus, October 4, 2007. Also Giorgi Lomsadze, "Georgia Plans Anti-Corruption Commission," Eurasianet, October 10, 2007, http://www.eurasianet.org/departments/insight/articles/eav101007c.shtml.

Hungary

by Balázs Áron Kovács and Bálint Molnár

Capital:	Budapest
Population:	10.1 million
GNI/capita:	US$16,970

The social data above was taken from the European Bank for Reconstruction and Development's *Transition Report 2007: People in Transition*, and the economic data from the World Bank's *World Development Indicators 2008*.

Nations in Transit Ratings and Averaged Scores

	1999	2001	2002	2003	2004	2005	2006	2007	2008
Electoral Process	1.25	1.25	1.25	1.25	1.25	1.25	1.25	1.75	1.75
Civil Society	1.25	1.25	1.25	1.25	1.25	1.25	1.25	1.50	1.50
Independent Media	2.00	2.25	2.25	2.25	2.25	2.50	2.50	2.50	2.50
Governance*	2.50	3.00	3.00	2.50	2.50	n/a	n/a	n/a	n/a
National Democratic Governance	n/a	n/a	n/a	n/a	n/a	2.00	2.00	2.25	2.25
Local Democratic Governance	n/a	n/a	n/a	n/a	n/a	2.25	2.25	2.25	2.25
Judicial Framework and Independence	1.75	2.00	2.00	1.75	1.75	1.75	1.75	1.75	1.75
Corruption	2.50	3.00	3.00	2.75	2.75	2.75	3.00	3.00	3.00
Democracy Score	1.88	2.13	2.13	1.96	1.96	1.96	2.00	2.14	2.14

* *With the 2005 edition, Freedom House introduced separate analysis and ratings for national democratic governance and local democratic governance to provide readers with more detailed and nuanced analysis of these two important subjects.*

NOTE: The ratings reflect the consensus of Freedom House, its academic advisers, and the author(s) of this report. The opinions expressed in this report are those of the author(s). The ratings are based on a scale of 1 to 7, with 1 representing the highest level of democratic progress and 7 the lowest. The Democracy Score is an average of ratings for the categories tracked in a given year.

EXECUTIVE SUMMARY

Following the riots of the previous year, 2007 was marked by polarized party politics, radicalization of the extreme Right, and half measures to implement reforms. Since the systemic changes of the early 1990s, Hungary has successfully introduced a free-market economy, albeit with significant involvement from the state mostly in the redistribution of resources and human services. Following his reelection in 2006, Prime Minister Ferenc Gyurcsány and his second government set out to launch reforms in central administration, education, and health care. The laws required to implement the reforms were passed during the year, but most of them were watered-down versions thanks in part to resistance from Gyurcsány's own Socialist Party caucus.

Despite these difficulties, Hungary is a stable parliamentary system in which two parties—the Hungarian Socialist Party (MSZP) and the right-wing Young Democrats Alliance–Hungarian Civic Association (Fidesz)—dominate the legislature, with three minor parties forming independent factions. The country's democratic institutions are robust and likely to hold together despite reckless party politics and radicalization. Public opinion surveys show, however, that the political elite are losing touch with the public as they compete for power and disregard the need for substantial reforms. Political leaders have done little to reconcile the divisions between Left and Right, and illiberal rhetoric still pesters political life in Hungary.

While there have been some minor clashes between the police and extreme right-wing rioters, and antigovernment protests have become a staple of Hungarian politics, there were no incidents during the year similar to the September–October 2006 unrest. The tensions released in 2006, however, were built up over a longer period and stem from several factors, including the lack of fundamental reforms, the state's central role in offering services beyond its capacity, and public reliance on the state instead of the private and nongovernmental sectors. The country's unresolved Communist legacy, including the role of secret services before transition and the management of privatization, still haunts the sociopolitical landscape.

National Democratic Governance. The lowered intensity of street demonstrations in 2007 did not mean that the crisis of 2006 was over. The country spent much effort bracing for the 2008 referendum, likely to be won by the opposition if the turnout is sufficiently high. The strengthening of political extremism—including the formation of an openly racist "paramilitary" group (Jobbik's Hungarian Guard) and violent attacks on coalition politicians, their property, and the police—is a worrisome factor. The government began some of its promised reforms, but their fate is uncertain facing the 2008 referendum and resistance from rank-and-file

Socialist parliamentarians. The Fidesz party's allusions to the referendum as a means of forcing early elections may weaken the country's democratic governance. *Hungary's rating for national democratic governance remains at 2.25.*

Electoral Process. Hungary's electoral system ensures free and fair elections in which political parties can alternate in power at both national and local levels. The year was marked by preparations for the referendum on the government's reforms, involving a series of legal battles in front of the National Electoral Committee and the Constitutional Court. *Hungary's rating for electoral process remains unchanged at 1.75.*

Civil Society. Hungary's legal framework is generally hospitable to civil society, but tax regulations and other administrative requirements may threaten its long-term sustainability and development. A worrisome trend is the growing reliance of nongovernmental organizations (NGOs) on state funding. Additionally, the 2007 amendments to the tax code limiting tax-deductible charitable donations impede the ability of NGOs to diversify their funding. The strengthening presence of illiberal radical views in Hungarian civil society continued from 2006, with the establishment of the far-right Hungarian Guard. *Hungary's civil society rating remains unchanged at 1.50.*

Independent Media. Hungarian media are generally free and diverse. The market is dominated by commercial outlets in both broadcast and print media. Public service media continue to struggle with lack of funding and occasional political meddling, but some signs point to increasing stability and sensible reforms in programming on public TV and radio. Hungarian journalists broke impressive news stories related to politicians and public servants in 2007, some of which led to resignations and changes in policy. Political polarization in the media, however, continued to reflect the division of the country as a whole. Notably, some Hungarian media owners have used their outlets to pursue political agendas. *Hungary's rating for independent media remains at 2.50.*

Local Democratic Governance. The local governance sphere in Hungary struggles with efficiency issues, overfragmentation, and a lack of human and financial resources in many small municipalities. Despite nominally significant independence, local self-governments are overdependent on the central government as a result of the high level of redistribution of local taxes and other revenues. There is a hollowing-out process under way at the territorial level, with counties steadily losing their relevance as an effective tier of self-governance. The introduction of regions and small regions has only complicated matters further. The distribution of European Union development funds in the coming years will necessitate a more efficient system of regional and local self-government. *Hungary's rating for local democratic governance remains at 2.25.*

Judicial Framework and Independence. Fundamental civil and political rights are guaranteed by an independent judiciary, the Constitutional Court, and the ombudsmen. There is no systematic torture or ill-treatment of defendants in Hungary. The professionalism of the police came under heavy criticism from the opposition following the 2006 clashes with extreme right-wing rioters, resulting in criminal procedures against policemen. A series of scandals further eroded the credibility of the police and resulted in a leadership purge of the national and capital police forces. The long overdue debate on the accountability of the judiciary begun in 2006 continued in 2007 and may improve judicial practices. *Hungary's rating for judicial framework and independence remains unchanged at 1.75.*

Corruption. While continuous legislative efforts have brought Hungary's anti-corruption legal framework closer to international standards, the lack of effective implementation and political will in such areas as party finance reform means that the country continues to struggle with high-level corruption. Although the government launched an ambitious and comprehensive anticorruption initiative in 2007, the year also saw the breakdown of four-party talks on campaign finance reform and a number of high-profile corruption scandals, resulting in a mixed picture at year's end. *Hungary's corruption rating remains unchanged at 3.00.*

Outlook for 2008. The most important emerging issue will likely be the Fidesz-proposed referendum on the reforms of the government scheduled for 2008. Fidesz leader Viktor Orbán aims to force the government to repeal the reforms and maintain the status quo, eventually forcing an early election. Whether this is only rhetoric remains to be seen. Nevertheless, a crushing defeat as predicted by several opinion polls may paralyze the government until the 2010 elections. Radicalization will probably continue, and the foreseeable legal actions against the ultranationalist party, Jobbik's Hungarian Guard, will not stem the tide. Despite this, there is no likelihood of extremists threatening the country's democratic system or influencing political decision making in 2008 or the near future.

Main Report

National Democratic Governance

1999	2001	2002	2003	2004	2005	2006	2007	2008
n/a	n/a	n/a	n/a	n/a	2.00	2.00	2.25	2.25

Hungary's constitutional system overall ensures stable, democratic governance. Following general elections, the Parliament elects by absolute majority the prime minister, who is responsible for governance. Ministers are not subject to no-confidence votes, and the Parliament can remove the prime minister and cabinet only through the process of "constructive no confidence," which requires not only a vote of no confidence, but the previous nomination of and vote on a new prime minister. This method ensures that the new head of the executive will also hold the support of the majority of members of Parliament (MPs). As a consequence, the opposition has very little chance to oust an incumbent prime minister between general elections. The Constitutional Court, with its broad powers to control legislation and the executive's decisions, provides effective checks. The president of the National Audit Office, the president of the Supreme Court, the chief prosecutor, and members of the Constitutional Court are elected by the Parliament, usually after reaching a broad consensus.

The top legislative organ in Hungary is the 386-member unicameral Parliament (*Országgyűlés*). The government and ministries may pass lower-level legislation that must conform to laws in force. The work of the Parliament is mostly transparent, with easy access to information through the media, interactions with MPs, and a frequently updated, easy-to-use website,[1] although there are some restrictions on live television broadcasting. In 2006, the Társaság a Szabadságjogokért (Hungarian Civil Liberties Union, HCLU) sued the Ministry of Justice and Law Enforcement to publish the draft of the new Constitution, and a court of first instance ruled that the ministry must publish the material.[2] The appeals court, however, overturned the verdict and upheld the claim of the minister of justice and law enforcement, József Petrétei, that the document is a preparatory one and as such does not need to be published.[3]

Even though the country's political system and democratic institutions are stable, public confidence is low. According to a survey by the polling agency Tárki published at the beginning of 2007, public confidence in political institutions has decreased—in December 2006, only 23 percent of respondents expressed full confidence in the president of the republic, less than 10 percent trusted the government entirely, and only 3 percent trusted political parties. The only institution to gain trust, according to the survey, was the judiciary.[4]

The trend of losing faith in politicians and institutions continued throughout 2007. According to a Tárki survey published in December, only 47 percent of respondents expressed a willingness to vote in the elections.[5] According to another survey conducted by Medián in the same period, only two prominent politicians, President of the Republic László Sólyom and Debrecen mayor Lajos Kósa, had approval ratings over 50 percent.[6] While this represents a slight increase from January 2007, when no politician had approval ratings over 50 percent, the overall picture is rather bleak. These trends are due largely to the controversy around the government's reform package, corruption scandals, and the tone of politics in Hungary. What makes these tendencies worrisome is the discernible popular alienation from mainstream politics.

Hungary's political leaders, most of whom gained experience in the 1970s and 1980s, appear unable to deliver on promises made or to effectively transform major state services.[7] Since the first free elections in Hungary in 1990, two major parties—the Hungarian Socialist Party (Magyar Szocialista Párt, MSZP) and Young Democrats Alliance–Hungarian Civic Association (Fiatal Demokraták Szövetsége–Magyar Polgári Szövetség, or Fidesz)—emerged to dominate the political landscape. The high costs of forming a viable new political party effectively inhibit any challenge to the current status quo. The result of the lack of a realistic third option in Hungarian politics has been that politicians in both major parties do not engage in substantive matters, nor do they appear compelled to respond voter feedback.

In 2006, the second government of Prime Minister Ferenc Gyurcsány pledged to carry out substantial reforms in education, health care, and social security. In the Hungarian parliamentary system, the opposition's chances to scuttle government-initiated legislation are minimal. Owing to the 2006 scandal connected to lies admitted by Gyurcsány, however, Prime Minister Gyurcsány lost his grip on the Socialist Party caucus, and the MSZP parliamentary bloc shattered the program.

Discontent with the reforms, fueled partly by Fidesz and trade unions, and the perceived decline in living standards, protests against Prime Minister Gyurcsány, his government, and the coalition parties became a political staple in Hungary in 2007. More worrisome was the associated radicalization of elements in the political opposition. There were several violent attacks on the prime minister, as well as on the Socialist and Liberal parties, politicians, and other authorities. On December 11, Sándor Csintalan, former Socialist politician turned right-wing media personality, was attacked in his garage.[8] A relatively unknown, extreme right-wing group (Magyarok Nyilai Nemzeti Felszabadító Hadsereg—Arrows of the Hungarians National Liberation Army) claimed responsibility for the attack. The existence of the group, however, has not been verified.[9] In February, unknown perpetrators fired on the headquarters of the national police with an AK-47 assault rifle.[10] In December, two shots were fired at Minister of Education István Hiller's home.[11] Molotov cocktails were thrown at the residences of János Kóka, president of the Alliance of Free Democrats (Szabad Demokraták Szövetsége, SZDSZ), and Socialist MP László Ecsődi, as well as an MSZP office in Budapest.

Extreme right-wing party Jobbik launched its "self-defense" group, Magyar Gárda (Hungarian Guard), in August. The Hungarian Guard has held racist marches in Tatárszentgyörgy,[12] Kerepes,[13] and Érpatak.[14] Mainstream political parties have condemned the formation of the group, and the Office of the Prosecutor filed a request with the Budapest Municipal Court to withdraw the group's registration. Independently, several municipalities declared that the Hungarian Guard will not be granted permission to demonstrate in their jurisdiction.

Hungarian law enforcement agencies and security services were under effective civilian control during 2007. Owing to the autumn 2006 events, the services had been severely criticized by the opposition and human rights groups. In November 2006, the government appointed a committee of prominent law enforcement experts and academics, chaired by former ombudsperson Katalin Gönczöl, to investigate police practices during the September–October riots. The committee's findings, released on February 5, 2007, indicated that responsibility was shared between the governing coalition, opposition parties, the police, and extremist groups.[15] Amnesty International expressed agreement with the findings.[16] Three former Constitutional Court justices, however, attacked the report as political and qualified it as exonerating the government from responsibility.[17] The Committee of Civil Jurists, an ad hoc group of lawyers opposed to the government, released its own report with findings contradictory to those of the Gönczöl committee.[18]

Electoral Process

1999	2001	2002	2003	2004	2005	2006	2007	2008
1.25	1.25	1.25	1.25	1.25	1.25	1.25	1.75	1.75

Members of Parliament are elected for four-year terms in a two-round mixed electoral system. In the first round, voters may select candidates running in 176 single-seat constituencies and regional party lists from which 152 candidates may win seats based on proportional representation. Only those constituencies where no single-seat candidate won with an absolute majority in the first round go on to hold second-round elections. The remaining 58 seats are filled from the national party lists on a proportional basis, with a 5 percent electoral threshold. Hungarian elections are considered fair and free.

Following the 2006 national elections, the MSZP had 190 members and 49 percent of the seats and formed a coalition government with the SZDSZ, which controls 5 percent of the seats with 20 representatives. The center-right Fidesz secured 139 members and 36 percent of the seats. Fidesz ran in an electoral coalition with the Christian Democratic People's Party (Kereszténydemokrata Néppárt, KDNP), which secured 6 percent of the vote, or 22 seats. Yet the relationship between Fidesz and KDNP remained so close that one may question the independence of the KDNP faction. The Hungarian Democratic Forum (Magyar Demokrata Fórum, MDF) had the smallest faction with 11 members, or 3 percent of seats. There are currently three independent MPs in the Parliament. With 85 percent of the seats held by the two major parties, coupled with KDNP's close relationship with Fidesz, Hungary has become a de facto two-party system.

Following the two heated polls (national elections in the spring and municipal elections in October) and the riots of 2006, the opposition's insistence on a referendum on the government-proposed reforms became one of the main themes in Hungarian politics in 2007. To call a referendum, the proponent must collect at least 200,000 valid signatures, and the result is binding on the Parliament and the government. The opposition party proposed seven referendum questions to counter the government's reform package and maintain the status quo in the social and educational sectors. The initiative started an avalanche of counterquestions mostly from citizens, which escalated to comic proportions. Following a series of legal battles and several verdicts by the Constitutional Court, the National Electoral Committee approved six of Fidesz's questions: to maintain state ownership of hospitals and health service providers; to allow only pharmacies to sell drugs; to grant preference to family farmers in the purchase of farms and farmland; to exempt students in higher education from paying tuition fees; to abolish the visiting fee in hospitals and doctors' offices; and to abolish the hospital fee.[19]

According to a Gallup survey published in December and quoted by HírTv, 60 percent of respondents were expected to participate in the referendum, which would make the result binding[20] (referendums are successful and binding if 50 percent of registered voters cast a valid vote and at least 25 percent give the same answer to the question).[21] According to a Marketing Centrum survey, 44 percent responded that they would participate.[22] Both surveys predicted an overwhelming approval of Fidesz's questions. The referendum is scheduled for 2008, and if the results correspond to the surveys, the ruling coalition will find itself in a precarious situation.

While political parties are active and often successful in mobilizing supporters, actual membership is low at about 1 percent of the population. Forming parties in Hungary is relatively easy, and according to the National Election Office, approximately 200 political parties are registered. Most of them, however, do not have enough support and resources to run in elections.[23]

Minority representation at the national level is still unsatisfactory. From the 2006 spring elections, only 40 women and 3 Roma gained seats in the 386-member Parliament. By constitutional requirement, the Parliament should have ensured real representation for ethnic minorities by 1992. Yet in November, the Parliament voted against a proposed law that stipulated 30 percent of the government and 50 percent of the electoral party list be women.[24]

The president of the republic is elected by the Parliament for a five-year term and can be reelected once. In the first two rounds of the election, a qualified majority is required; if it cannot be reached, a third round is held where the candidate with a simple majority is elected. Presidential elections are usually heated but fair. The last presidential elections were held in 2005 and resulted in the election of László Sólyom, former president of the Constitutional Court and a political outsider from the civil society organization Védegylet (Protect the Future), nominated by Fidesz. While the Constitution limits the president to mostly ceremonial functions, Sólyom has tried to stretch these boundaries with a mixed record.

Civil Society

1999	2001	2002	2003	2004	2005	2006	2007	2008
1.25	1.25	1.25	1.25	1.25	1.25	1.25	1.50	1.50

Hungarian law effectively facilitates the registration and administration of non-governmental organizations (NGOs), and there are no legal obstacles to the work of civil society organizations. At the same time, tax regulations put a significant burden on NGOs and in the long run may threaten their viability and sustainability.

In 2005, there were 56,694 NGOs in Hungary, according to data from the National Statistics Office. Forty percent of NGOs are foundations, while the rest are registered as associations, including both public benefit companies and public benefit associations. Two-thirds of registered foundations were active in education, social services, and culture, with the majority focused on sports and other recreational activities.[25] In addition, a range of influential human rights organizations, think tanks, and political foundations attest to the maturity and breadth of Hungarian civil society.

Despite steady growth over recent years, only about 1 percent of employed Hungarians work in the civil sector.[26] The high payroll tax makes human resource development increasingly difficult for NGOs, and some international NGOs based in Hungary have relocated to neighboring countries, such as Slovakia, to keep operational costs down.[27] Volunteers are increasingly seen by NGOs as an attractive addition to paid labor, and the public's interest in volunteering is also growing. However, the percentage of Hungarians who volunteer is still only half of the European Union (EU) average of 33 percent.[28]

In spite of growing overall incomes in the civil society sector, financial sustainability remains a serious problem. According to the National Statistical Office, the total income of the Hungarian nonprofit sector in 2005 was 854 billion forint (US$4.9 billion). Of this, the share of nonprofit organizations (mostly foundations and public benefit corporations) created by the government or by various municipalities was 497 billion forint (US$3.1 billion), or close to 60 percent.[29]

One discernible and potentially worrisome trend is the steady increase in state funding for the nonprofit sector. While state funding between 2000 and 2005 grew by 8 percent for private foundations and 18 percent for private associations, it increased by 85 percent for government or municipality-founded nonprofit organizations. Even more worrying, the share of private funding dropped in the same period, from 16 to 13 percent.[30] These numbers underscore the disproportionate reliance of the Hungarian civil society sector on central or local government–related funding and the still feeble nature of private philanthropy in Hungary.

Changes to the tax code in 2007 related to charitable donations—specifically, lowering the annual income ceiling for tax-deductible private donations—eliminated important incentives for private giving, especially for potential major donors. This decision further reduced the room for civil society organizations to diversify their funding sources and to decrease their dependence on state and municipal funding.

An increasingly important source of funding for NGOs is the annual 1 percent donation citizens can designate from their income tax. In 2007, the growing amount of 1 percent donations to civil society organizations reached 8 billion forint (US$40 million).[31] These contributions, however, represent supplementary revenue for the majority of beneficiaries and are a dominant source of income for only a small segment of the sector.[32] With only about half of taxpayers actually designating their 1 percent for NGOs, further publicity is needed to utilize the full capacity of the law to support the functioning of independent civil society.

Another important source of funding is the National Civil Fund (NCF) initiated in 2003. The NCF is a budget-financed program to match the total funds contributed by taxpayers every year through 1 percent donations. By law, the funds transferred annually to the NCF program cannot be less than 0.5 percent of the personal income tax actually paid by citizens in the previous budgetary year.[33] The NCF operates on an application basis and provides both project and organizational funding to NGOs. The NCF's various decision-making colleges (11 in total) are made up of civil society representatives, while its 15-member council includes both NGO delegates and delegates from the government. Despite being a vital source of funding for Hungarian civil society, the NCF has been criticized for paternalistic and non-meritocratic funding policies and inadequate control in conflicts of interest within the decision-making colleges and the council.[34]

There are six major trade union alliances in Hungary in addition to other labor-interest groups, such as vocational chambers and professional associations. Unions most of which have low membership and are seen as politically affiliated, have further increased their reputation for partisanship with high-profile participation in protests and strikes against the government's various reform measures. In December the League of Independent Trade Unions (Liga Szakszervezetek) announced an indefinite general strike, which was seen as politically motivated.[35] The strike, which fizzled after only a day, was the seventeenth strike action in 2007 to protest the Gyurcsány government's reforms in health care, transportation, education, and public services.

The trend in politicization and radicalization of civil society that was observable in 2006 continued unabated in 2007. With the political parties eager to attach themselves to any potentially popular cause, the room for effective advocacy for civil society organizations shrank in 2007, while new organizations with unabashedly radical platforms were registered. Of these, the Hungarian Guard, formally registered as a cultural association by the far-right Jobbik, stood out as the most virulently illiberal in its racist, homophobic, and anti-Semitic views.

Independent Media

1999	2001	2002	2003	2004	2005	2006	2007	2008
2.00	2.25	2.25	2.25	2.25	2.50	2.50	2.50	2.50

Hungarian media are mostly free and reflect a variety of views and interests. The vast majority of media outlets are controlled by private companies, many of them multinational, although a growing number are owned by Hungarian corporate interests, such as the influential outlets Index, *Napi Gazdaság*, Echo TV, InfoRadio, and *Magyar Hírlap*.[36] Despite the diverse media scene, political interference is not uncommon, although it is practiced in less direct and obvious ways than in the late 1990s.

While the 1996 Law on the Media introduced commercial broadcasting and broke up the state-controlled broadcasting monopoly, it has been constantly criticized for not creating the proper legislative and financing framework for the transformation of these outlets into genuine public service broadcasters. As a result, public broadcasters have become the battleground for intense political struggles, through closely-controlled connections to state financing and government agendas.

Half of the board members of the public service broadcasters are appointed by governing political parties, the other half by the opposition. For additional civilian involvement and control, the Law on the Media allows NGO representatives to sit on the boards. However, many of the NGOs that delegate these members are considered to be closely connected to political parties.

The National Television and Radio Board (ORTT), a regulatory and supervisory body, was also established in 1996 with a board comprising delegates from political parties. ORTT monitors the activities and programs of public and commercial broadcasters and also grants licenses and broadcasting frequencies.

One of the most important and controversial media-related stories of 2007 was the July decision by the Constitutional Court to abolish the jurisdiction of ORTT to act against broadcasters that violate the Law on the Media in their programming.[37] The decision removes ORTT's previous jurisdiction to levy fines or suspend the broadcasting of television and radio stations. The decision leaves a significant vacuum in the enforcement mechanism of the Law on the Media.[38]

The restructuring of public service radio—initiated by its new chairman, György Such, who was elected in 2006—elicited criticism from employees, some of whom expressed their extreme resistance by hunger striking.[39] These sweeping reforms aimed at streamlining production, reducing staff, and revamping programming to increase market share.

Hungarian broadcast media are dominated by commercial channels, most of which are foreign owned, although in 2007 the trend of Hungarian commercial interests entering the media market continued. A notable earlier development in this area was the 2005 creation of a media portfolio by entrepreneur Gábor Széles with the purchase of the daily *Magyar Hírlap* and the founding of Echo TV.

Széles is considered an opponent of Prime Minister Gyurcsány, and his medi outlets exhibited clear and growing partisanship in their news and commentar in 2007.

Besides the three state-supported channels, two commercial stations— RTL Klub (affiliated with the Belgian–French RTL–UFA) and TV2 (owned b a Hungarian–American–Scandinavian consortium)—also reach the entire popu lation. There are over 200 local or regional public, commercial, nonprofit, an cable radio stations, most limiting their programming to entertainment withou significant news content.

While Hungarian journalism generally strives for high standards and journalist are trained professionals, the lines between factual information, analysis, an commentary are often blurred. The media scene largely mirrors the deep politica divisions of the country, often impairing journalistic objectivity.

Libel and state secrecy laws are among the most noticeable burdens on th press. Hungarian court rulings in libel cases have consistently demonstrated th weaknesses of the system. The courts effectively curtailed the ability of journalist to quote controversial remarks about public figures, since, according to the crimina code, libel constitutes not only statements that damage an individual's reputation but also the act of publicizing derogatory statements.

In an encouraging development, investigative journalist Antónia Rádi wa acquitted in December after a four-year trial for disclosing state secrets. Rád had been on trial since 2003 for reporting to news weekly *HVG* on a crimina case.[40] However, her acquittal was the result of a technicality and not of change in legislation—which, according to Miklós Haraszti, media freedom representativ of the Organization for Security and Cooperation in Europe (OSCE), "allows fo the acquittal of journalists who report on state secrets only if the classification wa not carried out properly, or the officials compromised the classification procedur in other ways."[41]

Though leading media figures have argued that Hungarian journalism lack agreed-upon ethical standards and norms,[42] some media outlets were successful i revealing corruption or unethical behavior among politicians and public servants providing encouraging examples of professional journalism. The leading online new portal, Index, succeeded in forcing a court decision against the Ministry of Industr to reveal details of a contract with the South Korean tire manufacturer Hankook The contract detailed the amount and nature of state subsidies (15 billion forint, o US$92 million) provided to the company in setting up its new manufacturing plan in eastern Hungary, information the ministry initially withheld, citing busines confidentiality.[43]

In December, Richard Pimper, deputy chief of staff of the Office of the Prim Minister, was forced to resign after another prominent online news portal, Origo revealed that he ordered payment of 6 million forint (approximately US$35,000 for a poorly prepared study on regional development, commissioned by the Offic of the Prime Minister. In addition to Pimper's resignation, the company tha produced the study was ordered to repay the sum.[44]

Another notable journalistic scoop published by *Manager Magazin* reported that the leading Hungarian telecom company, Magyar Telekom, was entangled in an apparent bribery case through its Montenegrin subsidiary. As a result of this and subsequent reports in the magazine and other Hungarian media, the chairman of Magyar Telekom, Elek Straub, was forced to step down. For her work on the investigative series, Éva Vajda, then deputy editor in chief of *Manager Magazin*, received the 2007 Göbölyös Soma Award for Investigative Journalism.

While there is no systematic pressure on journalists by law enforcement authorities, the arrest of two journalists covering an unauthorized demonstration and its dispersal by police in November resulted not only in protests from human rights watchdogs, including Freedom House,[45] but also in criticism from OSCE media freedom representative Miklos Haraszti.[46]

In Hungary access to the Internet is free of governmental interference and monitoring. According to the Central Statistics Office, 32.3 percent of Hungarian households had access to the Internet in 2007 (up from 22.1 percent in 2005). Broadband penetration has shown significant growth in recent years (68.2 percent of all Internet access was broadband in 2006)[47], which in turn led to the proliferation of independent online news sources, some of which, like Index.hu, have become genuine competitors to both print and electronic media.

Local Democratic Governance

1999	2001	2002	2003	2004	2005	2006	2007	2008
n/a	n/a	n/a	n/a	n/a	2.25	2.25	2.25	2.25

Meaningful decentralization was essential to the transformation of Hungary's political system after the transition, and its core element was the development of a highly-devolved system of local self-government. The system's main pillars are enshrined in the Constitution and the Act of Local Self-Governance of 1990, whereby local communities are entitled to directly elected self-government to manage local affairs.

Hungary's territorial division is also defined in the Constitution, creating a two-tier self-government system: At the regional level, 19 counties serve as the main administrative units, while cities and villages with their own elected legislative bodies and executive organs function as the local units of self-government. There are no hierarchical relations between regional and local self-governments.

The welcome process of decentralization, however, led to a dramatic increase in the number of local political units that can elect their own representatives and executive. As a result, the local governance sphere in Hungary struggles with efficiency issues owing to overfragmentation: Most small villages with populations under 1,000 (54 percent of the smallest settlements) maintain full-fledged municipalities, most of which suffer from a lack of human and financial resources.[48] Despite their legally-enshrined autonomy, local self-governments suffer from overdependence on the central government's redistribution of local taxes and other revenues.[49]

Hungary's local and regional self-government structure has been further complicated by successive waves of reform since the mid-1990s, some related to Hungary's EU accession and the envisioned systems for the distribution of EU development funds.[50] The main thrust of these reforms was twofold. On the one hand, the creation of small regions—cooperative associations of small municipalities within the same county—aimed to ameliorate problems stemming from weak local capacity and scarcity of resources. The small regions serve three main functions performance of local public services, management of state administration task where local knowledge and expertise are necessary, and operation of development functions.[51] On the other hand, the formation of regions—seven in total, si of which comprise three counties each, while one includes the capital and Pes county—was intended to bring Hungary's regional governance system in lin with existing EU policies, which envision "a community of regions," and enabl more effective implementation of large-scale, EU-funded regional developmen programs.[52]

But without systematic reform of the existing two-tier system, the designatio of 174 small regions (sub-county units) and seven development regions (supra county units) essentially created additional levels of local self-governance withou sufficiently elaborating their jurisdiction and competences. This situation is part a result of the government's failure to pass legislation in 2006 to replace counti with regions as the main units of regional self-governance and in 2004 to make mandatory for small municipalities to belong to designated small regions.

Counties therefore remain important political factors thanks to their elect county assemblies and the county electoral lists in the national elections. Y as functional components of local governance, they have little influence jurisdiction.[53] This hollowing out at the county level is further exacerbated the increasingly important role played by the seven regions, which are the ma conduits for processing EU cohesion funds.

The capital, Budapest, presents a unique challenge to effective local governanc The city is divided into 23 districts, which, with their elected assemblies a mayors, enjoy rights equal to those of other municipal self-governments. Th makes citywide policy making extremely difficult and limits the ability of the c assembly and mayor to govern effectively.

In 2007, the various levels of regional and local self-governance receiv attention for their intended role in channeling significant EU development fun Between 2007 and 2013, Hungary is entitled to 24 billion euros (US$38 billi for development projects, and a significant portion of these funds will be manag through seven regional development councils (RDCs), made up of representati from relevant ministries, the heads of county assemblies, mayors of major cit and delegates of small regions.[54]

Owing to the overwhelming victory of opposition candidates in the Septem 2006 municipal elections, there is ample room for political friction in the RD

Not surprisingly, the opposition has criticized the government for attempting to influence decision making through the main national coordinating body of EU development funds, the National Development Agency (Nemzeti Fejlesztési Ügynökség).[55]

Yet party politics so far have exerted less influence over the functioning of the RDCs than previously feared. The need to roll out viable development programs that can bring significant funds to a given region might account for this uncharacteristically consensus-seeking atmosphere in most RDCs.[56] It remains to be seen whether this trend will continue in the coming years, when the amount of funding is set to increase.

Hungary's 13 recognized national and ethnic minority groups have the right to establish national and local minority self-governments. Financed by the state budget, minority self-governments can maintain institutions that help to preserve their culture and ethnic identity. As a result of 2005 amendments to the 1993 Law on the Rights of National and Ethnic Minorities, candidates for seats in minority self-governments may now run only with the nomination of minority civil society organizations and are required to declare their familiarity with the language, culture, and traditions of the given minority. The amendments were instituted to prevent non-minorities from holding positions in minority self-governments as a way to gain personal or business advantage, but some critics voiced concern over a registry that would display sensitive ethnic data.

Judicial Framework and Independence

1999	2001	2002	2003	2004	2005	2006	2007	2008
1.75	2.00	2.00	1.75	1.75	1.75	1.75	1.75	1.75

The Hungarian Constitution recognizes and protects the equality of its citizens before the law, as well as fundamental political, civil, economic, and social rights. The primary safeguard of human rights in the country is the four-tier judicial system, organized in local courts, county courts, the highest appeals courts, and the Supreme Court. Citizens can also turn to four ombudsmen (two newly elected in 2007), functioning independently from the judiciary. The ombudsmen are elected by the Parliament and protect privacy rights, ethnic and national minority rights, and the right to life and a healthy environment. Ombudsmen have no legal authority, but through their reporting to the Parliament they provide an effective complementary mechanism to protect human rights. The Ministry of Education and Culture employs a commissioner to protect student rights within the educational system.

The 11-member Constitutional Court, working since 1990, has shaped the legal framework of Hungary. Its members are legal scholars elected by the Parliament, with three new justices and one reelected justice in 2007. The Court's primary function is to safeguard human rights through its interpretation of the Constitution and control of legal norms. Lacking an effective enforcement mechanism, however, some decisions, most notably on the representation of minorities in the legislature, have not been implemented by the Parliament.

The judiciary functions as an independent branch of power. Since the reform of 1997, it is self-governed by the 15-member National Judicial Council. The head of the council is the president of the Supreme Court, currently Zoltán Lomnici. Nine members are elected by and from among judges; the other members are the minister of justice and law enforcement, the chief prosecutor, the chairman of the Hungarian Bar Association, and one delegate each from the Parliament's judicial and financial committees. The chief prosecutor is nominated by the president of the republic and elected by the Parliament.

The judiciary came under serious criticism in 2006, particularly from Mária Vásárhelyi of the weekly *Élet és Irodalom (Life and Literature)* and Zoltán Fleck, a leading sociologist of law, who urged the reform of the judiciary to overcome its alienation from society, intolerance of criticism, and lack of transparency and accountability.[57] While there was no visible improvement in 2007, the public discussion of this matter was a positive development.

Another area that needs more transparency is the judiciary's recruitment mechanism. According to László Gatter, president of the Capital Court, the county court of Budapest, relatives of judges are favored in the selection process for vacancies,[58] and promotions depend on personal connections rather than merit. The recent launch of a training academy for judges is an effort to increase professionalism and quality of work within the branch. Judges are not permitted to discuss cases with the press. The rationale for this rule is that the press often targets judges who pass important or controversial verdicts, and judges cannot defend themselves in public. But the practical result is it serves to reduce the already low transparency of the courts' functioning.[59]

To increase transparency and accountability, Judge Janos Cserni created a new association within the judiciary (Association for an Honest Judiciary Administration Association—Tisztességes Bírósági Igazgatásért Közhasznú Egyesület, or Tibike). The association immediately became a subject of controversy among judges and drew attacks on Cserni.[60]

Intolerant views against minority groups are well entrenched in Hungarian society, including discrimination against Roma. Amnesty International's 2007 *Report on Hungary* duly criticizes the country for discrimination against and segregation of Roma, particularly children in the educational system.[61] The Jászladány case, in which non-Roma parents led by the mayor created a private school with public resources that excluded Roma children, has not been settled despite nearly six years of protest by a local civil rights group and widespread outrage.[62]

After the riots of autumn 2006, the credibility of police was further challenged by events in 2007. A policeman was caught stealing 460,000 forint (US$2,700) following the shooting of a hostage-taker in a failed bank robbery in Budapest.[63] The policeman was sentenced to one year and eight months (suspended for four years).[64] Three policemen were detained in a kidnapping case in Kisvárda, allegedly part of a gang war among cigarette smugglers.[65] In May, a 21-year-old woman accused five policemen of raping her during a routine traffic control.[66] In response, the prime minister sacked Budapest police chief Péter Gergényi, national police chief László Bene, and Minister of Justice and Law Enforcement József Petrétei.[67] The Office of the Prosecutor dropped the rape case in December 2007, however, owing to lack of evidence against the policemen.[68]

Corruption

1999	2001	2002	2003	2004	2005	2006	2007	2008
2.50	3.00	3.00	2.75	2.75	2.75	3.00	3.00	3.00

On paper, Hungary's institutional anticorruption framework looks impressive, owing largely to reforms and legislative initiatives to reach EU standards. In 2001, the government adopted a Comprehensive Strategy Against Corruption, introducing a range of mandatory instruments on conflicts of interest and financial disclosure along with a host of punitive measures to deter corrupt practices.

In the following years, the State Secretariat on Public Finance was created to monitor public procurement and the handling of public finances, and the Glass Pocket Act was passed in Parliament, with unanimous support, to provide additional mandatory disclosure mechanisms on public spending. In 2006, the Law on Lobbying was enacted to inject transparency into lobbying efforts by special interest groups. However, implementation of anticorruption laws and regulations is patchy at best, owing to a lack of human and financial resources, as well as political will.

Parliamentarians, judges, and various other public officials are required to declare their assets annually, although many are suspected of transferring assets to family to avoid this legality. MPs are not restricted from engaging in business activities or assuming positions at state-owned companies before or after their mandate.

Instead of a designated independent body, a number of state institutions are empowered to fight corruption. The main investigative law enforcement body is the police, while high-level corruption (involving MPs, ministers, and heads of public departments) and organized crime cases fall under the jurisdiction of the Central Investigation Department of the National Office of the Prosecutor. Additional institutions with enforcement authority, such as customs and tax agencies, also have separate units to combat corruption.

The State Audit Office (Állami Számvevőszék, ÁSZ), the financial and economic audit organization of the Parliament, is the state's supreme audit organization to monitor public spending and ensure transparency in public finance processes. The president and vice president of the ÁSZ are elected by Parliament for 12 years, with supportive votes of two-thirds of all MPs. The Constitution requires a two-thirds vote from a parliamentary quorum to pass (and amend) an act on the ÁSZ and its operational guidelines. Because of its mandate and high level of independence, the

ÁSZ plays a key role in anticorruption efforts. However, its recommendations are not binding and therefore are often ignored by lawmakers and law enforcement authorities.[69]

In its National Integrity Systems study, published in 2007, Transparency International identified four critical weaknesses in Hungary's anticorruption legislation: a lack of protection for whistle-blowers, improper and weak conflict-of-interest regulations, lack of transparency in recruitment at public institutions, and restrictions on the availability of public interest information. The study pointed at party financing, corruption among police and other law enforcement authorities, and public procurement as the most acute areas of corruption.[70]

In all three areas, 2007 provided examples that underscore the study's findings. Toward the end of the year, separate cases highlighted inadequate safeguards surrounding public procurement. After the *Hungarian Post* acquired 4,800 bicycles for its delivery staff in a public tender, the selection of the tender's winner and the price paid (1.1 billion forint [US$6.86 million]) for the bikes were both widely criticized.[71] The deputy chief of staff of the Office of the Prime Minister was forced to resign after it was revealed that under his supervision, 6 million forint (approximately US$35,000) was paid for a substandard study produced by an outside contractor.[72]

In a statement referencing both cases, Transparency International stressed that the public procurement mechanism in Hungary is open to serious corruption and that despite highly regulated procedures, only about 10 percent of public procurements were conducted properly. The statement specifically criticized the use of "confidential business information" as a way to limit transparency in public procurement tenders.[73] It is estimated that corruption increases the cost of public procurement by approximately 25 percent.[74]

Police corruption also remained a recurrent topic in 2007 media reports, such as revelations that the new national police chief, József Bence, paid bonuses to a girlfriend while she was his subordinate at his previous position at the Customs and Finance Guard.[75] Allegations of corruption also reached high into the government when a former business associate of Minister of Finance János Veres was sentenced to three and a half years in prison for tax evasion and false accounting between 1991 and 1994. Veres claimed to have no knowledge of his business partner's wrongdoing.[76]

In September, MSZP politician Janos Zuschlág was arrested for using fake nonprofits to defraud the National Civil Fund of monies earmarked for civil society groups and channeling them to the Socialist Party.[77] The ongoing investigation touched even the prime minister, who was interviewed by the police. Gyurcsány served as minister of youth and sport during the time Zuschlág's faux NGOs received funds from the ministry.[78] Tamás Deutsch, minister of youth and sport in the Fidesz cabinet between 1998 and 2002, was also questioned by police as a witness.

A sprawling international investigation into bribes paid by the defense company BAE Systems to politicians in various countries in return for defense contracts reached Hungary when it was reported by Swedish and U.S. media that in 2001, Hungarian political parties received millions of dollars as payment for the purchase of Gripen fighter jets.[79]

Spending by Hungarian political parties is way above the declared income from state support and donations. According to a recent study by the Eötvös Károly Public Policy Institute, parties spent as much as 10 times the allowable limit of 385 million forint (US$2.4 million) for national election campaigns.[80] While parties must report their finances annually, the ÁSZ does not carry out its own investigations, even when discrepancies appear between the declared expenses and the price of services procured by the parties, as is the case with TV ads and street posters.[81] The 2007 roundtable negotiations among all parliamentary parties on a proposed reform package, including party and campaign financing, got off to a promising start but collapsed in August.[82]

During 2007, the government also launched an ambitious initiative to tackle corruption in a comprehensive and strategic manner by tasking the minister of justice and law enforcement to elaborate a long-term strategic document and a short-term program of action.[83] To coordinate this newest effort, the Anticorruption Coordination Body (AKT) was established in August. The AKT, which also included civil society representatives in its deliberations, designated four priority areas to combat corruption: EU development funds, party financing, public procurement, and the administrative authorization process. A National Strategy and Action Plan to combat corruption was expected to be completed by early 2008.

▮ Authors: Balázs Áron Kovács and Bálint Molnár

Balázs Áron Kovács is an instructor in the International Peace Studies dual campus program of the United Nations mandated University for Peace in Costa Rica and Ateneo de Manila University in the Philippines. Bálint Molnár is deputy director of Freedom House Europe in Budapest.

---

1   See http://www.mkogy.hu.

2   "Vesztett Petrétei—15 napon belül nyilvános az alkotmánytervezet" [Petretei Lost—Draft Constitution Public Within 15 Days], October 3, 2006, *MNO,* http://www.mno.hu/index. mno?cikk=377043&rvt=2.

3   "Pert nyert Petrétei a TASZ ellen" [Petretei Won Against HCLU], January 12, 2007, Index, http://index.hu/politika/belhirek/295536. Retrieved: December 12, 2007.
     Lencsés Károly, "Ma még láthatatlan alkotmány—Miért vesztett másodfokon a TASZ?" [The Constitution Is Still Invisible—Why Did HCLU Lose in the Second Instance?], January 15, 2007, *Népszabadság,* http://www.nol.hu/cikk/431485. Retrieved: December 12, 2007.

4   "Tárki: Csökkent a bizalom a politika iránt" [Tárki: Trust in Politics Has Decreased], January 5, 2007, Index, http://index.hu/politika/belfold/tarkei8827. Retrieved: December 12, 2007.

5   "Tárki: Mélyponton a választási hajlandóság" [Tárki: Willingness to Vote Is Plunging], *HVG Online*, December 19, 2007, http://hvg.hu/itthon/20071219_tarki_median_szonda.aspx. Retrieved: December 20, 2007.

6   "Medián: Stabilizálódó Fidesz-előny, Szili mélyrepülése folytatódik" [Medián: Stabilizing Fidesz Lead, Szili's Fall Continues], *HVG Online*, December 19, 2007, http://hvg.hu/itthon/20071219_median_fidesz_mszp_szdsz.aspx. Retrieved: December 20, 2007.

7   Publius Hungaricus, "A féltudású elit alternatívája" [The Half-Ignorant Hungarian Elite], Index, November 26, 2007, http://index.hu/velemeny/jegyzet/feltud2. Retrieved: January 19, 2008.

    Publius Hungaricus, "A féltudású magyar elit" [The Alternative of the Half-Ignorant Elite], Index, March 26, 2007, http://index.hu/velemeny/jegyzet/feltud070321. Retrieved: January 19, 2008.

8   "Megtámadták Csintalan Sándort" [Sándor Csintalan Assaulted], *Népszabadság Online (NOL)*, December 11, 2007, http://www.nol.hu/cikk/474578. Retrieved: December 19, 2007.

9   "Nem utal semmi arra, hogy az adott szervezet bántalmazta Csintalant" [Nothing Indicates that the Named Organization Attacked Csintalan], December 16, 2007, HírTV, http://www.hirtv.hu/belfold?article_id=190560&highlight_text=csintalan. Retrieved: December 19, 2007.

10 "Rálőttek a rendőrpalotára" [Bullets Fired at the Police Palace], Index, February 13, 2007, http://index.hu/politika/bulvar/teve3545. Retrieved: January 17, 2008.

11 "Két golyót eresztettek Hiller lakásába" [Two Bullets fired into Hiller's Apartment], December 19, 2007, Index, http://index.hu/politika/belfold/hiller4834. Retrieved: December 19, 2007.

12 "Mégis vonulhat a Magyar Gárda" [Hungarian Guard May Still March], Index, December 9, 2007, http://index.hu/politika/belfold/mgar071209. Retrieved: December 21, 2007; "Disznólopásból lett gárdafelvonulás?" [From Pig Theft to Guard March?] Index, December 9, 2007, http://index.hu/politika/belfold/gar071209. Retrieved: December 21, 2007

13 "Újabb cigányellenes tüntetés" [Another Anti-Gypsy Demonstration], Index, http://index.hu/politika/belfold/cigany7726. Retrieved: December 21, 2007.

14 "A Magyar Gárda Érpatakon demonstrál" [Hungarian Guard Demonstrates in Érpatak], Index, http://index.hu/politika/belhirek/336432. Retrieved: December 21, 2007.

15 "Mindenkit kioszt a Gönczöl-bizottság" [Gönczöl Committe Scorns Everybody], Index, February 6, 2007, http://index.hu/politika/belfold/gonczol2022. Retrieved: December 26, 2007. Homepage of the Gönczöl Committee, http://www.gonczolbizottsag.gov.hu/jelentes/gonczolbizottsag_jelentes.pdf. Retrieved: December 26, 2007.

16 "Az Amnesty International elégedett a Gönczöl-jelentéssel" [Amnesty International Content with Gönczöl Report], Index, February 8, 2007, http://index.hu/politika/belfold/0209aigyk. Retrieved: December 26, 2007.

17 Péter Bohus, "Volt alkotmánybírók agyagba döngölik a Gönczöl-bizottságot" [Former Constitutional Court Judges Slam Gönczöl Committee], Index, http://index.hu/politika/belfold/alk0220h. Retrieved: December 26, 2007.

18 Report on the Violation of Human Rights in September and October 2006 by the Committee of Civil Jurists Set Up for the Investigation of the Violent Acts of 23 October 2006, Committee of Civil Jurists Website, http://oktober23bizottsag.hu/CJB_teljes2_20070301EN.doc. Retrieved: December 26, 2007.

19 "Egyetért-e Ön azzal, hogy az egészségügyi közszolgáltató intézmények, kórházak maradjanak állami, önkormányzati tulajdonban?" [Do you agree that public health facilities and hospitals remain in public (state, municipal) ownership?].

"Egyetért-e Ön azzal, hogy gyógyszereket csak gyógyszertárban lehessen árusítani?" [Do you agree that drugs can only be sold in pharmacies?]

"Egyetért-e Ön azzal, hogy a—2002. június 15-i állapot szerint hatályos termőföldről szóló 1994. évi LV. törvény szerinti—családi gazdálkodót első helyen illesse meg elővásárlási jog termőföld vagy tanya vásárlása esetén?" [Do you agree that family farmers (as defined by Law LV of 1994) on agricultural land as of 15 June 2002 be given first priority in the purchase of farms or farmland?]

"Egyetért-e Ön azzal, hogy az államilag támogatott felsőfokú tanulmányokat folytató hallgatóknak ne kelljen képzési hozzájárulást fizetniük?" [Do you agree that students continuing state-sponsored studies do not pay educational fees?]

"Egyetért-e Ön azzal, hogy a háziorvosi ellátásért, fogászati ellátásért és a járóbeteg-szakellátásért a jelen kérdésben megtartott népszavazást követő év január 1-jétől ne kelljen vizitdíjat fizetni?" [Do you agree that for family medical attendance, dentistry and out-patient care no visiting fees be paid from 1 January of the year following this referendum?]

"Egyetért-e Ön azzal, hogy a fekvőbeteg-gyógyintézeti ellátásért a jelen kérdésben megtartott népszavazást követő év január 1-jétől ne kelljen kórházi napidíjat fizetni?" [Do you agree that from 1 January of the year following this referendum, no daily fees be paid for in-patient care?]

Fidesz website, http://www.fidesz.hu/index.php?Cikk=80169. Retrieved: January 15, 2008.

20   Dosszié 2007, HírTV http://www.hirtv.hu/?tPath=/view/videoview&videoview_id=4964.

21   The Constitution of the Republic of Hungary, the Constitutional Court's website, http://www.mkab.hu/hu/alkotm.htm.

22   K. B., "Nagyon kevés lesz a nem szavazat" [There will be very few "No" votes], Index, January 17, 2008, http://index.hu/politika/belfold/mc5340. Retrieved: January 17, 2008.

23   National Election Office website, http://valtor.valasztas.hu/valtort/jsp.

24   "Leszavazták a női kvótát" [Female Quota Turned Down], Index, http://index.hu/politika/belfold/noikvota3679. Retrieved: January 17, 2008.

25   "A nonprofit szektor legfontosabb jellemzői 2005-ben" [Most Important Characteristics of the Nonprofit Sector in 2005], Statisztikai Tükör 1, no. 15, May 30, 2007, National Statistics Office, http://portal.ksh.hu/pls/ksh/docs/hun/xftp/stattukor/nonprofit05.pdf.

26   Ibid.

27   The international charity, Habitat for Humanity, moved its regional headquartes from Budapest to Bratislava in 2007; https://www.habitat.org/hw/sept_2007/notes.html.

28   NGO Sustainability Index 2007, United States Agency for International Development (USAID) (prepublication draft), USAID, Washington, D.C..

29   "A nonprofit szektor legfontosabb jellemzői 2005-ben" [Most Important Characteristics of the Nonprofit Sector in 2005], Statisztikai Tükör 1, no. 15, May 30, 2007, National Statistics Office, http://portal.ksh.hu/pls/ksh/docs/hun/xftp/stattukor/nonprofit05.pdf.

30   Ibid.

31   NGO Sustainability Index 2007, (prepublication draft).

32   Éva Kuti, "Hungary's 1% System: Ten Years On," 2007, http://www.onepercent.hu/Dokumentumok/KUTI2007web.pdf.

33   2003 évi L. törvény a Nemzeti Civil Alapprogramról [Law of 2003 on the National Civil Fund Program], http://www.nca.hu/?page=lawsource/list&ftr_id=3.

34   NGO Sustainability Index 2007, prepublication draft.

35   "Megállapítottuk, hogy egyetértünk—Gaskó István a Liga Szekszervezetek és a VDDSZ Elnöke" [We Determined that We Agree—István Gaskó, President of Liga Trade Unions and VDDSZ], Magyar Narancs XIX. évf. 49. szám, 2007-12-06.

36   "Milliárdosok a médiában" [Billionaires in the Media], Figyelőnet, June 26, 2007, http://www.fn.hu/media/20070625/milliardosok_mediaban.

37 "Sóhivatal lesz az ORTT" [What Does ORTT Become?], Index, July 24, 2007, http://index. hu/kultur/media/ortt5996.

38 "ORTT: még lehet panaszkodni," [ORTT: You Can Continue Complaining], *Népszabadság Online*, December 29, 2007, http://www.nol.hu/cikk/476157.

39 "Tiltakozó éhezés a rádió előtt" [Protestors Starving in Front of the Radio], *Népszabadság Online*, July 25, 2007, http://www.nol.hu/cikk/457580.

40 "Felmentették a HVG újságíróját" [HVG Journalist Acquitted], hvg.hu, December 19, 2007, http://hvg.hu/itthon/20071219_radi_antonia_hvg_allamtitoksertes_varga.aspx.

41 "OSCE Media Freedom Watchdog Welcomes Acquittal of Hungarian Journalist in Secrecy Case, Urges Legislative Reforms," press release, December 19, 2007, http://www.osce.org/ fom/item_1_28999.html?print=1.

42 László Seres, "A nagy félreértés" [The Big Misunderstanding], *Élet és Irodalom*, no. 11, March 16, 2007.

43 "Elsőfokon nyilvános a Hankook szerződés" [Hankook Contract Public at First Instance], Index, September 4, 2007, http://index.hu/politika/belfold/hank070904.

44 "Fej hullott a fércmű miatt" [Head Rolls Because of Hack Job], Origo, December 12, 2007, http://www.origo.hu/itthon/20071212-tavozik-posztjarol-pimper-richard-a miniszterelnoki-hivatal-kabinetfonokenek-helyettese-az.html.

45 "A Freedom House Europe elítéli a rendőrség fellépését a média képviselőivel szemben" [Freedom House Condemns Police for Action Against Representatives of the Press], press release, November 20, 2007, http://www.freedomhouse.hu/index.php?option=com_content &task=view&id=119.

46 "At Demonstrations, Full Freedom to Report Is as Important as Reporters' Visibility, Say OSCE Media Freedom Watchdog," press release, November 27, 2007, http://www.osce.org fom/item_1_28337.html?print=1.

47 "A magyarországi háztartások infokommunikációs (IKT) eszközellátottsága és az egyéb használat jellemzői, 2006" [IT Equipment in Hungarian Households and the Characteristic of Usage in 2006], Hungarian Central Statistical Office, Budapest 2007, http://portal.ksh hu/pls/ksh/docs/hun/xftp/idoszaki/ikt/ikt06.pdf.

48 Ilona Pálné Kovács, "A kistérségek a területi igazgatás komplex összefüggésrendszerében" [Microregions in the Complex Context of Regional Administration], www.cipp.hu download.php?frm_id=7368149773.doc&frm_category_id=212.

49 "Fejre vagy talpra" [Heads or Heels], *HVG*, 2006/48. szám.

50 Márton Gellén, "A közigazgatási rendszer átalakítása és az önkormányzatok helyzete" [The Transformation of the Administration and the Situation of Municipalities], Századvég Közigazgatási Akadémia, 2007. április, http://www.szazadveg.hu/kozig/elemzes/onkor pdf.

51 Ibid.

52 Péter Kovács, "A regionális fejlesztési tanácsok és elnökeik—Eurók a kapu előtt" [The Region Development Councils and Their Presidents—Euros at the Gates], *Magyar Narancs*, n XIX, 49, December 6, 2007.

53 Márton Gellén, "A közigazgatási rendszer átalakítása és az önkormányzatok helyzete" [T Transformation of the Administration and the Situation of Municipalities], Századv Közigazgatási Akadémia, 2007.

54 Bálint Mészáros, "Döntések az uniós források elosztásáról—transparency national" [Decisio on the Distribution of EU Sources—Transparency National], *Magyar Narancs*, no. XIX, 3 August 9, 2007.

55 Ibid.

56 Ibid.

57 Zoltán Fleck, "Igazságszolgáltatás reform közben" [Judiciary in Reform], http://www.ajaj. hu/downloads/fleck-igazsagszolg-reform.doc.

Mária Vásárhelyi, "Jogszolgáltatás vagy igazságszolgáltatás I" [Administration of Law or of Justice I], http://www.es.hu/pd/display.asp?channel=PUBLICISZTIKA0634&article=2006 -0828-0200-56MGWR; Mária Vásárhelyi, "Jogszolgáltatás vagy igazságszolgáltatás II" [Administration of Law or of Justice II], http://www.es.hu/pd/display.asp?channel=PUBLI CISZTIKA0635&article=2006-0903-2048-42CSWO.

58 László Gatter, "A bírósági fogalmazóképzés szerepe a jogászok felkészítésében" [Court Training's Role in the Education of Lawyers], http://www.ajk.elte.hu/index.asp?URL=http:// www.ajk.elte.hu/tudomanyosprofil/kiadvanyok/bibliothecaiuridica/jogaszkepzes.html.

59 András Király, "Az egész világ egy nagy Cserni János" [The Whole World Is a Big Janos Cserni], Index, May 17, 2007, http://index.hu/politika/belfold/bjtbszit3608. Retrieved: January 19, 2007.

60 Károly Lencsés, "Alternatív bírói egyesület születik" [Alternative Judge Association Being Born], Népszabadság, November 19, 2007, http://www.nol.hu/cikk/472017. Retrieved: January 19, 2008.

61 Amnesty International Report on Hungary 2007, http://www.amnesty.org/en/region/ europe-and-central-asia/eastern-europe/hungary.

62 Judit Doros, "Jászladány: a járhatatlan folyosó—Nem nyugszanak a kedélyek a településen" [Jászladány: The Unpassable Corridor—Tensions Still High in the Village], Nepszabadsag, January 26, 2007, http://www.nol.hu/cikk/432974. Retrieved: January 19, 2008.

63 "Lopott egy rendőr a Széna téri túszejtés helyszínén" [A Policeman Stole at the Scene of the Széna tér Hostage Taking], Index, http://index.hu/politika/bulvar/lopp0512. Retrieved: December 26, 2007.

64 "Megbánta tettét az OTP-ből pénzt lopó rendőr" [Policeman Stealing from OTP Regrets What He Committed], Index, May 24, 2007, http://index.hu/politika/bulvar/rendor0515. Retrieved: December 26, 2007.

65 "Letartóztatták az emberrabló rendőrök társait" [The Partners of the Kidnapper-Policeman Arrested], Index, May 24, 2007, http://index.hu/politika/bulvar/ksvrd9522. Retrieved: December 26, 2007.

66 "Ha a rendőrök tényleg megerőszakolták Zsanettet" [If the Policemen Really Raped Zsanett], HVG, May 17, 2007, http://hvg.hu/velemeny/20070516_zsanett_rendorseg_eroszak.aspx. Retrieved: December 26, 2007.

67 "Személycserék: a botrány csak ürügy" [Personnel Swaps: The Scandal is Only an Excuse], HVG, May 24, 2007, http://hvg.hu/hvgfriss/2007.21/200721HVGFriss9.aspx. Retrieved: December 26, 2007.

68 "Zsanett-eset: hamis vád?" [Zsanett Csae: False Charges?], HVG, December 12, 2007, http:// hvg.hu/hvgfriss/2007.50/200750HVGFriss19.aspx. Retrieved: December 26, 2007.

59 "Corruption Risks in Hungary—National Integrity System Country Study," Hungary 2007, Transparency International, http://transparency.hu/drupal/files/active/0/Hungary_NIS_ final.pdf.

70 Ibid.

71 "Kerékpár-gate" [Bicycle Gate], Hírszerző, January 8, 2008, http://www.hirszerzo.hu/cikk. kerekpar-gate_a_fidesz_gondolkodni_fog.54586.html.

72 "Fej hullott a fércmű miatt" [Head Rolls Because of Hack Job], Origo, December 12, 2007, http://www.origo.hu/itthon/20071212-tavozik-posztjarol-pimper-richard-a-miniszter elnoki-hivatal-kabinetfonokenek-helyettese-az.html.

3 "Állásfoglalás a közbeszerzések helyzetéről" [Statement on Public Procurements], press release, January 10, 2008, Transparency International Magyarország, http://transparency.hu/drupal/ hu/node/50.

74 "A korrupció 25 százalékkal drágítja a közbeszerzéseket" [Corruption Makes Public Procurement 25% More Expensive], *Figyelőnet*, January 10, 2008, http://www.fn.hu/uzlet/ 20080110/korrupcio_25_szazalekkal_dragitja.

75 "New Top Cop Tainted by Whiff of Corruption," *Budapest Times*, June 11, 2007.

76 "Rozsdaövezet—Kabai Károly és Veres János fémbiznisze," *HVG*, no. 2007/41.

77 "A Zuschlag ügy és az MSZP—Róka fogta csuka" [The Zuschlag Case and the MSZP], *Magyar Narancs*, no. XIX, 37, September 13, 2007.

78 "Gyurcsány tavasz óta tudott a Zuschlag ügyről" [Gyurcsany Knew About the Zuschlag Case Since Spring], hvg.hu, October 11, 2007, http://hvg.hu/itthon/20071011_gyurcsany_ zuschlag_ugy.aspx.

79 "Payload: Taking Aim at Corporate Bribery," *New York Times*, November 25, 2007.

80 "A pártfinanszírozás alapelvei" [Fundamental Principles of Party Financing], *Eötvös Károly Közpolitikai Intézet*, June 26, 2006, http://ekint.org/ekint_files/File/tanulmanyok/apartfinan szirozasalapelvei.pdf.

81 "Corruption Risks in Hungary—National Integrity System Country Study," Hungary 2007, Transparency International, http://transparency.hu/drupal/files/active/0/Hungary_NIS_ final.pdf.

82 "Megállapodás-tervezet a párt- és kampámyfinanszírozás átalakításáról" [Draft Agreement on the Reform of Party and Campaign Financing], *Eötvös Károly Közpolitikai Intézet*, http:// ekint.org/ekint/ekint.news.page?nodeid=159.

83 "Munkához lát az antikorrupciós testület" [Anti-Corruption Body Starts Working], hvg.hu, September 5, 2007, http://hvg.hu/itthon/20070905_antikorrupcio.aspx.

Kazakhstan

by Bhavna Dave

Capital: Astana
Population: 15.4 million
GNI/capita: US$8,700

The social data above was taken from the European Bank for Reconstruction and Development's *Transition Report 2007: People in Transition*, and the economic data from the World Bank's *World Development Indicators 2008*.

Nations in Transit Ratings and Averaged Scores

	1999	2001	2002	2003	2004	2005	2006	2007	2008
Electoral Process	6.00	6.25	6.25	6.50	6.50	6.50	6.50	6.50	6.75
Civil Society	5.00	5.00	5.50	5.50	5.50	5.50	5.75	5.75	5.50
Independent Media	5.50	6.00	6.00	6.25	6.50	6.50	6.75	6.75	6.75
Governance*	5.00	5.00	5.75	6.25	6.25	n/a	n/a	n/a	n/a
National Democratic Governance	n/a	n/a	n/a	n/a	n/a	6.50	6.75	6.75	6.75
Local Democratic Governance	n/a	n/a	n/a	n/a	n/a	6.25	6.25	6.25	6.25
Judicial Framework and Independence	5.50	5.75	6.00	6.25	6.25	6.25	6.25	6.25	6.25
Corruption	6.00	6.25	6.25	6.25	6.50	6.50	6.50	6.50	6.50
Democracy Score	5.50	5.71	5.96	6.17	6.25	6.29	6.39	6.39	6.39

* *With the 2005 edition, Freedom House introduced separate analysis and ratings for national democratic governance and local democratic governance to provide readers with more detailed and nuanced analysis of these two important subjects.*

NOTE: The ratings reflect the consensus of Freedom House, its academic advisers, and the author(s) of this report. The opinions expressed in this report are those of the author(s). The ratings are based on a scale of 1 to 7, with 1 representing the highest level of democratic progress and 7 the lowest. The Democracy Score is an average of ratings for the categories tracked in a given year.

EXECUTIVE SUMMARY

K azakhstan's rich natural resources, rising oil exports, and small population base have turned it into the most prosperous and stable state in Central Asia. Having held the top office since 1989 under Soviet rule, President Nursultan Nazarbaev has continued to build a strong and personalized presidential regime by adopting a new Constitution in 1995 that granted unchecked powers to the presidency. In 2007, Nazarbaev indicated his desire to become president for life after the Parliament removed a two-term limit on the first president. His party, Nur Otan, obtained all 98 seats in the August parliamentary elections to the Mazhilis, the lower house.

Maintaining firm control over the country's key resources and using patronage to disburse power and privileges to family, friends, and clients, President Nazarbaev has allowed much economic freedom to the country's budding entre-preneurs and offered rapid career mobility to the growing class of skilled professionals, technocrats, and top bureaucrats. He has allowed an inner circle of close family and business associates to exert formal and informal influence over vital economic resources and political office. Although his skilled management of revenues from Kazakhstan's oil and mineral base, promotion of economic reforms, and top-down political and ethnic control have ensured significant material well-being and social stability, these have also led to a considerable undermining of democratic process, civic activism, and media independence. This concentration of wealth and power in a narrow social stratum of elites has marginalized a significant number of citizens.

Kazakhstan obtained the Organization for Security and Cooperation in Europe (OSCE) rotating chair for 2010 (a year later than it had bid for) despite its failure to hold free and fair parliamentary elections in 2007. This decision was a result of its successful diplomatic lobbying and pledge to play a constructive role in reconciling the differences between Russia and other OSCE member states, old and new.

National Democratic Governance. A package of constitutional amendments swiftly passed by a pliant Parliament before announcing elections two years ahead of schedule, removed the two-term limit on the first president. Nazarbaev has continued to eliminate all challenges to his leadership, whether from independent actors, ruling elites, or even within his own family. This includes the removal of all legal barriers to establishing a life presidency and the lack of mechanisms to allow independent deputies or those belonging to parties other than the ruling Nur Otan to partake in the formal political process and institutions of representation. Although Kazakhstan's economy continues to grow, the benefits of its rising prosperity are monopolized by the narrow circle of kin, clients, and powerful financial group and a limited stratum of government officials, technocrats, and entrepreneurs. *Kazakhstan's rating in national democratic governance remains at 6.75.*

Electoral Process. Despite the realization that gaining the chairmanship of the OSCE depended heavily on Kazakhstan holding genuinely competitive, free, and fair elections, the 2007 Mazhilis polls resulted in Nur Otan, headed by the president, capturing all seats in the Parliament. By requiring all candidates to be party members, setting a high 7 percent electoral threshold for political parties, and allowing no provision for independent candidates to contest, the Nazarbaev leadership effectively legalized the exclusion of non-regime parties and individuals from the political process. *Owing to amendments to electoral procedures and the legislative framework that have erected a one-party system, Kazakhstan's rating for electoral process deteriorates from 6.50 to 6.75.*

Civil Society. Kazakhstan has used its rising economic revenues, political control, electoral mandate, and 2007 success in attaining the OSCE chair for 2010 to portray itself as a promoter of civil society and the nongovernmental sector. By removing limits that prevented the state from funding nongovernmental organizations (NGOs), the government stepped up financial aid to NGOs engaged in social and infrastructure development. The government disbursed such aid through government-organized NGOs (GONGOs) in order to establish a pliant civil society. The Ministries of Justice and the Interior, together with the National Security Service, have intensified monitoring of ethnic groups, religious congregations, the opposition, and independent NGOs engaged in civil rights advocacy. *Owing to the government's efforts to involve civil society in various development projects and improved transparency regarding its functioning (to secure the OSCE chair), Kazakhstan's rating for civil society improves from 5.75 to 5.50.*

Independent Media. Kazakhstan's privately owned media are in fact almost entirely under the control of major financial groups affiliated with key members of the ruling elite. The existing Media Law and other provisions within the criminal code and National Security Law criminalize criticisms of leading government figures and render a small number of independent media outlets noncompetitive. The media coverage of the August 2007 parliamentary elections remained biased in favor of the ruling Nur Otan as the opposition received considerable negative publicity. The government sought to censor the media and Internet following the release of transcripts of taped conversations among state officials about campaign financing, posted on opposition Web sites. *Kazakhstan's independent media rating remains at 6.75.*

Local Democratic Governance. In Kazakhstan's unitary administrative framework, the central government exerts top-down control over regional and local levels, with the president maintaining full control over the appointment of all heads (akims) of regions and districts. Nazarbaev has refused to consider demands for the election of *akims*. The local administrative authorities are also facing increasing pressure from ordinary citizens and civic rights groups over property legalization, which is seen as more favorable to state officials than to ordinary citizens. *Although the constitutional amendments in 2007 granted a greater voice to local legislators in the appointment and removal of akims, the dominance of Nur Otan at all levels of governance makes such measures ineffective. Therefore, Kazakhstan's rating for local democratic governance remains at 6.25.*

Judicial Framework and Independence. Under the country's strong executive system based on presidential patronage, the judiciary, like the legislative branch, has remained loyal to the regime. The judiciary has continued to protect the interests of the state and its functionaries rather than those of individuals, minorities, and the weaker strata of society. In 2007, the judiciary responded once again to the command from above by conducting an *in absentia* trial of the president's now deposed son-in-law, Rakhat Aliev, and his associates, sentencing them to 20-year jail terms. The Austrian authorities have refused to extradite them by averring that they will not receive a fair trial in Kazakhstan. *Despite continuing improvement in wages and professional training for judges and the introduction of jury trials, the judiciary's record in handling cases related to civil liberties and human rights remains poor. Kazakhstan's judicial framework and independence rating remains at 6.25.*

Corruption. All inquiries into official corruption are handled by the prosecutor general, appointed by the president and working in conjunction with the Ministries of Justice and the Interior as well as the National Security Service. The president regularly launches anticorruption programs and appoints anticorruption bodies and members of the financial police, who report to the president. The government has invested some effort in developing civic awareness about corruption and has increased the salaries of public sector employees as long-term solutions to corruption. *While improved governance, salary increases, and more effective monitoring of corruption by government bodies may have helped at lower and middle levels of bureaucracy, the continuing absence of an independent media and judicial system make it impossible to launch an impartial inquiry into cases of corruption at top levels and deters ordinary citizens or independent public bodies from filing corruption charges against high-ranking state officials. Therefore, Kazakhstan's corruption rating remains at 6.50.*

Outlook for 2008. Having maintained almost 10 percent economic growth since 2000, Kazakhstan aspires to become the fifth-largest exporter of oil by 2015 and emerge as the "Kuwait of the region." Kazakhstan revised its economic growth projections from 9 percent to about 5 percent in 2008 owing to the delay in starting commercial oil production in the Kashagan oil field, which has also made the government lower its projected oil export target by some 20 percent.[1] The promise of rising prosperity, which has allowed Nazarbaev to muster considerable popular support and legitimacy, will be harder to deliver in 2008, when Kazakhstan begins to repay substantial foreign loans. Inflation, currently at 18 percent, is likely to soar as prices of essential commodities and real estate continue to increase. An economic setback could spur the generally pro-government lower strata of the population to demand greater material and social security, shaking up Kazakhstan's "stable" political system.

As Kazakhstan prepares to play a more visible role within the OSCE after acquiring its rotating chair for the year 2010, its ruling elites also seek a more prominent role in Europe on the basis of the country's growing strategic and economic partnership with the European Union. The government is likely to face more domestic and international pressure to liberalize its restrictive Media Law and amend electoral provisions to allow inclusion of other political parties in the Parliament.

MAIN REPORT

National Democratic Governance

1999	2001	2002	2003	2004	2005	2006	2007	2008
n/a	n/a	n/a	n/a	n/a	6.50	6.75	6.75	6.75

After attaining the chairmanship of the Organization for Security and Cooperation in Europe (OSCE) for 2010, Kazakhstan made a new pledge at the OSCE meeting in Madrid in November 2007 to maintain the unity of the 45-member organization, to protect its election-monitoring mandate, to build democracy and civil society, and to carry out reform of the legislation on media, elections, and political parties in conformance with OSCE recommendations. Pursuing these objectives within a legal framework that has pushed political competition out of the legislative process is a challenge that both Kazakhstan and the OSCE will continue to tackle.

Kazakhstan may become the "Kuwait of the region," but its leaders have yet to demonstrate a genuine commitment to establishing a democratic polity that respects human rights, civil liberties, tolerance, and the development of civil society.[2] International organizations such as Human Rights Watch and International Helsinki Federation for Human Rights, as well as independent media and civil society activists, have deemed Kazakhstan unfit to assume the leadership of the OSCE and pointed to the failure of the government to abide by the OSCE procedures at home since it made the bid to head the organization. Despite its poor democratic and human rights credentials and the failure to hold free and fair parliamentary elections in August 2007 (ruling Nur Otan won 100 percent of the seats), Kazakhstan still succeeded in attaining the rotating OSCE chairmanship for 2010, a year later than what it had expected.

This "success" was the result of hectic diplomatic lobbying by the Kazakhstani government and its tactful balancing between Russia and Western European states. In an organization where decisions are made by consensus, the initial opposition by the United States and United Kingdom to Kazakhstan's bid on the basis of its poor human rights record and weak democratic institutions led to the postponement of the decision on the 2009 chairmanship until late 2007. The United States withdrew its objections in Madrid after Kazakhstan distanced itself from Russia's criticism of the election observation missions headed by the Warsaw-based Office of Democratic Institutions and Human Rights (ODIHR) and the proposal to place the ODIHR under the direct supervision of the OSCE Permanent Council.

While maintaining a pro-Western orientation and coveting international acclaim for Kazakhstan's economic success and stability, President Nursultan Nazarbaev has continued to eliminate all major challengers to his leadership by using or sanctioning a repertoire of undemocratic tactics reminiscent of Soviet-era practices. The late rival to be eliminated was the president's eldest son-in-law, Rakhat Aliev. Ironically, as deputy foreign minister and then as Kazakhstan's ambassador to Austria, Aliev had played an active role in lobbying support for Kazakhstan's OSCE chairmanship bid. In a dramatic move in June 2007, Kazakhstani authorities charged Aliev and a number of his associates with forming an "organized criminal group" engaged in money laundering, extortion, and kidnapping. In 2007, Kazakhstani courts tried Aliev *in absentia* and numerous co-defendants, sentencing them to 20 years in prison, after Austrian authorities refused to extradite Aliev on the grounds that he was unlikely to receive a fair trial in Kazakhstan.

The case against Aliev also ended the domestic and international speculation that his wife, Dariga Nazarbaeva, aided by her husband's growing economic and political influence, was consolidating her position as the most likely successor to her father. Nazarbaeva, who became a parliamentary deputy in 2004, was not on the list of candidates nominated by Nur Otan in the 2007 Mazhilis elections. Her party, Asar, founded in 2004, merged with the largest party, Otan, two years later. Two other pro-regime parties, Civic Party of Kazakhstan and Agrarian Party of Kazakhstan, also merged with Nur Otan in 2007. The constitutional clause that the president is to be above party politics was amended in 2007, clearing the way for Nazarbaev to assume party leadership. Otan thus renamed itself Nur Otan in early 2007 and elected Nazarbaev as its leader.

A number of major financial groups closely associated with the president have coalesced on the broad-based platform of Nur Otan, which now controls the Parliament. These groups exert indirect influence over legislative organs at both central and regional levels and also control the network of prominent privatized media channels. Their financial success and political influence depend on a demonstration of loyalty to the president.

The Aliev-Nazarbaeva group, which owned numerous businesses and shares in leading banks, media channels, and other privatized sectors, received a drastic setback following the arrest warrant against Aliev. Nazarbaeva's control over the national media is challenged by other powerful figures and financial interests within elite circles.

Timur Kulibaev, head of KazEnergy and the president's second son-in-law, wields control over major oil and pipeline businesses as well as major banking and financial groups, notably Kazkommertsbank, the largest commercial bank in the country. In what may be an important signal to domestic and international observers that Nazarbaev is not preparing to hand over power within the family, in September 2007 Kulibaev was removed from the presidency of the newly-formed holding company Samruk, which manages the top energy companies of Kazakhstan. However, there is no evidence of a decline in his economic influence.

The president appoints the prime minister, who heads the government and bears responsibility for enacting and implementing all policies but has little independent power to formulate policies or initiate legislation. Karim Masimov, a technocrat proficient in Chinese, Arabic, Turkish, and English, and of mixed Kazakh-Uighur lineage, at 39 became the youngest person to hold the office, replacing Prime Minister Daniyal Akhmetov in early 2007.

The May 2007 amendments empower Parliament to nominate two-thirds of the members of the Constitutional Council, Central Election Committee, and Audit Committee. The president exerts a firm control over military and security services and nominates their heads and key members. The role of the security services has acquired greater public attention since the conviction of former security officers in the murder of opposition leader Altynbek Sarsenbaev in February 2006.

The Nazarbaev leadership has delivered considerable material well-being and security to Kazakhstan's citizens, and it argues that only prolonged social stability and economic growth can provide a basis for building democracy.

Electoral Process

1999	2001	2002	2003	2004	2005	2006	2007	2008
6.00	6.25	6.25	6.50	6.50	6.50	6.50	6.50	6.75

Although Kazakhstan has regularly held multicandidate parliamentary and presidential elections, none of these have been recognized as free and fair by observers of the OSCE/ODIHR, the most prominent international election-monitoring body.

The Senate (upper house of Parliament) is composed of 47 deputies. Of these, 32 are selected through indirect elections by 14 oblast (regional) assemblies, and assemblies from Astana (the capital) and Almaty (the former capital). The May 2007 amendments increased the number of Senate deputies appointed by the president from 7 to 15. Senators serve six-year terms, with half of the elected senators facing elections every three years. After winning the December 2005 presidential elections, Nazarbaev began a rapid process of bringing major pro-regime political parties under the umbrella of his Nur Otan party.

Elections to the Mazhilis (lower house of Parliament) were held in August 2007, two years ahead of schedule, after the Constitution was amended to allow all seats to be elected by party list on a proportional basis. The ruling party, Nur Otan, captured all 98 seats, as no other party was able to cross the 7 percent electoral threshold. These elections were not deemed free and fair, though it was understood that Kazakhstan's bid for the OSCE chairmanship depended heavily on it.

The OSCE/ODIHR preliminary report on the elections criticized "a combination of restrictive legal provisions" that hindered the development of "a pluralistic political party system" and decreased "accountability of elected representatives to voters" in Kazakhstan, while pointing to some "progress" in moving "forward in its evolution toward a democratic country."[3]

The package of constitutional amendments in May 2007 removed clauses limiting the first president of Kazakhstan to no more than two terms, leaving little doubt that the 67-year-old Nazarbaev is planning to remain president for life. Apart from reducing the presidential term from seven to five years, the amendments increased the number of seats in the Mazhilis from 67 to 107, of which 98 are elected by party list on a proportional basis and 9 are selected from the Assembly of the Peoples of Kazakhstan (APK).

Nur Otan obtained 88.5 percent of the votes, whereas six other parties—Ak Zhol, Aul, Democratic Party of Kazakhstan, Party of Patriots, Rukhaniyet, and the opposition Social Democratic Party supported by Nagyz Ak Zhol—failed to cross the 7 percent electoral threshold. The Social Democratic Party, with a paltry 4.6 percent, came second; Ak Zhol was third with 3.2 percent; Aul and the Party of Patriots obtained 1.58 percent and 0.75 percent, respectively. The Communist Party of Kazakhstan boycotted the elections.

A survey by the Center for Social and Political Research (TSiPR) reported that 10.3 percent of respondents supported the Social Democratic Party and only 63.6 percent supported Nur Otan, which casts doubt on official figures that show Nur Otan's dominance and the failure of the opposition to cross the 7 percent threshold. According to the Central Election Committee, the election turnout was 65 percent. Turnout was high in most rural areas and small towns, but only 22.5 percent in Almaty and 40.5 percent in Astana. The TSiPR survey suggests that turnout was only 16.5 percent in Almaty, which also questions the legitimacy of the elections. In the absence of a level playing field, the pro-government forces have been able to use administrative and media resources to deny opposition parties representation in the Parliament.

Taskyn Rakhimbekov, head of the National Network of Independent Observers, reported vote-counting violations in nine regions. The Social Democratic Party claims that it won the seats in Almaty and has filed hundreds of election-related lawsuits with the Office of the Prosecutor General and the Central Election Committee.[4]

Independent analysts and critics of the ruling establishment see the rise of Nur Otan as a "resurrection of the Communist Party of Kazakhstan." Like the old Communist Party, Nur Otan is becoming the all-encompassing party that has pushed out all other parties from the political arena. It has exploited its incumbency and control over the administrative resources and propaganda channels to appeal to state officials, media, prominent businesses, public figures, and university and school administrators. Nazarbaev and key figures within the ruling authorities claim that a one-party system is perfectly conducive to providing stability and aiding democratization.

Although Kazakhstan has liberalized the procedures for registering political parties and contesting elections, the opposition parties Atameken and Alga have not been allowed to register. Kazakhstan has not adopted any of the substantive recommendations made by the OSCE/ODIHR in its final report on the 2004 parliamentary elections concerning improvements to the Law on Elections.

As a result of the May 2007 amendments, elections in Kazakhstan are increasingly less democratic. The requirement that all candidates be elected according to a party list on a proportional basis has eliminated elections by single-mandate vote. Such a system privileges loyalty to the party over accountability to the electorate. Second, in requiring candidates to be members of parties, citizens are denied the right to seek election as individuals or as independent nominees. Third, the 7 percent threshold is too high in a country where the ruling party already controlled all but one seat in the previous Mazhilis elected in 2004. Finally, the provision to reserve nine seats for ethnic minorities to be elected by the APK fails to provide for a democratic method of representing ethnic minorities. The APK is an appointed body under the chairmanship of the president that has no legislative power or popular mandate.

Civil Society

1999	2001	2002	2003	2004	2005	2006	2007	2008
5.00	5.00	5.50	5.50	5.50	5.50	5.75	5.75	5.50

After bringing the Parliament, political parties, and regional and local governments under its control and driving the opposition out of the formal political process, the Nazarbaev government is now focused on co-opting independent nongovernmental organizations (NGOs) and other civil society groups in support of its agenda.

The National Commission on Democratization and Civil Society appointed by the president holds periodic meetings with pro-regime parties and quasi-governmental NGOs as it urges all parties and NGOs to engage in "constructive cooperation" with the government. Nazarbaev has emphasized the need to establish an "efficient cooperation between state bodies and NGOs to lay a firm foundation for the development of civil society" in Kazakhstan.

The head of the presidential human rights commission and a parliamentary deputy, Sagynbek Tursunov, pledged to adopt a five-year national plan of action on "protecting human rights on the basis of OSCE recommendations."[5] In making such a pledge, the government presented itself as a staunch champion of democracy, human rights, and civil society while treating the opposition, genuinely independent NGOs, and civil society groups as either causing disruption in the pursuit of these aims or simply incapable of devising effective policies.

According to the president's official Web site (www.akorda.kz), there are about 5,000 registered NGOs in Kazakhstan. Most of these are quasi-governmental, propped up to compete with independent NGOs in obtaining grants. Only about 1,000 are active, and only about 150 of these are able to make a positive impact. Official figures, which exaggerate the activities and contribution of the nongovernmental sector, mention that about 200,000 people are involved in the NGO sector, of whom about 40,000 are full-time employees; in addition, about 1 million are volunteers and about 2 million receive various services. The largest proportion of NGOs are environmental (15 percent), followed by children and youth (13.6 percent), women's rights (13.3 percent), health and medical (13.1 percent), and education (12.5 percent). NGOs active in civil rights issues have a smaller share, about 7.6 percent.[6]

The United States Agency for International Development (USAID) has been the largest single-country donor, providing over US$500 million in programs to develop Kazakhstan's economic sector, health care system, and democratic institutions. In 2007, it invested about US$15 million, with half going toward the development of the economy, whereas 17 percent was allocated to human development and about 34 percent to democratic governance.[7]

The NGO sustainability index for Eurasia released by USAID in May 2007 showed a marked improvement in the financial viability of NGOs in Kazakhstan, their public image, and the legal environment but also noted relatively poor infrastructural capacity and advocacy. Kazakhstan's score remained at 4.1 (on a scale of 1 to 10, a higher score representing lower sustainability).[8]

Within the corporate sector, Kazkommertsbank, the country's largest bank, offers funds to aid NGOs and civil society. The dependence of the corporate sector and private businesses on government patronage pressures them to fund government-organized NGOs (GONGOs) or to invest in social or community development projects. However, there are reports of private businesses covertly funding civil rights advocacy campaigns and independent media channels.

Less than 10 percent of NGOs are engaged in civil liberties, human rights, and minority protection issues. Since the so-called color revolutions in Georgia and Ukraine, and the opening ("Tulip Revolution") in Kyrgyzstan, human rights NGOs have become targets of considerable negative publicity by the national media. Nazarbaev has warned NGOs obtaining foreign funding that they will be "closely watched," an instruction followed diligently by the National Security Service and the prosecutor general.

Although Kazakhstan's political establishment takes credit for preserving "interethnic peace and reconciliation," it tightly regulates public expression of ethnic and religious claims by placing restrictions on the right to public assembly. Ethnic groups are encouraged to organize into "official" national-cultural centers, which are required to work closely with the APK, chaired by the president.

Ethnic Kazakhs form slightly less than 60 percent of the population. Their share is increasing as the share of Slavs and other Russian-speaking groups, currently about a third of the population, declines. Kazakhstan's political elite, government, and administrative structures do have a multiethnic profile; however, the fact that non-Kazakhs may hold positions in the government or administration is no indicator of influence, since these individuals do not truly represent their ethnic constituencies. Instead, a willingness and ability to operate within the regime-controlled patronage networks is crucial to acquiring a prominent public post.

Kazakhstan's self-acclaimed record of "ethnic harmony" began showing cracks during the year as local clashes in rural areas escalated into ethnic conflicts. Clashes between Kazakhs and Kurds in the village of Mayatas in south Kazakhstan forced most local Kurds to flee the village as the local authorities failed to provide security and protection to the minorities.[9]

In the village of Malovodnoe in the Almaty oblast, a minor brawl between an ethnic Kazakh and a Chechen grew into a street fight involving 200 people from the two communities, with 5 dead and a large number of Chechens fleeing the village. The district court imposed severe prison sentences on 3 men convicted of hooliganism but spared local officials. In both cases, the complicity of local officials exacerbated social tension and brought the ethnic factor into focus.

Using the rhetoric of religious goodwill and tolerance, Nazarbaev has built a new Catholic Church, a synagogue, a Russian Orthodox Church, and a giant mosque in the new capital, Astana. The multimillion-dollar Pyramid of Peace and Reconciliation in Astana is the latest and most ostentatious monument to Kazakhstan's tolerance, but the reality on the ground is rather different. In September 2006, local authorities of Karasai region in the Almaty oblast razed 13 houses on a farm belonging to members of Kazakhstan's local Society for Krishna Consciousness (SKC). Local sources suggest that a member of the president's family had plans to acquire the plot to develop a commercial center.[10] SKC members have sought mediation from the Almaty Helsinki Committee, OSCE, and other international organizations. Ninel Fokina of the Almaty Helsinki Committee noted that while the state may show a greater tolerance for Sunni Islam and Orthodox Christianity, all other religious congregations are looked upon as undesirable and constituting a threat.[11]

Like political parties, all NGOs, public associations, and religious bodies are required by law to register with the Ministry of Justice. The National Security Service monitors pro-opposition political parties and journalists, independent or foreign-funded NGOs, religious bodies, and missionaries. It has intensified surveillance over non-traditional religious practices and congregations, which include the Hare Krishna community, Jehovah's Witnesses, a number of Protestant and Catholic denominations, and Muslim groups not affiliated with the Spiritual Administration of Muslims of Kazakhstan.[12] The Ministries of Justice and the Interior, together with the National Security Service, have created special divisions to work with various religious denominations.

Some 30 suspected members of the banned Islamist group Hizb ut-Tahrir went on trial in Karaganda on charges of attempting to overthrow the government to create an Islamic caliphate, though the group has insisted it uses nonviolent means. Many members have reportedly cooperated with the authorities and pledged to renounce the group's ideology and abandon the party.[13] It is hard to ascertain if such cooperation indeed occurred or whether the defendants were arrested without any substantive evidence and then released.

Independent Media

1999	2001	2002	2003	2004	2005	2006	2007	2008
5.50	6.00	6.00	6.25	6.50	6.50	6.75	6.75	6.75

Most of the media in Kazakhstan are privately owned but not independent. The leading financial groups entrenched in the ruling circles own an overwhelming proportion of the country's mass media and seek to render the small number of independent media outlets noncompetitive. These business interests attempt to lure away talent from independent media channels through offers of greater material and personal security, and they portray pro-opposition media as lacking in responsibility and professionalism. Although media outlets may compete intensely with one another, they do not engage in genuinely investigative work and do not criticize the president, his close family, or other top figures within the regime.

By exerting firm control over the country's resource base and legal framework, the Nazarbaev regime has enacted favorable laws and adopted numerous other informal mechanisms of wielding control over the national media. The restrictive Media Law of 2005 and subsequent amendments in 2006 impose further limits on the modicum of independent media in the country. If in the past various banned media had resurfaced under new names, the 2006 amendments—criticized by local and international press and human rights organizations, the OSCE, and the international nonprofit Committee to Protect Journalists—closed those loopholes and allow the government to deny registration to news outlets.[14]

Other legal provisions, such as the Law on National Security passed in 2005 and the criminal code of Kazakhstan, already contain severe limits on the independence of media. Article 318 of the criminal code penalizes a person who "insults the honor and dignity of the president" and is used routinely to prosecute independent journalists by bringing charges of defamation. Influential members of the government have successfully won libel suits against pro-opposition media. Kazakhstan's highly restrictive Media Law and compliant judicial system fully protect top members of the government as they render independent and pro-opposition media highly vulnerable.

Further amendments to the law have sought to criminalize any public criticism of Kazakhstani officials as slander. By urging for measures to make journalists responsible for spreading discrediting information, the Ministries of the Interior and Culture and Information are seeking to further strengthen the clauses protecting government officials from public inquiry or criticism. While censorship is banned by the Constitution, Kazakhstani authorities continue to monitor all media and Internet activities and have erected numerous legal and informal mechanisms protecting against any threat that a truly independent media might pose.[15] Article 164 of the criminal code banning public calls for social hatred was invoked several times to restrict election campaigns.

Competition among leading financial groups for control of the media market became more intense after the ouster of Aliev and the political marginalization of Nazarbaeva. Nazarbaeva founded the privatized but state-controlled news agency Khabar in 1996, serving initially as its director and then as a board member. Kazakhstan's minister of culture and information, Ermukhamet Ertysbaev, has reiterated plans to nationalize the Khabar television channel by suggesting that the state may buy back all privately held shares. However, he has come under sustained criticism for his unrelenting attacks on independent media.

According to the 2007 Worldwide Press Freedom Index of the international media watchdog Reporters Without Borders, Kazakhstan ranked 131 out of 167 countries (behind Tajikistan and Kyrgyzstan, though ahead of Uzbekistan and Turkmenistan).[16]

Reporters Without Borders and the OSCE/ODIHR expressed concern at the biased media coverage of the August 2007 parliamentary elections and noted numerous cases of pressure, self-censorship, violations of electoral legislation, and bias in favor of the ruling party.[17] Although the government for the first time provided broadcasting of debates with all parties represented on the public TV Kazakhstan 1 and Khabar, the broadcasts credited Nur Otan with achieving the country's high degree of economic success and stability and portrayed the opposition as bent on causing social upheaval through misguided calls for reforms and change. The Social Democratic Party, the leading opposition party, received very little coverage on the public TV stations.

In 2007, an Internet scandal involved the sensational posting of recorded conversations purportedly among top government figures discussing illicit campaign-financing methods on pro-opposition Web sites (www.kub.kz and www.inkar.kz, an internet radio outlet). The tapes contain a voice purported to be Nazarbaev's, instructing an aide to induce some of the country's most influential entrepreneurs to make large-scale "donations" to Nur Otan.[18] A third site (www.geo.kz) published the transcripts. The government reacted by imposing de facto censorship over the Internet. Two of the sites changed names (www.kub.info and www.inkar.info), and all three have been unavailable to users inside Kazakhstan by normal means, though they can be accessed through proxy servers.

The opposition newspapers *Svoboda Slova*, *Vzglyad*, *Taszhargan*, and *Respublika*, which also published articles on the leaked transcripts, underwent numerous inspections ranging from tax and audit to fire and safety, and were unable to secure a printing house for their next issues. Vyacheslav Abramov of the Coalition for Torture Prevention in Central Asia noted that the media crackdown was unprecedented in its intensity and scale and extended to more media outlets than similar actions in the past.[19]

According to estimates by the *CIA World Factbook*, Kazakhstan had about 1.24 million Internet users in 2006.[20] As Kazakhstan's urban middle class and student population increasingly turn to the Internet to obtain news, the Kazakhstani authorities have made various efforts to control the spread of information on the Internet. Kazakhstan's law requires all Internet domain names to be registered in Kazakhstan (.kz), mentioning that non-Kazakh domains may be denied registration.

The state-owned Kazakhtelecom and its six subsidiaries are the monopoly Internet service providers, which regularly block access to opposition Web sites and apply technical controls. Kub and other popular Internet sites publishing materials by the opposition, are registered outside of Kazakhstan.

Bloggers publishing items critical of the government have been charged under clauses protecting the president's "honor and dignity." Nurlan Alimbekov, a philosophy teacher in south Kazakhstan, has been subjected to psychiatric examination since his arrest for allegedly inciting "interethnic hatred" in various e-mail correspondences. His defenders claim that he is being persecuted for having posted materials on the Internet site www.centrasia.ru, which offers widespread coverage to the views of independent and opposition journalists.[21]

Local Democratic Governance

1999	2001	2002	2003	2004	2005	2006	2007	2008
n/a	n/a	n/a	n/a	n/a	6.25	6.25	6.25	6.25

Kazakhstan has a unitary administrative framework, with the central government exerting top-down control over regional and local bodies. The Constitution does not provide for elections of oblast, regional, or local administrative heads (*akims*). All *akims* are part of the unified system of executive power, are appointed by the president and the government of the republic, and may, regardless of the level they occupy, be dismissed by the president at his discretion. The *akims* at lower administrative levels (towns and villages) report to their superior administrative heads.

In theory, local legislative councils, or *maslihats*, whose members are elected for a five-year term, serve as the only outlet for civic participation; in practice, they are accountable to the appointed *akims*. *Maslihats* serve primarily as rubber-stamp bodies to approve acts by local executives. This top-down control allows patronage and personal influence to define the powers of the incumbent. It is estimated that about 44 percent of Kazakhstan's rural population lack any say in local affairs.[22] Each oblast *maslihat*, and those of Almaty and Astana, nominate two members each to the Senate.

In August 2007, *maslihat* elections were held in 3,334 constituencies: 550 in oblasts, Astana, and Almaty; 625 in cities; and 2,159 in regions. These were held simultaneously with the parliamentary elections. Not only did this create some confusion among voters who took part in two different polls on the same day, but it resulted in the local elections being overshadowed by the parliamentary ones.

At the regional level, *akims* are appointed on the approval of *maslihats*. Under the constitutional amendments adopted in May 2007, regional and city *maslihats* now have the right of refusal when the president nominates an *akim* of a province or city. The number of no-confidence votes required to oust a sitting *akim* has been reduced from two-thirds to one-fifth of *maslihat* members. Given the nominal role assigned to *maslihats* in regions and the patronage exerted by *akims*, it is unlikely that *maslihats* play any significant part in defining the composition of local government.

As Nazarbaev remains opposed to holding direct elections for local and regional *akims* and granting local autonomy, discussion on the subject is virtually moot. Galymzhan Zhakiyanov, founder of the opposition Democratic Choice of Kazakhstan and a popular former *akim* of Pavlodar jailed for alleged misuse of office, has been the most prominent advocate of direct elections of *akims* and greater autonomy for oblasts.

Even if direct elections were introduced under the current framework, they are unlikely to have a democratizing effect as long as a single party dominates the entire political landscape. In addition, the incumbent *akims* and their patrons, together with members of the Central Election Committee and the District Election Committee, wield enormous influence in the nomination of candidates.

The lack of financial autonomy for local bodies is another serious limitation. The central government determines taxation rates and budgetary regulations. Although regional governments own over 80 percent of all state enterprises, the law limits local governments' control over the rates for local taxes, including property and vehicle taxes. Local governments are allowed to keep all fines for environmental pollution but are required to transfer other revenues to their higher authorities. Oblasts are not allowed to keep their surplus budgets, which are forfeited to needier ones.

The *akims* in oil-rich oblasts, which have attracted the most foreign investment, exert a greater control over budgetary matters mainly by extracting significant contributions from investors to various "social and welfare projects" and thus informally negotiating revenue-sharing rates with the central government. But this arrangement appears to be based largely on the personal standing of the *akim* and has no institutional repercussions. The oblast *akims* have shown no inclination to share powers or revenues with the lower-level city and village governments.[23]

The government's measures to promote "legalization of property," which in theory enables citizens to legalize private houses and *dachas* built in past years when a proper legal framework for ownership did not exist, have produced numerous disputes between citizens and local authorities on their actual interpretation and implementation. The inhabitants of the Shanyryk and Bakay shantytowns in Almaty continued their civic and legal action against the local *akimat* (council) decision to demolish their "illegal" settlements in 2006. More than 100 houses were torn down, but the residents have yet to receive any compensation, and the standoff between the poor squatters and the city administration continues.

Settlement dwellers and local civil rights groups blame the city administration for illegally clearing the slums to acquire the land for large commercial complexes. Aron Atabek, a religious activist and a longtime critic of the government, set up a group called the Land and Dwelling Committee, dedicated to promoting the rights of the homeless, and led protests in Shanyrak and Bakay in 2006. He was sentenced to 18 years in prison in October 2007 for disrupting law and order, allegedly triggering the death of a policeman during the protests.

Civil rights activists point out that while the local administration has allowed members of the elite to legalize houses and *dachas* built in posh parts of Almaty without obtaining proper authorization, poor residents have faced obstacles from local authorities in legalizing their dwellings. Almaty's *akim*, Imangali Tasmagambetov, offered up to US$4 billion in compensation to some 2,000 owners of luxury homes on the mountain slopes of Almaty, which are within an area now defined as a conservation zone and will be demolished to prevent further environmental damage.[24]

Judicial Framework and Independence

1999	2001	2002	2003	2004	2005	2006	2007	2008
5.50	5.75	6.00	6.25	6.25	6.25	6.25	6.25	6.25

Kazakhstan's strong executive system based on presidential patronage recognizes the separation of the three branches of power. Yet in practice, both the judiciary and the legislature remain loyal to the executive headed by the president. The judiciary seeks to protect the interests of the state and its functionaries rather than those of individuals, minorities, and the weaker strata of society.

Kazakhstan's Constitution makes formal mention of the independence of the judiciary without providing any mechanisms for safeguarding it. The Constitution spells out an elaborate procedure for appointing judges in which the president proposes nominees for the Supreme Court, who are then approved by the Senate. These nominees are recommended by the Supreme Judicial Council, which comprises the chair of the Constitutional Council, the chair of the Supreme Court, the prosecutor general, the minister of justice, senators, judges, and others appointed by the president. The president may remove judges, except members of the Supreme Court, on the recommendation of the minister of justice.

In order to combat deeply entrenched corruption within the judicial system, Kazakhstan has continued to invest efforts and resources in improving the training of judges and increasing their remuneration. Supreme Court judges receive higher salaries than government ministers. The two main associations of independent lawyers are the Association of Lawyers of Kazakhstan and the Legal Development of Kazakhstan.

All judges are required to attend the Judicial Academy, set up with help from the OSCE/ODIHR in 2004. Having advocated the introduction of jury trials, the OSCE academy is working to reform the criminal justice system and penitentiary legislation. Among the major proposals currently under discussion is the transfer of powers of arrest from the prosecutor's office to the judiciary.[25]

Kazakhstan began holding jury trials in April 2007. The jury of 11 is selected by a computer program from a list of eligible persons, with several exceptions (such as public servants, police officers, military personnel, lawyers, persons, criminal history, those who know the accused personally, and those who are under 25 years old). Kazakhstan has adopted the continental, or Franco-German, model in which the presiding judge reviews the case along with jurors and joins them in the final decision-making process.

If conducted properly, jury trials can play a vital role in reducing graft and corruption, reduce the waiting period for cases, and help to establish judicial independence, transparency, and accountability in a system where citizens tend to distrust the courts. So far, no jury selection mechanism exists to balance language, gender, and ethnic criteria, and the number of criminal cases involving juries is still limited.

Kazakhstan has a National Human Rights Commission headed by the ombudsman, who has the right to participate in court review of cases but is officially barred from any "interference with the work of either the police or the judicial system." As a presidential appointee, the ombudsman lacks an impartial image or the support of civil society and human rights activists.

While Kazakhstan's criminal justice system is undergoing important reforms, the judiciary continues a checkered record in handling cases related to civil liberties, political freedom, independent media, and human rights issues. It has convicted all major political or public figures brought to trial on politically motivated charges (the trial *in absentia* of ex-premier Akezhan Kazhegeldin in 2000, opposition leaders Ablyazov and Zhakiyanov and journalist Sergei Duvanov in 2003) without credible evidence or proper procedures.

In December 2006, the Supreme Court upheld the verdict of a regional court that found former security officer Rustam Ibragimov guilty of killing opposition leader Altynbek Sarsenbaev and two of his aides and resulted in a death sentence. It also sentenced Ibragimov's nine co-defendants to prison terms of 3 to 20 years. Since Kazakhstan has now abolished the death penalty, Ibragimov is likely to serve a life sentence. The trial *in absentia* of Aliev and his associates brought the role of the judiciary under scrutiny once again.

Corruption

1999	2001	2002	2003	2004	2005	2006	2007	2008
6.00	6.25	6.25	6.25	6.50	6.50	6.50	6.50	6.50

According to the 2007 Corruption Perceptions Index (CPI) published by Transparency International, Kazakhstan's score of 2.1 put it on a par with Azerbaijan, Belarus, Kyrgyzstan, and Tajikistan, though behind Russia. In the 2006 edition of the CPI, Kazakhstan's score of 2.6 was better than that of resource-rich Russia,

Azerbaijan, and the rest of the Central Asian states. Nonetheless, these differences are marginal, since any score of 5.0 or below indicates a serious corruption problem. The index defines corruption as the abuse of public office for private gain and measures the degree to which corruption is perceived to exist among a country's public officials and politicians.

The National Security Service and Office of the Prosecutor General intensified efforts in 2007 to expose a vast array of corrupt practices and arrested officials at various levels of the administration. It claimed to have "uncovered" 657 cases of corruption in 2007, in which 469 officials faced "administrative and disciplinary charges." That figure includes 95 local government officials, 2 judges, 2 court administrators, and 5 prosecutors. The corruption cases resulted in administrative punishment of 102 officials and criminal convictions of another 128. Its year-end report also noted significant success in curtailing the activities of "organized criminal groups" engaged in illegal transnational trade and claimed that its special operations had also foiled a major smuggling operation of "luxury cars stolen from European states and Russia."[26] It also uncovered a case of embezzlement involving the alleged misuse of 142 million tenge (over US$1 million) within the Defense Ministry's main intelligence directorate.

Top officials in the National Security Service and the Office of the Prosecutor General are appointed by the government and remain under the control of the president, which makes it impossible for them to function as independent bodies. Charges of corruption and misuse of office tend to be leveled against highly placed government figures only after these individuals enter into a personal or political rivalry with ruling elites or attempt to challenge Nazarbaev's authority.

The focal point of anticorruption inquiries in 2007 was the various financial scandals afflicting Nurbank, the country's fourth-largest bank, and Rakhat Aliev, the president's son-in-law. The authorities charged Aliev and his associates with the "disappearance" of about 11 billion tenge (US$90 million) from the bank, among other criminal activities. Aliev had been a highly controversial figure who alienated top political elites and rival financial groups by using his family connections to rapidly accumulate wealth and political influence. A group of entrepreneurs—including former opposition leader Mukhtar Ablyazov, now chairman of TuranAlem bank, and Grigory Marchenko, former head of the National Bank—urged the president to take action against Aliev and his associates, who they claimed were terrorizing and victimizing various businesses.

Aliev has claimed that the government illegally seized his assets worth US$300 million. Kazakhstan's Financial Oversight Agency authorized the transfer of 36 percent of Aliev's shares in Nurbank to Dariga Nazarbaeva and the couple's son, Nuraly, aged 23, who is chairman of Nurbank. With the Nazarbaev family remaining in charge of the bank's assets, prospects of an independent and impartial investigation are remote. As a regime insider, Aliev may also prove critical in the "Kazakhgate" trial, in which the American businessman James Giffen is accused of passing US$80 million from U.S. oil companies to Nazarbaev and top officials in exchange for lucrative oil contracts in Kazakhstan. The trial has been marred by repeated delays but is set to reopen in early 2008.

The Kazakhstani government has joined various international anticorruption initiatives. These include the Anticorruption Initiative for Asia and the Pacific, launched by the Asian Development Bank and Organization for Economic Cooperation and Development, which also advocates working closely with NGOs and civil society groups.[27]

Kazakhstan established the National Oil Fund in 2001 to protect the economy from volatility in oil prices and to aid transparent management of oil revenues. While these grew to almost US$20 billion in 2007,[28] vital issues of transparency, management, and redistribution of fund revenues have not been addressed. The Parliament has no authority to investigate an audit of oil funds or to determine how and under what conditions the funds are to be used.

Kazakhstan has joined the Extractive Industries Transparency Initiative. However, it has yet to make a mandatory disclosure of oil revenues received by the treasury from leading oil companies or to involve independent NGOs in overseeing how oil revenues are managed. Kazakhstan Revenue Watch and others have criticized the government for insufficient backing of the initiative.

Combating Corruption Through Civic Education, a joint initiative of Transparency Kazakhstan, the local branch of Transparency International, and the Interlegal Foundation for Political and Legal Research, has had positive results in enhancing awareness about corruption at the grassroots level. The absence of an independent judicial system makes it impossible for ordinary citizens or independent NGOs to file corruption charges against high-ranking state officials. The prosecutor general, appointed by the president and not accountable to the government, handles inquiries into official corruption, in conjunction with the Ministries of Justice and the Interior.

▌ AUTHOR: BHAVNA DAVE

Bhavna Dave is a lecturer in the Department of Politics and chair of the Center on Contemporary Central Asia and the Caucasus at the School of Oriental and African Studies, University of London. She is the author of Kazakhstan: Ethnicity, Language, and Power *(RoutledgeCurzon, 2007).*

1   Vladimir Socor, "Kazakhstan's Oil Export Picture Detailed," *Eurasia Daily Monitor* 4, no. 190 (October 15, 2007), http://www.jamestown.org/edm/article.php?article_id=2372502, accessed on November 28, 2007.

2   "Kazakhstan: OSCE Chairmanship Undeserved: Kazakhstan's Chairmanship for 2010 Places OSCE Human Right Principles at Risk," Human Rights Watch, http://hrw.org/english/docs/2007/11/30/kazakh17458_txt.htm, accessed on November 28, 2007.

3   "Kazakh elections: progress and problems," OSCE, http://www.osce.org:80/item/25959.
     html, accessed on August 23 2007.

4   Yaroslav Razumov, "Oppozitsiia analiziruet itogi vyborov," [Opposition Analysis Results of
     the Elections], *Panorama*, August 31 2007, http://www.panorama.kz, accessed on September
     3, 2007.

5   "Kazakhstan, OSCE to Continue Election Cooperation," November 6, 2007, http://www.
     rferl.org/featuresarticle/2007/11/20f6c86f-ebff-4f62-ba1f-37a2548405b9.html, accessed on
     November 10, 2007.

6   "Non-governmental Organizations in Kazakhstan," Official site of the President of the
     Republic of Kazakhstan, http://www.akorda.kz/www/www_akorda_kz.nsf/sections?Open
     Form&id_doc=1FAF925742420565462572340019E82A&lang=en&L1=L1&L2=L1-5,
     accessed on December 10, 2007.

7   *The 2006 NGO Sustainability Index*, Kazakhstan, USAID, Washington, D.C., http://www.
     usaid.gov/locations/europe_eurasia/dem_gov/ngoindex/2006/kazakhstan.pdf; and http://
     centralasia.usaid.gov/page.php?page=article-73, accessed on December 12, 2007.

8   Ibid.

9   "Kazakhstan: Ethnic Clash a Worrying Sign," Institute of War and Peace Reporting,
     November 23, 2007, http://iwpr.net/?p=rca&s=f&o=340846&apc_state=henprca, accessed
     on November 30, 2007.

10   Igor Rotar and Felix Corley, "Kazakhstan: How far does tolerance of religious minorities go?"
     Forum 18 News Service. http://www.forum18.org/Archive.php?article_id=839, accessed on
     December 20, 2007.

11   Rinat Saidullin, "Izmenieniia v zakon a svobode veroispovedaniia vyzvali v Kazakhstane vplesk
     presledovanii posledovatelei netraditsionnykh religii" [Changes in the Law on Freedom of
     Conscience Evoke Persecution of Followers of Non-Traditional Religious Groups], Ferghana.
     ru. June 8, 2007, http://www.ferghana.ru/article.php?id=5176&print=1.

12   Ibid.

13   Roger McDermott, "Kazakhstan Cracking Down on Hizb-Ut-Tahrir," Eurasia Daily
     Monitor, http://www.jamestown.org/edm/article.php?article_id=2372390; "Central Asia:
     Hizb Ut-Tahrir Gains Support from Women," rferl.org, July 11, 2007.

14   "Kazakhstan: President Signs Restrictive Media Bill," Committee to Protect Journalists,
     http://www.cpj.org/news/2006/europe/kazakh05july06na.html.

15   Gulnoza Saidazimova, "Kazakhstan: More Media Silenced as High-Stakes Feud Continues,"
     Eurasianet.org, November 11, 2007, http://www.eurasianet.org/departments/insight/articles
     /pp111007_pr.shtml.

16   "East Asia and Middle East Have Worst Press Freedom Records," Reporters Without Borders,
     http://www.rsf.org/article.php3?id_article=11715.

17   "Kazakhstan's OSCE Presidency Opposed After Heavily Biased Election Coverage," August
     22, 2007, http://www.rsf.org/article.php3?id_article=23360.

18   Joanna Lillis, "Kazakhstan: Appearance of Damaging Audiotapes Perhaps Linked to Aliyev
     Trial," Eurasianet.org, November 19, 2007, http://www.eurasianet.org/departments/insight/
     articles/eav111907_pr.shtml.

19   Elina Karakulova, "Kazak Media Crackdown Counterproductive," IWPR, November 23,
     2007, http://iwpr.net/?p=rca&s=f&o=340842&apc_state=henprca.

20   The Central Intelligence Agency World Factbook, Kazakhstan. https://www.cia.gov/library/
     publications/the-world-factbook/geos/kz.html.

21   Rinat Saydullin, "Kazakhstan: molodoi filosof obvinyaetsia v razzhiganii rozni posredstvom
     lichnoi perepiski" [Kazakhstan: Young Philospher Is Accused of Inciting Discord Through
     Personal Correspondence], Ferghana.ru. http://www.ferghana.ru/article.php?id=5509.

22   Marianna Gurtovnik, "Decentralization Reforms in Kazakhstan and Kyrgyzstan: Slowly and Unsteadily," International Assessment and Strategy Center. http://www.strategycenter.net/research/pubID.116/pub_detail.asp.

23   Rustem Kadyrzhanov, "Decentralization and Local Self-Government in Kazakhstan: An Institutional Analysis," Paper presented at Indiana University Workshop in Political Theory and Policy Analysis, Spring 2005, www.indiana.edu/~workshop/colloquia/papers/rustem_paper.pdf, accessed on December 19, 2007.

24   Yaroslav Razumov, "Kazakhstan: One Law for the Rich," Institute of War and Peace Reporting, October 19, 2007, http://iwpr.net/?p=rca&s=f&o=339987&apc_state=henprca, accessed on December 20, 2007.

25   "OSCE Centre Supports Judicial Reform in Kazakhstan," OSCE, http://www.osce.org/item/27406.html, accessed on December 12, 2007.

26   "Kazakh National Security Body Uncovers Embezzlement in Defense Ministry," RFE/RL Newsline, December 28, 2007.

27   "ADB/OECD Anticorruption Initiative for Asia and the Pacific: Under the Action Plan's 3rd Implementation Cycle (2006–2009): Kazakhstan," OECD, http://www.oecd.org/dataoecd/2/30/36780320.pdf, accessed on December 12, 2007.

28   "Kazakh Oil Fund Seen at $26 bln at Year-end," Reuters. November 12, 2007, http://uk.reuters.com/article/oilRpt/idUKL1242527520071112.

KOSOVO/UNMIK-Administered

by Ilir Deda

Capital: Pristina
Population: 1.9 million
GDP/capita: US$1,990

The economic and social data above were taken from the *UNMIK Factsheet 2007.*

Nations in Transit Ratings and Averaged Scores

	Yugoslavia				Kosovo				
	1999	2001	2002	2003	2004	2005	2006	2007	2008
Electoral Process	5.50	4.75	3.75	3.75	5.25	4.75	4.75	4.75	4.50
Civil Society	5.25	4.00	3.00	2.75	4.25	4.00	4.25	4.25	4.00
Independent Media	5.75	4.50	3.50	3.25	5.50	5.50	5.50	5.50	5.50
Governance*	5.50	5.25	4.25	4.25	6.00	n/a	n/a	n/a	n/a
National Democratic Governance	n/a	n/a	n/a	n/a	n/a	5.75	5.75	5.75	5.50
Local Democratic Governance	n/a	n/a	n/a	n/a	n/a	5.50	5.50	5.50	5.50
Judicial Framework and Independence	5.75	5.50	4.25	4.25	6.00	5.75	5.75	5.75	5.75
Corruption	6.25	6.25	5.25	5.00	6.00	6.00	6.00	6.00	5.75
Democracy Score	5.67	5.04	4.00	3.88	5.50	5.32	5.36	5.36	5.21

* With the 2005 edition, Freedom House introduced separate analysis and ratings for national democratic governance and local democratic governance to provide readers with more detailed and nuanced analysis of these two important subjects.

NOTES: The ratings reflect the consensus of Freedom House, its academic advisers, and the author(s) of this report. The opinions expressed in this report are those of the author(s). The ratings are based on a scale of 1 to 7, with 1 representing the highest level of democratic progress and 7 the lowest. The Democracy Score is an average of ratings for the categories tracked in a given year.

In *Nations in Transit 2008*, Freedom House provides separate ratings for Serbia and Kosovo in order to provide a clearer picture of processes and conditions in the different administrative areas. Doing so does not indicate a position on the part of Freedom House regarding Kosovo's status during the study year.

EXECUTIVE SUMMARY

F ollowing the NATO air campaign against Serbian forces in the spring of 1999, which ended the war in Kosovo, the province was placed under the administration of the United Nations. Kosovo's institutional arrangements are governed by United Nations Security Council Resolution 1244, which established an interim international civilian administration: the United Nations Interim Administration Mission in Kosovo (UNMIK). The security of Kosovo is the responsibility of NATO's Kosovo Force (KFOR). The Constitutional Framework for Provisional Self-Government of Kosovo divides responsibilities between UNMIK and the Provisional Institutions of Self-Government (PISG) to develop self-government pending the final settlement of Kosovo's status.

Beginning in 2000, UNMIK worked with the political leadership of Kosovo to develop this framework, which enabled the holding of five democratic elections and the development of Kosovo's institutions. The outbreak of interethnic violence in March 2004—which led to 19 dead, the destruction of Kosovo Serb property, churches, and monasteries, and 4,000 displaced Serbs—worsened relations between Kosovo Albanian and Kosovo Serb communities. Serbia filled the vacuum by tightening its grip on Kosovo Serbs and strengthening parallel institutions in health care, education, and the judiciary. The violence also virtually ended Kosovo Serb participation in Kosovo's institutions. As a result, UNMIK began accelerating the transfer of competences to PISG, a process that was ongoing throughout 2007, and the international community began taking serious steps to finalize Kosovo's status.

Throughout 2007, Kosovo continued to be governed by UNMIK, KFOR, and the PISG. The year's top priorities were preserving stability, containing radical Kosovo Albanian elements, preventing violence, and maintaining political unity in Kosovo. The ongoing process of final status resolution overshadowed almost all other activities apart from general, municipal, and mayoral elections held on November 17, 2007. These elections changed Kosovo's political landscape and resulted in a triumph for the Democratic Party of Kosovo (PDK) and its leader, Hashim Thaqi.

National Democratic Governance. The negotiation process to determine Kosovo's political status was society's main focus during the year. At the center of the process were the UN-mandated *troika* (U.S., EU, and Russia) and the negotiating Unity Team, composed of the four main Kosovo Albanian political parties in the government and the opposition. The team was challenged by the Vetevendosje (Self-Determination) movement and war associations for failing to deliver a status resolution. The government, although weak, maintained stability and unity of the government and political parties through extensive efforts from the international community, especially the U.S. and EU diplomatic offices in Pristina. Nevertheless, 2007 saw the most open debates in the Parliament, with an increasing independence of parliamentarians debating beyond their party agendas. Overall, internal government functioning and coordination were strengthened. *Owing to the activities of the legislature and the improved functioning of government institutions, Kosovo's rating for national democratic governance improves from 5.75 to 5.50.*

Electoral Process. General, municipal, and mayoral elections were held on November 17, 2007 and were considered free and fair by observers. Some 40 percent of the Kosovar electorate voted, but there was virtual boycott by the Kosovo Serb community. These elections changed the political landscape of Kosovo. Hashim Thaqi and his PDK were the most-voted political leader and party, garnering 34.3 percent of the ballot. The late president Ibrahim Rugova's Democratic League of Kosovo (LDK) won 22.6 percent, losing for the first time after 18 years of being the largest Kosovo Albanian political party. A new electoral law featuring civil society's longtime vision for open electoral lists was adopted. The Transition Working Group on Elections, which included representatives from the government, the opposition, and civil society, agreed on the new electoral principles. Kosovo remained a single district, with open lists at both central and local levels; a 5 percent threshold to gain seats at the central level was established for Kosovo Albanian political parties; and for the first time, direct mayoral elections took place. For the first time since the end of the war, Kosovo saw immense involvement of civil society in monitoring the elections and in the entire electoral process. *Following changes to electoral laws in line with civil society demands, the elections were held in conformity with the Constitutional Framework, and independent Kosovar and international organizations deemed the entire process generally free and fair; thus, Kosovo's electoral process rating improves from 4.75 to 4.50.*

Civil Society. Kosovo's tradition of nongovernmental organizations extends back to 1989, when the Council for the Defense of Human Rights and Freedoms and other political organizations created a parallel system to oppose Serbia's oppressive policies. In 2007, Kosovo's civil society, showing increased vibrancy, actively promoted participation in elections and did not limit its activities solely to monitoring the election process. For example, Youth Initiative for Human Rights held public campaigns in most Kosovo municipalities encouraging youth to participate in the elections. The Democracy in Action coalition, apart from monitoring, undertook a public campaign to explain the benefits of voting. Civil society groups continued with their activities in the anticorruption field by monitoring the government and implementation of laws (especially the Law on Access to Public Documents), compliance with human rights, and the electoral process. *Owing to the sector's increased activities and impact, Kosovo's civil society rating improves from 4.25 to 4.00.*

Independent Media. The Independent Media Commission approved several pieces of secondary legislation, including an advertising code and regulations on cable broadcasting in Kosovo. The Press Council of Kosovo continued its restructuring to better prepare the institution for future operations. Journalists and editors are increasingly adhering to the council's code of conduct and its statute. However, 2007 was the first year that the government undertook steps to control the media, primarily the public broadcaster Radio Television of Kosovo, by terminating the service contract to collect the public broadcast fee from citizens. *Despite the continuing development of the legal framework and the birth of the Press Council of Kosovo, political pressure on the media by the government increased and offset the achievements; therefore, Kosovo's independent media rating remains at 5.50.*

Local Democratic Governance. Municipal assemblies and mayors changed after the municipal and mayoral elections on November 17, 2007. The PDK won relative or absolute majorities in 17 municipalities, LDK in 5, and the Alliance for the Future of Kosovo (AAK) in 3. After the mayoral runoff ballot on December 8, PDK won 16 mayoral posts, LDK 6, and AAK 3. LDK held on to power in the capital, Pristina, while other urban centers went to PDK and AAK. The weakness of local governance in Kosovo continued in 2007, with no increase in the independence of local authorities. Furthermore, the relationship between the central level and the municipal level needed to be further defined in terms of competences. Parallel administrative structures sponsored from Belgrade continued to operate in most predominantly Kosovo Serb municipalities, particularly in the fields of justice, education, health care, and the postal service. The split in the LDK and establishment of the Democratic League of Dardania reduced the majority that the former enjoyed in many municipalities, which worsened the functioning of a number of assemblies. The Kosovo Serb community at large relied on Serbia's institutions in Kosovo instead of the PISG. *Kosovo's rating for local democratic governance remains at 5.50.*

Judicial Framework and Independence. The strengthening of the judiciary in Kosovo continued in 2007. The process of promulgating laws improved, but implementation remained a chronic problem. The body of applicable laws in Kosovo is still a tangle of divided areas; this hampers the delivery of justice, as judges are not always certain of the legal basis for their decisions. The court system still features an insufficient number of judges and a weak Office of the Prosecutor General. Nevertheless, steps were taken in 2007 to improve the protection of witnesses, the Office of the Special Prosecutor was created, and several high-profile public cases were initiated. Procedures were not respected during the election of a Kosovar ombudsperson, causing concern and opposition from both Kosovar and international human rights organizations. *Kosovo's rating for judicial framework and independence remains at 5.75.*

Corruption. Corruption remains widespread in Kosovo. The Office of the Auditor General continued publishing reports on massive abuse of public funds and procedures at PISG- and UNMIK-controlled institutions. The Anticorruption

Agency (AKK) became operational and submitted 47 cases to the Office of the Special Prosecutor. The AKK solved 61 cases, while 16 were pending at year's end. The AKK took steps to conform with the Law on Public Procurement and annulled tenders amounting to €7 million (US$10.3 million) where regulations had been violated. The UN Office of Internal Oversight Services began investigating top UNMIK officials, while UNMIK police and the Kosovo Police Service arrested high-level PISG officials suspected of money laundering. *Despite the general lack of political will to fight corruption, 2007 featured some of the most concrete anticorruption activities and successes to date in Kosovo; thus, the corruption rating improves from 6.00 to 5.75.*

Outlook for 2008. The new Assembly of Kosovo will declare independence in 2008. The new PDK-LDK coalition government led by Hashim Thaqi will face many challenges, which must be tackled with the help of NATO-led KFOR troops in the security sector and the new EU mission of rule of law and security. Further challenges will come from the reaction of Serbia and Kosovo Serbs to Kosovo's declaration of independence, the containment of Kosovo Albanian radical groups, and possible social unrest. In other sectors, the government must tackle corruption, strengthen the functioning of institutions, and take decisive steps to lay a foundation for economic development. The position of civil society and the media vis-à-vis Kosovo's new leadership will be a crucial independent voice outside of government institutions, in light of the currently weak political opposition.

MAIN REPORT

National Democratic Governance

1999	2001	2002	2003	2004	2005	2006	2007	2008
Y u g o s l a v i a				n/a	5.75	5.75	5.75	5.50

Kosovo began 2007 awaiting the resolution of its final status. The United Nations Interim Administration Mission in Kosovo (UNMIK) and the government of Kosovo began preparations for the handover of UNMIK responsibilities, including the formation of five technical working groups in the areas of law, governance, civil administration, legislation, economy, and property. At the same time, preparatory work began on a post-UNMIK constitutional arrangement and elections. The Special Representative of the UN Secretary General in Kosovo (SRSG) chaired the local steering group on future international arrangements, which included representatives from the Office of the Special Envoy of the Secretary General for the future status process for Kosovo, the preparation teams of the future International Civilian Office, and the future European Security and Defense Policy Mission.

The Assembly of Kosovo showed progress in its work in 2007. There were no major violations of Assembly rules and procedures, while an increased number of plenary debates, public hearings, interpellations, consultations, and opposition comments on draft laws were received. This increase in activity occurred thanks to newly elected Assembly Speaker and longtime Democratic League of Kosovo activist Kole Berisha. Under his leadership, the Assembly also strengthened the scrutiny of its budgetary expenditures. During this time, the Assembly adopted 25 laws and reviewed 11 draft laws.

In March 2007, the UN Special Envoy for Kosovo, former Finnish president Martti Ahtisaari, presented his plan for Kosovo's final status to the secretary general. This plan comprised two documents: *Report of the Special Envoy of the Secretary General on Kosovo's Future Status* and the *Comprehensive Proposal for the Kosovo Status Settlement*. Ahtisaari recommended that "Kosovo's status should be independence supervised by the international community."[1] The plan envisaged the end of UN Resolution 1244, hence the end of Serbia's sovereignty over Kosovo. It provided for UNMIK's departure and transfer of its remaining competences to the Kosovo government and mandated the European Union (EU) to deploy a political mission to oversee implementation of the settlement—the International Civilian Office/European Union Special Representative—and a police and justice mission to strengthen the rule of law, as well as a continuing military mission to guarantee overall security under a NATO-led International Military Presence.

Kosovo Serbs would enjoy a high degree of autonomy within their municipalities and relations with Belgrade, while religious and cultural sites would be protected with the creation of special zones around churches and monasteries of the Serbian Orthodox Church. The Kosovo Protection Corps—a civilian emergency force viewed as a future army by Kosovo Albanians—would be disbanded and a new protection force created. The International Civil Representative (ICR) would have the power to ensure Kosovo's implementation of its obligations by correcting or annulling inappropriate laws and sanctioning or removing disobedient officials. The ICR would also vet the appointment of some key Kosovo officeholders, while the office's deputy would command the EU Security and Defense Policy Mission (comprising police, justice, customs, border control, and prison service personnel). The ICR would have the authority to step in directly to ensure the maintenance and promotion of the rule of law, public order, and security where necessary. After two years, an International Steering Group, consisting of the Contact Group (United States, United Kingdom, France, Germany, Italy, and Russia), the EU Council, the European Commission, and NATO, would review progress and the ICR's mandate.

The Vetevendosje (Self-Determination) movement, Kosovo Liberation Army (KLA) war veterans' associations, and other Kosovo Albanian radical groups capitalized on Ahtisaari's concerns over the proposed disbandment of the Kosovo Protection Corps and decentralization. Some Kosovo Albanian and all Kosovo Serb groups rejected the settlement proposal, though for opposite reasons. For Kosovo Albanians, the proposal did not offer a clear independence and created a dysfunctional state owing to decentralization and other minority provisions, while Kosovo Serbs argued that the proposal contained insufficient minority protections and clear independence.

On February 10, Vetevendosje held a protest against the plan, the Kosovo negotiating team, UNMIK, and the future-envisaged International Civilian Office, with a stated violent intent. Thousands of protesters attacked the police and attempted to enter Kosovo government buildings. Two protesters died from rubber-bullet wounds to the head by the Romanian UNMIK police members. (The police commissioner subsequently banned the use of rubber bullets in Kosovo, and the UN Department of Peacekeeping Operations temporarily suspended the use of rubber bullets in all peacekeeping missions worldwide pending the outcome of the review.) In a rare move of accountability, Minister of the Interior Fatmir Rexhepi and the UNMIK police commissioner resigned, while Vetevendosje leader Albin Kurti was arrested and placed under house arrest. Vetevendosje rallies in March and June had low attendance and were peaceful.

Kosovo's Unity Team fully accepted the Ahtisaari proposal, and on April 5, the Assembly of Kosovo approved the future status report, stating that it represented "a fair and balanced solution in accordance with the will of the people of Kosovo." The Assembly committed itself to full implementation of the settlement proposal, adding that if it was endorsed by the Security Council, it would be considered legally binding for Kosovo. Assembly members also pledged to cooperate with the future international civilian and security presences envisaged in the proposal. On April 14, Unity Team members President Fatmir Sejdiu, Prime Minister Agim Ceku, Assembly Speaker Kole Berisha, and Democratic Party of Kosovo (PDK) and Reformist Party (ORA) leaders Hashim Thaqi and Veton Surroi signed the Pocantico Declaration, in which they agreed to remain united during the 120-day transition period envisaged in the settlement proposal. Further, on June 13, the Assembly announced a public design competition for the flag and emblem of Kosovo, following criteria drafted by the U.S. diplomatic office in Pristina.

Russia's threat to use its veto at the UN Security Council prevented the adoption of the Ahtisaari proposal for supervised independence for Kosovo. Russia claimed that Kosovo's case could not be viewed as *sui generis*. Further, Russia claimed that the Ahtisaari plan did not have the backing of Serbia and that no territory of a sovereign state can become independent without the consent of the mother state. The United States and the European Union claimed that Kosovo's case was unique owing to the disintegration of Yugoslavia, discrimination of the 1990s and Milosevic's policies of ethnic cleansing, NATO's intervention, and the period of UN administration. The Contact Group and the secretary general called for a new 120-day negotiation period beginning August 1 between Serbia and Kosovo about the status. These new negotiations were mediated by a U.S.-EU-Russian *troika* to secure a compromise solution between Pristina and Belgrade.

The Unity Team came under increasing pressure to resign and was criticized by the media, civil society, KLA veterans' associations, and intra-party factions for not having achieved results on the independence of Kosovo. Vetevendosje continued with inflammatory rhetoric, claiming that the Unity Team would lead to Kosovo's reintegration with Serbia. At the same time, divergences appeared within the team on which steps Kosovo should take. Prime Minister Agim Ceku and opposition ORA leader Veton Surroi called for Kosovo's institutions to set a date and declare independence by December 2007, opposed by President Fatmir Sejdiu and PDK leader Hashim Thaqi. KLA veterans' associations issued threats of a new war. While Thaqi engaged in pacifying the KLA organizations, Surroi undertook a "long walk" throughout Kosovo during August 2007, explaining to citizens the stages of the final status process. Prime Minister Ceku continued with the rhetoric of a unilateral Kosovar declaration of independence, and the Unity Team and the SRSG agreed on holding Kosovar general, municipal, and mayoral elections on November 17, 2007.

Electoral Process

1999	2001	2002	2003	2004	2005	2006	2007	2008
Y u g o s l a v i a				5.25	4.75	4.75	4.75	4.50

With the final status process deadlocked, the question of the legitimacy of Kosovo's institutions after November 2007 arose. According to the Constitutional Framework for Provisional Self-Government of Kosovo, the mandate of Kosovo's Assembly would expire in November, while the municipal elections were overdue for the past year. The SRSG and the Unity Team, after consultations with international representatives in Kosovo and abroad and the Organization for Security and

Cooperation in Europe (OSCE), authorized the start of technical preparations for elections by Kosovo's Central Election Commission (CEC) and scheduled the elections for November 17. The ruling Democratic League of Kosovo (LDK) and the Alliance for the Future of Kosovo (AAK), as in 2006, were in favor of postponing the elections but accepted the decision, as did the PDK and Democratic League of Dardania (LDD). The ORA did not have a clear position.

The November elections changed the political landscape of Kosovo. The PDK won 37 out of 120 seats in the Assembly. The LDK gained 25 seats; Alliance for New Kosovo (AKR), 13; LDD, 11; and AAK, 10. The ORA did not pass the 5 percent threshold. The rest of the seats were split among the Kosovo Serb community (10 reserved seats) and other minority communities (10 reserved and 2 gained).

The elections were marked by low voter turnout of about 40 percent and a near complete boycott by the Kosovo Serb community; only about 2,000 Kosovo Serbs south of the Ibar River participated in the ballot. Some 97 political entities were certified to run, including 33 Kosovo Serb political entities, despite pressure from Belgrade to boycott the elections. Following pressure and intimidation, 4 Kosovo Serb political entities withdrew from the race on October 31.

Observers claimed that the elections were generally free and fair. However, the Elections Complaints and Appeals Commission (ECAC) invalidated ballots in 1.3 percent of the polling stations owing to fraud and voting manipulations, as well as 34,000 mailed votes. The ECAC did not organize a new round of voting at those stations, claiming that the re-vote would not influence the final results. Close to 3,000 observers from the nongovernmental organization (NGO) coalition Democracy in Action monitored the elections and were the first to publish the preliminary results with no observed major irregularities. However, other parties did report irregularities, and the CEC recounted the entire ballot to avoid accusations of fraud and manipulations.

In terms of party participation, for the first time, Kosovo Albanian political parties campaigned on issues of economic development. The PDK agreed to a pre-electoral coalition with four smaller parties—the Liberal Party of Kosovo, Democratic Alternative of Kosovo, Social-Democratic Party, and the more radical National Movement of Kosovo. The once dominant electorate of the LDK under Ibrahim Rugova split in four ways. Half voted for LDK, others for AKR and LDD, while some voters abstained. The LDK incorporated a part of the Christian Democratic Party of Kosovo within its ranks. LDK, AAK, and ORA ran a negative campaign, hoping to diminish AKR's growing popularity owing to its populist promise of new jobs. The ORA gained 4.1 percent of the votes, but despite faring well in the largest urban centers, it did not pass the 5 percent threshold, although it was represented in most municipalities.

The new governing coalition, as many Kosovo analysts speculated, was formed by PDK, LDK, and minority parties. Some diplomatic offices in Pristina attempted to bring in the AAK and create a broader coalition, which failed. Kosovo media reported that the PDK coalition formula would leave the post of president to the LDK and prime minister and Assembly Speaker to the PDK. The government would have two deputy prime ministers, one each from the PDK and LDK, while the PDK would have seven ministerial posts, the LDK five, and the minority parties three (two for Kosovo Serb parties and one for other minorities). The government was not yet created by the end of 2007 because of internal LDK conflicts.

The civil society's longtime vision for open electoral lists was adopted in early 2007. The Transition Working Group on Elections, which included representatives from the government, the opposition, and civil society, agreed on the new electoral principles. The SRSG promulgated three key regulations changing the existing electoral legislative framework. These regulations—on the CEC, on elections for the Assembly of Kosovo, and on municipal elections in Kosovo—took into account both the provisions in the Comprehensive Proposal for the Kosovo Status Settlement and the recommendations of the Transition Working Group on Elections.

A new CEC was formed with 12 members composed of the following: chairperson—deputy SRSG for institution building (head of the OSCE mission); deputy chairperson—nominated by the president of Kosovo from judges of the Supreme Court or district courts of Kosovo; 6 members nominated by the proportionally-largest political entities in the Assembly of Kosovo; 1 member nominated by consensus from the political entities representing the Kosovo Serb community; and 3 members nominated by the political entities representing other communities.

At the central level, Kosovo remained a single electoral district, with a proportional electoral system, open lists, and a 5 percent threshold required for Kosovo Albanian political parties to gain seats in the new Assembly. One hundred seats were directly elected, while 20 seats were reserved for political entities representing Serbian, Bosniak, Turkish, and REA (Romany, Balkan Egyptian, and Ashkali) communities. Voters were able to cast their ballots for political entities and up to 10 candidates on a single political entity's candidate list. There were two levels of municipal elections: the municipal assembly and mayor. The electoral system was the same as for the Kosovo Assembly but without a threshold. Mayoral elections were direct for the first time in Kosovo, using a two-round system if no candidate received more than 50 percent of the vote in the first round.

Civil Society

1999	2001	2002	2003	2004	2005	2006	2007	2008
Y u g o s l a v i a				4.25	4.00	4.25	4.25	4.00

Kosovo's civil society has developed in four main phases. The first began in 1989 as a reaction to Serbia's oppressive policies, featuring the creation of the Council for the Defense of Human Rights and Freedoms (CDHRF), the activities of Mother Theresa's Missionaries of Charity, and the organization of independent trade unions. The main focus of these organizations at the time was the protection of human rights and humanitarian efforts. The second phase began in 1995 with the creation of think tank organizations such as Riinvest and Kosovo Action for Civic Initiatives (KACI) as well as expanded humanitarian work by women's organizations and associations. The third, "post-conflict" phase in 1999 was distinguished by the creation of a large donor market and the mushrooming of NGOs. The fourth and current phase is the professionalization of civil society as well as the struggle for NGOs to gain financial sustainability. NGO registration is easy and performed at the Ministry of Public Services. Among Kosovo's 3,000 registered NGOs, only a small number are active. Despite its plurality, Kosovo's civil society faces a developmental lag in stability, sustainability, independence, and activities.

In 2007, Kosovo's civil society engaged in vibrant and accelerated activities, a contrast from previous years. The Vetevendosje movement staged rallies in opposition to the final status negotiation process, while its leader, Albin Kurti, was in detention or under house arrest for most of the year. Kurti's actions divided civil society; the CDHRF called his arrest politically motivated. The CDHRF stepped closer to politics and held a somewhat softer line than Vetevendosje on the Ahtisaari proposal but actively opposed the provisions for minority protections and decentralization. Other NGOs, apart from Cohu! (the Organization for Democracy, Anticorruption, and Dignity), did not engage in debates about Kurti and the Vetevendosje elections-boycott campaign. Youth Initiative for Human Rights (YIHR) was very active in monitoring Kosovo's institutions for human rights compliance, implementation of antidiscrimination legislation, and public use of the official (Serbian) language.

Cohu! continued its anticorruption activities throughout 2007, beginning by planting an "anticorruption Christmas tree" in front of the government building. Other activities included placing a large, symbolic candle in downtown Pristina in April to "shine light on corruption" and to receive messages from citizens about corruption. Cohu! continually questioned the credibility of the Kosovar Anticorruption Agency and its reports. During the summer, Cohu! and other organizations created the Coalition for a Clean Parliament, which created a public roster of allegedly corrupt candidates running for the Assembly and municipal elections. While ORA and PDK provided their candidate lists to the coalition and agreed to comply fully with its recommendations and analysis, LDK, AAK, LDD, and AKR did not. Cohu!'s roster of candidates suspected of corruption and other illegal acts included 21 names from LDK, 14 from AAK, 10 from LDD, 8 from PDK, and 2 from AKR (2 candidates from PDK and 1 from AAK presented counterevidence to Cohu! and their names were subsequently removed from the "corrupt candidate" roster).

According to the roster, only ORA candidates were considered fit for the Kosovo Assembly, leading to accusations that Cohu! sided with the ORA. The AAK accused Cohu! and its leader, Avni Zogiani, of directing a campaign against political parties, particularly the AAK. Officials from the Ministry of Public Services turned up at Cohu! offices to conduct a financial audit. Other civil society organizations saw this as politically-motivated pressure, while the CDHRF called on the candidates on Cohu!'s roster to seek redress in the courts and not engage in revenge against the organization.

Ten Kosovar regional organizations led by the Kosovar Institute for Policy and Research Development joined Democracy in Action to monitor the entire electoral process and undertook activities to strengthen the legitimacy of elections, educate the public on the new voting system, and organize and participate in public debates. YIHR launched the activist network *Nisma Ime* (My Initiative) to increase the number of youth voters. YIHR also undertook human rights activities with other NGOs, from criticizing the Kosovar Assembly for its failure to follow procedures in electing ombudsperson candidates to monitoring institutional compliance with the Law on Access to Official Documents.

Independent Media

1999	2001	2002	2003	2004	2005	2006	2007	2008
Y u g o s l a v i a				5.50	5.50	5.50	5.50	5.50

There was progress in Kosovo's media regulatory framework in 2007, as well as a decrease in the arbitrary use of force against journalists. The media in general criticized the Unity Team, especially in late spring and summer, owing to the final status process and the Kosovar delegation's lack of accountability and transparency. The media also criticized the government for corruption and other forms of mismanagement of public funds. In response, there were government attempts to influence the public broadcaster.

In August, the Kosovo Energy Corporation (KEK)—controlled by AAK minister for energy and mining Ethem Ceku and under pressure from AAK members of the government—decided to terminate the service contract permitting collection of the public broadcast fee for Radio Television of Kosovo (RTK) along with electricity bills. The termination effectively cut-off funding for RTK and was a breach of the RTK–KEK agreement, which required a six-month notice prior to cancellation. The company said that the six-month notice period was too short for RTK to develop an alternative and sustainable fee collection mechanism. This move by KEK was the result of RTK's reports criticizing the government and ministers from the AAK and the government's desire to control the broadcaster. In another attempt to gain control over RTK, the government in October asked the RTK board to "reevaluate and change its editorial policies during the electoral campaign, and in return the government would reinstate the KEK service fee."[2] Another attack on the media came from PDK secretary general Jakup Krasniqi, who stated that all media in Kosovo were controlled by "dirty money."[3] Krasniqi's remarks were directed at an editorial in the daily *Express* that criticized the PDK.

The Association of Professional Journalists of Kosovo (APJK), on the other hand, continued to request maximum adherence to the Law on Access to Official Documents by public institutions. The APJK sent an open letter to the government stressing that the only credible way for it to fight corruption was by ensuring public access to official documents and through increased transparency. In 2007, APJK reported 19 cases of journalists prevented from carrying out their duties, physical assaults, and overall attacks on the media by governmental and other officials.

The work of the regulatory Independent Media Commission continued with the approval of several pieces of secondary legislation, including an advertising code and regulations on cable broadcasting in Kosovo. However, the license fees for broadcasters set by the adopted regulation could pose a heavy financial burden on stations. The commission, which is funded by the Kosovo consolidated budget, still lacks adequate resources to carry out its tasks fully.

In May 2004, the OSCE began the process of establishing a multiethnic self-regulatory media body—the Press Council of Kosovo—that would include the editors in chief of all local newspapers in Kosovo, regardless of the print language. In 2007, the Press Council continued its restructuring to better prepare the institution for future operations. Journalists and editors were increasingly adhering to the council's code of conduct and statutes. By early June, the council had received a total of 38 complaints, 26 of which had been adjudicated. Starting in May, *Infopress* published lists of Kosovo Serbs who were allegedly drafted into the Yugoslav army during the 1998–1999 conflict, and the council took up the issue. In June, the council discussed breaches of the code of conduct by *Infopress*. The issue caused a crisis within the council, and its activities were temporarily blocked. *Infopress* continued to publish controversial articles throughout July and August despite heavy international criticism. The OSCE mission in Kosovo continued to mediate among Press Council members on this issue, without apparent results. The matter was not resolved by the end of 2007.

Local Democratic Governance

1999	2001	2002	2003	2004	2005	2006	2007	2008
Y u g o s l a v i a				n/a	5.50	5.50	5.50	5.50

Kosovo's weak state of local governance continued throughout 2007, with no increase in the independence of local authorities. Administrative and planning capacities at the municipal level are insufficient, for example, in developing medium- to long-term economic development strategies. Furthermore, the relationship between the central government and municipal governments needs further definition in terms of competences. Parallel administrative structures sponsored from Belgrade continue to operate in most predominantly Kosovo Serb municipalities, including in the fields of justice, education, health care, and the postal service.

In the first half of the year, the government undertook planning activities to redraw municipal boundaries in accordance with the Ahtisaari plan. Also, activities and planning were focused on creating protection zones around Serbian Orthodox churches and monasteries. With the failure of the UN Security Council to adopt the Ahtisaari plan, the government halted these preparations, although publicly it committed to decentralization obligations outlined in the plan.

The northern Serb-controlled municipalities of Zvecan, Zubin Potok, and Leposavic continued their boycott of the central government and increased their dependence on Belgrade. The other two Serb municipalities, Novo Brdo and Strpce, did not take the same steps but faced pressure from Serbia's government to reduce cooperation with Kosovo institutions, resulting in Serbia's resolute pressure to prevent local Serbs from participating in the municipal elections. Kosovar Serbs from these two municipalities feared that in the case of a boycott, they would lose power and hand over their municipalities to Kosovo Albanian political parties. Novo Brdo's mayor, Petar Vasic, warned that in such a case, Kosovo Serbs would lose everything and have to collectively leave Kosovo.[4] Other Kosovo Serb leaders urged Belgrade to reconsider the boycott of municipal elections. In the end, Kosovo Serbs did not take part in the ballot, while Belgrade claimed that any participation in the elections would legitimize the new Kosovo institutions and the declaration of independence.

SRSG Joachim Rucker used his executive authority under UN Security Council Resolution 1244 to temporarily extend by six months the mandate of the 2002-elected Kosovo Serb municipal officials in four out of five municipalities where Kosovo Serbs constituted a majority. In Novo Brdo, Rucker allowed the Kosovo Albanian–elected mayor to take office, while the majority of the members of the municipal assembly would be Kosovo Serb delegates. Novo Brdo's mayor rejected the decision, saying that Serbs would not accept a municipality run by a Kosovo Albanian, who could in turn block the work of the municipal assembly. The northern Kosovo Serb municipalities defied the SRSG, stating that Kosovo Serbs would continue to hold the majority in the five municipalities. The Kosovo Albanian media, political parties, and government did not pay much attention to this event, while silently accepting Rucker's decision. Meanwhile, Serbia's government used this opportunity to further assert its control over the municipalities and other Kosovo Serb settlements via its "parallel institutions."

Through most of 2007, municipal governance was challenged by the split in the LDK and the establishment of the LDD, which reduced the majority that the LDK had enjoyed in many municipalities. This in turn worsened the functioning of a number of assemblies and affected the terms of service of board members, including chief executive officers. Municipal assemblies became dysfunctional, and the appointment of senior civil servants was perpetually delayed. An attempt by Minister of Local Governance Lutfi Haziri and PDK deputy Rrustem Mustafa to forge a power-sharing agreement in six municipalities and thus provide stability failed owing to objections from local branches and resistance at central party levels. These agreements led to speculations that the LDK and PDK had also reached a secret deal to create a new coalition government at the central level.

The introduction of direct mayoral elections raised hopes for an improvement in transparency and municipal work overall. The political parties nominated their prominent members for mayoral races, promising functional local governance and lowering corruption. Consistent with changes in the electoral system, UNMIK enhanced the executive powers of mayors. On October 16, 2007, the SRSG promulgated Regulation 2007/30, enhancing mayoral powers beyond the moderation of municipal assemblies to include such executive responsibilities as appointing municipal boards of directors, proposing the budget, implementing municipal regulations, and maintaining control over municipal finances.

Judicial Framework and Independence

1999	2001	2002	2003	2004	2005	2006	2007	2008
Y u g o s l a v i a				6.00	5.75	5.75	5.75	5.75

The judiciary is considered to be one of the weakest links in Kosovo's rule of law. This was recognized in the Ahtisaari proposal as well as in the plan on establishing EU police and the justice mission to strengthen the rule of law in Kosovo. Eight years after the creation of UNMIK, the judicial system is still being established. The body of applicable laws in Kosovo remains a series of divided areas between UNMIK regulations, laws adopted by the Assembly (and promulgated by the SRSG), and certain Yugoslav laws still in force in Kosovo that in turn should be made fully compliant with the highest international human rights norms and standards. This continues to hamper the delivery of justice, as judges are not always certain of the legal basis for their decisions.

Kosovo's highest constitutional act is the Constitutional Framework for Provisional Self-Government, based on UN Security Council Resolution 1244. The framework observes international standards on human rights, from the Universal Declaration of Human Rights to the Framework of the Council of Europe for Minority Protection. Also, Kosovo's Ministry of Justice has limited competences (along the lines of the reserved powers for UNMIK) and does not administer the judiciary and courts. In early 2007, UNMIK began transferring competences related to penal management, missing persons, and forensics to the Ministry of Justice. While the process of promulgating laws by the Assembly has improved, their implementation remains a chronic problem.

The judicial system of Kosovo recognizes the following types of courts: minor offense courts, municipal courts, district courts, commercial courts, and the Supreme Court of Kosovo. Within the Supreme Court is the Special Chamber on Constitutional Framework Matters, as Kosovo does not have a constitution or constitutional court. In addition, the Kosovo Judicial Council (KJC) is a professional body under the authority of the SRSG; apart from appointing judges, lay judges, and prosecutors and implementing disciplinary measures for judicial misconduct, the KJC has begun to supervise court administration.

The process of electing a Kosovar ombudsperson, which failed in 2006, became even more complicated in 2007. Following amendments to UNMIK Regulation 2006/06, which provided the legal basis for a Kosovar ombudsperson to be appointed by and report to the Kosovo Assembly, new recruitment proceedings were initiated at the end of June. From 20 applicants interviewed in October by the Assembly, three candidates with no human rights experience were short-listed: a lawyer, a journalist, and a businessman, supported by LDK, PDK, and AAK, respectively.

Considering their political ties and lack of human rights experience, the candidates did not appear to fulfill the requirements for ombudsperson laid down by the UNMIK regulation, which states: "The Ombudsperson and the Principal Deputy Ombudsperson shall be eminent figures of high moral character, impartiality and integrity, who possess a demonstrated commitment to human rights and who are habitual residents of Kosovo." Civil society and international reactions followed almost immediately, with calls for new candidates and accusations of politicization and manipulation of the recruitment process. As a result, the process was annulled and will be repeated in 2008.

In 2007, the civil court backlog increased to 47,105 cases, in addition to over 36,000 criminal cases and several hundred war crimes cases. The backlog reflects the poor state of Kosovo's judiciary; many judicial positions remain vacant, execution of judgments is weak, and judges are hesitant to deal with tougher cases such as organized crime and war crimes. Similarly, local populations show an unwillingness to testify. Domestic war crimes trials are handled exclusively by international judges and prosecutors, where 8 war crimes trials are under way and 48 are under investigation. In a sign of frustration, Rexhep Haxhimusa, president of the Supreme Court of Kosovo and the KJC, complained that owing to lack of implementation of the laws on administrative procedure and administrative disputes, two Supreme Court judges were in charge of 2,890 cases that belonged in the lower-level courts.[5]

A memorandum of understanding among the EU, UNMIK, and the U.S. on the funding and reappointment of judges and prosecutors was signed and is under review. In March, the KJC approved the allocation of 326 new judicial positions for the Supreme Court and the district, municipal, and minor offense courts. A number of judicial staff have been transferred from low-volume to high-volume courts as part of this process.

Since early April, the Police Task Force—established in 2006 to investigate the violence in March 2004 that led to 19 dead, destruction of property, and approximately 4,000 displaced Kosovo Serbs—investigated 1,526 cases, of which 754 were under review, 177 remained open, 315 were closed, 120 were under active investigation, and 160 were being investigated by the Kosovo Police Service. By December, the international prosecutors had indicted 36 people for the most serious March riot-related offenses, resulting in 30 convictions and 1 acquittal. Nine defendants in three cases are awaiting trial. Local prosecutors have brought over 300 criminal charges, resulting in 145 convictions, with another 19 persons currently under investigation.

Legislation on witness protection is still being finalized. With support from the United Kingdom and United States, all district courts in Kosovo are equipped with witness protection capabilities, which will improve the ability of the Kosovo justice system to conduct investigations and prosecutions in a variety of sensitive cases. In July, an international prosecutor filed an indictment against two Kosovo Albanians suspected of murdering a witness to war crimes and the attempted murder of another witness in the same case. At the same time, UNMIK finally succeeded in making the Kosovo Office of the Special Prosecutor operational. Six special prosecutors were appointed, and the office secured convictions in two cases related to drugs and weapons. At the same time, UNMIK and the Provisional Institutions of Self-Government (PISG) established the Legal Aid Commission in July 2007, an independent body responsible for the provision of free legal assistance. This will be the first state-funded legal aid agency in the entire Balkans region.

Corruption

1999	2001	2002	2003	2004	2005	2006	2007	2008
Y u g o s l a v i a				6.00	6.00	6.00	6.00	5.75

Corruption is prevalent in Kosovo, undermining the proper functioning of institutions, yet some progress was noted in 2007. Kosovo is not party to the main international conventions in the field of anticorruption. However, the provisions of these legal instruments have been partially integrated into Kosovo legislation, such as the provisional criminal code of Kosovo and the Law on the Suppression of Corruption. The European Commission claimed in its 2007 report that the number of cases of organized crime investigated in Kosovo increased substantially in the first half of 2007.

The Anticorruption Agency (AKK), with a staff of around 30, has been operational since February 2007. A two-week anticorruption campaign in December 2006 publicized a confidential hotline to report corruption; the AKK received 160 calls and 31 cases submitted directly by citizens. Out of 124 cases (of which it solved 61), 47 were submitted to district public prosecutor offices, the Office of the Special Prosecutor, UNMIK Police, KPS, and the Financial Intelligence Unit, while 16 are in procedure. Out of the 732 senior officials at the central government level, 713 have declared their properties and assets in accordance with the anticorruption legislation. However, these steps do not tackle the corruption within institutions. Still, the AKK managed to annul tenders of €7 million (US$10.3 million) that violated the Law on Public Procurement. Its biggest ongoing challenges are insufficient staff, low wages, budgetary constraints, and lack of coordination with public prosecutors.

In September, UNMIK's Financial Intelligence Center (FIC) released information on 124 ongoing analyses or cases. In November, the Ministry of Public Services and FIC signed a memorandum of understanding aiming to preempt illegal NGO activities. This foresees strengthening cooperation, information exchange, and inspection of NGO activities, primarily to uncover money laundering and financing of terrorism, but also to prevent irregularities in NGO financing and abuse of donations.

UNMIK and the Kosovo Police Service took a robust action in January and March 2007 by arresting AAK member Jahja Lluka, serving as political adviser to Prime Minister Agim Ceku, and Milazim Abazi, head of Kasabank in Pristina, both for money laundering. The police also raided the headquarters of the AAK in Pristina, collecting documentation on the defense fund for Ramush Haradinaj (leader of the AAK and a former KLA officer) following his return to the International Criminal Tribunal for the Former Yugoslavia for the continuation of his war crimes trial. The AAK subsequently accused UNMIK of politically-motivated arrests aimed at harming the party. In June, the authorities arrested eight people, including former members of the Bank for Business board of directors and clients, on suspicion of making harmful deals and misusing authorization that cost the bank more than €10 million (US$1.473 million).

The largest public support for combating corruption came on September 4, when approximately 5,000 people protested in Pristina in reaction to the killing of Kosovo Police Service officer Triumf Riza. Government officials joined the protest, promising institutional "zero tolerance" in combating corruption. The protest was the first of its kind in postwar Kosovo. Cohu! accused government officials and Prime Minister Ceku of hypocrisy and questioned the credibility of Anticorruption Agency head Hasan Preteni. At the same time, the agency launched its second media campaign to promote its toll-free number and new Web site.

The Office of the Auditor General published 2006 reports on the Assembly of Kosovo, Kosovo Office of the President, and Kosovo Police Service. These audits demonstrated massive problems with financial management, including public procurement. While these reports were widely covered by the media, the Office of the Prosecutor General did not prosecute the offices for misuse of public money. UNMIK and the PISG remained silent, while no dismissals of high-level public officials were reported. At the local level, 14 of the 30 municipalities audited in 2006 were revisited to determine whether they had adopted mandatory action plans (only 3 had done so in full). Four ministers of Ceku's government, all members of the AAK, were investigated for corruption in 2007.

Some of the most politically sensitive and high-profile investigations were those by the UN Office of Internal Oversight Services (OIOS) against SRSG Joachim Rucker, his principal deputy, Steven Schook, and the head of the legal office, Alexander Borg-Olivier. Kosovar media reported that OIOS investigators confiscated the computers of the three top UNMIK officials; allegedly Schook was being investigated for criminal acts and for his role in the Kosova C project (the building of a new, 2100 megawatt lignite-fuelled power plant), while Borg-Olivier according to the media, was under investigation for his role in the Kosova C project and Pristina Airport fuel tenders. In September, Schook held a press conference confirming OIOS investigations against him based on misconduct, unprofessional behavior, his involvement in the Kosova C project, and closeness with AAK minister for energy and mining Ethem Ceku and Ramush Haradinaj. In light of these investigations, Schook left Kosovo in December without making a statement, his contract not renewed.

▮ AUTHOR: ILIR DEDA

Ilir Deda is the Head of Special Research Projects of the Kosovar Institute for Policy and Research Development in Pristina. He has contributed to the work of the UN Development Programme's Bureau for Crisis Prevention and Recovery in New York; the Independent Diplomat in New York; the Geneva Center for Security Policy; former Kosovo prime minister Bajram Rexhepi; and the International Crisis Group in Kosovo.

---

[1]   Ahtisaari argued that supervised independence was the only option, because reintegration into Serbia was not viable and continued international administration was not sustainable.

[2]   "Qeveria kercenon RTK'ne" [The Government Threatens RTK], *Gazeta Express*, October 31, 2007, http://www.gazetaexpress.com.

[3]   "Mediat dhe parate e pista" [Media and Dirty Money], *Gazeta Express,* October 13, 2007.

[4]   "Sta ako Albanci osvoje vlast?" [What If the Albanians Gain Power?], *B92,* October 28, 2007, http://www.b92.net.

[5]   "Afer tre mije lende per dy gjyqtare!" [Around Three Thousand Cases for Two Judges!], *Lajm,* October 29, 2007, http://www.gazetalajm.info.

Kyrgyzstan

by Erica Marat

Capital: Bishkek
Population: 5.1 million
GNI/capita: US$1,790

The social data above was taken from the European Bank for Reconstruction and Development's *Transition Report 2007: People in Transition*, and the economic data from the World Bank's *World Development Indicators 2008*.

Nations in Transit Ratings and Averaged Scores

	1999	2001	2002	2003	2004	2005	2006	2007	2008
Electoral Process	5.00	5.75	5.75	6.00	6.00	6.00	5.75	5.75	6.00
Civil Society	4.50	4.50	4.50	4.50	4.50	4.50	4.50	4.50	4.50
Independent Media	5.00	5.00	5.75	6.00	6.00	5.75	5.75	5.75	6.00
Governance*	5.00	5.25	5.50	6.00	6.00	n/a	n/a	n/a	n/a
National Democratic Governance	n/a	n/a	n/a	n/a	n/a	6.00	6.00	6.00	6.25
Local Democratic Governance	n/a	n/a	n/a	n/a	n/a	5.75	6.25	6.25	6.50
Judicial Framework and Independence	5.00	5.25	5.25	5.50	5.50	5.50	5.50	5.50	6.00
Corruption	6.00	6.00	6.00	6.00	6.00	6.00	6.00	6.00	6.25
Democracy Score	5.08	5.29	5.46	5.67	5.67	5.64	5.68	5.68	5.93

* *With the 2005 edition, Freedom House introduced separate analysis and ratings for national democratic governance and local democratic governance to provide readers with more detailed and nuanced analysis of these two important subjects.*

NOTE: The ratings reflect the consensus of Freedom House, its academic advisers, and the author(s) of this report. The opinions expressed in this report are those of the author(s). The ratings are based on a scale of 1 to 7, with 1 representing the highest level of democratic progress and 7 the lowest. The Democracy Score is an average of ratings for the categories tracked in a given year.

EXECUTIVE SUMMARY

In March 2005, President Askar Akayev was forcefully ousted by opposition forces on allegations of large-scale corruption. Akayev was replaced by then opposition leader Kurmanbek Bakiyev. However, Bakiyev failed to meet public expectations, quickly succumbing to corruption himself and increasing his authoritarianism over competing political forces. Following two years of political instability, Kyrgyzstan was submerged in fierce competition among political leaders throughout 2007.

Lacking checks and balances, the new Constitution enabled Bakiyev to appoint the government and judges and to secure a majority for his Ak Zhol party bloc in the Parliament. Forceful suppression of opposition demonstrations in April and persecution of independent journalists further marred Bakiyev's regime in public opinion. Bakiyev also showed little ability or wish to curb corruption in government structures and the business sector. Overall, these events were reminiscent of the crucial mistakes made by former president Akayev and the subsequent fall of his regime to the opposition in 2005. Bakiyev has given signs of becoming an even more authoritarian and corrupt leader, driven by short-term goals to centralize his power while failing to design viable economic and political policies.

Still, the president was able to prevail over opposition forces in Kyrgyzstan throughout 2007. He created the powerful pro-regime bloc Ak Zhol, which facilitated Bakiyev-desired results in the constitutional referendum. Ak Zhol controls all state structures and enables the president to hold on to power. Yet Bakiyev faced competition from opposition blocs that challenged the president at the snap parliamentary elections on December 16 and set another opportunity in the 2010 presidential election.

National Democratic Governance. In late 2007, Bakiyev followed other neighboring states by designing a strong pro-regime political bloc to alienate competing political forces from decision making in the government and Parliament. The Constitution (endorsed through a referendum on October 21) allowed Bakiyev to prevail over opposition forces. The president took virtually full control and promoted his newly formed political bloc, Ak Zhol, to Parliament thanks to his leverage over the Central Election Commission and law enforcement agencies. Kyrgyz society, although largely disappointed with Bakiyev, had already experienced a high level of fatigue from the country's political turbulence; a few local civil society activists mobilized protests to Bakiyev's referendum but were forcefully dispersed by law enforcement agencies. At the December 16 snap parliamentary elections, 12 political parties competed for 90 seats distributed by proportional representation. Although at least 3 opposition parties showed ability to win representation, Ak

Zhol won over 70 percent of seats. Kyrgyzstan's political opposition and civil society groups hope to challenge the president during presidential elections in 2010. *With the adoption of a new Constitution designed primarily by Bakiyev, Kyrgyzstan's national democratic governance rating worsens from 6.00 to 6.25.*

Electoral Process. The referendum on October 21, which amended the Constitution and electoral legislation, was marked with widespread falsifications. Hours after the poll, Bakiyev announced a date for parliamentary elections. Although the new electoral legislation encouraged the formation of political parties, the new Constitution granted the president extensive powers over the Parliament, government, and judicial system. The new electoral law contains statutes that set hidden hurdles to parliamentary representation for regional parties, and local nongovernmental organizations (NGOs) called the referendum the "most cynical" in Kyrgyzstan's history. The December 16 parliamentary elections showed falsifications by the pro-regime Ak Zhol party, allowing it to prevail over the largest opposition parties—Social Democratic Party of Kyrgyzstan, Ata Meken, and Asaba. *Bakiyev's mobilizing of state forces to his advantage in the constitutional referendum worsens Kyrgyzstan's electoral process rating from 5.75 to 6.00.*

Civil Society. Several local NGOs were among the most active opponents of Bakiyev's October 21 constitutional referendum. The NGO Interbilim and coalition For Democratic Reform and Civil Society reported mass falsification of referendum results and condemned the president for undemocratic governance. A number of NGO activists joined opposition parties in protest. However, NGOs also played a somewhat negative role by rejecting the World Bank and International Monetary Fund's Heavily Indebted Poor Countries initiative in Kyrgyzstan in January. In mass protests organized by NGOs, local activists appealed largely to emotional arguments against the initiative rather than encouraging rational debate on its economic benefits, and political populism is on the rise among civil society groups. *Kyrgyzstan's civil society remains a strong political force in the country and is able to challenge the government and Parliament thanks to its connections to grassroots and regional representatives; therefore, the civil society rating remains at 4.50.*

Independent Media. A number of mass media outlets experienced difficulties with law enforcement agencies in 2007. Two well-known journalists from Piramida TV requested political asylum abroad, and one journalist from the newspaper *Bely Parokhod* was sued for libeling the government. The brutal killing of freelance journalist Alisher Saipov in October, allegedly organized by Uzbek intelligence and security forces, showed that local journalists are increasingly under threat. About a dozen journalists were attacked by unknown criminals throughout the year. Bakiyev also continued his tactics of appointing opposition journalists to diplomatic posts abroad. Although several newspapers publish daily news and opinion pieces on the latest developments in the country, Kyrgyzstan still lacks mass media outlets that produce analytical reports. The local media market is dominated by Russian-language outlets. *The government continues to suppress independent mass media, and more journalists fear attacks from the criminal underworld; therefore, Kyrgyzstan's independent media rating worsens from 5.75 to 6.00.*

Local Democratic Governance. In September–October, Bakiyev reshuffled local government members and appointed a new mayor of Bishkek. These extensive changes secured his desired outcomes at the referendum as local government members sought to prove their loyalty to the regime by falsifying voting results. Local government elections took place on October 7 with evidence of widespread falsification of voting results. The local government facilitated Ak Zhol's victory in the December 16 parliamentary elections, thus displaying its disinterest in serving the needs of the local population. *Kyrgyzstan's rating for local democratic governance declines from 6.25 to 6.50.*

Judicial Framework and Independence. In 2007 the Constitutional Court actions demonstrated that judicial independence had deteriorated to a new level. The Court annulled two previous constitutions (those adopted in November and December 2006) only days before President Bakiyev unveiled his own constitutional project. The Parliament expelled three Constitutional Court judges for cooperating with the president and insisted their activities were illegal. The Constitutional Court's chairwoman Cholpon Bayekova's inclusion as one of top five candidates for the largest pro-presidential political party list raised further questions about the court's independence. *Owing to pro-presidential actions by the Constitutional Court, Kyrgyzstan's rating for judicial framework and independence worsens from 5.50 to 6.00.*

Corruption. Bakiyev gained popularity after the regime change in March 2005 owing to his anticorruption slogans. However, three years past the ouster of former president Askar Akayev, corruption rates in public institutions and major economic sectors have been on the rise. The Bakiyev government brokered a number of opaque deals with domestic and foreign investors in the country's major economic areas. The energy sector, a vital source of Kyrgyzstan's gross domestic product, is deeply corrupt, as is the customs service, which benefits only a few government elites. Corruption in the energy sector is often discussed by local media. *Since the scale and number of corruption incidences were on the rise in 2007, Kyrgyzstan's corruption rating worsens from 6.00 to 6.25.*

Outlook for 2008. Kyrgyzstan's ongoing political turmoil is more a sign of the desire of the president and his allies to grab maximum power than an indication of the state's incentive to divide power for more efficient and transparent governance. The goals promoted by the leaders of the Tulip Revolution are becoming a distant reality. Since Bakiyev was unable to conduct a constitutional reform that reflected consensus among political forces, confrontation among various state structures and political parties will likely increase. Furthermore, corruption rates will continue to stall economic development. The government shows little incentive for designing long-term economic policies and guaranteeing efficient investment in the country's key economic sectors such as hydropower and gold mining. Based on a poor record of fighting corruption and increasing his own powers through a constitutional referendum, Bakiyev will continue to face strong opposition in 2008 in the run-up to the next presidential elections in 2010. His political bloc, Ak Zhol, won the majority of parliamentary seats and occupies the bulk of government positions.

Main Report

National Democratic Governance

1999	2001	2002	2003	2004	2005	2006	2007	2008
n/a	n/a	n/a	n/a	n/a	6.00	6.00	6.00	6.25

Kyrgyzstan's political turbulence, begun in early 2005, continued throughout 2006 and 2007. On December 30, 2006, the Kyrgyz Parliament adopted yet another Constitution that came only weeks after the previous version was endorsed in November. While the November Constitution was achieved after protests in central Bishkek organized by the For Reforms opposition bloc, the December version was concluded rapidly by the Parliament under pressure from President Kurmanbek Bakiyev. Unlike the November Constitution, which secured stronger powers for the Parliament and was regarded as the most liberal among Central Asian states, the December version returned key powers to the president. The Constitutional Court facilitated Bakiyev's consolidation of powers by annulling both the November and December 2006 constitutions and allowing the president to come up with his own constitutional project in September 2007.

Bakiyev was able to use inconsistencies in the November Constitution to his benefit. On December 19, he forced the resignation of the government including Prime Minister Felix Kulov. This made the Parliament de jure incapable of functioning, since according to the November 2006 Constitution, only a Parliament consisting of 90 members (not 75) had the right to form the government. Furthermore, the Parliament could do so only if one party represented a simple majority. Both provisions did not exist when the government resigned. To avoid its own dismissal, the Parliament was forced to quickly adopt Bakiyev's version of the Constitution.

Following approval of the December 2006 Constitution, both the Parliament and Bakiyev were interested in removing Kulov permanently. Most Parliament members, especially the For Reforms bloc, were dissatisfied with Kulov's passive stance against Bakiyev during his run as prime minister. According to the December 2006 Constitution, Parliament was allowed no more than three attempts to approve a prime minister or it would be dissolved. Although Bakiyev twice nominated Kulov to head the government, Parliament rejected the choice in both cases. Had Bakiyev named Kulov a third time, Parliament would have had to approve him to escape its own dismissal. But Bakiyev selected Azim Isabekov, former minister of agriculture and largely unknown to a broader public. Parliament was bound to vote in favor of Isabekov to avoid dismissal, thus ending the two-year Bakiyev-Kulov political tandem.

As an extremely weak political leader, Isabekov lasted only two months as Prime Minister and was succeeded by Almazbek Atambayev. In April, For Reform pushed the president to sack First Deputy Prime Minister Daniyar Usenov, who had a reputation for being corrupt. Usenov is notorious for using his vast financial strength to leverage control over regime members and key business sectors in the country. He was replaced by former Minister of Education Nur uulu Dosbol and in October 2007 appointed Mayor of Bishkek.

Kulov's reluctance to support the opposition in the November 2006 protests tarnished his popular approval rating. After being dismissed from the government, he quickly moved into the opposition and formed the United Front bloc, calling for immediate and radical actions against the president. The United Front's plans to organize open-ended mass protests in April and dismiss Bakiyev worried many in the country about the possibility of a civil conflict. Kulov still enjoyed some degree of support among law enforcement structures, with former interior minister Omurbek Suvanaliyev being his closest ally. Some members of the For Reforms bloc joined the United Front in April 2007; however, most expressed concern that should Bakiyev use violence against the opposition, an armed conflict would be inevitable. The Kyrgyz opposition was divided into two camps—those who wanted the president to resign in April and those who preferred to further negotiate on constitutional reform.

The United Front's protests began on April 11 and were forcefully suppressed by the police on April 19. Numerous protesters were arrested and a dozen wounded, while the United Front was not able to achieve any of its goals. Kulov claimed that the government organized a group of provocateurs to disperse the crowds. However, Atambayev and many other opposition and pro-regime politicians blamed Kulov for poor management of the crowds. The clashes led to a split among opposition leaders and a weakening of Kulov's party. The For Reforms bloc also sought to disassociate itself from the April 19 violence. The leader of For Reforms, parliamentarian Omurbek Tekebayev, argued that the opposition had clearly suffered a defeat. In October, two members of United Front were convicted of organizing mass clashes in April and sentenced to four years in prison.

In the months following the April demonstrations, Kyrgyzstan's economy faltered and the country endured steadily rising food prices. The cost of bread in Bishkek increased from an average of 6 soms to 9 soms (US$0.17–0.25). The government's 10 percent raise in pensions and public salaries could not compete with 30 percent inflation for food products. This demonstrated that the government was unable to foresee price hikes related to inflation in neighboring Kazakhstan and Russia. The government also showed that it lacked a coherent economic strategy even for the short term.

In September 2007, Bakiyev presented his draft Constitution, which was passed by referendum on October 21. The Constitution substantially increased his powers, and most local political observers agreed that the regime likely falsified the final vote tally. Bakiyev made an illusion of having developed his constitutional project as a result of protracted legal debates. With some restrictions, the president is now able to dissolve the Parliament, while presidential impeachment is possible only with an

80 percent vote of Parliament. As soon as Bakiyev set the date for the constitutional referendum, political parties began mobilizing for snap parliamentary elections.

The October 21 referendum was largely reminiscent of former president Askar Akayev's maneuvering in 1994, 1996, 1998, and 2003, when he tailored the Constitution according to his own interests. Although most Kyrgyz experts agreed that the party list system reduced regional divides among political elites and their constituencies, some worried that such a system would in fact exacerbate social cleavages. Prior to the referendum, Kyrgyz voters were not familiar with any party's program and had little experience in differentiating conservative or liberal views. Most voters continued to associate political parties with their leaders, since the party-building process was still conducted from the top down. Furthermore, most political parties were concentrated only in the large cities of Bishkek and Osh.

Kyrgyzstan's Parliament, elected in 2005, had been the most powerful in the country's history. It was able to form strong opposition blocs to the president. However, it also showed its fear of being dissolved through constitutional changes. The Parliament had an opportunity to resist Bakiyev's referendum but decided to allow it to take place, while individual members of Parliament (MPs) increased their political party activities. Following the referendum, Bakiyev promised to form a Parliament and government based on the new Constitution by the end of 2007.

On December 16, Kyrgyzstan held snap parliamentary elections. Twelve political parties competed for 90 seats distributed on the basis of proportional representation. Bakiyev's Ak Zhol won the elections with 48.82 percent of the vote. Although less than half of voters showed their support for Ak Zhol, the new proportional system allowed the pro-regime party to occupy over 70 percent of Parliament seats. The pro-regime Parliament formed a new government composed mostly of old faces who survived the numerous reshuffling efforts of former president Akayev, the change of presidents in March 2005, and the December parliamentary elections. Like Akayev, Bakiyev surrounded himself in the new government with loyal political supporters interested primarily in the continuity of the current political regime.

Electoral Process

1999	2001	2002	2003	2004	2005	2006	2007	2008
5.00	5.75	5.75	6.00	6.00	6.00	5.75	5.75	6.00

The new Law on Elections encouraged the formation of political parties, since elections were changed from a majoritarian system to a party list structure with a 5 percent nationwide electoral threshold. MPs supporting the president and willing to be reelected in the next elections set hidden hurdles in the new Law on Elections to keep competing forces from winning the parliamentary elections. A party must earn 0.5 percent (or 13,500 votes) support in each of the country's seven administrative regions and its two largest cities, Bishkek and Osh, to be represented in the Parliament.[1] This restrictive threshold, called a regional barrier potentially limits the chances for political parties that are concentrated in certain regions to gain representation in the Parliament. For instance, Bakiyev's most ardent opponent, Felix Kulov, and his party enjoy support mostly in northern Kyrgyzstan. In a similar manner, political parties supported mainly by ethnic Uzbeks living in southern Kyrgyzstan are unknown to the population in the north.

Bakiyev allowed only one month for Kyrgyz voters to get acquainted with the new Constitution and Law on Elections. This short period of time prevented the opposition from persuading the public about the imbalanced powers the president would receive as a result of the referendum. The ballots contained two questions: only one regarding the Constitution, and one on the Law on Elections. Voters had a choice of either "yes" or "no," with no voting permitted per each constitutional article. For the snap parliamentary elections on December 16, 2007, voters had to familiarize themselves with competing political party programs within a matter of weeks.

On December 3, Edil Baisalov, a member of the opposition Social Democratic Party of Kyrgyzstan (SDPK), published a sample ballot on his personal blog (http://baisalov.livejournal.com). In response, the Central Election Commission (CEC) announced its decision to invalidate all ballot papers and create new ones. Baisalov was charged with two criminal allegations: "Impeding the implementation of voting rights and work procedures of the electoral commission" and "Causing material losses by fraud and abuse of trust". Although no trial took place by year end, the SDPK was fined the equivalent of $570,000.

Outdated records of registered voters indicated that Bishkek had some 330,000 voters, while most experts claimed that roughly 1.2 million people live and work in the capital city. Also, the existing voter lists did not take into consideration the fact that up to 500,000 migrant laborers, roughly 10 percent of the voting population, are currently residing in Russia and Kazakhstan. Although special voting precincts were organized in the largest cities in Russia and Kazakhstan, most migrants never register with Kyrgyz diplomatic missions abroad and therefore are unable to vote. Such logistical issues facilitated falsification of results by the government.

Bakiyev appointed Klara Kabilova, former head of the International Institute for Strategic Studies under the president of the Kyrgyz Republic, as the CEC head. Kabilova's close association with Bakiyev indeed worked in the president's favor. According to the CEC, the October 21 referendum had a 82 percent turnout, with 76 percent supporting the new Constitution and 76 percent supporting the new Law on Elections.[2] However, the turnout was lowest in Bishkek (roughly 74 percent), where about 20 percent of the country's total five million residents reside. Since more than 50 percent of voters participated in the referendum, its results were recognized by the government.

Roughly 180 international observers were present at the referendum. Commonwealth of Independent States (CIS) observers, along with their counterparts from the Shanghai Cooperation Organization (SCO), supported the referendum results. These assessments should be taken with caution, as members of both organizations have their own substantial problems with democratic elections. Unlike the CIS and

SCO observers, local nongovernmental organizations (NGOs) reported violations and intimidation, including that in the Bishkek suburbs, voters were transported en masse, with the highest turnout noticed at precincts located at schools. The Association for Monitoring Elections and Referenda in the Kyrgyz Republic: Taza Shailoo (Clean Elections)—a new election monitoring network of domestic NGOs, launched in August—expressed "strong doubts about the results of the referendum due to the large number of serious and systematic violations of the laws of the Kyrgyz Republic."[3] The NGO coalition, For Democracy and Civil Society, discovered that members of local voting committees brought up to 600 ballots to ballot boxes.[4] The coalition also reported that the local governments were instructed to ensure at least a 65 percent turnout in their precincts. Cases of single persons having multiple ballots were also widespread. The NGO Interbilim called the October referendum the "most cynical" in the history of Kyrgyzstan.[5]

For Bakiyev, it was vital to show that the majority of the population in Bishkek was in favor of the referendum. In November, he appointed former first deputy prime minister Daniyar Usenov, his close political ally, as mayor of Bishkek, removing Arstanbek Nogoyev. Usenov's first decision was to ban public protest in the city. He was able to facilitate results desirable for Bakiyev in Bishkek but complained that the population was much more passive than had been the case with the 2003 referendum.

Bakiyev dissolved the Parliament hours after the referendum and announced that elections would be held on December 16. Several parties showed potential to become the opposition to Bakiyev: Asaba, led by MP Azimbek Beknazarov and former foreign minister Roza Otunbayeva; Ata Meken, led by MPs Omurbek Tekebayev and Bolot Sherniyazov; and the Social Democratic Party of Kyrgyzstan, led by then Prime Minister Almazbek Atambayev. However, only the Social Democrat and Communist Party were able to win a modest parliamentary representation in the December 16 elections. Except for a few candidates, most of the new Ak Zhol MPs have little experience in political or economic issues at the national level. Its top five members include the former chair of the Constitutional Court, Cholpon Bayekova, renowned surgeon Ernest Akramov, and Vladimir Nifad'yev, dean of the Kyrgyz-Slavic University.

Before the 2007 parliamentary elections, the absence of women in Parliament was one of the major concerns among Kyrgyz NGOs. There were both advocates and opponents of setting a special quota for women in the new Law on Elections. The law introduced a 30 percent quota on the candidate lists for female representatives, 15 percent for ethnic minorities, and 15 percent for candidates under 35 years of age. Most political parties preferred to appoint young females with non-Kyrgyz backgrounds to meet all three requirements.

Essentially, the new Constitution endorsed in October did not provide an effective system of government checks and balances. The December election demonstrated that the fully proportional system failed to eradicate the weaknesses of the majoritarian system, and wealthy candidates still had disproportionate chance of winning. Although political parties will be represented in the Parliament and can form the government, the president has the right to dissolve both the Parliament and the government, as well as form and annul state institutions. Bakiyev's Constitution does not represent the goals of Kyrgyzstan's Tulip Revolution and fails to foster political development in the country. On the contrary, it will likely provoke new political crises.

Civil Society

1999	2001	2002	2003	2004	2005	2006	2007	2008
4.50	4.50	4.50	4.50	4.50	4.50	4.50	4.50	4.50

Kyrgyzstan's civil society is the most vibrant in the region. The regime change in March 2005 showed that the state is no longer able to ignore civil society, let alone curtail its activity. Kyrgyzstan's civil society groups have learned to effectively voice their concerns over the government and Parliament's actions and organize peaceful mass demonstrations to promote their ideas. Often NGO leaders are more professional and skilled in voicing ideas than government officials. Civil society representatives are regularly invited to testify before the Parliament and are surveyed by local and foreign mass media outlets. However, the government and civil society groups still lack effective ways of communicating together constructively and continue to view each other as confrontational and competing actors.

Civil society activists were at the forefront of discussions on constitutional reform in November and played a vital role in pushing the government and president to adopt their version of the Constitution. Local civil society groups also showed that they were able to fund-raise domestically and were thus less dependent on foreign investors. The November 2006 protests were financed largely by local businessmen, though business circles cooperating with civil society activists often remain unknown to the larger public.

Local NGOs sent their own observers to the referendum on October 21 and parliamentary elections on December 16. The NGO For Democracy and Civil Society was especially active during the elections. As the electoral process in Kyrgyzstan changed to a party list system, some nationally known activists moved into political parties to participate in the parliamentary elections. These activists were especially welcomed for their experience in the NGO sector, connections at the grassroots level, and nationwide recognition. Several NGOs regularly publish independent reports on local and national elections. The NGO Institute for Public Policy, which acts as a local think tank, was prolific in publishing analytical works on political and economic developments in the country in 2007.

Civil society groups organized a series of actions to prevent the October 21 referendum. The Green Party, composed mostly of young activists, organized a demonstration in central Bishkek with the slogan "'No' to the Dictator." Local NGOs were especially concerned that the new Constitution suppressed freedom of speech. According to Maxim Kuleshov, an NGO activist and ardent critic of the referendum, the formation of a strong pro-presidential bloc could signify the beginning of widespread challenges to freedom of speech in Kyrgyzstan.[6]

However, along with high civic activism, Kyrgyzstan is awash in political populism voiced by various civic and political groups as well as individual advocates. Populism among the NGO community is indicative of its ability to effectively formulate and spread its message. However, Kyrgyz NGOs are sometimes susceptible to emotional and irrational nationalist calls produced by individual leaders within the community. For example, civil society activities contributed to a rise in nationalist feelings after the killing of a Kyrgyz citizen by a U.S. Marine in December 2006. In the months that followed the incident, various civil society groups called for expelling the U.S. military from the country. This gave rise to nationalist moods condemning the West and favoring Russian political and economic engagement in Kyrgyzstan. Also, mass protests organized by NGOs against the World Bank and International Monetary Fund's Heavily Indebted Poor Countries initiative appealed largely to emotional arguments rather than rational debate on the initiative's economic benefits.

The emergence of NGOs promoting a greater role for Islam in state affairs is another trend in Kyrgyz civil society. The most notable such religious movement Mutakalim, claims to have 30,000 members and successfully lobbied a law allowing women to wear a *hijab* (headscarf) on passport photographs.[7] The movement also speaks against the celebration of Western holidays, such as St. Valentine's Day or February 14, alleging that these undermine moral values among younger generation and harm social cohesion.

With all their criticism against the government, Kyrgyz NGOs do not always play the role of opposition. Cooperative relations between the state and civic society are noticeable within the Ministries of Defense, Education, Environment and Health Care. While civil society groups are only beginning to gain strength in neighboring states, NGOs in Kyrgyzstan have moved to defend the rights of sexual minorities and paid-sex workers. More than 7,000 members are registered with the NGO Oasis, which promotes the rights, health issues, and social acceptance of sexual minorities. Oasis also has a representative office in southern Kyrgyzstan. Several youth organizations promoting political participation have also emerged NGOs dealing with gender issues, civic education, and conflict prevention are especially widespread in Kyrgyzstan. However, although the share of female leader in the NGO sector is high, they are largely underrepresented in state structures.

Independent Media

1999	2001	2002	2003	2004	2005	2006	2007	2008
5.00	5.00	5.75	6.00	6.00	5.75	5.75	5.75	6.00

Like its civil society groups, Kyrgyzstan's mass media outlets enjoy greater freedom than in neighboring states. After Bakiyev came to power, the government forcefull assumed control over several TV channels and newspapers. However, a number of independent outlets still publish analytical and informative articles on developments in the country. Online news agencies such as Akipress.kg and 24.kg publish a wide variety of information on all aspects of local life.

As political struggle intensified after Bakiyev announced the constitutional referendum, local media became a common forum for public debates among political parties and their leaders. Government pressure on independent journalists was evident in the cases of Kairat Birimkulov and Turat Bektenov, reporters from the Piramida TV channel who sought political asylum in the West. Piramida was among the first mass media outlets forcefully returned to the government's indirect control by Bakiyev's regime in December 2005.[8] The popular channel is known nationwide for its news and entertainment programs.

The most shocking development in 2007 was the brutal killing of journalist Alisher Saipov on October 24. A Kyrgyz citizen and ethnic Uzbek, Saipov was known for his austere criticism of the policies of Uzbek president Islam Karimov. According to the Ferghana.ru news agency, Saipov was assassinated by contract killers allegedly hired by the Uzbek regime. Saipov's death raised panic among local journalists, and most of his colleagues in Kyrgyzstan accused the Kyrgyz government of failing to protect independent journalists. Ilim Karypbekov of the Media Institute in Kyrgyzstan claimed that the government has been ignoring the widespread abuse of journalists. During 2007, a total of 12 attacks were reported; in most cases, journalists were severely beaten, and local law enforcement agencies failed to investigate these crimes.[9] The international community called Saipov's death a grave infringement on the freedom of speech.

Bakiyev neutralized a number of opposition journalists by appointing them to the foreign service. Three widely known journalists, Zamira Sydykova, Rina Prizhivoit, and Kuban Mambetalieyv, were appointed as Kyrgyz ambassadors to the United States, Austria, and the United Kingdom, respectively. These journalists were ardent critics of Akayev's corrupt politics, calling for international attention to the lack of democracy under his leadership. They supported Akayev's ouster in March 2005, but their new foreign service positions quickly turned them from critical journalists into political actors with diplomatic responsibilities.

The Kyrgyz newspaper *Bely Parokhod* is known for publishing controversial articles on corruption among top officials. The newspaper's leading journalist, Elena Avdeyeva, is among the most vocal reporters on embezzlement scandals in state structures, but the newspaper began experiencing difficulties in September 2007. Avdeyeva was persecuted by law enforcement, and she claims that her family has experienced difficulties while traveling internationally. *Bely Parokhod* is one of the few Kyrgyz media outlets (along with Akipress.kg and 24.kg) to earn revenues from advertising and subscriptions.

Like civil society activists, Kyrgyz journalists have learned ways to voice their concerns during periods of political pressure. For instance, Piramida employees staged rallies when their journalists were persecuted by law enforcement, while *Bely Parokhod* threatened to draw the attention of the entire international community to its problems with government suppression. The Kyrgyz government is not able to muzzle all unwanted reporters or media outlets. On the contrary, the government's attempts to suppress popular independent media have damaged its image and lowered public trust. Although Kyrgyz journalists function in relative freedom, they do not yet promote their interests through professional networks. An association of Kyrgyz journalists does exist but is largely ineffective in protecting reporters or conducting regular activities.

Most of Kyrgyzstan's mass media are published and broadcast in Russian language; only a handful of newspapers and TV channels use Kyrgyz as their main language. The government heavily controls Kyrgyz Television and Radio (KTR), the only media outlet broadcast across the entire country. About a dozen Russian TV channels enjoy widespread popularity in the capital, Bishkek. Russian ORT and RTR TV are widely watched in Bishkek, where more than 20 percent of Kyrgyzstan's five million residents live. Most Kyrgyz get their international news from these two channels, which also broadcast popular entertainment programs. In October, the Kremlin announced it will subsidize the transmission of additional outlets in Kyrgyzstan—RTR-Planeta, Kul'tura, and Radio Rossii.

Since most Russian mass media outlets, especially state-run ORT and RTR TV, usually promulgate pro-Kremlin views, the Kyrgyz public's perceptions of world affairs are similar to those of Russian citizens. Russian mass media were especially successful in building pro-Kremlin attitudes toward the U.S.-led wars in Afghanistan and Iraq, the color revolutions in Georgia and Ukraine, and the war in Chechnya. They also propagate Russian President Vladimir Putin's image as a strong-minded, pragmatic politician. Owing to the pervasive presence of Russian media, the Kyrgyz public's knowledge and trust in Russian policies in Kyrgyzstan and Central Asia is higher compared with their views toward the West.

Very few citizens have access to Western media. Most Western analysis is presented through Russian and, in rare instances, Kyrgyz translations. Although local cable TV providers offer international news channels, they remain largely unpopular. Kyrgyz-language newspapers still lack analysis and critical views of current events. Few outlets, except for the newspaper Agym, KTR, and the local broadcast of Radio Free Europe, enjoy wide popularity. The Uzbek service of Voice of America broadcasts in southern Kyrgyzstan.

Kyrgyzstan has the region's highest per capita Internet access, and Web forums are an important medium for opinion exchange. Loosely regulated online discussions at Akipress.kg and Parahod.kg contain a range of anonymous viewpoints and unofficial information on developments in the political, economic, and social spheres of the country. These outlets regularly conduct public opinion surveys, but their forums are often full of libel, which is poorly controlled by either media or legal channels. Although Kyrgyz law enforcement sometimes prosecutes libel in the mass media, news outlets are never held accountable for information posted on their forums.

Local Democratic Governance

1999	2001	2002	2003	2004	2005	2006	2007	2008
n/a	n/a	n/a	n/a	n/a	5.75	6.25	6.25	6.50

Following the announcement of the referendum in September, Bakiyev began the swift reappointment of local governors. The president redistributed positions among members of the pro-regime bloc Ak Zhol. His first major reshuffle began with the appointment of Daniyar Usenov as mayor of Bishkek, replacing Arstanbek Nogoyev, and Svetlana Kulikova, a representative of Moya Strana (part of Ak Zhol), as deputy mayor. Besides facilitating Bakiyev-desired outcomes in the referendum and parliamentary elections, both Usenov and Kulikova restricted mass demonstrations by political parties prior to the referendum (the Green Party sued Usenov on this count). Usenov also prohibited demonstrations on the Bishkek central square, allowing mass gatherings only in remote parts of the city.

Bakiyev also reshuffled a number of local governors, and new governors were forced to join political parties belonging to the pro-presidential Ak Zhol bloc. On October 21, governors were present at voting precincts to personally control the activity of local electoral committees and secure favorable results. Local governors also forced all public employees, from schoolteachers to police, to be present at voting precincts. Furthermore, schoolteachers were instructed to persuade parents to vote in favor of the referendum. Newly appointed governors risked losing their jobs if they failed to meet the regime's demands. Former president Askar Akayev had used similar techniques, appointing new governors before elections to increase the chances of winning.

Local elections were held on October 7 in 3 cities, 1 town, and 14 *keneshes* (village councils)—a total of 296 mandates—and competition was fierce in most precincts. Voter participation was lowest in Jalalabad oblast with 47 percent and highest in Batken oblast with 63 percent.[10] The local elections were followed by numerous court appeals by unsuccessful candidates. Reports of widespread falsification of election results were reported in the cities of Osh and Tokmok. The competition was fiercest in Tokmok, with 123 candidates competing for 30 seats and several candidates violating the Law on Registration. In Osh, voter lists were outdated and incomplete. The CEC criticized Osh mayor Zhumadyl Isakov for poor management of the elections and referendum.[11] Falsification at other precincts was reported by some observers but poorly documented.

Judicial Framework and Independence

1999	2001	2002	2003	2004	2005	2006	2007	2008
5.00	5.25	5.25	5.50	5.50	5.50	5.50	5.50	6.00

The Constitutional Court played a vital role in the protracted Constitution changes in 2005–2007. Cholpon Bayekova, head of the Constitutional Court, has served in this position since 1993; she is known for her cooperation with former president Askar Akayev and supported him in organizing referendums during his reign. She also showed an inclination toward Bakiyev's changing the Constitution to strengthen his own powers. The Constitutional Court openly supported legal reforms initiated by Akayev and has quickly become a backup for the Bakiyev regime.

By showing support for the executive, the Constitutional Court has often confronted the Parliament. On September 18, Parliament expelled three Constitutional Court judges, Chinara Kurbanova, Omurzak Mamyrov, and Svetlana Sydykova, insisting their activities were illegal as they facilitated the Constitutional Court's cancellation of the November and December 2006 constitutions and approved Bakiyev's decision to hold a referendum. But on October 10, all three judges won their cases at the Parliament's court appeal, indicating that the judicial system is consolidated within itself against the Parliament. After the referendum, Parliament Speaker Marat Sultanov admitted that the Constitutional Court was the most difficult state institution for the Parliament to collaborate with.[12]

Trust in Constitutional Court activities has been extremely low among state structures and the general public since Kyrgyzstan's independence. A number of politicians have expressed their concern that the Constitutional Court is a major source of political instability in the country because of its service to the corrupt regimes of Akayev and Bakiyev, and the Parliament has called for an independent commission to investigate the work of the Court.

Regional courts also display a strong dependence on the president. In October, the Sverdlov Regional Court charged well-known journalist Elena Avdeyeva with libel against Saparbek Balkibekov, former General Director of public hydropower company Energeticheskie Stancii, and currently a Minister of Energy and Fuel Resources. Avdeyeva claimed that the court passed sentence without her presence and that Balkibekov pressured the court.[13] The total fine for Avdeyeva and her newspaper, *Bely Parokhod,* was 50,000 soms (US$12,000), a high sum by local standards.

Bakiyev's regime used the judicial system to expel unwanted MPs following the March 2005 regime change. Local courts dealt with numerous appeals over contested parliamentary seats following the controversial elections in February–March 2005. A few pro-Akayev MPs, including the president's son Aidar and daughter Bermet, were accused of falsifying election results and stripped of their mandates by local and regional courts.

The right to appoint and dismiss local judges was fiercely contested between the president and Parliament during the November and December 2006 discussion about the constitution. However, in the latest Constitution Bakiyev acquired this right, which will allow him to better control local government and secure desired outcomes where Parliament seats are contested. With the Constitutional Court showing loyalty to the president, local judges will be dependent on Bakiyev as well, thus the president has been able to usurp control entirely over the judicial branch.

Corruption

1999	2001	2002	2003	2004	2005	2006	2007	2008
6.00	6.00	6.00	6.00	6.00	6.00	6.00	6.00	6.25

The two years since the regime change in March 2005 have been marred with a rise in crime in Kyrgyzstan. Parliamentarians and government members openly blamed one another for connections with the criminal underworld and their negative repercussions on political stability. Days after the regime change, the rate of contract killings increased, with three MPs assassinated in July–November 2005. Like his Georgian and Ukrainian counterparts, Bakiyev was able to score a sweeping win in the July 2005 election thanks largely to his anticorruption slogans. But his popularity was short-lived as it became clear that the Bakiyev government was not implementing any policies to curb corruption. Frequent reshuffling of government members and confrontations between the president and Parliament over constitutional reform contributed to the rise of corruption at all levels of public institutions.

Hydropower is one of Kyrgyzstan's strategic economic sectors, but it is plagued by large-scale corruption and mounting tensions. The sector produces 12–14 million kilowatt-hours annually, which amounts to a profit of roughly US$1.2–1.5 million. After the regime change, the energy sector became even more corrupt, with key figures pocketing almost half of all profits in an elaborate graft scheme. In 2006, the energy sector was nearly 8 billion soms (about US$20 million) in debt, whereas in 2002 the debt was only 2.5 billion soms (about US$5 million). World Bank and International Monetary Fund observers estimated that annual commercial losses amount to 25–30 percent, or about US$30 million, though official records report only half that amount. The rest is attributed to lost profits, the public's failure to pay utility costs, or hidden profits gained via the difference in official and unofficial tariffs. According to reports by the Kyrgyz special antimonopoly committee, losses in the energy sector amount to roughly 17 percent (and not the reported 45–50 percent), while public payment losses approach 73 percent (not 50 percent, as reported by energy sector officials). The difference between real and forged indicators is allegedly explained by embezzlement surrounding the energy sector.

Reports of corruption are often voiced in local mass media outlets or on Internet forums. However, these reports, although revealing controversial information about particular political figures, raise little reaction among law enforcement agencies or the prosecutor general. This hints that most corrupt government officials and parliamentarians are able to prevail over law enforcement agencies. Corruption in the energy sector was one of the reasons behind Kyrgyzstan's decision in February to reject membership in the World Bank and International Monetary Fund's Heavily Indebted Poor Countries initiative, as membership would have required reforms and strong efforts to clean up corruption

Given that Kyrgyzstan is a significant regional transit for Chinese goods, its control of the customs service represents a profitable business and another major contributor to the state budget. However, Kyrgyz experts estimate that approximately half of taxes collected are pocketed by the State Customs Committee. The corruption scheme includes three main pillars: tax evasion, money laundering through importing and exporting illicit goods and services, and the protection of highly illegal activities, principally drug trafficking. Customs officers in Osh are especially corrupt, as they provide cover to drug smugglers on the Kharog-Osh-Bishkek route. They allow virtually unhampered passage for drugs imported from Tajikistan to other Central Asian states.

Since Bakiyev's government has failed to implement any visible political or economic changes, most Kyrgyz experts speculate that he will likely be replaced in the presidential elections in 2010. With a government that failed to fulfill the hopes of the Tulip Revolution and a politically charged local public that has proved its ability to impact the state, the upcoming elections in Kyrgyzstan will entail more political, economic, and social turbulence.

▮ AUTHOR: ERICA MARAT

Erica Marat is a research fellow with the Central Asia-Caucasus Institute & Silk Road Studies Program Joint Center, which is affiliated with Johns Hopkins University-SAIS and the Stockholm-based Institute for Security and Development Policy. She specializes in military institutions, state-building processes, and organized crime in Central Asia and beyond and has authored numerous publications in various policy and academic journals.

1   See Nurshat Ababakirov, "Problematic Threshold Angers Political Parties in Kyrgyzstan," Central Asia–Caucasus Institute, November 28, 2007, http://www.cacianalyst.org/?q=node/4751/print.

2   See the official results at the Kyrgyz Republic's Central Commission For Elections and Conducting Referenda, http://www.shailoo.gov.kg/show.php?tp=tx&id=341.

3   Preliminary Statement of Taza Shailoo on the October 21st Referendum in the Kyrgyz Republic, October 22, 2007, http://www.accessdemocracy.org/library/2336_kg_prelimref_engpdf_08082008.pdf.

4   "O faktah massovogo podvoza i podvornogo obhoda soobshchaet Koalitsiya" [Coalition Reports Facts of Mass Transportation (of Voters) and Visits to Each Neighborhood], Akipress. kg, October 21, 2007.

5   "Tsentr Interbilim: Takih tsinichnyh vyborov ne bylo eshche nikogda" [Interbilim Center Such Cynical Elections As Never Before], Akipress.kg, October 22, 2007.

6   Author's personal communication with Kyrgyz human rights activist, Maxim Kuleshov, Bishkek, October 2007.

7   "Zhenskie religioznye NPO Kyrgyzstana trebuyt razreshit; fotografirovat'sya im na pasport v hidzhabah" [Women Religious NGOs of Kyrgyzstan Demand the Right to Be Photographed in Hidjabs for Passports], 24.kg, October 6, 2006.

8   "Kirgizskii zhurnalist poluchil politicheskoe ubezhishche v Shveitsarii" [Kyrgyz Journalist Received Political Asylum in Switzerland], *Zona KZ,* October 3, 2007.

9   "Kto i za chto ubil oshskogo zhurnalista?" [Who and for What Was Osh Journalist Killed?], *Deutsche Welle,* October 28, 2007.

10   "Predvaritel'nye svedenya o vyborakh deputatov v mestnye keneshi Kyrgyzstana" [Preliminary Data on Local Government Elections to Keneshes in Kyrgyzstan], *CIS News,* October 9, 2007.

11   "Chlen TsIK J. Joldosheva: Spiski izbiratelei na vybory v Oshsky gorkenesh byli podgotovleny ne v dolzhnoy mere" [CEC Member J. Joldosheva: Electoral Lists to Osh City Kenesh Were Prepared Poorly], Akipress.kg, October 11, 2007.

12   "Toraga M. Sultanov: edinstvennoe, chto u nas ne poluchilos'—vzaimodeistviya s Konstitutsionnym sudom" [Parliament Speaker M. Sultanov: The Only Thing We Were Not Able to Achieve—Collaboration with the Constitutional Court], Akipress.kg, October 22, 2007.

13   "Zhurnalist E. Avdeeva schitaet, chto sud vynes nespravedlivoe reshenie, obyazav vyplatit' 50 tysyach somov v pol'zu energetika S. Balkibekova i podaet apellyatsiu" [Journalist E. Avdeeva Thinks That Court Made an Unfair Decision Obliging Her to Pay 50,000 Som to Power Engineer S. Balkibekov and Is Placing an Appeal], Akipress.kg, October 11, 2007.

Latvia

by Juris Dreifelds

Capital:	Riga
Population:	2.3 million
GNI/capita:	US$14,840

The social data above was taken from the European Bank for Reconstruction and Development's *Transition Report 2007: People in Transition*, and the economic data from the World Bank's *World Development Indicators 2008*.

Nations in Transit Ratings and Averaged Scores

	1999	2001	2002	2003	2004	2005	2006	2007	2008
Electoral Process	1.75	1.75	1.75	1.75	1.75	1.75	1.75	2.00	2.00
Civil Society	2.25	2.00	2.00	2.00	2.00	1.75	1.75	1.75	1.75
Independent Media	1.75	1.75	1.75	1.75	1.50	1.50	1.50	1.50	1.75
Governance*	2.50	2.25	2.25	2.25	2.25	n/a	n/a	n/a	n/a
National Democratic Governance	n/a	n/a	n/a	n/a	n/a	2.25	2.00	2.00	2.00
Local Democratic Governance	n/a	n/a	n/a	n/a	n/a	2.50	2.50	2.50	2.25
Judicial Framework and Independence	2.00	2.00	2.00	2.25	2.00	1.75	1.75	1.75	1.75
Corruption	3.50	3.50	3.75	3.50	3.50	3.50	3.25	3.00	3.00
Democracy Score	2.29	2.21	2.25	2.25	2.17	2.14	2.07	2.07	2.07

* *With the 2005 edition, Freedom House introduced separate analysis and ratings for national democratic governance and local democratic governance to provide readers with more detailed and nuanced analysis of these two important subjects.*

NOTE: The ratings reflect the consensus of Freedom House, its academic advisers, and the author(s) of this report. The opinions expressed in this report are those of the author(s). The ratings are based on a scale of 1 to 7, with 1 representing the highest level of democratic progress and 7 the lowest. The Democracy Score is an average of ratings for the categories tracked in a given year.

EXECUTIVE SUMMARY

L atvia's road to a fuller democracy, a functioning market economy, and an improved civil society has been made much easier by the country's historical exposure to two decades of independence won in 1920. While there was political turbulence and a certain alienation from political institutions in 2007, there were also positive signs of democratic consolidation. The increasing awareness of the value of nongovernmental organizations (NGOs) and liberal Internet access to all types of government information have slowly built a sense of democracy and a more informed electorate that is willing to press government for desired changes. The highly competitive Latvian mass media are proving to be reliable sources of information and watchdogs against governmental abuses of power.

National Democratic Governance. The four-party coalition following the October 2006 elections has maintained a solid majority of 59 deputies in the 100-member Parliament. However, through a series of unclear decisions, cavalier responses to the president and the opposition, and unresponsiveness to public opinion, this coalition squandered the trust expressed last year by a majority of voters. Three of the coalition parties, in the fall of 2007, were no longer able to surpass the required 5 percent threshold to gain seats in Latvia's Parliament. *The rating for national democratic government remains at 2.00.*

Electoral Process. Latvia is a parliamentary democracy, with elections to the 100-member Parliament (Saeima) held every four years. The most recent parliamentary elections took place in October 2006 and were considered by the Organization for Security and Cooperation in Europe to have been "administered transparently and professionally in a competitive and pluralistic environment." However, major distortions in electoral spending were introduced by third-party advertising. Voting turnout in four years declined from 71 percent to 62 percent. Presidential elections by Parliament on October 29, 2007, created widespread dismay because of the last minute choice of an unknown surgeon who was selected in secrecy (at the Riga Zoo) by four members of the coalition and the Latvian politician and business oligarch Andris Šķēle. The elected president, Valdis Zatlers, is turning out to be a relatively active and independent officeholder, increasingly gaining the respect of the population. *The rating for electoral process remains at 2.00.*

Civil Society. NGO activity is in a state of flux because of the loss of financing by foreign donors and reorientation to self-sustainability. Government funding and especially seed money to access European Union (EU) funds have provided some relief. Many ministries have stepped away from their apparent friendliness to NGOs prior to the elections and have discontinued certain former financial support initiatives, now deemed luxuries. At the same time, popular activity levels to counter threatening government initiatives, such as the dismissal of the anticorruption head, forced a retreat by government on many fronts. *The rating for civil society remains at 1.75.*

Independent Media. Latvian mass media have remained diverse, competitive, and buoyant. Almost all private media in Latvia continued to fall under foreign control, creating unease in the population. Many people also have access to television programs from other EU countries. Latvian public TV is losing its audience share, although public radio is still dominant. When public television LTV1 aborted a previously scheduled program about Russia, much criticism ensued charging that political pressure prevented the story from going on the air. Over 55 percent of the population is engaged in regular use of the Internet. *Owing to pressures against public television, Latvia's rating for independent media worsened from 1.50 to 1.75.*

Local Democratic Governance. After a decade of discussions, Latvia finally accepted the restructuring of 530 municipal units into a more manageable 105 self-governments, to be effected by the end of 2009. *Owing to the rationalization associated with territorial reforms and general activism of municipal politicians, the rating for local democratic governance improves from 2.50 to 2.25.*

Judicial Framework and Independence. The status, pay, and number of judges in Latvia continue to increase. Administrative courts are now planned to expand to all four major regions of Latvia, easing the pressure on the single court situated in Riga. Modernization of the court system is progressing rapidly, yet trust ratings remain low, with only 25 percent giving a positive rating against a 63 percent negative rating in September 2007. In August 2007, a published transcript of 1998–2000 pre-trial telephone conversations between a leading law firm and judges created much criticism from the public and soul-searching in the judiciary. Ethics committees have now been proposed for judges and lawyers. Funding for the Ministry of Justice, and especially its court administration sector, has more than doubled since 2004. *The rating for judicial framework and independence remains at 1.75.*

Corruption. While all signs indicate relatively limited corruption at the middle and lower levels of the administration and courts, the pinnacle of politics appears tainted. Latvia's anticorruption organization, the Corruption Prevention and Combating Bureau (KNAB), is becoming more sophisticated and has accelerated its investigations, increasingly catching "big fish" in its net. Leading oligarch Aivars Lembergs was jailed in March 2007 for alleged corruption, and another oligarch, Andris Šķēle, is under scrutiny. KNAB is now one of the most trusted organizations in Latvia, and people are more willing to inform officials about observed corruptive activities. Prime Minister Aigars Kalvītis tried to dismiss the head of KNAB in

September, but pressure from the public led instead to the prime minister's resignation. *Latvia's rating for corruption remains at 3.00.*

Outlook for 2008. In 2008, Latvia will continue to consolidate its position in the EU and NATO. There will be many bitter feelings regarding the distribution of EU funds. The government will no longer feel as confident and willing to ignore public opinion, and changes in the complexion of coalition parties can be expected. Russian-Latvian relations within the republic are presently relaxed, but group animosity might grow in spite of generally friendly personal interactions. This animosity might be fueled by the Russian-language media and by nationalist elements in Russia. Rapid economic growth in the heartland and the current high rate of inflation will create even more discontent in the hinterlands, where stagnation will deepen. More individuals are expected to leave Latvia to work abroad. Many of these, especially Russophones, will not return to Latvia.

MAIN REPORT

National Democratic Governance

1999	2001	2002	2003	2004	2005	2006	2007	2008
n/a	n/a	n/a	n/a	n/a	2.25	2.00	2.00	2.00

Classic democracy has been established in Latvia, and the country has become a model for other former Soviet republics in attuning national legislation to European Union (EU) standards. The Latvian president's Strategic Analysis Commission for several years has assembled specialists to evaluate the level of 14 separate components of democracy in the republic. In 2005, the commission judged the average score to be 3.02 (on a scale of 1–5, with 5 the highest). Two years later, the situation had changed very little, and the average was listed at 3.07.[1]

During 2007, Latvia's Parliament and government functioned according to the Constitution (which was established in 1922), adhering to laws and regulations and court decisions. There was no fear of extra-parliamentary armed or mob activities, and the elected deputies functioned, for the most part, within the parameters of their mandate and party discipline. The turbulence in politics in 2007 highlighted the viability of the institutional checks and balances that prevented the undue aggrandizement of executive power and finalization of sometimes hastily made decisions by the prime minister and his cabinet. In spite of the low levels of trust accorded Latvian democratic institutions, there is a general acceptance of the legitimacy of national authorities. More legal loopholes are being closed, although many still remain.

Prime Minister Aigars Kalvītis was in office longer than any other Latvian prime minister. He took over cabinet leadership on December 2, 2004, and retained his position until December 5, 2007, when he resigned. He was replaced by Ivars Godmanis, who was the first post-independence prime minister and recently served as cabinet minister of the Interior Ministry. Godmanis was selected as a candidate by newly chosen President Valdis Zatlers and confirmed by a vote of 54 to 43 in Parliament on December 19, 2007.

The 59 deputies of the four-party coalition voted almost unanimously in 2007 on most important legislation and official appointments. While such stability is a positive attribute, at times this cohesive majority gave rise to a high degree of intolerance toward the opposition, a dismissal of popular opinion, and a lack of attention to legitimate presidential requests and warnings. A series of unpopular decisions led to a perceptible gap between legislators and the electorate, peaking in September and October. Many citizens and journalists felt that the coalition was not working for the increased welfare of the entire nation, but for the interests of a narrow group of oligarchs. This concern about the misplaced focus of Parliament was a catalyst for a special public address at Riga University by the U.S. ambassador to Latvia, Catherine Todd Bailey, in mid-October. Her main message was that governmental authorities should work for "all the people" and not just "a small part."[2] Her speech was widely acclaimed but dismissed by the governmental coalition as irrelevant.

Three oligarchs in particular have been singled out in public discussions, especially because each held sway in separate coalition parties. One of the oligarchs, Aivars Lembergs—mayor of Ventspils and in October 2006 a nominee by the Union of Greens and Farmers Party for the position of prime minister—was arrested in mid-March and imprisoned, although he was later placed under house arrest.[3] Ainars Šlesers, founder of Latvia's First Party, was implicated in the attempted bribery of the mayor of Jurmala, publicized in early 2006. He was forced to resign his post as minister of transportation but returned to the post after the October 2006 elections. The other oligarch, Andris Šķēle, a former prime minister, was under increased suspicion of having been the mastermind of what has become known as "the Kempmayer affair," related to the digitalization of Latvia's media but involving the legally questioned appropriation of the republic's share of the largest mobile telephone company, LMT. Many of Šķēle's close associates have already been charged.

Without a doubt, Šķēle has been a masterful political tactician, but people are beginning to associate many of the decisions of the parliamentary coalition with the personal economic interests of this individual. This has been especially true of the attempted dismissal of Aleksejs Loskutovs, head of the Corruption Prevention and Combatting Bureau (*Korupcijas noversanas un apkarosanas biroja—*KNAB), by Prime Minister Kalvītis on September 24. The prime minister's basis for dismissal concerned limited bookkeeping errors in KNAB discovered by state control personnel. According to Inguna Sudraba, the key controller who wrote the report on KNAB, almost all ministries and agencies have had accounting issues of far greater import without having led to the dismissals of their leaders. Procurator General Janis Maizitis, after chairing a special investigative commission on this issue, found no basis for such a drastic measure.[4] The issue mobilized a growing and active opposition against Kalvītis and the coalition and, indeed, many deputies of the governing coalition openly protested such a move. Foreign Affairs Minister Artis Pabriks resigned in protest on October 19. Under much public pressure, Loskutovs' dismissal was abrogated by the government on November 1.[5]

The dismissal of Loskutovs was only one of a series of events that raised popular opposition toward the parliamentary coalition. One of the most important confrontations focused on two laws concerning national security restructuring, both passed on March 1. After several unsuccessful attempts by the President Vaira Vīķe-Freiberga to convince the coalition to tighten these laws, she finally resorted to the drastic option of Section 72 of the Constitution, a confrontational veto allowing a two-month period to organize a petition with the signatures of at least 10 percent of the electorate and then, if successful, a referendum on the issue. The president felt that these two new laws were going to extend access to secret information by parliamentary aides and other political personnel which could endanger NATO secrets, secret criminal investigations, and information about witnesses.[6] In spite of the speedy withdrawal of these laws, 337,000 citizens cast their ballots; many did so more as a protest against the direction of Parliament. Although a "victory" would have required the approval of one-half of all electors (453,730), voters were pleased with the mobilization of such large numbers.[7] Moreover, in the process of atonement, the government removed Section 81 of the Constitution. This section, included in the Constitution since 1922, had allowed the cabinet to vote into law any measures it deemed of immediate significance while Parliament was not sitting. This was also the section used to pass the notorious laws on security restructuring.[8]

President Vaira Vīķe-Freiberga received accolades for her bravery in vetoing the law. It was a fitting finale for her two terms and eight years as president, with her mandate ending on July 7. Her esteem as a people's president was visibly accentuated by the vast demonstration of support and emotions when thousands of people brought flowers in the city of Sigulda to form a "sun of flowers." The president's popularity on the international scene was in evidence when she received the Davos Forum award.

As a last contribution to Latvia's democracy, Vīķe-Freiberga also managed to strengthen the law concerning the process of presidential succession. The search for her successor once again created strains between the general population and the coalition. While many candidates were considered, only two remained on the final short list. At the last moment, in a surprise move, the coalition decided to pick an unknown, politically inexperienced individual who had been a surgeon and administrator of a hospital. Valdis Zatlers was chosen by four members of the coalition together with Andris Šķēle at a secret rendezvous at the Riga Zoo, where interference with them was less likely.[9] The opposition chose the retired head of the Constitutional Court, Aivars Endziņš. According to polls, a majority of people supported Endziņš. Nevertheless, in a secret ballot, Parliament chose Zatlers with 58 votes, whereas Endziņš received 39 votes.[10] Controversy also surrounded the appointment process for the ombudsman and for the Constitutional Court, with the media playing a large role in mobilizing public opinion.

The problems for the coalition led to signs of instability. Four ministers left the cabinet in the fall of 2007. One of these, Aigars Štokenbergs, was fired for insubordination. He claims that he displeased the People's Party leader, Andris Šķēle, when he tried to thwart his business ambitions in the processing of Riga garbage. Štokenbergs was also dismissed from the People's Party.[11]

Another embarrassment for the coalition was the bizarre behavior of former prime minister and longtime Speaker of Parliament Indulis Emsis. He made erroneous statements to the Procurator General's Office after the theft of his satchel in the parliamentary cafeteria. The bag contained US$6,000, but he initially claimed to have lost US$10,000.[12] The carrying of large sums of cash in Parliament raised the suspicion of many that Emsis was one of the "stipend" recipients of imprisoned oligarch Aivars Lembergs. Indeed, in 2007, evidence was found that Lembergs had in the past, and was still, secretly financing several political parties and deputies. At this point, the Office of the Procurator General is not divulging names until it has assembled sufficient evidence. Ironically, Emsis was replaced as Speaker in September by a close colleague of the oligarch Lembergs, a relatively unknown physician from Ventspils, Gundars Daudze.

The political coalition was formed by four parties: the People's Party, the Union of Greens and Farmers, the Union of First Party and Latvia's Way, and Fatherland and Freedom. They have managed to squander their relatively high public standing with the electorate in the space of one year. While they received over one-half of all votes in October 2006, three of the four coalition parties would receive less than 5 percent support at the end of October 2007, the threshold for representation in the Parliament.[13]

The judiciary is independent of direct government pressure once Parliament confirms a judge's candidacy. However, judges are dependent on the Ministry of Justice for their wages, administrative support, offices, and instructions on new laws and procedures.

People now have the option of suing state organs for compensation of losses incurred by their actions or inactions. The well-developed administrative courts allow for the resolution of cases between inhabitants and various state bodies. People can also turn to the Constitutional Court for reversal of policies or state decisions. Starting this year, as well, there is an Office of the Ombudsman that can help resolve certain complaints.

The Latvian civil service functions according to traditional standards of efficiency and public service and is monitored by various financial and other control and audit institutions, including the Civil Service Board. Unfortunately, its salary levels are relatively low compared with those in the private sector. A major problem is the annual 30–40 percent turnover rate of workers.

The Latvian military is well integrated with civilian authorities, and the president is commander in chief of the armed forces. Beginning in 2007, Latvia changed to an all-volunteer military service. The prestige of the military has grown with increased pay and financing. The holding of a NATO summit conference in Riga at the end of November 2006 further raised the prestige of Latvia's armed forces, and their participation in Iraq and Afghanistan has provided a degree of experience in real combat.

Electoral Process

1999	2001	2002	2003	2004	2005	2006	2007	2008
1.75	1.75	1.75	1.75	1.75	1.75	1.75	2.00	2.00

Latvia is a parliamentary democracy, and elections to the 100-member Parliament are held every four years. Deputies are elected proportionally from party lists in five large electoral districts.

The elections to the ninth Parliament were held on October 7, 2006, with the participation of 19 party lists with 1,027 candidates. The most far-reaching and significant change was the effort to circumvent party spending limits by orchestrating the financing of advertising by individual organizations under the guise of freedom of speech. The People's Party and Latvia's First Party were the leaders in such initiatives, gaining many votes in the process. Voter participation rate, however, was significantly lower than in 2002, decreasing from 70.3 percent to 62.28 percent.[14]

The elections were closely observed by a delegation from the OSCE's Office for Democratic Institutions and Human Rights. In their view, the election had been "administered transparently and professionally and the campaign took place in a competitive and pluralistic environment.[15]

The perceived big winner of the elections was the People's Party with 23 seats. The perceived big loser was the New Era Party, which in 2002 was elected with 26 seats but this time received only 18 seats. Of the 7 winning parties, only the above 2 were not coalitions. The seat distribution in the other parties was as follows: Union of Greens and Farmers 18, Harmony Center 17, Union of First Party and Latvia's Way 10, Fatherland and Freedom 7, and For Human Rights in a United Latvia 6.

Latvian presidents are chosen for a term of four years by the Parliament and require 51 votes to be elected. In the May 29, 2007, presidential elections, Valdis Zatlers, the coalition's candidate, won with 58 votes, while 39 votes supported Aivars Endziņš, the opposition's candidate.

Latvia joined the EU on May 1, 2004, and became a participant in the third supranational level of elections, to choose 9 deputies out of a total of 732 for the European Parliament. Elections were held on June 12, 2006. Voter participation was relatively low at 41.23 percent, which was close to the overall average for the 25 EU states (45.3 percent).

Civil Society

1999	2001	2002	2003	2004	2005	2006	2007	2008
2.25	2.00	2.00	2.00	2.00	1.75	1.75	1.75	1.75

Nongovernmental organizations (NGOs) are regulated and defended by the Latvian Constitution, the 1992 Law Concerning Public Organizations and Their Associations, and two subsequent laws on public organizations passed in 2003 and 2004. There have also been various mid- and long-term national programs outlining the duties of government in the strengthening of civil society. In particular, the Ministry of Special Issues and Social Integration has undertaken a leading role in dealing with NGOs. Similarly, the Ministry of Foreign Affairs signed a cooperation agreement on March 19, 2007, with major groups to coordinate various joint projects on EU matters. At the same time, many ministries have only paid lip service to cooperation and have not provided any contact personnel or Web sites for interaction with relevant groups. In 2007, most ministries halved their funds slated for interaction with NGOs, reflecting a perception of such activity as a "luxury."[16]

The early part of 2007, half a year after Latvia's October 2006 elections, was somewhat somnolent. The need to react to government actions, however, created a rise in participative fervor. The president's veto of the two laws on national security restructuring mobilized citizens both in the collection of signatures required for a referendum and in the July 7 referendum itself. Following the summer doldrums, the public was energized by the September dismissal of Aleksejs Loskutovs, head of the KNAB. Many people rose to protest until Loskutovs's dismissal was reversed on November 1.

A study for Eurobarometer (a social research survey series for the European Commission) published in 2007 has indicated that 65 percent of people in Latvia considered it important to help others and to work in volunteer organizations; the average for the EU was 78 percent. Active participation in volunteer work was supported by 20 percent in Latvia, but 33 percent on average in the EU.[17]

The 2006 NGO Sustainability Index by USAID provides a decade of assessments of group sustainability on a scale of 1 (perfect consolidation) to 7 (low sustainability). Latvia, with an average of 2.6, was one of the leading countries with respect to group viability in Eastern and Central Europe, ranking 4 out of 29 countries evaluated. In the same study, Latvia's weakest showing was in financial ability and organizational capacity.

The years since Latvia's accession to the EU in May 2004 have been marked by turbulence in the NGO sector. Most NGOs have lost financing by foreign donors and have required a reorientation to self-sustainability. The Latvian government provides grants to specific NGOs as "seed money" for receiving larger EU grants and is especially generous to groups involved in providing greater ethnic cooperation and understanding. The other major funding by the state is achieved through its tax policy. Donations to groups designated as having "public benefit status" are 85 percent tax deductible. In 2007, there were 940 such groups. In 2005, the donated sum to all NGOs was over 28 million lats (US$62 million). The lion's share (47.76 percent) went to cultural organizations, followed by sports groups (31.9 percent). Those active in the social realm claimed only 1.26 percent of the total. Thus, groups advocating a cleaner environment, gender equality, and transparency of governmental processes are mostly ignored by large donors.[18] Indeed, the Latvian chapter of Transparency International (Delna) could not afford to pay the salary of its director, and its accumulated debt threatened its very existence.

Latvian NGOs face many problems besides financing. Organizational capacity is low. Most are small groups composed of about two dozen individuals who often lack basic training in financial, legal, administrative, and public relations skills. They are dependent primarily on part-time volunteers who do not have the time or energy to plan and focus on long-term strategies. Even those groups that have paid staff often find themselves tied to the life of specific projects rather than having a continuous source of personnel financing. As one activist claimed, this "Russian roulette" financing prevents long-term planning. Another problem has been the exodus of many thousands to Ireland and other EU countries. While many left for economic reasons, a substantive group left because of frustration with Latvian institutional inertia and failings and are not planning to return.

Various ethnic groups have created their respective cultural and advocacy organizations. Most recently, the Latvian government has expended much effort to provide support systems for the "Cigani," or Roma, including a new Internet portal (http://www.romi.lv).[19] On March 24, 2006, the first Arab Cultural Center in the Baltic states was established in Latvia.

Perhaps an index of a certain measure of success of Latvian NGOs has been their invitation by several post-Soviet states, including Georgia, to provide advice on strengthening civil society.

Independent Media

1999	2001	2002	2003	2004	2005	2006	2007	2008
1.75	1.75	1.75	1.75	1.50	1.50	1.50	1.50	1.75

The Latvian media are free to disseminate information and views, limited only by libel considerations and the pressures of the market. Investigative journalists are free to pursue various sensitive topics, including government waste and corruption, but such initiatives are costly and limited in scale. The mass media generally enjoy editorial independence, although certain news items may be difficult to obtain from government sources in spite of the Freedom of Information Act passed in November 1998. The leading newspapers are available free of charge on the World Wide Web, and several print editions are distributed without charge.

In 2007, almost all private Latvian-language media in the country became foreign-owned. Rupert Murdoch's company News Corp Europe on May 8 purchased the leading Latvian TV station, LNT, and 70 percent of TV5. The Britain-based Swedish company Modern Times Group (MTG) controls TV3 and the Russian-language 3+, as well as several radio stations, including Star FM. The major newspaper *Diena* is owned by the Bonnier Group, a multinational Swedish company. This company also controls about one-third of local papers and the Baltic News Service. The newspapers *Neatkariga Rita Avize* and *Vakara Zinas* have been controlled by the owners of Ventspils Nafta, which appear to have moved offshore. Another leading newspaper, *Latvijas Avize,* is controlled through Ventbunkers, which in turn is under the direction of a foreign-owned corporation based in the Netherlands. The most watched and used Internet news source and interaction Web site, Delfi, was purchased by the Estonian Ekspress Grupp on August 2, 2007. Delfi news is available in the local Baltic languages and also in Russian. It also operates a news portal in Ukraine in Ukrainian.

The Russian-language First Baltic Channel (PBK), a Baltic-wide television network, is based in Riga, and the leading Russian-language newspapers (*Segodnya, Chas,* and *Telegraf*) appear to be locally owned. Their limited audiences and profit margins have not yet enticed foreign firms to buy them out.

The state-subsidized public LTV1 and LTV7 (Russian language) are struggling to maintain their audiences, which in the entire year of 2007 stood at 11.4 percent and 3.9 percent of the population, respectively. LNT was in the lead with 19 percent of total viewing time, followed by TV3 at 18 percent. The Russian-language PBK claimed 10.4 percent, and the station 3+ had 4.9 percent. In line with the new thrust of cultural globalization, the three most popular programs in September were *Singing with the Stars, Shrek,* and *Shrek 2.* In addition, a quarter of TV viewing time (24.2 percent) was focused on foreign broadcasts. However, the public station LTV1 attracted large audiences with its news and public affairs shows *Panorama* and *Kas Notiek Latvija? (What Is Happening in Latvia?).* Public broadcasting was surprisingly competitive in radio, garnering over one-half of total audiences.[20]

In total, people in Latvia spent over seven hours a day in media-related activities in early 2007. Television claimed 3 hours and 29 minutes (3:29) on weekdays and 5:10 on weekends. The other media received less attention—radio, 2:36 weekdays and 1:56 weekends; Internet, 1:21 and 1:32; newspapers, 0:43 and 0:47; and magazines, 0:29 and 0:38.[21] Internet usage has become a constituent part of life for a majority of people. The Central Statistics Bureau reported that Internet was available to 51 percent of households in the first quarter of 2007. In a poll also during the first quarter, 55 percent of respondents claimed to have used the Internet in the previous three months. Usage varied by age group: Among those 16–24, it was 94 percent; for those 25–34, it was 78 percent. Usage decreased with each subsequent age decade—63 percent, 44 percent, and 25 percent, respectively, but only 6 percent among those aged 65–74.[22]

The Latvian media advertising market is growing rapidly, up by 24 percent in 2007 compared with 2006. The bulk of advertising revenue went to TV (35 percent), newspapers (22 percent), magazines (17 percent), radio (10 percent), outdoor (9 percent), Internet (6 percent), and cinema (less than 1 percent).[23]

In 2007, there were several controversial issues connected to the media. The Latvian post office abruptly decided to increase the price of newspaper delivery. After much debate, a compromise was reached, allowing for a rate hike in 2008 by the amount of inflation plus 15 percent. A May 10 Latvian court decision shocked the Latvian Press Publishers Association when journalist Uldis Dreiblats of the newspaper *Neatkariga Rita Avize* was fined for not revealing one of his sources. While the primary- and secondary-level courts ruled against Dreiblats, the highest-level court (the Criminal Case Department of the Senate) absolved him entirely on December 4, 2007.[24] In another case, a journalist from the newspaper *Diena,* Aivars Ozolins, was supported by the European Court of Human Rights (ECHR) in his defense of press freedom. Indeed, the government of Latvia was forced to pay Ozolins €10,292 (US$16,000) for unfounded interference by the Latvian courts, which had forced *Diena* to retract its statement about privatization abuse by the economics minister, and also had to pay for moral damages. Much criticism ensued after Latvian TV1 decided to cancel a previously scheduled film critical of Russian president Vladimir Putin just before the Russian Duma elections in December. Many felt that this was a case of censorship by Latvian politicians in order not to antagonize its neighbor and not to interfere in the choices made by local Latvian Russians having voting rights. This interference precipitated the resignation of the head of Latvian TV, Zanis Holsteins.

Journalists in Latvia have almost no protection vis-à-vis their employers. Their unions are weak or nonexistent, and their remuneration is small and based on a low basic salary, with extra payments calculated per article or presentation. Many journalists are forced to moonlight at several jobs in order to survive. While earnings vary widely according to the journalist's professional experience and the size of the employing media outlet, the Latvian Union of Journalists estimated that monthly average earnings for a journalist in 2007 were 300–400 Latvian lats (US$600–US$900) before income taxes of 25 percent. Consequently, there is a large turnover of reporters. Many experienced reporters leave journalism to work in public relations firms and are replaced by an influx of young, inexperienced journalists who possess neither the time nor the acquired skills necessary to undertake major investigative initiatives. In spite of such issues, the media are the most trusted institutions in Latvia. Encouragingly, there is tremendous competition to enter journalism schools. The glamour of this profession and the levels of public trust for the media are strong in Latvia.

Local Democratic Governance

1999	2001	2002	2003	2004	2005	2006	2007	2008
n/a	n/a	n/a	n/a	n/a	2.50	2.50	2.50	2.25

In contrast with Estonia and Lithuania, Latvia has approved a Constitution that does not include the rights and principles of local governments, and the rectification of this omission has been one of the constant demands of the Union of Latvia's Self-Governments. Nevertheless, Latvia has several laws that apply to municipalities, with the main legislation being the Law on Local Governments, passed May 19, 1994, and amended more than 10 times since then.

The most important development for local governance in Latvia during the year was the cabinet's acceptance in September of the plan for territorial reform. After a decade of discussions, the territorial reform of Latvia's 530 local governments into 96 districts and 9 cities was approved. The more manageable number should increase the viability of local governments. This reorganization is to occur by the end of 2009.[25]

Territorial reform will not significantly alleviate the problem of financing. Local budgets are formed by property taxes and the retention of 79 percent of local income taxes (to be increased to 80 percent starting January 1, 2008). For many years, Latvia has implemented a so-called equalization fund to compensate poorer districts. This fund depends in part on state coffers (about 7 million lats [US$15.5 million]), but the largest contributors are the wealthy municipalities; the capital city of Riga alone accounted for the lion's share of the contributions. Not surprisingly, Riga has balked at growing assessments, noting that large numbers of out-of-town individuals contribute to the city's road congestion, partake of its infrastructure, study in Riga schools, and send children to the city's kindergartens.

In 2007, 59 local governments paid into the fund; 41 were neither contributors nor recipients, but 427 districts and 26 regional councils were recipients.[26] It should be noted that Latvia will receive 3.2 billion lats (US$7.05 billion) from the EU between 2007 and 2013, and a large part of this sum will be directed to upgrade municipal infrastructures, including roads.

Municipalities carry a large share of local governance responsibilities. Their competences include primary and secondary education, most social assistance (except pensions and family care benefits), health care, water supply and sewage works, county roads, solid waste collection and disposal, and about one-fifth of all housing in Latvia to which they hold legal title. Processes of governance vary according to the size of the municipality, but all are based on fundamental democratic foundations, which include openness of council and committee meetings and availability of their minutes, access to deputies and the executive by local residents, procedures for review of complaints and suggestions, public discussions, and audited annual reports or reviews of budget fulfillment, spending, assets, and activities. Citizens also have recourse to municipal elections every four years. Elections are free and democratic, with a turnout of 52.85 percent in the last elections, which were held on March 2, 2005. The next elections are slated for March 2009.

Judicial Framework and Independence

1999	2001	2002	2003	2004	2005	2006	2007	2008
2.00	2.00	2.00	2.25	2.00	1.75	1.75	1.75	1.75

Latvia's Constitution provides protection for fundamental political, civil, and human rights, and on the whole these are respected by authorities and the general population. Latvians are guaranteed equality before the law, but not all Latvians have equal access to justice in practice. Over 80 percent of litigants in civil cases act without the help of lawyers, but state legal aid is made available in all criminal cases.

On January 1, 2007, Latvia's Law on the Ombudsman came into force. After much controversy and a failed first round of candidates, all parliamentary parties agreed on the choice of Romans Apsitis, a former minister of justice and retired deputy chair of the Constitutional Court. The Office of the Ombudsman incorporates the duties of the former State Human Rights Bureau and extends its authority to all government institutions at both municipal and national levels. In the first half of 2007, the office reported receiving 2,861 complaints. About 20–30 percent were considered valid and within the scope of the ombudsman's mandate.[27] Apsitis had requested that the ombudsman's position be strengthened by extending appointments from four to five years and by formally including the position in the Constitution. An amendment by the Parliament allowed for the five-year appointment, but it was to be applied from January 1, 2010. As yet, the ombudsman has no constitutional protection. The state is also held accountable by the Latvian administrative court system and by the EU and its various institutions. Administrative courts adjudicate disputes and conflicts between the population and national or local public servants, including policemen. State bodies and state workers can be fined or asked for restitution of lost assets as a result of actions or inactions. A major step to expand administrative courts to the four Latvian regions by 2008–2009 will lessen the pressure on the single administrative court located in Riga, which now has a backlog of one year or longer.

The ECHR also considers cases after they have wound their way through the Latvian court system. Several successful litigations against Latvia have sensitized the administration and court judges to the fundamental civil rights of the EU population.

The judicial system is being consolidated and, indeed, much has been done to improve the working conditions, support systems, salaries, and pensions of judges. If a decade ago candidates for the judiciary were difficult to find and the salary gap between private law practice and the bench was enormous, then in the last several years, the scales between the two have narrowed significantly. There is now intensive competition for each opening in the judiciary, and the two-year probationary period has allowed for better long-term screening and more highly-qualified candidates.

Another new courthouse was opened in Riga in 2007 in order to increase the hearing of trials. Computerization in the courts of all cases has been completed. In an attempt to reduce the formidable turnover of court clerks and other court-related personnel—especially in the city of Riga—salaries were increased by 33 percent in 2007. The minister of justice has promised to include even greater increases in the 2008 budget. The court administration section of the Ministry of Justice, created in 2004, is in charge of over 2,000 court workers whose responsibility is to ensure that judges only need worry about the case verdicts. The budget allocation for the section has grown rapidly. In 2004, it was 14.39 million lats (US$31.7 million), but in 2007, it was 29.26 million lats (US$64.5 million). In 2007, its share of the Ministry of Justice's total budget was 27 percent.[28] According to the head of one Riga district court, all court cases are processed expeditiously and there is no significant backlog. Moreover, by the end of 2007, all cases will be assigned to different judges electronically to avoid any semblance of bias.

In spite of the evident progress, the courts suffer from a public perception problem. A poll by TNS Latvia published in January 2007 indicated that in Latvia, only 17 percent of people trusted the court system. In the EU, the average level of trust for courts was 46 percent.[29] A September 2007 poll by SKDS marketing and public opinion research center gave the following responses regarding trust of courts: trust entirely (1.9 percent); tend to trust (more or less) (23.3 percent); tend to distrust (35.5 percent); totally distrust (27 percent); and no position or answer (12.3 percent).[30] A major blow to the credibility of the court system occurred in August 2007 when illegal transcripts of old phone conversations (1998–2000) between Latvia's best-known senior lawyer, Andris Grutups, and half a dozen judges were published in a book titled *Tiesasanas ka Kekis* (*Legal Proceedings as a Kitchen*).

Names were slightly altered in the book to prevent prosecution of the publisher, but the media indulged in a "feeding frenzy," using the full names of the judges involved. The transcripts, which were validated as authentic by Procurator General Janis Maizitis, included ethically questionable, pre-trial discussions and referred to "tea for two" meetings between Grutups and judges to discuss specific cases in which he was involved.[31]

The best-seller engendered much soul-searching in the legal community and prompted an extraordinary meeting of judges on November 2, attended by 393 of Latvia's 520 judges. One of the key resolutions of this meeting was to establish an ethics committee that would be responsible for overseeing the implementation of the existing code of ethics. In reaction to the crisis, President Zatlers expressed his hope that judges would attempt to dissipate the widespread worries that "adjudication in Latvia is determined outside the halls of justice." Many people argued that these telephone conversations occurred almost a decade earliere, that the courts have now become much more immune to such cozy relationships between lawyers and judges, and that these Soviet-era practices are rare among the post-Soviet generation, which has been steeped in Western practices.[32]

The Latvian prison population is decreasing with the institution of new methods of dealing with lawbreakers (especially young offenders), such as suspended sentences, probation, and parole systems. In 2007, more than 12,000 cases were processed by the probationary service. However, a high rate of pre-trial detention remains a problem. In February 2007, there were 6,490 people incarcerated in Latvia's prisons; of these, 25.8 percent were awaiting trial. Prisons have become breeding grounds for various diseases such as resistant tuberculosis and AIDS. Indeed, one source claims that about half of all prisoners suffer from hepatitis C. New programs for prisoner employment and support systems for those discharged have been instituted.[33] Large sums have been earmarked in the state budget for the modernization of prison facilities.

The Latvian Constitutional Court is trusted by the public more than other courts, as indicated by all polls on institutional trust. The seven justices are appointed for a single term of 10 years. Three appointments can be nominated by a minimum of 10 parliamentary deputies, two by cabinet, and two by the Supreme Court "plenary" of about 50 justices. In 2006, four judges from the court retired. Much controversy surrounded the nominees for their replacements. The quality of two judges in particular was widely criticized. Nevertheless, one of these judges Viktors Skudra, was appointed by the Saeima in spite of opposition from its Justice Committee. The objection to Skudra was because he was graduated from university in 1973, and had neither pursued a higher academic degree nor attended international seminars or other courses.[34] Another judge, Zaiga Vrubļevska, withdrew her nomination after her questionable judgments regarding the petroleum company Ventspils Nafta were publicized.[35] Vrubļevska also was connected to the controversial telephone conversations with Grutups that were published in August.

Corruption

1999	2001	2002	2003	2004	2005	2006	2007	2008
3.50	3.50	3.75	3.50	3.50	3.50	3.25	3.00	3.00

A 2006 report by a respected specialist on corruption in Latvia, Valts Kalniņš, described Latvia as "slowly becoming similar to several west European states, where the civil service and court system are relatively noncorrupt, but politics is corrupt." In the report, Kalniņš observed: "Improvements are occurring in the justice environment and in the state bureaucracy, but in the political arena I do not see any visible improvements." With considerable prescience, Kalniņš noted that if the Latvian anticorruption bureau KNAB became a greater threat to political corruption, it would receive a "counterblow."[36] Indeed, the counterblow came from the prime minister, Aigars Kalvītis, who tried to dismiss the head of KNAB in September 2007. Public pressure and pressure from within his own party forced Kalvītis to rescind this order on November 1 and led to his own retirement from office in December.

KNAB has now become what has been commonly described as a "well-oiled machine" that in five years of existence has been able to weld its team of 136 "young and eager" specialists into a dedicated team in the fight against corruption. It has made efficient use of its modest budget of 3.5 million lats (US$7.7 million). If in its first year it focused on small and middle levels of corruption, in the last two years it has been able to deal successfully with corrupt officials, judges, leading police personnel, customs administration, top-level politicians, and illegal party financing.[37]

One of the most discussed events was the arrest of prominent oligarch Aivars Lembergs in mid-March 2007. Lembergs was charged with large-scale bribery, money laundering, blackmail, and abuse of authority. In August, documents surfaced that proved Lembergs had surreptitiously financed several political parties including the Social Democratic Party. In addition, it is widely believed that over 30 parliamentary deputies were on his payroll.[38]

According to Aleksejs Loskutovs, the biggest achievement of the KNAB has been the increase in public understanding about corruption risks and harm; this has been demonstrated by people's increased willingness to report corrupt practices. Indeed, the broad regard and respect for KNAB's efficient work was demonstrated immediately after Lostukovs's dismissal. Thousands of people demonstrated in the middle of Riga on multiple occasions, and despite adverse weather conditions. Some news sources even dubbed this overt opposition "the umbrella revolution." Latvia had not experienced such critical opposition to government and such cohesion and solidarity since the days of the Latvian Awakening and "singing revolution" in 1989. In 2006, KNAB registered 11,988 documents connected to possible corruption activities. This bureau also participated in reviewing legal drafts (providing 123 recommendations) and initiated 19 normative drafts connected to various aspects of corruption control.[39]

KNAB is but one of several organizations dealing with crime and corruption. According to Procurator General Maizitis, in 2006 KNAB was responsible for about one-third of corruption cases included in criminal process proceedings. The State Revenue Service, for example, has focused on criminal activities associated with illegal cigarette, alcohol, and gasoline contraband. In 2006, it was able to nullify or seriously hamper the activities of 11 organized criminal associations. Other corruption-seeking organizations include the financial police and the Money Laundering Prevention Division of the Office of the Procurator General.

By year-end 2007, many major investigations and cases of actual or potential corruption remained in progress. Greatest attention has been focused on the resolution of the Kempmayer affair, involving the other major oligarch, Andris Šķēle. The whereabouts of 46 million lats (US$101.3 million) that disappeared from the state-controlled Latvian Shipping Company drew wide public attention because both Lembergs and Šķēle were associated with this company.

In 2007, the courts charged three individuals involved in the 2006 bribery attempts in the seaside city of Jurmala, widely known as "Jurmalgate." Juris Hlevickis was found to be the organizer and was sentenced to five years in prison. The whereabouts of the two others charged, however, are unknown.

In sum, while more corruption cases are being uncovered, anticorruption efforts are improving. This is especially the result of greater public vigilance and willingness to become involved in reporting corrupt practices. Moreover, the pressure put by NGOs and the public on perceived political corruption has mitigated the governing coalition's tendency to cater to the interests of a few wealthy individuals and turned government's attention toward the broader public good.

▮ AUTHOR: JURIS DREIFELDS

Juris Dreifelds teaches political science at Brock University in Ontario, Canada. He is the author of many book chapters and articles on the Baltic area. His book Latvia in Transition *was published by Cambridge University Press in 1996.*

---

[1] "Petijums: pedejos divos gados demokratizacijas pakape Latvija nav butiski mainijusies" [Report: In the Last Two Years Level of Democratization in Latvia Has Not Essentially Changed], Delfi, September 28, 2007.

[2] "Beilija aicina tautu pretoties pastavosai varai" [Bailey Invites the Nation to Oppose the Existing Powerholders], TVNET Zinas, October 16, 2007.

[3] "Lembergs ievietots Matisa cietuma" [Lembergs Placed in the Matis Prison], *Diena*, March 17, 2007.

4   "Sudraba sasutusi par selektivo attieksmi prêt VK atzinumiem" [Sudraba Is Perturbed About the Selective Attitude to VK (State Control) Decisions], TVNET Zinas, October 23, 2007; "Maizitis: Loskutovs nebija jaatstadina no amata" [Maizitis: Loskutovs Did Not Have to Be Dismissed from His Position], TVNET Zinas, October 16, 2007.

5   "Valdiba atsauc lemumu par Loskutovu" [The Government Abrogates Its Decision Regarding Loskutovs], Diena, November 1, 2007.

6   "Izmainas valsts drosibas likumos var but saistitas ar oligarhu interesem" [Changes in the State Security Laws Could Be Connected to the Interests of the Oligarchs], TVNET Zinas, March 10, 2007. The two laws involved were similar in wording: Grozijumi Nacionalas drosibas likuma [Changes in the National Security Law] and Grozijumi valsts drosibas iestazu likuma [Changes in State Security Institution Law]. Also see "Vike Freiberga aicina pilsonus piedalities referenduma" [Vīķe-Freiberga Invites Citizens to Participate in the Referendum], Delfi, July 5, 2007.

7   "Balsu nepietiek, bet signals izskan" [The Number of Votes Are Not Sufficient, but a Signal Is Sounded], Diena, July 9, 2007.

8   "Saeima dzes Satversmes 81.pantu" [Saeima Erases the Section 81 of the Constitution], Dienas Bizness, May 4, 2007.

9   "Zooligisko darzu ka apspriedes vietu politikiem ieteicis Emsa padomnieks" [The Zoo, as a Location for Discussion by Politicians, Was Suggested by an Adviser to Emsis], TVNET Zinas, October 22, 2007.

10   "Ka vakar balsoja deputati—Dienas aptauja" [How Deputies Voted Yesterday—Query by Diena], Diena, October 30, 2007.

11   "Stokenbergs sodits par Šķēles biznesa kavesanu" [Stokenbergs Punished for Delaying Šķēles Business], TVNET Zinas, October 20, 2007.

12   "Saeimas priekssedetaja amata ievelets Daudze" [Daudze Elected as Speaker of the Saeima], Delfi, September 24, 2007; "Emsis nepatiesas liecibas sniedzis pec naudas nozagsanas" [Emsis Gave False Testimony After the Theft of Money], Delfi, October 15, 2007.

13   "Saeima ieklutu tris partijas, TP zem 5 percent barjeras" [Only Three Parties Would Make It into the Saeima, TP Under 5 Percent Barrier]," Diena, October 30, 2007. (The only coalition party with over 5 percent support was the Union of Greens and Farmers.)

14   "9.Saeimas velesanas" [9th Saeimas Elections], on Central Election Commission Web site: http://www.cvk.lv/pub/public.

15   OSCE Parliamentary Assembly Press Statement, "Latvian Election Transparent and Professional but Issue of 'Noncitizens' Remains," http://www.osce.org.

16   "Foreign Minister Pabriks: Improving Co-operation with NGOs Will Reduce Public Estrangement from Government," Ministry of Foreign Affairs of the Republic of Latvia, March 19, 2007, http://www.mfa.gov.lv. Rasma Pipike, "Saeimas kuga iegrime sadarbiba ar nevalstiskajam organizacijam" [The Saeima Boats Drag in Cooperation with NGOs], Diena, May 28, 2007.

17   "Piekta dala Latvijas pilsonu iesaistas dazados brivpratigos darbos" [A Fifth of Latvian Citizens Participate in Various Voluntary Initiatives], TNS Latvia, April 17, 2007.

18   Elmars Barkans, "Sabiedrisko labumu atbalsta valsts" [The State Supports Social Benefit], TVNET Zinas, July 19, 2007.

19   "Atklaj portalu ciganiem" [A Portal for Gypsies Opened], Diena, March 22, 2007.

20   "Share of TV Channels and TOP Programmes, September 2007," TNS Latvia, October 8, 2007.

21   "Internets—izaicinajums vai bieds drukatajiem medijiem" [The Internet, Challenge or Bugbear for Printed Media], TNS Latvia, archive #13. See http://www.tns.lv/newsletters/2007/13.

22 LR Central Statistical Bureau, "In the 1ˢᵗ Quarter of 2007 the Internet Was Available to 51 Percent of Households," October 10, 2007. See http://www.csb.gov.lv.

23 "Latvian Media Advertising Market Has Increased By 24% During 2007 Reaching 93.94 Million Lats," TNS Latvia, February 27, 2008. In Estonia it increased by 28 percent and in Lithuania by 15.6 percent. Ibid.

24 The abrogation of the criminal proceedings against journalist Uldis Dreiblats by the highest court on December 4, 2007, occurred a day before Prime Minister Kalvitis resigned his post; hence very little publicity surrounded the court decision. "Senats izbeidz kriminalprocesu prêt zurnalistu Dreiblatu" [The Senate Ends the Criminal Process Against Dreiblats], *Zemgales Zinas,* December 4, 2007.

25 Andris Grinbergs, "Aiz novadu kartes—cilveks" [Behind the Map of Regions—People], *Latvijas Avize,* September 18, 2007.

26 Daina Vesko, "Turigakas joprojam uztures vajakas" [The Rich Will Sustain the Weakest], October 30, 2007; "Rigas dome nevelas palielinat iemaksas pasvaldibu izlidzinasanas fonda" [The Riga Council Does Not Want to Increase Payments into the Municipal Equalization Fund], *Diena,* September 10, 2007.

27 "Aptuveni 20–30% sudzibu Tiesibsargam bijusas pamatotas" [About 20–30% of Complaints to the Ombudsman Were Valid], *Diena,* July 11, 2007.

28 "Tiesu administracija neatbilstibas par miljoniem" [In Administrative Courts, Insufficiency in the Millions], *Diena,* November 8, 2007; "Rindu mazinasanai tiesas" [To Shorten Lines in Court], *Diena,* November 8, 2007.

29 "Latvija vismazak uzticas politiskajams partijam un tieslietu sistemai" [In Latvia Lowest Trust Given to Political Parties and Court System], TVNET Zinas, January 9, 2007.

30 "Sabiedribas attieksme prêt tiesam" [Society's Orientation to Courts], SKDS, September 2007. The results varied by ethnicity. Among Latvians, the first positive categories were supported by 2.5 percent and 27.1 percent, whereas among non-Latvians it was 1.2 percent and 18.3 percent.

31 Mike Collier, "Wiretapping Sparks This Season's Scandal," *Baltic Times,* August 21, 2007.

32 Ilze Nagle, "Sevi tiesat nav viegli" [To Judge Oneself Is Not Easy], *Latvijas Avize,* November 3, 2007; "Zatlers cer ka tiesnesi kliedes bazas, ka tiesa Latvija tiek spriesta arpus tiesas zales" [Zatlers Hopes That Judges Will Dissipate Worries, That Adjudication in Latvia Is Determined Outside the Halls of Justice], TVNET Zinas, November 2, 2007.

33 Risina Valsts kontroles cietumu parvalde atklatos trukumus" [Solving the Revealed Shortcomings of the Prison Administration], *Diena,* January 31, 2007; "Pern vairak neka tresdala no tiesato-agrak soditi" [Last Year More Than a Third of Those Judged—Recedivists], Delfi, March 16, 2007.

34 "Saeima apstiprina Satversmes tiesas tiesnesus-papildinata" [Saeima Confirms Constitutional Court Justices], TVNET, December 14, 2006.

35 "Par rupjiem Vrublevskas parkapumiem rosina sakt disciplinarlietu" [Disciplinary Proceedings Are Called for Vrublevskas Serious Mistakes], *Diena,* February 16, 2007.

36 Valts Kalnins, "Korupcija-perversija vai norma?" [Corruption—A Perversion or the Norm?], *Latvijas Vestnesis,* May 25, 2006.

37 "Savejiem Loskutovs dargs, jo netrauce" [Among His Own, Loskutovs Is Valuable Because He Does Not Disturb], *Diena,* October 20, 2007.

38 "Bribery Allegations Against Lembergs Spark Rumours of Widespread Graft in Parliament," *Baltic Times,* March 21, 2007.

39 "Loskutovs: Negodigam amatpersonam zud nesodamibas sajuta" [Loskutovs: Dishonest Officials Are Losing Their Feeling of Immunity], TVNET Zinas, June 29, 2007.

Lithuania

by Aneta Piasecka

Capital: Vilnius
Population: 3.4 million
GNI/capita: US$14,550

The social data above was taken from the European Bank for Reconstruction and Development's *Transition Report 2007: People in Transition*, and the economic data from the World Bank's *World Development Indicators 2008*.

Nations in Transit Ratings and Averaged Scores

	1999	2001	2002	2003	2004	2005	2006	2007	2008
Electoral Process	1.75	1.75	1.75	1.75	1.75	1.75	1.75	1.75	1.75
Civil Society	2.00	1.75	1.50	1.50	1.50	1.50	1.50	1.75	1.75
Independent Media	1.75	1.75	1.75	1.75	1.75	1.75	1.75	1.75	1.75
Governance*	2.50	2.50	2.50	2.50	2.50	n/a	n/a	n/a	n/a
National Democratic Governance	n/a	n/a	n/a	n/a	n/a	2.50	2.50	2.50	2.50
Local Democratic Governance	n/a	n/a	n/a	n/a	n/a	2.50	2.50	2.50	2.50
Judicial Framework and Independence	2.00	1.75	2.00	1.75	1.75	1.75	1.50	1.75	1.75
Corruption	3.75	3.75	3.75	3.50	3.50	3.75	4.00	4.00	3.75
Democracy Score	2.29	2.21	2.21	2.13	2.13	2.21	2.21	2.29	2.25

* *With the 2005 edition, Freedom House introduced separate analysis and ratings for national democratic governance and local democratic governance to provide readers with more detailed and nuanced analysis of these two important subjects.*

NOTE: The ratings reflect the consensus of Freedom House, its academic advisers, and the author(s) of this report. The opinions expressed in this report are those of the author(s). The ratings are based on a scale of 1 to 7, with 1 representing the highest level of democratic progress and 7 the lowest. The Democracy Score is an average of ratings for the categories tracked in a given year.

Executive Summary

Seventeen years after regaining independence, Lithuania enjoys well-established political rights and civil liberties. Since 2004, Lithuania has been a member of NATO and the European Union (EU), and the public's support for Western integration remains strong. In December 2007, Lithuania joined the Schengen visa-free zone. The country remains one of the fastest-growing economies in the region. Although having achieved impressive gains and recognition in the foreign policy arena, political life within the country appears to be backsliding away from further reforms. Public apathy and alienation from the political process has deepened, and trust in major democratic institutions, including the Parliament, government, political parties, and courts, is critically low. Recent elections were held with record low turnouts. The current Parliament is widely regarded as the most inefficient and disorganized in Lithuania's post-independence history. Public confidence in the media has fallen dramatically, too. Civil society is not growing as rapidly as was expected a decade ago, and large-scale labor migration has taken a toll on the country's political and civic developments.

Lithuania's fourteenth administration, led by Gediminas Kirkilas, brought a modicum of stability to the country's fractured political arena, but it was criticized for dragging its feet on long overdue reforms in health care and education. The government remained secure owing to formal support from the opposition Homeland Union–Lithuanian Conservatives, the country's largest center-right force, which terminated their support in September 2007. Local government elections in February brought victory to the Lithuanian Social Democratic Party (LSDP), Lithuania's most influential political party, followed closely by its ideological rival, the Conservatives. The elections were surrounded by controversy involving the Constitutional Court and rulings allowing non-party-list candidates. The dismissal of embattled security chief Arvydas Pocius for incompetence and politicking ended a prolonged security crisis. The media market saw increased consolidation of media ownership among a few influential business groups. The spread of corruption finally slowed, but a lack of political will to pursue effective programs impeded further progress in combating corruption.

National Democratic Governance. In the first half of 2007, the State Security Department (SSD) remained engulfed in a crisis of leadership, corruption, and energy security matters. Confrontations between besieged security chief Arvydas Pocius and lawmakers over top government ties with energy business interests exacerbated the crisis. In May 2007, Pocius was removed from office. The prolonged resolution of the crisis threw the SSD into disarray, created political tension, and reinforced concerns over inadequate parliamentary oversight. In 2007, lawmakers failed to override a presidential veto on legislation proposing to extend a ban on public service employment to include former KGB reserve officials. *Owing to the modestly successful resolution of the security crisis, Lithuania's rating for national democratic governance remains at 2.50.*

Electoral Process. Lithuania's first minority government survived for a year and a half thanks to formal support from the opposition Conservatives. In September 2007, in what was seen as an early start to the 2008 election campaign, the Conservatives terminated their support agreement but continued to back the government on an informal basis. The Kirkilas administration remained preoccupied with its survival and showed no reform commitment, while the Parliament was troubled by political battling and weak and ineffective leadership. Despite this, both the ruling minority and the fractured opposition were set to preserve the status quo. *Lithuania's rating for electoral process remains at 1.75.*

Civil Society. The legal framework governing nongovernmental organizations (NGOs) and the general atmosphere in the country are both supportive of civil society. Yet greater progress in civic developments has been curbed by low public awareness and lack of support of NGOs. During 2007, nongovernmental groups increasingly sought to adjust their activities to qualify for EU support. EU funding and the public's growing awareness of the need to collectively address local concerns have spurred a proliferation of organized communities. Independent policy advocacy has been strengthened in recent years through the rise of several active center-right public policy groups. The proportion of people using income tax deductions to support NGOs is growing, but the bulk of these funds goes to underfunded municipal institutions, such as schools. *A lack of visible change in public perceptions and low support of the nongovernmental sector leaves the rating for civil society unchanged at 1.75.*

Independent Media. Lithuania's media remain competitive and vibrant despite continued consolidation of media ownership among a few influential business and media groups. In 2007, there were several major takeovers of media outlets by leading market players, including MG Baltic, Lietuvos Rytas Group, and newcomer Hermis Capital. There are indications that increased ownership concentration plus the wide use of disguised public relations tools are affecting media quality and independence. Public confidence in the media hit a record low of 40 percent— a marked drop from several years ago. Online media, and in particular Internet news portals, have been expanding rapidly in the past two years and are expected to enhance media transparency and objectivity. Internet use is growing at a rapid pace. In the first half of 2007, a total of 40 percent of households (primarily in urban areas) were connected to the Internet, up dramatically from just 2 percent in 2000. *The rating for independent media remains at 1.75.*

Local Democratic Governance. The February 2007 local government elections drew a record low turnout of 40 percent. The LSDP won the largest number of municipal council seats (302 out of 1,550), while the Conservatives came in second with 256 seats. The Liberal-Center Union and impeached president Rolandas Paksas's Order and Justice Party (Liberal Democrats) followed with 182 and 181 seats, respectively. The recent elections attracted heightened interest from political parties, owing mostly to the EU's injection of 10.4 billion euros (US$15.2 billion) for municipal development over the next six years. Two weeks before the elections, the Constitutional Court passed a watershed ruling allowing non-party-list candidates to run for municipal councils, thus abolishing party monopoly in local elections. In June, constitutional amendments to legitimize direct mayoral elections passed the first reading in Parliament. *Owing to the controversy surrounding the recent municipal elections, Lithuania's rating for local democratic governance remains at 2.50.*

Judicial Framework and Independence. A long overdue revision of the legal framework governing the judiciary, including the central Law on Courts, was postponed on several occasions. A lack of agreement and political will for reform has suppressed the need to address weaknesses in appointment procedures, the insularity of the courts, and a growing shortfall of judges. Lawmakers have been grappling with the problem of dual citizenship after the Constitutional Court found in late 2006 that citizenship legislation allowing dual citizenship was unconstitutional. Courts continue to rank among the least trusted institutions. In 2007, Lithuania incited an international clamor as Vilnius city authorities banned antidiscrimination campaigns promoting the rights of gays and lesbians. *Lack of progress in the long overdue revision of court legislation, a persistently low public trust in courts, and the society's biased attitudes toward ethnic and other minority groups leave Lithuania's judicial framework and independence rating unchanged at 1.75.*

Corruption. While most people in Lithuania increasingly believe that bribes can help in dealings with the authorities, the perceptions and attitudes of the business community are improving and the growth of corruption seems to have been curbed, according to the latest opinion polls. The exposure and investigation of corruption and conflict-of-interest allegations have become more open. Still, there is little follow-through toward effective anticorruption policies amid numerous corruption allegations. Also, 2007 provided ample evidence of double standards and leniency for wrongdoers on the part of authorities. Proposals to tighten political party and campaign finance regulations have stalled in the legislature since 2006. The government has embarked on an ambitious program to reduce corruption, but results have yet to be seen. *Despite a persistent lack of political will to strengthen anticorruption measures, greater openness in exposing, investigating, and discussing conflict-of-interest allegations, a recent curb in corruption growth, and marked improvements in the perceptions of the business community merit improvement in Lithuania's corruption rating from 4.00 to 3.75.*

Outlook for 2008. National legislative elections in fall 2008 will be the central event of the year. In the run-up to the polls, new party mergers and coalitions will be likely. The February 2007 municipal elections showed that certain shifts in political power might be anticipated. The minority Social Democrat–led government is expected to survive until the upcoming elections as major players on the political scene will try to maintain the status quo. Constitutional amendments stipulating direct mayoral elections are set to go through the final voting in Parliament, and the legislature will still have to agree on the powers of directly elected mayors. It remains to be seen whether lawmakers will revise the court legislation and tighten political campaign funding before the upcoming legislative elections. Equally newsworthy will be specific decisions regarding the creation of a national investor for the construction of a new atomic power plant that is to replace the Ignalina unit. There are concerns over the transparency of deals between the government and private business titans that will participate in creating a single mega-utility for the project.

MAIN REPORT

National Democratic Governance

1999	2001	2002	2003	2004	2005	2006	2007	2008
n/a	n/a	n/a	n/a	n/a	2.50	2.50	2.50	2.50

In 2007, political and public attention was riveted on solving the crisis that had engulfed the State Security Department (SSD) since fall 2006. Lithuania's main security agency was thrown into disarray after Vytautas Pociūnas, a security officer who had formerly headed the SSD's economic and energy security office, died mysteriously in August 2006 in Belarus. The story provoked suspicion over the SSD's leadership problems, politicization of security personnel, and the energy market's role in national security.

After a months-long investigation into the operation of the SSD, revealing possible corruption ties between high-ranking government and security officials and pro-Russian business groups, the parliamentary National Defense and Security Committee (NDSC) concluded that security chief Arvydas Pocius was unfit to lead the department. Observers severely criticized Pocius for politicking, manipulating information to discredit top politicians, and challenging the Parliament's duty to oversee security matters. Pocius officially resigned in December 2006, but amid the turmoil he managed to garner support from lawmakers and the president and remained in office, only to be dismissed five months later. In June 2007, Povilas Malakauskas, former head of the Special Investigation Bureau (SIB), replaced Pocius as security chief. Yet the security agency is still struggling to bring its operation back to normal.

Political analysts claimed that the prolonged security crisis was not limited to the SSD's problems, but engulfed the whole political system. The security chief's "rebellion" against the legislature was understood as an attempt by the top functionaries mentioned in the NDSC investigation to reinforce their political influence. The crisis mounted as flustered lawmakers appeared to be ignorant of their duties and unable to react adequately to the predicament. The president's office and the government both took a passive stance, drawing intense criticism from observers.

In October 2007, a long debated new Law on Lustration was passed, but President Valdas Adamkus vetoed it over procedural violations. The new law defined the status of KGB reservists and set career restrictions on KGB officials and collaborators who failed to confess. It also redefined procedures for composing the lustration commission. Earlier in the year, lawmakers failed to override a presidential veto on lustration legislation that would have banned former KGB reserve officials from public service. But given the strong support from members of Parliament (MPs), the new law is expected to pass the Parliament without further debates over its substance.

Lithuania's Parliament operates in an open manner, and all legislative documents and records are posted on the Internet. Public policy and interest groups may take part in the political process through policy advocacy, advising, and lobbying. Yet draft legislation is not always readily available to the public, and the mechanism for consulting legal experts and interest groups does not always function properly. The number of adopted laws has decreased, but their inconsistency and frequent amendments reveal systematic flaws in the lawmaking process.

The Lithuanian executive branch is less transparent than the legislature. Executive authorities often propose bills or adopt new regulations without prior notice or public scrutiny, though they are required by law to announce policy proposals via the Internet. Yet the current administration has started to provide systematic public access to government meeting agendas, and since August 2006, cabinet sessions have been broadcast live on the Internet.

The past few years have seen a sharp increase in the bureaucratic apparatus. The number of civil servants (excluding statutory officials) rose from 18,993 in July 2003 to 25,598 in July 2007. Over the past year, the number increased by 1,693.[1] The European Union (EU) has been a popular argument to boost bureaucracy. New positions are opened to allegedly meet the growing EU membership workload despite a large number of existing vacancies. In the meantime, public service is faced with an increasing shortfall of workers, caused mainly by large-scale labor migration in recent years. The most severely affected, and underpaid, sectors are education and health care, courts, police, and fire services. In light of Lithuania's continued economic growth and increasing budget revenues, the government is criticized for boosting public spending and failing to balance the budget. The 2007 and 2008 budgets both stipulate a deficit and revenue growth of about 33 percent per year.

Progress in delivering public services online has slowed over the past year, from an estimated 68 percent in 2006 to 64 percent in 2007, far behind the EU average of 76 percent. Full online availability in Lithuania was 35 percent in 2007.[2] Among the least advanced online services are building permits, car registration, health care services, and marriage and birth certificates.

In the energy arena, the Parliament passed a crucial law in July 2007 to build a new atomic power plant to replace the Ignalina unit, which will be closing in 2009 under EU obligations. Four countries—the three Baltic states and Poland—will participate in the project. The first reactor is scheduled to be completed around 2015. The new power grid will allow Lithuania to remain a nuclear energy producer and exporter and help guarantee energy independence. Despite the magnitude of the project, the law was adopted in some haste and with very little public discussion.

Electoral Process

1999	2001	2002	2003	2004	2005	2006	2007	2008
1.75	1.75	1.75	1.75	1.75	1.75	1.75	1.75	1.75

Lithuania's first post-independence minority government led by Social Democrat Gediminas Kirkilas remained secure in fall 2007. The center-left coalition was formed by the Lithuanian Social Democratic Party (LSDP), the National Farmers

Union (NFU), the Civil Democracy Party (CDP), and the Liberal-Center Union (LCU) in summer 2006 after months of political crisis and intrigue. With 57 seats in the Parliament in mid-2007, the minority government functioned largely thanks to the formal support of the opposition Conservatives. Yet political cleavage, inefficient legislature, and the prolonged resolution of the security crisis led analysts to speak of an imminent crisis in the country's political and governance system.

Most commentators agreed that Prime Minister Kirkilas, a political old-timer, brought the country some stability. Still, the administration was criticized for dragging its feet on reforms in health care and education, slowne s and inefficiency in making use of EU assistance funds, and its failure to meet the 2010 target for introducing the euro. Instead, the government was preoccupied largely with its own survival. It withstood two interpellations for several of its ministers and lost only one cabinet member. Unlike those of previous administrations, Kirkilas's cabinet was composed mainly of political appointees, including the prime minister himself, rather than technocrats. Seven ministerial posts belonged to LSDP, three to NFU, two to LCU, and one to CDP.

In September, the Conservatives, the largest right-of-center party with 24 MPs, terminated its yearlong formal support for the minority government reportedly over growing corruption and prolonged security problems. This was widely seen as a fictitious move aimed at preserving their political image before the 2008 legislative elections. The Conservatives are expected to informally support the minority government in order to prevent other forces from entering the coalition before the upcoming elections. LSDP is also hanging on to this partnership. Its plans to replace the Conservatives with the Labor Party failed after the Laborites upheld legislation fixing gas price mark-ups, an issue that was severely opposed by the government.

The current Parliament, considered the worst in Lithuania's post-independence history, is increasingly criticized for a lack of efficiency and organization. Continuous scandals and splits, multiple ad hoc commissions, and the incompetence of many political freshmen have distracted lawmakers and paralyzed important legislative debates. With the Conservatives supporting the minority government, the parliamentary opposition is as polarized and weak as ever despite its sizable composition and fairly broad statutory powers. Parliamentary Speaker Viktoras Muntianas, a former Laborite and founder of the CDP, lacks authority and has faced two no-confidence votes for failing to organize the Parliament's work.

Blurred boundaries among parties, unexpected and controversial coalitions, and party splits and infighting have long led analysts to speak of a moral and structural backslide in Lithuania's political party life. The Social Democrats, the foundation of the left-wing bloc, are leaning toward liberal economic policies, while liberal forces show a lack of loyalty and unity. Shifting party affiliation has become a routine practice, mainly as many of the recent ad hoc political projects have failed. In 2007, there were 38 registered political parties in Lithuania, with some 25 active players on the political scene. Membership requirement for political parties was lowered to 1,000 people in 2004. Several parties failed to meet this requirement but continued to exist owing to costly reorganization and liquidation procedures. Most parties rally around one leader and lack a clear ideological identity.

Fall 2007 saw an early start to the 2008 election campaign as parties began merger and coalition talks. The Conservatives called on right-wing forces to unite and create a stronger alternative to the ruling Left. In November, the Conservatives merged with the non-parliamentary Lithuanian National Union, and initiated merger talks with the Christian Democratic Party. Any stronger cooperation on the fractured liberal flank—represented by LCU, the Liberal Movement, the Social Liberals, and the Order and Justice Party (Liberal Democrats)—is improbable.

The Parliament and political parties remain the most unpopular public institutions, supported by only 10 and 5 percent of the population, respectively.[3] Passive public engagement in political life is reflected by low party membership and voter turnout; as few as three percent of Lithuanian citizens belong to political parties,[4] and the current Parliament was elected on a record low voter turnout of 44.3 percent. Observers attribute such attitudes to growing party insularity and the public's alienation from the political process. In a research study released in December 2006, the Civil Society Institute (CSI) concluded that the public has little confidence in its collective power and lacks a tradition of engaging in political and public life.[5] Large-scale labor migration has also taken its toll on public attitudes.

Despite tightened restrictions on campaign financing and advertising, the framework governing political parties contains serious flaws, and the mechanisms for ensuring compliance and transparency are inadequate. New proposals to prohibit businesses from donating to political parties and to ban political advertising on radio and television have stalled in the Parliament. Reportedly, radio and television advertising absorbs the bulk of campaign funds, so the proposed prohibition is expected to reduce political costs, corruption, and illegitimate party spending. At present, restrictions are applied only to outdoor political advertising.

Civil Society

1999	2001	2002	2003	2004	2005	2006	2007	2008
2.00	1.7.	1.50	1.50	1.50	1.50	1.50	1.75	1.75

Lithuania's legislative framework does not pose any serious barriers to nongovernmental organizations (NGOs), but public awareness and involvement in civil society remain low. The organizational and managerial capacities of Lithuanian NGOs are quite good, but weak constituency building and lack of public outreach are still problems. Nongovernmental groups have increasingly adjusted their activities to qualify for EU funding, but this drive to attract EU donations has distracted many from their normal work and core objectives.

Lithuanian society remains poorly organized. Although the number of NGOs grew from 9,250 in 1999 to 16,250 in 2005,[6] the level of public participation in their activities remained almost unchanged. According to a 2005 survey by the CSI, one-fifth of the population belonged to NGOs or participated in civil movements over the past six years. Sports and leisure groups have the largest membership, 3.5

percent of the population, while participation in educational, cultural, youth, or religious organizations does not exceed 2.5 percent. People with higher education are the most organized (29 percent).[7]

The most common reasons for nonparticipation are a lack of interest and confidence in NGOs plus their low public outreach and weak financial condition. Civil society organizations have failed to widen their range of activities or increase membership and thus remain largely unknown to the general public. A survey conducted in autumn 2007 by Transparency International's Lithuanian chapter showed that a majority of civil society representatives consider Lithuanian NGOs to be transparent.[8] A lack of clear criteria for NGO support provided through state and municipal tenders is considered to be the most frequent transparency problem, but financial disclosure is not seen as a key measure to enhance NGO transparency. Fundraising and finding qualified employees were cited as the most serious difficulties. Additionally, Lithuania lacks a strong tradition of volunteerism and charitable giving. Volunteerism has also been discouraged in the past by regulations, which were eased a few years ago but still place excessive bureaucratic constraints on volunteer work.

The past few years saw a massive proliferation of organized village communities. This trend was spurred largely by EU structural funds and ongoing rural Internet projects. Growing community awareness and joint efforts to address local concerns have also boosted these numbers. Community organizing has been stimulated by forceful land-planning and construction processes: On a number of occasions, both formal and informal local groups have intervened in official decisions where private construction sites allegedly violated public interests. The most resounding case involved the construction of the notorious Kazokiskiu waste dump, a project that provoked outrage from the local community.

The establishment of several center-right groups has reinforced independent policy advocacy in recent years. In June 2006, Piliečių Santalka, an informal network of citizens and organizations promoting civil society, was established. The network's focus areas are public administration, courts, and self-government. The CSI and the Human Rights Monitoring Institute, founded by the Open Society Fund–Lithuania in 2003 and 2004, respectively, have already gained recognition thanks to their active engagement in public policy.

Lithuanian nonprofits are required to pay a 15 percent profit tax on commercial proceeds exceeding approximately US$9,000. Companies can donate up to 40 percent of their annual taxable profits to NGOs, while Lithuanian taxpayers may contribute 2 percent of their income tax to private or public nonprofit entities. Yet most NGOs lack permanent sources of income and sufficient fund-raising capacities. NGOs may bid for government contracts, but this practice is rather uncommon owing to a complex administrative process.

The 2 percent income tax deduction, meant originally to boost civil society, goes mostly to underfunded municipal institutions and schools. In 2007, 36 percent of the 2 percent donations were transferred to municipal organizations, 32 percent to associations, 14 percent to public institutions,[9] 8 percent to charity and sponsorship funds, 6 percent to traditional religious communities, and 4 percent to state-run budgetary institutions. More than 12,000 organizations received donations. The number of donors rose from 370,000 in 2005 to 500,000 in 2007, or 33 percent of the working population.[10] While the 2 percent option helps to shore up NGOs, some worry it discourages philanthropy and leaves room for abuse by fictitious organizations.

Trade unions enjoy wide powers and rights by law and are quite influential, although they claim only about 15 percent of the workforce. Large-scale labor migration and a decreasing labor pool may further bolster their influence. Together with employers and the government, unions make recommendations on national labor policy. By law, unions sign collective agreements with employers on behalf of all employees, and the labor code requires all employers to comply. Members of a union's elected governing body may not be dismissed or penalized by their employers without the union's approval. The Lithuanian Confederation of Trade Unions, Lithuanian Labor Federation, and Employees Union are coalitions of labor groups.

Business associations and trade unions are the most active and influential NGOs in the policy-making arena making use of advocacy, advising, and lobbying—and, the media are receptive to public policy groups as reliable sources of information. However, government cooperation and consultation with NGOs has not been fully established. In 2007, there were only 13 registered lobbyists in Lithuania, of which 11 were active.[11] Observers note that such negligible formal lobbying activity may be attributed to extensive informal representation of special interest groups and legislative corruption. In current law, the concept of lobbying is defined quite broadly and can be applied to any publicly-aired opinions on legislation or policy research. NGOs worry that this discredits public policy groups that actively express their opinions. New lobbying legislation, which was presented before the Parliament in autumn 2007, fails to clarify the fuzzy boundaries between paid lobbying and advocacy.

Lithuania's education system is generally free of political influence, but school administrations are reportedly under pressure by local authorities. There are 25 private secondary schools, and 12 of the country's 28 higher education colleges and 7 of the 22 universities are private. Private schools account for a negligible 3 percent of all educational institutions.[12] The growth of private education has stagnated in recent years despite the country's basket principle of allocating funds per student. The cost to comply with high professional qualifications and cleanliness requirements for new establishments are one reason for this. In addition, state-run schools receive additional financial injections, which are not available to the private sector.

Independent Media

1999	2001	2002	2003	2004	2005	2006	2007	2008
1.75	1.75	1.75	1.75	1.75	1.75	1.75	1.75	1.75

There were important developments in Lithuania's media market in 2007, including several major outlet takeovers and an expansion of online news portals, digital

TV, and mobile broadcasting services. With recent acquisitions and increased consolidation of media ownership, the partition of the media market is drawing to an end, raising concerns over the effect of these processes on free media. Internet usage and online media are increasing, and media giants are set to exploit this growing popularity. Media outlets in Lithuania are privately owned, with the exception of the state-owned Lithuanian Radio and Television.

Lithuania's leading private equity concerns Achema Group and MG Baltic are now the most active players in the Lithuanian media market. MG Baltic, owner of the national broadcaster LNK (plus TV1), launched the news portal www.alfa. lt in August 2006 and took over UPG Baltic, which publishes about 30 journals in various markets. Another large concern, Hermis Capital, purchased a regional daily, *Kauno Diena,* from the Norwegian Mecom Press in 2006; bought the regional Žemaitijos TV in mid-2007; launched a new daily, *Vilniaus Diena,* in October; and is set to start the news portal www.diena.lt. Achema Group owns the national daily *Lietuvos Žinios*; the fourth largest national commercial television station, Baltijos TV; several radio stations, including the popular RC2 and Radiocentras; and two publishing houses.

The Lietuvos Rytas company, owner of the largest national daily, *Lietuvos Rytas*, and a TV production company, Spaudos Televizija, took over the Vilnius television station Penktas Kanalas from Rubicon Group in October 2007. Also during the year, the Respublika Group, publisher of the national daily *Respublika*, abandoned its news portal (delfis.lt) after evidence of plagiarism provoked outrage from other media outlets and journalists. According to 2003 regulations, online media are subject to self-regulation, which is performed by the same independent supervisory institutions in charge of the press, radio, and television.

In recent years, public confidence in the media has fallen. In 2007, it reached a record low of 40 percent.[13] Only five years ago, the media topped popularity rankings among various institutions, with public trust in the media standing at 70 percent of the population.[14] Observers say that this decline is related largely to increased penetration of industrial capital into the media market, media ownership concentration among a few influential domestic business groups and minimized foreign ownership in Lithuanian television.

These processes are already having an influence on media quality and independence, with both political and business interests receiving biased coverage in the media. Despite this, the media market remains competitive and vibrant. Lithuania has no sector-specific regulation of media ownership concentration, but competition legislation sets a general limit at 40 percent of the market share.

Public trust in the media is being damaged by a decline in responsible journalism and the growing use of hidden PR articles and reports by political and business interests. Lithuania's opinion leaders assert that media independence is limited chiefly by advertising contractors and media owners.[15] In a recent survey from Transparency International (TI),[16] more than half of Lithuania's CEOs and top executives claimed that the media were corrupt. An overwhelming majority (91 percent) believe that adverse reports in newspapers and TV can damage one's business or personal life.

National newspapers are considered to be the most corrupt, while news agencies are seen as the most transparent. Greater disclosure of media finances, management, circulation, and audience data is seen as the key to enhanced transparency.

The rapid growth of Internet media is expected to change public attitudes by enhancing media credibility. Lithuania's leading Internet news portal, www.delfi.lt, has increased its writing staff and in-house production, including recorded video materials. Other top Web sites are www.one.lt, www.plius.lt, and www.lrytas.lt.[17] Mobile TV broadcasting and digital TV are already available. In 2007, the country's mobile operators also started offering mobile video news.

There is a wide diversity of print and electronic media at national and local levels. The newspaper market is dominated by two large Lithuanian media concerns, Lietuvos Rytas and the Respublika Group. There are five national daily newspapers: *Lietuvos Rytas* (with a reported circulation of approximately 60,000), *Vakaro Žinios* (75,000), *Respublika* (33,000), *Kauno Diena* (34,000), and *Lietuvos Žinios* (20,000). In 2006, a total of 340 newspapers and 418 journals were published in Lithuania.[18] Several new intellectual magazines have been launched recently. The newspaper distribution system is privately owned.

The television market comprises 30 commercial stations and 1 public service television, Lithuanian Television, broadcasting two national programs, LTV1 and LTV2.[19] Out of four national broadcasters, the leading operators are TV3, owned by the Scandinavian Modern Times media group, and LNK, owned by MG Baltic. These two channels captured 28 and 22 percent of viewers, respectively, according to September 2007 data. LTV and Baltijos TV follow with 13 and 7.5 percent, respectively.[20]

There are 48 radio stations in Lithuania, of which 10 commercial stations and 1 public broadcaster (with 3 stations, LR1, LR2, and LR3) operate nationwide, 7 regionally, and 30 locally.[21] The state-run Lithuanian Radio has the largest audience (22 percent in summer 2007); other popular stations are Lietus (13 percent), M-1 (10 percent), Russkoje Radio Baltija (9 percent), Pūkas (9 percent), and Radiocentras (7 percent).[22] Žinių Radijas should be mentioned as a select radio project offering news and serious commentary enjoying a significant audience among businesspeople and intellectuals. The largest commercial radio stations are owned by four major groups, three of which are locally owned. So far, radio has been dominated by small local shareholders, but it is increasingly attracting large industries and other commercial interests.

Use of the Internet continues to grow rapidly. By mid-2007, the number of Internet subscribers rose by 60 percent.[23] In the first quarter of 2007, 40 percent of households were connected to the Internet, compared with 2.3 percent in 2000. Yet a gap between urban and rural connectivity exists: Every second urban household has an Internet connection, compared with every fourth rural household.[24]

Lithuanian media are self-regulated but supervised by the Commission of the Ethics of Journalists and Publishers, composed of media association members and public leaders, and the Office of the Inspector of Journalists Ethics.[25] Publications may be closed and journalists penalized only by court order.

Local Democratic Governance

1999	2001	2002	2003	2004	2005	2006	2007	2008
n/a	n/a	n/a	n/a	n/a	2.50	2.50	2.50	2.50

Lithuania's local elections on February 25, 2007, were won by LSDP, with the Conservatives coming in second. The turnout was a record low 40 percent of the country's 2.7 million electorate. Two weeks before the municipal elections, the Constitutional Court passed a groundbreaking ruling stating that non-party-list candidates may run for municipal councils. And later in the year, the Parliament made a first step toward direct mayoral elections, an issue debated in the country for almost a decade.

A total of 24 parties and a record 13,000 candidates contested for 1,550 seats in local government councils. LSDP won the most seats with a majority in 19 cities, although the party came in second in total number of votes. The Conservatives received the largest number of votes but were second in number of seats won. LCU came in third, followed by the Order and Justice Party. Ten major political parties gained more than 50 seats each. Ten other parties and coalitions secured representation with a negligible number of seats. Only 5 of the country's 60 municipalities saw any party winning an absolute majority. Municipal councils are elected for a four-year term. To place members on a city council, a party must receive no less than 4 percent of votes from residents of the municipality.

2007 Municipal Election Results

Party	Number of seats won in municipal councils
Lithuanian Social Democratic Party	302
Homeland Union-Lithuanian Conservatives	256
Liberal and Center Union	182
Order and Justice Party (Liberal Democrats)	181
National Farmers Union	141
Labor Party	111
New Union-Social Liberals	97
Lithuanian Christian Democrat Party	95
Lithuanian Polish Electoral Action	53
Liberal Movement	51
Other	81

Source: Central Electoral Committee of the Republic of Lithuania

The unprecedented interest from political parties in the 2007 elections wa explained by the financial assistance coming from the EU: During the next si years, Lithuanian local governments will absorb 10.4 billion euros in structur; assistance, and the newly-elected councils will be responsible for doling out th bulk of these funds.

A major surprise for most election observers was the successful performance of impeached president Rolandas Paksas's Order and Justice Party. Having struggled for a place in Lithuania's political arena, the party won almost one-third of the seats in the capital city of Vilnius. After prolonged coalition talks, the party managed to rally enough support to ensure victory in the mayoral vote. Juozas Imbrasas, an ally of Paksas, became mayor of Vilnius.

Lithuania's municipal elections were tainted with fraud. The Central Electoral Committee canceled election results in two municipalities because of "grave violations" of electoral laws, but later this decision was overruled in court. There were reports of vote buying, use of administrative resources for election agitation, and pressure on local electoral committees. To decrease electoral fraud, popular voting by mail in local government elections was outlawed in 2006 (except for voters in detention, the military services, and health care professions).[26] In the 2007 municipal elections, the proportion of vote by mail was 3.66 percent.[27]

Just two weeks before the local government elections, the Constitutional Court dramatically lifted the prohibition on non-party-list candidates, which the Court deemed unconstitutional. Though these new conditions could not be guaranteed across the board for the 2007 elections, the Court declared that postponing the elections would "inflict much greater damage to the expectations of voters and to the stability of not only local self-government, but the whole system of public power."[28] This statement provoked much controversy. Observers and political analysts criticized the Constitutional Court for exceeding its competence, interfering in administrative governance matters, and violating the principle of separation of powers. Many claimed that elections conducted under unconstitutional legislation could not be free and democratic. Others claimed that direct participation in elections was not a universal human right and the choice of an election system was a political, not a legal, decision.

In June 2007, an absolute majority of lawmakers voted for constitutional amendments in favor of direct mayoral elections, an issue that had been debated in the country for almost a decade. A second vote was scheduled for fall 2007, but it was postponed over disagreements on how much power directly-elected mayors should wield. At present, mayors are elected by municipal councils, whose members in turn are chosen in general elections through a proportional party-list ballot. Executive powers are vested in the municipal council and administration, which is led by a director appointed by the municipal council at the suggestion of the mayor. Yet some would like mayors to be an executive institution, with councils led by their elected chairs. Opponents of direct elections insist they would bring the rise of populists and that such mayors would be less resistant to corruption.

Polls over the last seven years consistently show that only a third of the population trusts local government.[29] Lithuanians recognize the importance of self-government and want community affairs to be tackled by local authorities, but they also doubt their powers to influence local decision-making, according to a survey by the CSI. Experts conclude that "self-government in Lithuania obviously lacks content."[30] It also lacks transparency. Legal acts by municipal councils are rarely available on the Internet, and decisions are not known to the public until their enactment. Cooperation with local constituencies revolves mostly around land-planning issues. Online availability of municipal services is low.

Lithuania has one level of local government, which encompasses 60 municipalities led by elected councils and 10 regional administrations governed by central appointees. In certain areas, such as land planning, health care, and education, both central and local authorities are involved. Ambiguities in power division have impeded decentralization, the distribution of fiscal allocations for municipalities, and transparent and accountable governance at the municipal level. From time to time, political parties propose abolishing regional administrations, especially before elections. However, regional governors remain influential political officials, so the removal of this tier of governance is unlikely.

Municipal governments have a limited degree of financial independence and are burdened with politicking and mismanagement. They generally lack funds to meet their obligations, and misuse of funds is widespread. Only a third of financial and performance audits are conducted correctly, according to the National Audit Office in 2006.[31] Financial discipline is also weak in regional administrations, as national audits revealed in 2007.

Municipal budgets, which range from 5 million to €223 million (US$7.3 million to US$327 million),[32] are composed of ever-shrinking central government subsidies and independent revenues collected from personal income tax, property and land taxes, and local fees. In 2007, central budget allocations to local governments stood at 42 percent, down from 58 percent in 2004.[33] The trend toward increasing independent proceeds is due largely to an increase in personal income tax revenues. Municipalities with over 19 percent revenue growth are required to transfer part of these funds to the state budget for the purpose of leveling wide disparities in revenue volumes across municipalities.

A large share of independent proceeds goes to the central government wage fund and utility payments, so in reality municipal councils are free to distribute only from 2 to 10 percent of municipal budgets.[34] For investment purposes, municipalities may take loans ranging from 35 to 50 percent of municipal budgets, but with the government's approval they may borrow 100 percent and more. Local governments are increasingly likely to use this right as they co-finance EU assistance projects.

Judicial Framework and Independence

1999	2001	2002	2003	2004	2005	2006	2007	2008
2.00	1.75	2.00	1.75	1.75	1.75	1.50	1.75	1.75

Despite intense public debates over the weaknesses of Lithuania's judiciary lawmakers lacked the political will to tackle long overdue institutional reforms The most pressing needs are to increase transparency of courts, to revise judges appointment procedures, and to administer the growing caseload amid a shortag of judges. A new Law on Courts has stalled in the Parliament for the past two years, while in 2006 the Constitutional Court found over 30 provisions of the functioning legislation unconstitutional. Recurrent scandals around the appointment of judges have highlighted a lack of procedural transparency and confirmed that the president and Parliament have up to now played only a symbolic role in the process.

In early 2007, President Valdas Adamkus called on lawmakers to adopt new rules for appointing court chairs to fill 29 vacancies.[35] The proposed procedure stipulates shortening tenures and establishing a rotation among court chairs, which are seen as necessary conditions for greater transparency and effectiveness. Yet experts warned of the growing shortfall of judges, who are overworked and underpaid, causing numerous vacancies particularly in the lower-tier courts. Shortcomings in court administration add to the problem. Judges and court chairs perform administrative functions, which not only impairs their performance but raises doubts about their independence and the level of transparency in assigning cases.

Pursuant to the 2006 ruling of the Constitutional Court, the Council of Judges, a body that advises the president on the appointment, promotion, and dismissal of judges, was recomposed. Politicians and government officials were removed from the council to make courts less prone to political pressure. Also, the powers of the Supreme Court chair were narrowed. The president nominates—and the Parliament approves—the chair and judges to the Supreme Court and the court of appeals. The president also appoints district court judges. Unlike judges and chairs of other courts, those on the Supreme Court are appointed and dismissed at the recommendation of the Supreme Court chair rather than the Council of Judges.

Public trust in the courts is consistently low, standing at one-fifth of the population.[36] Lower-tier courts are trusted the least, but only a small percentage of verdicts are appealed. The insularity of the court system, lengthy investigations and trials, judge bias in favor of the prosecution, and corruption explain the ingrained public mistrust of the court system.

The issue of dual citizenship has become a headache for the Lithuanian legislature since the Constitutional Court ruled in 2006 that dual citizenship must be a rare exception. Prior to the ruling, dual citizenship was granted on a fairly routine basis. While the country's politicians puzzle over how to satisfy a growing need for dual citizenship, over 600 persons were reportedly stripped of their Lithuanian passports in 2007.[37]

The Constitutional Court provoked much criticism and controversy in 2007, such as the rulings on dual citizenship and the 2007 municipal elections. Some observers claimed the Court exerted influence on the political process, interfered in administrative matters, and freely interpreted the Constitution. Debates also continued on whether to allow private individuals to file a petition with the Constitutional Court. Currently, this right is vested in the president, at least one-fifth of MPs, the government, and the courts. The Constitutional Court delivers about 20 rulings per year.

In response to growing public complaints, notary office hours were extended, real estate transaction procedures were simplified, and fees for such transactions were lowered starting in 2007. Disproportionately large fees for court bailiffs, who act as a private institution, continued to irritate the public, even though the costs of recovering small amounts were limited in 2005.

The criminal law reform of 2003 has not been as effective as expected. Criminal court proceedings have not shortened, nor has the average time spent in detention or prison decreased. The average time suspects spend in pre-trial detention was one month, according to the Office of the Prosecutor General.[38] Although the reform was meant to loosen criminal penalties and broaden alternatives to custodial sentences, these have in fact increased in number and duration, especially for juveniles.

Road safety has become a central concern as the number of accident fatalities has soared. Lithuania has the worst road safety record in the EU, posting 223 deaths per million people in 2006.[39] This issue topped the policy agenda in 2007 and lawmakers were set to tighten criminal measures for offenders. Amid these debates, Lithuania was shaken in November by a tragic car accident in which an off-duty police officer killed three children and fled the scene. This incident led to the resignation of Interior Minister Raimondas Šukys and Police Commissioner General Vytautas Grigaravičius. Lithuania also tops the EU list for suicides and on-the-job fatalities.

Public awareness of rights and opportunities has grown noticeably in recent years. Citizens increasingly report rights violations to the parliamentary and equal opportunity ombudsmen. The most frequent complaints concern land ownership and restitution issues, arbitrary arrests, illegally prolonged detention, and unsatisfactory detention conditions. Although the era of land ownership restitution is drawing to a close, the process has been severely protracted in the most marketable areas, such as Vilnius and Kaunas; owing to legislative loopholes and weaknesses, land has been parceled beyond the ability to resolve unsettled ownership issues for true land owners.

Although necessary legal protections for ethnic minorities are in place, Lithuania is troubled with persistent ethnic intolerance. Opinion polls show the public is biased against minority ethnicities and cultures, especially Roma, Jews, and immigrants, and these attitudes have soared since 1990.[40] An increase in hate speech against minorities, particularly Jews, has been recorded in the past two years, according to the Office of the Prosecutor General.[41] This is attributed more to the rise of new forms of electronic communication than to a growing incidence of hate speech. Also, social consciousness on the issue is increasing, so there is now more likelihood that a complaint will be filed when hate speech occurs. The media are criticized for contributing to the atmosphere of hostility toward minorities, as are the political elite for failing to react to instances of intolerance.

In May 2007, Vilnius city authorities incited an international clamor when they denied a permit for a Europe-wide antidiscrimination campaign rally in Vilnius over fears that the event would spark unrest. This EU-backed rally was aimed at promoting tolerance toward minority groups, including gays and lesbians, and informing citizens of their rights under EU and national antidiscrimination law. Earlier in the month, bus drivers in the country's two largest cities refused to drive vehicles bearing advertisements of a tolerance campaign for gays and lesbians. And again in October, the municipal authorities of Vilnius forbade a rainbow flag event during an annual conference of the International Lesbian and Gay Association. In the meantime, the headquarters of a new European gender-equality institute was scheduled to open in Vilnius by the end of 2007.

Corruption

1999	2001	2002	2003	2004	2005	2006	2007	2008
3.75	3.75	3.75	3.50	3.50	3.75	4.00	4.00	3.75

Transparency International's 2007 Corruption Perceptions Index showed that Lithuania made no visible progress in reducing corruption over the past three years, a report that made headlines. Lithuania maintained a score of 4.8 on the 0–10 scale, where 10 is the best possible score (perceived as least corrupt).[42] Prime Minister Gediminas Kirkilas, who upon taking office in July 2006 pledged to resign if corruption in Lithuania did not decline, criticized the index and insisted that the government worked openly. Although anticorruption efforts appeared to be stagnant, the latest opinion poll showed a turn for the better, since the spread of corruption was finally curbed—in other words, if not better, at least not worse.

According to the *2007 Lithuanian Corruption Map*, a survey of citizens and businesspeople commissioned by the Special Investigation Bureau (SIB) and conducted by TNS Gallup since 2000, most respondents believe that the corruption situation stabilized in 2007.[43] Although the level of corruption remains high, significant improvements were observed in the perceptions and attitudes of the business community. The proportion of citizens prepared to give bribes remained at 57 percent, while the business community showed a marked decline from 55 to 42 percent. Likewise, a consistent amount of people (28 percent) said they had given bribes over the past 12 months, while businesspeople reported a drop from 20 to 17 percent. Although Lithuanian society censures graft, an absolute majority (85 percent of the population) believe that bribes may help in dealings with authorities, and this proportion is growing (up from 75 percent in 2002). Most often bribes are offered to road police, medical workers, customs officials, and land-planning authorities.

Lithuania has a solid legal and institutional basis for fighting corruption, but there is little follow-through on corruption allegations. Ten years after its inception, the SIB, an independent institution in charge of investigation and prevention activities, has been increasingly criticized for ineffectiveness in high-profile corruption cases. Such concerns even spurred proposals to merge the SIB with the Financial Crime Investigation Service.

Notably, implementation of the broad national anticorruption program, adopted in 2002, has stagnated. As an illustration, bills on tightening electoral campaign financing and advertising have stalled in Parliament for over a year, and proposals to set up a separate authority for controlling political party financing have dwindled. Oversight of the administration of EU funds has not been strengthened, despite continuing allegations of misappropriation. In March 2007, Finance Minister Zigmantas Balcytis resigned over his son's involvement in mishandling EU funds.

The Kirkilas administration has renewed a program for curtailing bureaucracy under the so-called Sunset Commission, first launched in 1999, yet with difficulty. Starting from September 2007, ministries and other central and local government agencies were obligated to install a one-stop system in handling citizens' requests, but no mechanism or methodology was prepared for implementation. The Sunset Commission has also suggested dissolving numerous ministry-subordinate organizations that receive independent budget allocations and are largely uncontrollable, but only 2 out of 13 ministries responded to this proposal.

The year 2007 brought leniency for wrongdoings at the top level. Cases included Lithuania's agricultural minister, Kazimira Prunskienė, who remained in office although she was embroiled in conflict-of-interest violations over using public funds for a political and personal publicity campaign. Another incident involved Kęstutis Sabaliauskas, director of the real estate Register Center, who received only a written scolding for paying large illegal bonuses to himself and colleagues. In theory, official punishments for abuse of office include fines, denial of the right to hold certain positions, and imprisonment of four to six years.

The legislation on reconciling public and private interests in state service prohibits conflicts of interest and requires financial disclosure by politicians, CEOs and their spouses. Civil servants and politicians must submit private interest declarations when taking office or assuming leadership in political parties. These are posted on the Supreme Official Ethics Commission Web site, yet incomplete declarations are still a problem.

Graft and cronyism continue to plague the public procurement system. A majority of businesspeople say public procurement tenders are crafted for connected firms, and the winners are known in advance,[44] reported Transparency International (TI) in its March 2007 survey of 98 companies. Equally notorious are ownership restitution and land-planning procedures. An opinion poll conducted by TI in late 2007 showed that one-third of Lithuanian citizens who had built or reconstructed their homes had given bribes to officials or politicians.[45] The majority believe that unofficial payments help in land purchases, land-planning permits, and approval procedures. In 2007, two municipal officials in Vilnius faced graft and influence peddling allegations relating to land-planning decisions; one of them was indicted in October. Accepting or demanding a bribe is punishable by barring offender from certain professional positions and imprisonment of two to eight years.

Corruption remains pervasive in Lithuania's extensive regulatory system. Since direct state participation in the economy has been minimized through large-scale privatization, the regulatory system is the chief way that state officials intervene in the economy, which includes setting quality standards, requiring numerous permits and inspections, prescribing a mandatory minimum wage, regulating energy prices and so forth. Corruption-prone areas include environmental services; health, sanitation, and food inspections; and fire and building inspections. There are 152 regulatory agencies in Lithuania, and a total of 330 permissions are required for various businesses.[46] In a 2008 World Bank ranking of economies and their ease of doing business, Lithuania slipped in position from 16 to 26 owing to stagnating regulatory reforms.[47]

▌ AUTHOR: ANETA PIASECKA

Aneta Piasecka is a senior policy analyst at the Lithuanian Free Market Institute (LFMI), a nonprofit think tank based in Vilnius. Giedrius Kadziauskas, also a senior policy analyst at LFMI, assisted in the research for this report.

1   Civil Service Department, http://www.vtd.lt/index.php?-1902143909.

2   *The User Challenge Benchmarking: The Supply of Online Public Services*, 7th Measurement, September 2007, prepared by CapGemini for European Commission.

3   *Lietuvos Rytas*, "Politinės rietenos smukdo valdžios autoritetą" [Political Ruckus Undermines Government Authority], April 7, 2007; "Politikų rikiuotė—nerimo ir nusivylimo atspindys" [Politicians' Ranking Reflects Anxiety and Disappointment], October 20, 2007.

4   Rūta Žiliukaitė, Aistė Ramonaitė, Laima Nevinskaitė, Vida Beresnevičiūtė, Inga Vinograd-naitė, "Neatrasta galia: Lietuvos pilietinės visuomenės žemėlapis" [Undiscovered Power: Map of the Civil Society in Lithuania], Civil Society Institute, Vilnius, 2006, page 30.

5   Žiliukaitė et al., op. cit.

6   These figures include civic organizations and associations, charity and sponsorship funds, trade unions and public institutions, including budgetary schools, kindergartens, hospitals, research institutes, and so on. The number of civil society groups (excluding the aforesaid public budgetary institutions) is lower and was estimated at about 14,000 in 2005. Žiliukaitė et al., op. cit., page 22.

7   Žiliukaitė et al., op cit., pages 22–30.

8   Transparency International Lithuanian Chapter, "NVO sektoriaus skaidrumo skatinimas" [Promoting a Transparent NGO Sector], December 12, 2007, http://www.transparency.lt/new/images/tils/_nvo_spaudoskonf.pdf.

9   Public institutions are property-based nonprofit organizations. They include private and public research or public policy groups; educational, scientific, cultural, sport, and other organizations; and budgetary establishments such as schools, hospitals, research institutes, and so on. The Law on Public Institutions, I-1428, Seimas of the Republic of Lithuania, September 12, 2000.

10 State Tax Inspectorate, "Paramai šiemet skirta per 53 su puse mln. litų" [Over 53 Million Litas Go for Donations This Year], November 15, 2007, http://www.vmi.lt/lt/?itemId=10145460.

11 Chief Official Ethics Commission, http://www.vtek.lt/lt/disp.php/lt_lobby/lt_lobby_info.

12 Department of Statistics to the Government of the Republic of Lithuania, http://www.stat. gov.lt/lt/pages/view/?id=1336.

13 *Lietuvos Rytas*, "Populiariausių veikėjų lenktynės—be intrigos" [Race of Most Popular Public Figures Shows No Intrigue], June 16, 2007; "Politikų rikiuotė—nerimo ir nusivylimo atspindys" [Politicians' Ranking Reflects Anxiety and Disappointment], October 20, 2007.

14 *Lietuvos Zinios*, "Lietuvos gyventojų autoritetai nekinta" [Lithuanian People's Authorities Do Not Change], November 5, 2003.

15 Putelytė Giedrė, "Lietuviškos žiniasklaidos magnatai" [Lithuanian Media Tycoons], *Veidas*, May 24, 2007, pp. 16–20.

16 Transparency International–Lithuanian Chapter, "Skaidresnės žiniasklaidos link" [Toward Greater Media Transparency], May 2007, http://www.transparency.lt/new/images?media_ skaidrumas_www.pdf.

17 Gemius Audience, http://www.audience.lt, September 2007.

18 *Veidas*, August 17, 2006, page 4.

19 Radio and Television Commission of Lithuania, *Radio and Television in Lithuania: Guide to Audiovisual Sector 2005/2006*, 2006, page 42.

20 TNS Gallup, "TV kanalų auditorijos pasiekimas ir struktūra pagal žiūrėtą laiką" [Outreach and Structure of TV Audience by Viewing Time], October 15, 2007, http://www.tns-gallup. lt/lt/disp.php/lt_surveys/lt_surveys_117?ref=/lt/disp.php/lt_surveys.

21 Radio and Television Commission of Lithuania, *Radio and Television in Lithuania: Guide to Audiovisual Sector 2005/2006*, 2006, page 15.

22 TNS Gallup, "Radijo auditorijos pasiekimas ir struktūra pagal klausytą laiką" [Outreach and Structure of Radio Audience by Listening Time], September 25, 2007, http://www.tns-gallup.lt/lt/disp.php/lt_surveys/lt_surveys_117?ref=/lt/disp.php/lt_surveys.

23 Communications Regulatory Authority, "RRT skelbia elektroninių ryšių rinkos 2007 m. II ketvirčio duomenis" [CRA Announces Electronic Communications Market Data for II Quarter 2007], September 17, 2007, http://www.ivpk.lt/main-stat.php?cat=62&n=85.

24 Information Society Development Committee, "Ketvirtadaliu per metus padidėjo interneto prieigą turinčių namų ūkių skaičius" [Number of Households with Internet Access Grows by One-Fourth on Year], August 10, 2007, http://www.ivpk.lt/main-stat.php?cat=62&n=82.

25 The inspector of journalists' ethics is appointed by the Parliament for a five-year term at the recommendation of the Commission of the Ethics of Journalists and Publishers.

26 Law on the Election of Local Government Councils, No I-532, Seimas of the Republic of Lithuania, July 7, 1994, revision No. X-1001, December 21, 2006, http://www3.lrs.lt/pls/ inter2/dokpaieska.showdoc_l?p_id=289819&p_query=&p_tr2=.

27 Central Electoral Committee of the Republic of Lithuania "Rinkėjų aktyvumas balsuojant paštu" [Voter by Post Turnout], 2007.02.24," http://www.vrk.lt/balsavimas/balsavimas_ pastu/pastu_2007-02-24.html.

28 The Constitutional Court of the Republic of Lithuania, Ruling "On Election of Municipal Councils," February 9, 2007, http://www.lrkt.lt/dokumentai/2007/r070209.htm.

29 Civil Society Institute, "Lietuviai savo šalyje pasigenda tikros savivaldos" [Lithuanians Desire Genuine Self-Government], July 13, 2006, http://www.civitas.lt/lt/?pid=72&id=14. Baltic News Service, "Savivaldybių tarybų rinkimams abejingi daugiau kaip pusė rinkėjų, rodo apklausa" [More Than a Half of Voters Are Indifferent to Municipal Council Elections], February 2, 2007.

30 Civil Society Institute, "Lietuviai savo šalyje pasigenda tikros savivaldos" [Lithuanians Desire Genuine Self-Government], July 13, 2006.

31 National Audit Office of the Republic of Lithuania, *Report on External Review of Audits Conducted by Municipal Controllers (Municipal Control Services)*, November 28, 2006, http:// www.vkontrole.lt/dokumentai/apie/savivaldybiu_isorines_prieziuros_ataskaita.pdf.

32 Finance Ministry of the Republic of Lithuania, http://www.finmin.lt/dinmin.lt/failai/ savivaldybiu_finansiniai_rodikliai/2007_pagr_rodikliai_2_lent.pdf.

33 Seimas of the Republic of Lithuania, "Lietuvos Respublikos 2007 metų valstybės biudžeto ir savivaldybių biudžetų finansinių rodiklių patvirtinimo įstatymas" [Law on Approval of Financial Indicators of 2007 State Budget and Municipal Budgets], December 7, 2006, No. X-963. Ministry of Finance of the Republic of Lithuania, "Savivaldybiu biudžetu prognozuojamos pajamos ir dotacijos 2007 m." [Projected Municipal Budget Revenues and Subsidies in 2007], http://www.finmin.lt/dinmin.lt/failai/savivaldybiu_finansiniai_rodikliai/ 2007_pagr_rodikliai_3_lent.pdf.

34 Kučinskaitė Jonė, "Merų aukso amžius" [Mayors' Golden Age], *Veidas*, March 22, 2007.

35 Press Department of the Office of the President of the Republic of Lithuania, "Prezidentas su Seimo pirmininku aptarė Teismų įstatymo rengimo procesą" [President Discusses the Law-Drafting Process on the Law on Courts with Parliamentary Speaker], February 20, 2007.

36 *Lietuvos Rytas*, "Politinės reitenos smukdo valdžios autoritetą" [Political Ructions Undermine Government Authority], April 7, 2007; "Politikų rikiuotė—nerimo ir nusivylimo atspindys" [Politicians' Ranking Reflects Anxiety and Disappointment], October 20, 2007.

37 Klusas Mindaugas, "Valstybė išsižada savo piliečių" [The State Renounces Its Citizens], *Lietuvos Zinios,* October 24, 2007.

38 Prosecution Service of the Republic of Lithuania, "Nutrauktuose ikiteisminiuose tyrimuose vidutinė asmens suėmimo trukmė—mėnuo" [Average Time of Detention in Suspended Pre-trial Investigations Is One Month], May 30, 2007, http://www.prokuraturos.lt/Aktualijos/ Prane%C5%A1imaispaudai/tabid/71/ItemID/718/Default.aspx

39 European Transport Safety Council, "Road Safety Performance Index," October 10, 2007, http://www.etsc.be/documents/PIN%20Flash%2006.pdf

40 Civil Society Institute, "Lietuvių tolerancija bendrapiliečiams maža" [Lithuanians' Tolerance Toward Fellow Citizens Shrinks], February 2, 2006.

41 Prosecution Service of the Republic of Lithuania, "Daugėja nusikaltimų, kurių priežastis— neatsakinga saviraiškos laisvė" [Crimes Caused by Irresponsible Freedom of Self-Expression on the Rise], July 13, 2007.

42 Transparency International Lithuanian Chapter, "Transparency International korupcijos suvokimo indeksas 2007" [Transparency International Corruption Perceptions Index 2007], September 26, 2007, http://www.transparency.lt/new/images/cpi2007_info.pdf.

43 Special Investigation Bureau, *Lietuvos korupcijos žemėlapis 2007 [Lithuanian Corruption Map 2007]*, December 2007, http://www.stt.lt/lt/file/sociologiniai_tyrimai/korupcijos_ zemelapis_2007.pdf.

44 Transparency International Lithuanian Chapter, "12 įžvalgų apie viešuosius pirkimus Lietuvoje" [Twelve Insights into Public Procurement in Lithuania], March 5, 2007, http:// www.transparency.lt/new/images/vp_spaudos_konf.pdf.

45 Transparency International Lithuanian Chapter.

46 Ministry of Economy of the Republic of Lithuania, "Verslo teisinis reglamentavimas: leidimų, sertifikatų ir kitų panašaus pobūdžio dokumentų, reikalingų vykdant ūkinę veiklą, analizė" [Business Regulation: Analysis of Permissions, Certificates and Other Similar Documents Necessary for Doing Business], research study by Jurevičius, Balčiūnas&Bartkus, December 2006, http://www.ukmin.lt/strategija/doc/study_v5_06_12_20_lt.pdf, p. 4.

47 World Bank, *Doing Business 2008,* http://www.doingbusiness.org/ExploreEconomies/? economyid=114.

Macedonia

by Vladimir Misev

Capital:	Skopje
Population:	2.0 million
GNI/capita:	US$7,850

The social data above was taken from the European Bank for Reconstruction and Development's *Transition Report 2007: People in Transition*, and the economic data from the World Bank's *World Development Indicators 2008*.

Nations in Transit Ratings and Averaged Scores

	1999	2001	2002	2003	2004	2005	2006	2007	2008
Electoral Process	3.50	3.75	4.50	3.50	3.50	3.00	3.25	3.25	3.25
Civil Society	3.50	3.75	4.00	3.75	3.25	3.25	3.25	3.25	3.25
Independent Media	3.75	3.75	3.75	4.00	4.25	4.25	4.25	4.25	4.25
Governance*	3.00	3.75	4.25	4.50	4.00	n/a	n/a	n/a	n/a
National Democratic Governance	n/a	n/a	n/a	n/a	n/a	4.00	3.75	3.75	4.00
Local Democratic Governance	n/a	n/a	n/a	n/a	n/a	4.00	3.75	3.75	3.75
Judicial Framework and Independence	4.25	4.25	4.75	4.50	4.00	3.75	3.75	3.75	4.00
Corruption	5.00	5.00	5.50	5.50	5.00	5.00	4.75	4.75	4.50
Democracy Score	3.83	4.04	4.46	4.29	4.00	3.89	3.82	3.82	3.86

* With the 2005 edition, Freedom House introduced separate analysis and ratings for national democratic governance and local democratic governance to provide readers with more detailed and nuanced analysis of these two important subjects.

NOTE: The ratings reflect the consensus of Freedom House, its academic advisers, and the author(s) of this report. The opinions expressed in this report are those of the author(s). The ratings are based on a scale of 1 to 7, with 1 representing the highest level of democratic progress and 7 the lowest. The Democracy Score is an average of ratings for the categories tracked in a given year.

EXECUTIVE SUMMARY

In the 17 years since the Republic of Macedonia regained its independence in 1991, interethnic relations and minority rights have been at the forefront of the domestic political agenda. In 1993, Macedonia gained admission to the United Nations—albeit under the interim name of the Former Yugoslav Republic of Macedonia, a concession to a name dispute with Greece. This "name issue" has been the topic dominating domestic interest. Macedonia is a multiethnic state; the majority of the population (64 percent) is ethnic Macedonian, and the largest minority group (25 percent) is ethnic Albanian, with populations of Turks, Serbs, Roma, Bosniaks, and Vlachs as other minority communities. Following ethnic clashes during the 1990s over issues including the basic concept of a state, a crisis in the first half of 2001 was concluded with the signing of the Ohrid Framework Agreement (OFA), and Macedonia amended the 1991 Constitution to clarify the position of national minorities in the legal system. In 2005, the country became a European Union (EU) candidate and applied for NATO membership.

By 2007, all Macedonian political parties had reached consensus that a market-based democracy should be the foundation of the country's economic and political system and that Macedonia should become a member of the EU and NATO. It is widely understood that political moderation and ethnic tolerance are important to Macedonian politics. Yet interethnic disputes also characterized 2007.

National Democratic Governance. The national political system in Macedonia is free from such threats to stability as insurgency or war. In March 2007, the largest ethnic Albanian political party, Democratic Union for Integration (DUI), claimed that the provisions of the OFA were not met. DUI left the Parliament, and for two months negotiations were held with the governing party from the ethnic Macedonian political bloc. The finale of the negotiations was an agreement between Prime Minister Nikola Gruevski and the leader of DUI. The agreement and its context in the following period was the subject of serious disputes between the ethnic Macedonian parties and ethnic Albanian parties but also affected the intraethnic dialogue, especially in the ethnic Macedonian political parties. *Owing to the low representation of ethnic minorities in state institutions, the departure from Parliament of DUI over the poor implementation of the OFA, and a general lack of cooperation between the government and President Branko Crvenkovski, which drew sharp criticism from the international community, Macedonia's rating for national democratic governance worsens slightly from 3.75 to 4.00.*

Electoral Process. Macedonia has universal and equal suffrage, with regular, free and fair elections conducted by secret ballot. The electoral system is free of major barriers to political organization and registration and is multiparty-based, with the public engaged in the political life of the country. Since independence, power has rotated among different party coalitions representing competing interests and policy options. In 2007, the government proposed amendments to the electoral code that guaranteed 10 parliamentary seats for smaller ethnic minorities: 4 seats for Turks, 2 for Serbs, 2 for Roma, and 1 each for Bosniaks and Vlachs. The proposal was welcomed by the representatives of the ethnic communities but was met with strong opposition from the largest ethnic Albanian opposition party, DUI. The party claimed that the introduction of guaranteed seats for the other ethnic communities was an attempt to weaken the ethnic Albanian political bloc in Parliament. Three additional guaranteed seats were also proposed for the diaspora community living abroad. *Macedonia's electoral process rating remains at 3.25.*

Civil Society. After independence in 1991, Macedonia became fruitful ground for civil sector development, with a current total of around 5,800 nongovernmental organizations (NGOs). Still, citizen participation is low, and there is a general perception that the Macedonian public does not trust the civil sector. A recent survey reported that only 45 percent of the population has confidence in NGOs. Nevertheless, there have been positive developments in the sector in recent years. Several think tanks were established and gave significant input on a range of government and public policies. The Center for Economic Analysis and the Institute for Democracy work actively on the economic and political development of the country. A network of think tanks was established in 2006 to support the government with qualitative and science-based proposals and suggestions. Most NGOs in Macedonia are financed by the EU and the United States, but the development of much of the civil sector is hampered by a lack of resources. *Macedonia's rating for civil society remains at 3.25.*

Independent Media. The Macedonian public enjoys a diverse selection of print and electronic sources of information at both national and local levels, representing a range of political viewpoints. The weekly political journal *Aktuel* was discontinued owing to a small circulation, but in April 2007, the Westdeutsche Allgemeine Zeitung (WAZ) group introduced a new weekly periodical, *Globus*, which focuses on current affairs and politics. In October 2007, there were several physical attacks on members of the media, one involving the opposition ethnic Albanian party DUI and another involving the special police unit, Alpha. The government held a news conference at which the entire press corps turned their backs on the prime minister in protest of the events. *Macedonia's rating for independent media remains at 4.25.*

Local Democratic Governance. In 2007, a new Law on Balanced Regional Development was enacted by the Parliament, to be implemented in early 2008. Also in preparation is the Law on Inter-Municipal Cooperation, which aims to reduce regional disparities in local economic development. One of the most visible events to affect decentralization in 2007 was the change of the minister for local self-government. In June, the minister resigned as a result of negotiations between Prime Minister Gruevski and the leader of the Party for Democratic Prosperity

(PDP) (Abduladi Vejseli). In the same month, PDP joined the government coalition and filled the ministerial position. Another important event was the continuation of fiscal decentralization to municipalities, yet only half of the municipalities fulfilled the criteria for entering the second phase. A very positive development in the field of local government was the reduction of municipal debt by half. *Macedonia's rating for local democratic governance remains at 3.75.*

Judicial Framework and Independence. Improving the independence and efficiency of the judiciary continues to be a major challenge, yet no consensus has been reached between the government and the opposition on implementing reforms. Discussions on needed changes to the 2004 Law on Public Prosecutors have proved futile. The composition of the Judicial Council has also been an area where all sides of the political spectrum have been unable to reach an agreement. The Parliament elects members to the council with a two-thirds majority, but currently that requires the support of the opposition parties. After feuding much of the year, the parties finally reached an agreement on council nominees in October 2007. On October 23, the Constitutional Court ruled on the constitutionality of the 2005 Law on the Use of Cultural Symbols by Ethnic Communities, which found that certain articles in the law regulating the public display of flags by ethnic communities were unconstitutional. The ruling was strongly condemned by ethnic Albanian parties, with the governing Democratic Party of Albanians (DPA) accusing the opposition DUI of influencing members of the Court. *Owing to serious delays in reforms in this sector, Macedonia's rating for judicial framework and independence worsens from 3.75 to 4.00.*

Corruption. The new government has declared the fight against corruption to be a priority. Since its election, there have been a number of initiatives in this field. In September 2007, the government launched a major public anticorruption campaign entitled Macedonia Without Corruption, accompanied by glossy print and electronic advertising. The purpose of the campaign is to encourage the public to report corruption to the authorities using a special "199"-telephone line; around 100 calls were received in the first week. The government also made several high-profile arrests, but the public display of these arrests on broadcast media appears to challenge the right of citizens to be treated fairly and with a presumption of innocence until proven guilty. *Owing to progress made by the new government in tackling corruption and making anticorruption efforts a policy priority, Macedonia's rating for corruption improves from 4.75 to 4.50.*

Outlook for 2008. In 2008, the decision will be made whether to extend an invitation to Macedonia for NATO membership, which will be important for the stability of the country in light of an impending decision on the final status of Kosovo. With respect to the EU, the government will push for a date on the beginning of accession talks, which are likely to occur in the second half of the year. Overall, 2008 will be a critical year for the government to demonstrate leadership in tackling reforms and moving Macedonia further toward EU standards.

Main Report

National Democratic Governance

1999	2001	2002	2003	2004	2005	2006	2007	2008
n/a	n/a	n/a	n/a	n/a	4.00	3.75	3.75	4.00

The Republic of Macedonia was established in 1991 after the breakup of the Socialist Federal Republic of Yugoslavia and a referendum for the country's independence that drew overwhelming citizen support. On November 21, 1991, the Macedonian Parliament (*Sobranie*) adopted the first Constitution of the newly independent state. After the conclusion of the Ohrid Framework Agreement (OFA) in August 2001, Macedonia acquired a new profile on the domestic and international front, becoming a positive example for post-conflict government and the successful functioning of a multiethnic state.

According to the Constitution, legislative power is vested in the Parliament. The government and the president represent the executive branch, while the Constitutional Court, Supreme Court, and public prosecutor are the judicial authorities in the country. The Parliament is a unicameral legislative organ composed of 120 members elected by universal and direct suffrage. Macedonia is divided into six election districts with each district electing 20 members of Parliament (MPs). The organization and functioning of the Parliament, as well as parliamentary bodies and procedures, are detailed in the rules of procedure. Provisions in the Constitution regarding the Parliament have been largely harmonized with international standards in areas such as the election of MPs in direct and free elections and the division of power among the legislative, executive, and judiciary.

In 2007, the Parliament passed 150 laws, including legislation to harmonize national laws with EU law; implementation of this particular legislation, and the laws that require double majority, has been delayed. Even though the Parliament is formally the strongest institution in the system (can only be dissolved by Parliament itself), in practice its work is dependent largely on the government. Most MPs belong to the governing parties and maintain a subordinate position toward the government. On the one hand, such an attitude enhances efficiency in adopting legislation; on the other, it directly affects the independence of Parliament and the legislative process overall.[1]

Although from a formal point of view executive power is shared dually between the president and the government, in effect it is the government that executes legislative acts. One of the main developments of the state in the last 10 years (after the assassination attempt on Macedonia's first president, Kiro Gligorov) has been an increase in the power of the executive. By introducing 95 percent of the draft legislation into Parliament, the executive has become a legislative body in its own right.

Since independence, it has been a common practice for the government to be multiethnic in its composition. Currently, the Macedonian government is composed largely of ethnic Macedonians (five political parties from the Macedonian political bloc) and ethnic Albanians (two parties from the Albanian political bloc). The Democratic Party of Albanians (DPA) split off from the (ethnic Albanian) Party of Democratic Prosperity (PDP) in the middle of 1990s. Members of other communities, such as Turks, Vlachs, and other smaller ethnic groups, also participate in the government.

The president is elected by universal and direct suffrage, serving a period of five years with a two-term limit. In this semi-presidential system, the strong position of the president is characterized by having the right to veto legislation adopted by a simple majority in the Parliament. The current president, Branko Crvenkovski, succeeded Boris Trajkovski, who died in a fatal air crash. In 2007, the international community expressed concerns over the lack of cohabitation between the prime minister and the president. Namely, considering the importance of Macedonia's Euro-Atlantic aspirations, the president and the prime minister were warned by NATO and European Union (EU) officials that they should cooperate to push forward reforms and accelerate integration of the country into these international institutions. On several occasions, the prime minister and the president had grave disputes over their mutual competences and responsibilities. Cohabitation between the government and the president was seriously interrupted when the president's proposed nominees for ambassadors and members of the Judicial Council were refused.

The OFA was a turning point for improvements in local democratic governance and the preservation of Macedonia's cultural identities, while also acting as a catalyst for the country's entrance into Euro-Atlantic institutions. Still, representation of the country's multiethnic communities in state institutions is low. According to data from 2006, there is serious underrepresentation in many institutions, especially in the police, army, and judiciary. For instance, ethnic Albanians represented 8 percent of the judicial administration and judges, and other communities (combined) accounted for less than 3 percent. On the other hand, representation in educational institutions is proportional to the census data.[2] For 2008, the government has projected €2.5 million (US$3.8 million) for accelerating the process of reform and representation of all communities.[3]

The process of interethnic dialogue was intermittent during 2007. In March, the largest ethnic Albanian political party (Democratic Union for Integration [DUI]) claimed that OFA provisions were not being met and left the Parliament; this was followed by two months of negotiations with the governing party from the ethnic Macedonian political bloc. The finale was an agreement between Prime Minister Nikola Gruevski and the leader of DUI in the presence of the EU representative and endorsed by the U.S. Embassy in Skopje. According to the agreement, five points were to be negotiated: 1) preparing a list of 46 laws to be passed (evaluated against the so-called Badinter Principle); 2) drafting a new law for the composition of the Parliamentary Commission for Relations Between Communities; 3) securing social and material support for the victims of the conflict from 2001 within the framework of existing laws; 4) drafting a new law for the usage of languages in compliance with OFA and the Constitution; and 5) continuing discussions on increasing the multiethnic character of the state. The governing party stated that consensus was reached only on the first two points of the agreement, while DUI insisted that agreement was reached on all five issues.

Electoral Process

1999	2001	2002	2003	2004	2005	2006	2007	2008
3.50	3.75	4.50	3.50	3.50	3.00	3.25	3.25	3.25

Macedonia has universal and equal suffrage, with regular, free, and fair elections conducted by secret ballot. Moreover, the electoral system is free of major barriers to political organization and registration. In the years since independence, the electoral system has been multiparty-based, with the public engaged in the political life of the country. Power has rotated between different party coalitions representing competing interests and policy options. Although the field of political contenders is generally free from domination by different power groups, the lack of financial transparency of political parties and election campaigns remains a serious issue.

The 120 MPs are elected by proportional representation. There are six electoral districts comprising 20 members each. Parties or electoral coalitions nominate a list of candidates for each district. Votes are cast for a list rather than for individual candidates, and the number of candidates elected from a party's list in each district depends on their share of the vote. There is no minimum threshold for representation in Parliament.

On July 5, 2006, parliamentary elections were held in Macedonia and evaluated by international observers as largely meeting international standards. Yet there was some violence during the campaign and a few irregularities, including ballot stuffing, family voting, and voter intimidation. The Office of the Public Prosecutor initiated procedures against 20 persons suspected of committing election irregularities. The State Anticorruption Commission and the State Audit Office found that campaigns had exceeded the spending limits set by law and that many unreported donations had been received, in particular in the form of underpriced media advertising.

The parliamentary elections brought changes to the composition of the government and the Parliament. The new government coalition is led by VMRO-DPMNE and includes the Democratic Party of Albanians (DPA) as the main coalition partner, together with a number of smaller parties. This coalition holds 63 seats in Parliament.

In 2007, the government proposed amendments to the electoral code that will guarantee 10 parliamentary seats for smaller ethnic minorities: 4 seats for Turks, 2 for Serbs, 2 for Roma, and 1 each for Bosniaks and Vlachs. The proposal was welcomed by the representatives of the ethnic communities but strongly opposed by the ethnic Albanian opposition party DUI, which claimed that guaranteed seats for other ethnic communities is an attempt to weaken the ethnic Albanian political bloc in Parliament. The reforms mean that ethnic Albanians will have a reduced majority among non-Macedonian MPs. This is particularly significant considering the "double majority" principle required for passing some laws (that is, a majority of MPs overall, as well as a majority of the MPs belonging to ethnic communities).

Three additional guaranteed seats were also proposed for the diaspora community living abroad: one seat for Australia, one for North America, and one for Europe. Under these changes, Macedonian citizens residing abroad would elect their representatives. There was some criticism over exactly how voting would be controlled on foreign territories. As a result of the proposed changes, the number of MPs would increase from 120 to 133. These changes would come into effect at the next parliamentary elections, to be held no later than August 2010.

According to the Organization for Security and Cooperation in Europe, the most recent presidential elections (held in April 2004) were free and fair and generally complied with international standards, with only a few election irregularities, such as proxy voting, political violence, the presence of unauthorized personnel at polling stations, and voter intimidation. The next presidential elections, as well as municipal elections, are due to be held in 2009.

Civil Society

1999	2001	2002	2003	2004	2005	2006	2007	2008
3.50	3.75	4.00	3.75	3.25	3.25	3.25	3.25	3.25

After independence in 1991, Macedonia became fertile ground for the development of the civil sector, with around 5,800 nongovernmental organizations (NGOs) established in only 16 years.[4] Although there are numerous NGOs, the level of citizen participation is low, and the general perception is that Macedonian citizens do not trust the civil sector. According to a recent survey by Citizens' Platform of Macedonia, only 45 percent of the population has confidence in NGOs. By comparison, NGOs have a higher approval rating than trade unions but lower than religious institutions. One explanation is that citizens, to a large degree, believe that NGOs are misused by political parties.

Regarding the legislative framework, Macedonian civil society is free of state pressure. The sector is regulated by the Constitution, the Law for Citizens Associations and Foundations, and other bylaws and regulations. The Law for Citizens Associations and Foundations was adopted in July 1998 and amended in September 2007. Some NGOs had serious criticisms of the adoption process and content of the law. The Foundation Open Society Institute Macedonia (FOSIM) and Macedonian Center for International Cooperation (MCMS) under the Citizens' Platform of Macedonia organized a regional conference on the NGO legislative framework, which noted the strict regulations on organizational organs. According to the amendments, employees are prohibited from participating in the executive bodies of NGOs. However, the main criticism noted that the law does not provide a clear definition or regulations for organizations of public benefit.[5]

In the last few years, there have been some positive developments in Macedonia's third sector. Several think tanks were established and now give significant input to the government on public policy issues. There are many organizations that work actively on the economic and political development of the country. A network of organizations was established in 2006 to provide qualitative and science-based proposals and suggestions to the government.

The adoption of the Strategy for Cooperation of the Government with the Civil Sector is another important recent development. The document proposes concrete measures in legislative and financial areas that will enhance the progress of civil society. According to the strategy, changes will be made to the legislation on capital gains, value added tax, property, and the like. A reduction in the personal income tax from 15 to 12 percent is also foreseen.

Most NGOs in Macedonia are financed by two sources: the EU and U.S. private foundations. However, the general development of the civil sector is hampered by a lack of resources. MCMS and FOSIM are the largest domestic organizations that are financially viable in the long term. Some of the biggest recipients of state aid include the Trade Union Federation, Association of Veterans of World War II, and Association of Women. The most serious obstacles for the further development and improvement of Macedonian civil society are the taxation framework, lack of transparency, corruption, and the highly centralized state.

The links between the media and NGOs strengthened during 2007. It is now common practice for the media to broadcast press conferences or other events organized by NGOs. Also, experts from think tanks are regular guests on news programs and talk shows. Several research initiatives for cooperation between these two sectors were undertaken by the Macedonian Institute for Media (MIM), which organized conferences on EU topics to assist future journalists in understanding EU terminology. Additionally, MIM, in cooperation with different national and local TV and radio broadcasters, launched *Sunday Interview,* where young journalists interview political leaders on various topics of public interest.

Macedonian civil society is technically well equipped, despite the lack of financial resources. NGOs are generally composed of young and well educated persons and are active in a broad range of public interest areas, including health care, the economy, politics, and issues related to trafficking.

Independent Media

1999	2001	2002	2003	2004	2005	2006	2007	2008
3.75	3.75	3.75	4.00	4.25	4.25	4.25	4.25	4.25

Article 16 of the Macedonian Constitution, adopted in 2004, guarantees freedom of speech and access to information. Journalists and media outlets are able to form their own professional associations, and the Association of Journalists and MIM are particularly active. The 2007 World Press Freedom Index by Reporters Without Borders ranked Macedonia 36th out of 168 nations, an increase of 10 places over the 2006 ranking and better than neighboring Albania, Bulgaria, and Serbia.

The Macedonian public enjoys a diverse selection of print and electronic sources of information at both national and local levels, representing a range of political viewpoints. The distribution of privately controlled newspapers and the media's editorial independence and news-gathering functions are free of direct government interference.

In the overcrowded broadcast media arena, hundreds of private outlets compete for audiences. A few television stations are considered to be politically influenced since the owners are also presidents of political parties. A1 Television is owned by Velija Ramkovski, leader of the newly established Party for Economic Renewal, and Sitel TV is owned by Goran Ivanov, son of Ljubisav Ivanov, president of the Socialist Party. Channel 5 is owned by Emil Stojmenov, son of Boris Stojmenov, leader of the VMRO-Vistinska Party. The owner of Telma TV is Makpetrol, a large oil distribution company, while an ethnic Albanian businessman, Vebi Velija, owns the fifth station, Alsat TV.

Since 2004, the country's three best-selling newspapers, *Utrinski Vesnik*, *Vest*, and *Dnevnik*, have been owned by the German media giant Westdeutsche Allgemeine Zeitung (WAZ). The weekly political journal *Aktuel* was discontinued owing to its small circulation. In April 2007, WAZ introduced a successful new quality weekly periodical, *Globus*, which focuses on current affairs and politics.

In 2006, Parliament adopted new freedom of information legislation abolishing imprisonment as a punishment for defamation and libel. Previously, the lack of such legislation not only limited the media's ability to undertake investigative reporting, but, by limiting the factual information available, also contributed to the prosecution of journalists for defamation. Along with changes to the criminal code, Macedonia began implementing the Law on Free Access to Information in the autumn of 2006, but its implementation needs improvement. A report released in late 2007 by the Open Society Institute found that approximately 50 percent of all information requests in the preceding year had been ignored by state institutions.

In the broadcasting arena, only a thorough implementation of the law and regular collection of citizens' fees for the Public Broadcasting Company will secure its funding and raise standards. The Broadcasting Council grants licenses to media outlets and oversees their compliance with regulations and established standards. However, the council is ineffective and subject to political influence. The collection of broadcast licensing fees broke down entirely in early 2007.

Some journalists faced violent incidents and threats in 2007. In May, in response to an opinion piece by Iso Rusi in the Albanian-language daily *Koha*, the DPA (a member of the governing coalition) released a statement containing ethnic and religious slurs, as well as threats of violence. There were two physical attacks on members of the media in October. On the same day that a scuffle broke out in Parliament, a journalist from A1 Television was struck in the face by a DUI party activist. The next day, a cameraman from Alsat TV was beaten by members of the special police unit, Alpha, for recording members of Alpha at a checkpoint. The next day, the government held a news conference and the entire press corps turned their backs on the prime minister in protest of the events.

Local Democratic Governance

1999	2001	2002	2003	2004	2005	2006	2007	2008
n/a	n/a	n/a	n/a	n/a	4.00	3.75	3.75	3.75

In Article 8 of Macedonia's 1991 Constitution, legislators enumerated the right of local government as a basic value. Municipalities are the basic units of local government, with no intermediary levels between municipalities and the central government. Additionally, citizens have the right to establish local communities within municipalities, which oversee this process. Participation in local government takes the form of democratically elected representatives as well as referendums, where citizens may make decisions directly on a particular question.

The process of decentralization in Macedonia has been perceived as a vital step toward improving long held interethnic tensions in the country. The quest for real decentralization, unfortunately, ended with a violent civil conflict in Macedonia, culminating in 2001 with the OFA, which gave a legal basis for changes to legislation related to local government. According to the Congress of Local and Regional Authorities of the Council of Europe Recommendation 217 (2007), on local democracy in the Republic of Macedonia, "The measures taken by the authorities since 2001, and more particularly 2005, represent a significant change and marked progress towards better local democracy, and local authorities have, on the whole, coped satisfactorily with their new responsibilities, and standards of local service have improved."[6]

The conclusion of the OFA and the regulations therein present a turning point for the progress of local government. Broad competences and a strong emphasis on the identity of communities in local government units distinguish the Macedonian local government system. Additionally, the implementation of decentralization has been important for Macedonia's integration into the EU.

The main laws regulating local government are the Law of Local Self-Government, stipulating the main aspects of local government; the Law on Territorial Organization of Local Self-Government, by which municipal boundaries were revised and the number of municipalities reduced from 124 to 84, with the city of Skopje as a separate unit; the Law on Local Financing of Self-Government Units, regulating the financing of municipalities through their own revenue sources and fiscal decentralization implemented in phases; and the Law on the City of Skopje, defined as a separate unit of local self-government.

Municipalities are assigned numerous competences but remain financially dependent on the central government. A new Law on Balanced Regional Development was passed by Parliament and is due to be implemented in January 2008. Also in preparation is a separate Law on Inter-Municipal Cooperation, which aims to reduce regional disparities and enhance local economic development in rural areas.

One of the most visible events in 2007 was the naming of a new minister for local self-government. In June, the former minister resigned as a result of negotiations between Prime Minister Gruevski and the leader of PDP, Abduladi Vejseli. In the same month, PDP joined the government coalition and filled the ministerial post. The replacement was reportedly a result of a political deal struck among the new coalition partners. In another development, fiscal decentralization to municipalities (begun in 2006) entered its second phase in 2007, with only half of municipalities fulfilling the criteria for the second phase. On a more positive note, municipalities reduced their debt by half in 2007.

Still, areas of local governance that need improvement include local efforts to improve services for citizens, mayors fully implementing decentralization measures, and the central government following up transfers of competences with adequate funds to fulfill these responsibilities. Decentralization remains a subject of political disputes instead of being a policy for improving the lives of citizens at the local level.

Judicial Framework and Independence

1999	2001	2002	2003	2004	2005	2006	2007	2008
4.25	4.25	4.75	4.50	4.00	3.75	3.75	3.75	4.00

Improving the independence and efficiency of the judicial system continued to be a major challenge in 2007. Although the judiciary is still dependent on politics, in the last months of the year there was evidence of progress in this sector, a point also acknowledged by the international community. According to the Ministry of Justice, around 55 laws related to the judicial system were adopted in 2007, but their implementation is still pending. Apart from the legislation, which in general is in accordance with recommendations of the Council of Europe and the EU, there was a loud public debate among domestic experts over the interference of political parties in the composition of the Judicial Council and the nomination of judges.

The Judicial Council is composed of 13 judges elected by their peers, along with the Minister of Justice and the president of the Supreme Court as ex officio members. The new Judicial Council began operating in January 2007 with 10 of its 15 members. In October, an additional 4 members were appointed. Following completion of the council there began the recruitment of judges to the new administrative court and the new court of appeals in Gostivar. However, the new administrative court, which became legally competent for administrative cases as of May 2007, could not become operational since its judges were not yet appointed.

In December 2007, the Law on Public Prosecution and the Law on the Council of Public Prosecutors—the two final laws needed to complete the legislative framework set out in the constitutional amendments of December 2005—were adopted.

The Academy of Judges and Prosecutors was established and became operational. The director and executive director were appointed, and continuous training begun. The program council of the academy was established, and the managing board adopted the implementing legislation for entry tests. The initial training program started in September. Ensuring the function of the academy and promoting continuous training remain essential to improving the professionalism and competence of the judiciary. The 2006 Law on Mediation, which aims to lower court workloads via alternative dispute resolution, also entered into force.

In October 2007, the Constitutional Court ruled on the constitutionality of the 2005 Law on the Use of Cultural Symbols by Ethnic Communities. The ruling found unconstitutional certain articles in the law: specifically, those that regulated the public display of flags by ethnic communities. The ruling was strongly condemned by ethnic Albanian parties, with the governing DPA accusing the opposition DUI of influencing members of the Court. Similar accusations were made by DUI. Three days later, the president of the Constitutional Court and another ethnic Albanian judge resigned in protest over the decision.

Corruption

1999	2001	2002	2003	2004	2005	2006	2007	2008
5.00	5.00	5.50	5.50	5.00	5.00	4.75	4.75	4.50

Given that few cases of corruption have actually been resolved in the 16 years since independence, it is clear that Macedonians have come to accept corruption as part of public life. For experts and citizens alike, the perception is that corruption remains widespread, holding back economic development and weakening social cohesion. International reports and surveys indicate that corruption in Macedonia is a serious and widespread problem that affects many aspects of social, political, and economic life despite the intensification of efforts to fight it and increased awareness of its negative impact on the country.

The new government has declared the fight against corruption to be a priority. The issue was a major theme in the opposition's campaign in the 2006 parliamentary elections, and since it came to power there have been a number of initiatives in this field. In 2007, the government launched a public campaign entitled Macedonia Without Corruption, accompanied by glossy advertising and electronic media to convey the government's message. The purpose of the campaign was to encourage the public to report corruption to the authorities. A special "199"-telephone line was established for this purpose, and about 100 calls were received in the first week.

There have been several high-profile arrests involving misappropriation of public funds and bribery. Some of these cases involve what the media often calls "revenge" or "partisan" arrests against persons close to former government officials (now in the opposition). The government has been accused of selectively arresting and charging individuals in the opposition, while turning a blind eye to corruption scandals involving their own cadres.

One point of concern in 2007 was the public spectacle made of some arrests. In several cases, video footage of arrests was released and broadcast by the media. Such a practice does not conform to international standards regarding the right of citizens to be treated fairly and with a presumption of innocence until proven guilty.

Nevertheless, progress has been made in the fight against corruption and organized crime. In its 2007 Corruption Perceptions Index, Transparency International ranked Macedonia 84th out of 179 countries surveyed, a significant improvement over its ranking of 105th in 2006. The improvement was also noted by the European Parliament in its 2007 progress report on Macedonia. The report called for the government to continue with reforms, especially in implementing anticorruption legislation and reform of the judiciary.

▌   AUTHOR: VLADIMIR MISEV

Vladimir Misev is executive director of the Institute for Democracy Societas Civilis, a think tank based in Skopje.

---

1   A public opinion survey about citizens' views on political parties and party leadership, conducted twice in 2007 (February and September) by the Institute for Democracy Societas Civilis (IDSCS), showed that public opinion toward Parliament had not changed during the year. The average grade that the citizens gave for the work of the Parliament was 2.3 in both surveys (on the 1–5 scale, with 1 worst, 5 best). See http://www.idscs.org.mk/upload/news/IDSCS-Soopstenie_za_javnost-anketa_septemvri.pdf.

2   Last official data published on the Web site of the Sector for Implementation for Ohrid Framework Agreement, SIOFA, www.siofa.gov.mk.

3   "Pet godini po ramkovniot dogovor—Pravicnata zasapenost e pod 20%" [Five Years After the Framework Agreement—Equal Representation below 20 Percent], *Dnevnik*, September 11, 2007.

4   According to the 2003 Index of Civil Society from CIVICUS, in 2003 the total number of citizens associations was 5,769.

5   Information about the Regional Conference On Legislative and Fiscal Framework of NGOs, September 24–25, 2007, Foundation Open Society Institute–Macedonia, available at http://www.soros.org.mk and http://www.gpm.net.mk.

6   Recommendation 217 (2007) on local democracy in "the Former Yugoslav Republic of Macedonia," adopted by the Congress of Local and Regional Authorities of the Council of Europe on June 1, 2007 (see document CPL(14)2REC, draft recommendation presented by J.-C. Frécon [France, L, SOC]).

Moldova

by George Dura and Liliana Vitu

Capital: Chisinau
Population: 3.4 million
GNI/capita: US$2,660

The social data above was taken from the European Bank for Reconstruction and Development's *Transition Report 2007: People in Transition,* and the economic data from the World Bank's *World Development Indicators 2008.*

Nations in Transit Ratings and Averaged Scores

	1999	2001	2002	2003	2004	2005	2006	2007	2008
Electoral Process	3.25	3.25	3.50	3.75	4.00	4.00	3.75	3.75	3.75
Civil Society	3.75	3.75	4.00	3.75	4.00	4.00	4.00	3.75	3.75
Independent Media	4.00	4.25	4.50	4.75	5.00	5.00	5.00	5.25	5.50
Governance*	4.50	4.50	4.75	5.25	5.50	n/a	n/a	n/a	n/a
National Democratic Governance	n/a	n/a	n/a	n/a	n/a	5.75	5.75	5.75	5.75
Local Democratic Governance	n/a	n/a	n/a	n/a	n/a	5.75	5.75	5.75	5.75
Judicial Framework and Independence	4.00	4.00	4.00	4.50	4.50	4.75	4.50	4.50	4.50
Corruption	6.00	6.00	6.25	6.25	6.25	6.25	6.00	6.00	6.00
Democracy Score	4.25	4.29	4.50	4.71	4.88	5.07	4.96	4.96	5.00

* *With the 2005 edition, Freedom House introduced separate analysis and ratings for national democratic governance and local democratic governance to provide readers with more detailed and nuanced analysis of these two important subjects.*

NOTE: The ratings reflect the consensus of Freedom House, its academic advisers, and the author(s) of this report. The opinions expressed in this report are those of the author(s). The ratings are based on a scale of 1 to 7, with 1 representing the highest level of democratic progress and 7 the lowest. The Democracy Score is an average of ratings for the categories tracked in a given year.

EXECUTIVE SUMMARY

Following its declaration of independence on August 27, 1991, and a short civil war provoked by Russophones from the region east of the Nistru River in 1992, Moldova embarked on a political and economic reform process throughout the 1990s and succeeded in holding several rounds of largely free elections. With most heavy industry based in the breakaway Transnistria region, Moldova's gross domestic product, based primarily on agriculture, plummeted by the late 1990s. The resultant internal political crisis saw the Communists return to power in 2001. Until 2003–2004, the Communist leadership held a distinct pro-Russian foreign policy course, but after formulation of the European Union (EU) Neighborhood Policy in 2003, Moldova eventually made European integrity a priority and signed an Action Plan with the EU in February 2005.

Moldova has continued the reform process throughout 2007. However, the pace of reforms has been slowing down, partly because in the first half of 2007, most political efforts were geared toward the June local elections. Electoral support for the Party of Moldovan Communists (PMC) dropped significantly compared with the 2005 parliamentary elections (from 46 percent to 34.4 percent). In 2007, the Moldovan government also continued to implement the EU-Moldova Action Plan. However, the EU urged Moldovan authorities to take further action to tackle problems concerning the judiciary and related to the fight against corruption and as a result decided to extend the Action Plan (due to expire in February 2008) for another year.

Moldova's first year as an EU neighbor following Romania's accession to the EU on January 1, 2007, provoked embarrassing diplomatic exchanges between Chisinau and Bucharest surrounding questions of visas and passports. Romania's introduction of visas affected the ability of Moldovans to travel to and study in Romania and the EU. The delayed signature of a basic treaty between both countries was a further cause of deteriorating relations. However, the partial lifting of the Russian ban on Moldovan wine and confidential bilateral talks taking place throughout 2007 on a plan for the resolution of the Transnistrian conflict demonstrated that relations between Chisinau and Moscow are on the mend.

National Democratic Governance. Moldova's national governance continues to be marked by tight presidential control over the legislature, executive, and judiciary. Officials no longer refuse to release public information as they had in the first years following passage of the Law on Access to Information. Instead they release standard, non-informative answers to citizens' requests. The security services still need reforming in order to come under full civilian control. Opposition parties and civil society organizations lack oversight of government policies. No progress was made on a resolution of the Transnistrian conflict, despite a plan by President Vladimir Voronin to demilitarize Moldova and implement a series of confidence-building measures with Transnistria. *Owing to little progress made in domestic political processes during the election year, Moldova's rating for national democratic governance remains at 5.75.*

Electoral Process. Local elections held in June 2007 were considered generally free and fair by international institutions (the OSCE and the EU), but shortcomings and abuses were noted mainly during the electoral campaign. Most significant, the PMC lost ground to the main opposition parties in this year's local elections. Moldova's electoral legislation did not change much in 2007, except for the adoption of a new law on political parties. The electoral code is expected to be fine-tuned prior to the 2009 parliamentary elections to address problems identified in previous nation-wide elections pertaining to voter registration, voting privacy, registration of parties and electoral candidates, existence of equal campaign opportunities, and access to media. *Although the scale of electoral abuse recorded during the 2003 local elections was not repeated during the 2007 local elections, owing to procrastination by Moldovan authorities on electoral code reforms and persistent shortcomings throughout the electoral campaign, Moldova's rating for electoral process remains unchanged at 3.75.*

Civil Society. Abundant and fragmented, nongovernmental organizations (NGOs) are beginning the complicated process of consolidation. Civil society remains for the most part more preoccupied with its survival and the attraction of funding than with social problems. However, in certain cases the Moldovan government has undertaken efforts to involve civil society in the drafting of laws. The number of non-active organizations is significant, and only certain NGOs have the capacities to contribute to public policies. Lobbying and advocacy activities are developing slowly but lack impact. At the same time, monitoring efforts did not bear the expected results. Dependence on donor support makes NGOs vulnerable and poses the key challenge to the sector's development. Until NGOs become transparent and open to working with the media, they will lack credibility in their mission to promote democratic values. *Despite certain improvements, civil society did not manage to increase its influence over governmental policies and to establish itself as a vibrant component of the public sphere supported by constituents. The rating for civil society remains unchanged at 3.75.*

Independent Media. This electoral year saw a setback for media and press freedom. The public broadcaster Teleradio Moldova is still under excessive government influence, as is the Broadcasting Coordination Council. Self-censorship was common among journalists, particularly those covering the electoral campaign. Journalists investigating corruption, as well as their sources, were intimidated and harassed. While prison sentences can no longer be issued in libel cases, Parliament refuses to set a clear ceiling for libel fines. Teleradio Moldova has made little progress toward becoming a genuine public broadcaster. Diversity of opinion remains acutely limited owing to political pressure and economic restraints on independent, non-state newspapers. Media concentration in the hands of people closely affiliated to the PMC also raises concerns for plurality in Moldovan media. Media outlets continue to struggle to ensure their financial sustainability, hindered by constant political influence. On the eve of local elections, journalists from two non-state TV stations were prohibited from filming an opposition march. *The rating for independent media worsens from 5.25 to 5.50, as abuses and harassment, especially during local elections, resulted in an atmosphere of fear and self-censorship among journalists.*

Local Democratic Governance. Despite a wide range of rights, centralization of powers remains the key issue undermining the development of autonomously run regions in Moldova. Local authorities remain dependent on central authorities for funding and access to other resources. At the same time, the government clearly favors local communities led by representatives of the PMC and interferes with the prerogatives of the local authorities. The large number of candidates in local elections reflects not a wide range of political programs, but rather the fragmentation and intense fights at the local level, which draws attention from communities' interests. Journalists report the views of local civic groups in relation to local government policy, and a fair number of partnerships have emerged in such towns as Balti, Cahul, and Ungheni. Central authorities exercise control over local authorities mainly through the discriminatory distribution of budgets, whereby the central government clearly favors the Communist-led regions. *Because local governments continue to face excessive political control while centralization hinders the design and implementation of sound policies, the local democratic governance rating remains unchanged at 5.75.*

Judicial Framework and Independence. Moldova continues its reform efforts in the field of the judiciary, especially with respect to its organization, financing, independence, and proper functioning. Moldovan authorities work closely with experts from the Council of Europe (COE) and have agreed to submit all legislative proposals emanating from the Parliament for COE review. The Strategy on the Reform of the Judicial System for 2007–2008 was drafted with the help of the COE. The National Institute of Justice, which provides training for judges and prosecutors, opened in November 2007. However, independence is still not guaranteed with regard to the nomination and appointment of judges and prosecutors. The lack of sufficient financial resources, though partially addressed this year, is still a cause for corruption and does not create optimal conditions for effective trials. Moldova's penitentiary system is being reformed, but living conditions and treatment in prison are still degrading. *Throughout 2007, Moldova has continued to put in place a sound legal framework for its judiciary, which despite shortcomings is expected to yield results. Until then, Moldova's rating for judicial framework and independence remains at 4.50.*

Corruption. Throughout 2007, authorities aimed to implement the National Anticorruption Strategy for 2007–2009, but little real progress was recorded toward enforcement or closing off special immunity, as claimed by select groups (parliamentarians). A code of conduct for public officials, a Law on Conflict of Interest, and legislation on transparency in the decision-making process are still needed. Alongside the Center for Fighting Corruption and Economic Crime, the lead government agency, civil society organizations and the media are involved in the fight against corruption. According to Transparency International, Moldova is sliding back in the 2007 Corruption Perceptions Index despite the international assistance Moldova receives to fight corruption. *Moldova's authorities have continued in their efforts to implement a more effective legal framework to combat corruption and are increasingly cooperating with international organizations. However, recurrent shortcomings and the slow pace of implementation do not justify an improvement in the rating, which remains unchanged at 6.00.*

Outlook for 2008. This is a pre-electoral year, and competition among the ruling party and opposition will intensify. The PMC will most likely use its political influence to intimidate opposition leaders, especially those with the potential to consolidate smaller parties around their leadership. Pressure on the media will increase, and direct or indirect attacks on journalists cannot be ruled out. NGOs will attempt to monitor the government's actions. However, they are still weak and highly dependent on donors. Externally, Moldova and Romania will attempt to normalize their relations by signing a basic treaty on bilateral relations and by cooperating on EU integration. Russia may maintain the pressure to resolve the Transnistrian dispute, possibly leading to a controversial or detrimental quick-fix solution before the end of President Voronin's mandate. In 2008, Moldova will benefit from the system of autonomous trade preferences with the EU, and Moldovan citizens will benefit from facilitated visa travel to the EU. Moldova's Action Plan will be renewed for another year, until February 2009.

Main Report

National Democratic Governance

1999	2001	2002	2003	2004	2005	2006	2007	2008
n/a	n/a	n/a	n/a	n/a	5.75	5.75	5.75	5.75

European values and international democratic principles are enshrined in the Moldovan Constitution, which establishes the country as a parliamentary republic. Nevertheless, in practice the executive has sizable power and exerts pressure on the judiciary, as attested to by the number of cases lost by the state of Moldova at the European Court of Human Rights.[1]

In an attempt to enhance transparency and accountability, the Parliament has set up a Web page inviting nongovernmental organizations (NGOs) to submit amendments to legislation in process. Nevertheless, the site is not up-to-date and the archive is poor in resources. Also, the legislature suspended the obligatory broadcast of its sessions by the public broadcaster in March 2007, after only three months of broadcasts. Public broadcaster Teleradio Moldova presents regular reports on parliamentary sessions but tends to avoid opposition views.[2] The Accounting Chamber controls how public money is spent, but state bodies do not follow up with serious investigations on reports of malpractice.

The Law on Government defines the role of the executive. Appointments are political rather than career-based, non-transparent, and outside of public competitions. For example, only 6 of the 23 Moldovan ambassadors have diplomatic backgrounds, and knowledge of a foreign language is not required.[3] While it is common to mix career diplomats and political appointees as ambassador positions, for Moldova the balance is tilted heavily in favor of politicians that lack professional qualifications. In contrast to Western diplomacy where political appointees are backed by professional support and oversight, Moldovan Embassies are often a 2–3 person mission: a structure that supports inefficiency and opportunities for rent-seeking.

Journalists, despite the establishment of a press room, have limited access to decision makers in the government. Opportunities to meet with cabinet ministers are limited to days when the government sits. Public officials and journalists are based in Chisinau, but the access is so limited that the major possibility for journalists to "catch" a minister is at the weekly session of the government. Opposition media have even less access. The Law on Access to Information ensures access within 15 working days to data held by the government, except for data on national security, commercial secrets, or of a private nature. However, a number of reports revealed that the law is rarely enforced in practice.

Moldovan political life following the April 4, 2005 reelection of President Vladimir Voronin has been marked by a period of 'stability stagnation.' The political consensus that supported his reelection (the Democratic Party, Social-Liberal Party, and Christian Democratic People's Party) collapsed after local elections in the summer of 2007, with President Voronin threatening to "resume the most primitive political path between the two forces: Communists *versus* entire opposition."[4] Nevertheless, the population continues to support national authorities and their policies.

In law, the Security and Information Service (SIS) and the Ministries of the Interior and Defense are placed under parliamentary oversight, yet not in practice by the government. The security sector (ministries of Interior, Defense, and Justice, plus the Supreme Security Council), especially the Ministry of the Interior, is widely perceived as corrupt, and the judiciary system as politically-controlled, which heightens public concerns about guarantees for the respect of civilian rights and freedoms[5].

Moldovan citizens are in agreement with the government regarding the European prospects of the country. Over 70 percent of the population would support the country's EU membership in a referendum, and up to 30 percent support joining NATO.[6] In its report on the implementation of the EU-Moldova Action Plan in December 2006, the EU noted that despite steady implementation, shortcomings persist with regard to the judiciary, corruption, respect of human rights, and freedom of the media.

The EU extended the mandate of the EU Border Assistance Mission on the Moldova-Ukraine border until December 1, 2008. An EU common visa center opened on April 25, 2007, at the Hungarian embassy in Chisinau to issue Schengen visas for a number of EU states without representatives in Moldova.[7] In addition, a visa facilitation and readmission agreement with the EU will enter into force on January 1, 2008.

Throughout 2007, Moldovan officials held a number of high-level meetings with their Russian counterparts regarding the possibility of negotiating a settlement over Transnistria. Such negotiations in the OSCE have stalled since early 2006. In October 2007, President Voronin also proposed disarmament and demilitarization for Transnistria in return for the removal of Transnistria's border and customs guards on the Nistru River.

Relations with Romania proved tumultuous throughout 2007. After joining the EU, Romania introduced new visa requirements that were frustrating for Moldovans. Romanian president Traian Basescu, however, offered fast-track Romanian citizenship to over half a million Moldovan citizens, a move seen by Moldova's government as an attack on the sovereignty of the country. In retaliation, the Moldova government expelled four Orthodox priests of Romanian nationality for allegedly not holding valid residence and working permits. The Romanian government adopted the emergency decree 87/2007 on September 5, 2007 amending the 1991 law on granting Romanian citizenship. There were some procedural changes meant to streamline (but not necessarily speed up) the process, but the essence of the 1991 law was not changed. By the end of 2007, there were more than 450,000 applications for Romanian citizenship lodged by Moldovan citizens.

Moldova held confidential talks with Russia during 2007 on the issue of solving the Transnistrian conflict. Moldova showed its readiness to make a number of concessions to Russia in this field (guarantees of permanent neutrality and of not joining NATO) and this contributed to an improvement of relations between both countries (including on ending the Russian embargo on wine imports from Moldova). However, no consensus was reached on the withdrawal of the remaining Russian troops in Moldova, a move which Russia currently opposes. Russia was eager to show Georgia, and the international community in general, that it can have a constructive attitude in the resolution of the frozen conflicts in the post-soviet space (in Moldova) if Russia's concerns are seriously taken into account.

Electoral Process

1999	2001	2002	2003	2004	2005	2006	2007	2008
3.25	3.25	3.50	3.75	4.00	4.00	3.75	3.75	3.75

Moldova is a parliamentary republic. President Voronin is also the president of the Party of Moldovan Communists (PMC)—the largest parliamentary faction. Furthermore, as Moldova's territory represents a single electoral district, the activities of individual members of Parliament (MPs) are not scrutinized by local constituents. Thus, MPs answer to their faction or party leader, rather than directly to their constituents or electors.

The electoral code dates back to 1997 and has been amended a number of times. According to the OSCE, it "provides an adequate basis for the conduct of democratic elections, if implemented in good faith."[8] In 2007, a new Law on Political Parties complementing the electoral code was drafted and submitted to the Venice Commission. Adopted on December 21, 2007, the law aims to regulate the registration, functioning, and financing of political parties and seeks to make the electoral system more transparent and less prone to abuse; however, it also creates a number of restrictions. For example, only Moldovan citizens can become members of a political party or hold certain public offices, whilst the practice recommended by European community is to allow citizens of other countries to become party members.[9]

Local elections held on June 3 and 17 were the main electoral events in 2007. Voters elected 899 mayors and 11,967 council members at all levels (*raions,* municipalities, towns, communes, and villages). Voting did not take place in most of the the Transnistrian region owing to the separatist conflict that prevents Chisinau from extending its authority to Transnistria. However, in the Corjova commune, a Moldovan-administered part of Transnistria, the Transnistrian militia used force to prevent the opening of the polling station.

The elections were monitored by international election observers from the OSCE and the Council of Europe (COE), as well as the domestic Civic Coalition for Free and Fair Elections—Coalition 2007, which comprised 7 core Moldovan NGOs (3 of whom were umbrella groups, which included approximately 150 organizations). Although the elections were considered generally free and fair, and voters were given real electoral alternatives, the COE concluded that "some aspects of the electoral process still fall short of European standards for democratic elections."[10] However, the COE Parliamentary Assembly notes that the outcome of the local elections has "contributed to the increase of political diversity at local level,"[11] owing to the formation of coalitions.

Most electoral abuses, including intimidation and pressure on opposition candidates by the ruling party, lack of access to the media by opposition candidates, and intense media coverage of the PMC candidates, occurred during the electoral campaign. A public debate between the two candidates for the post of mayor of Chisinau, the capital, did not take place because of the refusal of Veaceslav Iordan, the PMC candidate, to meet with his main opponent, Dorin Chirtoaca. Additionally, in the first round of elections, observers cited problems pertaining to the secrecy of the vote as well as the counting and tabulation of election results.

Of the 28 political parties registered with the Ministry of Justice, 24 participated in the local elections. One party, the European Action Movement, was prevented from participating. This was due to the fact that the Ministry of Justice registered the organization on April 12—after the electoral period began.

The most significant outcome of the 2007 local elections was the PMC's sharp decline in support, which dropped to 34.4 percent from 46 percent at the 2005 parliamentary elections. The decline in support was most noticeable, though, in Chisinau, where the PMC had never won a majority. In the second round, PMC-backed mayoral candidate Veaceslav Iordan (with 38.83 percent), lost to Liberal Party candidate, Dorin Chirtoaca (61.17 percent), despite taking the lead in the first round (with 27.62 percent compared with 24.37 percent for his Liberal Party opponent). Overall, in the Chisinau municipality, the PMC obtained 26.6 percent of the votes, compared with 43.7 percent in the 2003 local elections, pointing to a decline of the PMC. Voter turnout also declined from 58.7 percent in 2003 to 52.3 percent, according to the Central Electoral Commission.

Civil Society

1999	2001	2002	2003	2004	2005	2006	2007	2008
3.75	3.75	4.00	3.75	4.00	4.00	4.00	3.75	3.75

Civil society is far from representing a vibrant aspect of Moldova's public space. According to the USAID 2006 Stability Index, nearly half of the 7,000 registered NGOs exist only on paper. John Balian, public affairs officer at the U.S. Embassy in Chisinau, (which includes a grant-giving program), noted that many NGOs are formed to acquire grants, and few embrace professional standards.[12] Civil society organizations lack constituencies that could serve as a base of support, and voluntary work remains undeveloped.[13] Almost 90 percent of national NGOs are concentrated in the capital, Chisinau. In 2006, local community organizations were as numerous as national NGOs thanks to increased funding in community development. The 2007 UNDP–Moldova's Study on NGOs Development in Moldova indicates that half of all NGOs work in social and educational fields.[14] More than half of all NGOs work to address social and poverty-related issues, with 60 percent of these activities focusing on children and youth. Pensioners, veterans, and women follow as primary beneficiaries in terms of NGO work. Only Proriv, an organization from Transnistria that has an anti-Moldovan/Western agenda, could be considered an organization promoting social unrest or extremist views.

A new Law of Public Associations was passed reluctantly, amid criticism in its final reading on July 20, 2007. According to the same UNDP study, state contributions represent 5 percent of civil society's budgetary resources, as opposed to more than 30 percent worldwide. Legally, it takes a group of at least three people to register an NGO. The process is free of excessive bureaucracy; however, the legal framework is rather confusing regarding the economic activities of NGOs. Additionally, the tax framework does not encourage companies and individuals to make donations. At the beginning of 2007, civil society organizations drafted the Law on Noncommercial Organizations and the Law on Public Utility Organizations to address these issues. The draft laws were submitted to the Ministry of Justice for revision, and it is expected that they will be passed by the Parliament in the second part of 2008.

The institutional capacities of local NGOs remain weak in Moldova. Less than half of local organizations have computers, photocopy machines, and access to the Internet, compared with over 80 percent of national NGOs. The majority of regional/local organizations claim to need training in accessing funding in order to diversify financial resources and community involvement. In terms of available personnel, the UNDP study revealed a disparity in levels of education between urban and rural areas—the countryside boasts fewer workers with higher education (by 20 percent, when compared with urban workers).[15]

Management structures within NGOs often resemble a "one-man show." Civil society organizations rely heavily on foreign funding; membership fees represent an important source of funding for local organizations only. NGOs do not face obstacles from the state in accessing donors' funds, but government procurement is limited to government-operated NGOs. Businesses avoid the politically sensitive element of such support. Financial sustainability resides in ensuring continued access to grants and not in diversifying activities or services to generate income. Monitoring and evaluation is absent in NGO work, a fact undermining their credibility among the public. The tax environment is not favorable, either; NGOs can seek nonprofit tax status by acquiring a certificate of public utility, yet only a few bother, owing to excessive bureaucracy in obtaining tax exemptions.

The government is steadily opening to cooperation with civil society, especially to provide expertise or services where the government lacks qualified people or funds. A number of advocacy groups united in 2007 to increase their efficiency and impact. Named Coalition 2007, the largest ever domestic Moldovan advocacy group, monitored the electoral campaign and saw its reports used by the Broadcasting Coordination Council to address pro-government bias at Teleradio Moldova during the campaign. Cooperation between state bodies and NGOs was imposed from the outside as a condition to foreign assistance, and as a result, the government reluctantly cooperates in a non-engaging manner. Moreover, Prime Minister Vasile Tarlev became critical of independent monitoring, accusing the "so-called experts whom we did not ask to be experts" for "disinformation and manipulation" regarding the pace of reforms under the EU-Moldova Action Plan.[16]

Mass media display a negative attitude toward civil society groups and depict them as donor-driven, money-laundering machines that mushroom with the prospect of grants. Their main criticism is directed toward the lack of communication and lack of financial transparency. This criticism is backed by data: Over 70 percent of registered NGOs never undertook an external audit, and around 30 percent have never undergone any type of audit—internal or external.[17] Few NGO leaders are referred to as experts by the media. To a large extent, there is a limited understanding of the advantages cooperation with media could bring for NGOs.

The state maintains tight control over trade unions. The Confederation of Free Trade Unions, Solidaritate (Solidarity), is widely recognized as loyal to the government and ruling party, while the National Confederation of Trade Unions is weak in terms of organization and credibility.

The education system is placed de facto under the ideology of the PMC, promoting the concept of a Moldovan statehood, Moldovan language, and Moldovan nation (developed under Stalinist rule). Such concepts oppose any likely references to the Romanian language and the common past shared with Romania. As the European Commission noted in its Report on Racism and Tolerance of April 29, 2008, the new textbooks—which the Moldovan authorities had begun to prepare—were accused of being politically biased and of denying the role of ethnic Romanians in the historic Moldovan identity—and even contained anti-Romanian sentiments. The same sort of discrimination was noticed when it came to state funding for various cultural and scientific programs.

Independent Media

1999	2001	2002	2003	2004	2005	2006	2007	2008
4.00	4.25	4.50	4.75	5.00	5.00	5.00	5.25	5.50

The Constitution guarantees freedom of opinion and expression. It condemns censorship and ensures editorial independence. The Law on Access to Information, Law on the Press, and broadcast code provide a set of additional rights to journalists. However, implementation remains a key issue in terms of legal guarantees. For example, in 2007, two cases concerning freedom of expression appeared before the European Court of Human Rights (ECHR); they were won by *Kommersant Moldovy,* a Russian-language weekly, and *Flux,* a Romanian-language daily.[18]

Investigative journalists remain particularly vulnerable to political actors, businesses, and other powerful interest groups that may easily accuse them of under defamation and libel. In February 2007, three journalists who wrote an investigative article for the weekly *Cuvintul* about abuses during the privatization of public properties were acquitted by a local court after the local government of Rezina (a town) demanded an amount equivalent to US$320,000 for "moral damages." This case, however, was seen as an exception to the rule, with self-censorship among journalists worsening in 2007.

Editorial duties are still subject to government control and interference by owners. The failure to reform the national broadcaster Teleradio Moldova into a genuinely independent public service outlet appears to be the most pressing issue on the media landscape.[19] The ruling party reluctantly continues to open the public broadcaster to those who may express opinions critical of their conduct.[20] The OSCE Mission to Moldova expressed concern in a statement on February 19 about the pace of reforms at Teleradio Moldova, which "has made almost no progress towards becoming a truly independent public service broadcaster since its formal transformation in August 2004."[21] Moreover, the Observers Council of Teleradio Moldova was constantly criticized by media watchdogs for polishing the government's image, serving the ruling party's interests, and applying double standards when appointing the new management of the public broadcaster.[22] On World Press Freedom Day, international organizations and foreign embassies noted that Moldova "may not be able to meet its international obligations without a correction in this trend."[23]

Significant restrictions to information pluralism existed during 2007. Three TV channels have nationwide coverage in Moldova: Moldova 1, TVR1 (Romanian public channel), and ORT (Russian public channel). In a controversial act in late September, the Broadcasting Coordination Council (BCC) informed Romanian Television Society (RTS)—the Romanian TV that owns TVR1, TVR2, TVR Cultural & TVR International—that it would be revoking its license to rebroadcast TVR1 on grounds that the payment arrangement (contract) for retransmission expired in June and was not extended.[24] The license and contract are two different things, authorized and signed by two different bodies; the BCC awards licenses and the Ministry of Telecommunications signs retransmission contracts. Without investigating details—RTS claimed it had sent a letter to the Ministry ahead of the June expiration requesting to extend its contract; the Ministry claimed it never received such a letter—and without delay, the BCC cancelled the license to RTS and re-awarded the license to Telefe International, an offshore company that partially re-broadcasts another Romanian entertainment TV channel. Technically, a delay is not grounds for an annulment; first some negotiation is required and only afterward can a license be revoked. RTS took the council to court, claiming that the decision was illegal and that its license is valid until 2011. This raised suspicions that the scenario was premeditated (on the side of the Ministry and BCC) and that regulatory body gave in to direct state pressure, adding another issue to the list of disputes with Romania.[25]

Also in September, the ruling PMC managed to maintain its control over the Broadcasting Coordination Council by using "technical" tactics to nullify the election of an opposition-affiliated council chairman.[26] Earlier, a member of the council had been detained by a state body, the Center for Fighting Corruption and Economic Crime, and another three were questioned on suspicion of taking bribes. These attacks came a week after the Broadcasting Coordination Council issued the first warning letters to government-controlled media outlets for failing to report on local elections in a balanced way.

According to IREX's Media Sustainability Index (2006 and 2007), since 2006, print media have enjoyed the diversity of 27 Romanian-language newspapers, 24 Russian-language newspapers, and about 40 regional newspapers, half of which are subsidized by local governments. Advertising revenues directed to media that are loyal to the ruling party, discriminatory fees used by the state publishing house, and the Post of Moldova's monopoly over distribution are all factors that limit available revenue and reach for newspapers that are critical of the ruling party.[27]

Although the government ceased to act as the founder of *Moldova Suverana* and *Nezavisimaya Moldova*, Romanian- and Russian-language dailies, articles favorable to the president, Speaker of the Parliament, and prime minister appear prominently, while editorials praise official policies. New Ideas TV Company is run by the former director of Teleradio Moldova, Ilie Telescu, while N4 is run by the former adviser for the Communists' 2005 parliamentary election campaign, Alexandr Petkov. After the controversial privatization of the municipal Euro TV and Antena-C radio stations in January 2007, Antena-C completely changed its staff and editorial line in step with the ruling party.[28] In turn, Euro TV (now "EU TV") supports the Christian Democratic People's party platform. Also, the first independent news agency, BASA-press, was gradually taken over by Communist affiliates throughout the year; its editors and reporters worked at the same time for the government-founded MOLDPRES news agency.

Renewed attacks on media freedom occurred prior to the June local elections. On March 27, PRO TV and DTV crews were detained by policemen while filming a protest march organized by an opposition political party. The following day, the print run of the *SP* regional newspaper was confiscated on financial grounds. The Civic Coalition for Free and Fair Elections (Coalition 2007) said this series of events "leaves no room to doubt over regrettable accidents; on the contrary, it suggests that these actions were not random."[29]

Watchdogs joined together again in late October to express their concern over an armed threat on a PRO TV crew that took place while the reporters were filming two crews of policemen—one of regular police and the other a special unit called "Fulger" (Thunder)—attempting to forcefully evacuate a man from his house. The regular police unit gave a statement to the TV, while the special unit (brandishing Kalashnikov machine guns) ordered the journalists to stop filming.[30] When the journalists continued filming, the special unit accused the journalists of hindering the unit's work, but no harm was meted to the journalists and that was the end of the incident.

Local Democratic Governance

1999	2001	2002	2003	2004	2005	2006	2007	2008
n/a	n/a	n/a	n/a	n/a	5.75	5.75	5.75	5.75

The Law on Public Administration, along with the Moldovan Constitution, is the main legal framework for democratic local governance. The central government continues to play a direct role in designing local affairs and even decides the priorities of certain communities, despite often lacking accurate information and proper understanding of causes and ways to address local needs. Local authorities are under substantial pressure to accept decisions of the central authorities on issues such as budgets, investments, and development strategies. Most Moldovans are accustomed to news reports from the president of the Moldovan Parliament inaugurating a new heating system at a village school or from the prime minister about cleaning water wells in the countryside—all of which are the direct responsibilities of local mayors and town halls.

Citizens regularly and directly elect their local leaders, as outlined in the Constitution and electoral code. The last local elections took place in June 2007 on the basis of free, secret, and universal vote. Except for the Transnistrian region, where citizens were blocked from voting, elections were considered "mostly free, but only partially fair"[31] by international and domestic observers. According to opposition party leaders and local observers, the PMC and the central government made use of administrative resources and exerted pressure on candidates to quit the race or shift to the ruling party's lists, leading to many withdrawals. In ODIHR's final report from the election observation mission it noted that "several cases implicated senior public servants and some members of Parliament."[32]

Local authorities increasingly welcome input from civil society on community development policies, but the implementation of these recommendations continues to lag. Poverty-related issues, as well as social and health care concerns, are the main areas where local governments initiate partnerships with NGOs, primarily because of limited services and human resources. Other sensitive issues are skillfully avoided on technical grounds. Organizations representing minorities, women, and other groups with a particular interest are extremely active at the community level and have managed to establish better cooperation with local governments.

The degree of transparency and accountability of local public authorities differs from case to case. Legislation does not require mandatory public hearings; thus they are not held at regular intervals but rather are concentrated during pre-electoral periods.

Overall, the media have poor access to information held by local authorities owing to inefficient management of data and lack of knowledge of the Law on Access to Information.[33] As a result, journalistic investigations are rarely conducted.

Corruption is widespread in local communities because of kinship ties. Various groups with corrupt economic interests reportedly operate in towns and district centers. On August 6, the newly-elected Christian Democratic mayor, Andrei Buzu, was killed in the village of Drasliceni, allegedly by groups with economic interests.[34]

Local authorities face obstacles from the central government when exercising their powers. Although the Ministry of Local Public Administration has the mandate to promote increased decentralization, it instead demonstrates a lack of genuine political will to ensure financial autonomy to local governments. Non-PMC mayors who feel their rights have been infringed upon do not rely on judicial remedy given the extent of political control over the system. Most of the associations that aim to protect and promote the rights of local government remain politically-affiliated and have yet to achieve tangible results.

Following local elections, President Voronin promised "big problems to those districts led by opposition" and spoke of "financial self-isolation," saying that the "central power will concentrate budgetary resources for strategic development projects such as roads, irrigation, and water pipelines."[35] As a rule, large shares of money go to localities run by PMC mayors—regardless of land area, poverty rate, or population size.[36] Local governments have the right to collect taxes and fees, but owing to widespread poverty and lack of economic activities, revenues fail to reach the budget. Therefore, local government relies heavily on central funding. Furthermore, owing to insufficient resources, municipalities remain severely understaffed with largely unqualified personnel.

Judicial Framework and Independence

1999	2001	2002	2003	2004	2005	2006	2007	2008
4.00	4.00	4.00	4.50	4.50	4.75	4.50	4.50	4.50

Moldova established a legal framework supported by the 1994 Constitution, which guarantees the respect of fundamental freedoms. Moldova is a member (under monitoring) of the Council of Europe and of the OSCE. It cooperates with the EU in the field of judiciary reform within the European Neighborhood Policy framework.[37] In 2007, the Moldovan government agreed to submit all legislative proposals to the COE for review prior to submitting them to the Parliament.

Moldova is in the process of renewing its legal framework for freedom of association, freedom of religion, and parliamentary immunity, but the adoption and implementation of this framework has been delayed. For instance, a new law regulating the registration and management of religious groups entered into force on August 17,[38] but by year's end the president refused to ratify the law in response to pressure from the Christian Orthodox clergy who demanded a stronger legal status for the Orthodox Church due to the fact that 98% of Moldovans declare themselves to be Christian Orthodox.[39]

On July 19, a Strategy on the Reform of the Judicial System was adopted, along with an Action Plan covering 2007–2008. The strategy was drafted in consultation with experts from the COE and represents an overall reform of the judiciary (transparency, efficiency, access, and so on). In addition, in 2007 the Ministry of Justice adopted a strategy for a system to enforce judicial decisions. There are also plans to draft a law curbing the extensive powers of the Office of the Prosecutor General, notably with regard to overturning final judgments. This also led to criticism from the ECHR, which punished the Moldovan state with a fine.[40]

Despite reform efforts and new legislative strategies, the COE, which monitors the implementation, adamantly declared in September 2007 that the judiciary requires further reforms in order to "guarantee the independence of the judiciary and increase the effectiveness and professionalism of the courts; improve the enforcement of judicial decisions; and undertake institutional reform." In addition, there is a need to "improve the working environment of the judiciary, by improving the training and working methods and by eliminating corruption within the system."[41]

To ensure the professionalism of judges and prosecutors, and to provide training and seminars, the National Institute of Justice was officially and legally established on July 7, 2006.

In practice, judicial independence is not guaranteed owing to political interference in the nomination of judges and prosecutors, despite the existing system of open competition for their recruitment. Judges are often subject to political pressure in high-profile cases, such as in the judgments against Serafim Urechean, president of the political party Our Moldova Alliance; Valeriu Pasat, former Moldovan defense minister; Mihail Formuzal, governor of the Gagauz Autonomous Region; and Eduard Musuc, secretary of the Social Democratic Party.[42] To address this situation, the Superior Council of Magistrates approved the code of conduct of judges on November 29, 2007.[43]

The lack of financial resources that underlies many of the judiciary's short-comings is addressed in a draft Law on Funding of the Judiciary. Financing of the judiciary will be fixed at 1 percent of the annual state budget, up from 0.45 percent at the end of 2007.[44] However, according to the minister of justice, between 1.5 percent and 2 percent of state budget resources should be allocated to the judiciary to ensure its effective functioning and independence. For instance, a member of the Supreme Court of Justice has a monthly income the equivalent of US$572.

This situation leads to the widespread perception in Moldova that corruption persists throughout the judiciary: 64 percent of Moldovans believe that almost all judges and prosecutors take bribes. This figure remains unchanged since 2005.[45]

The Moldovan judiciary must also cope with a backlog of unenforced judicial decisions, despite a slight decrease in comparison with last year.[46] This remains an important factor leading Moldovan citizens to take action against the Moldovan state at the ECHR in Strasbourg. The Moldovan Parliament adopted a law that foresees publishing a summary of ECHR decisions against the Moldovan state in the *Official Bulletin* (*Monitorul Official*).[47]

Moldova is also engaged in reforming its penitentiary system, but many abuses of human rights, and even torture while in detention or (often illegal) pre-arrest, are reported. However, the number of deaths in prison continues to decline.[48] In the Transnistrian region, people still reportedly disappear or are detained illegally for long periods of time and are subject to torture and degrading treatment.[49]

Corruption

1999	2001	2002	2003	2004	2005	2006	2007	2008
6.00	6.00	6.25	6.25	6.25	6.25	6.00	6.00	6.00

Corruption is a widespread phenomenon in Moldova and presents an enormous challenge to the authorities and a permanent worry for Moldovan citizens. According to the Moldovan Ministry of Economy and Trade, the effects of corruption are particularly pervasive in law enforcement agencies, the judiciary, the health and education systems, the fiscal system, customs, and local public administration.[50]

Moldovan authorities are currently implementing the country's National Anticorruption Strategy (2004) through the December 21, 2006, adoption of the Action Plan for 2007–2009. On January 21, 2007, the Ministry of Education and Youth and the Center for Fighting Corruption and Economic Crime (CFCEC) adopted an Action Plan to fight corruption in the education system.[51] On April 24, 2007, the government approved the draft laws on adapting Moldova's normative framework to the UN Convention Against Corruption and the Additional Protocol to the Criminal Law Convention with regard to corruption and forwarded them to the president for approval.[52]

The Anticorruption Alliance comprises 26 Moldovan NGOs and is thus the largest civil society organization monitoring and contributing to the fight against corruption in close collaboration with the Moldovan authorities, most notably the CFCEC. Representatives from the press and the media are present at ongoing sessions of the monitoring group for implementation of the National Anticorruption Strategy in a bid to ensure the transparency of the anticorruption campaign.[53] However, investigative journalism into misuse of public funds is less appreciated by the authorities. For example, all journalists from the weekly newspaper *Ziarul de Garda* were detained at least once by the authorities while investigating cases of corruption.[54]

Moldova's score of 2.8 on Transparency International's 2007 Corruption Perceptions Index (on a scale of 1–10, with 10 as least corrupt) shows erosion from the 2006 score of 3.2, worse even than the 2005 score (2.9). Moldovans perceive corruption as a phenomenon generated by the low salaries of public officials, imperfect legislation, and an inefficient judiciary.[55] However, the level of tolerance of corruption has dropped from 57 percent in 2005 to 45 percent of the Moldovan population in 2007.

Further problems in the fight against corruption arise from the fact that Moldova's legislation has still not been brought up-to-date with international anticorruption conventions. In particular, there is still progress to be made with respect to the immunity of certain categories of people (such as MPs), the penal code, and enforcement of the liability of acts of corruption in general.

Moldova also receives international assistance to fight corruption: Moldova and the EU cooperate on fighting corruption within the framework of the EU-Moldova Action Plan. Moldova is also cooperating closely with the COE's Group of States Against Corruption (GRECO) and is currently implementing a series of 15 recommendations from the GRECO evaluation report (second cycle), adopted on October 13, 2006. All 15 recommendations must be adopted by May 31, 2008.

Moldova has also been fighting corruption within the framework of the MOLICO program of the COE since August 2006. This project against corruption focuses on money laundering and the financing of terrorism in the Republic of Moldova. The program, which lasts for three years and has a budget of €3.5 million (US$5.4 million), essentially supports implementation of the National Anticorruption Strategy. Additionally, in December 2006, Moldova and the United States signed a US$24.7 million Millennium Challenge Corporation Threshold Program agreement, which aims at reducing government corruption.[56]

Finally, according to the World Bank report *Doing Business 2008,* Moldova ranks 92nd out of 178 states, compared with 88th out of 175 for the previous year. Although the cost of doing business in Moldova is close to the world average, and Moldova has succeeded in reducing its taxes, especially on income and labor, certain legal provisions have become more constraining.

▮ AUTHORS: GEORGE DURA AND LILIANA VITU

George Dura is a researcher at the Centre for European Policy Studies in Brussels and a PhD candidate in political science at the Université Catholique de Louvain in Belgium. Liliana Vitu is a PhD candidate in political communications at Moldova State University and has worked as a political analyst for the BBC World Service and the Economist Intelligence Unit.

1   Corneliu Rusnac, "Şapte procese pierdute la CEDO într-o săptămână" [Seven Cases Lost at ECHR in One Week], BBC, October 24, 2007, http://www.bbc.md.

2   For example, reporters from Teleradio Moldova do not take interviews from opposition party leaders. Also, the right to reply is not observed by Teleradio Moldova. Association for Electronic Press APEL monitoring reports, 2007, http://http://www.apel.md.

³ "Moldovan Embassies: Promoting the Country's Image or Private Interests," Journalistic Investigations Centre, August 22, 2006, http://www.investigatii.md/eng/index.php?art=121.

⁴ Alexandru Canțîr, "Președintele Voronin în război cu opoziția" [President Voronin at War with Opposition], BBC, July 25, 2007, http://www.bbc.co.uk/romanian/news/story/2007/07/070725_moldova_voronin.shtml.

⁵ See Institute for Public Policy's Barometer of Public Opinion, May 21, 2007, http://www.ipp.md; For more details about corruption issue in Moldova, refer to http://www.transparency.md/documents.htm.

⁶ Institute for Public Policy, Barometer of Public Opinion, May 21, 2007, http://www.ipp.md.

⁷ At the time of this writing, the following countries were represented by the common visa center: Austria, Denmark, Estonia, Latvia, Slovenia, and Hungary, which hosts the center on its embassy's premises.

⁸ OSCE/Office for Democratic Institutions and Human Rights—Election Observation Mission, *Republic of Moldova—Local Election 2007—Interim Report No. 1—April 27–May 7, 2007*, May 2007, http://www.osce.org/documents/odihr/2007/05/24453_en.pdf.

⁹ Many politicians and officials are known to have dual Moldovan-Romanian, Moldovan-Russian, Moldovan-Ukrainian citizenship and it is feared that the law could be used to prevent the nomination of (opposition) politicians in key positions of power. More importantly, in the event of Transnistria's reintegration with Moldova, a large part of the political elite exclusively holds a Russian passport. The law would prevent not only political participation in the government but the population would be unable to participate in political parties.

¹⁰ Council of Europe Parliamentary Assembly, "Honouring of obligations and Commitments by Moldova", Doc. 11374, 14 September 2007, http://assembly.coe.int/Main.asp?link=/Documents/AdoptedText/ta07/ERES1572.htm.

¹¹ Ibid.

¹² John Balian, "Lessons for Moldovan NGOs, Civic Forum," *Monitorul Civic*, July 6, 2007, http://www.civic.md/en/interviews/lessons-for-moldovan-ngos-interview-with-john-balian-first-secretary-for-culture-and-press.html.

¹³ Ibid.

¹⁴ UNDP–Moldova, *Study on NGOs Development in Moldova*, December 2007, http://www.undp.md.

¹⁵ Ibid.

¹⁶ "Premierul Tarlev îi acuză pe experți de dezinformare" [Premier Tarlev Accuses the Experts of Disinformation], BBC, October 12, 2007, http://www.bbc.md.

¹⁷ Up to 30 percent of NGOs have a Web page, and a third of them refuse to disclose financial data. UNDP–Moldova, *Study on NGOs Development in Moldova*, December 2007, http://www.undp.md.

¹⁸ Independent Journalism Centre, Moldova Media News, Chisinau, January 30, 2007, http://www.ijc.md/eng/index.php?option=com_content&task=view&id=109&Itemid=34.

¹⁹ Independent Journalism Centre, Media Monitoring reports, http://www.ijc.md; Association of Electronic Press reports, http://www.apel.md.

²⁰ Prime Minister Vasile Tarlev criticized Teleradio Moldova for not covering governments' "accomplishments," and for being "unfair that the public is less and less informed about the great achievements of the central authorities," Info Prim Neo News-Agency, August 3, 2007.

²¹ OSCE Mission to Moldova, *Statement*, dated 19 February 2007, http://www.osce.org/item/23339.html.

²² Subjects that tackle social issues and poverty are largely absent in news programs; the tone and wording are rather more positive than neutral; only local governments are criticized, while reporters insert their own opinions and not facts. Our Moldova Alliance Party, *Monitoring Report of Teleradio Moldova Main News Broadcast*, February 2007.

23   "Joint Statement on the Occasion of World Press Freedom Day 2007," signed by multiple embassies and international organizations, Embassy of the United States, Chisinau, Moldova, May 3, 2007, http://moldova.usembassy.gov/050307.html.

24   "TVR nu mai emite direct în Republica Moldova" [TVR Does Not Broadcast Any Longer in the Rep. of Moldova], BBC, September 27, 2007, http://www.bbc.md.

25   The European Federation of Journalists denounced "political manipulation" of broadcasting in Moldova and called for a fair and transparent attribution of broadcasting frequencies in a statement on October 10, 2007, www.ifj-europe.org.

26   "Președintele CCA acuză 'Monitorul Oficial' de sabotaj" [President of Broadcasting Council Accuses Official Gazette of Sabotage], BBC, September 4, 2007, http://www.bbc.md.

27   Interview with Petru Macovei, executive director of the Association of Independent Press, September 21, 2007.

28   Raisa Lozinschi, "Încă o agenție de presă în media holdingul communist" [One More News Agency for the Communist Media Holding], *Jurnal de Chișinău*, June 17, 2007, http://www.jurnal.md/article/4071/.

29   Civic Coalition for Free and Fair Elections—Coalition 2007, *Statement on the Abuses of the Police Forces*, March 28, 2007, http://www.alegeri.md/en/2007/coalition2007.

30   Info-Prim-Neo News Agency, Chisinau, October 24, 2007.

31   Coalition 2007 Media Release, "Local Elections in Second Round: Largely Free but Partially Fair," Eurasia Foundation, June 18, 2007, http://www.eurasia.md.

32   "Republic of Moldova Local Elections June 3 & 17, 2007: OSCE/ODIHR Election Observation Mission Final Report," OSCE/ODIHR, http://www.osce.org/documents/odihr/2007/09/26372_en.pdf.

33   Lucia Candu, "Searching for Truth in Moldova," Public Policy Watch, October 20, 2007, http://publicpolicywatch.blogspot.com/.

34   DECA-press, "The Mayor of the Village of Drasliceni Was Killed," *Moldova Azi*, August 6, 2007, http://www.azi.md.

35   Alexandru Canțîr, "Președintele Voronin în război cu opoziția" [President Voronin at War with Opposition], July 25, 2007, http://www.bbc.md.

36   According to Deputy Mayor of Chisinau Mihai Furtuna, the country's second-largest city, Balti (which is run by a PMC affiliate) will get 30 percent more than Chisinau in 2008.

37   In February 2005, the EU and Moldova signed an Action Plan that foresees cooperation in a series of fields, such as the judiciary, where the EU provides assistance for reforms.

38   Council of Europe Parliamentary Assembly, "Honouring of Obligations and Commitments by Moldova," Doc. 11374, September 14, 2007.

39   Ibid.

40   Ibid.

41   Decision n. 366/15 of November 29, 2007.

42   Ibid.

43   Council of Europe MOLICO, "Perceptia si atitudinea fata de fenomenul coruptiei in Republica Moldova" [Project Against Corruption, Money Laundering and the Financing of Terrorism in Moldova], Public Opinion Poll by IMAS, July 2007, p. 8.

44   Euromonitor Nr. 6, "Planul de Acțiuni Uniunea Europeană—Republica Moldova: Evaluarea progresului în Trimestrul II, 2007"[European Union – Republic of Moldova Action Plan: Evaluation of the Progress in the Second Trimester of 2007], ADEPT, 2007, p. 26.

45   Ibid., p. 11.

46   Moldovan Ministry of Justice, "Delegatia Parlamentului European in vizita la Ministerul Justitiei" [Delegation of the European Parliament on a Visit at the Ministry of Justice], accessed on October 4, 2007.

[47] See, for instance, the case of *Pruneanu v. Moldova*, ECHR judgment, May 23, 2007.

[48] Interview with the deputy director of the Department for Penitentiary Institutions of the Ministry of Justice, in *Ziarul de Garda*, February 22, 2007.

[49] Interview with Andrei Invantoc, member of the Ilascu group, imprisoned illegally for over 15 years by the Transnistrian security services, in *Ziarul de Garda*, August 23, 2007.

[50] Ministry of Economy and Trade, National Development Plan 2008–2011, May 21, 2007.

[51] *Corruption in Higher Education in Moldova*, Alexandru Culiuc, AlmaMater, April 17, 2007, http://www.almamater.md/articles/2526/index.html.

[52] Report of the Center for Fighting Corruption and Economic Crime on the implementation of the EU-Moldova Action Plan, February 2007.

[53] Ibid.

[54] "Trei ani scanand coruptia" [Three Years Spent Monitoring Corruption], August 2, 2007, http://www.transparency.md/News/ro/20070802.shtml.

[55] "Around 40 Percent of the Population Would Take Bribes If They Were Public Servants with Small Salaries," Moldova Azi News Agency, July 20, 2007.

[56] Millennium Challenge Corporation, press release, December 15, 2006.

Montenegro

by Lisa McLean

Capital:	Podgorica
Population:	0.7 million
GNI/capita:	US$8,930

The social data above was taken from the European Bank for Reconstruction and Development's *Transition Report 2007: People in Transition*, and the economic data from the World Bank's *World Development Indicators 2008*.

Nations in Transit Ratings and Averaged Scores

	Yugoslavia				Montenegro				
	1999	2001	2002	2003	2004	2005	2006	2007	2008
Electoral Process	5.50	4.75	3.75	3.75	3.50	3.25	3.50	3.50	3.25
Civil Society	5.25	4.00	3.00	2.75	2.75	2.50	3.00	3.00	2.75
Independent Media	5.75	4.50	3.50	3.25	3.25	3.25	3.25	3.50	3.75
Governance*	5.50	5.25	4.25	4.25	4.00	n/a	n/a	n/a	n/a
National Democratic Governance	n/a	n/a	n/a	n/a	n/a	4.50	4.50	4.50	4.25
Local Democratic Governance	n/a	n/a	n/a	n/a	n/a	3.50	3.50	3.25	3.25
Judicial Framework and Independence	5.75	5.50	4.25	4.25	4.25	4.25	4.25	4.25	4.00
Corruption	6.25	6.25	5.25	5.00	5.25	5.25	5.25	5.50	5.25
Democracy Score	5.67	5.04	4.00	3.88	3.83	3.79	3.89	3.93	3.79

* With the 2005 edition, Freedom House introduced separate analysis and ratings for national democratic governance and local democratic governance to provide readers with more detailed and nuanced analysis of these two important subjects.

NOTE: The ratings reflect the consensus of Freedom House, its academic advisers, and the author(s) of this report. The opinions expressed in this report are those of the author(s). The ratings are based on a scale of 1 to 7, with 1 representing the highest level of democratic progress and 7 the lowest. The Democracy Score is an average of ratings for the categories tracked in a given year.

EXECUTIVE SUMMARY

In the 16 years since the introduction of a multiparty system, Montenegro continues to be dominated by the same political force confronted by a divided and weak opposition. Politicization in the public sector persists and limits the development of independent, nonpartisan civil service, police, judiciary, electoral administration, and media. It also interferes with the struggle against corruption. Much of its first full year as an independent, sovereign country with full control and responsibility over the development of its own institutions was spent establishing the institutions of the new state.

A key foundation of the state—its Constitution—was adopted with a two-thirds majority in Parliament in October and is expected to provide the basis for a civic state with full political, civil, and human rights and a healthy balance of powers among the three branches of government. In addition, Montenegro and the European Union (EU) signed a Stabilization and Association Agreement (SAA) as a first significant step toward EU membership. As part of its international obligations, the government began to implement measures to combat organized crime and corruption and to improve the administrative structure. Nonetheless, in Montenegro's small society, familial, friendship, and political connections undermine the establishment of the rule of law with equal opportunities for all. These connections also thwart the ability of civil society and the media to act as effective watchdogs and pressure groups for change.

National Democratic Governance. On October 15, the EU and the Montenegrin government signed the SAA, launching Montenegro's membership bid. Four days later, 55 of 81 members of Parliament (MPs) voted to adopt the new Constitution and a law on its implementation that met the Council of Europe's minimum standards. The ability to muster the necessary two-thirds majority in Parliament is a credit to the three opposition parties that voted for it, as well as the ruling parties. The reaction of those parties that voted against the Constitution was a disappointment and sign of competition within the opposition for primacy based on divisive issues of ethnicity. The new Constitution and the EU agreement should provide the basis for faster reforms, especially in depoliticizing parts of the public sector. The Parliament should continue to use the oversight instruments it began to use in 2007 to follow the reform process. *The Constitution—and especially its passage by a two-thirds majority in Parliament—is a significant development, signaling the thawing of political animosities in the interests of citizens and earning an improvement in Montenegro's rating for national democratic governance from 4.50 to 4.25.*

Electoral Process. In 2007, for the first time in seven years, there was no election held in Montenegro. Several provisions on the electoral process were enshrined in the Constitution, including the requirement for a high level of consensus, guaranteed representation of minorities in elected bodies, and residency requirements for voters and citizens. Most laws related to electoral processes must be harmonized with the Constitution by January 22, 2008—a process that had not begun by the end of the year. Cases of vote buying and pressure that surfaced as early as March 2006 remain tied up in court or in the investigation stage, lacking vigorous pursuit of all cases of illegal voter persuasion. The absence of sanctions in such cases fails to serve as a deterrent against such illegal methods of voter persuasion. *Although internationally recommended changes to the electoral laws are still needed, the new constitutional provisions mark a step forward. Thus, Montenegro's electoral process rating improves from 3.50 to 3.25.*

Civil Society. In 2007, the civil society sector had a number of significant accomplishments, demonstrating its growing credibility and effectiveness. First and foremost, working in cooperation with the government, a coalition of nongovernmental organizations (NGOs) managed to introduce changes to the NGO law that will limit NGO advantages to genuine NGOs. NGOs also ensured the inclusion of free access to information and consumer protection provisions in the Constitution and engaged actively in the public debate on a number of important long-term development strategies. Finally, the government opened an NGO liaison office. Still, some NGOs have complained that the success of their efforts have led to harassment and threats from the police and government bodies. *Given the growing effectiveness of the NGO sector and efforts made by a part of the government to establish good cooperation, Montenegro's civil society rating improves from 3.00 to 2.75.*

Independent Media. In 2007, two instances of journalist beatings threatened the independence of the media. Local observers believed that failure to find the perpetrators of these attacks demonstrated a lack of commitment on the part of the authorities to protect the freedoms of expression and the press recently enshrined in the new Constitution. Further, the continuing ability to sue journalists and media for unlimited sums of money in slander cases also limits the growth of true investigative journalism in Montenegro. In the meantime, public service television and radio lagged behind in its transformation process. A positive step was the improved government response rate to requests for free access to information. *The seriousness of the attacks on independent journalists results in a deterioration of Montenegro's independent media rating from 3.50 to 3.75.*

Local Democratic Governance. The new Constitution enshrines the principles of local self-government and autonomous operation and financing of local government. With a directly elected mayor accountable to the citizens, there were clear indications of increased municipal decision making in the interests of citizens rather than politics. Still, planning and local government financing continue to be a challenge. Many urban-planning decisions produce allegations of corruption, and national government concern about local financial management prevents decentralization of real authorities. *While a change in municipal management practices in the interests of citizens is a positive development, it is offset by continuing challenges to municipal financing and budgeting and suggests that Montenegro's local democratic governance has remained solidly at 3.25.*

Judicial Framework and Independence. The new Constitution paid special attention to establishing previously nonexistent fundamental political, civil, and human rights and institutionalizing the office of the ombudsman. Constitution drafting also focused on establishing the independence of the judiciary, which is much improved, although the parliamentary majority continues to be involved in some appointments. The weak state administration limited the ability of citizens to fully exercise their rights, and the length of court processes continued to be a problem. Legislation and the Action Plan for Judicial Reform were put in place by the end of the year to improve judicial administration. Efforts to hold police accountable for prisoner abuse and conclude the civil suit on Bosnian Muslim deportations are still under way. *Together, the Action Plan for Judicial Reform and the Constitution create the basis for improvements in judicial independence and improved protection of fundamental rights, leading to an improvement in Montenegro's judicial framework and independence rating from 4.25 to 4.00.*

Corruption. The government began implementation of its Action Plan for the Fight Against Corruption and Organized Crime and began to put in place the legal framework for that struggle. But no significant cases of corruption or organized crime were prosecuted successfully ending with a conviction and jail sentence. *Although the domestic and international public continue to criticize the lack of effective efforts to hold public servants accountable for their behavior, the establishment of the Anticorruption Commission and Action Plan for the Fight Against Corruption and Organized Crime merits a slight improvement of Montenegro's corruption rating from 5.50 to 5.25.*

Outlook for 2008. In 2006, Montenegro focused on regaining its independence; and, in 2007, the focus was on establishing the state framework. Montenegro's challenge in 2008 will be to make the established legal framework produce real change, especially the establishment of an independent judiciary, the struggle against corruption, and the strengthening of the state administration. These challenges place special importance on laws related to state administration, courts, the state prosecutor, and the Judicial Council. The Law on Minority Rights and Freedom, the definition of minority nations and national minorities, and other special minority rights defined in the Constitution may serve to raise tensions and divisions among different ethnic groups living in Montenegro, as will the presidential elections.

Main Report

National Democratic Governance

1999	2001	2002	2003	2004	2005	2006	2007	2008
Y u g o s l a v i a				n/a	4.50	4.50	4.50	4.25

On October 19, 2007, Parliament adopted a new Constitution and the law on its implementation. It was written in cooperation with the Council of Europe's Venice Commission, and its December opinion considered the new basic law as deserving of a "generally positive assessment" and found no measures that contradicted the Declaration of Minimal Principles signed in February by six of eight parliamentary groups and representing a promise to the Council of Europe.[1] The new Constitution provides for an 81-member Parliament that elects a prime minister, while the president is elected by popular vote. Civilian control of the armed forces and security forces is based on establishing a civilian Defense and Security Council, designating the president as commander in chief, and granting Parliament some authority in sending troops abroad and approving security and defense strategies.[2]

Importantly, the Constitution was adopted in Parliament by 55 of 81 MPs—that is, by a two-thirds majority. Initially, it had appeared that no one from the opposition ranks would support the draft the ruling parties advocated, which meant that the Constitution would have to be adopted in a referendum. But during the summer, the opposition negotiated a common platform of 29 demands that was used in negotiations with the ruling parties on the final draft. As the negotiations came to a conclusion, the People's Party, followed by the Serbian List, the Socialist People's Party, and the Democratic Party of Serbs, withdrew from the negotiations, dissatisfied with agreed solutions related to the name of the language, the definition of a civic state, and the lack of reference to the Serbian Orthodox Church.

In the end, Movement for Changes (PzP) led the way, together with Bosnian and liberal parties, in providing a high degree of consensus for the Constitution. Unfortunately, emotional issues about the country's language, its state symbols, the status of churches, and the civic nature of the state dominated the yearlong debate over the Constitution in an attempt by some political leaders to maintain divisions among the people and raise tensions. In a sign of the immaturity of the political system and the continued internal fight within the opposition for leadership of that bloc, PzP was severely criticized in parliamentary debate by its opposition colleagues for supporting the Constitution. A common accusation was that by cooperating with the ruling parties, PzP had failed to oppose, thereby betraying opposition voters. Those against the Constitution claimed that opposition to the document was necessary in order to bring down the regime.

In addition to working on the Constitution, Parliament was busy in 2007 debating and adopting a number of treaties and laws necessary for establishing the state and its institutions and for pursuing the goal of Euro-Atlantic integration. In addition, Parliament made tentative steps toward improving its oversight of government. The opposition advanced three interpellations on government policies related to energy policy, privatization, and telecommunications—adopting proposed conclusions in two of these cases. Also, parliamentary committees began to exercise oversight functions. Especially notable were actions by the Committee for Security and Defense and the Committee for International Relations and European Integration.[3] Finally, the prime minister's question hour, followed by MP questions to ministers, was held four times in 2007, which is significantly more regular than was the case in the previous parliamentary mandate.

Despite these achievements, the Parliament as a whole continued to function with less than adequate human resources and office space. Further, despite live broadcast of plenary sessions on public service television, Parliament's operations were far from transparent given (among other things) the lack of a regular schedule, a rarely updated Web site, and lack of public access to voting records without a lengthy request for access to information. At the end of the day, while there were improvements, Parliament continued to be a theater for the presentation of views and interests of politicians based on the topical issues of the day, rather than an institution through which political parties representing social groups articulate interests of the citizens and affect decision making in state institutions. Plagued by infighting, the opposition continually used strong attacks on government in Parliament to appeal to the public. The political machinations on both sides of the aisle blocked a number of reform processes and threatened to isolate Parliament as a significant branch of government in the eyes of the people.

A significant achievement in 2007 was the signing of the Stabilization and Association Agreement (SAA) with the European Union (EU). All political parties hailed the SAA, with governing parties defining it as a significant step toward EU membership and opposition parties as the introduction of an external monitor that will force reforms. As Montenegro embarks on its path to EU membership, a key challenge identified is weak administrative capacity. With the January approval of the EU partnership document, the government undertook to implement public administration reforms; ensure transparent employment, professionalism, and responsibility in the public service; and depoliticize public administration. Despite the existence of a formal system of examinations—such as language and computer knowledge—for attaining civil service jobs, there are continued accusations that party affiliation and familial and friendship connections are key qualifications for public sector employment. In October, the Council for Citizen Control of the Police—joined by other nongovernmental organizations (NGOs)—pointed out that throughout the state administration, the picture of the president of the Democratic Party of Socialists (DPS) hangs in official buildings, including at the Police Academy. The long-term challenge is to instill a sense of responsibility in the public on the part of public servants, to hold public servants accountable, and to make the evaluation of public servants' work transparent.

Electoral Process

1999	2001	2002	2003	2004	2005	2006	2007	2008
Y u g o s l a v i a				3.50	3.25	3.50	3.50	3.25

The year 2007 was the first since the new millennium that Montenegro did not hold an election. With political focus on the Constitution, it was that document that brought the most significant changes to the electoral process. At the insistence of opposition parties, a two-thirds majority of all MPs—that is, a high level of consensus—is required to adopt electoral laws. Also, the Constitution establishes residency requirements for voters and candidates. Eligible voters and candidates are now citizens who are at least 18 years of age and have resided in Montenegro for two years, while candidates for the presidency must be "a Montenegrin citizen residing in Montenegro for a minimum 10 of the past 15 years."[4]

Finally, the new Constitution's section on special minority rights says, "Persons belonging to minority nations and other minority national communities shall be guaranteed the rights and liberties, which they can exercise individually or collectively with others...." One of the listed rights is "the right to authentic representation in the Parliament of the Republic of Montenegro and in the assemblies of the local self-government units in which they represent a significant share in the population, according to the principle of affirmative action."[5] Like legislation related to the electoral system, legislation regarding special minority rights must be approved by a two-thirds majority of all MPs.

The European Partnership with Montenegro document adopted by the Council of the EU in January 2007 expects Montenegro, within the next two years, to bring its election legislation "in line with the recommendations of the Office for Democratic Institutions and Human Rights."[6] At present, since the current election system is the result of a carefully negotiated balance of individual political party interests, the new constitutional requirement of two-thirds support for changes may actually prevent some of the very changes that the EU expects. Furthermore, the guarantee for representation of minority nations and other minority national communities in Parliament and municipal assemblies will meet its first challenge with the need to define a minority nation and other minority national communities and decide which groups qualify for special minority rights.[7] The presidential elections that must be held by April 2008, along with two local elections, will be the first test of whether the international community's concerns about electoral legislation are addressed. By the end of the year, Parliament had adopted its own Law on Presidential Elections but had not made progress in addressing the legislation on elections of MPs and councillors and political party financing, which require intense political negotiations.

Until now, participation in elections in Montenegro has been high in comparison with other countries in Central and Eastern Europe. In campaign periods, political parties are quite active in mobilizing their activists and supporters. In the 2006 referendum, the Montenegrin style of political activism was caught on tape when two DPS activists tried to convince a neighbor to vote "yes" or abstain in exchange for payment of an electricity bill in the amount of €1,500 (US$2,052). The activists were quickly sentenced to 6 and 10 months in jail; but on appeal, the case was sent back to the basic court "because of important violations of provisions of the criminal procedure."[8] To date, no one has been punished.

In February 2007, a member of the border police transferred without his consent told Radio Free Europe that a DPS MP had forced him to get 34 of his neighbors to vote for DPS in the September 2006 elections. He explained that for nine years, he had worked on contract with the constant threat of not having his contract extended if he did not deliver the votes.[9] The ruling party denied the charges, and no official charges have been filed, although the policeman has since been dismissed from the service as part of its downsizing and reorganization.

The fact that the actors in the referendum video have not yet been brought to justice and that a policeman publicly states he agitated for the ruling party lends credence to the long held beliefs that political party activists exceed the legal limits in their efforts to convince voters. Establishment of a genuinely fair electoral process absolutely depends on the depoliticization—and the consequent professionalization—of the civil service, the police forces, the judiciary, and all other public servants.

Civil Society

1999	2001	2002	2003	2004	2005	2006	2007	2008
Y u g o s l a v i a				2.75	2.50	3.00	3.00	2.75

The 1999 Law on NGOs makes it easy to establish an NGO with five individuals and an address in Montenegro. Many small businesses register as NGOs because the profit of an NGO's economic activities currently is tax-exempt; as a result, a majority of the more than 3,800 registered NGOs function as cafés, kindergartens, taxi companies, or consulting firms, and only a few hundred can be considered genuine members of civil society. Not surprisingly, therefore, a poll in March found that 41 percent of respondents have either only a little or no trust in the NGO sector, and 31 percent were not sure whose interests NGOs represent.[10]

A number of NGOs conducted effective advocacy campaigns, watchdog programs, and civic education programs in 2007. A coalition of more than 200 NGOs, Together Toward the Goal, successfully brought together 147 NGOs on October 19 to sign a code of conduct and elect a seven-member self-regulatory body to enforce and monitor the implementation of the code. With the code, NGOs obliged themselves to submit their program and financial reports to the public, which should further the process of distinguishing between real and nominal NGOs and strengthen the credibility of NGOs. The same coalition has also worked with the government to prepare amendments to the Law on NGOs that limit tax-exempt status to organizations with an annual income of less than €4,000 (US$5,473). The amendment should cut drastically the number of registered NGOs, bring clarity to the civil society sector, and improve public perception.[11]

Other NGO activity is considered responsible for the inclusion of provisions on consumer protection and free access to information in the new Constitution. NGOs were additionally active throughout the year in public debates over important planning documents, such as the National Strategy for Sustainable Development, the Spatial Plan, the Energy Development Strategy, and municipal urban development plans. In public statements, NGOs raised a number of issues that put government representatives who prepared the plans and strategies on notice that people were watching. The debates in the news between the NGOs and the government helped raise awareness about the purposes of these strategies and plans.

One particular campaign—led by the Network for Affirmation of the NGO Sector (MANS) and joined by another 40 NGOs and some branch trade unions—raised the issue of the price consumers pay for electricity, comparing it with prices paid by two recently privatized companies. Entitled "KAP Spends, Who Pays?,"[12] the campaign forced the government to explain the differences, examined the reasons for the companies' government-guaranteed prices, and even eventually contributed to the cancellation of the privatization of the Thermo-Electric Plant and Coal Mine in Pljevlja. While the government continues to maintain that government-guaranteed prices are necessary to ensure successful privatization of these two companies and much larger investments, the public furor raised by the MANS campaign forced the government to explain itself, and citizens learned more about the economics of electricity pricing and privatization.

Another significant development in the civil society sector in 2007 was a split in the trade union confederation, whose former unity had made Montenegro unique in the region. While this split has not yet been formalized and while the government continues to consider the Confederation of Trade Unions of Montenegro its social partner, the breakaway confederation[13] has organized itself as a strong advocate for democratization of trade union governance and for workers' rights. If nothing else, its presence on the public scene has forced the leadership of the traditional confederation to take action in cases where it might not have ordinarily, such as when the prices of basic foodstuffs increased in the fall.

In terms of government-NGO relations, the government established in its first ever Office for NGO Cooperation in 2007 and appointed a national NGO coordinator who is considered to be open and committed to cooperation. Still, a report issued late in the year concluded that government has a "two track" approach to the nongovernmental sector. Cooperation is good when government wants to attract the interest of the international community and the topic is noncontroversial. However, when the issue is about transparency and accountability of government and when the NGOs present themselves as bodies with the right to know, to criticize, and to ask for accountability, the relationship is not so smooth.[14]

Also, some NGOs complained of government harassment in 2007 because of their activities. Human rights activist Aleksandar Zeković claimed to be the target of systematic surveillance, phone taps, blackmail, and death threats,[15] and he accused the police and its director of responsibility. Despite a stated commitment on the part of the police director to find the perpetrators, there had been no arrests by the end of the year.

In other cases, the Tax Administration has conducted extensive financial audits on NGOs that pursue particularly sensitive cases. The director of the Center for Civic Education and the director of MANS both believe that the thorough audits of four years of their respective finances in March and April, respectively, were intended to pressure the two organizations for their watchdog activities at the time.[16]

Independent Media

1999	2001	2002	2003	2004	2005	2006	2007	2008
Y	u	g	o s l a v i a	3.25	3.25	3.25	3.50	3.75

The new Constitution guarantees freedom of press and of expression and prohibits censorship. Importantly, the Constitution also guarantees everyone's "right to access information held by state authorities and organizations exercising public authority."[17] The opinion of the Venice Commission notes, however, that the focus of the freedoms of press and expression is on the "protection of 'dignity, reputation, and honour' and the provision of a remedy for the publication of untrue, incomplete, or incorrectly conveyed information"[18] and does not limit such freedoms only as "necessary in a democratic society."[19]

While the public enjoys a diverse selection of print and electronic sources of information at both national and local levels and privately controlled newspaper distribution, two beatings of journalists were quite disturbing. In addition to the September beating of Željko Ivanović, a founder of the highest-circulation daily *Vijesti*, Tufik Softić, a journalist for the daily *Republika* and Radio Berane, was beaten severely in the northern town of Berane in November. The victims consider the cases to be unsolved, although police have arrested two individuals who have apparently confessed to the attack on Ivanović. A lawyer from the NGO Action for Human Rights believes that "having failed to seriously investigate and punish murders, physical attacks, and threats directed to the critics of the government, the competent authorities have created an atmosphere of fear where only the courageous dare speak up, which is a drastic limitation of freedom of expression to the detriment of democratic society in Montenegro."[20]

According to current law, the penalty for slander in criminal cases can be up to €14,000 (US$19,156), while there are no limits for slander in civil suits.[21] DPS president Milo Đukanović filed a €1 million (US$1,368,325) civil suit against *Vijesti*, Ivanović, and the paper's editor for "mental injury" to his reputation and dignity owing to public statements by Ivanović and a strong editorial in *Vijesti* that blamed the DPS president for the attack on Ivanović.[22]

In 2007, there was little to no progress in the transformation of Radio Television Montenegro (RTCG) into a public service television station, a delay that many consider to be the result of a lack of political will.[23] Commenting on the public service news, journalist Duško Vuković said that "instead of inviting citizens to a critical dialogue about the issues that are of utmost importance for the community, our public service directs most of its energy to the promotion and propagation of the government's party line."[24] Officials in the public service claim that the problems with transformation are financing an overly complicated management structure, overstaffing, and lack of donor funding. Total expenditures in 2006 were almost €13 million (US$18 million) of which 62 percent was spent on "employee expenses"[25]; thus suggesting that downsizing could produce savings to help overcome lack of financing.

Unfortunately, the year ended with the breakdown of the independent management system created by the 2002 media reform, when Parliament failed to confirm nominees to the Radio and Television Council, leaving it without a quorum to make decisions on program issues. While NGOs insist that Parliament had a legal obligation only to "confirm" the independent sector's nominees, a majority in Parliament believes it also has the right not to confirm a nomination if it believes that the individual is not politically neutral or was nominated in a fraudulent process.[26] At a November roundtable, an analysis on the transformation of the public service noted that Parliament's role in the "election" of council members had brought the autonomy of the public service into question,[27] suggesting the need for introducing changes to the management system.

In terms of free access to information, two NGOs—Association of Young Journalists (AYJ) and MANS—have submitted about 90 percent of the requests and, as such, have been most instrumental in keeping the Free Access to Information Act alive.[28] The average response rate is now 60 percent, which is a concrete improvement over the 20–30 percent response rate achieved in 2006.[29] The other 40 percent of the state organs do not respond. Both organizations have submitted appeals to the administrative court, whose decisions have been positive, according to the two organizations, but take a long time given the limited capacity of the court.[30]

Local Democratic Governance

1999	2001	2002	2003	2004	2005	2006	2007	2008
Y u g o s l a v i a				n/a	3.50	3.50	3.25	3.25

The new Constitution guarantees the autonomy of local government in the performance of its duties and "the right of citizens and local self-government bodies to regulate and manage certain public and other affairs in their own responsibility and in the interest of the local population."[31] Importantly, the Constitution gives local self-governments the right to own property and enables the national government to dismiss the mayor or the municipal assembly only if either fails to perform requisite duties for a period of more than six months. All of these provisions are improvements and provide more explicit guarantees for the independent functioning of local self-government.

After four years under new local government laws, the functioning of local government has improved. Divided government in several municipalities, joint projects of opposition municipalities with the national government, and joint appearances of opposition municipal leaders and government ministers indicate that politicized management of the municipality is giving way to municipal administration based on all citizen interests. At present, 38 percent of the municipalities have Web sites that provide useful and timely information to the public about upcoming meetings of the municipal assemblies, decisions made, and public tenders issued and awarded. In two cases, even the 2007 budget is available on the Web site.[32] Especially in the last year, when mayors directly elected and directly accountable to citizens assumed office in each municipality, the local governments have exhibited an increased level of responsibility for the management and development of the municipalities—particularly in those municipalities with enough revenues to pay for development projects.

Local governments are free to collect taxes, fees, and other revenues, and they receive transfers from the national budget and an equalization fund, as well as subsidies for specific national development or investment projects.[33] In the first half of 2007—as was the case in 2006—the bulk of the local government budgets (83.3 percent in the first half of 2007 and 80 percent in 2006)[34] came from local revenues, especially land sales and construction taxes. Having valuable land for building, the three richest municipalities—Podgorica, Kotor, and Budva—raised 65 percent of the total local revenue collected throughout Montenegro and spent 56 percent of total expenditures, while the six poorest municipalities raised 1.7 percent and spent 2.5 percent.[35] More than half of these expenditures in the poor municipalities went to current expenditures, including salaries, compared with only 23 percent in the top three municipalities.[36]

In the effort to raise local revenues, some municipal administrations often fail to understand the concept of competition and drive away business interests or choke small- and medium-size enterprises with excessive regulations, taxes, and fees. A March 2006 study found that municipalities had defined 859 local taxes and fees, for an average of 41 taxes in each municipality, which represented a barrier to establishing and running a business.[37] In some cases, municipalities see an opportunity to wrest money from state-owned enterprises or regulated monopolies that have a hard time passing on the cost to the users. In 2007, the Electricity Company of Montenegro (EPCG) found its bank accounts blocked several times for failing to pay exorbitant municipal fees for services it believes it is charged for at the national level.[38] EPCG complained to the government that it was being used like a cash cow.[39] In 2007, the government recognized imbalances created by Montenegro's uneven economic development and planned to make changes in 2008 to the way equalization funds are distributed.

The fact is that the current real estate boom in Montenegro and successful 2007 tourist season created a significant windfall for some local governments. At the coast and in the capital, the urban-planning function has become especially important with the skyrocketing price of land and the focus on the tourist industry. Designating land for business development purposes has the potential to generate significant financial resources for a municipality that can be used to finance further development, but it also generates regular accusations of corruption, abuse of office, and irreversible environmental degradation from NGOs and ordinary citizens.

There are also signs of financial mismanagement at the local level and irrational spending; and the government, the State Audit Institute, and the European Commission have expressed concern about financial management, especially related to respect for the Budget Law, Law on Public Procurement, and Law on Wages of Public Employees, at the local level.[40] As a result, the national government is reluctant to decentralize public services and leaves in place (or creates new) systems to maintain national control over tasks in important sectors, such as tourism. It is likely to remain this way until the local administrations begin to demonstrate improved fiscal responsibility and administrative capacity.

Judicial Framework and Independence

1999	2001	2002	2003	2004	2005	2006	2007	2008
Y u g o s l a v i a				4.25	4.25	4.25	4.25	4.00

The new Constitution provides for equality before the law; freedom of thought, conscience, and religion; freedom of expression; guaranteed property rights; the right to work and to entrepreneurship; and gender equality. In the opinion of the Venice Commission on the Constitution of Montenegro, the adopted Constitution "meets most of the recommendations made by the Venice Commission...[and] provides for the direct applicability and supremacy of human rights treaties, including the European Convention on Human Rights."[41]

For the first time, the institution of ombudsman is included in the Constitution, although the Venice Commission expressed regret that its suggestions for strengthening the body's independence were not taken into account sufficiently. Thus, there is no explicit mention of its functional or budgetary independence, and the parliamentary majority holds the power to appoint and dismiss the ombudspersons.[42]

In the 2006 *Report of the Ombudsman,* almost 50 percent of complaints related to the slow court procedure, especially in civil suits, while others related to property rights and the rights to free access to information, to legal and nonpartisan treatment in state administration, to work and work-related benefits, and of children.[43] The 2006 report concluded that the state's weak administrative capacity has the effect of limiting the exercise of citizens' political, civil, and human rights.[44]

Preliminary figures for 2007 suggest a similar proportion of complaints about the slow judicial process.[45] The provisions in the new Constitution guaranteeing the "right to recourse" and "right to fair and public trial within a reasonable time before an independent and impartial court established by law," as well as the adoption in November of the Law on Protection of the Right to Trial Within a Reasonable Period, if applied in a meaningful way, may begin to address the long-standing problem of unreasonably long court proceedings.

Among the cases that saw little progress in 2007, but are important for the protection of fundamental human rights and freedom, are two in which the police were put under investigation for prisoner abuse related to arrests made in 2006.[46] By the end of 2007, two indictments in these cases had been issued, but there was no resolution in either case. Complete investigation of these cases and the handing down of disciplinary judgments in fair trial procedures would send a powerful message to the police force as it continues its effort to become a modern, professional body serving the public interest.

International and domestic public attention also focused in 2007 on accountability of the state and the police in the case of some 83 Bosnian Muslims who in 1992 were rounded up in Montenegro and deported to Foča, Bosnia-Herzegovina. Their subsequent disappearance has led most of the families of the victims to believe that they were killed, and they have filed a civil suit against the state that is still in the investigation stage, without any charges having yet been brought or damages awarded. The state prosecutor also launched investigation in two cases of potential war crimes from the wars of the Yugoslav succession. One relates to a concentration camp established in the coastal town of Morinj, where Croatian prisoners of war are said to have been abused and tortured; another relates to the massacre, arrest, and torture in Montenegro by the Yugoslav army of ethnic Albanians fleeing Kosovo in 1999. In neither case has anyone been arrested or charged with a crime.

The independence of the judiciary was a key topic in 2007, especially in the debate on the Constitution and in continued court vacancies. The mandate of the Judicial Council, tasked with nominating judges to the bench, expired in December 2006, and Parliament did not take up the issue of appointing a new Judicial Council in 2007. As a result, no vacancies were filled and no disciplinary action against judges took place.

The new constitutional provisions on the judiciary move the power to appoint judges to a Judicial Council with a balanced composition that, according to the Venice Commission, is "now suitable for preserving...the autonomy and independence of courts and judges."[47] It also provides judges only with functional immunity, which makes them more vulnerable to corruption charges. Nonetheless, Parliament has retained an influence in its power to elect the Supreme Court president, nominated jointly by the president, Speaker, and prime minister, which according to the Venice Commission leaves "the impression that the whole judiciary is under the control of the majority of the Parliament...which risks undermining the public confidence."[48] A simple parliamentary majority also appoints and dismisses the state prosecutor, the prosecutors, and members of the Prosecutorial Council, as well as all members of the Constitutional Court. This same parliamentary majority decides on the immunity of the president of the Supreme Court and the Constitutional Court judges.

The Venice Commission's opinion explained that "the Montenegrin political class is firmly convinced that [problems related to the effectiveness and impartiality] can be overcome only through oversight of the judiciary by Parliament."[49] While the commission accepted this argument, it expects a change once there are improvements in the judiciary. In the meantime, Parliament appointed a new president of the Supreme Court, who vowed to restore confidence in the judiciary but acknowledged that it would take time. In another positive step, in December the government adopted the Action Plan for Judicial Reform for 2007–2012, which defines concrete measures to improve the independence, autonomy, effectiveness, and public trust in the judiciary and a budget focused on capital investments rather than salaries, which is usually the case.

Corruption

1999	2001	2002	2003	2004	2005	2006	2007	2008
Y u g o s l a v i a				5.25	5.25	5.25	5.50	5.25

In February, the government established a National Anticorruption Commission to coordinate efforts to implement the Action Plan for the Fight Against Corruption and Organized Crime.[50] At the end of the year, Parliament passed a resolution expressing its "maximum readiness to build anticorruption legislation and establish strong international cooperation" in the fight against corruption.[51]

The National Anticorruption Commission met in July and December and adopted its first report on realization of measures on July 10. The conclusion of that report is that based on monthly reports of some 30 institutions, 25 percent of the two-year plan (69 of 280 measures) had been fully achieved from September 2006 until March 2007, including the adoption of a number of laws, the beginning of work on a new criminal procedure code, analyses on harmonization of legislation with international standards in the field of fight against organized crime, and work on a number of laws and amendments to existing laws and reform strategies. In addition, the various institutions tasked with a role in implementing the action plan established bilateral or multilateral cooperation with counterparts in the region and international institutions.[52] Thus, by the end of 2007, the responsible state organs had begun to put into place a framework for the struggle against corruption.

Still, in 2007, no major corruption case had concluded with a conviction. Charges against officials in state companies for abuse of office brought in 2006 and before were either still in the investigation stage or dismissed because of lack of evidence. In fact, in presenting the July report, the deputy prime minister who chairs the National Anticorruption Commission noted that "only based on verdicts can

I talk about the level of corruption because there is no other data. In Montenegro, in 2006, the courts handed down 442 verdicts on corrupt criminal activities, which are hard to prove. I hope that the Law on Criminal Procedure will be changed so that secret surveillance can be applied to a larger number of investigations, and the investigative organs can be more effective."[53]

The EU *Report on Montenegro* in November noted that "corruption is widespread and is a very serious problem…enforcement remains a problem…. There have been no improvements in activities to curb political corruption…. The situation calls for urgent action in order to achieve relevant results on the ground, especially in the area of high-level corruption."[54] Equally, the NGO MANS severely criticized the government for feigning its struggle against corruption[55] and brought many charges against public officials for violating the Law on Conflict of Interest—most of which were dismissed as unfounded. While the Commission for Determining Conflicts of Interest has sent five cases to the state prosecutor since 2005, no charges have yet been filed.[56] Further, the much criticized Law on Conflict of Interest was not amended in 2007, nor was any effort made to increase the transparency of political party financing, demonstrating a lack of political commitment to the anticorruption struggle.

There are regular media reports about corruption in public procurement, the management of state companies, construction, and privatization that remain in the realm of speculation without any charges filed and that leave the impression of corruption cases not pursued. The police, public prosecutor, and courts regularly exchange accusations about inefficiencies in corruption investigations, and a tripartite commission among these three institutions was established in October to address the problem and improve cooperation in the struggle against corruption.

In fact, corruption in Montenegro is as real as it is perceived. Public opinion surveys identify customs, health, judiciary, police, municipal services, and the public prosecution as the public institutions with the highest levels of corruption.[57] Yet the same public is considered to be a participant in official corruption in these sectors, and the high level of tolerance for and unwillingness to report official corruption help fuel Montenegro's culture of impunity.

Despite the bleak picture in the area of corruption, there is no doubt that the adoption of laws and pressure from NGOs and the public for implementation of those laws has begun to change behavior. As an example, the Property Administration made data about landownership available on its Web site, which MANS used to compare with the public declarations of assets and income of public officials available on the Commission for Determining Conflicts of Interest Web site. Thus, in 2007, 72 percent of the charges MANS filed against public officials were for incorrect data on their declarations—something that had been impossible to track in previous years. In 2005 and 2006, a majority of MANS's charges focused on unlawful membership in boards of public companies and multiple public functions.[58] Thus, as the framework detailed in the government's Action Plan for the Fight Against Corruption and Organized Crime continues to be put in place, public institutions will be forced to increase their transparency and accountability with the expectation of reduced conflicts of interest and corruption cases. But political will is still necessary in the coming year to pass the necessary laws to control official behavior and strengthen the capacity of the enforcement agencies to pursue abuses.

▌ AUTHOR: LISA MCLEAN

Lisa McLean is senior resident director of the Montenegro office of the National Democratic Institute, where she has served for the last nine years.

---

[1] The signatories to the declaration pledged to enshrine into the new Constitution the following provisions: 1) establishment of Montenegro as a civic state with equality of all persons and not of constituent peoples; 2) provisions to guarantee the independence of the judiciary; 3) removing the public prosecutor from the role of representing the state in civil cases to avoid conflicts of interests; 4) establishment of human rights guarantees at least on the level they had been in the Charter on Human and Minority Rights in the State Union of Serbia and Montenegro; 5) prohibition of the death penalty; 6) provisions for the retroactive applicability of human rights protection to past events; and 7) regulation of the status of the armed forces, security forces, and intelligence services and the means for parliamentary supervision, as well as establishment of a civilian as commander in chief. *Opinion on the Constitution of Montenegro* (Strasbourg: European Commission for Democracy Through Law, Council of Europe, December 20, 2007), 3.

[2] Ibid., 15.

[3] On a number of occasions, the police director, the head of the National Security Agency, and the minister of defense appeared before the Committee on Security and Defense to provide reports on organized crime and ordinary crime. Committee members also visited the police headquarters, Defense Ministry, and National Security Agency at the invitation of those bodies. The Committee for International Relations and European Integration invited the minister of foreign affairs to discuss the government's foreign policy priorities and the deputy prime minister to discuss EU integration efforts.

[4] Article 96, Constitution of the Republic of Montenegro, October 19, 2007.

[5] Article 79, §1, item 9, Constitution of the Republic of Montenegro, October 19, 2007.

[6] Those recommendations as summed up in the partnership document are "depoliticize the election administration, improve its functioning, in particular regarding announcement of results, codify election legislation, establish rules for media coverage of campaigns and introduce rules guaranteeing transparency for the allocation of seats in line with European standards; set up a transparent framework for campaign financing." Council Decision on the Principles, Priorities, and Conditions Contained in the European Partnership with Montenegro, 5047/07, Council of the European Union, January 17, 2007, 4.

[7] According to the 2003 census, 43% of residents identified themselves as Montenegrin, 32% Serb, 8% Bosniak, 5% Albanian, 4% Muslim, and 1% Croatian. Given this breakdown, it is hard to say who is a minority and who is entitled to special protections. Furthermore, within

the Serbian community, there is a dispute about whether Serbs are a minority in Montenegro and entitled to minority rights or whether Serbs and Montenegrins are the same people and together make up the majority population in Montenegro. Ethnic Albanians consider themselves a minority with special characteristics (for instance, distinctive language) that sets them apart from all other ethnic groups in Montenegro and entitles them to special considerations. Ethnic Bosniaks disagree with this interpretation.

8   D.B., "Jedno suđenje svim 'glumcima'" [One Trial for All 'Actors'], *Vijesti*, October 4, 2007, http://www.vijesti.cg.yu.

9   N.R., "Odradio 34 komšije da glasaju za DPS" [I Worked on 34 Neighbors to Vote for DPS], *Vijesti*, February 22, 2007, http://www.vijesti.cg.yu.

10 CEDEM Empirical Research Department, "Public Opinion in Montenegro, June 2007," *Newsletter 20*, March–June 2007, 10.

11 Interview with Claire O'Riordan, Chief of Party, USAID/ORT, Montenegro Advocacy Program (MAP), October 2007.

12 The campaign highlighted the reduced prices that the Aluminum Conglomerate (KAP) and steelworks companies pay compared with ordinary citizens and argued that taxpayers funded the difference between the government-guaranteed price and the market price.

13 Calling itself the Coordination Board, it claims to represent 27,000 workers, including from the education sector, from the populated towns of Nikšić and Bar, and from the Aluminum Conglomerate.

14 N. Nelević, "Dva lica saradnje, Intervju: Stevo Muk, autor izvještaja 'Odnos Vlade i državne uprave sa nevladinim organizacijama—2007'" [Two Faces of Cooperation, Interview: Stevo Muk, Author of the Report, 'Relations with Government and State Administration with Nongovernmental Organizations—2007'], *Građanin 53*, January 2008, 16–17.

15 Zeković believes that he became a target because of his efforts to investigate the case of Bosnian Muslims deported to Bosnia-Herzegovina in 1992 and the case of police brutality in the arrest of ethnic Albanians in September 2006 accused of plotting a terrorist incident.

16 Interviews with Daliborka Uljarević, director of Center for Civic Education, October 2007, and Vanja Čalović, director of MANS, January 2008.

17 It can only be limited in the "interest of: protecting life; public health; morality and privacy; criminal proceeding; security and defense of Montenegro; foreign, monetary, and economic policy." Article 51, Constitution of the Republic of Montenegro, October 19, 2007.

18 *Opinion on the Constitution of Montenegro* (Strasbourg: European Commission for Democracy Through Law, Council of Europe, December 20, 2007), 8.

19 Article 10, §2, European Convention on Human Rights, Council of Europe, Rome, November 1950. Article 51, Constitution of the Republic of Montenegro, October 19, 2007.

20 Vladan Zugić, "Politicians Must Tolerate Greater Criticism Than Ordinary Citizens," *EIC Bulletin*, no. 24, September 2007, 6.

21 M. Jovović, "Tuže novinare da ugase medije" [Journalists Sued to Extinguish Media], *Vijesti*, October 7, 2007, http://www.vijesti.cg.yu.

22 "Objective responsibility for all that [i.e., ineffective police and weak state], as well as for the attack on Ivanović...falls on the regime that Milo Đukanović led for 17 years, which he still leads, regardless in what form. He and his people are responsible from top to bottom for the atmosphere in which journalists, writers, and all those who dare to think and speak differently become victims." Editorial Department, *Vijesti*, "Neće nas uplašiti" [You Will Not Scare Us], *Vijesti*, September 2, 2007, http://www.arhiva-medija.com.

23 "After almost five years...practice has shown that the public service has not become a reality yet...partly because of the reluctance of some circles for reform that would make RTCG a real citizens' service and not a service for a group of individuals." M.B., "Još daleko od servisa građana: Učesnici okruglog stola o transformaciji RTCG ocijenili da je finansiranje

glavni problem te kuće" [Still Far Away from Citizens' Service: Participants in Roundtable on Transformation of RTCG Consider Financing to Be the Big Problem of that House], *Vijesti*, November 29, 2007, http://www.arhiva-medija.com.

24 Vladan Zugić, "Politicians Must Tolerate Greater Criticism Than Ordinary Citizens," *EIC Bulletin*, no. 24, September 2007, 4.

25 *Izvještaj o izvršenoj reviziji finanskih iskaza za 2006. godinu* [*Report on the Final Audit of the Financial Statement for 2006*] (Podgorica: Revizorska agencija "Auditor" DOO, May 2007), 2.

26 V. Radenović, "Krivokapić podmetnuo krivotvorenu izjavu: Doris Pak optužila Predsjednika Skupštine da je izmijenio tekst zajedničkog dokumenta, opozicija traži njegovu ostavku" [Krivokapić Put Aside Forged Statement: Doris Pack Accused President of Parliament of Changing the Text of the Joint Document, Opposition Seeks His Resignation], *Dan*, December 21, 2007, http://www.arhiva-medija.com.

27 M.B., "Još daleko od servisa građana: Učesnici okruglog stola o transformaciji RTCG ocijenili da je finansiranje glavni problem te kuće" [Still Far Away from Citizens' Service: Participants in Roundtable on Transformation of RTCG Consider Financing to Be the Big Problem of That House], *Vijesti*, November 29, 2007, http://www.arhiva-medija.com.

28 I.A., "Uvesti institut povjerenika: Asocijacija mladih novinara Crne Gore predlaže izmjene zakona o slobodnom pristupu informacija" [Introduce a Commissioner: Association of Young Journalists of Montenegro Proposes Changes to the Law on Free Access to Information], *Pobjeda*, November 1, 2007, http://www.arhiva-medija.com.

29 Interview with Claire O'Riordan, Chief of Party, USAID/ORT, Montenegro Advocacy Program (MAP), October 2007.

30 I.A., "Uvesti institut povjerenika: Asocijacija mladih novinara Crne Gore predlaže izmjene zakona o slobodnom pristupu informacija" [Bring the Institute of Representative: Association of Young Journalists of Montenegro Proposes Changes to the Law on Free Access to Information], *Pobjeda*, November 1, 2007, http://www.arhiva-medija.com.

31 Article 113, Constitution of the Republic of Montenegro, October 19, 2007.

32 Especially notable is Pljevlja municipality, which published its full 35-page budget with specific line items and a detailed 48-page budget of planned capital investments, http://www.pljevlja.cg.yu/budzet.html.

33 National budget transfers include a portion of the collected income tax, land sales tax, concession fees, and motor vehicle registration. The equalization fund makes transfers to municipalities based on the proportion of total residents to residents earning less than the average income in the municipality. *Bulletin IX* (Podgorica: Ministry of Finance, July–September 2007), 52–54.

34 Vladislav Karadžić and Gordana Radović, "Realization of Public Spending at the Local Level from January to June 2007," *Bulletin IX* (Podgorica: Ministry of Finance, July–September 2007), 52; and MINA Business, *Debts 1.7 Percent of GDP*, May 7, 2007, 1.

35 All located in the north, the six municipalities are Andrijevica, Mojkovac, Plav, Plužine, Šavnik, and Žabljak.

36 Vladislav Karadžić and Gordana Radović, "Realization of Public Spending at the Local Level from January to June 2007," *Bulletin IX* (Podgorica: Ministry of Finance, July–September 2007), 52–55.

37 Mina Business, "Opštinski propisi prepreka biznisu" [Municipal Regulations Are an Obstacle for Businesses], *Vijesti*, February 10, 2007, http:/www.vijesti.cg.yu.

38 The municipalities of Kolašin, Nikšić, and Pljevlja each blocked EPCG accounts at various times during 2007.

39 M. Milošević, "Za takse traže šest miliona" [For Taxes, It Asks Six Million], *Vijesti*, August 28, 2007, http://www.vijesti.cg.yu.

40   See MINA Business, "Opštine mnogo duguju: Vlada zabrinuta radom lokalnih vlasti [Municipalities Owe a Lot: Government Worries About the Work of Local Authorities]," *Vijesti*, May 7, 2007; "Municipalities Do Not Abide by Local Financing Decision," MINA Business, October 26, 2007, 3; and *Montenegro 2007 Progress Report* (Brussels: Commission of European Communities, November 6, 2007), 10.

41   *Opinion on the Constitution of Montenegro* (Strasbourg: European Commission for Democracy Through Law, Council of Europe, December 20, 2007), 5.

42   Ibid., 9, and *Interim Opinion on the Draft Constitution of Montenegro* (Strasbourg: European Commission for Democracy Through Law, Council of Europe, June 5, 2007), §103, http://www.venice.coe.int/docs/2007/CDL-AD(2007)017-e.asp.

43   *Izvještaj o radu za 2006. Godinu [Report of Work for 2006]* (Podgorica: Ombudsman, Protector of Human Rights and Freedom, March 2007).

44   N.M., "Crnovršanin: Ljudska prava kršena na svim nivoima: Ombudsman prošle godine primio 495 pritužbi, većinom na rad sudova i državne uprave" [Crnovršanin: Human Rights Violated at All Levels: Last Year, Ombudsman Received 495 Complaints, Mostly on the Work of the Courts and State Administration], *Dan*, June 5, 2007, http://www.arhiva-medija.com.

45   Šefko Crnovršanin, Speech at Press Conference on the Occasion of Human Rights and Freedom Day, December 10, 2007, http://www.ombudsman.cg.yu/aktuelnosti.php.

46   One case relates to the arrest of suspects accused of killing the head of the criminal division in the police and the other to the arrest of ethnic Albanian suspects accused of plotting a terrorist incident.

47   The president will now appoint a Judicial Council for a four-year term that will include the president of the Supreme Court, four judges elected by the Conference of Judges, two MPs (one each from the parliamentary majority and opposition), two renowned lawyers nominated by the president, and the minister of justice. The latter cannot vote in disciplinary proceedings against judges. *Opinion on the Constitution of Montenegro* (Strasbourg: European Commission for Democracy Through Law, Council of Europe, December 20, 2007), 14.

48   *Opinion on the Constitution of Montenegro* (Strasbourg: European Commission for Democracy Through Law, Council of Europe, December 20, 2007), 13.

49   Ibid., 12.

50   With 11 members including representatives from government anticorruption and crime-fighting agencies, one NGO and one opposition representative, the body's official name is the National Commission to Monitor Implementation of the Action Plan for Implementation of the Program for the Fight Against Corruption and Organized Crime.

51   D.M., "Da bitka ne bude samo formalnost: Skupštinski odbori utvrdili predlog rezolucije o borbi protiv korupcije i organizovanog kriminala" [That the Struggle Be Not Just a Formality: Parliamentary Committees Approved the Resolution About the Fight Against Corruption and Organized Crime], *Vijesti*, December 11, 2007, http://www.arhiva-medija.com.

52   National Commission to Monitor Implementation of the Action Plan for Implementation of the Program for the Fight against Corruption and Organized Crime, *The First Report on Realization of Measures from the Action Plan for Implementation of the Program for the Fight Against Corruption and Organized Crime* (Podgorica: July 10, 2007), 3–9.

53   D.P. and M.R., "Vanja ne razumije mnogo toga, ali je dragocjena: Gordana Đurović pozvala direktoricu MANS-a da se vrati u Komisiju za suzbijanje korupcije i organizovanog kriminala" [Vanja Does Not Understand Much of It, but She Is Well-Intentioned: Gordana Đurović Calls the Director of MANS to Return to the Commission for Fighting Corruption and Organized Crime], *Vijesti*, July 12, 2007, http://www.arhiva-medija.com.

54   *Montenegro 2007 Progress Report* (Brussels: Commission of European Communities, November 6, 2007), 12.

55 Ibid.

56 MINA News Agency, "Zaboravili na stanove i poklone: MANS optužio Tužilaštvo da podstiče prikazivanje prihoda i imovin" [They Forgot Apartments and Gifts: MANS Accuses Prosecution of Filing False Data on Income and Assets], *Vijesti*, January 17, 2008, http://www.vijesti.cg.yu.

57 CEDEM Empirical Research Department, "Public Opinion in Montenegro, June 2007," *Newsletter 20*, March–June 2007, 14.

58 N. Mrdak, "Za tri godine samo 15 odluka: Od osnivanja Komisije za konflikt interesa MANS prijavio 119 javnih funkcionera" [In Three Years Only 15 Decisions: Since Founding of the Commission for Conflict of Interest, MANS Charged 119 Public Officials], *Dan*, January 10, 2008, http://www.dan.cg.yu.

Poland

by Andrzej Krajewski

Capital: Warsaw
Population: 38.1 million
GNI/capita: US$14,250

The social data above was taken from the European Bank for Reconstruction and Development's *Transition Report 2007: People in Transition*, and the economic data from the World Bank's *World Development Indicators 2008*.

Nations in Transit Ratings and Averaged Scores

	1999	2001	2002	2003	2004	2005	2006	2007	2008
Electoral Process	1.25	1.25	1.25	1.50	1.50	1.75	1.75	2.00	2.00
Civil Society	1.25	1.25	1.25	1.25	1.25	1.25	1.25	1.50	1.25
Independent Media	1.50	1.50	1.50	1.75	1.75	1.50	1.75	2.25	2.25
Governance*	1.75	1.75	2.00	2.00	2.00	n/a	n/a	n/a	n/a
National Democratic Governance	n/a	n/a	n/a	n/a	n/a	2.50	2.75	3.25	3.50
Local Democratic Governance	n/a	n/a	n/a	n/a	n/a	2.00	2.00	2.25	2.25
Judicial Framework and Independence	1.50	1.50	1.50	1.50	1.50	2.00	2.25	2.25	2.50
Corruption	2.25	2.25	2.25	2.50	2.50	3.00	3.25	3.00	3.00
Democracy Score	1.58	1.58	1.63	1.75	1.75	2.00	2.14	2.36	2.39

* *With the 2005 edition, Freedom House introduced separate analysis and ratings for national democratic governance and local democratic governance to provide readers with more detailed and nuanced analysis of these two important subjects.*

NOTE: The ratings reflect the consensus of Freedom House, its academic advisers, and the author(s) of this report. The opinions expressed in this report are those of the author(s). The ratings are based on a scale of 1 to 7, with 1 representing the highest level of democratic progress and 7 the lowest. The Democracy Score is an average of ratings for the categories tracked in a given year.

EXECUTIVE SUMMARY

With the Kaczyński twins, Lech and Jarosław, at the nation's helm for 10 months of the year—as president and prime minister, respectively—2007 marked the second (and final) year of Poland's Fourth Republic. Under the Kaczyńskis in 2007, there were 60 laws introduced in Parliament and 115 bills prepared by ministers. Driven by a leadership that looked backwards into the specter of the Communist past, the secret services investigated actively, prosecutors waited on call, and fervent journalists engaged in lustrating the nation's intellectuals. The Constitutional Court and private media resisted state pressure with some success. Early elections in October proved that the methods used by the Fourth Republic were unacceptable for many Poles.

The political situation, polarized throughout the year, was a roller coaster. It was initially affected by the pope's nomination for Warsaw archbishop, followed by a break-up in the government coalition that led to a search for a government "conspiracy" (the specter of which brought the Kaczyńskis to power) that ultimately failed to materialize. In October, the ruling duo and their Law and Justice Party (PiS) lost the early elections they had called for owing to the recent record high 54 percent turnout, thus bringing the opposition Civic Platform (PO) to power in a coalition government with the Peasant Party (PSL). The more affluent, educated, and mobile Poles (with some voting from abroad) rebelled via the ballot box against the changes instituted during the Fourth Republic.

National Democratic Governance. In essence, there were two distinctly different governments and styles of national democratic governance during 2007. PiS, the ruling party for the first 10 months, was obsessed with uncovering conspiracies of the past connected to the present among politicians, wealthy people, secret services, and the mafia. Few of the connections were discovered, and of those, mainly in the ruling party's own political camp. PiS relinquished power democratically after losing the early elections called on October 21, 2007. The new government (led by Donald Tusk) stopped inquiring about the past and focus returned to present-day issues. *Owing to PiS's overusing state power to hunt for political opponents and allies, and further concentration of power in the executive branch, Poland's national democratic governance rating worsens from 3.25 to 3.50.*

Electoral Process. Despite erratic governing during most of the year, Poland proved to be a stable democracy, solving its political problems by early parliamentary elections—scheduled two years in advance by a vote that garnered support from both the ruling party and the opposition. There were no attempts to change electoral law.

The elections were held in October with international observers present. *Poland's rating for electoral process remains at 2.00.*

Civil Society. An overbearing manner of governing invigorated NGOs and civic-minded citizens alike to fight for their beliefs: protecting the pristine valley of Rospuda from intrusive road planning, maintaining the rights of professionals obliged to report on themselves, and upholding the freedom of information on farm subsidies. *These undertakings combined with government's refusal to further curtail civil society and civil freedoms improved Poland's civil society rating from 1.50 to 1.25.*

Independent Media. The year 2007 saw a continuation of attacks by authorities on the media, which the prime minister accused of being owned by "oligarchs." Similarly, attacks by authorities on journalists continued as reporters and editors were pressed to sign declarations about their Communist-era security connections, which were then widely covered by the media. Despite the government's pressure in the first part of the year on limiting press freedom and partisan usage of public media, freedom of speech in Poland was secured and new media outlets appeared in the market. The new government installed in November stopped pressuring the media and declared its will to depoliticize the public media. *Poland's independent media rating remains at 2.25.*

Local Democratic Governance. After the 2006 elections, local government work included applying for and using EU budgets, a process that was sometimes hampered by Warsaw's centrally-driven government. *Owing to the restricted scale of these hampering efforts and the stability of local governance, the rating for local democratic governance remains at 2.25.*

Judicial Framework and Independence. Administrative restrictions on courts' independence, steering of prosecutors' work by their superiors and the minister of justice, verbal attacks, and formal threats to the Constitutional Court were realities of 2007. Ruling politicians spent much of the year attempting to control the judiciary. *Administrative restrictions on the judiciary during much of the year worsens Poland's rating for judicial framework and independence from 2.25 to 2.50.*

Corruption. Last year's trumpeted war on corruption did not bring measurable progress. The secret services disregarded citizens' rights while looking for instances of corruption in former politicians—but found some within their own ranks. *Owing to the ineffectiveness of anticorruption measures and investigations, Poland's corruption rating remains at 3.00.*

Outlook for 2008. The early elections in October 2007, which brought the main opposition party to power with a strong, but not exclusive government, will set the tone for Polish politics in 2008. Cohabitation with the remaining brother, President

Lech Kaczyński, may be difficult, but it is unlikely that the newly opposition PiS could re-take power. PO will take a conciliatory stance toward improving Poland's relations with the rest of the EU; inside the country, PO will likely stop the lustration hunt and change the general political focus from one of looking backward to moving forward. The two currently active parliamentary investigative commissions may yet discover hidden illegal practices of the former PiS government. Public media should recover from their earlier PiS political dependency, attacks on the judiciary are likely to stop, and tolerance in public life and discourse should begin to make a comeback. But too much liberalism may cost PO support from voters, as two years of Kaczyński demagoguery has revitalized the right, awakened nationalism, and strengthened populism. There will be no easy way out from the Fourth Republic, especially with the new role of the Kaczyński duo: Lech the president refusing cohabitation with the government of the new prime minister, Donald Tusk, and Jarosław as the new opposition leader, criticizing every action and lack of action by his successor.

MAIN REPORT

National Democratic Governance

1999	2001	2002	2003	2004	2005	2006	2007	2008
n/a	n/a	n/a	n/a	n/a	2.50	2.75	3.25	3.50

The year 2007 began with a lustration scandal as the media accused conservative archbishop Stanisław Wielgus, appointed to run the Warsaw diocese, of collaboration with the Communist secret police. Although church officials are excluded from the Law on Lustration, the Vatican asked Wielgus to resign on the day of his inauguration, under unclear but obvious pressure from Warsaw. He did so despite loud protests, thus becoming the highest-ranking victim of the country's unchecked lustration. The lustration program began in earnest in 2005 when right-wing journalists published 170,000 suspected names taken from the Institute of National Remembrance (which was formed to archive and lustrate the Communist past). In Wielgus' case, the lustration by the media supposedly received support from the Kaczyński twins' state apparatus, opening speculation that it could influence even the Vatican. This was only the beginning of the 2007 political roller coaster, which ended abruptly with the October 21 early elections and change of government.

Poland is a parliamentary democracy. Its Constitution provides a balance among executive, legislative, and judicial powers. Broad changes to the nation's legislation were introduced in 2004 to meet requirements for European Union (EU) accession. Additional harmonization continued post-accession. Notably, in 2006, the Constitution was changed to accommodate the European Arrest Warrant Act, which allows for the deportation of Polish nationals who break laws abroad on the condition that the same crimes are punishable under Polish law.

The government is confirmed by a majority of the 460-member *Sejm*. Both chambers of Parliament—the *Sejm* (the lower house) and the *Senat* (the upper house)—work on new legislation and must agree on it, with the president then signing or vetoing it. The president's veto may be overridden by a two-thirds majority of the *Sejm*. The president may also send legislation to the Constitutional Court, whose 15 members are elected by the *Sejm* for a single nine-year term. The Constitutional Court can declare laws or parts of laws unconstitutional; its decisions are final and obligatory. The Parliament can form investigative commissions and impeach the president.

Following a vigorously contested campaign—one of the most heated and divisive since the Polish transition—the October 2007 early elections delivered a victory (42 percent) for the opposition Civic Platform (PO), which formed a coalition government with the Peasant Party (PSL; 9 percent). The *Senat* was divided between the PO (60 seats) and the Law and Justice Party (PiS; 39 seats), with a single independent, the left-wing former prime minister. Before the elections, the government was headed by PiS, which won 27 percent of votes in 2005 and formed a minority government under Kazimierz Marcinkiewicz. The populist Self-Defense League (Samoobrona) and the right-wing League of Polish Families (LPR) soon joined, as well. In mid-2006, Jarosław Kaczyński, the twin brother of President Lech Kaczyński, became prime minister, breaking his pre-election promise not to assume the post if his brother was elected president.

The most powerful political office in Poland is the prime minister, who can be recalled only by a constructive no-confidence vote. President Lech Wałęsa (1990–1995) greatly influenced the choice of ministers of defense, the interior, and foreign affairs, which led to restrictions on presidential powers in the Constitution adopted in 1997. His successor, Aleksander Kwaśniewski, who held the office from 1995 to 2005, had a lesser mandate and was more active abroad, garnering support for Poland's NATO membership in 1999 and EU membership in 2004. In October 2005, Lech Kaczyński (PiS) succeeded President Kwaśniewski with 54 percent of the popular vote, beating Donald Tusk (PO) and swinging Poland's political pendulum significantly to the right. Lech Kaczyński was internationally known for his anti-European and illiberal views.

All legislation is published in the *Official Gazette* and on the *Sejm*, *Senat*, and president's Web sites. *Sejm* proceedings and parliamentary investigative commissions are broadcast live on public television TVP Info and on TVN24, a private channel. Thanks to the Law on Freedom of Information, adopted in 2001, there is access to a significant amount of government, self-government, and other public documents. The law did not replace all earlier legislation dealing with this topic, however, and many items are still inaccessible.

Members of Parliament and all government officials must post their property annually. The Central Anticorruption Bureau (CBA), with 500 officers, is empowered to fight corruption at the highest levels by acting undercover and performing investigative and control functions. One of its duties is to review the property statements of politicians and officials.

Under the 1997 Law on Lustration, all public representatives, high-ranking government officials, and attorneys were required to declare if they had worked for Communist-era secret police or intelligence. Those who hid this information were punished with a 10-year ban on public service after trials in the lustration court initiated by the public interest prosecutor. These procedures often took years and were criticized as being too lenient. According to the new 2006 Law on Lustration, the Institute of National Remembrance (IPN) replaced the lustration court, the public interest prosecutor ceased to exist, and IPN files of all public officials were to be opened. About 700,000 people, including journalists, teachers, and university professors, would be required to declare past activities in accordance with the information contained in the files.

President Kaczyński signed the new law in 2006 but three months later introduced IPN-prepared amendments, eliminating the Information Sources Register (the roster of all persons enlisted as Communist secret police informants) but maintaining the declaration policy. The opposition brought the law to the Constitutional Court, while many well-known journalists, teachers, and academics, at risk of losing their jobs, announced that they would not sign the declarations. The rift between the country's elite and PiS became widened. In May 2007, on the final date for collection of declarations, a Constitutional Court verdict voided all of the declarations. The Catholic Church formed its own investigation commissions in dioceses, judging agents found among clergy. All churches were officially excluded from the Law on Lustration. A report on the military intelligence service, published in February 2007, listed names of alleged agents, including several well-known journalists. In autumn, IPN began publishing the first files of senior officials.

The shaky coalition of PiS, Samoobrona, and LPR finally collapsed in July, after a clandestine action against Deputy Prime Minister Andrzej Lepper. Two of his associates were arrested, allegedly for taking a bribe in a CBA-sting operation and Lepper was dismissed. The government lost its majority status under challenges from the opposition, including a PO motion to recall all ministers. This motion was unprecedented and legally dubious, made in lieu of a proposal from the new prime minister, which would result in a no-confidence vote. Jarosław Kaczyński's response was no less complex: He asked his brother to recall all 15 ministers and to nominate them again, whereby the first portfolio was returned the same evening. Constitutional Court chief Jerzy Stępień deemed this action illegal, stating that the ministerial vow must be taken personally in front of the president.[1]

Before the first autumn session of Parliament, the recalled minister of internal affairs, Janusz Kaczmarek, was accused of warning the Samoobrona leader about the CBA operation. Prosecutors showed a videotape of Kaczmarek, caught by a hotel security camera waiting for businessman Ryszard Krauze, who avoided arrest only by staying abroad.[2] "In their hunt for a conspiracy, PiS politicians found only the one established by themselves," ridiculed the opposition,[3] but soon it voted with PiS (377 out of 460) to dissolve the *Sejm* and the *Senat*.

The Supreme Chamber of Control audits all government institutions. Its head is nominated by the *Sejm* and approved by the *Senat* for a six-year term, which keeps the office less prone to political influence. The chamber audits institutional legality, efficacy, economic sense, and diligence at all levels of the central administration, the Polish National Bank, and state and local administrations. In 2007, Mirosław Sekuła, elected by the center-right Solidarity Electoral Action (AWS) coalition, was replaced by its former deputy Jacek Jezierski. Also, the head of the Polish National Bank was changed; Leszek Balcerowicz, author of the "shock therapy" approach for Poland's economy in the early 1990s, was exchanged for a low-level PiS official, Sławomir Skrzypek.

The early 1990s goal of creating a depoliticized, high-quality corps of civil servants throughout government was finally abandoned. In 2006, the State Cadres Reserve was formed; in 2007, all people holding the advanced academic degree of Ph.D. (about 120,000 people)—no matter the type or source of degree—were included, forcing former civil servants into lower positions. The law establishing the State Cadres Reserve has been challenged in the Constitutional Court. Meanwhile, younger, educated, alienated, entrepreneurial Poles have been immigrating to other European Union (EU) countries.[4]

The Polish economy is now mostly composed of private companies, but despite 18 years of privatization, the state still holds majority shares in 1,641 companies and owns 38 percent of Poland's territory.[5] In 2007, the process of changing management at the largest state companies was completed, though not without raising political questions. For instance: When the head of the national insurance company PZU, Jaromir Netzel, was dismissed in connection with the Kaczmarek affair, the media revived information about his murky past revealed a year earlier, which was ignored at the time by PiS. The extent to which the private sector is vulnerable to political maneuvering is exemplified by the business troubles of Ryszard Krauze, whose enterprises overnight lost over 600 million złoty (US$230 million) in stock value after news of his possible arrest.

The past successes of the *Sejm* investigative commissions, which toppled the left-wing (liberal) government of Leszek Miller in 2004, were not repeated in 2007. Likewise, the Investigative Commission to Study State Organs' Inaccuracies in the Process of Transformation of Certain Banks (Bank Commission) failed to conduct any important investigations during the year after the Constitutional Court found its prerogatives too vague.

Electoral Process

1999	2001	2002	2003	2004	2005	2006	2007	2008
1.25	1.25	1.25	1.50	1.50	1.75	1.75	2.00	2.00

In summer 2007, the ruling party PiS lost majority in the Parliament by dissolving its coalition with minor partners Samoobrona and LPR. Deputy Prime Minister Andrzej Lepper (leader of Samoobrona) was accused of involvement in bribe taking, which was the result of an investigation by the CBA. The opposition refused to form a government, and a majority of parliamentarians voted for earlier elections. The election results again followed the pattern that every election brings the opposition to power. This time, it happened after only two years. PO won with 42 percent of the votes, while the ruling PiS was second with 31 percent. Its former allies, LPR and Samoobrona, received less than 2 percent and were thus removed from the Parliament as well as excluded from the system of state subsidies for political parties.

Poland's multiparty parliamentary system with proportional representation was introduced in 1993. The electoral thresholds are 5 percent for parties and 8 percent for coalitions. These do not apply to national minorities; for example, the German community won one seat in the *Sejm* in 2007, although its voting power is less than 0.5 percent. The *Sejm* has 460 members, elected for four-year terms. The *Senat* has 100 members elected by majority vote on a provincial basis, also for four-year terms. Ahead of the 2007 fall elections, there was no attempt to make last minute changes in the electoral legislation (as had occurred in 2006). However, before the next elections there may be some changes to the law, because the PO promised to expand the majority vote and eliminate the *Senat*.

Poland's electoral system is considered free and fair. There are no instances of significant voting fraud or use of coercion, and complaints may be effectively filed with the Supreme Court. Perhaps this is why when former president of the Czech Republic Vaclav Havel proposed international monitoring of the 2007 elections, he was heavily criticized by Polish politicians and media alike.[6] Yet, Warsaw is home to the human rights office of the OSCE, which provides electoral oversight (through the Office for Democratic Institutions and Human Rights), and observers were quietly invited to monitor the early elections. ODIHR noted "occasional partisan interventions by institutions of the State."[7] Regarding the media, ODIHR drew attention to deficiencies in the structure and partisan composition and of the National Broadcasting Council, and expressed concern over: "a lack of qualitative balance by public television [and] ...the absence of effective mechanisms of oversight."[8]

Low voter turnout has been characteristic for all elections since the beginning of the Third Republic in 1989, when a record 62 percent voted. Subsequently, the rate has decreased steadily, from 52 percent in 1993 to 41 percent in 2005. The all-time low was 21 percent in 2004 in the European Parliament election. Given the 46 percent turnout in local elections in 2006 and the 54 percent turnout in the 2007 early elections, it would appear there may be a reversal in the trend. Or these recent higher numbers may simply reflect the high emotions caused by the Kaczyńskis' administration.

Civil Society

1999	2001	2002	2003	2004	2005	2006	2007	2008
1.25	1.25	1.25	1.25	1.25	1.25	1.25	1.50	1.25

The most successful, widespread, and spontaneous civil society action in 2007 was the protest against a highway construction project in the Rospuda valley peat bogs near Augustów, in northeastern Poland. For years ecologists had been fighting this project, even offering an alternative route, but local and central authorities insisted, with support from Augustów residents frustrated by the heavy truck traffic through the city center. After marches and volunteer sit-ins, actors and TV anchors wearing green "Save Rospuda" ribbons, and huge media support, especially by *Gazeta Wyborcza*, the European Commission asked the European Tribunal of Justice to halt construction on the site while it reviews the case.

Poland's civil society is based on the traditions of the Solidarity trade union and other anti-Communist opposition movements of the 1970s and 1980s, as well as social activity by the religiously dominant Catholic Church. Frequent changes of government in the 1990s helped to establish civil society structures: foundations, think tanks, and analytical centers which support the current opposition until the political pendulum replaces the incumbent with the opposition. Since 2004, the Law on Public Benefit Activities and Volunteering has given nongovernmental organizations (NGOs) the option to register as "public benefit organizations," allowing tax breaks and 1 percent personal income tax donations, but also imposing stricter rules on salaries and an obligatory annual audit.

More than 50,000 associations and 7,000 foundations are registered as active in sports, recreation, tourism, culture and art, education, social help, and health protection. In total, these organizations report eight million members, and one million are noted as volunteers. The main sources of financing are member dues, self-government donations, private donations, and funding from institutions. Some of the major donors to the sector are the Polish American Freedom Foundation, Stefan Batory Foundation, Agora Foundation, and Kronenberg Foundation. This and other information supporting Poland's third sector is available on the Klon/Jawor Association's NGO information portal, which supports the third sector (http://english.ngo.pl).

Freedom of association is secured in Article 58 of the Polish Constitution and the Law on Associations. There are prohibitions against groups promoting Nazi, Fascist, and Communist ideology, racial and national hatred, secret membership, or the use of power to overthrow the authorities. However, the government itself has not fully supported these freedoms.

In May 2007, the European Court of Human Rights (ECHR) in Strasbourg decided the case of *Bączkowski and Others v. Poland*, dealing with the Warsaw ban on a Lesbian, Gay, Bisexual, and Transgender Pride Parade two years earlier. Poland was reprimanded for violating several articles of the Human Rights Convention, and Lech Kaczyński, then mayor of Warsaw, was personally criticized for his homophobic remarks. "Public officials should be restrained in expressing their opinions, realizing that their words may be treated as instructions by their subordinates," wrote ECHR judges.[9] Their criticism did not influence public officials, however. In an education bill prepared by Minister of Education Roman Giertych, schools are obliged to protect students against the "promotion of homosexuality," defined as "presentation of homosexual relationship in a form convincing to have one," arguing that teens may change their sexual preferences under this influence. "Such ignorance proves that this bill was filled with homophobia and intolerance, therefore being outright discriminatory," wrote Professor Wojciech Sadurski in an Institute of Public Affairs (Instytut Spraw Publicznych: ISP) report on the state of democracy in Poland.[10]

Poland lost another strategic case in the ECHR during the year, that of Alicja Tysiąc, who was denied the right to an abortion. In September 2007, she was granted compensation of €25,000 (US$39,000), and the Polish government was instructed by the ECHR to construct a mechanism to decide whether abortion is available when permitted by law. It was Deputy Prime Minister and Minister of Education Roman Giertych again who talked about the overturned verdict as running against the rules upon which Polish society is built and demanded Poland's withdrawal from the European Convention on Human Rights. On a more positive note, in July the government quietly gave in to the request to disclose farm subsidies data, which the Helsinki Foundation for Human Rights had been requesting in the administrative and civil courts. After two years of legal battles, when the ruling coalition collapsed in late 2007, the agency handling farm subsidies promptly published the names of 1.5 million beneficiaries on its Web page.

In the autumn, Leszek Balcerowicz, former Polish National Bank president, started the Citizens' Development Forum, a new watchdog NGO aimed at verifying politician declarations and promises. The Stefan Batory Foundation also ran several watchdog projects in public education, access to information, ecology, and other areas. There was even an initiative to recall President Kaczyński in a call for a national referendum that collected half a million signatures.

The most high-profile Polish charity action was the annual New Year's telethon of the Wielka Orkiestra Świątecznej Pomocy (the Great Orchestra of Christmas Charity); 120,000 youth volunteers collected 29 million złoty (US$9.7 million) from street donations and auctions, and the proceeds went to purchase medical equipment for handicapped children. However, the minister of education was directed to verify whether the action was, in fact, voluntarily supported by youth, and public TV downgraded its coverage of the event. Polish Humanitarian Action continued to help victims of natural disasters and armed conflicts in Chechnya, Palestine, Iraq, Sri Lanka, and other countries, as well as indigent children and refugees in Poland. The largest charity organization in Poland is Caritas, which feeds the poor and shelters the homeless on behalf of the Catholic Church.

The trade union movement has good standing in Poland thanks to the tradition of Solidarność (Solidarity), which in 1981 boasted 10 million members. Today's Independent and Self-Governing Trade Union Solidarity, while still one of the two largest trade unions in Poland, is only a shadow of its former strength, with fewer than 1 million members. The largest trade union is the All-Poland Trade Unions Agreement, with about 1.5 million members. The majority of both unions' members are from state-owned factories, steel mills, mines, railways, and budget-funded health care and education facilities. In March 2007, the two unions launched a campaign to protest a minimum monthly wage of 936 złoty (US$424) and to secure higher wages. In the state-run health care system, the year was marred by strikes of doctors and other health care personnel over low pay, resulting in some cases in the evacuation of patients. During a two-month protest, nurses set up tents in front of the Office of the Prime Minister, who took an early summer holiday and avoided the protesters. There was some movement toward a resolution between the Trilateral Social Commission and the unions before the dissolution of Parliament late in the year.[11]

Independent Media

1999	2001	2002	2003	2004	2005	2006	2007	2008
1.50	1.50	1.50	1.75	1.75	1.50	1.75	2.25	2.25

Prime Minister Jarosław Kaczyński's intolerance towards the media outlets that were critical of the PiS-led government continued throughout 2007, especially in the lustration of journalists. Kaczyński stated that the "majority of media are under oligarchs' control,"[12] comparing *Gazeta Wyborcza* to the Communist Party daily

Trybuna Ludu of 1953. Agora, the publisher of *Gazeta Wyborcza*, took the prime minister to court for the remark. In the Reporters Without Borders 2007 survey of world press freedom, Poland for the second year was ranked 56, last among EU countries. Poland's low ranking was attributed to the pressuring of private media by the government, attempts to control media by the secret services, and a proposed work ban on journalists under the Law on Lustration. During the year, public media were under the political control of PiS and its allies, and private media were increasingly politicized and divided, with tabloids frequently supporting the authorities.

The importance of free media is well understood in Poland, where fighting censorship and a tradition of an underground free press go back to the nineteenth century. According to the Constitution, the state "shall ensure freedom of the press and other means of social communication,"[13] but other legal acts still contain traces of authoritarian rule that threaten this basic freedom.

Article 133 of the penal code provides up to three years' imprisonment for persons who "publicly insult the Polish Nation or the state," though the statute has not been used in recent years. In 2007, a new form of "insulting the Polish Nation" was added as Article 132a: "Anyone publicly insulting the Polish Nation for participating in, organizing of, or responsibility for Nazi or Communist crimes may be punished up to three years in jail." The dangers to free speech presented by this article prompted the ombudsman to challenge it in the Constitutional Court. The prosecutor in Kraków initiated an investigation but dropped it in a short time.[14]

Libeling the president can carry a sentence of up to three years in jail. Libeling members of Parliament or government ministers is punishable by two years in jail and libeling other public officials by one year.

Libel suits against media professionals are common, but those found guilty are usually only fined. The Constitutional Court upheld the constitutionality of the penal code article that penalizes 'defamation' in the media (even if determined to be an expression of facts and opinions) with up to two years in prison; however, three justices, including the chair, wrote dissenting opinions, emphasizing that the truth of questioned statements protects the journalist against the defamation charge only if it safeguards "a socially protected interest." In addition, they pointed out, the article runs counter to the verdict of the ECHR in Strasbourg, which ruled that a requirement of truth concerning opinions is an impossibility and therefore an infringement of the freedom of speech.[15]

In 2007, further changes occurred in the state media (that is, Polish Television TVP, Polskie Radio PR, state news agency PAP, and *Rzeczpospolita* daily, half-owned by the state). The TVP presidency, held from April 2006 by right-wing journalist Bronisław Wildstein, was transferred in February 2007 to Andrzej Urbański, former journalist and President Lech Kaczyński's first chief of staff. On the closely controlled news program *Wiadomości*, 80 percent of the political reporters were changed. In the last week before the elections, TVP twice changed its program to repeat accusations brought by the CBA against opposition parliamentarians. In other public media, close control by PiS became the rule during the year.

According to the Stefan Batory Foundation, TVP's 2006 local elections coverage strongly favored PiS, and TVP devoted more attention to the government than to the opposition. In local TVP programs, the incumbents were shown preferentially, but only if they were from PiS. In towns with mayors from other parties, their TVP presence was less than those with PiS-connected mayors. In Warsaw, governed by a PiS mayor, the coverage of the incumbent was overwhelming.

Polish electronic media are controlled by the National Broadcasting Council (KRRiT), a body elected by the Parliament and the president. Before the 2005 elections, the KRRiT was composed almost completely of left-wing nominees. The new Law on Radio and Television, signed by President Kaczyński in 2005, reduced the KRRiT from nine to five members (two nominated by the *Sejm*, one by the *Senat*, and two by the president). KRRiT was again politicized, but this time by PiS and its allies; the KRRiT chair resigned to become a PiS parliamentarian following the 2007 early elections.

TVP, the public station, has a dominant position with both viewers and advertising markets with its three ground channels (TVP1, TVP2, and TVP Info with 16 local branches), satellite channels (TVP Polonia, TVP Kultura, TVP Sport, TVP History), and potentially more with digital Webcasting. TVP's strong position comes at the price of commercialization and political influence on programming, formerly from the Left and since 2006 from the Right. The extent to which TVP's supervisory board has become political was made obvious in January 2007, when the election of its two new members by KRRiT was tied directly to the minority coalition parties' approval of the new Polish National Bank president. TVP's executive board has also been composed along party lines.

Two-thirds of TVP's income comes from advertising, the rest from license fees. TVP looks in prime time exactly like its private competitors (movies, soap operas, and talk shows), while documentaries, education, and cultural programs are shown late at night. The new ruling PO proposes to stop the collection of license fees, unpaid by 20 percent of households and 95 percent of enterprises, and to eliminate KRRiT, which requires a change in the Constitution.[16]

TVP's main private television competitors include Polsat TV, TVN holding (which includes TVN24), the Canal+ cable channel, and Father Tadeusz Rydzyk's Trwam TV, a religious satellite channel broadcast from Torun.[17] TV digital platforms are Cyfra+, Cyfrowy Polsat, and N. The ITI Group owns N and TVN. News Corporation, owned by Rupert Murdoch, bought 24.5 percent of TV Puls, which launched new commercial programming in the fall of 2007 after KRRiT agreed to allow the station to change its religious character (which had been largely devoted to Catholic issues).

Among radio stations, the public Polskie Radio—with 6 Warsaw-based channels and 17 local radio stations—has a strong position, but private competitors Radio ZET and Radio RMF FM are leaders in audience and advertising revenues. Radio Maryja, founded by Father Rydzyk in 1991 together with Trwam TV, has been the favorite government outlet, despite occasional rifts between PiS and Father Rydzyk caused by his anti-presidential and anti-Semitic remarks. The president refused interviews with Rydzyk media during the year, but his brother, the prime minister, defended Rydzyk against criticism from Roman Catholic bishops, arguing that "there would be no Radio Maryja without its founder."

Major newspapers *Gazeta Wyborcza* (circulation 419,000 copies; owner Polish Agora), *Rzeczpospolita* (144,000; owner British Mecom), and *Dziennik* (176,000; owner Axel Springer) gained a fourth competitor in October 2007: *Polska* (owner Neue Passauer Presse). The largest press circulation is maintained by tabloids *Fakt* (512,000 copies; owner Axel Springer) and *Super Express* (197,000; owner Bonnier with Polish capital).

There are three major opinion weeklies: the left-wing *Polityka* (172,000 copies; owned by a journalist co-op), the center *Newsweek Polska* (132,000; owner Axel Springer), and the right-wing *Wprost* (177,000; owner Agencja Reklamowa Wprost). *Nasz Dziennik*, a conservative nationalist daily, is part of the Father Rydzyk media empire. The Catholic liberal *Tygodnik Powszechny* has a strong intellectual reputation as the only independent (though censored) paper of the former Communist Poland. *Przekrój*, published by Edipresse, moved from Kraków to Warsaw and has skillfully become a voice of the younger generation. The private Polish weekly *Nie*, run by Jerzy Urban, former spokesman for President Wojciech Jaruzelski, is anticlerical, left-wing, and often provocative.[18] Two English weeklies (*Warsaw Voice* and *Warsaw Business Journal*) and a Russian weekly are also in publication.

The local press produces 3,000 titles, but media concentration has become a threat. The major press companies include Axel Springer, Agora, Mecom, and Polskapresse (Neue Passauer Presse). Media cross-ownership has not been regulated, but when Axel Springer attempted to buy 25.1 percent of Polsat TV in 2006, the purchase was stopped by the antimonopoly office, which argued that Springer already owned the tabloid *Fakt*, opinion daily *Dziennik*, and weekly *Newsweek Polska*. According to a leading journalist critical of the Kaczyński brothers, his dismissal from Polsat TV was demanded by the prime minister in order to facilitate the deal.[19]

Over 50 percent of Polish households have a computer and use the Internet. Child pornography is the only prosecuted Web offense. Naukowa Akademicka Sieć Komputerowa (Research and Academic Computer Network), a research and development organization, leading Polish data networks operator keeps a registry of sites, but there are no address restrictions. Print media have Web sites, and the number of personal and public Web sites, blogs, and video blogs has increased rapidly.

There are about 20,000 journalists working in Poland, but only a few hundred are members of the media trade unions (Journalists' Syndicate and a branch of Solidarity). Only a few thousand, mostly older professionals, are members of the Polish Journalists' Association or Republic of Poland Journalists' Association. These groups maintain ethics standards and lobby for new press legislation and changes in the penal code, but their authority is weak. There was no outcry when the telephones of several investigative journalists were tapped during 2007, which could have a chilling effect on the profession.[20] The majority of Polish journalists work without collective agreement or wage bargaining, and publishers keep salaries secret. Media strikes and other union actions rarely if ever occur in Poland.

Local Democratic Governance

1999	2001	2002	2003	2004	2005	2006	2007	2008
n/a	n/a	n/a	n/a	n/a	2.00	2.00	2.25	2.25

Self-government traditions are strong in Poland. This is especially true in the west and south, where more than a century ago, in the absence of a Polish state, local authorities worked with Catholic and Protestant clergy to maintain Polish schools and nurture Polish customs in choirs, folk dance, gymnastics groups, fire brigades, and credit unions. One of the first acts of the Solidarity government after 1989 was the restoration of local self-governance by re-creating the approximately 2,500 *gminas* (Poland's basic territorial division) that were canceled in the 1950s. Ninety thousand local officials were transferred from the state administration to local governments. In 1998, the number of regions was reduced from 49 to 16, and 314 counties and 65 cities with equal status were added.

According to the Constitution, local government is a permanent feature of the state based on the principle of subsidiarity. The powers and independence of local authorities are protected by the courts, and there is a presumption that *gmina* competences extend to all matters not reserved for other institutions of central administration. Local authorities are responsible for education, social welfare, local roads, health care, public transport, water and sewage systems, local culture, public order, and security. Municipalities are responsible for a majority of these tasks. Regional accounting chambers audit local authorities.

Local representatives are elected every four years. Mayors of cities and towns are elected directly, as are the members of local, county, and regional councils. County members elect the heads of *powiats (starosta)*, and members of regional assemblies elect the heads of the *voivods*. In the 16 *voivods,* elected heads (marshals) must cooperate with government-nominated *voievodas*, the national authority representatives outside Warsaw who control *gmina* resolutions by suspending them within 30 days if they contradict the law. Appeals of *voivod* decisions are filed with the regional administrative courts.

Two-thirds of councillors—elected in the 2006 elections to two levels of local councils (*gmina* and *powiat*, or town councils) and the 16 regional (*voivod*) assemblies—have no party affiliation. The strongest party representation (10 percent) is held by PSL. Among the regional councils, PO and the Lewica i Demokraci (LiD) were stronger in the more affluent, western part of Poland, and the PiS led in the poorer east and south. In cities, the incumbent mayors won easily, no matter what their political affiliation was, proving that in local elections the candidates' past record and personality counts more than party affiliation.

PiS-empowered *voievodas* with veto power over the decisions of regional assemblies, where the opposition PO has a majority of deputies, drew protests from the European Commission. Prime Minister Kaczyński promised to ask the *voievodas* to abstain from using the law and to take decisions himself. In response, the EU will not block funds allotted for Poland in the 2007–2013 timeframe (€67 billion [US$104 billion]) but may slow down their payments.[21] The same arguments figured into Education Minister Roman Giertych's decisions on EU education funds of €700 million (US$1.1 billion).[22] The most publicized example of political patronage was the allotment of €15 million (US$23.2 million) for a Torun media school run by Father Rydzyk, famous for his anti-European tirades.

The 1990 Law on Local Government introduced referenda as a tool of direct democracy on issues such as voluntary taxation for public purposes and the dismissal of local councils. At least 10 percent of voters must support the referendum motion, and it is valid with a minimum of 30 percent of voters participating. The majority of referenda, usually to recall local officials, have not rallied enough support to make it to a vote.

Municipalities are allowed to collect taxes on farms, properties, forests, pet registrations, and transportation. New taxes can be levied only via a referendum. Personal and corporate income taxes account for 75 percent of local government income. Taxes are redistributed from richer to poorer local governments.

The central government is obliged to consult local governments on every bill that may add costs to their budgets, but the time given to review budgets is often too short, and cost estimates are vague. Local self-governments must seek opinions from environmental organizations when granting building licenses, which may allow the blocking of some development plans.

Judicial Framework and Independence

1999	2001	2002	2003	2004	2005	2006	2007	2008
1.50	1.50	1.50	1.50	1.50	2.00	2.25	2.25	2.50

During 2007, the Constitutional Court repeatedly attempted to derail many of the laws already passed by the Parliament and signed by the president. In response, PiS frequently criticized the Constitutional Court as a body of political opposition, especially after the Law on Lustration decision, which the government fought to the end by slowing down the verdict's publication in the *Official Gazette*. In an attempt to avoid the Court, President Kaczyński did not send the Law on Lustration and the Law on Court Organization to the Constitutional Court, despite his own declarations about their unconstitutionality. The prime minister speculated about future Court decisions, called its past verdicts "legal circus tricks,"[23] and threatened to weaken its role. By autumn more than 20 Constitutional Court decisions were not being implemented.

Judges nominated by a majority of the National Judicial Council are appointed by the president. In 2007, for the first time, the president did not sign some of the nominations, which caused an uproar among lawyers. The 2007 law obliges the National Judicial Council to lustrate the courts, to help unify sentencing, and to prohibit all chief justices from being council members—which would eliminate 9 of its 23 members. The Constitutional Court rejected some of these changes.

As stated in the Constitution, the judiciary has full independence from the executive and legislative branches. The court system consists of the Supreme Court, 310 district courts, 43 regional courts, 11 appeals courts, 10 garrison courts plus 2 provincial military courts, 16 regional administrative courts, and the main administrative court. The Constitutional Court, elected by the lower chamber of Parliament, determines constitutional violations by the highest officials. The Constitutional Court analyzes the conformity of Polish and international laws to the Polish Constitution, adjudicates disputes of authority among central state bodies, and recognizes the temporary incapacity of the president to perform his or her office. Court decisions are final and applied directly. The *Sejm* elects Constitutional Court justices for a single nine-year term. In 2006, six vacancies were filled (all by coalition candidates).

Polish judges cannot be members of political parties or trade unions and cannot perform any public functions that might jeopardize their independence. They must be at least 29 years of age (27 for junior judges); there is no prerequisite of earlier work as prosecutors or lawyers. Judges cannot be arbitrarily dismissed or removed; however, the 2007 Law on Court Organization gives the minister of justice the right to reassign judges to different courts for six months, to arrest and strip judges of immunity in 24 hours, and to temporarily nominate a chief judge without soliciting the opinion of other judges. The head of the Supreme Court called these changes crazy and offensive; on his motion, the Constitutional Court will review the law.

Poles frequently appeal to the ECHR in Strasbourg: In January 2007, about 5,100 cases from Poland were pending in the ECHR, representing 5.7 percent of all 89,900 cases from the 46 countries of the Council of Europe to come before the Court.[24]

The computerization of Polish courts made advances in 2007. Protocols are being digitized, accessing criminal records takes two hours instead of two days, real estate records are being scanned, and courts have information pages on the Internet. In 800 halls, court procedures are audio recorded, and witness interrogations can be conducted via videoconference. However, judges are concerned about that the practice might make them susceptible to pressure from the Ministry of Justice.

Prosecutors are part of the executive branch. Experts argue that as long as the minister of justice is the attorney general, there is no chance for autonomous, non–politically motivated work by prosecutors. Before his arrest, former attorney general Janusz Kaczmarek revealed numerous examples of "hand steering" of attorneys by the minister of justice, Zbigniew Ziobro.

According to the penal procedures code, prosecutors have three months to present an indictment to the court; in practice, it takes three to four times longer than that. In the political case of lobbyist Marek Dochnal and heads of the "fuel mafia," the process took three years. Prosecutors do not have terms of office; they may be advanced or removed at any time. In the first 10 months of 2007, the minister of justice changed 10 out of 11 appeals prosecutors and half of the regional ones. Appeals by the Prosecutors' Association to "not give in to political pressure" led to an interrogation of its head, Krzysztof Parulski. In response, the leading NGO Helsinki Foundation for Human Rights called for passage of a whistle-blower's protection law.[25]

The justice minister's flagship program of 24-hour courts for petty crimes initiated in 2007 achieved little, except for costs. Other ministerial projects also failed to accomplish their goals—for instance, the attempted extradition from a Chicago prison of Edward Mazur, an American businessman of Polish descent accused of ordering the 2001 murder of a former Warsaw police chief; and Poland's attempt to gain access to Swiss bank accounts of corrupt post-Communist officials—both initiatives proved fruitless.

Corruption

1999	2001	2002	2003	2004	2005	2006	2007	2008
2.25	2.25	2.25	2.50	2.50	3.00	3.25	3.00	3.00

According to Transparency International's annual Corruption Perceptions Index (CPI), Poland is no longer the most corrupt country in the EU (following the entry of Bulgaria and Romania). In 2007, Poland's CPI rating was 4.2, while in 2006 it was 3.7 and in 2005 it was 3.4 (on a scale of 0–10, where 0 indicates highly corrupt). Transparency International acknowledges the following conditions as contributing to the lowered level of corruption in Poland: one-mandate election precincts, government officials taking responsibility for wrong decisions and delays in the decision-making process, legal definitions for conflicts of interest, anticorruption procedures in central and local governments, better quality of laws, and more transparent administration and public institutions.

However, according to Warsaw University sociologist Grzegorz Makowski, corruption is a convenient enemy for politicians to attack. They like public opinion polls, in which 90 percent of people say that corruption is overwhelming, but when asked whether they personally have ever given a bribe, less than 10 percent confirm it.[26] In fighting corruption, politicians put such a tough requirement on local council officials to produce wealth declarations that over 700 did not file them on time in 2007 and only the Constitutional Court saved these officials from losing their newly acquired posts. A PiS-proposed law would require all self-government workers, teachers, doctors, and other government employees to refuse any additional jobs, paid or nonpaid, and reveal all their property and past earnings. "Under the corruption fight banner, the government strives to watch citizens, breaking constitutional protections of privacy and freedom of assembly," notes Makowski.[27]

The much trumpeted bribery scheme involving Polish soccer tournaments, which started in 2005 and gained momentum in 2006, produced only a single court case in 2007. The two most spectacular CBA anticorruption cases ended futilely: Owing to a leak, agents failed to hand a "controlled bribe" to the deputy prime minister, which led to the arrest of the interior minister and eventually to the early elections. The second case, publicized a few days before the elections, revealed the opposition's main female member of Parliament taking a bribe from a CBA officer, which likely contributed to PiS's electoral failure, as Polish voters have been shown to dislike sting operations against political rivals.

When the laws allowing government agencies to conduct such operations were adopted, foreign experts warned that the thin line between voluntarily taking a bribe and doing it under pressure might be easily blurred by secret agents. Anticorruption expert Grażyna Kopińska stated the following: "CBA's priority should be corruption prevention, pointing out bribery-prone laws or positions in the administration, and not investigations. It does just the opposite."[28]

▌ AUTHOR: ANDRZEJ KRAJEWSKI

Andrzej Krajewski is a freelance journalist based in Warsaw, a former TVP correspondent in Washington, D.C., and a former editor in chief of Reader's Digest *Polish edition. In 2006, he worked for the Stefan Batory Foundation; in 2007, he resided in Colombo, Sri Lanka.*

[1] Ewa Siedlecka, "Kim jest Anna Fotyga? " [Who Is Anna Fotyga?], *Gazeta Wyborcza*, September 11, 2007.

[2] As an indication of Krauze's influence, see Wojciech Surmacz, "Szach cesarzowi" [Checkmate to Cesar], *Newsweek Polska*, September 9, 2007.

[3] Contrary to this opinion of Ryszard Kalisz from LiD, 52 percent of Poles believe in "conspiracy" existence, 36 percent do not: Piotr Semka, "Układ wstrząśnięty, nie zmieszany" [Conspiracy Shaken, Not Stirred], *Rzeczpospolita*, September 5, 2007.

[4] Jan Puhl, "Going West for the Good Life", *Der Spiegel* (online), March 28, 2007, http://www.spiegel.de/international/europe/0,1518,474167,00.html; and Krzysztof Cibor, "Hollow Land? On the Politicisation of Emigration from Poland", Migration Online (migrationonline.cz), http://aa.ecn.cz/img_upload/6334c0c7298d6b396d213ccd19be5999/KCibor_TheHollowLand.pdf.

[5] *2005 State Treasury Report*, Ministry of the Treasury, http://www.msp.gov.pl/index_msp.php?dzial=45&id=768.

[6] With notable exception of Jacek Żakowski. "Piraci i misjonarze" [Pirates and Missionaries], *Polityka* 5 (September 2007): 12.

[7] "Republic of Poland Pre-Term Parliamentary Elections 21 October 2007: OSCE/ODIHR Election Assessment Mission Final Report," OSCE/ODIHR, http://www.osce.org/documents/odihr/2008/03/30354_en.pdf.

8   Ibid.

9   *Bączkowski v Poland*, case 1543/06, par. 97, ECHR, May 3, 2007, http://www.statewatch. org/news/2007/may/echr-judgment-baczkowski-and-others-judgment.pdf.

10   Wojciech Sadurski, "Porządek konstytucyjny" [Constitutional Order], in Public Affairs Institute (ISP) report on state of democracy in Poland 2005–2007, www.isp.org.pl.

11   Witold Gadomski, "I ty zostaniesz oligarchą" [You Also Become an Oligarch], *Gazeta Wyborcza*, September 15–16, 2007.

12   Joanna Lichocka and Paweł Lisicki, "Wyciągam łosia z bagna" [I Am Taking Out Elk from the Swamp], interview with Jarosław Kaczyński, *Rzeczpospolita*, September 13, 2007.

13   Constitution of Republic of Poland, Article 14, http://www.sejm.gov.pl/prawo/konst/ angielski/kon1.htm.

14   "Gross przedstawił swoją wizję i ma do tego prawo, tak jak każdy autor" [Gross Presented His Version and Has a Right to That, as All Other Authors Do], Polskie Radio, http://www. polskieradio.pl/iar/wiadomosci/artykul37242.html.

15   Ireneusz C. Kamiński, "Polish Media Freedom in Law and Practice," Open Society Institute–International Policy Fellowships (OSI-IPF) Policy Paper, www.policy.hu/discus/messages/ 102/ceaserk-evalpolmedialaw.pdf; also http://www.trybunal.gov.pl/OTK/otk.htm.

16   Jarosław Kurski's interview with Donald Tusk, "Nie będzie koalicji z PIS Kaczyńskiego" [There Will Be No Coalition with Kaczyński's PiS], *Gazeta Wyborcza*, September 1–2, 2007.

17   *Television Across Europe: Regulation, Policy, and Independence*, Open Society Institute, Budapest, 2005, http://www.eumap.org.

18   All numbers are July 2007 sold copies; data from Press Distribution Control Association, https://www.teleskop.org.pl/dane_ogolnodostepne.php.

19   Andrzej Skworz, "Dojście do ściany" [Getting to Wall], interview with Tomasz Lis, *Press* monthly, January 2008.

20   Piotr Pytlakowski, "Życie na podsłuchu" [Taped Life], *Polityka*, September 1, 2007.

21   Maciej Kuźmicz and Konrad Niklewicz, "Rząd znowu chce weta" [The Government Wants The Veto Again], *Gazeta Wyborcza*, March 14, 2007.

22   Aleksandra Pezda and Maciej Kuźmicz, "Giertych myśli, że lepiej wyda miliony" [Giertych Thinks He Will Spend Millions Better], *Gazeta Wyborcza*, January 2, 2007.

23   Ewa Siedlecka, http://polishpress.wordpress.com/2007/03/14/tribunal-defends-local-council -members-and-mayors/. *Gazeta Wyborcza*, March 14, 2007, available at http://polishpress. wordpress.com/2007/03/14/tribunal-defends-local-council-members-and-mayors/.

24   See www.echr.coe.int/NR/rdonlyres/69564084-9825-430B-9150.

25   Ewa Siedlecka, "Tajemnicze śledztwo w sprawie prokuratorów" [Mysterious Investigation in Prosecutors' Case], *Gazeta Wyborcza*, July 31, 2007.

26   *Corruption Barometer*, 2007, p. 12; Stefan Batory Foundation, www.batory.org.pl, http:// www.batory.org.pl/doc/barometr-korupcji-2007.pdf.

27   Grzegorz Makowski, "Gra w czarnego luda" [Playing the Stupid], *Newsweek Polska*, September 30, 2007.

28   Krzysztof Burnetko, "Prawo i prowokacja" [Law and Provocation], *Polityka*, July 21, 2007.

Romania

by Alina Mungiu-Pippidi

Capital: Bucharest
Population: 21.7 million
GNI/capita: US$10,150

The social data above was taken from the European Bank for Reconstruction and Development's *Transition Report 2007: People in Transition*, and the economic data from the World Bank's *World Development Indicators 2008.*

Nations in Transit Ratings and Averaged Scores

	1999	2001	2002	2003	2004	2005	2006	2007	2008
Electoral Process	2.75	3.00	3.00	2.75	2.75	2.75	2.75	2.75	2.75
Civil Society	3.00	3.00	3.00	2.75	2.50	2.25	2.25	2.25	2.25
Independent Media	3.50	3.50	3.50	3.75	3.75	4.00	4.00	3.75	3.75
Governance*	3.50	3.75	3.75	3.75	3.75	n/a	n/a	n/a	n/a
National Democratic Governance	n/a	n/a	n/a	n/a	n/a	3.50	3.50	3.50	3.75
Local Democratic Governance	n/a	n/a	n/a	n/a	n/a	3.00	3.00	3.00	3.00
Judicial Framework and Independence	4.25	4.25	4.25	4.25	4.25	4.00	4.00	3.75	4.00
Corruption	4.25	4.50	4.75	4.50	4.50	4.25	4.25	4.00	4.00
Democracy Score	3.54	3.67	3.71	3.63	3.58	3.39	3.39	3.29	3.36

* With the 2005 edition, Freedom House introduced separate analysis and ratings for national democratic governance and local democratic governance to provide readers with more detailed and nuanced analysis of these two important subjects.

NOTE: The ratings reflect the consensus of Freedom House, its academic advisers, and the author(s) of this report. The opinions expressed in this report are those of the author(s). The ratings are based on a scale of 1 to 7, with 1 representing the highest level of democratic progress and 7 the lowest. The Democracy Score is an average of ratings for the categories tracked in a given year.

EXECUTIVE SUMMARY

Romania joined the European Union (EU) on January 1, 2007, having come a long way from Nicolae Ceauşescu's dictatorship. Its evolution is all the more remarkable considering it was the only Eastern European country with a bloody revolution (1,000 dead in still unclear circumstances) and a transition dominated by former Communists. Ion Iliescu, a reformed apparatchik with authoritarian tendencies, enjoyed three out of the first four presidential mandates. As there was no organized opposition under Ceauşescu's harsh regime, the challenger elite has had significant difficulty providing a viable political alternative.

In 2007, Romania had barely entered the EU when its political class started to undo the commitments undertaken to allow the country's accession. In the realm of anticorruption, matters worsened to the point that two deputy prime ministers resigned in one year, and most of the political class mobilized to change the legislation to decrease the power of prosecutors. The government even attempted to close down the National Anticorruption Directorate, Romania's independent anticorruption agency. A vicious fight erupted between the president and the Parliament, culminating in an attempt to impeach President Traian Băsescu. A real split between representatives and voters emerged when two-thirds of Parliament voted to have Băsescu deposed and two-thirds of the voters reinstated him in a referendum on May 19.

National Democratic Governance. In Romania, 2007 was a year of political instability, as the Parliament tried to impeach the president, despite a negative *avis* from the Constitutional Court. Voters later reinstated him in a referendum. The government continued to legislate by using emergency ordinances even after EU accession, when urgent need could no longer be pleaded. Other bad practices returned to the Romanian central government, from discretionary allocation of funds to special destination bills. *For these reasons, Romania's national democratic governance rating worsens from 3.50 to 3.75.*

Electoral Process. In 2007, Romania held its first European Parliament elections and two referenda, one for the impeachment of the president and another for the change of the voting system. All ballots were surrounded by important legal battles for influence, but once the rules of the game had been settled by the Constitutional Court, which played a major referee role in 2007, no irregularities were reported on voting days. *However, chronic problems with the potential to generate irregularities persisted and were not properly addressed by Romania's authorities (for instance, incomplete distribution of voter cards and unfinished correction of electoral lists); therefore, Romania's electoral process rating remains at 2.75.*

Romania ∎ 453

Civil Society. Romanian civil society showed signs of vulnerability both financially and politically in 2007. Attempts by politicians to corrupt or intimidate civil society were on the rise. *Despite real vibrancy in some sectors, and continuous potential to generate new coalitions on various topics, the influence of economic and political pressures on civil society continues to be significant; thus, the civil society rating remains at 2.25.*

Independent Media. The trend toward concentration of media ownership continued in 2007, with content still influenced by blackmail and defamation campaigns of every kind. The Romanian public television's news department again came under political attack with the change of the government coalition. On the positive side, Romania recorded for the first time the resignation of a reputed journalist owing to such practices, as well as some prosecutions of journalists for corruption. *By and large, there were no significant developments compared with the previous year, so the rating for independent media remains at 3.75.*

Local Democratic Governance. Decentralization made little progress in 2007 in Romania, despite the existence of new legislation. A new electoral law provides for county council heads to be elected directly, opening the door to increased legitimacy for regional government. Despite an increase in the discretionary allocation of funds from the central government, the public perceives Romanian local governments to be the most trusted and effective tier of government. *As there were no substantial developments compared with the previous year, the rating for local democratic governance remains at 3.00.*

Judicial Framework and Independence. The year marked a step back in the reform of the Romanian judiciary. After the February 2007 dismissal of Justice Minister Monica Macovei, trusted by both the public and the European Commission, her successor attempted without success to fire an anticorruption prosecutor and to close down the National Anticorruption Directorate. The prosecutors, who were protected by the magistrates' self-governing bodies, continued to indict top politicians; by autumn 2007, nine ministers of the government had been investigated. *Despite the good show of will by magistrates, repeated attempts of the government and some members of Parliament to subordinate the judiciary and terminate anticorruption investigations against politicians were a constant threat to the independence of the judiciary; thus, the rating for judicial framework and independence deteriorates from 3.75 to 4.00.*

Corruption. Romania's anticorruption activity remained high throughout 2007, with central and regional offices of the National Anticorruption Directorate indicting many key figures in Romania's political and business community. This activity, however, only exposed the weaknesses of the central government and its lack of will to continue anticorruption efforts after the departure of Minister Macovei. Ministers were recorded accepting bribes, and had to resign, once exposed. Courts are hesitant to decide major corruption cases and prefer procedurally motivated postponements. The media have continued to play a positive role in exposing corruption cases, and the public is well aware of the problem. Despite the strong counter-offensive of politicians to aggressive anticorruption campaigns, prosecutors backed by President Traian Băsescu, seemed intent on continuing Minister Macovei's work. *As these two divergent tendencies are quite balanced currently, the rating for corruption remains at 4.00.*

Outlook for 2008. In 2008, Romania will hold local and legislative elections that will include several firsts. Heads of county councils will be elected directly for the first time, which will strengthen the local tier of political parties and empower local politicians. Second, legislative and presidential elections for the first time will not run simultaneously, following a 2003 constitutional modification that lengthened the mandate of the president from four to five years. As the Romanian Constitution demands that a president be politically neutral, this de-synchronization is expected to boost the importance of party platform over leaders. However, the third positive step is that legislators will be elected in single-unit constituencies on the basis of a mixed electoral system, which will fragment the electoral campaign and craft party messages for local constituencies. Great expectations exist that these reforms will curb political corruption. What is more likely is that political parties will be further fragmented and undisciplined, with huge competition over public funds. The Liberal Democratic Party (*Partidul Liberal Democrat*, PLD), the president's party, is expected to win the elections, but not the absolute majority. As PLD's coalition potential is rather limited, Băsescu, who has the constitutional right to appoint the prime minister, will have to display strong skills as a political broker to hold together a majority government.

Main Report

National Democratic Governance

1999	2001	2002	2003	2004	2005	2006	2007	2008
n/a	n/a	n/a	n/a	n/a	3.50	3.50	3.50	3.75

Romania became a full member of the European Union (EU) on January 1, 2007. The accession treaty made clear that if there were serious shortcomings in the transposition and implementation of the EU *acquis* regarding the economy, domestic market, or justice system, then "safeguard measures" would be implemented for up to three years. Romania's accession was also accompanied by specific measures to prevent or remedy shortcomings in both judicial reform and the fight against corruption. For the past two years, a cooperation and verification mechanism had been in place to benchmark progress in this area. The purpose of this unprecedented mechanism was to assure Romanians and other EU member states that administrative, legislative, and judicial practices in Romania were in line with the rest of the EU. This entitled the European Commission to closely monitor Romania's progress or lack of progress in these areas. However, this strong EU conditionality did not prevent Romania from sliding back into old habits immediately after accession, including issues with corruption and an ongoing conflict between Prime Minister Calin Popescu Tăriceanu and President Traian Băsescu.

Romania is a semi-presidential republic. The president is directly elected by the voters but has limited powers, which include overseeing defense and foreign policy and appointing (but not dismissing) the prime minister. President Băsescu and Prime Minister Tăriceanu began as allies in the Truth and Justice Alliance formed by the Democratic Party (*Partidul Democrat*, PD) and the National Liberal Party (*Partidul Național Liberal*, PNL), but they fell out over Băsescu's wish to call early elections in order to secure a larger majority. (He appointed Tăriceanu in 2004 for the same reason). This divergence over tactics led to more serious disagreements, and coalition infighting gradually turned unmanageable.

Tăriceanu in turn began seeking parliamentary majorities backed by the opposition rather than the PD, while Băsescu started to evoke his constitutional powers to organize direct consultations in order to push his own agenda. Members of Parliament (MPs), fearful that the president might initiate constitutional reforms of the presidency and electoral system, reacted promptly by focusing on the referendum law, which sparked legal battles in the Constitutional Court and a war between Băsescu and the parliamentary majority. Tăriceanu eliminated his former PD allies and completed his government with more liberals and a junior ally, the Democratic Union of Hungarians in Romania (*Uniunea Democrată Maghiară din România*, UDMR). This minority government, through negotiations within Parliament, survived two no-confidence votes in 2007 and was frequently at odds with the president.

One of the chief characteristics of Romanian political life is that the country's history haunts its present. The phenomenon of digging into the past to level accusations against former Securitate "collaborators" continues to capture public attention and, to a large extent, corrodes the country's transformation and impedes progress. Following the elimination of the PD in March, the Parliament appointed a special committee to investigate alleged abuses of the Constitution by President Băsescu. Dan Voiculescu, president of the Conservative Party (*Partidul Conservator*, PC), chaired the committee. President Băsescu's past included a position as head of Nicolae Ceaușescu's Romanian foreign trade office in Antwerp. Voiculescu, now one of Romania's leading media tycoons, once worked for Dunarea, another Ceaușescu-era former foreign trade enterprise. As it turned out, the Council for the Study of the Securitate Archives (CNSAS), the authority screening the Communist archives, reported that Voiculescu also worked for Ceaușescu's secret service—another ember from Romania's past that continues to fuel political fires.

The special committee's report on Băsescu's alleged constitutional infringements was sent to the Constitutional Court to receive an *avis*. The Court ruled that there was no proof of a serious breach of the Constitution but on April 19 the majority of MPs voted for his suspension. A two-thirds majority (322) of MPs cast their vote to impeach Băsescu, with 108 against and 10 abstentions.[1] Nicolae Văcăroiu, the head of the Senate, became interim head of state. The Constitution, however, gave voters the right to directly sanction this decision in a referendum after a one-month campaign.

MPs tried to modify the referendum law to curb the president's constitutional powers. As Romania had elections for the European Parliament scheduled for May, the Parliament ruled that a referendum could not be organized three months before or after elections. The Parliament also ruled that a president can be dismissed with a majority of voters present if he was elected in the second round, but if he was elected from the first round with an absolute majority, then a majority from the absolute number of votes is required for dismissal. Additionally, the government rushed through an emergency ordinance to restrict the topics on which the president can call a referendum, excluding all constitutional matters.

Another amendment reversed an earlier decision that referendums are valid regardless of turnout (as elections in Romania fail to draw an absolute majority turnout, referendums are even less able to mobilize people). This meant that Băsescu could have remained impeached indefinitely if an absolute majority did not turn out to vote at the referendum. The Constitutional Court was overwhelmed in the space of a few weeks with motions contesting these amendments, and despite having a majority of members with Social Democratic Party (*Partidul Social Democrat*, PSD) ties, the Court overruled most of these initiatives as unconstitutional. The government postponed the European elections, declaring that the referendum on impeachment, which was held on May 19, would unnecessarily confuse voters.

The already weak policy formulation process in Romania underwent further degradation in 2007. The lack of a majority in Parliament meant that every bill had to be negotiated with each MP. Despite Romania's EU-sponsored department for policy formulation, legislative proposals reach Parliament that do not satisfy even minimal requirements. In an extraordinary blunder, the Parliament adopted a law increasing pensions even though Romania's pay-as-you-go system was already overstretched. The bill was rejected by the government and the parliamentary committee in charge of finance (led by an PSD politician), yet it reached the plenum and was adopted instantly.

The 2008 budget is for the first time based on the optimistic expectation that tax collection will improve. By the end of 2007, Romania had missed its inflation target and was downgraded for the first time in years by rating agencies like Standard & Poor's. Nevertheless, the Tăriceanu government survived two no-confidence votes. The last was initiated by the PSD, the largest opposition party, but it failed owing to defections within the party and with its PD partner.

The Tăriceanu government issued 130 emergency ordinances in 2007. These are laws applied immediately after their promulgation by the government, prior to their parliamentary approval. The practice is problematic because it further delays the Parliament's legislative backlog in which ordinances are delayed for months or sometimes years and frequently must undergo significant modifications before being brought for approval; thus creating continuous legal instability. As most of Romania's important legislation continued to be passed in this manner, even after the country's EU accession, the result is extremely confusing for legal practitioners.

Numerous proposals emerged in 2007 to amend the Constitution to allow a reshaping of Romania's executive. These proposals tended to be maximalist in nature (some argued for the restoration of the monarchy, for full American-style presidentialism, or for full parliamentarianism, giving up direct election of the president). Any constitutional modification must be approved by two-thirds of the joint chambers and by a popular vote. However, such proposals are unlikely to advance given the strict process for amending the Constitution and Romania's political environment, where productive dialogue and the capacity to compromise are in short supply.

Electoral Process

1999	2001	2002	2003	2004	2005	2006	2007	2008
2.75	3.00	3.00	2.75	2.75	2.75	2.75	2.75	2.75

On May 19, 2007, a solid 74 percent of Romanians voted against the impeachment of President Traian Băsescu. The Audio-Visual Council ruled that broadcasting time during the campaign was not divided equally among the "yes" and "no" camps but mirrored the proportion that political parties currently enjoyed in Parliament.

The European parliamentary elections were postponed from May to November 25. The electoral campaign was dominated by news that Romania's uncontrolled migration to Italy before and after EU accession (650,000 Romanians having moved to Italy over the last four years) had started to generate a negative reaction triggered by increased criminality—from petty begging to armed robberies.

There was no observable debate on European issues among politicians or the public during the year, yet a survey of political parties by the Romanian Academic Society showed political positions typical of the "new Europe," with an abundance of parties in the center-right camp (that is, Liberals, Liberal Democrats, Democrats, and Hungarian Democrats). The PSD positioned itself somewhat more to the left but also quite close to the center on economic issues. The small PLD declared itself against the current foreign and security policies. In total, 35 European MPs were elected by universal proportional suffrage, with an electoral threshold of 5 percent. Turnout was 29 percent. The PD came first with 32 percent, followed by the PSD with 21 percent, the PNL with 15 percent, and the PLD with 7 percent.

During his spring contest with MPs, Băsescu began to speak about a self-serving "political class" insensitive to voters' needs as the paramount problem in Romania.[2] The lack of integrity and professionalism of politicians, he said, was responsible for impeding Romania's successful European integration following its accession on January 1. Băsescu declared that ordinary people stood no chance of seeing any benefit from European funds under these circumstances where special interest groups ruled. Returning to the civil society language he had used in the 2004 campaign (and then dropped), he called for a "cleaning" of politics and politicians.

On the one hand, he encouraged prosecutors to continue corruption investigations against top politicians. On the other, he proposed changing the electoral system with the adoption of a single-unit constituency system, so that voters could easily trace responsibility to their MP. This topic has been debated for years, with unions and nongovernmental organizations (NGOs) collecting signatures for such a reform. In reality, NGOs lobbied for a uni-nominal system that could have been based either on a majority (simple or absolute) or on proportionality (within single constituencies). Băsescu himself had always been skeptical, but in February he defied the Parliament to adopt such legislation.

Parties have long competed for such a reform, despite the lack of evidence that irregularities are more closely related to proportional voting list systems. Several competitive projects have emerged in the Parliament, including the PSD proposal for a double-ballot majority vote (two rounds in a single constituency), which is already used in Romania to directly elect mayors. This system has the advantage of creating clear majorities and pushing parties into alliances between the two rounds (when a candidate does not win an absolute majority outright). Some cite a lack of representativeness as a disadvantage of this system. A second proposal (from the NGO ProDemocracy and supported by parties from the Truth and Justice Alliance) featured a mixed system. A third proposal allowed different systems for the Assembly and the Senate. Hungarians tended to oppose all three proposals, as any step away from proportionality threatens a reduced representation for this strong minority, which generally mobilizes its voters effectively and participates in government coalitions as minor partners.

President Băsescu set a summer deadline for the Parliament, but by the end of the session in July, MPs had not yet agreed on a project. The committee in charge of electoral legislation finally offered a version of the NGO proposal where half of the MPs would be elected from the first round, regardless of turnout, in single-unit constituencies. According to the parties' national performance, the other half of the seats would be distributed proportionally to losers in the first round. Although the system was inferior in terms of legitimacy to the current simple proportional formula (parties meeting the 5 percent threshold get seats proportional to votes), it preserved a strong proportional element. The proposal's potential to reform political parties is ambiguous, as few candidates would achieve absolute majorities and thus benefit from the direct gain of a seat.

Nevertheless, the Parliament did not approve the plan until Băsescu announced he would call a referendum to consult voters on the double-ballot system. The government then sent the proposal to Parliament in a procedure known as "assuming responsibility," where Parliament cannot vote against a bill without bringing down the government. As MPs feared the prospect of early elections, the government's project passed. Still, Băsescu announced the referendum and scheduled it for the same day as elections for the European Parliament. The Greater Romanian Party filed a motion to the Constitutional Court, but the Court ruled in line with its previous decisions, declaring there was no constitutional impediment to prevent two simultaneous ballots.

President Băsescu stated that he would not promulgate the government's bill until Romanian citizens had expressed their will by way of a referendum, and the fight over the voting system was the last of a series of fierce struggles between Băsescu and Prime Minister Tăriceanu in 2007. An absolute majority was needed but (predictably) not reached on November 25, when only 26.5 percent of voters showed up for the referendum. The "yes" vote came to 81.3 percent against a "no" vote of just 16.1 percent. One of the strategies of "no" supporters was to boycott the vote so as to invalidate the process.

Civil Society

1999	2001	2002	2003	2004	2005	2006	2007	2008
3.00	3.00	3.00	2.75	2.50	2.25	2.25	2.25	2.25

Owing to the intensity of political conflict in Romania, few prominent NGOs managed to keep an independent position in 2007. However, in the autumn a coalition of groups, including some trade unions, monitored the integrity of candidates for the European Parliament under the banner of the Romanian Coalition for a Clean Parliament. Otherwise, the general lack of funding, un- cooperative behavior of the government, and new defections of civil society activists into politics diminished the watchdog potential of civil society. Notoriously vocal Romanian NGOs, such as the Group for Social Dialogue and the Timisoara Society, lost their headquarters that had been rented from municipalities and had serious difficulties securing new offices.

Still other organizations have long courted public funds and worked in close partnership with government agencies, whose friendliness has been needed in order to access EU money. The list is long and includes NGOs that started out as government watchdogs. In a typical scenario, NGOs strongly criticize public agencies and then offer contractual services to remedy the situation. Political parties try to recruit intellectuals and civil society activists to stand as candidates for elections to the European Parliament. Renate Weber, former president of Romania's Soros Foundation, after years of work as an independent civil society activist, became a candidate for the European Parliament with the PNL.

Major businesspersons sponsor soccer clubs, which often thrive on fiscal evasion and are pursued in various courts by tax authorities. Sponsorship legislation is poor and outdated, and there are few attempts to revive it. Donations from the 2 percent deductible income tax category increased significantly as compared with 2006, but the total remains a meager €5 million (US$7.7 million) for all types of NGOs. The Foundation for Development of Civil Society, a resource center for NGOs created during Romania's EU accession, is lobbying to preserve funds for civil society, but the issue is still unresolved. While many incoming EU funds create opportunities for NGOs that act as service providers, the funds are distributed to the government at each tier (central, regional, local), so NGOs only have access through partnerships with authorities.

An institution with a brave record of political correctness in 2007 was the Romanian National Antidiscrimination Council (RNAC), an official agency whose members are independent and belong to various NGOs. The RNAC intervened in a dispute where a teacher sued a school over the excessive presence of Byzantine icons. In a wave of response, print and TV editorialists argued that it is crucial for Romania to safeguard its Christian Orthodox identity in the year of its accession to the "Catholic and Protestant" Europe. The Ministry of Education at first sided with the plaintiff but later shifted toward public opinion. The RNAC, whose powers include offering consultative opinions and issuing fines, ruled that the posting of Christian icons in public schools constituted discrimination toward students of other religions as well as nonbelievers. The ministry appealed the decision, and a populist politician and soccer club owner, George Becali, publicly insulted the RNAC head.

In a second decision, the RNAC fined President Băsescu when he called a journalist a "stinking Gypsy."[3] [The comment was captured on video on the journalist's cellular phone, which had been confiscated after the journalist refused to stop recording. Unwittingly, the video function remained engaged and recorded the private exchange between Băsescu and his wife; when the president later returned the phone to the journalist, with his apologies, the journalist found the recording and made it public. Likewise, Minister of Foreign Affairs Adrian Cioroianu made a verbal slip, saying Roma who committed crimes in EU countries should be sent to a camp in the Egyptian desert and he was similarly pursued by the RNAC.[4]

During 2007, the country's various public voices showed a lack of preparedness for joining the wider European discourse. Politics aside, the public sphere was dominated by identity debates highlighting Romania's apprehensions about "secular Europe." Many intellectuals in Romanian public life are practicing Orthodox Christians; in addition there is a growing attitude of bigotry and nationalism in the country. The general tone of public discussion in the media is often offensive to one group or another. Defenders of political correctness are few and generally come from professional civil society, thus carrying little credibility with the wider public, which appears to greatly enjoy the rough language from Băsescu and Becali. The expulsion of some Romanian Roma from Italy by the end of 2007 provoked a new round of identity debates and new expressions of racism, somewhat moderated by regulators like the Audio-Visual Council and RNAC.

Independent Media

1999	2001	2002	2003	2004	2005	2006	2007	2008
3.50	3.50	3.50	3.75	3.75	4.00	4.00	3.75	3.75

In 2007, Romanian media were increasingly concentrated in the hands of a few owners. Of the 12 Romanian dailies, 3 are owned by Swiss media corporation Ringier AG, 2 by Adrian Sarbu (who, in autumn 2007, became chief operating officer of Central European Media Enterprises), 2 by the politician and businessman Dan Voiculescu's family, 2 by the oil tycoon Dinu Patriciu, and 2 by investment fund manager Sorin Ovidiu Vântu. Vântu now owns 14 publications, 3 television stations, a radio station, and a news agency. Sarbu owns 5 television stations alongside 2 national dailies and a network of local newspapers. The Voiculescu family owns 3 television stations, 2 dailies, and several other smaller outlets. Ringier is the only important foreign company to enter the Romanian media market. There were 8 unaffiliated dailies two years ago; now there are only 2.

Corruption in the Romanian media, or *kompromat* (to borrow the Russian term), continues to be the main problem within the press. "Black and gray" PR has turned into a profitable industry in its own right. Full campaigns are funded against political or business opponents, and few newspapers are completely protected from such deals. During the campaign for the patriarchy of the Romanian Orthodox Church, for instance, newspapers lent their support to certain candidates and published defamatory materials against others. Even *Evenminentul Zilei*, Ringier's main quality newspaper, published an article describing the brother of the would-be patriarch Daniel as a secret service officer and a thief. The newspaper later reported on the election of Daniel without mentioning the claims of the earlier piece. Oligarchs under investigation for corruption devote generous space in their media outlets to insult-laden fights against magistrates. During his impeachment process, President Băsescu was criticized on most TV channels and accused of being a dictator threatening Romanian democracy.

The main political pressure in 2007 was on the Romanian public television outlet, SRTV, which includes the four channels TVR1, TVR2, TVR Cultural, and TVRi. During the highly sensitive period before the referendum on President Băsescu in May, tensions mounted between TVR general manager Tudor Giurgiu and TVR news director Rodica Culcer. The press and the opposition had criticized Culcer for her outspoken support of Băsescu during his 2004 election campaign, but her work as TVR news director had generally been praised. The administrative regulations of TVR are protective of employees, and Culcer refused to step down. In the meantime, Giurgiu lost the favor of the government and resigned on May 4, 2007. His replacement was Alexandru Sassu, proposed by the PSD. Like Giurgiu before him, Sassu tried to preside directly over newsroom meetings, replaced all producers, appointed Madalina Radulescu as news director and denied President Băsescu the right to appear on television to promote his referendum. There was only a weak show of solidarity among Romanian media and civil society for the TVR journalists.

Local Democratic Governance

1999	2001	2002	2003	2004	2005	2006	2007	2008
n/a	n/a	n/a	n/a	n/a	3.00	3.00	3.00	3.00

Of the 113 amendments to the electoral reform bill proposed by MPs in 2007, the government included 23 in the final version. The most important was the PSD proposal that heads of county councils should also be directly elected by majority ballot, which has the potential to overhaul regional politics and open the door to significant changes in Romania's administrative organization.

The importance of the county council grew rapidly during the years it functioned as the main relay in the fiscal decentralization process. Most funds from the central budget were traditionally distributed to county councils, which then had a large say over their distribution to communes and towns. This mechanism was curtailed by new legislation starting in 2004. County council presidents play a key role in the distribution of European funds. Most EU funds in 2006 were distributed by regional development boards, where the majority of county council heads have decisive power. This led to continuous struggles among parties to control this office. Normally, the county head is elected by the council following local elections (councils themselves are elected proportionally). As local elections in 2004 preceded general ones, and the electorate was split over Left and Right, in many counties forging a majority was extremely difficult. The situation was further complicated by squabbles and shifts of the majority within the government alliance. In many counties, this led to reelection of the county heads and continuous bargaining among parties over most projects.

Political migration was prohibited by law in 2006, but even where formal migration has not taken place, there has been instability and fluctuation on county councils. In many counties, the majority is not so much a political but a business majority, bargained among the actors with the strongest economic interests in the county. It is difficult for any company not networked to the political majority to win a county project, and mayors are continually pressed to switch parties in order to fulfill their promises (and be reelected). County heads are popularly called "local barons" and have emerged as real influence brokers in national politics. A rising star of the PSD, Liviu Dragnea, managed his considerable advance in the party from his position as president of the powerful association of county councils.

The direct election of county heads is not altogether a bad idea. It empowers citizens to vote out corrupt local characters and motivates county heads to invest in popular projects. It could provide stability instead of the current continuous bargaining and fluctuation. However, the idea was opposed by President Băsescu. As the twice former directly-elected mayor of Bucharest, Băsescu struggled in vain with a local council that maintained a different political majority and followed its own project agenda. In light of the power distribution in the current legislation, it is likely that regional bargaining would be followed by regional deadlock once county heads have a different constituency from that of the council members. Although Băsescu vowed not to promulgate the government's electoral reform bill until his referendum was held—and had not done so by year end 2007, he might be forced to accept it in the end, opening the door to new developments.

The decentralization legal package adopted in 2006 was not followed by real implementation, and mayors of smaller administrative units often faced shortages of funds owing to irregular transfers from the central government. Ministers were assigned the priority of proposing decentralization programs in their respective fields (for instance, education or the police), but no serious steps were undertaken in the last years. The influx of funds to the budget owing to Romania's positive economic growth offered the government resources to, in essence, return to bad practices. Despite the adoption in 2003 of clear criteria for distributing funds to subnational government, new programs were created by ministries to distribute by political criteria, especially to counties or mayors from the government party. Even mandatory payments from the central budget have at times been manipulated—for instance, penalizing schools in opposition counties by transferring maintenance funds late in the summer to leave schools unprepared for the coming academic year. Despite an increase in local budgets in 2007, the practice of discretionary allocation is a step back toward previous years.

There were other steps back in local governance during the year. Despite turning prefects into civil servants at the EU's request (formerly they were politically appointed), the Democrat prefects were fired once the government coalition split. This EU requirement was intended to prevent the politicization of prefects, but it failed completely. To avoid lawsuits by fired civil servants, which are generally won, the government offered other positions in the administration at a similar level. This strategy added to the growing group of tenured administrators who are politically appointed rather than hired through the professional training channels created for civil servants, such as the National Institute for Administration.

Judicial Framework and Independence

1999	2001	2002	2003	2004	2005	2006	2007	2008
4.25	4.25	4.25	4.25	4.25	4.00	4.00	3.75	4.00

In the immediate aftermath of Romania's accession to the EU in January, the battle began against Justice Minister Monica Macovei and anticorruption measures agreed upon with the European Commission. An ordinance meant to bring the powers of the Department to Counter International Organized Criminality and Terrorism (DIICOT) in line with the rest of the Office of the Prosecutor General was met with hostility from the general secretariat of the government, MPs, and the media. A provision in the ordinance allowing prosecutors to see telephone and e-mail lists without a warrant was considered particularly offensive. In the midst of the battle, the Senate voted on a motion against Minister Macovei, proclaiming justice reform a "failure."

As EU institutions considered Macovei a trusted minister[5] the motion was postponed until after Romania's accession. So on February 13, slightly more than a month following EU accession, 81 senators, including both governing and opposition members, voted to dismiss Macovei. The Romanian Parliament, however, may dismiss a minister only by dismissing the entire cabinet. The no-confidence motion in a minister is therefore constitutionally a "simple" motion whose result is not binding on the prime minister. The phrasing of the motion was particularly embarrassing for Romania, as it was for all intents and purposes an inventory of legislation passed to make the country acceptable to Brussels. As public opinion sided with Macovei, who also enjoyed huge support from international media and European institutions, she was not dismissed outright. Negotiations and pressures dragged on for weeks, with the European Commissioner for Justice Franco Frattini making public statements in Macovei's favor.[6] As ministers from the PD did not agree to continue without her, and the opposition threatened to bring down the whole government, the Truth and Justice Alliance eventually collapsed and all PD ministers were dismissed, including Macovei, who was succeeded by Tudor Chiuariu of the PNL as the new justice minister.

The departure of the minister for internal affairs, Vasile Blaga, was a second blow to the European Commission, as he had been the other most effective minister in transposing the European *acquis*. Blaga was replaced by Christian David of the PNL.

The Romanian justice system and the government's anticorruption efforts remained under close EU monitoring even after accession and were evaluated against a number of benchmarks set by the European Commission. The existence of this mechanism explains the puzzling behavior of the Romanian government, whose MPs frequently joined opposition MPs in 2007 in their reluctance to fulfill commitments to the EU (especially those calling for greater political accountability and increased powers to magistrates) but later had to promulgate ordinances to this effect (sometimes retrospectively), fearing that the safeguard mechanism would be activated otherwise. The result was continual confusion, resulting in a lack of legislative implementation.

In an ostensible effort to advance reform of the criminal and civil codes in 2007, Parliament began a review of newly-proposed procedures for the criminal code, which earlier had been posted for public debate on the Justice Ministry site under Minister Macovei. U.S. and British ambassadors, as well as the Romanian media and former minister Macovei, accused MPs of changing the bill to make the prosecution of corruption more difficult. Among the new practices introduced by MPs were notifying suspects in advance of domestic searches and identifying the precise object of the search, notifying suspects of wiretapping, and closing criminal investigations if they exceeded a length of six months. These provisions would make it impossible for Romania not only to prosecute domestic corruption, but also to cooperate effectively in international investigations of terrorism and organized crime.

The capacity of Romania's Superior Council of Magistrates (SCM) to ensure both accountability and control of magistrates has been one of the main concerns of the European Commission. Although it notes some progress, the European Commission also stated that "the accountability and ethical standards of the Council and its individual members remain issues of concern. The same applies for the potential conflicts of interest of the SCM members." Romanian civil society also complains about the lack of transparency of the SCM. In an open letter, magistrate associations as well as watchdog NGOs deplored the fact that SCM meeting agendas are not made public, despite the existence of a law to that effect. They also offered a number of proposals to improve SCM transparency, including observing a three-day advance posting of meeting agendas on the SCM Web site and publication of minutes or ex officio communication of meeting transcripts. In 2007, EU and U.S. diplomats attended important SCM meetings to assist the passage of crucial reform bills during the accession transition. Though still weak, with inspectors inherited from the Communist era and plagued by conflicts of interest, the SCM did make some progress in 2007 and was helped by an unprecedented endorsement from national and international public opinion for the protection of magistrates from political interventions.

Still, the quality of Romanian courts remains poor, and verdicts are seldom predictable. The European Commission, whose experts reviewed prosecutor files as part of the monitoring mechanism, was so puzzled by the frequent refusals to begin top-level corruption trials on various procedural grounds that it ruled to launch an investigation. In a defiant response, the Romanian High Court of Justice and Cassation stated that the EU is not allowed to interfere with the business of the Romanian judiciary.

Ironically, quality does not evolve with hierarchy in the Romanian judiciary, and sometimes the reverse is true. Most judges recruited after 1989 are still in the lower courts. Appeals courts and the Supreme Court are staffed by many Communist-era senior magistrates. Attempts to appoint heads of courts on the basis of open competition have, so far, failed. In the upper-level courts most of the magistrates are political appointees from before 2005, and some have records of integrity that are, at best, controversial.

Corruption

1999	2001	2002	2003	2004	2005	2006	2007	2008
4.25	4.50	4.75	4.50	4.50	4.25	4.25	4.00	4.00

There were serious setbacks in Romania's anticorruption effort in 2007. In March—barely three months after it joined the EU—the Romanian government attempted to remove Monica Macovei, an independent justice minister who had shaken up the structure and accountability of the judiciary and the prosecutor's office in order to attack corruption head-on. Investigations by the National Anticorruption Directorate (DNA) had begun to reach the top levels of Romanian politics. In 2006, Deputy Prime Minister George Copos from the Conservative Party resigned under charges of corruption. In 2007, the same situation threatened Deputy Prime Minister Markó Béla, head of the Democratic Alliance of Hungarians (DAHR), and the ministers of economics and communications (members of the PNL and DAHR.

Tudor Chiuariu, member of the PNL, was named Macovei's successor. Romanian media voiced concern that PNL politicians would try to influence investigations concerning their party. Indeed, soon after his appointment Minister Chiuariu asked the head of the DNA, Daniel Morar, to put on hold criminal investigations of top politicians until the political struggle against President Băsescu and his referendum were finalized. This telephone conversation between them was witnessed by an official from the Anticorruption Department within the Ministry of Justice, who later resigned in protest.

By autumn 2007, nine ministers were under investigation by the DNA, but procedural snags held up all high-level corruption cases, and Minister Chiuariu had tried to fire anticorruption prosecutor Doru Țuluș for investigating his political sponsors. Most of the files concerning current and former dignitaries were investigated by Țuluș, who had already indicted eight MPs; in August, Minister Chiuariu announced Țuluș's dismissal. Under the ensuing public outrage, Chiuariu postponed his decision to rally support from the SCM, parliamentary members, the president of the Senate, the PNL, the tabloid media, and so forth. The final report brought no serious evidence justifying the dismissal of Țuluș, especially since the European Commission's May report had praised the DNA. The prosecutors' section of the SCM therefore voted against Minister Chiuariu, who was the only member to vote in favor of Ţuluş's dismissal.

For the first time in Romania, magistrates mobilized to defend the independence of the judiciary. About 60 DNA prosecutors, the National Union of Judges, and four other legal professional associations expressed their disapproval of the inappropriate way in which the minister of justice tried to remove DNA prosecutors from office. Following his request to dismiss Doru Ţuluş, the National Institute of Magistracy, the only body authorized to train magistrates, sent a letter to Justice Minister Chiuariu calling off an invitation to take part in a meeting with justice auditors. A few Ministry of Justice officials resigned in protest.

Politicians have continually tried to control the DNA's activity by modifying its legal status or scaling back legal anticorruption instruments. A new law was passed in late March 2007 decriminalizing certain aspects of bank fraud previously under the jurisdiction of the DNA. The law is likely to be applied retroactively to bank officers who received kickbacks for granting illegitimate loans, which will lead to the dismissal of numerous pending cases at the DNA. In October, an emergency ordinance initiated by Minister Chiuariu closed the advisory commission on the prosecution of current and former ministers. According to the Law of Ministerial Responsibility passed in 2005, this commission advised the president on the lifting of the immunity of cabinet members charged by the DNA. A Constitutional Court decision of 2007 extended its authority also over former ministers, answering an appeal by former prime minister Adrian Năstase. In the new formula proposed by the ordinance, investigation of former ministers would require parliamentary approval, and the advisory commission would comprise magistrates and would hear cases prior to the first instance The Constitutional Court ruled in the end that it was unconstitutional, but all investigations concerning current and former ministers had de facto been stopped for several months.

Romanian courts are extremely cautious in cases concerning top politicians and generally use any pretext to pass the decision to another court. While the European Commission praised the activity of anticorruption prosecutors, it also noted in its 2007 report that rigor in prosecution is not mirrored by judicial decisions. An analysis of sentences in corruption cases shows that penalties are typically not decisive, and in many cases of high-level corruption, judges grant suspended penalties. The European Commission expressed concern that this undermines recent progress in investigations and negatively affects public perception of the political commitment to tackle corruption. The public is exasperated that despite increased prosecutorial activity, courts do not bring cases to closure, and the level of corruption was perceived to have risen again in 2007. Transparency International rates Romania as the most corrupt EU member country.

Politicians investigated by the DNA invariably claim that these efforts constitute a political witch hunt.[7] A review of cases shows that no party was spared. Former PSD president Adrian Năstase was tried for accepting bribes, blackmail, and influence peddling; Şerban Mihăilescu (MP from PSD and former minister secretary general of the Romanian government) was tried for accepting bribes in the form of cash and hunting rifles; Ioan Stan (MP from PSD) was under investigation for exercising undue influence as a party leader; Miron Mitrea (MP from PSD and former minister of transport) was indicted for accepting bribes. Other MPs and PSD-affiliated mayors are also facing indictment. From the Democratic Party, the DNA charged Gheorghe Falcă (mayor of Arad and godson of President Băsescu) with accepting bribes and abuse of office; Ionel Manțog (former secretary of state) with accepting bribes and abuse of office; Stelian Duțu (MP) with abuse of office; Cosmin Popescu (former secretary of state) with intellectual forgery and helping a criminal; and other mayors and lower-ranked politicians with similar transgressions. At the beginning of the year, the National Liberal Party had only a few mayors and regional leaders under investigation.

Despite a report by the American Bar Association showing that Romanian legislation is still behind in granting sufficient powers to law enforcement agencies to investigate organized crime and corruption, anticorruption instruments adopted in previous years began to be dismantled in 2007. The Chamber of Deputies modified the criminal procedural code, limiting investigations to a maximum of six months and wiretapping to a maximum of 120 days, among other changes. The European Commission commented that "these amendments would seriously limit the potential of the investigators in collecting evidence, particularly when tackling well-established criminal groups or powerful governmental representatives deeply involved with corruption." An amendment calling for seven-year prison terms for journalists who publish leaks was first adopted, then dropped. The American ambassador in Bucharest joined the European Commission in its warning that such provisions are not suitable for an EU member country.

Equally telling is the embattled attempt to create the National Agency for Integrity (ANI). The draft law proposed by Monica Macovei was approved by the government in July 2006 and finally adopted by the Romanian Senate in May 2007. Under the law, the president and vice presidents of the agency are to be appointed (and can be recalled) by the Senate, upon proposal of the National Integrity Council, the agency's ruling body, for a four-year mandate. Concerns were expressed by the European Commission over the final version of the ANI. Originally, the goal was to set up an agency able to verify and take action in a zone not covered by any other institution in Romania—namely, wealth that cannot be justified by the income(s) of the verified person. However the adopted form of the ANI legislation replaced the concept of "illicit" wealth instead of "unjustified" wealth. An article in the Romanian Constitution claiming that "all wealth is presumed licit" has so far allowed the few defendants charged with illicit enrichment to file for non-constitutionality and escape prosecution. In fact, individuals have no legal obligation to preserve any records of how they acquired their wealth, and the burden of proof is on the prosecutors.

Precisely to avoid this problem, the ANI was originally designed to remain within the area of administrative procedure, much like its model, the U.S. Office of Government Ethics, but the Parliament scaled it back. At the European

Commission's suggestion, a government ordinance was again promulgated to revise the law (which went into force in June 2007), replacing "illicit wealth" with "unjustified wealth." Although establishing the ANI is part of an absolute EU conditionality and its failure can trigger the safeguard clause, the Romanian Parliament restored its preferred "illicit wealth" language when the ordinance came up for approval in the autumn.

The natural question is, why did the European Commission not activate the safeguard clause, which was created to protect the EU from such a breach of legal commitments? It was the first time such a tough post-accession mechanism was introduced, but the penalties proved inadequate to the monitoring mechanism. Activating the clause, at worst, would mean that Romania's judicial decisions would no longer be recognized in the EU. Bad publicity aside, this move would not hurt either the government or the Parliament as much as it would hurt European companies doing business in Romania. Although activation of the safeguard clause was discussed by the European Commission, it was promptly abandoned and relegated to the "lessons learned" chapter for further accessions.

▌ Author: Alina Mungiu-Pippidi

Alina Mungiu-Pippidi is founding president of the Romanian Academic Society and democracy studies chair at Hertie School of Governance in Berlin; she was a senior member of St. Antony's College in Oxford in spring–summer 2007. Cristian Ghinea is a political analyst with SAR and MSc candidate at London School of Economics.

---

1   "Romania's MPs Suspend President," BBC News, April 18, 2007, http://news.bbc.co.uk/2/hi/europe/6572003.stm.

2   "Discursul Presedintelui Traian Basescu adresat Parlamentului Romaniei" [Speech of President Traian Basecu Addressing Romanian Parliament], E–JURIDIC.RO Portalul lumii juridice din Romania [portal of the Romanian judicial world], February 15, 2007, http://www.e-juridic.ro/stiri/discursul-presedintelui-traian-basescu-adresat-parlamentului-romaniei-851.html.

3   "Clubul Roman de Presa discuta maine cazul 'Basescu—tiganca imputita'" [Romanian Press Club will Debate Tomorrow the Case "Basescu—Dirty Gipsy"], ROL.ro Romania Online, May 21, 2007, http://stiri.rol.ro/content/view/52528/2/.

4   "Cioaba condamna declaratia lui Cioroianu despre mutarea romilor in desertul egiptean" [Cioaba Condemns Cioroianu Statement Regarding the Move of the Roma Population in the Egyptian Desert], ROL.ro Romania Online, November 5, 2007, http://stiri.rol.ro/content/view/90491/2/.

5   See Judy Dempsey, "Reform Shouldn't Stop with EU Membership," *International Herald Tribune*, February 6, 2008, http://www.iht.com/articles/2008/02/06/europe/letter.php.

6   See the interview with commissioner Frattini in *Cotidianul*, March 13, 2006: "There would be a disaster for Romania if Mrs Macovei cannot enjoy the support from the political groups." http://ec.europa.eu/commission_barroso/frattini/news/archives_2006_en.htm.

7   Paul Cristian Radu, "Romania: Reporter's Notebook" Global Inegrity Report 2007 Assessment, http://report.globalintegrity.org/Romania/2007/notebook.

Russia

by Robert W. Orttung

Capital: Moscow
Population: 142.2 million
GNI/capita: US$12,740

The social data above was taken from the European Bank for Reconstruction and Development's *Transition Report 2007: People in Transition*, and the economic data from the World Bank's *World Development Indicators 2008*.

Nations in Transit Ratings and Averaged Scores

	1999	2001	2002	2003	2004	2005	2006	2007	2008
Electoral Process	4.00	4.25	4.50	4.75	5.50	6.00	6.25	6.50	6.75
Civil Society	3.75	4.00	4.00	4.25	4.50	4.75	5.00	5.25	5.50
Independent Media	4.75	5.25	5.50	5.50	5.75	6.00	6.00	6.25	6.25
Governance*	4.50	5.00	5.25	5.00	5.25	n/a	n/a	n/a	n/a
National Democratic Governance	n/a	n/a	n/a	n/a	n/a	5.75	6.00	6.00	6.25
Local Democratic Governance	n/a	n/a	n/a	n/a	n/a	5.75	5.75	5.75	5.75
Judicial Framework and Independence	4.25	4.50	4.75	4.50	4.75	5.25	5.25	5.25	5.25
Corruption	6.25	6.25	6.00	5.75	5.75	5.75	6.00	6.00	6.00
Democracy Score	4.58	4.88	5.00	4.96	5.25	5.61	5.75	5.86	5.96

* *With the 2005 edition, Freedom House introduced separate analysis and ratings for national democratic governance and local democratic governance to provide readers with more detailed and nuanced analysis of these two important subjects.*

NOTE: The ratings reflect the consensus of Freedom House, its academic advisers, and the author(s) of this report. The opinions expressed in this report are those of the author(s). The ratings are based on a scale of 1 to 7, with 1 representing the highest level of democratic progress and 7 the lowest. The Democracy Score is an average of ratings for the categories tracked in a given year.

Executive SUMMARY

Russia has faced numerous difficulties since the collapse of the Soviet Union in 1991. Upon coming to power in 2000, President Vladimir Putin has consistently sought to concentrate power, control electoral outcomes, reduce media freedom, and tighten constraints on nongovernmental organizations (NGOs). Like Boris Yeltsin before him, he has failed to make much headway in the battle against corruption.

The central political event of 2007 was Putin's selection of First Deputy Prime Minister Dmitry Medvedev as his successor, to be elected president March 2, 2008, and the subsequent announcement that Putin would stay on in power, serving as prime minister. Putin's action serves to extend his term in power for the foreseeable future. Pro-Kremlin parties won the vast majority of seats in the State Duma elections on December 2. In these elections, Putin and his allies used state resources, particularly state-controlled television, to support the pro-Kremlin parties and crush any conceivable opposition. The elections were neither free nor fair. The Russian authorities put in place such severe restrictions on foreign oversight that monitors from the Organization for Security and Cooperation in Europe (OSCE) refused to observe the elections.

National Democratic Governance. The key issue for 2007 was the presidential succession. Putin made it clear that he would not leave the political stage after the end of his constitutionally-mandated two terms in office. This decision leaves in place the current elite and allows them to continue managing the economic assets they gained control over during the last eight years. The system is characterized by intimidation and political passivity on the part of the population. *Russia's rating for national democratic governance drops from 6.00 to 6.25. Putin's decision to remain in power demonstrates that the political system is increasingly authoritarian, with little accountability to the population and few opportunities for substantial public participation in the decision-making process. While the system is stable in the short term, the mid- and long-term prospects are bleak because such a top-heavy government has little ability to understand what is going on in Russian society and react to social change effectively.*

Electoral Process. The State Duma elections were neither free nor fair, setting the stage for similarly controlled presidential elections in 2008. Russia placed such strict constraints on international observers that the OSCE monitors ultimately decided not to observe the elections. The campaign was skewed in favor of United Russia, the party of power, with the authorities making extensive use of state resources to ensure victory. Opposition parties were harassed at every step. The national television networks, under the control of the government, promoted pro-Kremlin parties through their news coverage, thereby creating a playing field that was not level. *Russia's rating for electoral process drops from 6.50 to 6.75. The 2007 parliamentary elections set a new level of state control over the electoral process in Russia and prepared the ground for equally undemocratic presidential elections in 2008.*

Civil Society. Russia's NGOs continue to face intense pressure from the Russian state, particularly in complying with the provisions of the 2006 Law on NGOs. The state applies the law more harshly against NGOs it does not favor, and many are having trouble meeting its onerous requirements. Kremlin-sponsored groups like Nashi harass the opposition and Moscow-based diplomats alike. *Russia's rating for civil society worsens from 5.25 to 5.50 because of the implementation of the Law on NGOs, increasing restrictions on the right to public protest, greater use of psychiatric hospitals against activists, and growing political propaganda in the education system.*

Independent Media. The state continues to exercise extensive control over television, radio, and the print media. Only a few exceptional outlets and the Internet remain open for political discussion. While the Kremlin has not limited the range of free discussion on the Internet, critics accuse it of funding online attacks against opponents, while regional authorities have filed criminal charges against some bloggers who criticize them. *Russia's rating for independent media remains at 6.25 as the state continues to put binding limits on free expression. Attempts to assert more control over the Internet do not bode well for the future.*

Local Democratic Governance. In an era of centralization, local government in Russia remains an afterthought. Putin used his power to appoint governors to shore up his political support in advance of the State Duma elections. Mayors are increasingly dependent on governors and the rest of the political hierarchy. The federal government has returned to a process of signing treaties with some regions, suggesting that federal laws do not apply equally to all. Chechnya has achieved relative calm, but at the cost of continued suppression of civil and political liberties. At the same time, violence continues to plague neighboring Dagestan and Ingushetia. *Russia's rating for local democratic governance remains at 5.75 because centralizing tendencies remain strong, denying the population much tangible influence in the conduct of local affairs.*

Judicial Framework and Independence. Russia's courts are subject to political manipulation and can be reliably counted on to return the decisions needed by the authorities. Major problems remain in terms of pre-trial detention, lengthy trials, the failure to implement court decisions, and the poor quality of the defense. The greatest indictment of the Russian court system is the large number of citizens who believe that they cannot get a fair hearing and seek redress at the European Court of Human Rights. Although there are provisions for jury trials, they are rarely used, and the decisions are often overturned by higher courts. *Russia's rating for judicial* *framework and independence remains at 5.25 because of the system's inability to assert greater independence. While some reforms have been implemented, such as increasing the role of judges, it will be a long time before these reforms change the way the system actually operates.*

Corruption. Bribery and other forms of corruption continue to pervade Russian society: Official efforts to address the problem have mostly amounted to politically driven campaigns to discredit opponents. *Russia's rating for corruption stays the same at 6.00 because in conditions where there is not a free press, energetic civil society, and independent judiciary, there are few prospects for making substantial progress in the battle against bribery and abuse of public office.*

Outlook for 2008. Putin has made clear that he will remain in power, serving now as prime minister along with his handpicked successor as president. Accordingly, the presidential elections are meaningless, as is the campaign leading up to them. This outcome means that there is little chance Russia's political process will open up or gain democratic legitimacy in the foreseeable future.

MAIN REPORT

National Democratic Governance

1999	2001	2002	2003	2004	2005	2006	2007	2008
n/a	n/a	n/a	n/a	n/a	5.75	6.00	6.00	6.25

Russia does not have a democratic political system. Instead, there is a facade of democracy, with a Constitution, formal elections, political parties, and other attributes typically found in democracies. However, without public accountability, a free media, and independent courts, the incumbent leadership can manipulate the entire structure to its benefit. Such a system may be able to maintain itself in power for decades, but ultimately it will lose touch with society and become unstable.

Quickly following the Kremlin's stage-managed victory in the December parliamentary elections, President Vladimir Putin announced that he would remain in power as prime minister, working with his handpicked successor as president, Dmitry Medvedev. With all the backing of the state's resources and the elimination of any potential opposition, Medvedev was set to win the presidency, presumably to serve in a ceremonial role, while Putin and the shadowy security, law enforcement, and military groups around him continue to call the shots. Putin had to settle for this inelegant solution because the Constitution rules out the possibility of a third consecutive presidential term. By choosing to remain in power, Putin has violated the spirit of the Russian Constitution, if not its letter. Putin's continuing role at the top of the country's hierarchy reflects the complete lack of institutionalization of the Russian political system and the absence of a functioning procedure for identifying new leaders in a democratic manner.[1]

The main beneficiaries of Putin's decision are the secret service representatives and other advisers around him who will also remain in power and continue to benefit from their incumbency at the top of the political system. More than half of the senior staff in the Kremlin have connections to the intelligence services, according to the estimates of sociologist Olga Khryshtanovskaya.[2] This elite is not monolithic, and there will be continuing struggles among the various Kremlin clans, perhaps stimulated further because Medvedev does not himself have a secret service background.

The central issue of Russian politics is the distribution of property in the country. Putin's decision to remain in power means that the current elite will continue to control the enormous monetary flows associated with Russia's increasingly state-dominated economy. In the current Russian system, property ownership is not as important as controlling state assets, such as the energy companies, and the revenues they create. Putin has overseen an enormous transfer of property, and now he must stay on to ensure the safety of that transfer. Formal property rights are of little significance.

Putin's continued tenure signals that the Constitution and Russia's political institutions have little practical meaning. The system is designed for one individual and the people surrounding him. While Putin and his supporters claim that his continued rule is based on his personal popularity, in the absence of fair elections, a free media, and a vibrant civil society, there is no way to measure his real popularity. All institutions outside the executive have been weakened—the Parliament has no power to oppose the executive branch, while the courts lack the independence to decide political issues.

Intimidation is now a central feature of the political system. With the collapse of the Soviet system at the end of 1991, most citizens felt free to speak and act in the political arena according to their conscience, but that is no longer true. Today, pressure by the authorities, combined with traditionally low levels of citizen participation and engagement, breeds political passivity. Rules are written so that they can be applied against anybody at any time. A selective application of repression makes for a very efficient system of management. By silencing a few key individuals, the regime is able to keep most of the rest of the population in line. People now understand that it is better to remain passive than to say anything negative about the political system. This atmosphere of repression explains the growing number of people who answer, "I don't know," in polls conducted by the Levada Center about the political system, according to Lev Gudkov, the center's director.[3]

In order to ensure conformity, the ruling elite constantly emphasize the threat of an outside enemy, which would menace society without the Kremlin's protection. For example, Putin told a November 21 campaign rally in Moscow that "those who oppose us do not want us to implement our plan....They need a weak nation, a sick nation...so that they can covertly work out their deals and receive their reward at our expense."[4] Likewise pursuing an aggressive foreign policy makes it possible to deflect attention from domestic issues.

The current system is self-maintaining and stable in the short term. Putin is very careful in his choice of personnel: When a high-level official is fired, he is moved into another job of generally equal importance. Putin is using this technique to avoid creating any enemies among the elite, as Boris Yeltsin and Mikhail Gorbachev did.[5] In a process that could last decades, this system will likely collapse as the incumbent leaders age and few new people will be brought in to implement necessary reforms. With a lack of open discussion, there is little chance that Russia's leadership or society will generate new ideas to address the challenges the country faces.

The Federal Security Service (former KGB known by its Russian initials as the FSB) and other law enforcement groups that surround Putin are calling for the imposition of a new regime, which would include increased state regulation of the economy and strict limits on political activities. Currently, these groups are fighting with one another over control of various agencies and assets. But Viktor Cherkesov, a key Putin ally who heads the antidrug agency, has made public appeals for all of the security agents to work together to serve their corporate interests while blocking the rise of other interests in Russian society.[6] Putin currently is the only arbiter among these feuding clans.[7]

Given its security service style of management, Russia is increasingly relying on giant state corporations to control strategic sectors of the economy. This trend is dangerous because it undermines the economic growth that Russia has achieved since the 1998 financial meltdown. Most economists agree that state corporations work less efficiently than private ones. They are also opaque and well positioned to secure subsidies and tax benefits from the government. Today, these corporations have extensive control over the energy sector, shipbuilding, aircraft construction, and nuclear energy and are likely to take over a wide variety of new areas, such as automobile production, drug manufacturing, and fishing.

Electoral Process

1999	2001	2002	2003	2004	2005	2006	2007	2008
4.00	4.25	4.50	4.75	5.50	6.00	6.25	6.50	6.75

The December 2, 2007, State Duma elections were neither free nor fair. They violated international norms and Russia's own declared commitment to free elections, calling into question the result's legitimacy. The parliamentary elections set the stage for the March 2008 presidential elections, which also will be managed from above with little room for voter participation beyond ratifying a choice made in the Kremlin.

In the 2007 Duma elections, the Kremlin used extensive state resources, including its control of television, radio, and many newspapers, to guarantee that it would win a supermajority of the seats.[8] Reports indicated that voters felt coerced to take part and the authorities sought to influence the way people voted through such tactics as workplace pressure, particularly on public sector employees.[9] The number of absentee ballots increased greatly over the 2003 elections, another indicator of suspicious activity in Russian conditions. Ultimately, four parties secured seats in the Parliament: United Russia (64 percent of the vote); Communist Party (12 percent); Liberal Democratic Party (8 percent); and Just Russia (8 percent). Three of these parties support the Kremlin, with only the Communists in nominal opposition. The pro-Kremlin parties won 393 seats and the Communists 57 in the 450-seat body.[10]

There was clear evidence of abnormalities in the vote counts from some regions. In Chechnya, Ingushetia, Kabardino-Balkaria, Mordova, Karachaevo-Cherkessia, Dagestan, Bashkortostan, and Tatarstan, turnout was far above the Russian average and support for the chief pro-Kremlin party ranged from 81 to 99 percent.[11] In the major urban areas, United Russia did not do as well, and there the elections were probably conducted more fairly.

The election proceeded according to Kremlin plans from the beginning. Eleven parties participated in the campaign, while Other Russia (Garry Kasparov) and

Great Russia (Dmitry Rogozin) were not allowed to compete. Critics charged that the registration service based its decision to remove these genuine opposition parties on a variety of technicalities, narrowing the field and making it easier for the pro-Kremlin United Russia to dominate.

The campaign itself lacked substance. United Russia, which brought together almost all of Russia's leaders from Putin to more than 60 governors, refused to participate in the campaign debates, dismissing them as nothing but "squabbles."[12] The authorities thus avoided addressing difficult questions from the electorate. The party instead ran on what it called "Putin's Plan," signaling a continuation of the status quo. The result was no debating of the government position, with the likely consequence of low-quality public policy.

The authorities blocked international and independent domestic observers from monitoring the elections in a substantive manner. Russian authorities made conditions so difficult for election observers from the Organization for Security and Cooperation in Europe (OSCE) that they decided not to monitor the elections because they did not have sufficient monitors or time for advance fieldwork to do a credible job of assessing the election's validity. Russia offered to admit 70 OSCE observers, down from 450 in 2003, and made visas available only one month before the voting, rather than the usual three months.[13] The OSCE rejected these conditions (foreshadowing its actions in the March 2008 presidential elections). The authorities also pressured independent domestic monitoring organizations like Golos, which is funded by the European Commission and United States Agency for International Development.[14] Nevertheless, Golos reported violations, such as illegal campaigning on election day and numerous efforts to block monitors from doing their job.[15] A Samara court blocked Russia's registration service from dissolving the Samara branch of the organization, which had declared the Duma elections undemocratic.[16]

Changes in the electoral law had a profound impact on the elections. The 2007 elections were conducted purely on the basis of party lists, eliminating the previous system whereby half of the seats were elected from single-member districts, which collectively represented all of Russia's regions. Without the district elections, the parliamentary campaign lost its connection to real local issues. Now Moscow has control of the party lists and can block the rise of unwanted regional politicians. The Kremlin directly created two of four parties now in the Parliament and seems to prefer to work with parties that it established rather than authentic parties that maintain some autonomy. Many of the big names on the party lists, including Putin and many of the governors, did not accept their seats, allowing the parties to fill them with lesser-known people who are beholden to the Kremlin leadership for their positions.[17]

A key element in the Kremlin victory was the hierarchy of electoral commissions. Vladimir Churov became head of the Central Electoral Commission on March 27. He had worked closely with Putin in the 1990s in St. Petersburg. Russia changed its legislation specifically for Churov, allowing people without law degrees to join the Central Electoral Commission. Since the Russian procurator general or a regional procurator must agree with charges against an electoral commission member, it is highly unlikely that such officials could ever be charged with the crime of vote rigging.[18]

On October 1, Putin agreed to personally lead United Russia, lending the party his personal popularity and the resources of the state. There were no limits on what the authorities would do to ensure victory. On October 22, Russia's largest food distributors "voluntarily" agreed to freeze the prices of milk, vegetable oil, cheese, bread, and other basic goods through the end of January 2008 in a thinly veiled effort to win popular support. United Russia also placed its symbol on state-owned vehicles, and election officials often spoke in favor of the party, according to a report on party activities in 40 regions prepared by Transparency International.[19] Leaders of government organizations and private enterprises were under pressure to mobilize their workers to deliver a high turnout for Putin's party. As noted earlier, turnout in many regions defied credibility. Additionally, the Center for Journalism in Extreme Situations released a report on November 12 showing that Russia's television stations devoted most of their coverage to Putin and United Russia. The report said that Channel One set aside 96.5 percent of its coverage to state bodies and pro-government political parties.

During the course of the campaign, Union of Right Forces leaders claimed that 10 million copies of their newspaper were seized and that an additional 4 million copies were being held at the printing houses where they were produced. Party leaders claimed that the authorities were preventing them from campaigning.[20] The Communists and Liberal Democratic Party of Russia (LDPR) also reported harassment: For example, police confiscated equipment from a printing plant in Omsk as it prepared to print material for the Communists.

Civil Society

1999	2001	2002	2003	2004	2005	2006	2007	2008
3.75	4.00	4.00	4.25	4.50	4.75	5.00	5.25	5.50

Russian nongovernmental organizations (NGOs) are under extreme pressure from the state. In fact, many Russian NGOs are finding it necessary to open offices outside of Russia to continue their activities. Examples include the International Protection Center, which opened in Strasbourg in July 2006 in order to handle Chechen cases at the European Court of Human Rights in case its Moscow office is closed.

The adoption of the new Law on NGOs in 2006 continues to complicate life for the organizations working in this sector. Between April 2006 and the beginning of November 2007, the Moscow Federal Registration Service directorate denied registration to 1,380 NGOs—11 percent of the 13,014 applications it received—because of "inconsistencies in the founding documents" and "their inappropriate completion," according to the head of the Moscow branch of the Federal Registration

Service, Ivan Kondrat.[21] The Moscow Helsinki Group reported that the authorities had closed 2,300 organizations by the end of 2007.[22] Registering an NGO is now three times as expensive as registering a business and takes longer, according to a study conducted by Moscow State University's Economics Faculty and the Higher School of Economics.[23]

Most NGOs are having difficulty meeting the requirements of the legislation. Before the 2006 law went into effect, Russia had more than 500,000 registered NGOs, though it is impossible to say how many were actually active and how many existed only on paper.[24] Currently, there are 216,000 domestic and 226 foreign-run NGOs in Russia.[25] Only 36 percent of the NGOs registered in Russia had reported the results of their work to the Federal Registration Service by September 1, meaning most were in violation of the law, according to Sergei Vasiliev, head of the Federal Registration Service.[26] Some NGOs have been hit with excessive demands. For example, St. Petersburg's Citizen Watch, which seeks to establish parliamentary and civic oversight over the police, security service, and armed forces, was asked to disclose its correspondence with everyone it had been in touch with for the period between July 2004 and July 2007, including e-mails.

Many human rights groups get their funding from Western sources since very few domestic sources are available. Now the Russian government is trying to provide more funding and awarded 1.25 billion rubles (US$51 million) to a variety of nongovernmental groups on November 6. The largest recipients included the pro-Kremlin nationalist youth group Nashi, which holds a summer youth camp each year. The authorities sought to show that they were being evenhanded by giving awards to authentic human rights defenders such as the Moscow Helsinki Group, Memorial, and For Human Rights. However, it later turned out that the national office of Memorial had not applied for funds, just the branch organizations in Vladimir and Ivanovo, without coordinating with the organization's leadership. For Human Rights, another group that received funding, was in fact a regional organization with a similar name to the better-known human rights organization but not connected to it.[27]

Pro-Kremlin groups like Nashi play a negative role in Russian society. They harass what little political opposition there is—for example, giving independent Duma member Vladimir Ryzhkov an American flag on his birthday, symbolizing their belief that he is not acting in Russia's interests. In 2007, activists from the group also hectored the Estonian and British ambassadors. Police have provided Nashi activists with training so that they can help counter demonstrations by opposition groups. Toward the end of the year, the Kremlin cut off most of Nashi's funding, pointing out that the group was no longer necessary since there was not likely to be a Ukraine-style Orange Revolution in Russia. Nashi's original purpose was to prevent such a grassroots uprising among young people.[28]

The state crackdown on officially-registered NGOs is creating a new phenomenon in Russia: unofficial organizations of citizens working together for specific purposes.[29] These groups address citizen concerns in areas such as deceived investors, rules of the road, environmentalism, and urban planning. Much of this activity takes place on the Internet. Accordingly, civic society capacity in Russia potentially remains strong, but many of its activities must now take place outside official institutions.

Citizens are also losing their right to engage in public demonstrations. The NGO Legal Team studied all of the public protests held across Russia during the first nine months of 2007 and concluded that the authorities had banned or dispersed almost every one of them.[30] While the law permits such demonstrations, the authorities' implementation of approval procedures makes such protest impossible in practice. In the past, protesters detained were given administrative fines; now they often face 15-day prison terms. On September 4, Moscow mayor Yurii Luzhkov issued a decree restricting demonstrations near historical or cultural landmarks, requiring the city's Cultural Heritage Committee to approve them. Since demonstrations typically take place near such monuments, the requirement amounts to an attempt to block such gatherings from taking place in well-populated downtown areas. The authorities also took action against prominent protesters: Opposition leader Boris Nemtsov was arrested on November 25—and released later that day—for participating in an unauthorized anti-Putin demonstration. Garry Kasparov was also arrested during the course of his campaign activities on November 24 and released five days later.

Russian authorities continue to use psychiatric hospitals as a form of punishment for critical activists. After she published an article on such practices in Murmansk, Larisa Arap was herself imprisoned for six weeks.[31] A court ultimately ordered her release. In custody, Arap found others sent to such hospitals for political reasons, as a result of business conflicts, or because they were inconvenient witnesses in criminal cases. In some cases, people seeking to take over the apartment of residents who do not want to sell can pay a bribe to have the resident declared insane, at which point the residents lose many of their rights, and it becomes much easier to take over their property.[32]

Ethnic intolerance remains a major problem. According to Sova, an independent NGO that tracks hate-crimes across Russia, there were 632 victims of such crimes in 2007—including 67 people who died.[33] The 2007 numbers marked an increase as the group counted 564 victims, including 61 deaths, in 2006. A Moscow Human Rights Bureau report on youth extremism in Russia claimed that there were 141 active extremist youth groups with approximately half a million members. Many of the groups are concentrated in Moscow and St. Petersburg. In its analysis of 2007, Sova found that, unfortunately, prosecutions of violent crimes dropped for the first time since 2003.

Independent trade unions have difficulty protecting worker rights. The largest trade union, the Federation of Independent Trade Unions, is closely associated with United Russia and the Kremlin and does little to help workers. Smaller trade unions have great difficulty in their efforts to secure better conditions for workers and striking to promote their members' aims. Although the Constitution protects the right to strike, carrying out labor actions is difficult in practice. According to the labor code, the first step in legally conducting a strike is calling a meeting of all enterprise employees, a feat that is extremely difficult to achieve. If a majority support a more forward, a list of demands must be presented to management. After the directors respond, there is a reconciliation process. A strike can legally begin only if this process fails. The courts typically side with employers in declaring strikes illegal, according to Elena Gerasimova, director of the Social and Labor Rights Center.[34] However, when strikes are held, they frequently result in higher salaries and better conditions.

There were numerous labor actions across Russia in 2007. Workers on the railroad have been staging "work to the rule" protests to avoid the possibility of the law being used against them. Additionally, workers at Russia's largest carmaker, AvtoVAZ, held a one-day strike on August 1 to demand higher wages. In that action, the authorities detained union official Aleksandr Dzyuban, who had taken a lead in organizing the strike. At the Ford plant in Leningrad oblast, workers held the first open-ended strike since Putin came to power.[35] The strike lasted 25 days in November and December before the workers voted to end it.[36] According to Federation of Independent Trade Unions head Mikhail Shmakov, there have been more strikes in Russia recently, even though it is almost impossible to strike legally.[37]

There is an increasing amount of political influence and propaganda in the education system. During the summer, there was an intensive discussion about a new high school history teachers' manual that painted a positive picture of the Stalin era and included an extremely laudatory picture of Putin's time in office, claiming that many of Russia's successes were connected with his name.[38] A new textbook, which was based on the manual and has been approved for classroom use, carried these themes forward by presenting the authorities' version of history without trying to instill abilities in the students critical thinking so that they could conduct their own analysis.[39]

The authorities have sought to stamp out some unwanted foreign influence in Russia. On December 12, they ordered the closure of British Council offices in St. Petersburg and Yekaterinburg. The British Council is devoted to promoting British culture and teaching English around the world.

Independent Media

1999	2001	2002	2003	2004	2005	2006	2007	2008
4.75	5.25	5.50	5.50	5.75	6.00	6.00	6.25	6.25

The federal authorities exert extensive control over Russia's television and radio broadcasters and much of the print media. Free speech remains in a few newspapers, on the Ekho Moskvy radio station, and over the Internet. But the situation is dismal. Reporters Without Borders ranked Russia 144 out of 169 countries studied in 2007.[40]

In recent years, Kremlin-connected oligarchs have been buying up the last outposts of media that still provide critical coverage. For example, Alisher Usmanov, who has close ties to Gazprom, now owns *Kommersant* and gazeta.ru. While he has not forced these outlets to take a pro-government line, he clearly has the power to do so if necessary. Under publisher and editor in chief Konstantin Remchukov, *Nezavisimaya Gazeta* has been able to criticize some aspects of the government's policies, including its takeover of the Russian Academy of Sciences and the Central Electoral Commission, though it is far from an opposition paper.[41] On September 14, the authorities arrested *Nezavisimaya Gazeta*'s deputy editor, Boris Zemtsov, on extortion charges—apparently in an attempt to limit the paper's criticisms.

Beyond influencing the actions of rich individuals, the Putin government has an extensive arsenal to use against the media, including frequent tax audits, complex reregistration procedures, orders to present the government in a positive light, blacklists of who cannot be allowed on the air, bans on live reporting and debate in talk shows, and public officials who tell companies not to advertise on certain stations.[42] Accordingly, most outlets are willing to toe the Kremlin line or focus on nonpolitical information, highlighting entertainment, business, and sports.

In July, Putin signed amendments to the Law on Extremism that make "public slander of state officials," "humiliating national pride," "hampering the lawful activity of state organizations," and "hooliganism committed for political or ideological motives" extremist acts. Critics claim that the provisions of the law are so broad that it can be used to stifle the political opposition and independent journalists. In one example of how the law is being used, Andrei Piontkovsky, a prominent member of the Yabloko party, was put on trial for extremism because of passages in his books, *Unloved Country* and *For the Motherland! For Abramovich! Fire!*, which allegedly stirred violence against Russians, Jews, and Americans.[43] The absurd nature of the case became clear when the prosecution was not able to cite concrete passages where Piontkovsky's books were "extremist." The court is currently seeking more information before ruling. Many observers see Piontkovsky's case as a warning to less prominent critics to be careful of what they say.

There are plenty of cases of regional officials working to keep local publications in line. For example, on May 11 the police in Samara investigated the local office of *Novaya Gazeta* for allegedly using pirated software and confiscated three computers.[44] The use of illegal software is common in Russia, and investigating such charges is a favorite ploy of the authorities against opposition groups. The special services thus kill two birds with one stone—shut down the opposition by confiscating their computers and show the West that they are combating software piracy, at least selectively.

The Internet is the last frontier for free media in Russia. One-quarter of Russian adults are now online, marking a slow increase over previous years.[45] So far, the authorities have not imposed explicit bans on Internet speech. However, many opposition parties and other activists accuse the authorities of using various forms of cyber-warfare to block their sites. Such efforts are more effective and less costly than outright censorship since it is impossible to identify the source of the attacks. In a similar vein, Internet users were particularly concerned when Kremlin-connected magnate Aleksandr Mamut purchased the LiveJournal blogging site from its original San Francisco–based owners.⁴⁶ Critics fear that he will institute free speech limits on the site. In addition, the Kremlin is creating a series of pro-government Web sites and a network of friendly bloggers.

At the same time, local officials have filed criminal cases against a number of bloggers outside of Moscow. These individual cases are not part of a federally organized crackdown. Typically, these online commentators offended local officials. Examples include Savva Terentyev, a Syktyvkar resident, who faces charges filed August 9 under Article 282 of the criminal code, inciting hatred or enmity and humiliating a person's dignity, with a maximum sentence of two years for denouncing the local police in explicit language, calling for them to be burned in a public square. Terentyev was angered because the police had removed computers from the office of *Iskra*, a local opposition newspaper, and found pirated software on them.

Because of its location in the volatile Caucasus, the federal government seems to be playing a greater role in the campaign against Ingushetiya.ru, which publishes frequent articles critical of the corruption and poor management of Ingushetia's leaders. Ingushetia's president, Murat Zyazikov, ordered two local Internet providers to block access to the opposition Web site Ingushetiya.ru, though they refused to implement the order. In October, the Russian procurator general reopened a 1999 case against the site's owner, Magomed Yevloyev. The site is also being investigated for inciting ethnic hatred. The authorities closed it in December, but it was able to resume operations within a few days.⁴⁷ Just before the end of the year, it conducted an investigation of the State Duma elections in the region, gathering data to show that the authorities had inflated turnout figures, and again courting official ire.⁴⁸

The authorities have also cracked down on foreign broadcasters trying to reach a Russian audience. They removed the BBC from the FM dial in August as part of a dispute with the United Kingdom over the murder of former FSB agent Aleksandr Litvinenko in London. Additionally, the authorities have been pushing local partners of the U.S. government-funded Radio Liberty to drop its programming from their schedules.

At least 14 journalists have been slain for their work in Russia since 2000, according to the Committee to Protect Journalists. The killings remain unsolved. The authorities have made several arrests in the case of Anna Politkovskaya, including that of a member of the FSB, but have not identified the person or group that ordered the assassination, and Prosecutor General Yury Chaika continues to insist on the theory that the shooting was organized abroad in order to discredit Russia's leaders. The authorities also closed the investigation into the March death of *Kommersant* military correspondent Igor Safronov, claiming that his fall from his Moscow apartment building window was a suicide. Safronov's colleagues believe that the investigators never really examined the theory that he was killed because of his work. Additionally, the Investigative Committee of the Prosecutor General's office has reopened the case of Yury Shchekochikhin, a Duma member and *Novaya Gazeta* journalist who investigated corruption, to see if he had been intentionally poisoned with radiation when he died in 2003. He apparently lost all of his hair before his death, which went unexplained at the time. The medical tests and autopsy results were sealed as "medical secrets."[49] In one sign of progress, a court in Tatarstan convicted five individuals for the murder of *Novaya Gazeta* journalist Igor Domnikov. This was the first case to hold people responsible for a journalist's murder during Putin's tenure. However, the authorities have yet to identify who ordered the assassination, having so far prosecuted only the people who carried it out.

This year, the Russian authorities shut down the Educated Media Foundation (EMF), the Russian legal successor to Internews, which had provided training for more than 15,000 broadcast journalists since 1992. The EMF suspended its work following a raid in April 2007 on its Moscow headquarters in which police seized numerous financial documents and computer servers. The search was ostensibly part of a criminal investigation of EMF president Manana Aslamazyan, who violated Russian law by failing to declare that she had slightly more than US$10,000 in cash when she returned from a trip abroad. Usually, the penalty for such transgressions is a fine, not closing down an entire organization.

Aslamazyan fled abroad, joining other journalists who felt it was too dangerous to work in Russia. The United States accepted as political refugees journalists Fatima Tlisova and Yury Bagrov. Both had run afoul of the Russian authorities for their reporting on the North Caucasus, including coverage of soldiers' abuses in Chechnya.

Despite the restrictions on free speech in the media market, spending on advertising is continuing to increase at a rapid pace. In 2007, the Group M advertising company expected media advertising sales to increase more than 25 percent to US$8.5 billion.[50] Advertising purchases on the Internet were also growing rapidly and expected to be up more than 75 percent in 2007, to US$330 million.

Local Democratic Governance

1999	2001	2002	2003	2004	2005	2006	2007	2008
n/a	n/a	n/a	n/a	n/a	5.75	5.75	5.75	5.75

While Russian law provides for regional and local government, Putin's policies of centralization have meant that subnational government has lost power and resources to the federal center since 2000. Regional and local officials complain that important funding sources have increasingly flowed from local control to Moscow. Local government reforms, adopted in 2003 and set to be implemented by 2006, were ultimately postponed until 2009, well after the 2007–2008 electoral cycle.

Putin took the power to appoint governors in September 2004, abolishing the Yeltsin-initiated practice of allowing them to stand for direct election. Initially, the president mainly used his new power to reappoint incumbents, largely continuing his tradition of leaving the elite intact. However, as the elections approached in 2007, he began replacing some key governors from the Yeltsin era, including Novgorod's Mikhail Prusak and Samara's Konstantin Titov, with people who will be unreservedly loyal to the Kremlin. Putin also replaced the governor of Sakhalin Oblast with Alexander Khoroshavin, who is close to the head of the state-owned energy company Rosneft, which now has lucrative contracts in the area. The changes seem to be part of the general plan to extend federal control farther into the regions, particularly ensuring victory in the elections and continuing to demonstrate Putin's overwhelming dominance.

The governors had not made a serious challenge to Putin's power when they were directly elected between 2000 and 2004. Under the new system, the governors have become more dependent on Moscow but have gained greater power vis-à-vis regional legislatures and the local governments in their jurisdictions. They are no longer accountable to the population in their constituency, depending instead on the president's favor to remain in office. Ironically, the governors also have greater abilities now to lobby for resources in the presidential administration since they are in fact a part of that administration, according to an analysis by Oklahoma University's Paul Goode.[51]

At the bottom of the "hierarchy of power," mayors have little power and little access to funding. They hope to use the federal government as a lever against the governors who stand above them and often control all of the local financial assets, but they have little access to Putin and the highest levels of the federal government.

The federal authorities used their coercive and law enforcement capacities to bring unruly mayors into line in the run-up to the 2007 elections. Yakutsk mayor Ilya Mikhalchuk resigned unexpectedly on September 10; Vologda mayor Aleksei Yakunichev faced criminal charges for abuse of power and taking bribes; while Arkhangelsk mayor Aleksandr Donskoi was convicted of forging a diploma and engaging in illegal commercial activity, according to reports summarized by Radio Liberty. All of these local officials had come into conflict with federal or regional authorities. For example, Donskoi angered his superiors when in 2006 he announced plans to run for president.

In some places, the Kremlin does not have the authority to remove regional leaders because their local power bases are too strong and therefore must compromise with them. Tatarstan is a case in point. After ending the Yeltsin-era practice of signing power-sharing treaties with the Russian regions and abolishing those treaties, the Putin administration in 2007 reversed its past practices and signed such a treaty with Tatarstan. Critics pointed out that the 10-year treaty gives Tatarstan special status among Russian regions and violated both the Russian and Tatarstan Constitutions because it requires that the president of Tatarstan speak both Russian and Tatar. The Federation Council, the upper house of the Russian Parliament, had initially refused to ratify the treaty, fearing that other regions would begin to demand similar treaties for themselves.

The North Caucasus continues to present the greatest difficulties for local government in Russia. In Chechnya, Ramzan Kadyrov was inaugurated as president on April 5. He has long headed a variety of armed groups that international observers have linked to numerous assassinations, incidents of torture, and myriad other crimes. Since taking office, he has worked hard to secure his personal power, reduce

Moscow's reach into the region, and increase his access to resources. A referendum held on December 2 extended his term from five to seven years, increased parliamentarians' terms from four to five years, established a unicameral Parliament with 41 members, added Chechen as a state language, and allowed the Parliament to adopt future constitutional amendments without direct popular input.

Although active fighting in Chechnya has come to an end and there has been some progress in the rebuilding effort, Kadyrov's leadership remains extremely problematic. He is inspiring a cult of personality, and it is not clear that he has given up violence in pursuit of his goals. Corruption is pervasive, particularly among officials helping citizens secure restitution for property they lost during the fighting.[52] In September, Kadyrov ordered female civil servants to wear head scarves on the threat that they would otherwise lose their jobs. Russian law separates religion and state and guarantees equality to both sexes. Earlier, Kadyrov had ordered all NGOs working in Chechnya to move their headquarters there, but the organizations pointed out that he had no legal basis for doing this and ignored the demand.

In contrast with the relatively peaceful Chechnya, Ingushetia and Dagestan today are characterized by extensive violence. Numerous assassinations, kidnappings, and other crimes are committed in both republics on a daily basis. Amnesty International reported that law enforcement agents had carried out executions in Nazran, Malgobek, and Karabulak.[53] There is now a loose network of autonomous violent groups, operating in Ingushetia, Dagestan, Karachaevo-Cherkessia, and Kabardino-Balkaria.[54]

Judicial Framework and Independence

1999	2001	2002	2003	2004	2005	2006	2007	2008
4.25	4.50	4.75	4.50	4.75	5.25	5.25	5.25	5.25

Numerous problems remain in the exercise of Russian justice. Above all, the courts remain subject to political caprice and can be reliably counted on to serve political goals when required to do so. Chief Arbitration Justice Anton Ivanov has complained that executive branch bodies intervene in judicial matters that affect their interests.[55] The authorities are moving ahead with plans to move the Constitutional Court to St. Petersburg in May 2008, likely reducing its influence.[56] Additionally, there are numerous problems with lengthy pre-trial detentions, court cases that drag on too long, and a frequent failure to implement court decisions—problems that are not unique to Russia.[57]

Thanks to continuing reform efforts, there are three positive developments in the Russian judicial system, though these developments often reveal the depth of the problems the court system still faces. First, there are more opportunities to bring abuses to the attention of judges, though the nature of the response naturally then depends on the professionalism of the judge. A judge must make decisions on pre-trial detention, which judges frequently use. Currently, a person who is arrested must see a judge within 48 hours. Under the old system, it could have been many months before an arrested person saw a judge. Most judges are from the prosecutor's office or the police and are very conservative. Nevertheless, if a defendant becomes a victim of torture as the police try to extract information or a confession from him, he has the opportunity to show his wounds to the judge, who may or may not take action in regard to this evidence. Such a provision makes torturing prisoners more difficult, though it is far from abolishing such practices. Despite these reforms, many people spend considerable time in pre-trial detention.

Second, Article 125 of the criminal procedure code (adopted in 2001, with numerous subsequent amendments) allows the defendant to complain to the judge about the actions or inactions of the investigators and prosecutor working on his case. This provision is useful because it gives the defendant a chance at the very beginning of the case to say that the prosecutor is not working fairly. Allowing the defendant to struggle against the charges against him from the beginning often makes a big difference in the outcome of the case. A good defense attorney will start this process as soon as possible.

A third improvement is the possibility of having a jury trial. Despite considerable attention given to this possibility, less than 2 percent of trials are eligible for juries since juries hear only serious charges. In fact, sometimes prosecutors deliberately reduce charges so there is no chance for a jury trial. Such trials offer a greater likelihood for acquittal, though higher courts can overturn juries' decisions as many times as necessary to obtain the "correct" decision.

Part of the problem in improving the functioning of the justice system is that the quality of the defense remains extremely poor in Russia and may even be deteriorating. Often the defense attorney is not prepared because he has not seen the case file or has not visited the prisoner in custody. Some even confuse the defendant's name during the trial. According to the Russian Constitution, defendants are entitled to free legal representation. But the bar association is supposed to provide these free lawyers, and it does not have the resources to do so. Not surprisingly, defense lawyers have extremely low salaries and are often overworked. Additionally, many started their careers in the prosecutor's office or the police and lack a basic understanding of the duties of a lawyer, nor do they want to defend people they believe are guilty.[58]

Perhaps the greatest indictment of the Russian court system is the large number of people who appeal to the European Court of Human Rights (ECHR) in Strasbourg because they believe they cannot get a fair trial in Russia.[59] Russia is bound by the ECHR's decisions since it incorporated the European Convention on Human Rights into its 1993 Constitution. More Russian citizens file cases with the ECHR than any other country in the Council of Europe. The ECHR's documents show that as of January 1, 2007, of some 90,000 cases pending before the Court, approximately 20,000 originated in Russia. More than 10,500 applications were logged in 2006 alone, double the 2003 figures and an increase of more than 400 percent over 2000.[60] Unfortunately, rather than address the problems causing citizens to appeal to the ECHR, the Russian authorities are looking for ways to limit Russian citizens' access to it. Such steps, including a proposal by Constitutional Court chairman Valery Zorkin, have gone nowhere because they would violate Russia's international obligations.

While the Russian authorities always pay the penalties assessed in individual cases, they rarely make structural changes to address the underlying issues in each case. In 2007, the ECHR made several rulings against Russian actions in Chechnya, including a determination that state agents had "extrajudicially executed" Zura Bitiyeva, a local human rights activist in Chechnya, along with three others in her home after she had appealed to the ECHR. The case was the first in which someone had apparently been slain for appealing to the ECHR. In July, the ECHR ruled that Russian soldiers had killed 50 civilians in the Chechen village of Novye Aldy in 2000 and ordered the government to pay US$200,000 to relatives of the deceased.

Anecdotal evidence suggests that conditions are deteriorating in Russian prisons.[61] The number of prison inmates in Russia reached 890,000 in the first half of 2007, according to the Federal Penitentiary Service Web site, the highest figure in five years.[62] The system has "slipped away from public, and even law enforcement, control almost entirely and increasingly bears the hallmarks of a repressive camp system of the totalitarian type," according to For Human Rights executive director Lev Ponomarev's analysis.[63] He argues that "those who find themselves remanded to a pre-trial detention center (SIZO) likely will be subjected to torturous conditions in overcrowded facilities, where there is a very real risk of contracting tuberculosis, HIV, hepatitis, or some other dangerous disease with far less than adequate medical care."

Corruption

1999	2001	2002	2003	2004	2005	2006	2007	2008
6.25	6.25	6.00	5.75	5.75	5.75	6.00	6.00	6.00

Russia lacks a coherent strategy to combat corruption. Putin has openly admitted that he has made little progress in this area, and Medvedev has declared that he will make the issue a priority. Nevertheless, in practice, few groups in society are interested in fighting corruption. The failure of both state and society to address the problem means that the situation is getting worse. In Transparency International's 2007 Corruption Perceptions Index, Russia was ranked 143 out of 180 countries, with an absolute score of 2.3 on the 0–10 scale, where 10 is the best possible score (perceived as least corrupt).[64] This is a drop from 2006, when Russia had a 2.5 score. Anticorruption campaigns in Russia are mostly attempts to discredit political opponents. An effective effort against this scourge would require a free media and a vibrant civil society that included many watchdog groups exercising oversight over public officials.

Russia faces many problems. Bribery is part of the culture now because as much as 40 percent of Russians see it as a useful way to solve problems, according to a poll conducted by the Levada Center in October.[65] About one-quarter of all money allocated for state purchases is stolen each year, according to a study by the National Association of Electronic Traders and the NGO Against Corruption. Many members of the organized crime groups prominent in the 1990s have now moved into business, where they often continue to function according to the old rules. Additionally, there is extensive corruption throughout Russia's law enforcement agencies. This problem used to apply mainly to the Ministry of Internal Affairs, but now an increasing number of criminal cases are being filed against employees of the FSB and the Office of the Procurator General.[66] While some evidence suggests that low-level corruption is decreasing, corruption at the highest levels of the political system and business is increasing, according to former economics minister Yevgeny Yasin.[67]

Part of the problem is a growing bureaucracy. When Putin came to power, Russia had approximately 1.14 million public officials—slightly fewer than were employed at the end of the Soviet era. In 2004, when administrative reform was launched, one of its main slogans was "Fewer bureaucrats!" As a result, according to Russia's Federal Statistics Service (Rosstat), perversely there are now almost 1.6 million officials in Russia,[68] plus approximately 3 million so-called *siloviki*—policemen, soldiers, and law enforcement and security agents.[69] Bureaucrats' salaries are increasing with their numbers: They were up 22.9 percent in the first six months of 2007, reaching an average of 23,029 rubles (approximately US$925) a month, according to Rosstat.[70] These higher salaries have apparently not made an impact on bribe taking.

Government efforts to address the problem have gone nowhere. In February 2007, an interdepartmental anticorruption working group, chaired by presidential aide Viktor Ivanov, was established. The group is supposed to amend current legislation in accordance with the UN and Council of Europe anticorruption conventions and define the functions and powers of a special anticorruption body. The group will also design mechanisms for requiring mandatory declarations of assets, preventing the legalization of criminal income, and avoiding conflicts of interest by public officials. The task group was supposed to come up with its proposals by August 1, 2007.[71] However, on August 14, President Putin moved the deadline to July 1, 2008.[72]

The appointment of the Viktor Zubkov government has raised concerns about the current extent of nepotism in Russian politics. Putin refused to accept the resignation of Defense Minister Anatoly Serdyukov after his father-in-law was appointed prime minister. There are many such family ties at federal and regional levels in Russia.[73] Federal Security Service Director Nikolai Patrushev's elder son handles loans to oil companies at Vneshtorgbank, while his younger son advises Rosneft chairman Igor Sechin.

Conditions for corruption seem to be proliferating. During the year, the authorities created several state corporations that have the ability to spend from the public budget with little oversight.[74] These noncommercial state entities include RosNanoTech, the Development Bank, and Dmitry Medvedev's Housing and Communal Services Reform Fund. They are not subject to the usual audit by the tax authorities or law enforcement. RosNanoTech will be directly subordinate to the president and cabinet and accountable only to them.

There is also a flagrant use of Russia's political institutions for provocative purposes. In one of the most pugnacious cases, the Liberal Democrats' list included Andrei Lugovoy, accused by the United Kingdom of murdering Aleksandr Litvinenko with polonium. Since the LDPR successfully crossed the 7 percent barrier, Lugovoy gained a seat in Parliament and immunity from prosecution.

▌ AUTHOR: ROBERT W. ORTTUNG

Robert W. Orttung is a senior fellow at the Jefferson Institute and a visiting scholar at the Swiss Federal Institute of Technology's Center for Security Studies.

---

[1]   Andrey Ryabov, "One Law for Two People: Dualism of Power After March Elections Will Inevitably Necessitate Amendments to Constitution," Gazeta.ru, December 26, 2007.

[2]   Francesca Mereu, "Putin Made Good on Promise to FSB," *Moscow Times*, February 8, 2008.

[3]   Viktor Khamrayev, "Russian Citizens Adapting to the Electoral System," *Kommersant*, November 12, 2007.

[4]   He went on to say: "And, unfortunately, we still have people in the country who live by begging at foreign embassies and foreign diplomatic missions. They count on the support of foreign funds and governments, rather than the support of their own people." Vladimir Putin, "Speech to a Gathering of Supporters of the President of Russia," November 21, 2007, http://www.kremlin.ru/eng/speeches/2007/11/21/1735_type82912type84779_153676. shtml.

[5]   According to sociologist Olga Khryshtanovskaya. See Vitali Tseplyaev, "All-Purpose Cadres," *Argumenty i Fakty*, 45 (November 7, 2007).

[6]   Viktor Cherkesov, "Nel'zya dopustit', chtoby voiny prevratilis' v torgovtsev" [We Must Not Allow Warriors to Turn into Traders], *Kommersant*, October 9, 2007.

[7]   See Peter Reddaway's work for detailed analyses of the *siloviki*. A recent summary was "Kremlin Politics and the Upcoming Election Cycle," remarks presented at Russia's Future and the 2007–2008 Elections, a conference at George Washington University, November 13, 2007.

[8]   Oleg Panfilov, "Elections of the Absurd," Index on Censorship Web site, http://www.indexoncensorship.org/?p=128, December 20, 2007.

[9]   "Independent Report Lists Numerous Irregularities in 2007 Russian Duma Election," Interfax, January 30, 2008.

10   "Udar po autoritetu 'Yedinoy Rossii'" [The Authority of 'United Russia' Takes a Hit], Gazeta.
     ru, December 24, 2007, http://www.gazeta.ru/politics/elections2007.

11   See Hans-Henning Schroder, "Sufficient Legitimation for a 'Shadow President'?" *Russian
     Analytical Digest* 32 (December 14, 2007).

12   Channel One and Russian Television aired the debates at 7:05 a.m. and 10:50 to 11:20 a.m.,
     respectively. The stations said that viewers have very little interest in them.

13   Jean-Christophe Peuch, "Russia: Moscow Targets Vote Monitors in Bid to Overhaul OSCE,"
     Radio Free Europe/Radio Liberty, November 5, 2007, http://www.rferl.org/featuresarticle/
     2007/11/5586be84-4c61-4367-977f-abd1293a4149.html.

14   "Russia: Rights Activists Worried by Pressure on NGOs During Election Campaign,"
     Interfax, November 13, 2007.

15   "Predvaritel'nye rezul'taty nablyudeniya v den' golosovaniya na osnove soobshchenii ot
     korrespondentov gazety *Grazhdanskii golos* i soobshcehnii s Goryachei linii" [Preliminary
     Results of Observing Election Day on the Basis of Communications from Correspondents
     of the Newspaper *Civil Voice* and Communications from the Hot Line], http://golos.org/
     a1036.html.

16   "NKO Exodus: The Number of Nonprofits in Russia Has Declined Sharply," *Nezavisimaya
     Gazeta*, December 28, 2007.

17   Nikolai Petrov, "Great Shell Game in Duma," *Moscow Times*, December 18, 2007.

18   Leonid Kirichenko, "A Free Pass for Elections," *Novaya Gazeta*, November 29, 2007; and
     Leonid Kirichenko, "The Regime's Victories Are Always Legal," *Nezavisimaya Gazeta*, January
     18, 2008.

19   Robert Coalson, "Transparency International Criticizes Pro-Kremlin Parties," RFE/RL
     Newsline, October 31, 2007, citing *Vedomosti*, October 31, 2007.

20   "SPS Charges Government Prevents It from Campaigning," RFE/RL Newsline, November
     8, 2007.

21   "Over 1,000 NGOs Refused Registration in Russia—Official," Interfax, November 8,
     2007.

22   "NKO Exodus: The Number of Nonprofits in Russia Has Declined Sharply," *Nezavisimaya
     Gazeta*, December 28, 2007.

23   Anastasiya Kornya and Yekaterina Kudashkina, "Dorogoi al'truizm" [Expensive Altruism]
     Vedomosti, July 18, 2007.

24   "Over 600 NGOs Closed in Russia This Year," *Kommersant*, August 20, 2007.

25   Nikolaus von Twickel, "NGOs Buried by Mountain of Paper," *Moscow Times*, August 24,
     2007.

26   "Only 36 Percent of Russian NGOs Reported Working Results," ITAR-TASS, September
     11, 2007.

27   "NKO Exodus: The Number of Nonprofits in Russia Has Declined Sharply," *Nezavisimaya
     Gazeta*, December 28, 2007.

28   Interview with Nashi leader Nikita Borovikov, "Russia Must Be a Global Leader in the 21st
     Century," *Izvestia*, February 7, 2008.

29   Yevgeniy Gontmakher, "New Unofficial Organizations—Nonpolitical Self-Organization Is
     the Russian Middle Class's Last Outlet for Civil Activity," *Nezavisimaya Gazeta*, December
     14, 2007.

30   Andrei Kuzenko, "Demokratiyu ne puskayut na ulitsu [They Do Not Allow Democracy on
     the Street]," *Kommersant*, October 12, 2007.

31   Nora Boustany, "Rights Activist Tells of Detention in Russian Psychiatric Institutions,"
     Washington Post, October 22, 2007.

32   Mark Franchetti, "Putin Brings Back Mental Ward Torment," *Sunday Times*, August 26,
     2007.

33 Galina Kozhevnikova, "Radikal'nyi natsionalizm v Rossii i protivodeistvie emu v 2007 godu" [Radical Nationalism in Russia and Efforts Against It in 2007], February 7, 2008, available at http://xeno.sova-center.ru/29481C8/A91EC67, accessed February 14, 2008.

34 Tatyana Lvova, "ON STRIKE: Labor Unrest Sweeps Russia," *Versiya* 30 (August 6, 2007).

35 Boris Kagarlitsky, "A New Era for Labor Unions," *Moscow Times*, December 6, 2007.

36 'Tovarish' Kasrils, "Priostanovlenie zabastovki" [Strike Postponed], *Ford-Profsoyuz*, December 15, 2007, http://www.ford-profsoyuz.ru/content/view/479/1.

37 "Legal Strikes Almost Impossible in Russia—Union Leader," ITAR-TASS, January 29, 2008.

38 Peter Finn, "New Manuals Push a Putin's-Eye View in Russian Schools," *Washington Post*, July 20, 2007. See also the discussion in Edward Lucas, *The New Cold War: Putin's Russia and the Threat to the West* (New York: Palgrave Macmillan, 2008), pp. 107–108.

39 The textbook is entitled *The History of Russia, 1945–2007* and was written by Aleksandr Filippov, Anatoliy Utkin, and Aleksandr Danilov. Yuliya Taratuta, "Sovereign Democracy Will Be Taught in the Schools," *Kommersant*, December 27, 2007.

40 Reporters Without Borders Press Freedom Index, http://www.rsf.org/article.php3?id_article=24025.

41 Robert Coalson, "Russia: *Nezavisimaya Gazeta* Is Worth Watching Again," Radio Free Europe/Radio Liberty, September 3, 2007.

42 Jamey Gambrell, "Putin Strikes Again," *New York Review of Books* 54 (July 2007): 12.

43 Peter Finn, "Russia Turns New Law Against Kremlin Critics," *Washington Post*, September 26, 2007.

44 C. J. Chivers, "Eviction Notice Is Latest Russian Move Against Journalists," *New York Times*, May 19, 2007.

45 Anton Troianovski and Peter Finn, "Kremlin Seeks to Extend Its Reach in Cyberspace," *Washington Post*, October 28, 2007; and "Number of Internet Users in Russia Grows 40% to 35 Mln in 2007," ITAR-TASS, February 11, 2008, citing Minister of Information Technologies and Communications Leonid Reiman.

46 "Six Apart Announces New Home for LiveJournal," December 3, 2007, http://news.livejournal.com/104520.html; and Helen Womack and Will Stewart, "Oligarch in the Blogosphere," *Sunday Telegraph*, January 6, 2008.

47 American Committee for Peace in the Caucasus Weekly News Update, December 4–10, 2007.

48 Ibid., December 20, 2007–January 9, 2008.

49 See Committee to Protect Journalists, "Attacks on the Press in 2007," http://www.cpj.org/attacks07/europe07/rus07.html.

50 Heidi Dawley, "Russian Media: Blossoming, If Bloody," *Media Life Magazine*, July 12, 2007.

51 J. Paul Goode, "The Puzzle of Putin's Gubernatorial Appointments," *Europe-Asia Studies* 59, no. 3 (May 2007): 365–399.

52 Liz Fuller, "Chechnya: Kadyrov Completes First 100 Days in Office," Radio Free Europe/Radio Liberty, July 11, 2007.

53 Amnesty International Press Release, "Russian Federation: Do Not Repeat Mistakes Made in Chechnya," October 25, 2007.

54 Domitilla Sagramoso, "Violence and Conflict in the Russian North Caucasus," *International Affairs* 83, no. 4 (2007): 681–705.

55 Kira Latukhina, Yelena Ivanova, "Oligarchs' Wishes," *Vedomosti*, February 1, 2008; and "Chief Arbitration Justice Admits to Pressure from Authorities," ITAR-TASS, February 1, 2008.

56 "Constitutional Court to Move to St. Pete by Spring—Kozhin," ITAR-TASS, January 16, 2008.

57   See the evaluation of European Court of Human Rights president John Paul Costa in "Top Strasbourg Judges Comment on Russian Justice System's Failings, Improvements," Interfax, August 3, 2007.

58   This analysis is based on the comments of Russian lawyer Karinna Moskalenko, director of the Center for International Protection, at Freedom House, and the Carnegie Endowment for International Peace, September 29, 2007.

59   See, for example, the complaints by official human rights ombudsman Vladimir Lukin in Boris Yamshanov, "Judicial Error," *Rossiiskaya Gazeta*, February 8, 2008.

60   Iva Savic, "The Russians and the Courts," *International Herald Tribune*, August 10, 2007, http://www.iht.com/articles/2007/08/10/opinion/edsavic.php?page=1.

61   Elena Borisova, "Durnaya beskonechnost" [Evil Eternity], Ekspert online, October 19, 2007, http://www.expert.ru/articles/2007/10/19/bunt.

62   Anastasia Kornia and Alexei Nikolsky, "Imprisoned Russia," *Vedomosti*, July 30, 2007.

63   Lev Ponomarev, "Revival of the Gulag?: Putin's Penitentiary System," *Perspective* XVIII, no. 1 (November–December 2007).

64   *Corruption Perceptions Index 2007*, Transparency International, http://www.transparency. org/news_room/latest_news/press_releases/2007/2007_09_26_cpi_2007_en.

65   Kira Vasilieva, "Bribes as Salary Supplements," *Novye Izvestia*, October 11, 2007.

66   See the analysis by former procurator general Yury Skuratov in "Time of Werewolves: To Suggest That Organized Crime Has Been Defeated in Russia Is to Dangerously Mislead Our Citizens," *Nezavisimaya Gazeta*, September 19, 2007.

67   Aleksei Shcheglov, "U Rossii ukrali eshche odin trillion" [They Stole Another Trillion from Russia], *Nezavisimaya Gazeta*, October 17, 2007.

68   Nadezhda Ivanitskaya, "The Number of Public Officials Has Grown 7.9 percent," *Vedomosti*, April 24, 2007.

69   "Voorujennie sily nefti i gaza" [Armed Forces of Oil and Gas], *Novaya Gazeta*, July 20, 2007, http://www.novayagazeta.ru/data/2007/color27/01.html. See also Nikolaus von Twickel, "Red Tape Reaching Its Soviet Heights," *Moscow Times*, August 7, 2007, http://www. themoscowtimes.com/stories/2007/08/07/001.html.

70   Olga Gorelik, "Salaries Rise–Queues Remain," *Izvestia*, September 17, 2007.

71   Natalia Melikova, "All to Fight Corruption!" *Nezavisimaya Gazeta*, March 2, 2007.

72   "Putin prodlil deyatelnost gruppy po protivodeystviyu korruptsii" [Putin Prolonged Activity of the Anti-Corruption Group], *Delo*, August 14, 2007, http://delo.ua/news/politics/world/ info-46849.html.

73   "Relatives in Power," *Kommersant-Vlast*, 37 (September 2007).

74   Andrei Lavrov, Yevgeny Belyakov, "Budget Money to the Negative Ninth Degree," *Gazeta*, July 4, 2007.

Serbia

by Slobodan Markovich

Capital:	Belgrade
Population:	7.5 million
GNI/capita:	US$9,320

The social data above was taken from the European Bank for Reconstruction and Development's *Transition Report 2007: People in Transition*, and the economic data from the World Bank's *World Development Indicators 2008*.

Nations in Transit Ratings and Averaged Scores

	Yugoslavia				Serbia				
	1999	2001	2002	2003	2004	2005	2006	2007	2008
Electoral Process	5.50	4.75	3.75	3.75	3.50	3.25	3.25	3.25	3.25
Civil Society	5.25	4.00	3.00	2.75	2.75	2.75	2.75	2.75	2.75
Independent Media	5.75	4.50	3.50	3.25	3.50	3.25	3.25	3.50	3.75
Governance*	5.50	5.25	4.25	4.25	4.00	n/a	n/a	n/a	n/a
National Democratic Governance	n/a	n/a	n/a	n/a	n/a	4.00	4.00	3.75	4.00
Local Democratic Governance	n/a	n/a	n/a	n/a	n/a	3.75	3.75	3.75	3.75
Judicial Framework and Independence	5.75	5.50	4.25	4.25	4.25	4.25	4.25	4.25	4.50
Corruption	6.25	6.25	5.25	5.00	5.00	5.00	4.75	4.50	4.50
Democracy Score	5.67	5.04	4.00	3.88	3.83	3.75	3.71	3.68	3.79

* With the 2005 edition, Freedom House introduced separate analysis and ratings for national democratic governance and local democratic governance to provide readers with more detailed and nuanced analysis of these two important subjects.

NOTES: The ratings reflect the consensus of Freedom House, its academic advisers, and the author(s) of this report. The opinions expressed in this report are those of the author(s). The ratings are based on a scale of 1 to 7, with 1 representing the highest level of democratic progress and 7 the lowest. The Democracy Score is an average of ratings for the categories tracked in a given year.

In *Nations in Transit 2007*, Freedom House provides separate ratings for Serbia and Kosovo in order to provide a clearer picture of processes and conditions in the different administrative areas. Doing so does not indicate a position on the part of Freedom House on Kosovo's future status

EXECUTIVE SUMMARY

Serbia's democratization processes continued to encounter challenges in 2007, and political commitment to consolidate previous advances was in weak evidence. In February 2007, the International Court of Justice (ICJ) made the first-ever ruling on the application of the 1948 Genocide Convention, and in the case of *Bosnia and Herzegovina v. Serbia and Montenegro,* found that Serbia had not committed, conspired to commit, or been complicit in genocide during the Bosnian war; but that it violated the Convention by not using its influence on the Republica Srpska leaders to prevent genocide from happening in Bosnia-Herzegovina. The court also stated that Serbia was in breach of its obligations by its failure to transfer Ratko Mladić for trial and cooperate fully with the ICTY.[1]

The judgment was received well among Bosnian Serbs (but not by Muslims in Bosnia) and mainstream political parties in both Serbia and the Republica Srpska, but some NGOs in Serbia severely criticized this judgment claiming that it was in insult to victims. Cooperation with the International Criminal Tribunal for the Former Yugoslavia (ICTY) improved in 2007 in terms of supplying the court with documentation, although Serbia did not arrest the chief suspects (General Ratko Mladić and Radovan Karadzic), which was the court's primary demand. Negotiations with the EU continued, half-heartedly—and did not result in a Stabilization and Association Agreement (SAA)—and the status of Kosovo remained the key issue that increasingly influenced domestic politics.

National Democratic Governance. In January 2007, the parties of the democratic bloc won the elections, but it took three months of negotiating to form a new government. The center-right minority government led by Vojislav Koštunica and the Democratic Party of Serbia (DSS) was replaced by a coalition of two centrist parties—G17plus and the Democratic Party (DS)—and one center-right party: Koštunica's DSS. The DS and G17plus had been unable to form a majority in the parliament and through "horse-trading" the position of prime minister were able to bring in the DSS, which had been negotiating with the Serbian Radical Party (SRS), and achieve the necessary majority. After political maneuvers that included the brief appointment of the leader of the nationalistic Serbian Radical Party as speaker of parliament, Prime Minister Koštunica thus secured another appointment as Prime Minister. However, his coalition won significantly fewer votes than the Democratic Party led by Serbia's president Boris Tadić. It was May when the Democratic Party, the Democratic Party of Serbia (DSS), and G17plus formed the new government, but the rivalry between DS and DSS remained throughout 2007. Negotiations with the EU were resumed and progressed, but the main political obstacle—the inadequacy of Serbia's co-operation with the ICTY—made these relations ambiguous. Two more indicted persons were transferred to The Hague, but four are still demanded from Serbia. The government made the status of Kosovo the major domestic issue and allowed it to derail the completion of many other important reforms. *Owing to the difficulties encountered during the several months it took to form a government, and political leadership that chose to let the Kosovo issue derail major reforms, Serbia's national democratic governance rating worsens from 3.75 to 4.00.*

Electoral Process. In 2007 general elections were held in Serbia, and the parties of the democratic bloc won 145 seats. The January 21 elections were held in accordance with democratic principles and under more objective media coverage than in earlier elections. Elections were observed by leading domestic and foreign observers and were assessed as free. Marking a minor improvement, previously enacted legislation enabled better representation of women through quotas placed on party list candidates, and a return of minorities to the National Parliament. Presidential elections were postponed until the beginning of 2008. *Serbia's electoral process rating remains at 3.25.*

Civil Society. The law on NGOs was prepared but not enacted in 2007, and an ombudsperson for citizens was finally appointed in June 2007. Leading NGOs found themselves in opposite camps regarding the question of the conditionality of Serbia's SAA negotiations with the EU. NGOs successfully opposed a neo-Nazi march in Novi Sad and campaigned against a state tax of 5 percent on donations to NGOs. But overall, neither political space nor civil society's scope of influence was broadened. *Serbia's rating for civil society remains at 2.75.*

Independent Media. Television remained the most influential among Serbian media options, and tabloids maintained their quantitative dominance over quality dailies. State television was ordered to broadcast sessions of the parliament, and the state television found itself in a dilemma on whether to meet demands by SRS to broadcast the ICTY court proceedings against the president of the Serbian Radical Party, Vojislav Šešelj. An assassination attempt was made on the journalist Dejan Anastasijević of *Vreme*, a national independent weekly. *As the attempted assassination of a prominent journalist is symptomatic of the intimidation and overall environment surrounding those who engage in investigative journalism, Serbia's independent media rating worsens from 3.50 to 3.75.*

Local Democratic Governance. The concession for the Horgos-Požega highway caused major disputes between the autonomous province of Vojvodina and central authorities in Belgrade. Laws enacted at the end of 2007 brought no new improvements to the field of regionalization, which was not debated much during the year. Local elections were discussed to a greater degree, and the proportional system with a possibility of "envelope resignations" was accepted. This is likely to have a negative effect on local governance in the future. Some important initiatives that would give local property to municipalities were initiated in 2007, which may be enacted in 2008. *Serbia's rating for local democratic governance remains at 3.75.*

Judicial Framework and Independence. The Constitutional Court was not in session from October 2006 through December 2007. This was detrimental to the rule of law in Serbia. The Ministry of Justice initiated the first prosecution of judges whose neglect of their duties over a long period of time led to the cancellation of several cases. The ministry also initiated an analysis of the duration of court cases in Serbia, which often extend beyond a reasonable length of time. On May 23, and despite ongoing reports of political interference in the work of prosecutors of the case since it began in 2003, the verdict and sentencing were delivered in the former Prime Minister Zoran Đinđić assassination trial. Nevertheless, slight progress in the judiciary is countered by the lack of an operational constitutional court in 2007. *Owing to the lack of a functional constitutional court for all of 2007, Serbia's rating for judicial framework and independence worsens from 4.25 to 4.50.*

Corruption. The question of monopolies was widely debated for the first time in Serbia in 2007. Police arrested an organized group connected to cigarette smuggling. A study by independent analysts established some progress in fighting corruption over the last seven years, but also insufficient political will. *There were some improvements but insufficient progress overall, therefore Serbia's rating for corruption remains at 4.50*

Outlook for 2008. Resolution of the final status of Kosovo is likely to influence the stability of the current government in Serbia. The current pro-reformist president Boris Tadić and the pro-Russian leader of the Serbian Radical Party, Tomislav Nikolić, will compete in the presidential elections in 2008. Tadić's victory is likely, unless the Kosovo crisis provokes national radicalization in Serbia. After Kosovo's independence, cohabitation between the president and the Prime Minister will become more complicated, and their coalition government will experience a serious test. The Prime Minister's party may decide to abandon the current coalition to join the bloc of parties from the Milošević era. Cooperation with the ICTY will depend on political will in Serbia following Kosovo's proclamation of independence. Serbia may accelerate or temporarily abandon efforts to become a member of the EU, depending on the coalition in power.

Main Report

National Democratic Governance

1999	2001	2002	2003	2004	2005	2006	2007	2008
Y u g o s l a v i a				n/a	4.00	4.00	3.75	4.00

In Serbia, the year began with parliamentary elections in which the parties of the democratic bloc won the majority of seats. The negotiations on forming a government between the two principal actors—Prime Minister Vojislav Koštunica, leader of the center-right Democratic Party of Serbia (DSS), and President Boris Tadić, leader of the centrist Democratic Party (DS)—did not go well. Koštunica and Tadić disagreed on who would be the new Prime Minister or head major ministries. The third party participating in the negotiations, the liberal G17plus, headed by Mladan Dinkić, announced that it would accept any Prime Minister acceptable to DS and DSS. Finally, the smallest party of the democratic bloc, the Liberal-Democratic Party, rejected cooperation with any government that would include G17plus and particularly DSS, and thus excluded itself from further negotiations.

The Serbian parliament has a total of 250 seats. DS won 64 seats, DSS 47, and G17plus with 19 seats, secured a majority, and enough to form a government. Differing views on who should be the next Prime Minister bitterly divided DS and DSS. DS suggested an economist, former finance minister Božidar Đelić; DSS wanted to keep Koštunica as Prime Minister.

At the center of the Serbian political spectrum, Prime Minister Koštunica negotiated a coalition with DS and G17plus, as well as the extreme nationalists from the Serbian Radical Party (SRS) with the largest number of seats in parliament. Following almost three months of official and unofficial negotiations between DSS and DS, Koštunica allowed the leader of SRS, Tomislav Nikolić, to become speaker of the parliament on May 8, 2007. Nikolić surprised all when he announced a day later that the parliament might introduce a state of emergency because of circumstances in Kosovo.

The situation looked gloomy for the democratic bloc, and the Belgrade Stock Exchange suffered a tremendous decline. In this atmosphere of uncertainty, Tadić decided to yield. On May 11, Tadić and Koštunica made an agreement permitting Koštunica to form a new government. On May 13, Nikolić resigned from his post. The parliament confirmed the government on May 15, only 50 minutes before the constitutional deadline. Had this deadline been breached, the president would have been obliged to call new elections. A compromise between DS and DSS was made in such a way that DSS kept the position of prime minister but DS and G17plus got the majority of cabinet ministers.

Nikolić's posting had threatened to undermine Serbia's Chairmanship of the Committee of Ministers of the Council of Europe, which coincidentally began just when Nikolić became Speaker of the Parliament. After his resignation, relations with the Council of Europe immediately improved, and the 1,000th meeting of the Committee of Ministers of the Council of Europe was held in Belgrade on June 22, 2007.

Following Montenegro's independence, the government used the dissolution of the State Union to focus Serbian public opinion even more closely on the issue of Kosovo's status, though Serbian political players continued to avoid preparing the public for the probable independence of Kosovo. Although the plan for the resolution of the status of Kosovo was prepared by UN envoy Martti Ahtisaari at the end of 2006; its publication was postponed until after the Serbian elections. The Ahtisaari plan envisaged independence for Kosovo, although the word independence was not explicitly mentioned. What gradually became obvious in the first half of 2007 was that Russia was ready to use its veto to block a UN resolution that would lead to Kosovo's independence. At the end of March 2007, the Serbian Prime Minister openly expressed his conviction that Russia would veto Ahtisaari's plan. The plan, in several drafts, met with fierce opposition from Serbian officials.

Finally, negotiations between Belgrade and Pristina were resumed by a team consisting of representatives from the EU, Russia, and the United States. On December 7 the troika submitted a progress report to the UN and concluded that four months of negotiations between Belgrade and Pristina had ended without results. While the American side held that, should negotiations fail, supervised independence should be given to Kosovo, Russia claimed that negotiations should be continued as long as the two sides lacked an agreement. The presidential elections in Serbia were called on December 12 and were scheduled for January 20, 2008.

At the beginning of 2007, six persons were still wanted by the ICTY, and Serbia was held responsible for at least five of them, especially the onetime military leader of the Bosnian Serbs, General Ratko Mladić. Two persons were arrested during 2007: in May, Zdravko Tolimir, a commander in the Bosnian Serb army was arrested, followed by Vlastimir Đorđević, a senior Serbian police officer, in June.

The European Commission postponed negotiations with Serbia on the Stabilization and Association Agreement (SAA) on May 3, 2006, due to Serbia's non-cooperation with the International Criminal Tribunal for the Former Yugoslavia (ICTY). Within the EU, the Member States disagreed about whether an SAA should be signed with Serbia before Serbia arrests and extradites General Mladić to the ICTY, which is the court's principle demand. Some say ICTY compliance should be a precondition for an SAA, while others favor signing the SAA agreement with Serbia without preconditions related to the ICTY, in a nod to pro-Western leadership within Serbia.

Technical negotiations between Serbia and the EU on the SAA were resumed in June 2007. In July the two sides harmonized the SAA, and the final round of technical negotiations was successfully completed in Brussels in September. However, the signing of the agreement was postponed. On November 6, Chief Prosecutor from The Hague Carla Del Ponte informed EU enlargement commissioner Olli Rehn that "Serbia had made sufficient progress in cooperation with the Tribunal to merit initialing of the agreement," and the Agreement was initialed but not signed on November 7, 2007.

Important agreements with the EU were reached in September 2007, including the signing of Visa Facilitation and Readmission Agreements. These should enter into force on January 1, 2008. Officials in Belgrade expressed their hopes that these agreements would accelerate Serbia's road toward a visa-free regime with EU countries. At the very end of 2007, in an article written for Belgrade daily *Danas*, Rehn concluded: "The year 2008 will be crucial for the European future of Serbia," and said that signing the SAA was "within arm's reach."[2]

The February 2007 judgment of the International Court of Justice in The Hague (not to be confused with the ICTY) regarding *Bosnia and Herzegovina v. Serbia and Montenegro* stirred great debate among NGOs. It confirmed that the Srebrenica massacre was a case of genocide conducted by Bosnian Serb forces, but rejected claims that genocide was committed everywhere on the territory of Bosnia and Herzegovina. It also stated that Serbia was not directly responsible for the genocide in Srebrenica, but found Serbia was guilty of failing to prevent genocide.

Serbia became a member of the Partnership for Peace at the NATO summit in Riga on November 29, 2006. While the Democratic Party (DS) supports Serbia's future membership in NATO, the Democratic Party of Serbia (DSS) opposes it.

The Exoneration Bill enacted in 2006 was implemented in some key cases in 2007. The law was intended to exonerate victims who were convicted by Communist and other authorities between 1941 and 2006 for political or ideological reasons. Still victims cannot yet demand restitution of confiscated property as a bill on restitution has yet to be enacted.

The 2006 constitution introduced the ombudsperson as a constitutional category. In June 2007, the parliament enacted the Law on supplements to the Law of the Protector of Citizens originally enacted in 2005, and then appointed Saša Janković to be the first Protector of Citizens in Serbia. The office was fully operational by the end of 2007.

Serbia's economy continued to improve. The IMF office in Belgrade recorded relatively low inflation (7.4 percent in September 2007), while economic growth of 6.7 percent was expected in 2007, following a high level of foreign direct investment in 2006. However, the IMF warned Serbia about overly rapid wage and credit growth, which is connected to high trade and current account deficits. Recognition for achievements in this field came from the London-based *Euromoney*, which named minister of economy and former finance minister Mlađan Dinkić "Finance minister of the year 2007."

Electoral Process

1999	2001	2002	2003	2004	2005	2006	2007	2008
Y u g o s l a v i a				3.50	3.25	3.25	3.25	3.25

Parliamentary elections were held on January 21, 2007. These were the third elections for the Parliament of Serbia since the pro-democratic revolution in

October 2000, and they were held in accordance with electoral legislation amended in February 2004. The elections were proportional with a minimum threshold of 5 percent. Parties of national minorities had no electoral threshold and could gain a seat in parliament with 0.4 percent of votes (8 seats were won by national minority candidates). Amendments obliged all parties to put forward electoral lists with 30 percent women candidates, although they were not obliged to follow an equal percentage when appointing MPs. The Serbian Parliament had only 30 women, or 12 percent of total MPs, in the period 2003-2006, but this percentage increased to 20.4 percent in 2007. "Pro-democratic" parties won 145 seats (DS—64, DSS—47, G17plus—19, and the coalition headed by LDP—15); while parties of the former regime of Slobodan Milošević won 97 seats (SRS—81 and SPS—16).

Table 1.
Results of the January 2007 Elections for the Parliament of Serbia

Political Party	Popular Votes	Number of MPs
Ruling Coalition		
Democratic Party (DS)	915,854	64
Democratic Party of Serbia—New Serbia (DSS/NS)	667,615	47
G17plus	275,041	19
Coalition List for Sanjak*	33,823	2
TOTAL	1,892,333	132
Others		
Serbian Radical Party (SRS)	1,153,453	81
Socialist Party of Serbia (SPS)	227,580	16
Coalition headed by the Liberal Democratic Party (LDP)	214,262	15
Union of Hungarians of Vojvodina*	52,510	3
Coalition of Albanians of the Presevo Valley*	16,973	1
Union of Roma of Serbia*	17,128	1
Roma Party*	14,631	1
TOTAL	1,664,778	116

* Parties of national minorities

The leading Serbian NGO for monitoring elections, the Center for Free Elections and Democracy (CeSID), supervised 5,000 polling places and reported that "the elections were mainly conducted in accordance with rules, democratic standards, and principles." Elections were observed by a range of foreign observers including OSCE and the Council of Europe who assessed them as free. In the municipality of Presevo in southern Serbia, CeSID recorded violations of election rules and noted overall some remaining problems, primary among them: insufficient mechanisms for controlling campaign financing. Although the State Register of Voters was improved since 2001, it also remained a problem since many voters who left the country or even died abroad are still in the list, and voters who have changed their place of residence are often registered at their former addresses.

Almost all 250 MPs followed the orders of their parties in 2007, an effect of "pre-submitted" or "envelope" resignations. This means that an MP at the beginning of his/her tenure may be asked by his/her political party to sign a resignation, which the party keeps on file and may produce whenever it wishes to rid itself of a problematic MP. This practice was instituted in 2006 as a reaction to an earlier state of affairs, when some MPs were ready to sell their party allegiance. Proponents of "envelope resignations" claimed that it was better to restrict MP freedoms in decision-making rather than permit an open market on votes in the parliament.

Civil Society

1999	2001	2002	2003	2004	2005	2006	2007	2008
Y u g o s l a v i a				2.75	2.75	2.75	2.75	2.75

In October, the government of Serbia adopted a version of the Law on Associations, which was not yet accepted by the parliament by the end of 2007. The draft law was well received in the Serbian NGO community, since it aimed to introduce European standards in the field. In 2007, NGOs tried but failed to prevent the imposition of a 5-percent tax on donations to NGOs.

Demonstrating the civil sector's vibrancy, in 2007 a group of leading NGOs hotly debated the continuation of SAA negotiations and called on the EU not to continue until persons indicted by the ICTY were transferred to The Hague. Another group of NGOs issued a different appeal claiming that it was precisely the continuation of negotiations between Serbia and the EU that would facilitate the full cooperation of the Serbian government with the ICTY.

Neo-Nazi groups continued to be active in Serbia during the year and tried to organize an October march in Novi Sad with foreign neo-Nazis groups. The application to march, submitted to the police by Goran Davidović of the Serbian branch of National Storm, was rejected. Key political parties in Serbia, including the mayor of Novi Sad from SRS, condemned the march. Numerous NGOs and liberal and social-democratic political parties organized an anti-fascist rally in Novi

Sad on the same day. Davidović and members of his group heckled the anti-fascist marchers and were arrested.

Serbian Ombudsman Saša Janković expressed concern (in a press release on the 60th anniversary of the International Human Rights Day in December 2007) that in Serbia "there is still no culture of respect of human rights, and consideration and tolerance for differences of everyone with no exception".[3] He also pointed out that excesses are still present that affect freedom of speech. An important example of these tendencies—widely commented on and covered by the media—was the disruption of programming and cancellation of events of the popular B92 radio show Peščanik (Hourglass).

Peščanik, run by two prominent Serbian journalists Svetlana Lukić and Svetlana Vuković, is known for its criticism of the government, especially of Prime Minister Koštunica. Strong opposition to events to promote the show and related publications led to a series of confrontations, cancellations, and protests. In the provincial town of Aranđelovac the director of the local cultural center cancelled a panel discussion intended to launch a publication of the program. The local TV station Šumadija, in a special broadcast, urged the public to turn out and protest the release of a Peščanik publication. Physical clashes and a barrage of insults resulted when several dozen supporters from nationalist political parties forcibly broke up a promotion at Aranđelovac's House of Culture.[4] The president in the municipality of Topola (from the governing party New Serbia) organized around 200 protestors who entered the town center and prevented the panel discussion from taking place.[5] Svetlana Lukić said that the problem is that in many provincial areas of Serbia "local political parties took full control of everything and there is now limited space for liberal views."[6]

Not only in the provinces, but also in the Parliament of Serbia an incident took place. On November 14, inside the hall of the Parliament of Serbia, opposition SRS MPs were selling copies of a book entitled *Afera Hrtkovici i Ustaška Kurva Nataša Kandić* [Hrtkovci Affair and Ustasha Whore Nataša Kandić]. After the intervention by the speaker of the parliament they stopped selling it but continued to distribute it. This book has been written by the leader of SRS Vojislav Šešelj (currently tried for crimes by the Hague Tribunal), and the aim of the book has been to attack and offend Nataša Kandić, executive director of the Humanitarian Law Center in Belgrade. Additionally to this incident, MPs of SRS often misused discussions in the Parliament throughout 2007 to attack various public figures of liberal orientation in Serbia.

In November, after campaigning by student groups, the post-validation of "basic studies" diplomas converting them into master degrees was approved after some hesitation by the parliament. However, the University of Belgrade opposes post-validation and has announced that it will only implement the decision with numerous restrictions.

Associations advocating property restitution were active in 2007. After many years of hesitation, the state finally proposed a draft Law on Denationalization in September that gives advantage to natural restitution of private property confiscated in communist regimes. But it also allows substitution of property where possible, and monetary compensation where the first two possibilities are not applicable. Serbia remains the only post-communist country in the region that has yet to enact a law on the restitution of nationalized private property. During 2007, the Agency for Privatization continued to sell real estate that had been nationalized during the period of Communism despite the fact that previous legal owners or their heirs were officially registered in 2005–2006 in accordance with the Law on the Registration of Confiscated Property. These violations roused the European Parliament, which called on Serbian authorities to adopt restitution laws "as a matter of urgency."

Independent Media

1999	2001	2002	2003	2004	2005	2006	2007	2008
Y u g o s l a v i a				3.50	3.25	3.25	3.50	3.75

Serbian media represent a diverse range of opinions, but among print outlets, tabloids have dominated journalism for years. The most popular are the soft tabloids *Vecernje Novosti* (pro-government) and *Blic*, followed by the hardcore tabloids *Kurir* and *Press*. The hardcore tabloids have a tendency to publish sensationalistic articles that are light on facts (or omit them completely). The moderately pro-government *Politika* has no competition among quality dailies, while the liberal *Danas*, the provincial Novi Sad *Dnevnik*, and *Privredni Pregled* (an economic paper) have much smaller circulation. All leading newspapers are private with the exception of *Politika*, half of which is owned by the German Westdeutsche Allgemeine Zeitung (WAZ) and half by the state.

The leading quality weeklies are the conservative *NIN* and the liberal journal *Vreme*. The role of WAZ was a subject of debate in Serbia in 2007. The main distribution network of kiosks in Serbia is half owned by WAZ and half owned by a controversial Serbian tycoon, Stanko Subotić. In June, Serbian police announced that Subotić was on the list of individuals accused of smuggling cigarettes and issued a warrant for his arrest, but he happened to be outside of Serbia at the time.

Television remains the most influential among Serbian media. A survey conducted by Strategic Marketing Research in April 2007 found that 83 percent of respondents relied on television as their main source of information. The most important TV stations are: the state-owned Radio Television of Serbia (37 percent); and the privately-owned TV B92 (24 percent), and TV Pink (18 percent). Only 8 percent of respondents said their main source of information was print dailies, while 4 percent named radio. Respondents had the highest confidence in TV 92 (47 percent), followed by TV Pink (36 percent) and RTS (35 percent). Among print media, *Vecernje Novosti* (33 percent) and *Blic* (31 percent) recorded the highest confidence, followed by *Politika* (24 percent). Among radio stations, the highest confidence was given to Radio B92 (22 percent), closely followed by the state-controlled Radio Belgrade 1 (19 percent).

The same survey found that 56 percent believed that journalism is an important profession, while 11 percent believed it is not important. At the same time, only 41 percent of respondents believed that journalists were well paid, and 37 percent believed that journalists were corrupt. For Serbia's roughly 8,000 journalists, this was a very positive ranking in comparison with perceptions of corruption regarding politicians (85 percent) and judges (75 percent).

In 2007, the Serbian Radical Party and the Socialist Party of Serbia insisted that Radio Television of Serbia (RTS) broadcast parliamentary sessions in their entirety on the television's second channel. The director of RTS opposed this, but the Republic Broadcasting Agency (RBA) issued a general binding instruction in September obliging RTS to broadcast all regular parliamentary sessions (a win for the Serbian Radical Party). Since RBA members have a reputation of being close to the Democratic Party of Serbia, the decision was seen as a concession made by the Prime Minister to the Serbian Radical Party.

Another dilemma appeared over whether RTS should directly broadcast the ICTY war crimes trial of Vojislav Šešelj, who is indicted for war crimes and crimes against humanity by the ICTY but is also still the president of the Serbian Radical Party, the largest party in the Serbian Parliament. Slobodan Milošević and Vojislav Šešelj (both lawyers by profession) refused to have barristers at the Hague tribunal and were allowed by the Tribunal to defend themselves personally. Therefore SRS and Vojislav Šešelj have seen a possibility to promote their own party policies through direct broadcasts of Šešelj trials. During 2007, the SRS collected more than 700,000 signatures on a petition demanding that RTS provide simultaneous broadcast of the entire trial, and said the party believed that broadcasts of the trial would increase its popularity and strengthen public distaste with the ICTY. RTS demanded an opinion on the broadcast of the trial from RBA, but the agency declined to make a decision and left the matter up to RTS, which decided to broadcast extensive excerpts of Šešelj's prosecution.

In the early hours of April 14, a bomb exploded in the apartment of Dejan Anastasijević, a leading journalist from the liberal weekly *Vreme*. A second (unexploded) bomb was later found in the apartment. Anastasijević is known for his coverage of war crimes and criminal activities in Serbia, and he indirectly accused two persons indicted by ICTY for the attack: Vojislav Šešelj, leader of SRS, and Jovica Stanisic, former chief of the Serbian secret police during the Milošević era, who is on trial at the ICTY. Anastasijević claimed that Šešelj had prepared a list of potential witnesses who should be intimidated or eliminated, including himself.[7] By year end, no perpetrators for the bombing were found. This incident illustrates that a pattern used during Milošević's era of intimidating journalists by attacks—and even murders—is still used. Moreover, the murder of an influential journalist, Slavko Ćuruvija, which was committed in 1999, still was not resolved by the police by the end of 2007.

On International Human Rights Day in December 2007, Serbian ombudsman Saša Janković noted that there were still issues that affect freedom of speech in Serbia. Svetlana Lukić, a prominent Serbian journalist critical of the Koštunica government, claims that in many provincial areas of the country "local political parties [have taken] full control of everything and there is now limited space for liberal views."[8]

However, coverage of the issue of Kosovo's status in quality dailies and weeklies and in major digital media provided a range of opposite views. The positions of the major international powers were presented accurately, often more accurately than by Serbian politicians. Outside the quality press, the issues were presented quite differently, with nationalistic views and jingoism predominating.

In its annual index of press freedoms, Reporters Without Borders ranked Serbia 67 among 169 countries surveyed in 2007, a significant step backwards compared to Serbia's ranking of 48 in 2006.

Local Democratic Governance

1999	2001	2002	2003	2004	2005	2006	2007	2008
Y	u	g	o	s	l	a	v	i	a	n/a	3.75	3.75	3.75	3.75

For most Serbian political parties, decentralization was one of the key slogans in the electoral campaigns of 2003 and 2007. Minister of Public Administration and Local Self-Government, Milan Marković, called decentralization a priority and identified the instability of local self-government and the over-politicization and lack of professionalism in local bureaucracies as the main obstacles to decentralization in Serbia.

Decentralization in Serbia remains an issue because of the autonomous province of Vojvodina, as well as Kosovo, which came under UN rule in 1999. The 2006 constitution permits the formation of new autonomous provinces, but there were no serious discussions about this in 2007. There was much more debate over which towns in Serbia should receive the legal status of cities. At the end of 2007, a total of 23 municipalities received the status of cities but with only one additional competence, that of communal police.

A construction concession for a major highway through Vojvodina produced open conflict between the Speaker of Parliament of Vojvodina, Bojan Kostreš, and the Minister for Capital Investments in the government of Serbia, Velimir Ilić. Kostreš demanded the cancellation of a concession agreement signed with the consortium FCC and Alpina. When Kostreš was denied access to the contract, he took legal action, but Minister Ilić defied his appeals, and it was several months before the contract was made public. The Executive Council of Vojvodina formed its own Commission for Concessions in August, which determined that Vojvodina should receive compensation of €220 million (US$342 million). No agreement was reached by year's end.

The organization of elections was another problem at the local level, with DS favoring majority elections and DSS advocating for proportional elections. The consequence of proportional elections has been that local parties are able to "smuggle" names onto the list, since voters vote for parties, not for individuals.

Also, rural areas tend not to be represented in the proportional system, which privileges local councilors, elected based on party loyalties. At the end of 2007, the Law of Local Elections instituted the proportional system, which is likely to worsen local democratic governance in Serbia in the future. On a more positive note, municipalities demanded the transfer to municipal control of local property (now owned by the state). The major political parties agreed with this initiative, which may transfer property to municipalities as soon as 2008.

In 2007 the two municipalities in southern Serbia with an Albanian majority (Presevo and Bujanovac) remained relatively stable. However, the situation in the southwestern Sandzak region has proven to be very fragile. Sandzak consists of 6 municipalities, and there is also a part of Sandzak in northern Montenegro. Bosniaks make up the majority of the local population in three municipalities in the Serbian part of Sandzak (Sjenica, Tutin and Novi Pazar). There are two Bosniak parties in this region of Serbia: the liberal Sanjak Democratic Party (SDP), an ally of President Tadić since 2005, and the Conservative Party of Democratic Action (SDA), headed by Sulejman Ugljanin, ally of PM Koštunica since 2004. A conflict between these parties has bitterly divided Bosniaks in the region and has led to incidents and fights.

The situation in Sandzak was further complicated by the emergence of Wahabis, a group of Islamists who were arrested on March 17 in their camp near Novi Pazar. Serbian police found large quantities of ammunition in the camp. On September 14, fifteen arrested members of the group were charged with terrorism, and their trial is expected to take place in 2008. This group has been in conflict with local Islamic leaders but has not been connected to either of the two Sandzak parties.

On December 29, 2007, the Serbian parliament adopted four laws: the Law on Local Self-Government, the Law on Local Elections, the Law on the Capital City, and the Law on the Territorial Organization of the Republic Serbia. As a result, mayors will no longer be directly elected, but chosen by local councils. The reasons behind this change are that political parties were not able to control some mayors and some parties wished to prevent independent candidates from winning local elections. Moreover, the Law on Local Elections (article 47) now permits "envelope resignations," which is likely to strengthen party loyalty at the local level. These newly adopted laws may worsen local democratic governance in the future, particularly after the local elections scheduled for May 11, 2008.

Judicial Framework and Independence

1999	2001	2002	2003	2004	2005	2006	2007	2008
Y u g o s l a v i a				4.25	4.25	4.25	4.25	4.50

The Serbian constitution of 2006 redefined important elements of the judicial framework. An important novelty is that the tenure of judges is no longer unlimited. Every judge is now elected for a period of three years by the Serbian Parliament on the proposal of the High Judicial Council. After the first tenure of three years, the High Judicial Council may appoint the same person to be a permanent judge of the same or higher court (article 147). It is still not clear how this procedure will be implemented.

The Constitutional Court of Serbia, a nine-person body defined by the Constitution of 1990, ceased to operate on October 10, 2006, when its president retired. The old court could not perform since it had no quorum and no president, and a new one with fifteen judges was not appointed for more than a year. This meant that Serbia was without an authority capable of judging the constitutionality of laws for more than fourteen months.

The government submitted the Law on the Constitutional Court to the parliament on October 5, 2007, and the law was enacted on November 24. In accordance with the constitution, five judges were appointed by the parliament on November 24, and five were appointed by the president on December 7. Thus a legal quorum for sessions was obtained. The Constitutional Court finally became operational on December 26, when the president of the court was elected. The long delay arose from the inability of the ruling political parties to make a deal on who would be appointed to the court. Needless to say, the party inclinations of future judges played an important role in determining who would fill these important positions

The Ministry of Justice announced in September that it had started to work on the Law on Confiscation of Property obtained through Criminal Acts. This law should cover a wide range of cases, including organized crime, crimes against humanity, and corruption, which is a serious problem within the Serbian judicial system.

The Minister of Justice initiated an investigation of the conduct of judges of the District Court and the Supreme Court after they missed the deadline to bring a judgment in a child abuse case against a Serbian Orthodox monk. The Grand Personnel Council of the Supreme Court suggested that parliament remove two judges from the Supreme Court for their neglect in the case. If parliament accepts this suggestion in 2008, it will be the first instance in which judges of the Supreme Court have been dismissed for neglecting their duties.

On May 23, and despite ongoing reports of political interference in the work of prosecutors, the verdict was delivered in the former Prime Minister Zoran Đinđić assassination trial. Human Rights Watch commended prosecutors and judges, saying they "demonstrated the courage to bring 12 individuals to justice despite political pressure"[9] The most prominent person among the accused, leader of the Zemun Clan, Milorad Luković Ulemek (Legija), was sentenced to 40 years in prison. Đinđić was assassinated in 2003.

Overall, the Serbian judiciary is inefficient, and disputing parties must often wait for years until judgments are brought and enforced. Yet in 2007 the making and enforcement of judgments was more closely analyzed by the Ministry of Justice than ever before. Mediation has also gained some ground, facilitating the work of courts. The new Criminal Procedure Code came fully into effect on June 1, 2007.

Consequently, criminal cases are bringing quicker verdicts, but civil procedures remain unsatisfactorily long, particularly in so-called old cases. These are cases that have been before the courts for years, sometimes over a decade, with no judgment issued.

Corruption

1999	2001	2002	2003	2004	2005	2006	2007	2008
Y u g o s l a v i a				5.00	5.00	4.75	4.50	4.50

Corruption remains one of the primary problems in Serbia's transition. In 2007, the main corruption debates focused on the question of monopolies. The Anti-corruption Council spent much time disputing the sale of C Market, a major retailer purchased by Delta Holding through the Cyprus-based Hemslade Trading Ltd. Hemslade is the owner of several other leading retailers in Serbia and is owned by a leading Serbian tycoon Miroslav Mišković, who was Deputy Prime Minister of Serbia during the Milošević years.

The president of the council, Verica Barać, delivered an October report on C Market claiming that the sale indicates a clear case of corruption. In an allusion to Mišković, Barać pointed out that if an individual has great wealth, political factors "will endeavor to meet his demands."[10] In an obvious reference to this report, Minister of Trade, Predrag Bubalo, declared that he could not support those who give "unfounded estimates" that there were monopolies in Serbia. Mišković struck back by filing a law-suit against Verica Barać on November 5.

However, Barać replied that the Commission for the Protection of Competition has still not completed its procedures for permitting the merger of C Market and Delta Holding.[11] The Commission for the Protection of Competition rejected the demand for the merger on July 10, 2006, but the Supreme Court cancelled this decision due to procedural reasons. The Commission again rejected the merger on November 26, 2007, claiming that the merger of three supermarket chains owned by Hemslade Trading Ltd. covered 55.5 percent of all consumer purchases in Belgrade, of which C Market alone had 32 percent.[12] A decision by the Supreme Court of Serbia is expected in 2008.

Concerns over the role of Delta Holding were also voiced by politicians, particularly the Liberal-Democratic Party. In September 2007, MPs from this party accused Mišković of being "the leader of the cigarette mafia" and demanded his arrest. In the 1990s, Serbia was one of the major sources of cigarettes smuggled into Western Europe. On June 7, the police arrested eight suspects in an operation referred to as a "network," although the main suspect, Stanko Subotić, could not be apprehended since he was in Switzerland.

A study entitled *Corruption in Serbia: Five years later* estimated that indirect government policies were "mildly positive." The reduction of corruption over the previous seven years had been fostered by foreign trade liberalization, the reform of public finances, and liberalization in general. On the other hand, no major improvement resulted from direct policies of the government, which is attributed to a lack of political will. For this reason the Minister of Economy Mlađan Dinkić announced plans to introduce a new set of anticorruption laws that may be of great importance.

In November 2007, the parliament ratified the Civil Law Convention on Corruption enacted by the Council of Europe in 1999 and the Additional Protocol to the Criminal Law Convention on Corruption adopted by the Council of Europe in 2000. Serbia made further advances in Transparency International's Corruption Perceptions Index, moving from a score of 2.8 in 2005, to 3.0 in 2006, and 3.4 in 2007, on a 0–10 scale where 10 indicates the lowest level of corruption.

▌ AUTHOR: SLOBODAN MARKOVICH

Slobodan Markovich is Assistant Professor at the Faculty of Political Science, University of Belgrade, and Advisor at the Belgrade Fund for Political Excellence.

[1] International Court of Justice, Press Release 2007/8, "The Court finds that Serbia has violated its obligation under the Genocide Convention to prevent genocide in Srebrenica and that it has also violated its obligations under the Convention by having failed fully to co-operate with the International Criminal Tribunal for the former Yugoslavia (ICTY)," February 26, 2007, http://www.icj-cij.org/docket/index.php?pr=1897&code=bhy&p1=3&p2=3&p3=6 &case=91&k=f4.

[2] Oli Ren, "Zajednički cilj vredan je svih napora" [A Common Goal is Worthy of All Efforts], *Danas*, December 30, 2007, http://www.danas.co.yu/20071231/vikend1.html#0 (Rehn's spelling is not a mistake. Serbs transliterate names even in Latin script. So, Rehn's name has been spelled here as in the original article that has been published in Serbian in Latin script.)

[3] Press release of Serbian Ombudsperson Saša Janković on the occasion of the Day of Human Rights, December 20, 2007.

[4] "Protestors Disrupt B92 Radio Program," B92, December 4, 2007, http://www.b92.net/ eng/news/society-article.php?yyyy=2007&mm=12&dd=04&nav_id=45918.

[5] "Sprečena promocija 'Peščanika'" [The Special Promotion of Pescanik], B92, December 3, 2007, http://www.b92.net/info/vesti/index.php?yyyy=2007&mm=12&dd=03&nav_category =11&nav_id=274916.

[6] From an author interview with Svetlana Lukić, editor of a popular radio-show Pescanik known for its criticism of the policies of Prime Minister Koštunica, conducted on January 31, 2008.

[7] Dejan Anastasijevic, "Ko mi je stavio bombe na prozor" [Who Placed Bombs Under My Window], *Vreme*, no. 876, October 18, 2007, http://www.vreme.com/cms/view.php?id= 516408.

8   From an author interview with Svetlana Lukić, editor of a popular radio-show Pescanik known for its criticism of the policies of Prime Minister Koštunica, conducted in Belgrade on January 31, 2008. Lukić encountered various barriers in her efforts to present her radio-show in many Serbian provincial places.

9   Serbia Events of 2007 in the World Report 2008, Human Rights Watch, http://hrw.org/ englishwr2k8/docs/2008/01/31/serbia17679.htm.

10   Verica Barac "Izveštaj o C marketu" [A Report on C Market], Savet za borbu protiv korupcije (the web-site of the Anti-Corruption Council), October 12, 2007, http://www.antikorupcija-savet.sr.gov.yu/view.jsp?articleId=545.

11   *Politika*, November 11, 2007.

12   The decision of the Commission for the Protection of Competition [Komisija za zastitu konkurencije], No. 6/0-02-138/07-15, brought on November 26, 2007, http://www.kzk. org.yu/download/DELTA-%20resenje%20u%20ponovnom%20postupku.doc.

Slovakia

by Grigorij Mesežnikov, Miroslav Kollár, and Michal Vašečka

Capital: Bratislava
Population: 5.4 million
GNI/capita: US$17,060

The social data above was taken from the European Bank for Reconstruction and Development's *Transition Report 2007: People in Transition*, and the economic data from the World Bank's *World Development Indicators 2008*.

Nations in Transit Ratings and Averaged Scores

	1999	2001	2002	2003	2004	2005	2006	2007	2008
Electoral Process	2.50	2.25	1.75	1.50	1.50	1.25	1.25	1.50	1.50
Civil Society	2.25	2.00	1.75	1.50	1.25	1.25	1.25	1.50	1.50
Independent Media	2.25	2.00	2.00	2.00	2.25	2.25	2.25	2.25	2.50
Governance*	3.00	2.75	2.25	2.25	2.25	n/a	n/a	n/a	n/a
National Democratic Governance	n/a	n/a	n/a	n/a	n/a	2.00	2.00	2.25	2.50
Local Democratic Governance	n/a	n/a	n/a	n/a	n/a	2.25	2.00	2.00	2.25
Judicial Framework and Independence	2.50	2.25	2.00	2.00	2.00	2.00	2.00	2.25	2.50
Corruption	3.75	3.75	3.25	3.25	3.25	3.00	3.00	3.25	3.25
Democracy Score	2.71	2.50	2.17	2.08	2.08	2.00	1.96	2.14	2.29

* With the 2005 edition, Freedom House introduced separate analysis and ratings for national democratic governance and local democratic governance to provide readers with more detailed and nuanced analysis of these two important subjects.

NOTE: The ratings reflect the consensus of Freedom House, its academic advisers, and the author(s) of this report. The opinions expressed in this report are those of the author(s). The ratings are based on a scale of 1 to 7, with 1 representing the highest level of democratic progress and 7 the lowest. The Democracy Score is an average of ratings for the categories tracked in a given year.

EXECUTIVE SUMMARY

After the collapse of the Communist regime in 1989, Slovakia embarked on a long and complicated transition to democracy. Milestones included systemic changes within the former Czechoslovakia between 1990 and 1992, the emergence of an independent Slovakia in January 1993, a struggle to preserve the country's democratic regime under nationalist and populist forces between 1994 and 1998, the elimination of authoritarian characteristics, and pro-democratic and pro-market reforms between 1998 and 2006. Following its accession to the Organization for Economic Cooperation and Development (2000), World Trade Organization (1995), European Union (EU), and NATO (2004), Slovakia may be considered a country with a consolidated democracy and functioning market economy.

Winning parliamentary elections in 2006, the self-declared social democratic Smer–Social Democracy (Smer-SD), radical nationalist Slovak National Party (SNS), and national populist People's Party–Movement for a Democratic Slovakia (ĽS-HZDS) formed a broad-spectrum coalition government. The inherited economic development created comfortable conditions for the new government led by Robert Fico, chairman of Smer-SD. In 2007, Fico's cabinet was not forced to adopt any austerity measures. The ruling coalition enjoyed a comfortable majority in the Parliament and put through its legislative proposals.

The following trends could be observed during 2007: increased state interventionism; deepening of the government's role in the economy, social policy, education, health care, and culture; appointments to government and public institutions based on political connections and party loyalty; increased ethnocentric elements in domestic politics; and changes in the government's declared foreign policy priorities, such as playing down the transatlantic dimension.

National Democratic Governance. In 2007, the system of power division in Slovakia remained sufficiently stable, and government institutions performed their duties relatively effectively. At the same time, the ruling coalition strove to use its dominant position to concentrate power and weaken opposition parliamentary parties, rejecting *a priori* all proposals submitted by opposition colleagues. The quality of adopted legislation was reduced indirectly by amending laws. Most top personnel changes in government institutions at central and regional levels were politically motivated, reflecting party loyalty or family bonds. To facilitate these sweeping personnel changes, the ruling coalition passed an amendment to the Civil Service Act. It also tried repeatedly to amend the law to restrict public access to information on government decisions. *Owing to nonconsensual elements in Parliament, concentration of power in the ruling coalition, politically motivated* *personnel changes in state institutions, and the overall confrontational relationship between the ruling coalition and the opposition, Slovakia's rating for national democratic governance worsens from 2.25 to 2.50.*

Electoral Process. In 2007, Slovakia did not hold any nationwide elections and no changes were made to electoral legislation, which provides adequate conditions for fair competition. Seats in the legislative assembly are divided among six political parties, three ruling and three opposition. Caucuses of parliamentary parties showed remarkable stability, and the opposition in the assembly has remained unchanged since the 2006 elections. The dominant ruling Smer-SD party failed to restore its affiliate membership in the Party of European Socialists (PES), which was suspended in 2006 as a result of the party's governmental cooperation with the radically nationalistic SNS. *Slovakia's rating for electoral process remains unchanged at 1.50.*

Civil Society. Slovakia's civil society is vibrant, and its public image is mostly positive. The legal and regulatory environment is free of excessive state pressures and bureaucracy; however, the current government is less open to nongovernmental organizations (NGOs) than previous administrations. While there are favorable taxation conditions for most NGOs, civil society actors in environmental protection and human rights lost the 2 percent tax support for more than a year (but restored in November 2007 under successful NGO pressure). The civic sector has a well-developed infrastructure, with competent training and research capacities; however, the incumbent government is not receptive to policy institutes, advocacy, and watchdog groups. Slovakia's education system is free of political influence, but the ruling coalition's efforts to foster "Slovak patriotism" are worrying. *Slovakia's rating for civil society remains at 1.50.*

Independent Media. Media outlets and journalists in Slovakia were free in 2007, although a court ruling threatened to undermine one leading periodical's financial stability and there was an assault on a journalist. The Slovak Supreme Court set a disturbing precedent in ignoring a European Court of Human Rights (ECHR) decision by sticking to its ruling that found a Slovak journalist guilty of libel. Tensions between government and public service media increased as well; after the new management of Slovak Television took office, one-third of its news employees quit, citing interventions in their editorial work. There is a trend toward increasing influence by the political elite over media content and operations, particularly in public service media. *Owing to persistent and even deepening problems (that is, deficient legislation, pressure on public service media, and attempts to undermine financial stability of media), Slovakia's rating for independent media worsens from 2.25 to 2.50.*

Local Democratic Governance. Thanks to reforms carried out between 2001 and 2005, Slovakia became a decentralized state with a relatively effective system of regional and local self-governance. The positive effects of decentralization continued to show throughout 2007, particularly as tax revenues of regional and local self-governments continued to increase. Yet the government failed to adopt legislation that would further strengthen local democracy and extend executive powers of self-governments; on the contrary, it passed amendments that cemented the position of central government institutions. Most legislative changes aimed to strengthen the ruling parties' power at regional and local levels. The administration adopted measures that undermined the principle of subsidiarity in Slovakia, provoking criticism from self-governance associations. *Owing to problematic trends in public administration and local democracy, Slovakia's rating for local democratic governance worsens from 2.00 to 2.25.*

Judicial Framework and Independence. While Slovakia saw some positive developments in human rights in 2007, negative trends prevailed. On the one hand, Parliament passed an amendment to the Antidiscrimination Act in compliance with EU Council recommendations; also, another amendment was drafted to this law that seeks to restore the principle of affirmative action for disadvantaged population groups; finally, the cabinet announced its intention to establish a special Council for Gender Equality. On the other hand, the Slovak Supreme Court ignored a ruling of the European Court of Human Rights, and Parliament introduced stricter conditions for registering churches and religious associations and establishing citizenship. There was evidence of government pressure on the Constitutional Court. Representation of ethnic Hungarians and Roma in the cabinet's advisory body was reduced in 2007. Experts say the code of criminal procedures drafted by the Ministry of Justice may impair government efforts to fight organized crime. *Owing to the above-mentioned negative developments, Slovakia's rating for judicial framework and independence worsens from 2.25 to 2.50.*

Corruption. Corruption continues to rank among the most pressing social problems in Slovakia. While earlier measures created favorable institutional conditions to fight corruption, the intensity of the government's anticorruption efforts declined in 2007. State interventionist actions extended the space for clientelism. The Parliament did not pass any anticorruption legislation, nor did the cabinet articulate a clear policy. Cabinet members involved in corruption scandals remained in office, thanks to strong political support. The government increased spending without strengthening anticorruption mechanisms. Consequently, transparency and competition in public tenders and procurements declined. *Slovakia's rating for corruption stagnates at 3.25.*

Outlook for 2008. It is likely that the etatist socioeconomic policies pursued by the ruling coalition of Smer-SD, SNS, and ĽS-HZDS will grow stronger in 2008. The incumbent administration will likely strive to make Slovakia part of the Eurozone; however, there are misgivings about Slovakia's ability to comply with Maastricht convergence criteria in the long term. Ethnocentric elements and tensions in Slovak-

Hungarian relations are likely to grow stronger in the country. Political parties will begin to prepare for the upcoming presidential elections scheduled for May 2009. It is likely that the incumbent president, Ivan Gašparovič, will announce his decision to run for reelection. Efforts by the opposition to nominate a joint candidate to challenge Gašparovič may eventually fail owing to strong party differences.

Main Report

National Democratic Governance

1999	2001	2002	2003	2004	2005	2006	2007	2008
n/a	n/a	n/a	n/a	n/a	2.00	2.00	2.25	2.50

The Slovak Republic is a stable democracy with a generally effective system of governmental checks and balances. The cabinet reports to the legislative assembly, which has the right to recall it. The president can veto laws adopted by the Parliament; in order to pass vetoed legislation, the Parliament must subsequently muster a qualified majority. The Constitutional Court acts as an independent judicial body. Citizens enjoy direct participation in the political process through elections and political party activities.

The Slovak Constitution guarantees the right to free retrieval, collection, and dissemination of information. In 2000, the Parliament passed the Law on Free Access to Information, but citizens often encounter bureaucratic resistance. Furthermore, since its inauguration in 2006, the administration has tried to restrict the law with respect to state administrative organs. In February 2007, a member of Parliament (MP) from Smer–Social Democracy (Smer-SD) proposed to amend the law so authorities could refuse to provide information in "apparently unreasonable" requests, but the proposal was successfully blocked by opposition parties and nongovernmental organizations (NGOs).

More than 90 percent of Slovakia's gross domestic product is produced by the private sector. Since 1998, the drive toward liberalization has been the chief development trend within Slovakia's economy. However, the current coalition government led by Prime Minister Robert Fico has championed a different approach by halting the privatization of state property and pursuing a policy of state interventionism, strengthening the position of executive organs, and limiting the space for market mechanisms. This was most perceptible in the areas of pensions and health insurance. While no cases of direct nationalization of private property were recorded in 2007, the cabinet-initiated amendment to the Law on Health Insurance, passed by Parliament in October 2007, bans private health insurance companies from generating profit. According to legal experts, this law creates conditions for indirect confiscation of private property by the government.

After parliamentary elections in June 2006, a new ruling coalition was formed comprising Smer-SD, People's Party–Movement for a Democratic Slovakia (ĽS-HZDS), and the Slovak National Party (SNS); the latter two parties were directly responsible for authoritarian tendencies from 1994 to 1998. The ruling coalition shows signs of using its dominant position to concentrate power and weaken the position of opposition parties. The administration repeatedly clashed with a broad spectrum of players in 2007, including opposition parties, businesses, the media, NGOs, civic initiatives, and self-governance associations.

The National Council (Parliament) is the sole legislative assembly and autonomous from the executive. It has sufficient resources and capacities for the creation and enactment of bills, as well as adequate control powers. Parliamentarians frequently interpellate cabinet members and exercise oversight of state and public institutions. Between January and December 2007, Parliament passed 143 pieces of legislation; a vast majority were amendments to existing laws. During the same period, President Ivan Gašparovič vetoed eight laws; seven were subsequently re-enacted by the Parliament.

Parliamentary deliberations are open to the public and media except for closed sessions on sensitive matters (such as intelligence and secret service issues). Public representatives may be present during deliberations of parliamentary committees if invited by their members. The entire legislative process is made public via the Parliament's website.

In 2007, Parliament rejected almost all legislative proposals submitted by opposition parties. Another disturbing trend was the use of so-called indirect law amending, where Parliament alters laws by amending provisions of other, often unrelated laws. Since the 2006 parliamentary elections, the assembly has frequently resorted to this practice. Examples include: the altered law on the Social Insurance Company through the amended pension system law, the altered competence and collective negotiations laws through the amended tripartite law, the altered law on public procurement through the amended commercial advertisement law, and the altered communities law through the amended trade and emission quotas law.

When deliberating on procedural issues, the ruling coalition also used "majority rule," as in the action against Justice Minister Štefan Harabin initiated by opposition deputies for his suspected violation of the Law on Conflict of Interest. The assembly's Committee for Incompatibility of Functions twice abandoned the action against Harabin when opposition proposals failed to muster sufficient support among committee members—a privilege used openly by the ruling coalition's majority on the committee.

Personnel changes in state administration at central and regional levels, as well as supervisory boards of government-supported enterprises, also continued in 2007. Most were politically motivated, and many appointments were based on party loyalty or family ties. In May, Parliament passed an amendment that gave the cabinet a free hand to make personnel changes in leading state administration posts. After taking office, Prime Minister Fico proposed to reduce the number of civil servants by 20 percent (about 30,000 jobs), but the number of state employees declined by only 2.5 percent in 2006 and held steady in 2007.

All state agencies are subject to control by the Supreme Bureau of Supervision (NKÚ), which regularly publishes violations of laws and bylaws. The Parliament elects the NKÚ chairman and vice chairmen for seven-year terms. Though funded by the state budget, the NKÚ is free from political influence. In March 2007, Parliament passed an amendment to the Law on the Supreme Bureau of Supervision that strengthened the NKÚ's financial independence. There were no attempts to politically restrict or influence the NKÚ's supervisory roles or question its findings during the year.

The reform of the armed forces implemented during the past decade has introduced civilian controls that are in line with NATO, which Slovakia joined in 2004. Judicial oversight of the military and security services is effective, and the Slovak army uses a system of martial prosecution with martial courts. The Parliament approves the military and security services budget, and spending is supervised by the Parliamentary Defense and Security Committee. Deputies, media, and the general public may access information on the activities of the military and security services, but certain types of information are classified.

Electoral Process

1999	2001	2002	2003	2004	2005	2006	2007	2008
2.50	2.25	1.75	1.50	1.50	1.25	1.25	1.50	1.50

The authority of the Slovak government is based on freely-exercised universal suffrage. Since 1989, Slovakia has held six parliamentary elections, five municipal elections, two regional elections (2001 and 2005), two presidential elections (1999 and 2004), and one election to the European Parliament (2004). International and domestic election monitors declared all of these elections free and fair.

The legislative framework provides for free and democratic competition, equal campaigning, fair voting, and the transparent scrutiny of votes. Election regulations create favorable conditions for political parties to perform their traditional functions: mobilizing public participation in democratic processes, mediating between civil society and the state, representing the interests of a variety of groups in society (including national minorities), and recruiting personnel for support within legislative and executive functions.

In Slovakia, the legitimacy of the government is based on the results of elections. Generally speaking, special interest groups respect this principle; however, some have attempted to influence policy making, building on their close ties with political parties. Most active in this respect are commercial groups that lobby individual representatives of political parties. The Confederation of Trade Unions of the Slovak Republic (KOZ), the largest trade union organization in Slovakia, openly supported Smer-SD before the 2006 elections; after the incumbent administration was formed, KOZ leaders positively evaluated its program goals. Representatives of the Catholic Church also encouraged citizens to support political parties that promoted "Christian values" (that is, primarily conservative parties).

Parliamentary elections are based on a proportional system with qualifying thresholds: 5 percent for single parties, 7 percent for coalitions of two or three parties, and 10 percent for coalitions of four or more parties. The electoral rules also include a system of preferential votes. A candidate who receives more than 3 percent of preferential votes is treated preferentially in the allocation of mandates. Elections to the European Parliament use a proportional system. The minimum quorum to qualify for the assembly is 5 percent of the popular vote, which applies to both individual parties and party coalitions. Elections to local and regional self-governments use a modified majority electoral model. Slovakia's president and regional governors are elected using a majority model with two rounds. In 2005, the Parliament passed the Law on Political Parties, which requires a party to submit a petition of 10,000 signatures to register for elections.

The Supreme Court may dissolve political parties whose statutes, program, or activities violate the Constitution, constitutional laws, or international treaties. Motions to dissolve a political party must be filed by the attorney general. In 2006, the Supreme Court ordered the dissolution of the Slovak Community–National Party, the first political party to be dissolved in Slovakia since 1989. The party advocated removing Slovakia's democratic system of government and openly promulgated racial discrimination.

The most recent parliamentary elections were held in Slovakia in June 17, 2006. Smer-SD, which portrays itself as a social democratic political force, received the most votes and won 50 seats in the Parliament. The new ruling coalition comprises parties formerly with the opposition (Smer-SD, SNS, and ĽS-HZDS) and currently controls 85 out of 150 seats, which gives it a comfortable majority.

The decision of Smer-SD to form a government with the nationalist SNS provoked harsh criticism from the Party of European Socialists (PES), which unites socialist and social democratic parties from European Union (EU) member states and prohibits its member parties from cooperating with far-right, extremist, and nationalistic parties. Smer-SD became a PES affiliate member in 2005 but was suspended in October 2006.

All parliamentary parties have functioning structures at the national, regional, and local levels and are represented in regional and local self-governments. Currently, five Slovak parties are represented in the European Parliament. The most recent presidential elections in Slovakia were held in April 2004. Ivan Gašparovič, a joint candidate of the Movement for Democracy (HZD), Smer (before the party became Smer-SD), and the SNS, obtained 59.9 percent of the popular vote in the second round and was elected president.[1]

Although citizens are quite active in Slovakia's political life, there has been an overall decline in voter participation. Traditionally, the highest turnout is recorded in parliamentary elections. The turnout in 2006 (54.7 percent) represented the lowest voter participation in parliamentary elections since 1990. In 2004, the presidential elections recorded turnouts of 47.9 percent (first round) and 43.5 percent (second round). Municipal and regional elections typically show lower voter turnout than national elections. In the 2005 municipal elections, the turnout was 18 percent (first round) and 11 percent (second round)—the lowest in Slovakia's modern history. Turnout of only 17 percent was recorded in the first elections to the European Parliament in 2004.[2]

Ethnic minorities encounter no institutional obstacles to participating in political processes. About 15 percent of Slovak citizens belong to various ethnic minorities. Ethnic Hungarians form the largest minority, making up nearly 10 percent of the total population.[3] Traditionally, ethnic Hungarians have a high rate of political mobilization; as a result, this minority is represented effectively, mainly through the Party of Hungarian Coalition (SMK). The party also enjoys a solid position in some regional and local self-governance organs. Following the parliamentary elections, SMK found itself in opposition, and many of its representatives have been removed from state administration posts by the new ruling coalition. Following a leadership change in 2007, SMK began to present its views more openly and radically. Recently, the party focused on evaluating certain historical events that have affected ethnic Hungarians in Slovakia.

By contrast, the Roma minority is under-represented. This is due to a number of social factors (such as low economic status, and inadequate education) and a virtual absence of political leaders, as well as the inability of the mainstream political parties to cooperate with Romany organizations. No Romany political parties have gained a foothold in executive or legislative organs at the national or regional level, but there are Roma representatives in local self-governance organs. The only registered political party, the Romany Initiative of Slovakia, struggles with a lack of credibility among Roma and a history of conflicts among Romany leaders.

Civil Society

1999	2001	2002	2003	2004	2005	2006	2007	2008
2.25	2.00	1.75	1.50	1.25	1.25	1.25	1.50	1.50

The Slovakian state respects the independent civic sector, which is dynamic and vibrant. Yet the mutual cooperation between government institutions and NGOs that had existed since 1998 started to disappear after the 2006 parliamentary elections. Still, the professionalism of Slovak NGOs continued in 2007, and the civil society sector can be described as heterogeneous and pluralistic, while relations between particular segments were complicated and sometimes tense.

In October 2007, the Ministry of the Interior listed 23,064 organizations that may be considered NGOs in a broad sense. Of these, 92.5 percent were civil associations (societies, clubs, associations, movements, trade unions, international NGOs, and various sports clubs), 1.4 percent were foundations, 2.5 percent were non-investment funds, and 3.6 percent were nonprofit organizations. The public opinion of NGOs is positive.

Most national minorities are represented by cultural and civic organizations. While the Hungarian minority is well represented at all levels, the number of Roma organizations is much lower (almost 20 times less than mainstream organizations). Churches play an important role in charitable activities, with all major religious groups (that is, Catholics, Greek Orthodox, Protestants, Jews) involved in these activities.

Openly extremist and racist organizations operate illegally in Slovakia. During 2007, the Slovak police continued systematic monitoring of neo-Nazi, right-wing, and left-wing extremist groups, yet racist attacks occurred frequently. Discussions were heated during the year over how to fight all forms of extremism, which proliferated on the Internet with discriminatory, racist, and biased content against minorities.

The legal and regulatory environment for civil society is free of excessive state pressures and unnecessary bureaucracy. The basic legislative framework is provided by the Constitution and guarantees freedom of expression (Article 29), freedom of assembly (Article 28), and freedom of association (Articles 29 and 37). NGO registration is easy, and both legal entities and private persons may establish nonprofit organizations. The Ministry of the Interior serves as both registry and supervising institution.

NGOs are exempt from gift and income taxes. In 2007, the government reduced opportunities to support domestic NGOs operating in policy development and democracy assistance abroad, creating instead more favorable conditions for private companies.

The Slovak civic sector has a well-developed infrastructure with adequate training and research, but there is a lack of technical resources. Numerous NGOs provide training for civil society activists by way of informal coalitions and networks (platforms) formed on an ad hoc basis. Information services for NGOs are provided via the Internet portal ChangeNet. NGOs receive mostly positive coverage from public and private media.

Assistance from Western democracies was instrumental in developing a vital Slovak civil society, and EU structural funds brought new opportunities as well as new challenges. One of the most pressing problems—that of cash flow—improved slightly. NGOs often must advance their own money for projects and then wait sometimes more than a year or two for reimbursement from the EU. As a result, the prevailing opinion of most NGOs is that the European Commission (EC), in spite of significant contributions, does not possess a sustainable model for supporting civil society activities. NGOs have worked to raise more money from local businesses, but the results are modest. Corporate social responsibility and philanthropy are relatively low, but in 2007, businesses and citizens could begin dedicating 2 percent of their income tax to benefit the public.

Restrictions on the types of NGOs approved to receive 2 percent tax contributions demonstrated the government's distrust toward some types of NGOs. Groups working in environmental protection and human rights were excluded in 2006, but their eligibility was restored in 2007 under pressure from a massive NGO campaign. The incumbent government is not receptive to policy advocacy activities. Think tanks and watchdog groups were perceived as a threat and verbally attacked by officials, including Prime Minister Fico. During 2007, there were attacks on environmental organizations that criticized the government's environmental policies.

Trade unions in Slovakia are free. Konfederácia Odborových Zväzov Slovenskej Republiky [KOZ SR], the country's largest trade union, represented 390,000 employees in 2007, but membership is shrinking annually. The image of trade unions was predominantly negative in all segments of the population in 2007, which might be attributed to KOZ SR's problematic involvement in politics and leadership style.

The country's education system is free of political influence and propaganda. The Ministry of Education continues, albeit rather slowly, to implement multicultural measures into primary and secondary school curricula. Prime Minister Fico speaks frequently about the need to strengthen patriotic feelings in Slovak youth. The nationalist SNS, one of the ruling parties, advocated changing the curricula in order to strengthen the "Slovak national identity," but these plans have not yet affected the nonpartisan character of Slovakia's education system.

Independent Media

1999	2001	2002	2003	2004	2005	2006	2007	2008
2.25	2.00	2.00	2.00	2.25	2.25	2.25	2.25	2.50

Freedom of speech is embodied in the Slovak Constitution and regulated by the (unsatisfactory) Press Act of 1966. A cabinet-initiated Press Act proposed in 2007 features provisions that strengthen the right to correction and the right to respond. While the former requires media to publish corrections of untruthful information, the latter requires them to publish reactions to any information without regard for its truthfulness. Furthermore, the bill lacks provisions to protect journalists, such as the right to pardonable error.

Slovak journalists are protected from victimization by powerful state or nonstate actors, and the country's legal system does not punish "irresponsible" journalism with respect to government organs. Yet 2007 brought a disturbing precedent when the Slovak Supreme Court ignored a ruling by the European Court of Human Rights (ECHR) by sustaining a decision against former journalist Martin Klein. In 2006, the ECHR ruled that the Slovak courts had violated Klein's freedom of speech by sentencing him to pay 15,000 Slovak koruna (US$650) or serve one month in prison after deeming his article "The Falcon Is Sitting in the Maple Tree: Larry Flint and Seven Slaps to the Hypocrite" to be defamation of nation, race, and religion. The ECHR subsequently indemnified Klein in the amount of 380,000 Slovak koruna (US$16,000).

Journalists and editorial offices are partly free of interference from government or private owners. While formal dependence of public service media on the government has not increased, their economic dependence has deepened with the government's hesitation to tackle financing issues. Shortly after the administration's inauguration, it proposed a redivision of public service media; in response to new Slovak Television management, more than one-third of the news department's employees quit, citing political and incompetent intervention in their editorial work.

In September 2007, the cabinet convened a special session to discuss the issue of "unethical behavior and unlawful practices of some journalists." In a resolution, the cabinet expressed astonishment that neither the Press Council nor the Council for Broadcasting and Retransmission had dealt with suspicions of journalists allegedly receiving gifts from subjects in the pension and insurance fields. The Slovak Syndicate of Journalists (SSN), the largest professional organization of journalists in Slovakia, rejected the cabinet's sweeping accusations and its efforts to usurp the regulation of media ethics.

Regional media inadequacies and the recent tendency to replace broadcast news with "infotainment" are both increasingly outweighed by the fast development of Internet news portals. Blogs and video news have significantly broadened the space for participation, including nonprofessionals as well. These developing platforms provide an alternative source of information that can be rebroadcast on more mainstream communication channels for a greater impact.

In Slovakia, all relevant media are in private hands. The only exceptions are public service media—Slovak Television (STV) and Slovak Radio (SRo)—which are controlled by councils appointed by Parliament and the state press agency TASR. In the private sphere, ownership concentration among Slovakia's top television outlets during 2007 could potentially jeopardize fair economic competition on the broadcast media market. The financial stability of nationwide private media in Slovakia is free of political intervention, but is affected by the size of media and advertising markets.

By contrast, in print media, a 2007 court ruling against the economic weekly *Trend* for failing to publish a correction may lead to the financial collapse of this respected periodical. Press distribution is controlled by the private sector and the state-run Slovak Post and showed no fundamental problems in 2007.

In the public service media, Parliament failed to pass a long-awaited bill on license fees to improve collections. As a result, STV piled up debt of approximately 300 million Slovak koruna (US$13 million) in 2007. This increased STV's and SRo's financial dependence on the ruling political elite, which began to treat the public service media "possessively." For instance, the cabinet announced plans to build a new complex that would place public service media under one roof, against the objections of STV, SRo, and both media councils (the only bodies lawfully empowered to make decisions regarding public service media property). In terms of successes, the Association of Independent Radio and Television Stations in 2007 incorporated provisions into the recently passed Law on Digital Broadcasting that will enable the two largest TV broadcasters to transition toward terrestrial digital broadcasting.

Access to the Internet is unregulated in Slovakia. The total number of Slovaks who use the Internet continues to grow in relation to the increasing availability of ever more affordable broadband services. According to a survey by GfK in August 2007, better than 40 percent of Slovak citizens regularly used the Internet. Almost half (46 percent) of all Slovak households own computers, but most Internet usage is limited to young people (93 percent for ages 15–19). In contrast, most Slovaks over 60 (94 percent) do not use the Internet.

Local Democratic Governance

1999	2001	2002	2003	2004	2005	2006	2007	2008
n/a	n/a	n/a	n/a	n/a	2.25	2.00	2.00	2.25

The Slovak Constitution and legislation provide an adequate framework for self-governance, with a dual system of public administration—state administration (organs of executive power) and self-governments (elected bodies). There are three levels of elected bodies: central (Parliament), regional (regional assemblies), and local (municipal councils). Public administration is based on the principle of "subsidiarity," or keeping public administration functions with smaller units when no major advantage exists for transferring them to larger ones.

The establishment of state and self-governance institutions is subject to laws passed by the Parliament. However, local self-governments may initiate non-state organizations that focus on aiding local development, such as agencies, associations, funds, and so forth. To communicate with central government institutions and present their priorities, self-governments use various associations, such as the Association of Slovak Towns and Villages, the Union of Slovak Towns, and the Association of Regional Capitals K–8.

As part of public administration reform, a massive set of powers was transferred in 2001–2005 from central government organs to local and regional self-governance bodies. These bodies now address issues in education, health care, social affairs, transportation, and the environment. In order for local and regional self-governments to perform their delegated responsibilities, the central government provided them with necessary funding through fiscal decentralization—in other words, the right to collect so-called local taxes. In the case of municipalities, this is the real estate tax; for regional self-governments, this is the motor vehicle tax. In 2004, the government began distributing income tax revenues to local and regional self-governments.

Although government institutions and self-governance organs cooperate in tackling many local and regional problems, in 2007 they differed on certain issues. For instance, representatives of local self-governments criticized the cabinet for the way it delegated responsibility to local self-governments for administering and financing the education system. The Union of Slovak Towns declared that the "cabinet measures jeopardize stability of the existing model of public administration and are aimed at undermining sovereignty of territorial self-governments."[4] In August, local representatives launched a petition to protest the cabinet's plans to reduce the number of registries and other local state administration offices and change the scope of their powers. In response, the Ministry of the Interior withdrew the amendment from cabinet deliberations.

In May, the Parliament passed legislation abolishing regional state administration offices. Property of the cancelled regional offices along with some employees were transferred to district state administration offices, while approximately 150 employees were laid off. In June, the ruling coalition passed a law that strengthened powers of regional governors with respect to regional assemblies. The amendment granted regional governors discretion to circumscribe their deputies' powers; previously, this discretion rested with the assemblies. Regional governors were also granted a power to alter already-approved regional budgets.

In the 2005 regional elections, representatives of ruling parties clinched all eight governor posts; however, five of them coexist with assemblies controlled by opposition parties. In June 2007, Parliament passed a bill to extend the powers of regional self-governments in the field of housing development at the expense of local self-governments; this was a clear intrusion upon the principle of subsidiarity, perhaps intending to strengthen regional governors close to the incumbent administration. An amendment to the legislation on budgetary rules passed in June strengthened the position of the central government by extending the scope of allocated items in self-governments' budgetary expenditures.

In 2002, the cabinet established the 25-member Government Council for Public Administration as an advisory body in public administration issues, with representatives of central and local state administration organs, regional and local self-governments, associations of towns and villages, regional assemblies, and academic experts. The council's chairman is the minister of the interior, and detailed information on council deliberations is published on the ministry website. The council analyzes implemented measures and assesses the potential impact of proposed legislation.

The Constitution allows citizens to exercise their right to suffrage at regional and local levels. Representatives of self-governments (deputies of municipal councils and regional assemblies, mayors of villages and towns, and regional governors) are elected in direct, free, and democratic competitions, which are open to political party candidates as well as independent candidates. Elections to local and regional self-governments are held every four years and are open to independent observers. Candidates represent a broad spectrum of opinions, and political parties play an important role in local elections. Apart from elections, local and regional governments give citizens a chance to take a much more active part in the administration of public affairs. Direct public participation in decision-making processes is regulated by the Law on the Municipal System of Government and the Law on Self-Governance of Higher Territorial Units.

The level of public participation in regional and local politics is similar to that in national politics; in the case of women and ethnic minorities (especially Roma), the rate of participation is higher locally than at the national level. In recent years, Slovak media have paid relatively close attention to issues of local democracy and self-governance. The most active in this respect are regional and local media outlets.

The increased attention reflects the greater social relevance and political importance that self-governance organs gained as a result of the public administration reform. Regional and local self-governments do not have the power to pass laws, but they can pass bylaws and regulations that apply exclusively to them. Self-governance bodies may turn to the courts to enforce their decisions. The law allows self-governments to form associations with other domestic and foreign self-governance institutions to cooperate in representing their interests and assisting one another to tackle local problems. Self-governance organs, especially the regions and larger municipalities, frequently cooperate with partners from abroad, particularly from neighboring countries.

Internal control of self-governments is entrusted to chief comptrollers who are appointed for six-year terms. Externally, the NKÚ controls all funds spent by self-government organs and supervises the financial management of legal entities established by self-government organs. Meetings of local and regional self-governance bodies are open to the public; results are posted on public notice boards, via the media, and increasingly on the Internet.

Judicial Framework and Independence

1999	2001	2002	2003	2004	2005	2006	2007	2008
2.50	2.25	2.00	2.00	2.00	2.00	2.00	2.25	2.50

The Slovak Constitution, Bill of Fundamental Rights and Freedoms, and other laws provide a framework for the protection of human rights. The Constitutional Court accepts complaints regarding violations of human rights and issues verdicts. An extensive 2001 amendment of the Constitution introduced a public defender of human rights.

As a member of the Council of Europe, Slovakia is part of the European system of human rights protection and has ratified all important international human rights documents. Citizens may turn to the ECHR if they believe their rights have been violated and Slovak judicial institutions have been unable to take action or provide a remedy to an alleged human rights violation. In 2007, the ECHR issued a number of rulings in favor of Slovak citizens. Most frequently, these cases involved drawn-out proceedings that violated citizens' constitutional right to a lawsuit without unnecessary delays.

In 2007, Parliament passed amendments that might improve implementation of human rights for certain population groups; at the same time, it adopted several laws that might make the exercise of certain civil rights and freedoms more difficult. The former include an amendment to the Antidiscrimination Act (the Law on Equal Treatment and Protection Against Discrimination), an amendment that simplified citizen access to criminal records, and an amendment reducing court fees for citizens. The latter includes an amendment to the Law on Freedom of Worship that introduces stricter conditions for registering churches and religious associations.

In June 2007, Parliament passed an amendment to the Citizenship Act that introduced stricter conditions for obtaining Slovak citizenship. Now, persons applying for citizenship must live in Slovakia uninterrupted for at least eight years. When justifying the need for tightening these conditions, the Ministry of the Interior cited its campaign against organized crime and international terrorism. Security arguments were also cited by initiators of an amendment to the Law on the Right of Assembly approved by Parliament in September 2007. The amendment forbids participants at public rallies from covering their faces to allow police to identify rally participants during police interventions.

The Constitutional Court is an independent institution, and its verdicts are legally binding. The right to appeal to the Constitutional Court rests with parliamentary deputies (at least 30 are required to launch an appeal), the president, the cabinet, courts of justice, the attorney general, and the ombudsman for human rights; in certain cases, local self-governments also enjoy this right.

Prime Minister Robert Fico has repeatedly urged the Constitutional Court to begin adjudication on the constitutionality of legislation on demonstrating the origin of property, arguing that the legislation is "important to the government." These public statements by Fico could be interpreted as indirect political pressure. As of December 2007, the Constitutional Court had not issued a ruling. Also during the year, some legal experts criticized the Constitutional Court for failing to comply with a law that obliges all courts of justice in Slovakia to assign cases randomly via electronic registry.

The Constitution guarantees all citizens equality before the law regardless of sex, race, skin color, language, religion, political preference, nationality, ethnicity, property status, or other categories. However, women and other groups are inadequately represented in public posts. While the general standard of minority rights in Slovakia did not deteriorate in 2007, slovak relations with some minority groups, in particular the ethnic Hungarians, worsened. This can be attributed to the radical nationalist SNS, whose representatives became part of the incumbent administration in 2006.

In July 2007, on the occasion of the fifteenth anniversary of adopting the Declaration of Sovereignty of the Slovak Republic, Prime Minister Fico mentioned "loyal" minorities, which drew criticism from ethnic minorities, particularly ethnic Hungarians, as it suggested there were also "disloyal" minorities. The tension further escalated in September when Parliament passed a resolution initiated by the SNS that proclaimed the Beneš Decrees as "unalterable"; many ethnic Hungarians interpret these post–World War II decrees as the state's adoption of the principle of collective guilt, discriminating against Czechoslovakia's population of Hungarian origin.

By joining the EU in 2004, the Slovak Republic undertook all related human rights obligations and passed the Antidiscrimination Act. According to the European Commission, the Slovak law features inaccurate terms and provisions that may restrict EU Council directives regarding the issue of equal treatment; the EC announced it would initiate an action for violation of the Treaty on Establishing the

European Community owing to these deficiencies, which meant that Slovakia could be brought before the European Court of Justice and face applicable sanctions. In reaction to the EC criticism, the Slovak government swiftly drafted an amendment to the Antidiscrimination Act that was passed by Parliament in June 2007. Dušan Čaplovič, deputy prime minister for European affairs, human rights, and minorities, subsequently announced that the cabinet would draft yet another amendment to the law to restore temporary equalization measures for certain population groups by exercising the principle of affirmative action on a social, not an ethnic, basis.

At the end of October, the cabinet approved an amendment that was positively evaluated by NGOs specializing in human rights. In the same month, the cabinet also endorsed a proposal to establish the Government Council for Gender Equality, which should begin to operate in January 2008. This time, NGOs criticized the council's inadequate civil society representation (only 3 out of 39 members).

Slovakia's Constitution guarantees the presumption of innocence, and the state is obliged to provide a defender to those who cannot afford one. Investigation of criminal offenses in Slovakia is conducted under a prosecutor's supervision. An accused person may be detained and arrested only if a judge has issued a written warrant. International conventions and other legal acts banning torture and maltreatment form an integral part of Slovakia's legal system. No cases of maltreatment were reported in 2007. However, there were several cases of racially motivated violence against Roma and physical assaults on civil society activists, mostly from neo-Nazi "skinhead" movements.

Slovakia has a three-level judicial system—the Supreme Court, 8 regional courts, and 45 district courts—administered jointly by the president, Parliament, Ministry of Justice, Judicial Council, and Supreme Court. The president appoints judges acting on proposals from the Judicial Council, which is the principal organ of self-governance within the judiciary. The Ministry of Justice appoints the chairmen and vice chairmen of particular courts. Slovakia's judicial system also includes three regional military courts and a higher military court, as well as the Special Court to Combat Corruption and Organized Crime.

International monitors have confirmed that the Slovak judiciary is independent to a satisfactory degree. However, the public's sense of legal safety continued to be impaired by court inefficiency, exacerbated by an overwhelming backlog of cases. Public trust is also undermined by a common belief that the judiciary is plagued by corruption.

Corruption

1999	2001	2002	2003	2004	2005	2006	2007	2008
3.75	3.75	3.25	3.25	3.25	3.00	3.00	3.25	3.25

Corruption ranks among the most pressing and deeply rooted social problems in Slovakia. Yet a positive turnaround can be observed since the end of the 1990s, when the country's leadership was replaced by democratic and pro-reform political forces. Administrations between 2002 and 2006 took a number of steps, including incorporating an anticorruption policy into the government's program framework; establishing the Special Court and Office of the Special Attorney; adopting a constitutional Law on Conflict of Interest; extending the supervisory powers of the NKÚ; increasing transparency in the public procurement process; improving the Corporate Register and enhancing its availability to the general public; improving the performance of judicial management; adopting legislation on labor in the public interest; strengthening supervision over regional and local self-governance organs; enhancing general awareness of the courts' activities; and increasing the number of exposed corruption cases.

The constitutional Law on Conflict of Interest bans the president, cabinet members, Constitutional Court justices, and other top officials from pursuing any business activities, receiving pay for brokering deals between the government and private entities, or receiving income generated by a side job or contract that exceeds the minimum wage. Other bills have sought to introduce the principle of zero tolerance for corruption among notaries and marshals, compulsory disclosure for customs officers, protection of whistle-blowers in the workplace and witnesses in court cases, and the post of comptroller in bodies of local and regional self-governance. All Slovak institutions financed from public funds are subject to the supervisory authority of the NKÚ, and its findings are made public via the media and Internet and often become the focus of vivid public debate.

Legislative activities aimed at combating corruption declined in 2007. The incumbent administration, formed in July 2006, presented a vague anticorruption strategy in its program manifesto, and Parliament did not pass any legislative measures aimed at curbing the space for corrupt practices during the year. Corruption and clientelism scandals involving high government officials did not result in personnel changes apart from the case of agriculture minister Miroslav Jureňa and chief of Slovak Land Fund Branislav Bríza, who were fired in November following a scandal related to restitutions.

The government increased public spending in 2007 without strengthening anticorruption mechanisms. Consequently, transparency and competition in public procurement declined rapidly, as many government contracts were awarded without proper public tenders. Most of these business subjects were clearly connected to representatives of ruling parties, particularly the dominant Smer-SD. The cabinet used excessive discretion in distributing subsidies to individual municipalities, allocating them in a nontransparent way and often based on the political closeness of local self-government representatives to ruling parties.

When making personnel changes at state posts, the administration often refused to advertise the post in a public competition and appointed family members of government officials. At the end of 2006, Parliament passed an amendment to the Civil Service Act that took effect in 2007; the amendment allows cabinet members to remove heads of state institutions without stating a reason and loosens the obligation to announce selection procedures when filling state posts.

The ruling coalition repeatedly attempted to amend the Law on Free Access to Information, provoking harsh criticism and protests from NGOs. Additionally, the administration's efforts to increase government regulation in certain economic sectors threatened to make clientelism and corruption more prevalent. The Ministry of Justice has drafted an amendment to the code of criminal procedures that seeks to abolish the institution of police *agents provocateurs* and the practice of sting operations; according to legal experts and the Office of the Attorney General, if approved, this will make combating corruption more difficult.

A handful of corruption scandals in 2007 involved cabinet members, members of regional parliaments and local councils, representatives of political parties, and functionaries of government agencies. In March, several of these functionaries were all caught taking bribes: Vladimír Wänke, secretary general of the Slovak Football Association; Jozef Molnár, member of a Bratislava district council (Smer-SD); and Ján Bukaj, head of the SNS district branch in Tvrdošín. In February, Minister of the Economy Ľubomír Jahnátek, in an interview for *Trend* weekly, attempted to justify corrupt methods used by state-run firms when selling arms to third world countries. Opposition parties called on Jahnátek to resign, but he was backed by Prime Minister Fico and MPs. The cabinet expressed full confidence in Jahnátek and called his activities a "mirror of political maturity, professional and life experience, and moral integrity."[5] The ruling coalition's majority in the Parliament rejected a motion of no confidence against Jahnátek in April.

Perhaps the greatest political furor in 2007 involved Viera Tomanová, minister of labor, social affairs, and family. The ministry wrongfully allotted a state budget subsidy to an organization, Privilégium, that had not paid contributions to the state-run Social Insurance Company for several years and also had tax arrears. Tomanová worked as a project manager at Privilégium prior to her appointment, and statutory representatives of the organization were connected to Smer-SD. Prime Minister Fico dismissed all accusations against Tomanová. Opposition deputies proposed a motion of no confidence, but that was rejected by the ruling coalition.

A number of independent NGOs are very active in fighting corruption and promoting transparency and accountability in public life, including Transparency International–Slovakia, the Alliance for Transparency and Fighting Corruption, the Alliance to Stop Conflicts of Interest, and Fair Play Alliance. There were no attempts by the state or private individuals to hinder the activities of these groups in 2007, although senior government officials questioned the accuracy and objectivity of their findings.

The police encourage citizens with information on corrupt civil servants or a personal experience of corruption to participate in exposing concrete cases. According to available statistical data from January to October 2007, a total of 186 criminal offenses of corruption were reported; 122 cases of corruption were cleared, and 9 persons were convicted.[6] Slovakia scored 4.9 in Transparency International's 2007 Corruption Perceptions Index (where 10 is least corrupt).[7]

Corruption is a frequent issue of public debate in Slovakia, and in opinion polls it trails only after living standards, unemployment, and health care as the most pressing social problem. A survey carried out by the FOCUS agency in August 2007 suggested that 22 percent of respondents recently gave bribes to public service officials; 74 percent said they did not bribe anybody; and 4 percent refused to answer the question.[8] According to a 2006 FOCUS survey, most citizens believe that excessive corruption exists in health care, the judiciary, ministries, police, and other sectors of public and private life.[9]

∎ AUTHORS: GRIGORIJ MESEŽNIKOV, MIROSLAV KOLLÁR AND MICHAL VAŠEČKA

Grigorij Mesežnikov is president of the Institute for Public Affairs (IVO) in Bratislava. He is the author and editor of numerous publications on Slovakia's political development and party system, including IVO's annual Global Report on the State of Society in Slovakia. *Miroslav Kollár is a senior analyst at IVO and a coeditor of the* Global Report on the State of Society in Slovakia. *He writes frequently about the media, culture, and the church. Michal Vašečka serves as an assistant professor at the Faculty of Social Studies of Masaryk University in Brno. He is the author of numerous works on civil society and ethnic minorities.*

1   See website of the Statistic Office of the Slovak Republic, http://www.statistics.sk.

2   For electoral statistics, see website of the Statistic Office of the Slovak Republic, http://www.statistics.sk.

3   See *Sčítanie obyvateľov, domov a bytov 2001* [*Population and Housing Census 2001*], http://www.statistics.Sk/webdata/slov/scitanie/namj.htm.

4   "Samospráva: Únia miest Slovenska je znepokojená krokmi vlády" [*Self-Government: The Union of Slovak Towns Is Concerned by the Steps of the Cabinet*], SITA news agency, February 2, 2007.

5   "Vláda: Aktivity Jahnátka sú zrkadlom politickej zrelosti a charakteru" [*Government: Jahnátek Activities are the Mirror of His Political Maturity and Character*], SITA news agency, April 11, 2007)

6   Emília Sičáková–Beblavá, "Korupcia," in Miroslav Kollár, Grigorij Mesežnikov, Martin Bútora, eds., *Slovensko 2007: Súhrnná správa o stave spoločnosti* [*Slovakia 2007: A Global Report on the State of Society*], Bratislava: Institute for Public Affairs, 2008, p. 663.

7   *Corruption Perception Index 2007*, Transparency International, http://www.transparency.org/policy_research/surveys_indices/cpi/2007.

8   "Každý piaty Slovák priznal, že dal úplatok" [One in Five Slovaks Admits to Having Given a Bribe], *Hospodárske Noviny* daily, August 15, 2007.

9   *Percepcia korupcie na Slovensku. Prieskum verejnej mienky pre Transparency International –Slovensko, Marec 2006* [*Perception of Corruption in Slovakia. Public opinion poll for Transparency International–Slovensko, March 2006*], http://www.transparency.sk/prieskumy/060424_perce.pdf.

Slovenia

by Sabrina P. Ramet and Damjan Lajh

Capital: Ljubljana
Population: 2.0 million
GNI/capita: US$23,970

The social data above was taken from the European Bank for Reconstruction and Development's *Transition Report 2007: People in Transition*, and the economic data from the World Bank's *World Development Indicators 2008.*

Nations in Transit Ratings and Averaged Scores

	1999	2001	2002	2003	2004	2005	2006	2007	2008
Electoral Process	2.00	1.75	1.75	1.50	1.50	1.50	1.50	1.50	1.50
Civil Society	1.75	1.75	1.50	1.50	1.50	1.75	1.75	2.00	2.00
Independent Media	1.75	1.75	1.75	1.75	1.75	1.50	1.75	2.00	2.25
Governance*	2.25	2.50	2.25	2.25	2.00	n/a	n/a	n/a	n/a
National Democratic Governance	n/a	n/a	n/a	n/a	n/a	2.00	2.00	2.00	2.00
Local Democratic Governance	n/a	n/a	n/a	n/a	n/a	1.50	1.50	1.50	1.50
Judicial Framework and Independence	1.50	1.50	1.75	1.75	1.75	1.50	1.50	1.50	1.50
Corruption	2.00	2.00	2.00	2.00	2.00	2.00	2.25	2.25	2.25
Democracy Score	1.88	1.88	1.83	1.79	1.75	1.68	1.75	1.82	1.86

* *With the 2005 edition, Freedom House introduced separate analysis and ratings for national democratic governance and local democratic governance to provide readers with more detailed and nuanced analysis of these two important subjects.*

NOTE: The ratings reflect the consensus of Freedom House, its academic advisers, and the author(s) of this report. The opinions expressed in this report are those of the author(s). The ratings are based on a scale of 1 to 7, with 1 representing the highest level of democratic progress and 7 the lowest. The Democracy Score is an average of ratings for the categories tracked in a given year.

Executive Summary

Slovenia joined the United Nations in 1992, the Council of Europe in 1993, and the European Union (EU) and NATO in 2004. It continued the momentum in January 2007 by joining the euro currency zone (replacing the Slovenian tolar) and in December entering the Schengen Agreement association of countries in Europe that have abolished passport controls at common internal borders. Slovenia launched the destruction of control points along its Italian border and planned tougher controls along its border with Croatia. At the close of the year, Slovenia was slated (on January 1, 2008) to become the first new member state to hold the presidency of the Council of the European Union.

In general, Slovenia's democratic institutions are consolidated. The state and ruling coalitions retain direct as well as indirect influence on the economy, while foreign investments in the country remain relatively low. Slovenia recorded the highest inflation in the euro zone in 2007, with an annual rate of 5.8 percent in November, up from 2.4 percent the previous year, a jump attributed to oil and food price increases, among other things.[1] At the same time, unemployment dropped from 8.6 percent in November 2006 to 7.3 percent in November 2007, and in December, for the first time in its 17 years of independence, Slovenia ended its budget year with a surplus.[2] This mixed result prompted the European Central Bank to warn Slovenian authorities of the risk of a "boom-and-bust cycle" and to suggest that wages in Slovenia were rising faster than productivity.

Minority rights discussions in 2007 focused on the "erased," the Roma, and gays and lesbians. Other issues discussed in Slovenia in 2007 included domestic violence, human trafficking, and gender inequality. Media independence remained a subject of controversy between the center-right government of Prime Minister Janez Janša and the center-left opposition.

National Democratic Governance. The Constitution of Slovenia guarantees rights and liberties without regard to nationality, race, sex, language, religion, political or other convictions, material state, birth, and social status. The system is highly stable, as demonstrated in 2007 in the wake of presidential elections conducted in October (first round) and November (second round), in which the prime minister's preferred candidate was defeated. The National Assembly subsequently held a vote of confidence, which the prime minister and his government survived. *Slovenia's rating for national democratic governance remains unchanged at 2.00.*

Electoral Process. In October 2007, a new political party, Zares, developed from the restructured political Left in Slovenia. In November, the National Assembly voted on a motion of confidence in the government at the request of the prime minister. Although the prime minister won the vote of confidence, he voiced disappointment with the opposition's lack of support in light of Slovenia's imminent assumption of the EU presidency. In the second round of presidential elections held at the end of 2007, Danilo Türk defeated Lojze Peterle with 68.03 percent of the vote. *Slovenia's rating for electoral process remains unchanged at 1.50.*

Civil Society. Discussions regarding the rights of gays and lesbians, Roma, and 30,000 persons erased from the registry of permanent residents in 1992 (who lost access to comprehensive health care, employment, and unemployment benefits) continued in 2007. Wages did not keep pace with inflation, and in mid-November, trade unions organized mass demonstrations of Slovenian workers to gain better living standards. *Slovenia's rating for civil society remains at 2.00.*

Independent Media. Controversy over press freedom escalated in 2007. The dismissal of editors and journalists of various newspapers led to accusations of government attempts to limit the freedom of the Slovenian press. In October 2007, 571 journalists signed and submitted to Speaker of Parliament France Cukjati a petition alleging that authorities were censoring and exerting pressure on the media to toe the government line. The European Federation of Journalists and the International Press Institute both expressed concern over developments in the Slovenian media. *Owing to these reasons, Slovenia's rating for independent media worsens from 2.00 to 2.25.*

Local Democratic Governance. In November 2007, the government passed the Act Establishing Provinces. Many experts, including coalition political parties, disagree with the bill's proposed division of Slovenia into 14 provinces. The bill also proposes regulation of the powers, structure, and financing of the provinces. By year's end, a group of 14 deputies had called for a public debate on the controversial bill. *Slovenia's rating for local democratic governance remains unchanged at 1.50.*

Judicial Framework and Independence. In May 2007, Slovenia joined the Academy of European Law. In October, outgoing president Janez Drnovšek proposed five new justices to the Constitutional Court, but the National Assembly approved only two of his five nominees. It will fall to President-elect Danilo Türk to nominate replacements for the unfilled positions. *As the judicial system remains overburdened and the issue of long delays in trials has yet to be resolved, Slovenia's rating for judicial framework and independence remains unchanged at 1.50.*

Corruption. In 2007, Slovenia adopted a series of measures to combat corruption, including a bill to monitor officials suspected of corruption. Slovenia also expanded its network of bilateral agreements for cooperation in combating corrupt practices. In July, the Working Group on Bribery of the Organisation for Economic Cooperation and Development warned that low public awareness about foreign bribery presented a problem in Slovenia and expressed concern over reports that Slovenia's Commission for the Prevention of Corruption faced abolishment. *Slovenia's rating for corruption remains unchanged at 2.25.*

Outlook for 2008. During 2008, Slovenia will continue to face pressure to resolve the controversies of the "erased," the treatment of the Roma population, and freedom of the press. The newly established political party Zares is expected to play an important role in the next regular parliamentary elections at the end of 2008. Slovenia will also assume new responsibilities during its six months presiding over the EU.

MAIN REPORT

National Democratic Governance

1999	2001	2002	2003	2004	2005	2006	2007	2008
n/a	n/a	n/a	n/a	n/a	2.00	2.00	2.00	2.00

The Constitution defines Slovenia as a democratic republic based on the rule of law. The separation of powers is provided through checks and balances among the legislative, executive, and judicial branches. (Although the executive is by law subordinated to the legislative, its de facto power is greater.) The country's system of government has achieved stability without coercion, violence, or other abuse of basic rights and civil liberties. Citizens may participate in decision-making processes, and referendums have become a stable feature in Slovenian politics. In 2007, for instance, the National Council (the upper house of Parliament) required a referendum on the amended Law on Ownership Transformation of Insurance Companies.

The Slovenian Parliament consists of the National Assembly and National Council. Owing to the limited powers of the National Council, however, the Parliament is sometimes referred to as a "one-and-a-half-chamber system." The National Assembly has 90 members, with a single representative each from the Italian and Hungarian national minorities. In general, the National Assembly is effective but overburdened, and there have been proposals to increase the number of members to 120.

Parliamentary documents and sessions are available to the public via the National Assembly's Web site, which also posts transcripts of parliamentary debates (a practice observed since the end of 1996). The public may attend all parliamentary sessions except those of the Commission for Supervision of the Intelligence and Security Services. Access to government information is ensured by Article 39 of the Constitution and by the Law on Access to Public Information and is overseen by the Office of the Information Commissioner, which was established in 2005. Implementation of this right, however, has occasionally proven difficult.

In Slovenia, the president's role is largely ceremonial, while the prime minister steers the ship of state. Yet during the presidency of Janez Drnovšek, the division of labor has not been entirely clear. Several soloist actions by President Drnovšek have triggered debates among experts about the de facto role of the president and the extent of his responsibilities, particularly regarding foreign policy issues. In some cases, the president's actions have contradicted the position of the Foreign Ministry as well as led to controversy in the appointment of judges.

A so-called constructive vote of no confidence ensures government stability. Accordingly, the prime minister may be removed from office only when the National

Assembly can simultaneously put forth a new prime ministerial candidate with a majority of votes. At the same time, the prime minister may require the National Assembly to vote on a motion of confidence in the government. On November 19, 2007, Prime Minister Janez Janša invoked this instrument, criticizing the opposition for "exhausting" the government coalition in the period just before Slovenia assumed the presidency of the Council of the European Union (EU). Janša claimed that some opposition parties broke the "agreement on the co-operation of political parties, the group of unconnected deputies and representatives of national minorities in the National Assembly of the Republic of Slovenia for the successful implementation of the preparation and presidency of the EU."[3]

After the second round of the presidential elections in November 2007, Prime Minister Janša reportedly considered submitting his resignation; instead, he called for a vote of confidence in what was interpreted as a move to shore up public and political support for his four-party coalition government.[4] Although Janša won the vote of confidence in the National Assembly with the support of his coalition partners, he expressed disappointment that the opposition had not supported him, especially in light of Slovenia's imminent assumption of the EU presidency. The government won the vote handily, with 51 deputies supporting the government and 33 opposing it.

In October 2007, a new leftist political party, Zares—Nova Politika (For Real—New Politics), was established. Former members of the Liberal Democracy of Slovenia, the major political force in Slovenia from 1992 to 2004, make up the core of Zares's membership. In the first half of December 2007, Zares merged with the non-parliamentary party Active Slovenia.

Electoral Process

1999	2001	2002	2003	2004	2005	2006	2007	2008
2.00	1.75	1.75	1.50	1.50	1.50	1.50	1.50	1.50

The Slovenian government gains its authority through universal and equal suffrage, and the will of the people is expressed by regular, free, and fair elections conducted by secret ballot. The electoral system is multiparty-based; political parties have equal campaigning opportunities, and the public's choices are free from domination by any specific interest groups. In 2007, there were two rounds of presidential elections (October and November), as well as elections to the National Council in November and a vote of confidence in the government.

Deputies to the National Assembly are elected on the basis of proportional representation with a 4 percent threshold. Only 200 signatures are required to establish a party, and there are few barriers to political organization, registration, and participation in elections. In practice, it is much easier for parliamentary parties to participate in elections, while non-parliamentary parties and independent candidates must obtain 50 signatures from eight electoral districts. According to the Constitution, professionals in the defense forces and the police may not be members of political parties. Similarly, members of the Office of the State Prosecutor and the judiciary may not hold office in a political party, as the Constitutional Court supervises political parties.

The Slovenian party system has achieved a high level of consolidation and stability through party competition without major electoral engineering.[5] By the end of 2007, eight deputy groups sat in the National Assembly. Continually declining voter turnout indicates that the public has been less engaged politically in recent years than it was during the late 1980s. In National Assembly elections, voter turnout declined from 85.8 percent in 1992 to 60.6 percent in 2004.[6] Turnout for presidential elections in 2007 was the lowest to date: 57.67 percent in the first round and 58.46 percent in the second round.

Italian and Hungarian national minorities have the right to an upbringing and education in their own language. Bilingual upbringing and education are assured in regions that are home to national minorities as defined by law. Both minorities have a seat guaranteed in the National Assembly independent of population size and the right to vote for other representatives. They are likewise directly represented in local self-government. Representation rights of minorities include the Roma community in Slovenia, but Roma are guaranteed specific seats only at the local level.

In 2007, seven candidates entered the presidential race. Incumbent president Janez Drnovšek decided not to seek reelection, citing personal reasons. In the first round of elections, Lojze Peterle, a member of the European Parliament, received the majority of votes (28.73 percent). His 4 percent victory over the second-place candidate was a considerably smaller margin than had been expected. Danilo Türk (24.47 percent), professor at the Faculty of Law of the University of Ljubljana who served as UN assistant secretary general for political affairs from 2000 to 2005, edged out Mitja Gaspari (24.09 percent), a respected economist and former governor of the Bank of Slovenia, to capture second place and a spot in the runoff election. All three candidates declared themselves independent during the campaign, but in general, the center-right (governmental) parties supported Peterle while center-left (oppositional) parties supported either Türk or Gaspari. Peterle's lead did not meet the minimum threshold to declare him the winner, since he did not receive an absolute majority. In the second round, Türk defeated Peterle with 68.03 percent of votes to become the new president of the Republic of Slovenia.

Overall, domestic observers have declared Slovenian elections free and fair and have not called for international election monitoring. However, during the 2007 presidential elections, controversy arose over mailing electoral material to voters who permanently reside abroad. Previously, only voters requesting to do so could vote by mail (fewer than 5,000 votes). In 2007, however, 40,000 ballots were sent to voters permanently residing abroad. Additionally, Zmago Jelinčič, another candidate who did not survive the first round, expressed dissatisfaction with access to television media, complaining that mass media favored Lojze Peterle, Danilo Türk, and Mitja Gaspari.[7]

During the second round of the presidential elections, a referendum was held regarding the amended Law on Ownership Transformation of Insurance Companies. The amended law suggested that in the course of privatizing the Triglav Insurance Company, about 750,000 persons previously insured by that company in 1990 would lose entitlement to 35.25 percent of the company's capital in the form of shares. The majority (71.12 percent) voted against the amended law. Unlike most other referendums in Slovenia, this one had a relatively high turnout (57.98 percent)—a result, it is believed, of having been held during the presidential election.

Elections to the National Council were held at the end of 2007. The National Council has 40 members, with fixed seats representing different local and functional interests elected indirectly by representatives of these interests. These elections again triggered the question of the status of the National Council in the legislative sphere. Some observers have called for it to be restructured, while others have simply suggested abolishing it.[8] The National Council may propose bills to the National Assembly, inform the assembly of its views concerning legislative matters, require that the assembly reconsider an adopted law prior to its promulgation, require the calling of a popular referendum, and initiate inquiries on matters of public importance, as specified in Article 93 of the Constitution.

Civil Society

1999	2001	2002	2003	2004	2005	2006	2007	2008
1.75	1.75	1.50	1.50	1.50	1.75	1.75	2.00	2.00

Thousands of associations exist in Slovenia, but most nongovernmental organizations (NGOs) are not involved in public affairs. The Center for Information Service, Cooperation, and Development of NGOs (CNVOS) was established in 2001 to empower NGOs to participate in public affairs through publications and an informational Web site. Demonstrating that it is receptive to input from civil society, in 2005 the government established an interministerial working body to facilitate cooperation with NGOs. However, cooperation remains poor, and the expectation that NGOs would become more engaged in public affairs following Slovenia's membership in the EU remains unmet. In September 2007, CNVOS and the Office of Government Communication signed an agreement defining relations between the two offices, which experts hope will stimulate better relations between the government and NGOs in the future.

In the Constitution, numerous rights and basic liberties are guaranteed without regard to nationality, race, sex, language, religion, political or other convictions, material state, birth, and social status. There was much national attention on human rights during 2007, particularly concerning the "erased," the Roma, and gays and lesbians.

The case of the "erased" involves roughly 30,000 natives of other Yugoslav republics who had been permanent residents of Slovenia but failed to file applications for Slovenian citizenship within the short period of time permitted. Subsequently, these individuals were erased from the registry of permanent residents in 1992 and lost access to comprehensive health care, employment rights, and unemployment benefits. Some 11,000 left the country, but 18,305 remained in Slovenia, where they have slid ever deeper into poverty.[9] While the number of the "erased" is not disputed, there is debate over (1) whether the government violated their human rights in erasing them; (2) whether their rights of citizenship should be restored by fiat or by instituting new procedures or not at all; and (3) whether those who failed to meet the deadline to register are somehow to blame for their situation. In 1999 and 2003, the Constitutional Court ruled the erasure unconstitutional. In its 2007 annual report, the Office of the Ombudsman noted that the Constitutional Court ruling had yet to be enforced.

On February 27, 2007, the Association of the Erased presented a draft compensation claim to the government that discussed the possibility of amending the Constitution to allow a case-by-case reinstatement of rights. Liberal Democrats and Social Democrats objected to the proposal and insisted on retroactively reinstating the rights of all 30,000 erased (upholding the Constitutional Court decision). On October 30, 2007, the government presented its proposed amendment under which erased persons would be eligible for restoration of permanent residence rights "only if they had asked for permanent residence before but [had been] denied the request"—hence on a case-by-case basis.[10]

Matevž Krivic, a former Constitutional Court justice acting as legal counsel for the Association of the Erased, declared the proposed law unconstitutional,[11] while Amnesty International issued a bulletin declaring that "in its present form the draft law continues to violate the human rights of the 'erased' and further aggravates their disadvantaged position. It maintains discriminatory treatment of the 'erased,' provides new legal grounds for more discriminatory actions by the authorities…and fails to retroactively restore the status of permanent residents of all the 'erased.'"[12]

Roma living in Slovenia face numerous problems, including high unemployment (more than 90 percent in some areas), lack of running water, poor sanitation, lack of electricity, and lack of sewers or waste removal services. Of the 105 Roma settlements in Slovenia, only 34 are legal.[13] Many Roma lost their status and rights in the 1992 erasure. The most up-to-date and available census data (from the 2002 census) report the number of persons living in Slovenia and declaring themselves Roma at 3,000, but Amnesty International estimates the real number to be between 7,000 and 12,000.

School attendance by Roma children varies from about 70 percent in the Prekmurje region to 39 percent in the Dolenjska region. Where Roma children are enrolled in schools, they are often placed in classes for the developmentally delayed and taught a reduced curriculum. There continued to be obstacles in 2007 to the inclusion of Roma children in school, and according to Amnesty International, only about 10 percent of Roma in Slovenia are literate. The government has resisted introducing bilingual education for Roma children on the argument that there is no standardized Romany language, and some Roma children who attend school are segregated from Slovene children.

Since 2001, gay and lesbian organizations in Slovenia have staged an annual Gay Pride Parade and homophobia has lessened somewhat. The seventh annual Gay Pride Parade took place in June 2007, with the support of local government authorities. There was sufficient police protection for the parade, but some bystanders shouted homophobic slurs, and there were instances of anti-gay graffiti on public walls. At a separate gay pride event, four men attacked a gay man, who had to be hospitalized. The Slovenian Press Agency did not report the attack, even though local gay activists brought it to their attention. While the annual report on human rights issued by the ombudsman in July 2007 addressed concerns of the "erased" and the Roma, it made no mention of homosexuality or of any intolerance toward homosexuals in Slovenia. This indicates the general invisibility of gays and lesbians in Slovenia. Same-sex couples are granted limited rights, including the right to register their partnership. There is no discrimination against gays in the Slovenian armed forces.

Other human rights issues were advanced throughout the year. In September, the government adopted a bill identifying five forms of domestic violence, including psychological and economic violence, human trafficking, and gender inequality in workplace compensation. In early October, the Foreign Ministry of the Republic of Slovenia joined the EU (with the exception of Poland) in calling for the abolition of the death penalty for all criminal acts. Later that month, the Slovenian government rejected an opposition demand for tougher penalties for hate speech and prison sentences for Holocaust denial.

As of 2007, there were 43 religious communities registered in Slovenia, according to the Office of Religious Communities. The Islamic community's multiyear endeavor to build a religious and cultural center in Ljubljana for Slovenia's approximately 47,000 Muslims came to a head in May. The new mayor of Ljubljana, Zoran Janković, said that the local community would not contribute any money to construct the center—with the sale of the building site and the grant of a construction permit, the municipality of Ljubljana would play no further role in the matter. This statement was not unusual, since the municipality does not give contributions to other religious communities.

The state respects the right to form and join free trade unions. In mid-November, trade unions (led by Association of Free Trade Unions of Slovenia) organized mass demonstrations of tens of thousands of Slovenian workers prompted by the country's high inflation and low wages (nearly 300,000 workers earn less than €500 [US$771] per month). Negotiations were not concluded by the end of the year. The demonstrations challenged the regulative capacity of the new social agreement for 2007–2009 signed in October 2007.[14]

Independent Media

1999	2001	2002	2003	2004	2005	2006	2007	2008
1.75	1.75	1.75	1.75	1.75	1.50	1.75	2.00	2.25

Media independence remained a point of controversy during 2007 between the center-right government of Janez Janša and the center-left opposition, reaching a peak in October with 571 journalists signing a petition of protest. The trend began after the October 2004 elections, when the center-right government passed a law enhancing government influence in the supervisory council of Radio-Television Slovenia (RTS). In 2005, the government fired the entire editorial council of RTS, its programming directors, and an editor at the daily newspaper *Delo*. In subsequent months, several journalists were either dismissed or reassigned under unclear circumstances. In late August 2005, Prime Minister Janša allowed the takeover of Mercator, a primary investor in *Delo*, which subsequently became very supportive of the Janša government, reversing its earlier more critical stance. By 2007, the takeover had become a matter of public scandal, with complex maneuverings on several sides.

In March 2007, the Slovenian Union of Journalists and the Slovenian Association of Journalists expressed their concern about developments at the regional newspaper *Primorske Novice*, pointing to the dismissal of editors and journalists and to the appointment of Vesna Humar as acting editor in chief without the approval and consultation of the editorial board, as required by law. There were also concerns that some journalists were required to register as freelancers.[15] The following month, journalists at *Delo* accused Danilo Slivnik, director of the Delo publishing house, and Peter Jančič, editor in chief of *Delo*, of using pressure and disciplinary measures to constrict journalists' freedom.[16] About the same time, the European Federation of Journalists joined the Slovenian Union of Journalists, the Slovenian Association of Journalists, and other bodies in protesting the premature recall of two *Delo* foreign correspondents, Matija Grah and Rok Kajzer (Kajzer was later reinstated).

Several protests followed, including a statement co-signed by the Slovenian Union of Journalists and Slovenian Association of Journalists against alleged encroachments on the ability of TV Slovenia journalist Vida Petrovčič to perform her duties for the station; a protest by members of the Slovenian Writers Association alleging that Peter Kolšek, chair of the journalists' working group at *Delo*, and Mija Repovž, president of the *Delo* branch of the Slovenian Union of Journalists, had been subjected to intimidation and unwarranted sanctions; and a protest from the Slovenian journalists' associations against the dismissal of Nataša Štefe from Radio Slovenia.[17]

These currents intensified in October 2007 when a petition signed by 571 journalists was submitted to Speaker of the Parliament France Cukjati. Initiated by radio journalist Matej Šurc and Blaž Zgaga of the daily *Vecer*, the petition, which alleged that the authorities were censoring the media and exerting pressure on newspapers and public broadcasters, quickly gained public attention. Among various allegations, the petition claimed that "the government has established an informal and influential decision-making pyramid" exerting undue influence in the media sector and asserted that the authorities did not "respect the autonomy of journalists" and actually censored journalists' texts.[18] The International Press Institute expressed concern about the situation and called for an impartial investigation; the European Federation of Journalists also expressed its concern and backed the journalists who signed the petition.

The government denied the charges and, in a statement posted on the prime minister's Web site, asserted that "the Government does not control the media, does not have ownership shares in media companies and does not impose censorship." It also noted that Reporters Without Borders, in its 2006 report, had ranked Slovenian media freer than U.S. media.[19] Although in its 2007 report the Paris-based NGO downgraded Slovenia from 10th to 21st place, Slovenia still remains well ahead of the United States, which ranked 48th out of 169 countries evaluated.

In response to the government, the Slovenian Association of Journalists and Slovenian Union of Journalists issued a joint statement repudiating the government's statement as "unacceptable" and highlighting "many protests by journalists in individual cases of being transferred, pettifoggery, interventions in journalists' articles, threats of being made redundant or having a contract of collaboration terminated, [and] editors' staff placements despite the clearly stated opposition of editorial boards, which we have witnessed in the last three years."[20] The two associations demanded the reinstatement of journalists who had been fired, the initiation of a serious dialogue about the situation of the media in Slovenia (which they described as a "crisis") as a first step toward changing existing legislation, and negotiation of a collective contract that would set down minimum rules and procedures for the resolution of conflicts between the editorial board and the publisher.[21]

The Office of the Prime Minister announced in late November that several journalists who had signed the petition claimed that the text they had signed was not the same that was later published and that they did not realize the petition would be used as part of an anti-government campaign.[22] Amid the controversy, several things became clear: First, the press could continue to report objectively about the petition and the ensuing controversy; second, the journalists who signed the petition retained their jobs; and third, the controversy reflected the left-right polarization in Slovenian politics. On the other hand, six citizens brought charges against the 571 journalists who had signed the petition, and by year's end these charges had not been dismissed.

Finally, in late December 2007, after the magazine *Mag* was purchased by the Salomon 2000 publishing house, the publication's editor was dismissed and replaced. The journalists of *Mag* issued a public protest, describing the turnover as a "deliberate political takeover," and criticized the incoming editor for allegedly opposing Slovenian membership in NATO.[23]

Local Democratic Governance

1999	2001	2002	2003	2004	2005	2006	2007	2008
n/a	n/a	n/a	n/a	n/a	1.50	1.50	1.50	1.50

In 2007, Slovenia consisted of 210 municipalities (*obcine*). The majority of central bodies at the national level were created in 1992; others—including institutional design at the local level—remained a part of the so-called communal system from the earlier Socialist era. The main institution of the communal system was the municipality, designated as a commune. In terms of status, it was an independent public entity with a directly elected, representative body that functioned relatively autonomously. These communes undertook the bulk of state administrative tasks. Thus, most of the territorial, functional, and organizational structure of the commune reflected the needs of the central administration.[24]

However, this old municipal system could not be taken apart by decree overnight; communes gained an extension until new municipalities became operative in 1995. The Law on Local Self-Government and the referendum on the establishment of municipalities led to the formation of these new municipalities. Although municipalities must, by law, contain 5,000 inhabitants, some have as few as 1,200, while the largest, Ljubljana, contains about 270,000. This inefficient and expensive system makes regional planning difficult. Furthermore, municipalities are incorporated into 12 overarching regions, which the EU would like to reduce to perhaps 3.[25]

In November 2007, the government passed the Act Establishing Provinces, which suggests dividing Slovenia into 14 provinces—a number that experts and coalition political parties argue is too large. The act had not passed in the National Assembly by the end of 2007. Fueling the controversy, a group of 14 deputies demanded a public debate on the proposed act, which also outlined the borders of provinces and regulation of their powers, structure, and financing. Municipalities are supposed to finance their operations from their own resources, but in less developed parts of Slovenia, local municipalities frequently rely on subventions from the central government.

In 1996, Slovenia adopted the European Charter of Local Self-Government and ratified it a year later. Under the Constitution, municipalities are responsible for the management of the economic sector and provision of social services in the territories within their jurisdiction. Elections are held at the local level every four years. Municipal councils range from 7 to 45 members, depending on the size of the population. Hungarian and Italian minorities are guaranteed the right to elect at least 1 member each into local councils in municipalities where they are represented among the local population. Members of these communities enjoy cultural, athletic, and other associations funded through their respective minority communities. In the Prekmurje region, bilingual education (in Slovenian and Hungarian) is available in primary and secondary schools; in the coastal region, bilingual education (in

Slovenian and Italian) is available in the corresponding institutions. The Roma community also has representatives on municipal councils.

Judicial Framework and Independence

1999	2001	2002	2003	2004	2005	2006	2007	2008
1.50	1.50	1.75	1.75	1.75	1.50	1.50	1.50	1.50

The Slovenian judicial system includes 44 local courts, 11 district courts, 4 courts of appeal, a Supreme Court, and a Constitutional Court. Judges are independent and may not belong to any political party. They are elected by Parliament from among nominees selected by the Judicial Council, a body of six judges chosen by their peers and five persons selected by the Parliament. Members of the Constitutional Court serve for nine years. Despite reform efforts, the judicial system remains overburdened with long delays in trials. Inexperienced judges also pose a problem. On May 25, 2007, Justice Minister Lovro Šturm and Wolfgang Heusel, director of the Academy of European Law (ERA), signed an agreement making Slovenia the 19th EU member state to join the ERA. The academy serves as a forum for discussions on European legal policy, and membership entails eligibility for the training of legal practitioners.

In 2007, conflicts continued to plague the appointment of the chair of the Ljubljana District Court, a position vacant since 2005. During this period, Justice Minister Lovro Šturm twice rejected the Judicial Council's nominee, Judge Andrej Žalar. On the third occasion, the council proposed two candidates, Andrej Žalar and Andrej Baraga. In the end, Baraga received the nod for the chair of the Ljubljana District Court, and Justice Minister Šturm was confronted with accusations of political motivation; even the administrative court called his treatment of Žalar's application discriminatory. In response, the minister lodged a complaint that had not been resolved by the end of 2007. At the end of March 2007, the Law on Criminal Procedure was adopted in the National Assembly, supported by 62 deputies. The end of the year saw the introduction of a new salary scale for judges that put them on the verge of organizing a strike; however, none had occurred by year's end.

Additionally in 2007, Slovenia faced problems in the election of Constitutional Court justices. The Court is composed of nine justices elected for onetime nine-year terms by the National Assembly on the proposal of the president. The Constitution declares that when their terms expire, justices may continue to perform their duties until the election of a new justice. In 2007, the terms of five justices expired between October and November, and President Drnovšek proposed new justices to the National Assembly on October 12. Although the Commission for Mandates and Elections of the National Assembly approved all five candidates, the National Assembly supported only two. Hence, three new justices must be elected to the

Constitutional Court in 2008. However, newly elected president Danilo Türk may propose as many as four new candidates since Justice Franci Grad indicated in mid-December that he would leave the Court before the expiration of his term.

Corruption

1999	2001	2002	2003	2004	2005	2006	2007	2008
2.00	2.00	2.00	2.00	2.00	2.00	2.25	2.25	2.25

In 2007, Slovenia adopted a series of bills to combat corruption, including the following: in March, a bill specifying 22 examples of deceptive business practices; in June, a bill on cooperation with the EU in criminal matters; and in November, a bill to monitor officials suspected of corruption. Slovenia also signed an agreement with Macedonia to train Slovenian experts to detect documents forged in Macedonia. The most typical forgeries involve passports and visas for women being trafficked into prostitution.

In October, Canadian authorities extradited to Slovenia former deputy minister of the economy Boris Šuštar. Šuštar had fled to Canada before being convicted of corruption and given a six-year sentence for receiving kickbacks from companies he assisted in obtaining state funding and loans during his time in office (1997–2000). In August 2005, the United States extradited Davorin Sadar, who had defrauded some 3,000 fellow Slovenes out of a total of US$116 million. He was arrested in Laredo, Texas, in October 2004 and returned to Slovenia in August 2005 to stand trial.

These developments notwithstanding, the Working Group on Bribery of the Organization for Economic Cooperation and Development (OECD) issued a report in June 2007 warning that the low level of public awareness about foreign bribery "could be a signal that the priority and commitment given to fighting corruption are declining in Slovenia." The Working Group on Bribery also expressed its concern that Slovenia's Commission for the Prevention of Corruption might be abolished.

Slovenian authorities rejected this criticism, stating that the anticorruption commission needed overhauling because it differed from similar commissions in other EU member states. According to the government, amendments to existing legislation were needed to bring the Slovenian Commission for the Prevention of Corruption in line with EU standards and introduce tougher controls on corruption. At issue have been EU standards in privatization and the financial sector. The authorities' rejection of the OECD criticism was not merely an excuse but reflected the serious commitment of the Slovenian government to combat corruption. For example, in January 2007 the Slovenian National Assembly adopted legislation establishing a new judicial police branch authorized to investigate allegations of misconduct on the part of judges, prosecutors, and police. The new system went into effect in November.

In March, the Constitutional Court declared parts of a Law on Anticorruption adopted in 2006 inconsistent with the Constitution. In April 2006, the Court had temporarily withheld the law by order. Elaborating the Court's decision in March 2007, discussion focused on the institutions responsible for implementing the law— namely, the Judicial Council (for judicial officials) and the National Assembly's commission (for all other officials). The Court said that the law's concentration of responsibility in the National Assembly for control over all branches of government except the judiciary did not comply with the principle of the division of power.

Consequently, on November 29, 2007, the government forwarded to the National Assembly a new anticorruption bill (the Law on Restrictions and Interdictions for Barriers of Public Functions). The 2007 law vested responsibility for control over public functions in different branches of the government. The bill also proposed extending the mandate of the Commission for the Prevention of Corruption to early 2009, after which it would be abolished. The bill also imposed restrictions on the participation of government officials in for-profit activities and makes their acceptance of gifts subject to public review. As of the end of 2007, the bill had not yet been adopted.

Transparency International's 2007 Corruption Perceptions Index ranked Slovenia 27 out of 179 countries surveyed. The index gives Slovenia a score of 6.6 on the 0–10 scale, where 10 is the best possible score (perceived as least corrupt), classifying it as comparatively less corrupt than Hungary, Czech Republic, Slovakia, Greece, Poland, and Croatia.

▌ AUTHOR: SABRINA P. RAMET AND DAMJAN LAJH

Sabrina P. Ramet is a professor of political science at the Norwegian University of Science and Technology in Trondheim and a senior research associate of the Center for the Study of Civil War of the International Peace Research Institute, Oslo. She is the author of 11 scholarly books and editor or coeditor of 21 scholarly books. Damjan Lajh is assistant professor at the Faculty of Social Sciences, University of Ljubljana, Slovenia, and a researcher in the Center for Political Science Research at the same faculty. He is author or coauthor of 5 scholarly books.

---

[1]   "High Slovenian Inflation Due to Oil, Food, Lack of Competition: Finance Minister," *EU Business,* at www.eubusiness.com/news-eu/1196738222.7, accessed December 14, 2007.

[2]   Official statistics of the Slovenian Statistics Office, as reported in Agence France-Presse, December 27, 2007, and January 16, 2008, topic@afp.com. The *Financial Times* offered a lower estimate of unemployment, reporting that the unemployment rate in December 2007 was just 4.9 percent. *Financial Times,* December 18, 2007, www.ft.com, accessed February 9, 2008.

3   This agreement, based on the earlier Agreement on Cooperation in the Accession Process with the EU signed in 1997, was prepared on the initiative of the Slovenian prime minister with the intention that in the period of the Slovenian EU presidency, all signatories would consider more demanding obligations of the government. As a result, the agreement was informally known as an "agreement on 'non-attacking' the government in the period of holding the EU Presidency." A decision concerning the agreement met with a relatively positive response from the majority of parties. With the exception of the oppositional Liberal Democracy of Slovenia and the Slovenian National Party, all parliamentary parties signed the agreement.

4   "Slovenian Government Mulls Resignation After Presidential Defeat," Agence France-Presse, November 13, 2007, from topic@afp.com, by subscription; and "Slovenian MPs to Hold Confidence Vote on Government Monday: Speaker," Agence France-Presse, November 16, 2007, from topic@afp.com, by subscription.

5   Danica Fink-Hafner, Damjan Lajh, and Alenka Krasovec, *Politika na območju nekdanje Jugoslavije* [*Politics in the Territory of Former Yugoslavia*] (Ljubljana: Faculty of Social Sciences, 2005).

6   Ibid., p. 103.

7   "Odzivi predsedniskih kandidatov na neuradne rezultate volitev" [Responses of Presidential Candidates to Unofficial Electoral Results], *Večer* (Maribor), October 21, 2007, http://213.250.55.115/Ris2007/default.asp?kaj=3&id=2007102105259193, accessed February 7, 2007.

8   Interview with Miro Cerar, expert on constitutional law, on Slovenian national television, *Dnevnik*, November 28, 2007, http://www.rtvslo.si/modload.php?&c_mod=rnews&op=sections&func=read&c_menu=1&c_id=158624, accessed December 6, 2007.

9   *Amnesty International Report 2007—Slovenia*, UNHCR, May 23, 2007, at http://www.unhcr.org/cgi-bin/texis/vtx/refworld/rwmain?page=printdoc&amp, accessed on November 27, 2007.

10   "Government Adopts Law on the Erased," in Republic of Slovenia, Government Communication Office, October 30, 2007, http://www.ukom.gov.si/slo/, accessed November 6, 2007.

11   "Krivic: Ustavni zakon o izbrisanih je protiustaven" [Krivic: The New Constitutional Law on the Erased Is Unconstitutional], *Vecer* (Ljubljana), October 31, 2007, http://www.vecer.si, accessed November 1, 2007.

12   "Slovenia: Draft Constitutional Law Perpetuates Discriminatory Treatment Suffered by the 'Erased,'" Amnesty International, November 2, 2007, http://www.amnestyusa.org/print.php, accessed December 1, 2007. Amnesty International's views were reported in *Dnevnik* (Ljubljana), November 2, 2007, http://www.dnevnik.si, accessed November 6, 2007.

13   "Roma Association Says Housing, Infrastructure Biggest Problems," in Republic of Slovenia, Government Communication Office, February 16, 2007, http://www.ukom.gov.si/slo/, accessed December 1, 2007.

14   "Podpisali socialni sporazum 2007–2009" [Social Agreement for 2007–2009 Signed], in *Delo* (Ljubljana), October 2, 2007, http://www.delo.si/index.php?sv_path=41,35,243184, accessed February 7, 2008.

15   "Threats to Editorial Independence and Existence of *Primorske Novice* [*Primorska News*]," http://www.novinar.com, accessed October 21, 2007.

16   "Slovenija: Novinari 'Dela' upozoravaju na pritiske" [Slovenia: *Delo* Journalists Warn of Pressure], *Vecernji List* (Zagreb), April 20, 2007, http://www.vecernji.hr, accessed June 7, 2007.

17   "A Demand for an End to Encroachments on the Rights of the TV Slovenia Journalist Vida Petrovcic," May 18, 2007; "Against Intimidation and Sanctions," May 25, 2007; and "Statement of Protest Against Actions of the Director of Radio Slovenija," July 9, 2007—

all three posted as attachments to the Web site of the Slovenian Association of Journalists, http://www.novinar.com, accessed October 21, 2007.

[18] Extracts from the petition, as quoted in "EFJ Supports Petition Against Censorship and Political Pressures on Journalists in Slovenia," in *Die medienhilfe* (Zürich), http://www.medienhilfe.ch/nc/news-updates/latest/c/463/?cHash=b2f5dfff00, last accessed December 3, 2007.

[19] "Information on the Media Situation in Slovenia," Republic of Slovenia, Prime Minister of the Republic of Slovenia, www.kpv.gov.si/index.php?id=225&L=1, accessed December 2, 2007.

[20] "Public Call to the National Assembly and the Government of the Republic of Slovenia," October 17, 2007, attachment posted to the Web site of the Slovenian Association of Journalists, http://www.novinar.com, accessed December 3, 2007.

[21] Ibid.

[22] "Kdo koga zavaja?" [Who Leads Whom Astray?], *Delo,* November 23, 2007, http://www.delo.si, accessed November 23, 2007.

[23] Igor Krsinar et al., "Public Protest by *Mag* Journalists," in *Mag* (Ljubljana), n.d., http://www.mag.si, accessed December 21, 2007. See also "Novi odgovorni urednik Maga je Veselin Stojanov" [The New Editor Responsible for *Mag* Is Veselin Stojanov], in *Vecer,* December 28, 2007, http://www.vecer.si, accessed December 28, 2007.

[24] Stane Vlaj, *Lokalna samouprava. Obcine in pokrajine* [Local self-government. Municipalities and provinces] (Ljubljana: Faculty of Social Sciences, 1998), p. 21.

[25] "Local Community," in Leopoldina Plut-Pregelj and Carole Rogel, *Historical Dictionary of Slovenia,* 2nd ed. (Lanham, Md.: Scarecrow Press, 2007), pp. 271–272.

Tajikistan

by Raissa Muhutdinova

Capital:	Dushanbe
Population:	6.6 million
GNI/capita:	US$1,560

The social data above was taken from the European Bank for Reconstruction and Development's *Transition Report 2007: People in Transition*, and the economic data from the World Bank's *World Development Indicators 2008*.

Nations in Transit Ratings and Averaged Scores

	1999	2001	2002	2003	2004	2005	2006	2007	2008
Electoral Process	5.50	5.25	5.25	5.25	5.75	6.00	6.25	6.50	6.50
Civil Society	5.25	5.00	5.00	5.00	5.00	4.75	5.00	5.00	5.50
Independent Media	5.75	5.50	5.75	5.75	5.75	6.00	6.25	6.25	6.00
Governance*	6.25	6.00	6.00	6.00	5.75	n/a	n/a	n/a	n/a
National Democratic Governance	n/a	n/a	n/a	n/a	n/a	6.00	6.25	6.25	6.25
Local Democratic Governance	n/a	n/a	n/a	n/a	n/a	5.75	5.75	5.75	6.00
Judicial Framework and Independence	5.75	5.75	5.75	5.75	5.75	5.75	5.75	5.75	6.00
Corruption	6.00	6.00	6.00	6.00	6.25	6.25	6.25	6.25	6.25
Democracy Score	5.75	5.58	5.63	5.63	5.71	5.79	5.93	5.96	6.07

* *With the 2005 edition, Freedom House introduced separate analysis and ratings for national democratic governance and local democratic governance to provide readers with more detailed and nuanced analysis of these two important subjects.*

NOTE: The ratings reflect the consensus of Freedom House, its academic advisers, and the author(s) of this report. The opinions expressed in this report are those of the author(s). The ratings are based on a scale of 1 to 7, with 1 representing the highest level of democratic progress and 7 the lowest. The Democracy Score is an average of ratings for the categories tracked in a given year.

EXECUTIVE SUMMARY

In June 2007, Tajikistan commemorated a decade of peace. Ten years earlier, an accord signed in Moscow between the government of Tajikistan and the Islamist-led United Tajik Opposition, brokered by Russia, Iran, and the United Nations, had led to the formal ending of a brutal civil war between the forces of the formerly Communist government and a coalition of Islamists, "democrats," and nationalists. Much progress was seen during this decade: The economy grew at an impressive rate (an average of 8.5 percent from 2003 to 2007), and poverty fell, albeit slowly (from a high of 83 percent in 1999 to an estimated 55 percent by the end of 2007). Macroeconomic stability was achieved owing to the maintenance of peace and security. The government did away with armed militias and bands that had festered in major cities and harassed the public. And as part of the peace accord, the ruling administration lifted the ban on most political opposition, including the Islamic Renaissance Party, which currently remains the only legal Islamic party in the Commonwealth of Independent States (CIS).

There have been setbacks, too. As the economy grew and stabilized, the country was beset by massive income disparity and corruption. The government turned a blind eye to human rights violations. Law enforcement bodies and the courts continue to function in an archaic and unjust manner. And despite the many prisoners granted amnesty since independence in 1991, detention conditions are rife with disease and abuse, and authorities have blocked prison visits by the International Committee of the Red Cross. Land reform, urged by international financial institutions, has instead become "land grab," and the blatant takeover of private property by city governments without adequate compensation is now routine. Despite government denials, vestiges of the Communist past are alive and well. For instance, the push for cotton production continues in spite of poverty-ridden cotton-farming communities and rising prices for grain and food.

National Democratic Governance. President Emomali Rahmon and the pro-government Peoples' Democratic Party (PDP) took the 2006 presidential victory as a mandate to further consolidate their power base. The partial political pluralism that was seen over half a dozen years in the post-peace accord period has largely faded, with the government exerting pressure on opposition parties and sacking former opposition figures from key government positions. During 2007, the government emphasized economic matters, in an attempt to attract foreign capital to several large-scale development projects. The government also focused on a series of cultural and nationalistic issues, some of which have been labeled by critics as distractions from more important topics, such as the population's access to justice, land reform, and the fight against corruption. *There was no evidence that political pluralism, stability, and democracy either improved or worsened during 2007. Thus, the rating for national democratic governance remains unchanged at 6.25.*

Electoral Process. Observation missions sent by the Organization for Security and Cooperation in Europe (OSCE) to monitor the 2005 parliamentary and 2006 presidential elections described them as having "failed to meet many key OSCE commitments and other international standards on democratic elections." During 2007, by-elections of the lower house of Parliament were held and informal monitoring by international organizations raised concerns, among them the existence of family and multiple voting, and undue influence by the pro-government PDP. Despite the fact that the OSCE has provided a comprehensive list of recommendations for amending the electoral legislation to conform to international standards and help ensure fair and pluralistic elections, there were no noticeable movements by the government's Central Election Commission or the Parliament in favor of amending the law. *Given the less than democratic procedures of the 2007 by-elections and the lack of progress by government organs and the Parliament toward increased pluralism and conformity with international standards, the rating for electoral process remains at 6.50.*

Civil Society. Two draft laws on civil society and freedom of association were reconsidered by the government in 2007: The Law on Civil Society Organizations was approved by the government in May, and the Law on Freedom of Conscience and Religious Associations was still to be voted on at the end of the year. The two laws restrict the freedoms of association, speech, and belief and contradict international agreements ratified by Tajikistan, including the International Covenant on Civil and Political Rights. The Law on Civil Society Organizations required all existing nongovernmental organizations (NGOs) to re-register with the Ministry of Justice. Anecdotal evidence shows that some NGOs were asked for inordinate and arbitrary information and illegal payments by the authorities. *Given the new Law on Civil Society Organizations, which has increased pressure on existing NGOs, and given the introduction of a draft Law on Freedom of Conscience and Religious Associations, which appears to restrict and even ban the activities of some religious associations, the rating for civil society worsens from 5.00 to 5.50.*

Independent Media. Like civil society entities, media outlets were required to re-register with the government in 2007. Despite this requirement, the year saw an overall loosening of what had become highly problematic pressure tactics and even closures of some outlets in previous years. No media outlet was reportedly closed by the authorities in 2007, while several new outlets were able to secure operating licenses. More important, the year saw a bolder approach in reporting by journalists with no major repercussions reported. Reporters Without Borders considered Tajikistan to have had the second freest press in Central Asia in 2007, ranking it 114 out of 169 countries surveyed. *More benefits than liabilities for Tajikistan's* *media were observed in 2007, with several new outlets receiving permission to operate and bolder and less restricted reporting by journalists. Given an apparent loosening of controls by the government, the rating for independent media improves from 6.25 to 6.00.*

Local Democratic Governance. Sixteen years into independence and 10 years after the signing of the peace accord, Tajik citizens are not yet able to elect their own leaders at subnational levels (that is, province, district, city, town, and *jamoat*). Instead, local leaders are selected via patronage and are accountable solely to the chain of command. During 2007, residents of the capital, Dushanbe, and outlying areas experienced harassment by the local government, which unilaterally redesigned the city's urban plan and began confiscating the property of mostly poor and middle-class residents with woefully inadequate compensation. Local courts sentenced ordinary citizens who refused eviction orders to jail terms. Though some local communities saw progress in infrastructure projects and economic development, such advancements were not necessarily a result of local democratic governance. Rather, they reflected the work of top-down Soviet-style command, direct intervention and funding by the president of the republic, and the normal benefits of an ongoing efficient distribution of wealth by nearly a million migrant workers (mostly working in Russia) sending regular remittances to families in Tajikistan. *An accelerated deterioration in citizens' property rights and the lack of legal protection were an added setbacks for local democratic governance during 2007, which worsen the rating from 5.75 to 6.00.*

Judicial Framework and Independence. Justice in Tajikistan is bought and sold. It is widely acknowledged that in the majority of court cases, receiving favorable verdicts requires illegal payments transferred to the prosecutor, judge, and intermediaries by advocates (many of whom work as "brokers" rather than lawyers). During 2007, there was some evidence that a government working group overseeing planned reforms to Tajikistan's criminal procedures code only remained active due to pressure—as well as technical and financial assistance—from the international community. Despite the rhetoric of reform, real progress during 2007 was nonexistent. Law enforcement agencies, nearly all of them under the tutelage of the Ministry of the Interior, remained unreformed and possibly responsible for violations of human rights abuses, especially in police-controlled temporary isolation cells. Similarly, pre-trial detention and prison conditions, under the control of the Ministry of Justice, continued to be off-limits to independent national and international observers (notably the International Committee of the Red Cross), with anecdotal reports of corruption and abuse, as well as the spread of tuberculosis and other diseases. *Owing to the lack of reform in the justice system, including the existence of endemic corruption in the courts and violations of detainee rights, Tajikistan's rating for judicial framework and independence worsens from 5.75 to 6.00.*

Corruption. In January 2007, the government created the State Financial Control and Anticorruption Agency, which claimed to have unraveled 300 corruption cases—albeit only low- and middle-level—and in the process was able to recover US$24 million of state funds during the year. One reason for the widespread corruption among government organs is the meager public salaries—the average monthly wage was the equivalent of US$53 in June 2007. Aside from petty corruption, allegations of high-level corruption and cronyism continue, particularly in the cotton and aluminum sectors (together making up 80 percent of Tajikistan's exports), both of which are plagued by intermediary companies that many claim illegitimately siphon off much of the profits. *Tajikistan's rating for corruption remains at 6.25.*

Outlook for 2008. Tajikistan is at a crossroads. The economy has shown impressive growth, poverty is slowly receding, and the government has also been able to improve the business climate by sticking to International Monetary Fund–recommended policies and putting into force strict regulations on banking. Significantly higher amounts of foreign investment have also been seen. The improving business climate, however, has not witnessed a concurrent improvement in political pluralism, improved human rights conditions, or a rising level of democratization. Thus, the challenge facing Tajikistan in 2008 is a widening economic gap is leading to a slowdown in democratic reforms that could in turn, lead to social and political instability. A concerted effort is needed by the government to bridge increased ethnic (Tajik) nationalistic rhetoric by the authorities; lack of progress in allowing the free functioning of existing and new political parties; and stagnation in human rights, including unfair trials and continued allegations of prisoner abuse.

Main Report

National Democratic Governance

1999	2001	2002	2003	2004	2005	2006	2007	2008
n/a	n/a	n/a	n/a	n/a	6.00	6.25	6.25	6.25

In 2007, Tajikistan celebrated the 15th anniversary of the appointment of Emomali Rahmon as president, an event that marked a turning point in the country's ethno-regionalist politics. Prior to 1992, Tajikistan had been run for half a century by Moscow-appointed technocrats from the northern Leninobod (now Sughd) province. Since 1992, however, southerners have held the reins. The power base in Tajikistan comprises traditional, patriarchal clan-based figures relying on patronage and networks of common ancestral ties.[1] President Rahmon, an ex-Communists who won three controversial elections in 1994, 1999, and 2006, has indulged in the same tradition. He has appointed a disproportionate number of individuals from Kulob, his home region, to key governmental positions. At the same time, other ethnic groups, such as the country's substantial Uzbek population, have been largely left out of the central and regional governments.

President Rahmon has nonetheless continued to enjoy a relatively high degree of popularity and legitimacy. One can even argue that he would probably legitimately win his current position if genuinely free and fair elections were held. Rahmon is liked by the population for several reasons but most of all for his role in achieving peace and stability after the civil war. In June 1997, the government led by Rahmon was able to secure a historic peace accord with the armed Islamist-led United Tajik Opposition, ending a five-year brutal civil war. As a result of the accord, the government lifted the ban on several political parties and their associated media, including the Islamic Renaissance Party (IRP), which remains the only Islamic political party in the former Soviet Union and Eastern Europe.

The partial political pluralism that existed in the post–peace accord period has now faded, with the government exerting pressure on opposition parties and sacking former opposition figures from key government positions. Concurrently, the opposition, which like all politics in Tajikistan tends to be personality-based, lacks direction and unity. A lack of alternatives to President Rahmon's rule and the pro-government Peoples' Democratic Party (PDP) is yet another reason for his popularity. The chances of a liberal so-called color revolution remain rather slim, as the population is generally depoliticized: some enjoying their economic gains and others worrying about daily subsistence. Also, the terrifying memories of the civil war are still fresh.

Hopes that Rahmon, secure in power after the November 2006 election, would implement major democratic policy changes in the post-election period have been dashed, although there have been tentative commitments to tackle corruption and rhetoric to reform the justice system, including a proposal to introduce a human rights ombudsman. The government has instead focused increasingly on Tajik culture and issues of national identity. As part of an ongoing streak of nationalism, in March 2007, for example, the president de-Russified his surname (changing it from Rahmonov to Rahmon). Though this practice has not been made into law, gradually more government officials have followed the president's lead in de-Russifying their family names as well. Other recent edicts of Tajik national identity have been the naming of 2006 as the "Year of the Aryans" and 2008 as the "Year of the Tajik Language." Some argue that such decisions promote a national identity that unites the population; other experts claim the government's "Tajik Aryan myth" is part of the overall "ethnicization of discourses on identity" currently taking place throughout Central Asia.[2]

Among other measures in 2007 was a May 30 parliamentary bill regulating ceremonies and celebrations, such as funerals, weddings, and even birthdays. As a result of the new law, *inter alia*, one cannot invite more than 150 guests to a wedding and no participants other than family members to a birthday party. Violators can be fined up to US$3,000. This law, though undemocratic in nature, has been well received by the population, as many felt social pressure to spend exorbitant sums on traditional ceremonies. The government estimates that regulation of ceremonies will save Tajikistan citizens hundreds of millions of dollars annually. Additionally, the Ministry of Education reinstated a previous order for students to wear proper clothing, which the authorities have interpreted as a ban on miniskirts, Islamic garb, and excessive jewelry for females. The president also banned the use of mobile phones and private cars for university students, arguing that such goods are signs of excess materialism. Some have argued that these new laws and regulations act as distractions from serious issues, such as lack of access to justice and endemic corruption.

The government has identified several key threats to the country's security, including "Islamic extremism." To combat the perceived threat, in April 2007 the authorities closed down several unauthorized mosques and religious centers in Dushanbe. Police have also been deployed to mosques to prevent attendance by youth (who, it is argued, should be in school). The government has also worried about the potential spread of extremism via outlawed groups, such as the Islamic Movement of Uzbekistan (IMU) and Hizb ut-Tahrir (Freedom Party). In recent years, there are estimates of hundreds of mostly young men who have been accused of membership in the groups, being arrested and hastily tried, and sentenced to long prison terms. The Islamic Renaissance Party (IRP) has claimed that the government has sought to equate piety with extremism. At least some of those arrested are likely to have been either innocent or merely sympathetic rather than outright militants. Several unexplained explosions during 2007, one killing a security guard, were labeled as acts of terrorism with possible connections to the IMU.

Tajikistan remains the poorest of the Central Asian republics, with real per capita income just one-tenth of Kazakhstan, the richest of the republics.[3] Toward the end of 2007, as a reaction to global markets, consumer prices saw a massive increase. The near doubling of bread prices intensified the argument for changing much of the country's agricultural production from cotton to wheat. At the national level, authorities have continued to emphasize the "strategic" nature of cotton, despite the large-scale poverty associated with cotton farmers, lack of transparency in deals made by cotton and other agricultural intermediary companies, and Tajikistan's resulting massive cotton debt (approaching US$500 million).

Electoral Process

1999	2001	2002	2003	2004	2005	2006	2007	2008
5.50	5.25	5.25	5.25	5.75	6.00	6.25	6.50	6.50

Though observers from the Commonwealth of Independent States (CIS) region endorsed both the February 2005 parliamentary and the November 2006 presidential elections, the OSCE was critical in its assessments, concluding that the 2005 elections "failed to meet many key OSCE commitments and other international standards on democratic elections" and were "not conducted fully in accordance with domestic law."[4] Regarding the November 2006 presidential election, the OSCE had similar comments, stating that it did "not fully test democratic electoral practices...due to a lack of genuine choice and meaningful pluralism, and revealed substantial shortcomings."[5] However, the OSCE also reported some positive elements of the elections. The fact that six political parties and many self-nominated candidates participated in the parliamentary elections was noted as positive, as were the use of transparent ballot boxes and the lack of election-related violence.

During both election processes, the ruling party held a disproportionate advantage over the opposition. The opposition, in turn, either did not field candidates for the presidential election (for instance, the IRP and Communist Party [CP]) or boycotted the election altogether (as did the Democratic Party [DP] and the Social Democratic Party [SDP]). The 2005 parliamentary elections resulted in the PDP gaining 75 percent of the votes and consequently control of 52 seats (out of 63) in the Council of Representatives (*Majlisi Namoyandagon*, the lower house of Parliament). Of the other parties running, only two won seats, the CP with 4 seats and the IRP with 2. There were also five independent candidates, some or all of whom were likely closet-PDP members.[6] A similar disproportionatily large victory occurred during the 2006 presidential election, where the incumbent President Rahmon was re-elected for the third time with over 79 percent of the vote, with a reported voter turnout exceeding 90 percent.

Prior to the parliamentary and presidential elections, the government took steps to ensure its party's dominance at the polls, including arresting potential presidential rival Mahmadruzi Iskandarov, leader of the DP. Iskandarov, who had criticized the electoral legislation, was arrested by Russian authorities in Moscow in 2004 on a Tajik warrant for alleged criminal charges, mysteriously renditioned to Dushanbe, and tried and sentenced to 23 years in prison. The authorities also obstructed independent media, aided the splitting up of opposition parties, and blocked the registration of new parties. Possibly fearing real or imaginary plots favoring regime change, the government's Central Election Commission (CEC) threatened de-registration of parliamentary candidates receiving financial support from abroad. Soon after the 2006 presidential election, some in the opposition unsuccessfully lodged an appeal with the CEC to rerun the poll in Dushanbe.

The 2006 presidential election was referred to by some experts as an "exercise in virtual politics," as the four candidates running against the incumbent were largely unknown figures and possibly brought together on an ad hoc basis to demonstrate an illusion of plurality. Despite the SDP's lack of a popular base, bold criticisms of the political system were issued by its leader, Rahmatullo Zoirov, and have been problematic for the regime.[7] In April 2007, the Justice Ministry announced its intention to seek a six-month suspension of the SDP for failing to file its party papers on time but later dropped the charges.[8]

In 2007, by-elections were held in March and May for five vacated seats in the lower house of Parliament, all of which were won by PDP candidates. The IRP contested the outcome in the southern Hamadoni district, where its candidate reportedly received just 2 percent of the vote. PDP candidates generally received around 90–95 percent of the vote, and voter participation was officially said to have been above 80 percent. But informal observers from international and Western diplomatic missions estimated voter participation to have been no more than 50 percent in most precincts.[9] Also, about 25 percent of registered voters conducted family or multiple voting (where an individual votes on behalf of all members of a household), which is illegal under electoral law. Family voting is likely the result of pressure by authorities on precinct heads to produce high turnout rates in order to lock in election results.[10]

Civil Society

1999	2001	2002	2003	2004	2005	2006	2007	2008
5.25	5.00	5.00	5.00	5.00	4.75	5.00	5.00	5.50

In February 2007, Tajikistan's Parliament approved a new Law on Civil Society Organizations, which many consider to be a threat to the freedoms of association and speech and a means for the government to restrict and control civil society groups. As is the case with many other laws in Tajikistan, this one is nearly identical to a similar law passed by the Russian Federation. Some of its provisions contradict international law and can be used to limit fundamental freedoms; some even contradict one another. Furthermore, the new law defines a public association as being an "initiative of the majority of residents at the place of residence" and thus discriminates against entities formed by a minority of citizens in a given locality.

Under a new re-registration requirement, the number of registered local nongovernmental organizations (NGOs) decreased in 2007 by nearly two-thirds, from 3,500 to 1,040. Registered foreign NGOs also fell, from 110 to 50.[11] The decrease was nonetheless expected, as most registered NGOs had existed only on paper. The new law, however, gives authorities undue powers of intervention, as it permits them to, among other things, sit in on the meetings of registered groups. Furthermore, as a means of control or harassment, the registration process allows the authorities to demand inordinate and arbitrary amounts of information from civil society entities. To re-register before the end of 2007, for example, one NGO was required to provide all of its project reports for the past seven years.

At the same time, a large proportion of NGOs operate primarily for personal gain, and cases of fraud among the NGO community are known to exist. NGOs also lack focus. In 2007, for example, one NGO sought funding from the same donor for a project on public legal assistance and another project on beekeeping.[12] Based on a 2007 study, a large proportion of the country's population has no knowledge about the activities of NGOs, and despite the presence of a relatively large number of potential donors, NGOs often see one another as competitors.[13]

Aside from the Law on Civil Society Organizations, Tajikistan revived its intention to adopt a highly restrictive Law on Freedom of Conscience and Religious Associations in 2007. Until recently, Tajikistan had been relatively tolerant of religious practices and groups, and its 1994 Law on Religion is considered to be quite liberal. One theory for the shift in the government's attitude toward religious groups has to do with the country's recent years of political stability and economic growth, which have allowed Tajikistan to take its post-independence nation-building project more seriously. The new trend toward restrictions on religious groups also has to do with the increasingly successful activity of (overwhelmingly Christian Protestant) missionary groups, which many local Muslim leaders and followers find offensive. Tajikistan remains a predominantly traditional society, and changing one's religion, although legal by law, remains a taboo. Though the proposed Law on Freedom of Conscience and Religious Associations does not ban individual conversions, it does forbid proselytizing.

The draft law also bans individuals who hold positions of authority in religious organizations from standing for elected office and, more importantly, in what may be a preparatory move to ban the IRP, it prohibits the formation of religiously-affiliated political parties. It also disallows religious education in private houses, a condition that could prevent the many minority religions with insufficient physical infrastructure from conducting their normal educational and devotional activities. The law also bans religious education for children under the age of seven and for children older than seven if it is against their will, thus taking away parental authority on religious matters.

Though the Law on Freedom of Conscience and Religious Associations was not yet ratified by the end of 2007, in October the Ministry of Culture banned the activities of Jehovah's Witnesses owing to the group's allegedly incomplete registration. Later, in a propaganda piece on state television, the authorities called

Jehovah's Witnesses "traitors," attacking their unwillingness to serve in the militaries of their respective countries. Foreign and local branches of Islamic groups have also been under scrutiny. During 2007, the authorities shut down a number of mosques. This prompted the leader of the IRP, Muhiddin Kabiri, to write an open letter to the president claiming that in its campaign to clamp down on religious extremism, the government is instead pursuing a policy of "secular extremism."[14]

Independent Media

1999	2001	2002	2003	2004	2005	2006	2007	2008
5.75	5.50	5.75	5.75	5.75	6.00	6.25	6.25	6.00

Nearly all forms of existing media in Tajikistan were introduced during the Soviet era, as prior to the Bolshevik Revolution the majority of the population was illiterate. According to the government, as of the end of 2006, there were 79 newspapers (mostly weeklies, with no daily papers available) and 101 journals and periodicals published, though the figures are likely exaggerated.[15] Radio broadcasting in Tajikistan commenced in 1932, and television made its debut in 1959. Today, there are around 30 radio and television stations, most privately owned, but no private television stations are allowed to broadcast in the capital city.

And while Tajikistan was the last country among the former Soviet Union and Eastern Europe to connect to the World Wide Web (by the mid-1990s), it currently has as many as a dozen Internet service providers. Still, given the continued economic turmoil, a deemphasis on scholarship in the post-independence era, and a quasi-authoritarian system that discourages independent investigation, the proportion of the population having access to and regularly reading the press is likely far lower than in the Communist era.

After the November 2006 presidential election, the authorities appeared to soften restrictions on the media. Notably, several new media outlets were approved in 2007, and no newspapers were shut down during the year. In its 2007 Worldwide Press Freedom Index, Reporters Without Borders considered Tajikistan to have the second most free press in Central Asia, assigning it a score of 37 (an improvement over 2006) and ranking it 114 out of the 169 countries surveyed (neighboring Kyrgyzstan ranked 100 and Russia 144, while Turkmenistan ranked among the worst at 167).[16]

Freedom of expression is guaranteed by the Law on Press and Other Mass Media, and Article 36 establishes liability for individuals forcing a journalist to disseminate (or to prevent from disseminating) information. Still, independent media in Tajikistan face many challenges, some owing to imperfect laws. Article 135 of the criminal code, for instance, makes defamation a criminal offense in cases where the dissemination of false information offends the honor and dignity of a person; and Article 137 stipulates a maximum of five years' imprisonment for defaming or insulting the president.

In July 2007, the Dushanbe Office of the Prosecutor General launched a criminal defamation case against the editor in chief and two correspondents of *Ovoza* (Rumors), a 'yellow press' weekly, involving an item published about the singer Rayhona, who in turn lodged a formal complaint over the unflattering coverage of one of her concerts. Though the case had yet to be decided by the end of 2007, what was of concern was the possibility that the journalists involved would be found guilty and face criminal conviction, exorbitant fines, and even prison sentences. Several international observers have rallied in the past for the decriminalization of defamation and insult. In 2007, however, the Parliament also passed an amendment to the libel and defamation legislation to include the Internet. Subsequently, both the Committee to Protect Journalists and Tajikistan's National Association of Independent Media unsuccessfully called on President Rahmon to veto the new amendment.

Taxes on media are another source of pressure; some outlets report taxes of between 30 and 50 percent of revenue. Journalists claim that they pay as many as 17 different taxes and fees (aside from the allegations that tax inspectors often ignore tax code violations in exchange for unofficial payments). Currently, Tajik media are generally considered unprofitable, and a 2007 OSCE study found that as much as 97 percent of all Tajik print media are unsustainable. High paper and printing prices are two reasons behind this, with an estimated 21 percent of the cost of print media going to purchasing paper, 20 percent for printing, 8 percent for taxes, and 25 percent for salaries and wages. Since revenues from sales account for 95 percent of print media's overall revenue, only three papers, which print over 10,000 copies on a weekly basis (*Asia Plus, Digest Press,* and *Reklamnaya Gazieta*), were thought to be financially sustainable.[17]

Not all problems related to Tajikistan's media are the fault of the government. In general, the profession of journalism has been significantly affected—not always positively—by the country's economic transition. The expansion of the economy has prevented standard practices and conflict-of-interest guidelines from taking root. In Tajikistan, print media follow the general pattern of the region, where editors and journalists often run paid or de facto public relations coverage, a violation of international codes of journalism ethics and a form of corruption. The average monthly salary of journalists is about the equivalent of US$100, and though above the country's average wage, it is still an unacceptable living standard.

Despite the availability of a variety of news sources, the public appears to be mostly passive in responding to specific events, demonstrating a withdrawal from public space, a condition likely due to a combination of factors ranging from the preoccupation of the average household with daily subsistence (with the average cost of a print weekly at one somoni, equivalent to the cost of *non*—the typical Central Asian bread); the fascination of much of the public (especially youth) with the material and nonpolitical benefits of globalization; fear of repercussions from the authorities; and continued mass trauma resulting from the civil war.

Tajikistan's Law on Press and Other Mass Media guarantees the right of minorities to use their mother tongue in the media of their choice. Aside from media outlets in Russian, which is the de facto second language for many and the lingua franca for Tajikistan, other minorities have few, if any, media outlets. Tajikistan is a multiethnic state; based on the official 2000 census, ethnic Tajiks make up 80 percent of the population, ethnic Uzbeks about 15 percent, and other ethnicities another 5 percent (including at least 5 percent ethnic Pamiris, which the government classifies as Tajiks although they speak what can be categorized as three separate languages).[18] Regardless of the country's ethnic diversity, the government has utilized a nation-building policy of propaganda to portray the state as a single ethnical unit. For example, 2006 was named the "Year of the Aryans" (according to the government, the Aryan type, or race, is ethnic Tajiks' progenitor). Right or wrong, the government's concentration on the supposed Aryan-ness of the Tajik population by default excludes and infringes upon on the rights of non-Tajik minorities.

Local Democratic Governance

1999	2001	2002	2003	2004	2005	2006	2007	2008
n/a	n/a	n/a	n/a	n/a	5.75	5.75	5.75	6.00

Local governments in Tajikistan are not directly elected, and many claim they have little or no legitimacy. Local government leaders are normally political appointees, picked for their allegiance and loyalty rather than administrative and management capabilities. Many are incapable of running an efficient city, municipality, or district and are perpetually short of funds, with large arrears in public employee wages. More important is the lack of democracy at the local level. Though provincial and district assemblies are elected by law, nomination of candidates is highly political, with many obstacles put in the way of opposition candidates or those who are not pro-regime or pro-PDP. Cronyism, incompetence, and corruption are widespread, given the lack of legitimacy and democracy at the local level. In nearly all districts, for example, there are illegal sales of agricultural lands, often to benefit local leaders.[19]

In the Soviet era, Communist planners created a series of political institutions responsible for social mobilization. This strategy assisted in Tajikistan's ensuing economic development and interethnic peace.[20] Among the institutions were territorial and administrative units. During pre-revolutionary Russia, when the territory of today's Tajikistan was part of the greater Turkistan under Russian tutelage, the region was divided mostly into *oblasti* (provinces; *viloyatho* in Tajik) and *volosti* (districts). The Soviets modified the old system, adding new entities, and Tajikistan's post-Communist Constitution of 1994 confirmed the Soviet administrative divisions, with Article 6 devoted to local administration and governance. Today in Tajikistan, there are 22 cities, 47 towns, 354 villages, and 3,570 settlements, and the country is divided into four provinces, with each province being subdivided into *rayoni* (districts; *nohiyaho* in Tajik). Three provinces (Khatlon, Sughd, and

Badakhshan) support their own regional governments and elect, at least on paper, the majority of their regional parliamentarians. The capital, Dushanbe, and a series of surrounding districts are equivalent to two additional provinces.

The subdivision within each district is known as the *jamoat*. According to the Law on Local Self-Governance in Towns and Villages, *jamoats* are institutions for "organizing public activities...autonomously and at their own discretion...directly or through their representatives." The president appoints provincial and district heads in consultation with governors and *jamoat* leaders through the head of their respective district *hukumat* (government). Though district council members can veto appointments, they seldom do. Not surprisingly, central government political organizations, such as the ruling PDP apparatus, almost always dominate provincial, district, and *jamoat* bodies. Local election commissions of the 2005 parliamentary and 2006 presidential elections, for example, were composed mainly of pro-government PDP members. Each *jamoat* normally comprises a number of settlements (*posiolki*) and villages (*qishloqho*). Below this level is where the semiformal entity of *mahalla* (neighborhood) lies.

Jamoats by law must be provided with "financial resources...to be used independently," but in reality they lack funds and independence. Many agricultural workers in the *jamoat* territory live under conditions described as "bonded labor" and "financial servitude." As such, local democratic governance for rural folk, who form the majority of Tajikistan's population, is in an extremely poor state or nonexistent. Local governments face serious budgetary constraints and have difficulty raising revenue through taxation owing to a lack of know-how, low income of rural citizens, and corruption. *Jamoats* are fully dependent on the district administrations and private donors, including *dehqon* (private) farmers, to fulfill their budgets.[21]

During 2007, the city of Dushanbe began forced confiscation of houses as part of a non-transparent urban-planning scheme, which envisages the forced removal of thousands of households and the sale of their properties to domestic and foreign developers, without consultations and with only limited compensation to those affected by the plan.[22] The Dushanbe government and its unelected powerful mayor have refused to publicly share its "genplan" (the new general plan for Dushanbe). Similar scenarios are playing out in other towns and cities across the country. According to NGOs specializing in legal assistance, cases of property disputes—both among civilians, and between civilians and local governments involved in unilateral urban renewal plans—surged in 2007. In the latter instance, the country's justice system and courts have nearly always taken the side of the local governments, with severe penalties and even imprisonment for civilians unwilling to comply with eviction orders.

Local communities in Tajikistan do not lack mobilizing capacities or even a tradition of volunteerism; both traits exist in the people's mostly Islamic faith and were reinforced by 70 years of communism. The population does, however, suffer from a "loss of direction, passivity, and the absence of economic resources."[23] According to a prominent local expert, the long-term solution to local mismanagement is the introduction of democratic elections for leaders and the consolidation and reformulation of districts and municipalities (given the low population density of many districts). Furthermore, local governments must introduce economic incentives to attract capital for investment in manufacturing and industry to supplement their mostly agrarian (and remittance-based) economies. Much of the outlying areas of Tajikistan are virtually cut off from the country's electricity grid during energy shortages in the winter. Local governments and communities have the potential to become economically self-sustaining via the production of much of their own energy requirements (such as the use of solar and hydropower).

Judicial Framework and Independence

1999	2001	2002	2003	2004	2005	2006	2007	2008
5.75	5.75	5.75	5.75	5.75	5.75	5.75	5.75	6.00

The 1994 Constitution is the main legal reference of Tajikistan, though it is poorly implemented. Tajikistan's criminal code, dating back to the Soviet era of 1961, is also problematic. Today, the public perception is that human rights violations are frequent, and the notion of "guilty until proven innocent" is commonly held.[24] Based on anecdotal evidence, toward the end of 2007, the prevalent human rights complaints in Dushanbe were violations of property rights, lack of access to lawyers, lack of fair trials, and violation of women's rights (nonpayment of alimony and violations of economic rights related to divorce, separation, and abandonment). In the northern part of the country, abuse by authorities (especially in police temporary holding facilities under the Ministry of the Interior) has been of public concern. Complaints related to agricultural land use and reform were also common. Many farmers, for example, tell of insufficient income and threats by authorities if they do not sow cotton.[25]

The most important problem facing Tajikistan's judicial system, one that brings about or is inextricably linked to other problems, is corruption. In judicial processes, this includes bribery and extortion as well as political influence on decisions by the executive and legislative branches of government.[26] Given Tajikistan's skewed economic development and low wages in the public sector, much of the prevalent corruption in the country is inevitable. With regard to the justice system, the state is obliged to pay public advocates representing clients in criminal cases, but such payments rarely occur or are insufficient. Law enforcement officials and judges can be intimidating and punitive or highly lenient, depending on the financial enticements. Consequently, trust in the judiciary remains low. According to a 2006 International Finance Corporation survey of small and medium-sized businesses, less than one percent of entrepreneurs in Tajikistan have used the court system to solve economic disputes. This is likely due to the belief that court processes are unfair, non-transparent, costly, and time-consuming.

In its legal and judicial reform agenda, released in summer 2007, the government announced its intention to: improve the abilities of the Constitutional Court; enhance citizen rights, including equal rights of court participants; require a court order for arrests, confiscation of property, and wiretapping; increase judicial powers to consider complaints against law enforcement bodies and prosecution; adopt a law of third-party arbitration; adopt new criminal procedure, civil, and family codes; and improve the material conditions of the courts, including higher pay for judges and court employees. Despite minimal progress, according to the UN Special Rapporteur on Independence of Judges and Lawyers, some "backward reform" has taken place in recent years, such as the increase of powers to the prosecutor manifested in the modified Law on the Office of the Prosecutor General.[27] According to the Constitution, judges are independent and interference in their activity is prohibited, but the notion of separation of powers in Tajikistan is nonexistent.

Under communism, judges and courts were subordinate to the executive branch. And today, the justice system takes its cues from the centers of power, including the executive and the wealthy. Judges are appointed by the executive branch and have a practical and financial dependence on it; this dependence negatively affects their objectivity. There also remains a gross inequality between the prosecutor and the defense counsel during the investigation phase and in court. This inequality is demonstrated in the low level of acquittals, estimated at only 0.5 percent.[28] The Constitution stipulates that individuals have the right to a lawyer of their choice from the moment of their arrest. In reality, one may be arrested, interrogated, tried, and sentenced to a multi-year prison term without proper legal representation.

Since independence, Tajikistan has ratified a plethora of international covenants, conventions, and agreements, including the Convention Against Torture (CAT, 1994) and the International Covenant on Civil and Political Rights (1999). There is no record, however, of a Tajik court nullifying a confession allegedly extracted under torture, and most victims are reluctant to report abuse to the police. In 2006, the UN committee overseeing the implementation of the CAT criticized Tajikistan for not providing satisfactory data and not having a proper definition of torture in its domestic legislation that would fully conform to CAT articles.[29]

In an April 2007 speech, President Rahmon expressed support for the creation of the institution of the human rights commissioner or ombudsman. Many international and civil society organizations agree that Tajikistan is not ready for such an institution. Critics argue that with the present state of affairs—when pluralism, power sharing, freedom of expression, and access to information and justice are heavily restricted, with the government treating the international and local communities' human rights concerns with disregard (such as rebuffing the request of the International Committee of the Red Cross to be granted access to detention centers and prisoners)—the role of a human rights ombudsman will be mere window dressing, serving as a muzzle on international criticism of rights violations. By the end of 2007, the draft Law on the Ombudsman was being reviewed by a pro-government, president-appointed working group and was expected to be approved by the Parliament in early 2008.

Corruption

1999	2001	2002	2003	2004	2005	2006	2007	2008
6.00	6.00	6.00	6.00	6.25	6.25	6.25	6.25	6.25

Corruption is widespread in Tajikistan. A 2006 UN-implemented survey by the Strategic Research Center conducted under the auspices of the president of Tajikistan found the public perceived corruption as widespread, identifying the courts, local administration, and law enforcement bodies as the most corrupt institutions. According to Transparency International's 2007 Corruption Perceptions Index, Tajikistan received a score of 2.1 on a scale of 0–10, with 10 indicating "highly clean." Requests for illegal payments are common, especially from civil servants, traffic police, tax officials, and even teachers, doctors, and prosecutors.

In January 2007, the government approved the creation of the State Financial Control and Anticorruption Agency, which consolidated nearly all anticorruption functions previously exercised by the State Tax Committee, the Office of the Prosecutor General, and other law enforcement bodies. The former head of the Committee on Constitution, Legislation, and Human Rights of the lower house of Parliament, Sherkhon Salimov, was assigned as its head, and by mid-2007, the agency had hired a staff of nearly 500. Despite shortcomings, the formation of this new agency marks a significant step forward in the fight against corruption in Tajikistan.

Prior to the newly formed State Anticorruption Agency, the State Tax Committee's anticorruption branch included only 47 investigators with 50 criminal cases in 2006. During 2007, the new agency claims to have initiated a total of 300 corruption cases and on the whole, put US$24 million back into government coffers. Criminal cases were opened against 14 employees of the State Tax Committee, 20 police officers, and several court employees. At the same time, in December 2007, the State Anticorruption Agency announced that 4 of its own employees had been penalized for corruption. It refused, however, to identify the individuals or the type and amount of corruption involved.

Allegations of corruption are not always clear-cut, as there are believed to be cases where innocent individuals are set up by officials. Anecdotal evidence suggests that a number of successful businesspeople may have run up against corrupt stakeholders who used allegations of bribery and other methods to eliminate them as business competitors.[30] Much of the corruption in Tajikistan is due to low public sector wages. Even the State Anticorruption Agency has complained about its low staff salaries, which range between 300 and 1,200 somonis (US$87–350) per month—yet, this is still much higher than the average wage in the country.[31]

Corruption allegations also revolve around the country's dual export commodities of cotton and aluminum, which together constitute over 80 percent of Tajikistan's export earnings. While in 2007 aluminum exports were estimated at just over US$1.1 billion and cotton fiber exports likely reached US$120 million, the economic benefit and impact of these commodities on the population is uncertain. Cotton farmers, for example, are known to be poorer than farmers involved in food production, and the cotton debt by the end of 2007 was estimated to be near US$500 million.[32] While the negative consequences of this debt will likely remain for a decade or two, a handful of local intermediary companies dealing with loans to cotton farmers continue to enrich themselves by acting as monopolies and monopsonies.

In recent years, the Tajikistan Aluminum Company (Talco, formerly TadAZ) has had a business relationship with Norway's Hydro Aluminum, which delivers raw alumina to Tajikistan and in return purchases processed aluminum. In between, however, there is a front company, Talco Management Ltd. (TML), that is registered in the British Virgin Islands and is owned 70 percent by the Tajik government and 30 percent allegedly by wealthy Tajik citizens. Another company of similar nature is CHD, which is also registered in the Caribbean and provides Talco with raw material and mechanical parts.[33] The World Bank reportedly stated in June 2004 that Talco "is not governed by a board of directors or any other type of executive committee [and] is under the sole command of its director, who reports only to the Tajik President...." The International Monetary Fund, in turn, reportedly indicated in April 2007 that Talco receives below one-fourth the international benchmark price from exports of its aluminum.[34] To dispel allegations of corruption against the aluminum industry, the government reportedly hired a British public relations firm in 2007.

Drug trafficking is another major source of corruption. Since the overthrow of the Taliban by U.S.-led forces in late 2001, there has been a massive upsurge in the cultivation and consequent trafficking of drugs from Afghanistan through Tajikistan en route to Russia and Europe. Ninety-three percent of the world's supply of illicit opiates, mostly in the form of heroin, originates from Afghanistan—where in 2007, over 7,000 tons of opium poppy were cultivated, a 17 percent rise over 2006. Given its nearly 1,400 kilometers (870 miles) of porous borders with Afghanistan, Tajikistan has one of the highest rates of drug trafficking and interception in the world. Like its Central Asian neighbors, soon after independence, Tajikistan ratified the 1988 UN Convention Against Illicit Traffic in Narcotic Drugs and Psychotropic Substances. And in 2004, the Tajik Parliament ratified the 1999 International Convention for the Suppression of the Financing of Terrorism and the 2000 UN Convention Against Transnational Organized Crime (aka Palermo Convention). Tajikistan is also a member of the Eurasian Group, a regional financial task force aimed at creating the legal and institutional framework to assist in preventing money laundering and combatting the financing of terrorism. In mid-2007, the World Bank and the UN Office on Drugs and Crime attempted to persuade Tajikistan to formulate a Financial Intelligence Unit, a governmental body gathering critical data on drug trafficking and terrorism financing for the purpose of sharing information. But, like other Central Asian republics (except Kyrgyzstan), Tajikistan has yet to set up such a unit.

▮ Author: Raissa Muhutdinova

Raissa Muhutdinova, an independent consultant, holds a graduate degree from the School of Public Administration at the University of Colorado.

1   Kirill Nourzhanov, "Saviours of the Nation or Robber Barons?: Warlord Politics in Tajikistan," *Central Asian Survey* 24, no. 2 (June 2005): 109–130.

2   Marlene Laruelle, "The Return of the Aryan Myth: Tajikistan in Search of a Secularized National Ideology," *Nationalities Papers* 35, no. 1 (March 2007): 51–70.

3   Per capita gross domestic product for Tajikistan was estimated to be a mere US$325 per year during 2005, as compared with US$3,460 for Kazakhstan. Tatiana Esanu, "Central Asia: Between Hope and Disillusion," *Conjuncture*, Economic Research, BNP Paribas, April 2006.

4   OSCE, *Republic of Tajikistan: Parliamentary Elections 27 February and 13 March, 2005—OSCE/ODIHR Election Observation Mission Final Report*, Office of Democratic Institutions and Human Rights, Warsaw, May 31, 2005.

5   OSCE, *Republic of Tajikistan: Presidential Election 6 November, 2006—OSCE/ODIHR Election Observation Mission Final Report*, Office of Democratic Institutions and Human Rights, Warsaw, April 18, 2007.

6   Ibid.

7   Nargis Haroboyeva, "SDPT Leader Considers Presidential Election Illegitimate," *Asia Plus*, Dushanbe, November 21, 2006, http://www.asiaplus.tj/en/news/17/12843.html.

8   EIU, *Tajikistan Country Report*, London, June 2007.

9   Ibid.

10   Interview with anonymous international observer, Dushanbe, November 14, 2007.

11   "Ministerstvo yustisii Respubliki Tadzhikistan priostanovit diyatelnost fsiekh organizatsii, nie proshedshikh pereregistratsiou" [Ministry of Justice of the Republic of Tajikistan Puts Hold on Activities of All Unregistered Organizations], *Tribun*, January 10, 2007, http://www.tribun.tj/news.php?n=4038&a=2.

12   Interview with anonymous international organization, Dushanbe, November 20, 2007.

13   Nigora Bukharizade, "*Neudovletvoritelno*—Todzhik NPO Eksperti dali otsenku deyatel'nosti NPO Tajikistana" [*Unsatisfactory*—Tajik NGO Experts Assess Activities of NGOs in Tajikistan], *Asia Plus*, January 1, 2007, http://www.asiaplus.tj/articles/50/1001.html.

14   EIU, *Tajikistan Country Report*, London, December 2007.

15   State Statistical Agency of Tajikistan, *Amori Colonai Jumhuriyi Tojikiston* [*Annual Statistics of the Republic of Tajikistan*], Dushanbe, 2007.

16   Reporters Without Borders, "Press Freedom Day by Day," December 2007, http://www.rsf.org/article.php3?id_article=24027.

17   BBC, "Mushkilate Nashriyehoye Tajikistan" [Problems of Tajikistan's Newspapers], December 19, 2007, http://www.bbc.co.uk.

18   Tatiana Bozrikova, *Problems of Ethnic Minorities in Tajikistan*, Tajik Branch of the Open Society Institute, Dushanbe, 2003.

19   Interview with anonymous local specialist, December 15, 2007.

20   Philip G. Roeder, "Soviet Federalism and Ethnic Mobilization," *World Politics* 43, no. 2 (1991): 196–242.

21 Muzaffar Olimov and Saodat Olimova, "Ethnic Factors and Local Self-Government in Tajikistan," in Valery Tishkov and Elena Filippova, eds., *Local Governance and Minority Education in the CIS* (Budapest: Open Society Institute, 2002), pp. 235–363.

22 EIU, *Country Report: Tajikistan*, London, March 2007.

23 Sabine Freizer, "Tajikistan Local Self-governance: A Potential Bridge Between Government and Civil Society?," in Luigi de Martino, ed., *Tajikistan at a Crossroad: The Politics of Decentralization* (Geneva: CIMERA, 2004), pp. 17–25.

24 Roger D. Kangas, "Legal Reform in Central Asia: Battling the influence of History," in D. L. Burghart and T. Sabonis-Helf, eds., *In the Tracks of Tamerlane: Central Asia's Path to the 21st Century* (Washington, D.C.: National Defense University, 2004).

25 Interview with anonymous international organization, Dushanbe, November 26, 2007.

26 Tom Blass, "Combating Corruption and Political Influence in Russia's Court System," *Global Corruption Report 2007: Corruption in Judicial Systems*, Transparency International, Cambridge University Press, 2007, pp. 31–34.

27 UN Economic and Social Council—Commission on Human Rights, Civil and Political Rights, Including the Questions of Independence of the Judiciary, *Administration of Justice, Impunity: Report of the Special Rapporteur on the Independence of Judges and Lawyers, Leandro Despouy—Addendum: Mission to Tajikistan*, E/CN.4/2006/52/Add.4, December 30, 2005.

28 UN, International Covenant on Civil and Political Rights, *Consideration of Reports Submitted by States Parties Under Article 40 of the Covenant: Concluding Observations of the Human Rights Committee*, July 18, 2005.

29 Convention Against Torture (CAT), *Consideration of Reports Submitted by State Parties Under Article 19 of the Convention: Conclusions and Recommendations of the Committee Against Torture: Tajikistan*, CAT/C/TJK/CO/1, November 20, 2006.

30 EIU, *Tajikistan Country Report*, London, December 2007.

31 Nosirjon Mamurzoda, "Tojikiston: Rishvatkhoroni Ozhonsi Muborizi bo Korrupsia" [Tajikistan: Bribe-taking by the Anti-Corruption Agency?] RFE/RL, December 12 2007, http://www.ozodi.org/content/Article/822696.html.

32 EIU, *Tajikistan Country Report*, London, December 2007.

33 John Helmer, "Global Tizz over Tajik Aluminum Deal," *Asia Times*, November 21, 2007.

34 ———, "Cover Off Tajikistan's Missing Millions," *Asia Times*, January 8, 2008.

Turkmenistan

by Annette Bohr

Capital:	Ashgabat
Population:	6.5 million
GDP/capita:	US$5,326

The economic and social data above were taken from the European Bank for Reconstruction and Development's *Transition Report 2006: Finance in Transition.*

Nations in Transit Ratings and Averaged Scores

	1999	2001	2002	2003	2004	2005	2006	2007	2008
Electoral Process	7.00	7.00	7.00	7.00	7.00	7.00	7.00	7.00	7.00
Civil Society	7.00	7.00	7.00	7.00	7.00	7.00	7.00	7.00	7.00
Independent Media	7.00	7.00	7.00	7.00	7.00	7.00	7.00	7.00	7.00
Governance*	6.75	6.75	6.75	6.75	7.00	n/a	n/a	n/a	n/a
National Democratic Governance	n/a	n/a	n/a	n/a	n/a	7.00	7.00	7.00	7.00
Local Democratic Governance	n/a	n/a	n/a	n/a	n/a	7.00	7.00	7.00	6.75
Judicial Framework and Independence	6.75	7.00	7.00	7.00	7.00	7.00	7.00	7.00	7.00
Corruption	6.00	6.25	6.25	6.25	6.25	6.50	6.75	6.75	6.75
Democracy Score	6.75	6.83	6.83	6.83	6.88	6.93	6.96	6.96	6.93

* *With the 2005 edition, Freedom House introduced separate analysis and ratings for national democratic governance and local democratic governance to provide readers with more detailed and nuanced analysis of these two important subjects.*

NOTE: The ratings reflect the consensus of Freedom House, its academic advisers, and the author(s) of this report. The opinions expressed in this report are those of the author(s). The ratings are based on a scale of 1 to 7, with 1 representing the highest level of democratic progress and 7 the lowest. The Democracy Score is an average of ratings for the categories tracked in a given year.

EXECUTIVE SUMMARY

Since the death in December 2006 of independent Turkmenistan's first president, Saparmurat Niyazov, the international community has waited and watched for signs of genuine reform. Under the leadership of President Gurbanguly Berdimuhamedov, Turkmenistan has witnessed varying degrees of change, notably in education, freedom of movement within the country, and the reinstatement of pension payments. The new Turkmen leader has also demonstrated a greater willingness to engage with regional cooperation structures and international organizations, such as agencies of the United Nations, OSCE, IMF, and the U.S. Center for Disease Control. However, while the new government's repudiation of certain of Niyazov's social and economic policies has inspired an initial degree of hope among the population, the reform process so far has been neither far-reaching nor systematically implemented.

Following his election to the presidency in February, President Berdimuhamedov consolidated his rule with surprising swiftness, and one-man rule was quickly reestablished in Turkmenistan within a few short months. In 2007, Turkmenistan under the new leadership retained many of the hallmark features of the Niyazov era, including the frequent purging of senior officials, control of the mass media, drastic restrictions on civil liberties and the continuation of the cult of the quasi-spiritual guidebook, the *Ruhnama* (*Book of the Soul*). Like his predecessor, Berdimuhamedov has persisted in using state revenue to fund grandiose construction projects. Perhaps most significantly, the new government has not increased budget transparency, and it remains unclear whether the vast amounts of export revenues that were concealed by Niyazov in foreign banks have been introduced into formal accounting mechanisms.

National Democratic Governance. In 2007 President Berdimuhamedov did not seek to change significantly either the structure of government or the command-administrative methods of rule employed by Niyazov. As was the case throughout Niyazov's rule, under Berdimuhamedov only the executive branch exercises any real power in practice, despite constitutional stipulations regarding the formal existence of executive, legislative, and judicial branches. Other than the government-sponsored Democratic Party of Turkmenistan (DPT) and the Galkynysh National Revival Movement, no parties or movements are legally registered in the country. Turkmenistan is a police state in which the activities of its citizens are carefully monitored by hypertrophied internal security and law enforcement agencies and the president's private militia, whose members receive favorable treatment relative to the rest of the population.

Having consolidated power with surprising swiftness, Berdimuhamedov began reshaping his cabinet within a few months of taking office. Purges were carried out throughout 2007, as the new Turkmen leader berated and summarily sacked over a dozen senior officials in publicized meetings. The work of the Ministry of Internal Affairs was held out for especially harsh criticism. During 2007 progress was made in the dismantling of Niyazov's extensive personality cult, although the new leadership showed no inclination to abandon the *Ruhnama* as mandatory reading. *Turkmenistan's rating for national democratic governance remains unchanged at 7.00.*

Electoral Process. Contrary to expectation, a smoothly orchestrated succession was carried out when an extraordinary session of the State Security Council and the Cabinet of Ministers appointed Berdimuhamedov as acting head of state within hours of the announcement of Niyazov's death. Within a few days an emergency session of the People's Council (*Halk Maslahaty*) had rubber-stamped the laws and constitutional amendments formalizing the arrangements for a presidential election to be held in February 2007. In keeping with tradition, the Turkmen Central Electoral Commission claimed that voter turnout for the presidential election was an unlikely 98.6 percent, of which Berdimuhamedov received 89.2 percent of the votes cast. Elections to 40-member people's councils in Turkmenistan's five regions and the city of Ashgabat took place in December. At the end of 2007, no opposition parties or movements were officially registered in Turkmenistan. Unrelenting harassment by the authorities had driven the relatively small Turkmen opposition either underground or into exile. *While multi-candidate, the February presidential election could not be deemed free and fair, given that media coverage was state-controlled, all six candidates were from the same political party (the DPT) and the opposition-in-exile was barred from participation. The elections in December of regional-level people's councils are unlikely to lead to devolution of power or authority to local governments. Turkmenistan's rating for electoral process remains unchanged at 7.00.*

Civil Society. Steady repression by government authorities has forced those independent non-governmental organisations (NGOs) that had managed to gain a foothold in the newly independent state either to dissolve, re-designate themselves as commercial enterprises, or merge with pro-government public associations. Little has changed on the ground for civil society under the new leadership, despite Berdimuhamedov's assertion during a visit to New York in September that the state imposes no restrictions on either foreign or domestic NGOs. As with political parties and public associations, all religious congregations are required to register with the Ministry of Fairness to gain legal status. According to the religious freedom watchdog Forum 18 News Service, since Berdimuhamedov became president, state officials have increased pressures on religious communities—especially Protestant congregations—"with threats, intermittent raids and fines, travel bans on prominent religious activists, denial of legal status and censorship of all religious literature". During a trip to Turkmenistan in August, a team from the U.S. Commission on

International Religious Freedom reported that harassment of both registered and unregistered religious groups was still in evidence. *Turkmenistan's rating for civil society remains unchanged at 7.00.*

Independent Media. In 2007, Turkmenistan's media organizations continued to uphold the ideological line of the state, which maintains its control over all forms of mass media. Aside from a few foreign short-wave radio broadcasts targeted specifically at Turkmen listeners, satellite television provides the only source of alternative information in Turkmenistan. While foreign printed matter remains generally unavailable, in December Berdimuhamedov announced that the ban on the importation and circulation of all foreign print media—introduced in 2005 by Niyazov—might soon be lifted to allow selected print publications from abroad to become available in the country. Despite the new president's pledge to make 'both the Internet and all other advanced communication technologies available for every citizen of Turkmenistan', access to the Internet remained strictly controlled by TurkmenTelecom, the country's sole Internet provider. New, state-run Internet cafes were reported to be virtually empty of users, primarily owing to high charges, while the resource centers sponsored by some Western embassies and international organizations, which offer free Internet access to the general public, provided a popular alternative. In 2007, inexpensive Chinese-made receivers were reported to have flooded the Turkmen market as people sought news about developments in their country, and mobile phones became more accessible than the Internet for the average Turkmen citizen. *Despite modest improvements in Internet access and mobile telephony, a substantive improvement in information liberalization is unlikely without changes in censorship policy, the establishment of a rigorous system for the training of journalists, and TurkmenTelekom giving up its role as the country's sole internet service provider. Turkmenistan's rating for independent media remains unchanged at 7.00.*

Local Democratic Governance. State power in Turkmenistan's five *velayats* (regions) and in the city of Ashgabat is formally vested in the largely decorative 40-member regional-level people's councils (*halk maslahaty*), which were elected for the first time in the history of independent Turkmenistan in December 2007. The right to appoint governors (*hakims*) was transferred from the president to the councils, which elect the governors from among their memberships in an open ballot, by a simple majority vote. However, the president not only proposes candidates for election to the post of governor, but also confirms their election and retains the right to propose and confirm their dismissal, thereby greatly diminishing any decentralizing effect. Of the reforms undertaken by Berdimuhamedov in 2007, those in the sphere of education were perhaps the most significant and far-reaching, despite the retention of the *Ruhnama* as a part of school curricula. Among several other substantive measures, a March presidential decree restored the tenth year of compulsory education and extended the period of higher education from two to five years beginning in September 2007. However, while teachers were granted a forty percent wage increase in theory, in practice the money reportedly was either not being paid or was manifested as a cut in hours, throwing into question how quickly and fully the proposed reforms will be implemented. *Owing to substantive reforms in the sphere of education, Turkmenistan's rating for local democratic governance improves from 7.00 to 6.75.*

Judicial Framework and Independence. The Office of the Prosecutor General dominates a legal system in which judges and lawyers play a marginal role. Although formally independent, the court system has no impact on the observance of human rights but rather acts as an important instrument of repression for the regime. Arbitrary arrest and detention remains a widespread practice in Turkmenistan, despite laws prohibiting it. In a clear effort to promote its image internationally before the president's trip to the U.S. in September, in August the Turkmen government pardoned 11 political prisoners held at the Ovan-Depe high-security prison, a few of whom had been convicted in connection with the failed 2002 coup attempt against Niyazov. Human rights organizations were disappointed when a list of more than 9,000 prisoners to be released under an annual amnesty held in October contained no additional names of prominent political prisoners. A meaningful reform enacted by the new Turkmen leadership was the easing of internal travel restrictions, which in practice meant a reduction in the number of roadside document checks and inspections between cities. Significantly, in July the president signed a decree abolishing the requirement to obtain a special permit in order to travel to the country's sensitive border regions. Berdimuhamedov's rule has seen a perceptible reduction in discrimination towards non-Turkmen ethnic minorities, as evidenced by the re-introduction of foreign languages, particularly Russian, into school curricula and public life. *Despite the easing of internal travel restrictions and the toning down of discriminatory practices towards some non-Turkmen ethnic minorities, Turkmenistan's rating for judicial framework and independence remains unchanged at 7.00.*

Corruption. The existence of patronage networks as the basis of power in Turkmenistan has inevitably given rise to a political culture of bribery, nepotism, and embezzlement. During the final years of Niyazov's rule, drastic cuts in pensions and public services, particularly in health and education, and the use of military conscripts as a source of free labor in various sectors of the economy all indicated that the state was having difficulty funding its huge public sector, despite official reports of record foreign trade surpluses. Although Niyazov sought to pin the blame for budget shortfalls on his subordinates by accusing them of mass embezzlement, a more likely explanation was the continued diversion by Niyazov of billions of dollars from gas, oil, and cotton revenues to off-budget accounts under his de facto personal control. According to the London-based international watchdog Global Witness, no information has been forthcoming from the new Turkmen leadership regarding the vast amounts of export revenues concealed by Niyazov in foreign banks. Despite a continued lack of budget transparency under Berdimuhamedov, there does appear to be some easing of the fiscal budget, as evidenced primarily by the reinstatement of pension rights and plans to improve local infrastructure. However, Berdimuhamedov has continued his predecessor's practice of using state revenue to fund grandiose construction projects. *Despite limited evidence that more state funds have been directed to social programs, most notably pension allowances, it remains unclear whether steps have been taken by the new Turkmen leadership to introduce the off-budget export revenues that were controlled by former president Niyazov into formal accounting mechanisms; consequently Turkmenistan's rating for corruption remains at 6.75.*

Outlook for 2008. As the new Turkmen leadership actively seeks to increase foreign direct investment and improve its international image, President Berdimuhamedov is likely to continue to implement reform in circumscribed areas, notably education, the improvement of the rural infrastructure, and the fight against the illicit drugs trade, while cutting short any attempt to create political pluralism or a vibrant civil society.

Main Report

National Democratic Governance

1999	2001	2002	2003	2004	2005	2006	2007	2008
n/a	n/a	n/a	n/a	n/a	7.00	7.00	7.00	7.00

Since his formal election in February 2007, Turkmen President Gurbanguly Berdimuhamedov has not sought to change significantly either the structure of government or the command-administrative methods of rule employed by former president Saparmurat Niyazov. Following the example of his predecessor, the new Turkmen leader kept the post of prime minister for himself when awarding positions in his new cabinet. In March, the country's highest ruling body, the 2,507-member People's Council (*Halk Maslahaty*), unanimously elected Berdimuhamedov as its chairman, and in August, in a vote with no opposing candidates, the Turkmen president was named the leader of the country's only legal political party and of its sole social movement. Thus, by August 2007, in similar fashion to Niyazov, Berdimuhamedov held the posts of president of the Republic, chairman of the *Halk Maslahaty*, chairman of the Council of Ministers (prime minister), chairman of the Council of Elders, head of the Council for Religious Affairs (*Genges*), supreme commander-in-chief of the National Armed Forces, chairman of the Higher Council of Science and Technology, and chairman of both the Democratic Party of Turkmenistan (DPT) and the National Revival Movement of Turkmenistan (Galkynysh).

Despite predictions that the sudden death of Niyazov, independent Turkmenistan's first president, would lead to internal power struggles and possible chaos given the absence of an heir apparent, the transfer of power to 49-year-old Deputy Prime Minister Gurbanguly Berdimuhamedov—who had survived innumerable purges since his appointment as health minister in 1997—was swift and orderly, indicating that a succession strategy had been worked out by Niyazov's inner circle in advance. The power brokers behind the agreement to appoint Berdimuhamedov as Niyazov's successor were most likely leading figures in the country's security agencies, who formed the most influential political force in the country at the time of Niyazov's death. Constitutional changes adopted in the immediate aftermath of Niyazov's death that granted greater authority to the State Security Council, a body including, *inter alia*, leading defense and security officials, lent support to this hypothesis.[1]

Turkmenistan is a police state in which the activities of its citizens are carefully monitored by hypertrophied internal security and law enforcement agencies and the president's private militia, whose members receive favorable treatment relative to the rest of the population, such as higher salaries and privileged accommodation.

The Ministry of National Security (MNB) has the responsibilities held by the Committee for State Security during the Soviet period—namely, to ensure that the regime remains in power through tight control of society and by discouraging dissent. The Ministry of Internal Affairs directs the criminal police, who work closely with the MNB on matters of national security. Both ministries abuse the rights of individuals and enforce the government's policy of repressing political opposition. Following the coup attempt in November 2002—when oppositionists led by Boris Shikhmuradov, a former long-serving foreign minister, sought forcibly to remove the president from power—greater powers were devolved to the President's paramilitary force, the Presidential Guard. Consisting of some 2,000 to 3,000 former security agents whose loyalty has been tested over time, the Presidential Guard is not subordinated to any security service and carries out a wide range of functions on the personal orders of the president. Both the Presidential Guard and the MNB operate with impunity.

As was the case throughout Niyazov's rule, under the new Turkmen leadership only the executive branch exercises any real power in practice, despite constitutional stipulations regarding the formal existence of executive, legislative, and judicial branches. The Parliament (Majlis) has been transformed into a presidential appendage, and presidential decree is the usual mode of legislation. During his reorganization of political structures in 1992, President Niyazov created the *Halk Maslahaty* to recall the Turkmen "national tradition" of holding tribal assemblies in order to solve society's most pressing problems. According to a constitutional amendment and constitutional Law on the People's Council, which were passed by that same body in August 2003, the council was elevated to the status of a "permanently functioning supreme representative body of popular authority." The August 2003 law ascribed to the People's Council a number of legislative powers, including the passing of constitutional laws, thereby officially displacing the Parliament as the country's primary legislative body. All political parties are required by law to register with the Ministry of Justice (renamed the Ministry of Fairness in September 2003), thereby allowing the government to deny official status to groups that are critical of its policies. Other than the government-sponsored DPT and the Galkynysh National Revival Movement, no parties or movements are legally registered in the country. The Constitution proscribes the formation of parties with a religious or nationalist orientation (Article 28). However, since the government has prevented all parties other than the DPT from registering and functioning, this ban is of little relevance.

Having consolidated power with surprising swiftness, within a few months of taking office President Berdimuhamedov was secure enough in his new post to begin reshaping his cabinet. Perhaps the surest indication that the new leader had successfully created his own power network was the removal in May of 'grey cardinal' Akmurad Rejepov, head of the president's personal militia and the only senior official who had managed to retain his place in Niyazov's inner circle throughout Niyazov's presidency. A career KGB agent since Soviet times, Rejepov had provided personal security to Niyazov with unswerving loyalty since 1986, becoming head of the Presidential Guard in 1991. By removing Rejepov, who was indelibly linked to the *ancien regime*, Berdimuhamedov gained the ability to act with greater autonomy, particularly when appointing leading figures in the 'power ministries'. In July Rejepov was sentenced to 20 years' imprisonment on charges of corruption and abuse of office.

The purges carried on apace throughout 2007, as Berdimuhamedov removed over a dozen cabinet-level officials, including the Supreme Court Chairman, the Oil and Gas Minister, the Minister for National Security and two Ministers for Culture and Media. As the new President repeated his predecessor's pattern of berating and summarily sacking senor officials in publicized meetings, by October only six Niyazov appointees remained in the 30-member Cabinet of Ministers. The work of the Ministry of Internal Affairs, which saw its head replaced twice within the space of a few months (April and October), was held out for especially harsh criticism by the new regime. The Ministry for National Security did not come in for censure, and it is unclear whether Berdimuhamedov singled out the Interior Ministry for public lambasting in order to make that body more accountable for its actions, to put the Ministry more firmly under his own control, or to serve as a response to the deluge of complaints from members of the public that had been submitted to the newly formed police complaints commission.[2] Owing to a lack of transparency and contradictory reports, it is difficult to draw firm conclusions regarding the effectiveness of the police complaints commission, which was created as a presidential council in March 2007 for the purpose of uncovering abuse in the law enforcement agencies.

During 2007 progress was made in the dismantling of Niyazov's extensive personality cult. In March Niyazov's honorific title 'Turkmenbashi' was replaced in the state oath by the term 'President',[3] and in June the golden logotype of Niyazov's profile was removed from television screens and replaced by the profile of the new president, although only during news broadcasts. The appearance of Berdimuhamedov's portrait in public places coupled with the disappearance of many portraits and statues of Niyazov prompted speculation by some observers that the new president was in the process of establishing his own personality cult, while others noted that officials accustomed to servility as a way of seeking favor were responsible for perpetuating certain aspects of the cult.[4]

A major tool used to buttress Niyazov's lavish personality cult and to create a pseudo–state ideology was the *Ruhnama* (*Book of the Soul*), a national code of spiritual conduct ostensibly written by Niyazov. Published in two volumes, the *Ruhnama*—which was accorded the de facto status of a holy book on a par with the Koran—embodies Niyazov's personal reflections on Turkmen history and traditions as well as moral directives. Imams were required to display the *Ruhnama* in mosques and to quote from it in sermons, and the country's citizens were required to study and memorize its passages. In 2007, the new leadership stated that it did not intend to abandon Niyazov's quasi-spiritual guidebook, even sponsoring an international conference in April titled "Holy Ruhnama—Treasury of Knowledge and Youth of the World". The same month Berdimuhamedov announced the construction of a

Ruhnama University, which was to be a major science and education centre and a 'unique institution of higher learning'.[5]

Electoral Process

1999	2001	2002	2003	2004	2005	2006	2007	2008
7.00	7.00	7.00	7.00	7.00	7.00	7.00	7.00	7.00

Contrary to expectations, a smoothly orchestrated succession was carried out when an extraordinary session of the State Security Council and the Cabinet of Ministers appointed Berdimuhamedov as acting head of state within hours of the announcement of Niyazov's death on 21 December 2006. A constitutional coup was executed by the political elite in power at the time of Niyazov's death in order to secure the placement in power of the candidate of their choice: while the Constitution clearly stated that the parliamentary chairman was to fill in as president until a new leader was elected, the current chairman, Ovezgeldy Ataev, was removed on the same day and charged with criminal activity by the Office of the Prosecutor General.

Only five days later, on December 26, an emergency session of the *Halk Maslahaty* rubber-stamped the laws and constitutional amendments formalizing the arrangements for a smooth transfer of power, thereby ensuring stability in the short term. The Law on Presidential Elections was passed (this law had not been adopted under Niyazov owing to his "life presidency"), and the presidential election was set for February 11. In order to legitimate the appointment of Deputy Prime Minister Berdimuhamedov as interim president, the Constitution was amended to designate a deputy prime minister as acting head of state by a resolution of the State Security Council in the event that the president is unable to execute his duties. In a relatively quick procedure that did not reveal any latent power struggles, two candidates for president were nominated from each of the country's five regions and the city of Ashgabat, although only six ultimately received the requisite number of votes (two-thirds of the membership of the *Halk Maslahaty*). Aside from Acting President Berdimuhamedov, all candidates were lesser known bureaucrats lacking political weight. In a scenario reminiscent of Niyazov's rule, only Berdimuhamedov received the unanimous support of the *Halk Maslahaty*, which was an excellent indicator that his victory in the February 2007 election was a foregone conclusion.

In keeping with tradition, the Turkmen Central Electoral Commission claimed that voter turnout for the presidential election was an unlikely 98.6 percent, of which Berdimuhamedov received 89.2 per cent of the votes cast. While multi-candidate, the election could not be deemed free and fair, given that media coverage was state-controlled, all six candidates were from the same political party (the DPT) and the opposition was barred from participation. Despite these impediments, the campaign meetings preceding the presidential election offered the Turkmen electorate the chance to tentatively raise some issues regarded as taboo under Niyazov, which was an opportunity they had not been afforded since the perestroika years under Gorbachev.

No opposition parties or movements are officially registered in Turkmenistan. Unrelenting harassment by the authorities has driven the relatively small Turkmen opposition either underground or into exile. The opposition-in-exile remains small, weak, poor, and prone to internal division. Nonetheless, in the immediate aftermath of Niyazov's death, leading members publicly announced their intention to agree on a single candidate to run in the presidential election. Meeting in the Ukrainian capital of Kiev on December 25, the opposition-in-exile nominated former deputy prime minister and central bank chairman Khudaiberdy Orazov as their presidential candidate. In the event, Turkmen security agencies warned that opposition leaders would be arrested on arrival at any airport in Turkmenistan should they attempt to return.[6]

During Turkmenistan's 16-year history of independent rule, electoral officials have declared near 100 percent voter turnout rates for all elections and referendums. To achieve such spectacularly high participation rates, electoral officials have engaged widely in irregular procedures, such as stuffing ballot boxes and making door-to-door home visits during which voters were urged to cast their ballots. Pressure is exerted on all civil servants to vote, and failure to do so can lead to reprisals.[7]

The most recent elections of people's representatives—one from each of the country's 60 districts—to the national-level *Halk Maslahaty* (People's Council) were held in April 2003 amid a near total absence of information about the candidates or their platforms. Electoral officials claimed a 99.8 percent voter turnout. The next such elections are scheduled for December 2008. The country's third parliamentary elections in December 2004 were widely regarded as a purely ceremonial exercise, in line with previous elections to that body. Although 131 candidates vied for 50 seats, all had been approved by governmental authorities prior to the elections and were members of the DPT. The next elections to parliament are scheduled for December 2008. In July 2006, 5,320 deputies from a field of 12,200 contenders were elected to the village and town councils (*gengeshes*), which represented the lowest level of government. Despite multiple candidacies and the use of transparent ballot boxes for the first time, there was minimal pre-election campaigning, and all candidates still represented Niyazov's DPT.

In October 2005, the People's Council amended the Constitution to provide for the holding of direct elections to district, city, and regional people's councils (*halk maslahaty*). In December 2006, elections to 40-member district and city people's councils were held for the first time since independence, with 6,142 candidates vying for 2,640 seats.[8] As is standard practice in Turkmenistan, electoral officials accompanied by policemen made door-to-door visits urging voters to go to the polls. Voter turnout was officially reported at 96.9 percent. Candidates underwent the usual dual screening process by local governmental officials and officials from the MNB, according to the Institute for War and Peace Reporting.[9] Elections to people's councils in Turkmenistan's five regions and in the city of Ashgabat were held in December 2007. As in the days of President Niyazov, Turkmen state media reported a 98.8 percent voter turnout, declaring that domestic observers had characterized the elections as 'completely transparent'.[10]

Civil Society

1999	2001	2002	2003	2004	2005	2006	2007	2008
7.00	7.00	7.00	7.00	7.00	7.00	7.00	7.00	7.00

The state of civil society has changed little on the ground under the new Turkmen leadership. Nonetheless, during a visit to New York in September 2007, President Berdimuhamedov asserted that the state imposes no restrictions on either foreign or domestic non-governmental organisations (NGOs), which, he claimed, face no obstacles in either registering or carrying out activity.[11]

Although civil society has never thrived in Turkmenistan, steady repression by government authorities, since 2002 in particular, has forced those independent NGOs that had managed to gain a foothold in the newly independent country either to dissolve, re-designate themselves as commercial enterprises, or merge with pro-government public associations. According to the U.S. NGO Counterpart Consortium, in 2000 there were approximately 200 to 300 registered and unregistered NGOs in Turkmenistan.[12] By August 2006, that number had dwindled to fewer than 90,[13] the vast majority of which either supported the government or received funding from the government. There are no independent trade unions, and the successor to the Soviet-era Federation of Trade Unions remains linked to the government. Other government-organized NGOs include the veterans association, the youth association, and the journalists union. The women's union, which is dedicated to the memory of former president Niyazov's mother, is the only officially registered women's NGO.

As with political parties and public associations, all religious congregations are required to register with the Ministry of Fairness to gain legal status. Before 2004, the only religions that had managed to register successfully were Sunni Islam and Russian Orthodox Christianity, although they were still subject to tight government controls. In March 2004, President Niyazov issued a decree pledging to register all religious groups regardless of creed or number. As a result of these changes, a handful of minority religious groups have managed to gain registration since 2004.[14] Despite this minimal progress, many minority religious groups remain unregistered, such as the Catholic, Lutheran, Jehovah's Witness, Armenian Apostolic, and Jewish communities. More important, registration has not brought the promised benefits, as registered and unregistered groups alike continue to experience police raids, detentions, fines, and other forms of harassment. Especially outside Ashgabat, some minority religious groups have been prohibited from meeting, throwing into question the very purpose of the registration process.[15]

According to the religious freedom watchdog Forum 18 News Service, under Berdimuhamedov, state officials have increased pressures on religious communities—especially Protestant congregations—"with threats, intermittent raids and fines, travel bans on prominent religious activists, denial of legal status and censorship of all religious literature".[16] In 2007 two Baptist pastors were imprisoned, released and deported to Russia, while five Jehovah's Witnesses served suspended sentences for refusing compulsory military service (three of whom were amnestied in October). During a trip to Turkmenistan in August 2007, a team from the U.S. Commission on International Religious Freedom reported that, despite encouraging reports from the government on plans for reform, harassment of both registered and unregistered religious groups was still in evidence.[17]

Independent Media

1999	2001	2002	2003	2004	2005	2006	2007	2008
7.00	7.00	7.00	7.00	7.00	7.00	7.00	7.00	7.00

In 2007, Turkmenistan's media organizations continued to uphold the ideological line of the state, which maintains its control over all forms of mass media. Despite modest improvements in Internet access and mobile telephony, a substantive improvement in information liberalization is unlikely without changes in censorship policy and the establishment of a rigorous system for the training of journalists.

In addition to 23 newspapers and 17 journals, the four state television channels[18] and four state radio stations function as mouthpieces for government propaganda. There is a single information agency (TDH), which has a monopoly on the information provided to Turkmenistan's mass media. Foreign journalists are rarely allowed to enter the country, and those who do gain entry are closely monitored by the State Service for the Registration of Foreigners. Only the Russian news agency ITAR-TASS has its own accredited foreign correspondent in Ashgabat, while all other news agencies were required to rely on the services of freelance, unregistered stringers.

Aside from the programs of the Turkmen Service of Radio Liberty and the German Deutsche Welle in Russian, which are specifically targeted at Turkmen listeners, satellite television—in very widespread use throughout Ashgabat as well as in other cities—provides the only source of alternative information in Turkmenistan. However, in December 2007 the government announced that the mushrooming of satellite antennae was uglifying Ashgabat's landscape, proposing that the numerous antennae present on most apartment blocks be replaced by a "single powerful dish". Despite the leadership's claim of an aesthetic rationale, it is not yet clear to what extent this change might limit the population's viewing choices.[19]

Although Turkmen television began to rebroadcast some news and entertainment programs from Russian's Channel One TV in January, the content of the tapes are reportedly cleared by MNB officials beforehand. While foreign printed matter remained generally unavailable, in December President Berdimuhamedov announced that the ban on the importation and circulation of all foreign print media—introduced in 2005 by Niyazov—might soon be lifted to allow selected print publications from abroad to become available in the country.[20]

Despite the new president's pledge to make 'both the Internet and all other advanced communication technologies available for every citizen of Turkmenistan',[21] access to the Internet is still strictly controlled by the country's sole Internet provider, TurkmenTelecom. TurkmenTelekom has still not undertaken to connect private citizens to the Internet, with the consequence that only state agencies, embassies, international organizations, large foreign firms and some NGOs in the country's major cities have unhindered access to the Internet. According to the Internet World Stats directory, Turkmenistan had only an estimated 64,800 Internet users, or .91 percent of the population, as of August 2007. While a small number, this represented nearly a 100% increase over 2006 figures.[22]

As of late 2007, approximately a dozen state-run Internet cafes in Ashgabat and regional capitals had been set up. The cafes were reported to be virtually empty of users, primarily owing to high charges as well as concerns that Internet use could be monitored by the authorities. While from two to four thousand users were reported to have visited the state-run Internet cafes during the first half of 2007, the same number of users were registered in a two-week period at the resource centers sponsored by some Western embassies and international organizations, which offer free Internet access to the general public.[23] Most Internet websites critical of official government policy remain blocked by the authorities, although several major foreign news sites, such as the BBC or CNN, are accessible—a distinct change from the Niyazov era. In an apparent move towards greater freedom in public discourse, in October Turkmen authorities initiated a readers' comments feature on the official government website, but removed this feedback option only two days later after one posted comment called on the president to release all political prisoners.

In 2007, inexpensive Chinese-made receivers are reported to have flooded the Turkmen market as people sought news about developments in their country, and mobile phones became more accessible than the Internet for the average Turkmen citizen. In mid-2007, Turkmenistan's local company Altyn Asyr GSM was serving 43,000 customers, while Russia's MTS reported 240,000 subscribers, representing an increase of 96 percent over 2006 figures.[24]

Local Democratic Governance

1999	2001	2002	2003	2004	2005	2006	2007	2008
n/a	n/a	n/a	n/a	n/a	7.00	7.00	7.00	6.75

State power in Turkmenistan's five *velayats* (regions) and in the city of Ashgabat is formally vested in the largely decorative 40-member people's councils (*halk maslahaty*), which were elected in December 2007, following district and city people's councils contests in December 2006. In the villages, the 1992 Constitution provided for the replacement of local soviets by councils (*gengeshes*), whose members are directly elected for five-year terms. The more than 600 *gengeshes* are administered by *archins*, who are elected from among their respective memberships for three-year terms.

Perhaps more significant than the creation of new regional, district and city people's councils under the October 2005 constitutional amendment was the transfer of the right to appoint governors (*hakims*) at all levels from the president to the respective councils, which elect the *hakims* from among their memberships in an open ballot, by a simple majority vote, as was already the practice for village councils. Although in a less authoritarian state this transfer of power might have been hailed as a major step toward the devolution of authority from the center to local organs of government, in Turkmenistan all candidates for election to official posts are carefully vetted in a pre-election screening process designed to weed out any potentially disloyal deputies. In fact, according to the law "On Hakims", revised under President Berdimuhamedov, the hakims of regions, districts and cities are elected by their respective people's councils after being proposed as candidates by the president of Turkmenistan, who also subsequently confirms their election to the post. Similarly, the hakim of a region or the city of Ashgabat is removed from his/her post by a simple majority vote of the corresponding people's council at the proposal of the president of Turkmenistan, who also subsequently confirms the council's decision.[25]

Tribal identities remain strong in Turkmenistan and continue to play an important role in Turkmen society and informal local politics. The largest tribes are the Tekke in south-central Turkmenistan (Ahal Tekke and Mary Tekke), the Ersary near the Turkmenistan-Afghanistan border, the Yomud in western and northeastern Turkmenistan, and the Saryks in the southernmost corner of the country. In Turkmenistan tribalism manifests itself primarily in social practices, such as the maintenance of preferential networks, endogamy, and the persistence of dialects. Virtually all Turkmen have at least a minimal knowledge of their own tribal affiliation, which is still a relatively reliable indicator of birthplace. A disproportionate number of influential positions in central government tend to go to members of Niyazov's and Berdimuhamedov's own tribe, the Ahal Tekke.

From approximately 2000, Niyazov's government engaged in the systematic dismantling of key areas of the public sector, notably education, health care, and social security, with serious repercussions for the rural population in particular. In many rural schools, it was estimated that up to one-half of classroom time was allocated to the study of the *Ruhnama*. Class sizes increased and facilities deteriorated as state funds earmarked for education diminished.[26] In addition to other changes, the number of student places in institutes of higher education was cut by nearly 75 percent, and compulsory education was reduced from 11 to 9 years (a circumstance that complicated the entry of Turkmen students into foreign universities). The steady dismantling of the education system put in doubt the ability of the next generation of Turkmen to compete successfully in the global market.

Consequently, of the reforms undertaken by Berdimuhamedov in 2007, those concerning the sphere of education have been perhaps the most significant and far-reaching, despite the retention of the *Ruhnama* as a part of school curricula. Measures taken by the new government only months after coming to power to rejuvenate Turkmenistan's decaying educational system were widely hailed, both domestically and internationally. A March presidential decree restored the tenth year of compulsory education and extended the period of higher education from two to five years beginning in September 2007. High school students are no longer required to undergo two years' of practical work experience before applying to universities, foreign degrees are once again recognized and the university admission system is reported to have been made fairer.[27] Not least, in June Berdimuhamedov announced the re-opening of the defunct Academy of Sciences, which, before its closure in 1993, had acted as the mainstay of the scientific and academic community. He also decreed the establishment of a new presidential Higher Council on Science and Technology to coordinate the state's scientific and academic policy, and ordered the introduction of post-graduate and doctoral studies in certain higher educational establishments and scientific organizations.[28] Physical education, social sciences, art and foreign languages were restored to the national curriculum, the workload of teachers was reduced and limits placed on classroom size. More than 20,000 teachers, many of whom had lost their jobs under Niyazov, were expected to return to work in 2007. However, while teachers were granted a forty percent wage increase in theory, in practice the money reportedly was either not being paid or was manifested as a cut in hours.[29]

In addition to the education sector, health care services in Turkmenistan were systematically undermined under Niyazov. Despite a large cut in the number of state-employed health care workers in 2001,[30] 15,000 skilled health care workers (including doctors, nurses, midwives, and medical attendants) were dismissed in March 2004 and, in some cases, replaced by untrained military conscripts. In addition, the March "reforms" introduced fees for specialist services that had previously been free of charge, making treatment unaffordable for many patients.[31] In February 2005 President Niyazov announced a plan to close all hospitals outside Ashgabat, claiming that regional hospitals were "not needed." Under Niyazov's proposals, citizens in the country's regions were to visit medical diagnostic centers—which required payment for services—to obtain prescriptions and general advice, while those in need of hospitalization or specialist care were to be compelled to travel to Ashgabat. By late 2006 most rural district hospitals were reported to have closed, although hospitals in district and regional centers, which offered some specialist care, continued to operate.[32] With the exception of a large-scale vaccination program undertaken in cooperation with international bodies, there were no significant improvements in the area of healthcare in 2007, although the new government announced longer-term plans to construct a number of hospitals.

Judicial Framework and Independence

1999	2001	2002	2003	2004	2005	2006	2007	2008
6.75	7.00	7.00	7.00	7.00	7.00	7.00	7.00	7.00

On May 18, 1992, Turkmenistan's Parliament adopted a new Constitution—the first Central Asian state to enact such a document after the dissolution of the U.S.S.R.. The Constitution guarantees in theory the protection of basic rights and liberties, equality under the law, and the separation of religion and state.

Unchanged since the Soviet era, the court system in Turkmenistan consists of a Supreme Court, 6 regional courts (including 1 for the city of Ashgabat), and, at the lowest level, 61 district and city courts. In addition, the Supreme Economic Court hears all commercial disputes and cases involving conflicts between state enterprises and ministries. Because all military courts were abolished in 1997, criminal offences committed by military personnel are tried in civilian courts under the authority of the Office of the Prosecutor General. Although formally independent, the court system has no impact on the observance of human rights but rather acts as an important instrument of repression for the regime. The president appoints all judges for five-year terms without legislative review. The Office of the Prosecutor General dominates a legal system in which judges and lawyers play a marginal role. As in the former Soviet Union, convictions are generally based on confessions that are sometimes extracted by forcible means, including the use of torture and psychotropic substances.

Arbitrary arrest and detention remains a widespread practice in Turkmenistan, despite laws prohibiting it. Prison riots are a relatively common occurrence, apparently provoked by inhumane conditions, and human rights organizations have reported that inmates are routinely beaten and tortured. Turkmen authorities have refused consistently to grant the International Committee of the Red Cross unaccompanied access to prisons. Under an annual amnesty mandated by a 1999 law and presidential decree, the government releases thousands of inmates each year on the eve of the Muslim feast Gadyr Gijesi (Night of Forgiveness) in October, primarily to relieve overcrowding. The number of persons amnestied since 1999 totals more than 250,000.[33] Although individuals convicted of serious crimes are theoretically ineligible for amnesty, those who can pay bribes—excluding political prisoners—are generally freed, regardless of the type of crime for which they were imprisoned.

In a clear effort to promote its image internationally before President Berdimuhamedov's trip to the U.S. in September, in August the Turkmen government pardoned 11 political prisoners held at the Ovan-Depe high-security prison, some of whom were convicted in connection with the failed 2002 coup against President Niyazov. The prisoners reportedly were required to admit their guilt in the presence of relatives before being released.[34] The most well-known among the prisoners was Nasrullah ibn Ibadullah, who had served as Turkmenistan's chief religious leader from 1996–2003 before being sentenced in 2004 to 22 years in prison on treason charges. Upon his release Ibadullah thanked the President and accepted a post as adviser at the President's State Council for Religious Affairs, thus remaining under the close supervision of administration officials. Although human rights organizations and other observers held out hope that some of the remaining prisoners convicted in connection with the coup attempt would be freed under the annual October amnesty, when the government published the names of the more than 9,000 prisoners to be amnestied, the list contained no names of prominent political prisoners.

In January 2004 the exit visa regime, which required citizens of Turkmenistan to obtain visas—often at considerable expense—to travel to foreign states, was abolished, although in its stead the government implemented a number of unofficial measures to prevent free travel, such as the drawing up of an extensive "blacklist" of citizens who were prohibited from leaving the country and the arbitrary confiscation of passports. Under Niyazov's government, impediments also existed to travel within Turkmenistan owing to frequent roadblocks, checkpoints, and document checks throughout the country. A meaningful reform enacted by the new Turkmen leadership was the easing of internal travel restrictions, which in practice meant a reduction in the number of roadside document checks and inspections between cities. Significantly, in July the president signed a decree abolishing the requirement to obtain a special permit in order to travel to the country's sensitive border regions.

In line with other post-Soviet states, with the advent of independence Turkmenistan accorded a de facto higher status to its titular population, ethnic Turkmen, and legitimized the adoption of policies and practices that promoted their specific interests. (According to 2003 statistics, ethnic Turkmen constituted 85 percent of Turkmenistan's population, ethnic Uzbeks 5 percent, ethnic Russians 4 percent, and other ethnic minorities the remaining 6 percent.)[35] In 2000, Turkmen was introduced as the language of instruction in all the country's schools, including in regions where ethnic Uzbeks or Kazakhs were preponderant. Higher education and jobs in the public sector were effectively closed to non-Turkmen, and senior state officials needed to demonstrate ethnic purity by tracing their Turkmen ancestry back several generations. These discriminatory practices affected, among other minorities, the non-Turkmen Russian-speaking population, who witnessed a virtual ban on Russian-language publications and education as well as the bulldozing of the historic Pushkin Russian Dramatic Theater.

Berdimuhamedov's rule has seen a perceptible reduction in discrimination towards non-Turkmen ethnic minorities, as evidenced by the re-introduction of foreign languages, particularly Russian, into school curricula and public life. A newly created fourth radio station is to offer news and entertainment in Russian and English as well as Turkmen, marking the return of Russian to Turkmen radio airwaves for the first time since the suspension of transmission by Turkmen authorities in July 2004 of the highly popular Russian radio station "Mayak".[36] In March 2007 a Russian book fair was held in Ashgabat, which, according to the Open Society

Institute's Turkmenistan Project, "signalled a sea change in the government's policy of intolerance for Russian culture that had been the hallmark of President Niyazov's policy of promoting 'pure' ethnic Turkmen culture".[37] Additionally, the Russian government has agreed to participate in the construction of a branch of Moscow State University in the new Ruhnama University in Ashgabat.[38]

Corruption

1999	2001	2002	2003	2004	2005	2006	2007	2008
6.00	6.25	6.25	6.25	6.25	6.50	6.75	6.75	6.75

According to its Corruption Perceptions Index for 2007, Transparency International ranked Turkmenistan as one of the most corrupt countries in the world, giving it a score of only 2.0 (with 10 "highly clean" and 0 "highly corrupt"). Out of all Eastern European/Central Asian countries, only one was perceived as more corrupt than Turkmenistan: Uzbekistan.[39] In Turkmenistan, political elites have traditionally built up local power bases by allocating key posts and opportunities to their loyalists. These informal networks, which have survived the demise of the Soviet system, are frequently referred to as "clans," although they are based on patron-client relationships, often with links to extended families, rather than on actual blood ties. The existence of patronage networks as the basis of power has inevitably given rise to a political culture of bribery, nepotism, and embezzlement.

During the final years of Niyazov's rule, drastic cuts in pensions,[40] massive redundancies in government jobs, the introduction of fees for medical services, the closure of hospitals, the dismantling of the educational system and the use of military conscripts as a source of free labor in various sectors of the economy all indicated that the state was having difficulty funding its huge public sector, despite official reports of record foreign trade surpluses. Although President Niyazov sought to pin the blame for budget shortfalls on his subordinates by accusing them of mass embezzlement, a more likely explanation was the continued diversion by Niyazov of billions of dollars from gas, oil, and cotton revenues to off-budget accounts under his de facto personal control, which were located in European (primarily German) and other bank accounts. The London-based international watchdog Global Witness estimated that as much as 75 percent of government spending did not form part of the state budget.[41] In the aftermath of Niyazov's death, the German Deutsche Bank admitted holding accounts for Turkmenistan's Central Bank, although it denied holding any personal accounts for Niyazov.[42] However, according to the European Bank for Reconstruction and Development, the Turkmen government accounts managed by Deutsche Bank were under the "discretionary control of the president without proper regulation and transparency."[43] Global Witness has stated that no information has been forthcoming from the new Turkmen leadership regarding the vast amounts of export revenues concealed by Niyazov in foreign banks,[44] and it remains unclear whether any of the off-budget funds have been introduced into formal accounting mechanisms.

In June 2007 Berdimuhamedov signed a resolution ordering the liquidation and auditing of the Saparmurat Niyazov International Fund,[45] although no clarification was provided as to the whereabouts, purpose or size of this fund. To add to the confusion, according to both Deutsche Bank and Global Witness, the International Fund does not necessarily bear any relation to the off-budget accounts managed by the German bank and might well be located within Turkmenistan itself.[46] Whatever the case, if an audit of the fund has in fact been carried out, the results have not been made public. Similarly, in August the State News Agency of Turkmenistan declared that accounts of budgetary expenditures would henceforth be published in the mass media, although this does not appear to have happened in practice.[47]

Despite a continued lack of budget transparency under the new leadership, there does appear to be a certain easing of the fiscal budget under Berdimuhamedov, as evidenced primarily by the reinstatement of pension rights for approximately 100,000 citizens as well as the introduction of payments for the socially vulnerable. Additionally, in November Turkmen media announced a plan to allocate US$4 billion for the implementation of a national program to improve the country's infrastructure through the construction of hundreds of schools, hospitals, cultural and sports facilities and houses.[48] Limited evidence that more state funds are being directed to social programs is a possible indicator that fewer export revenues are being diverted to off-budget accounts, which could ultimately lead to a decrease in corruption levels. On a more pessimistic note, Berdimuhamedov has continued his predecessor's practice of using state revenue to fund grandiose construction projects, such as the transformation of the Caspian sea town of Turkmenbashi into a free economic zone and world-class resort—complete with an artificial river, a yacht club and an oceanographic centre—at the cost of US$1billion. Similarly, in July 2007 the government awarded the French company Bouygues a US$85 million contract to construct an officers' club and apartment buildings for employees of the much feared National Security Ministry.

Turkmenistan continues to act as an important trans-shipment point for illicit drugs from Afghanistan to Western Europe. Under Niyazov, the narcotics trade provided a significant source of unofficial income for a number of government officials, including employees of the security agencies and the border service.[49] Niyazov's departure has allowed for an improvement in Turkmenistan's drug related problems in two notable ways: first, in direct contrast to the former president, who denied outright the existence of a drug problem in Turkmenistan, President Berdimuhamedov has officially acknowledged problems related to narcotics trafficking and drug use in Turkmenistan, even declaring a 'large-scale war against this destructive threat";[50] and, second, he has engaged the help of outside agencies to aid in the public destruction and disposal of drugs. Furthermore, in March the Turkmen government signed an agreement with UNAIDS on the launching of a program to prevent the spread of HIV, which is to include an educational campaign to fight drug use. However, despite this sea change in relation to drugs-related issues, the bumper opium harvest in Aghanistan, with which Turkmenistan shares a 700 km border, appears to have offset any progress that might have been made in 2007 in combating the illicit drugs trade.[51]

█ Author: Annette Bohr

Annette Bohr is an associate fellow of the Russian and Eurasia Programme at the Institute of International Affairs in London (Chatham House). She is the author or coauthor of two monographs and numerous articles on Central Asian politics, contemporary history, and ethnic and language policies.

---

1   The constitutional changes gave the Security Council—a body that does not normally concern itself with matters of state administration—the right to choose a deputy prime minister to serve as acting president in the event that the president is no longer able to perform his duties. "Konstitutsionnyi zakon Turkmenistana" [Constitutional Law of Turkmenistan], Turkmenistan.ru, December 27, 2006, http://www.turkmenistan.ru/?page_id=4&lang_id=ru&elem_id=9060&type=event&sort=date_desc.

2   Maksat Alekperov and John MacLeod, "Special Report: Halting Progress on Turkmen Reforms," *Reporting Central Asia*, Institute for War & Peace Reporting, November 28, 2007, http://www.iwpr.net/?p=rca&s=f&o=340987&apc_state=henprca.

3   "Zakon Turkmenistana: O Natsional'noi kliatve Turkmenistana" [Law of Turkmenistan: On the National Oath of Turkmenistan] *Neitral'nyi Turkmenistan*, March 20, 2007.

4   Maksat Alekperov, "Mixed Reaction to Turkmen Birthday Bash," *Reporting Central Asia*, Institute for War & Peace Reporting, July 6, 2007, http://www.iwpr.net/?p=rca&s=f&o=336880&apc_state=henirca2007.

5   "10-story Turkmen-Russian school and International Ruhnama University to be Built in Ashgabat," centralasia.ru, April 30, 2007, cited in *Weekly News Brief on Turkmenistan*, April 27–May 3, 2007, Turkmenistan Project, available at http://www.eurasianet.org/turkmenistan.project/index.php?page=weekly&lang=eng.

6   Turkmen Opposition Seeks Single Presidential Candidate," Radio Free Europe/Radio Liberty, 25 December 2006, cited in *Weekly News Brief on Turkmenistan*, December 23, 2006–January 4, 2007, Turkmenistan Project, available at http://www.eurasianet.org/turkmenistan.project/index.php?page=weekly&lang=eng.

7   "Turkmen Election a Mockery," Reporting Central Asia, Institute for War & Peace Reporting, December 15, 2004, www.iwpr.net/?s=f&o=162094.

8   Changes to the legislation subsequently introduced by President Berdimuhamedov reduced the size of district and city people's councils from 40 deputies to 20. Similarly, the size of regional councils was reduced from 80 deputies to 20. "O vnesenii izmenenii i dopolnenii v Zakon Turkmenistana: 'O khiakimakh'" [On changes and additions to the Law of Turkmenistan: 'On Hakims'], Turkmenistan zolotoi vek [Turkmenistan: the Golden Century], http://www.turkmenistan.gov.tm/_ru/laws/?laws=88.

9   Turkmenistan's Tightly Controlled Election," *Turkmen Radio: Inside View*, Institute for War & Peace Reporting, December 4, 2006, http://www.iwpr.net/?p=trk&s=f&o=325918&apc_state=henptrk.

10   "V Turkmenistane sostoialiis' vybory velaiatskikh i stolichnogo khalk maslakhaty" [Elections to the Regional and Capital Khalk Maslakhaty Have Taken Place], Turkmenistan zolotoi vek [Turkmenistan: the Golden Century], December 9, 2007, http://www.turkmenistan.gov.tm/?idr=7&id=071209d.

11   Nikola Krastev, "Turkmenistan: President Says Press, NGOS Operate Freely," Radio Free Europe/Radio Liberty, Inc., September 24, 2007, http://www.rferl.org/featuresarticle/2007/09/96CBE108-BA4B-4B35-BA75-6B2D4064AE97.html.

12   *The 2000 NGO Sustainability Index for Central and Eastern Europe and Eurasia*, USAID, Bureau for Europe and Eurasia, http://www.usaid.gov/locations/europe_eurasia/dem_gov/ngoindex/2000/turkmenistan.pdf.

13   "Turkmen Civil Society Under Threat," *Reporting Central Asia*, Institute for War & Peace Reporting, August 11, 2006, http://iwpr.net/?p=rca&s=f&o=322914&apc_state=henprca.

14   Felix Corley, "Turkmenistan: Will Registration End Harassment of Religious Communities?," Forum 18 News Service, April 22, 2005, http://www.forum18.org/Archive.php?article_id=548.

15   Felix Corley, "It Seems the Bad Times are Coming Back," Forum 18 News Service, May 25, 2007, http://www.forum18.org/Archive.php?article_id=963.

16   Felix Corley, "Prayer Without State Registration Violates the Religion Law", November 21, 2007, http://www.forum18.org/Archive.php?article_id=1050.

17   "Turkmenistan: U.S. Commission on Religious Freedom Says Progress Is Heard, But Not Seen," Radio Free Europe/Radio Liberty, Inc., September 1, 2007, http://www.rferl.org/featuresarticle/2007/09/8e41750b-8de1-4de6-b28f-81ef835401be.html.

18   Turkmenistan's fourth television channel, the multilingual satellite television service TV-4 Turkmenistan, which was created in 2004 at an estimated cost of US$12 million, was a major propaganda effort undertaken to improve Turkmenistan's international image. It broadcasts programs in Turkmen and in six foreign languages: English, Chinese, Russian, French, Arabic, and Persian. A newly created fourth radio station is to offer news and entertainment in Russian and English as well as Turkmen.

19   Gulnoza Saidazimova, "Turkmenistan: a new obstacle for access to the airways," Radio Free Europe/ Radio Liberty, Inc., December 5, 2007, http://www.rferl.org/featuresarticle/2007/12/2E82F2BD-1E61-406E-81A4-F442BF6876D4.html.

20   Vladimir Soloviev, "Turkmeniya oformila podpisku na demokratiiu" [Turkmenistan has Subscribed to Democracy], Gundogar.org, December 10, 2007, available at http://www.gundogar.org.

21   "Turkmen President Wants to Bring Internet 'to Every Home'," BBC Monitoring Central Asia/TV Altyn Assyr, September 14, 2007.

22   Available at http://www.internetworldstats.com/asia/tm.htm.

23   "Internet in Turkmenistan", Gundogar.org, October 11, 2007, available at http://www.gundogar.org.

24   "Turkmenistan: New social policy yields first results," *Oxford Analytica*, November 2, 2007, http://www.oxan.com/display.aspx?ItemID=DB138304.

25   The removal of a regional hakim can also be proposed by the chairman of the Halk Maslahaty of Turkmenistan or by not less than one-third of the members of the people's council headed by the hakim in question. The removal of a district or city hakim is proposed by the corresponding regional hakim (or the hakim of the city of Ashgabat) or by not less than one-third of the members of the people's council headed by the hakim in question. "O vnesenii izmenenii i dopolnenii v Zakon Turkmenistana 'O khiakimakh'" [On Changes and Additions

to the Law of Turkmenistan 'On Hakims'], Turkmenistan zolotoi vek [Turkmenistan: The Golden Age], http://www.turkmenistan.gov.tm/_ru/laws/?laws=88.

26 *Turkmenistan: The Making of a Failed State*, International Helsinki Federation for Human Rights, April 2004, http://www.ihf-hr.org/documents/doc_summary.php?sec_id=3&d_id=3831.

27 "Special Report: Halting Progress on Turkmen Reforms," *Reporting Central Asia*, Institute for War & Peace Reporting, November 28, 2007, http://www.iwpr.net/?p=rca&s=f&o=340987&apc_state=henprca.

28 "Otechestvennaia nauka: vremia peremen" [Homeland Science: A Time of Change], *Neitral'nyi Turkmenistan*, June 22, 2007.

29 "What is New in Schools?" *Khronika Turkmenistana*, December 10, 2007, http://www.chrono-tm.org/?02550435410000000000000011000000; "Special Report: Halting Progress on Turkmen Reforms," *Reporting Central Asia*, Institute for War & Peace Reporting, 28 November 2007, http://www.iwpr.net/?p=rca&s=f&o=340987&apc_state=henprca.

30 Bernd Rachel and Martin McKee, "The effects of dictatorship on health: the case of Turkmenistan," BMC Medicine 2007, 5:21, http://www.biomedcentral.com/1741-7015/5/21.

31 Bernd Rachel and Martin McKee, *Human Rights and Health in Turkmenistan*, European Centre on Health of Societies in Transition (London: London School of Hygiene & Tropical Medicine, 2005), pages 24–25.

32 "Reform of the Health Care System," Turkmen Initiative for Human Rights, April 19, 2006, cited in *Weekly News Brief on Turkmenistan*, April 14–20, 2006, Turkmenistan Project, available at http://www.eurasianet.org/turkmenistan.project/index.php?page=weekly&lang=eng; "Turkmenistan Vulnerable to Public Health Catastrophe," *Eurasianet*, February 6, 2006, available at http://www.eurasianet.org.

33 Ashgabat Turkmen Television, October 16, 2006, cited in *Weekly News Brief on Turkmenistan*, 13–19 October 2006, Turkmenistan Project, available at http://www.eurasianet.org/turkmenistan.project/index.php?page=weekly&lang=eng.

34 *Weekly News Brief on Turkmenistan*, Part 1, August 10–16, 2007, Turkmenistan Project, available at http://www.eurasianet.org/turkmenistan.project/index.php?page=weekly&lang=eng.

35 *CIA World Factbook*, http://www.cia.gov/library/publications/the-world-factbook/index.html.

36 "Turkmenistan: New social policy yields first results," *Oxford Analytica*, November 2, 2007. http://www.oxan.com/display.aspx?ItemID=DB138304.

37 *Weekly News Brief on Turkmenistan*, Part 1, March 30–April 5, 2007, Turkmenistan Project, available http://www.eurasianet.org/turkmenistan.project/index.php?page=weekly&lang=eng.

38 Chemen Durdiyeva, "Berdimukhammedov enters a new phase of relations with Russia," The Central Asia-Caucasus Institute Analyst, May 16, 2007, available at http://www.cacianalyst.org/newsite.

39 Corruption Perceptions Index 2007, Transparency International, http://www.transparency.org/policy_research/surveys_indices/cpi/2007.

40 "Pension Payments Slashed and Withheld," January 16, 2006, *Weekly News Brief on Turkmenistan*, January 13–19, 2006, Turkmenistan Project, available at http://www.eurasianet.org/turkmenistan.project/index.php?page=weekly&lang=eng.

41 "Funny Business in the Turkmen-Ukraine Gas Trade," *Global Witness*, April 2006, http://www.globalwitness.org/reports/download.php/00297.pdf; Annette Bohr, "Independent Turkmenistan: From Post-Communism to Sultanism," in Sally N. Cummings, *Oil, Transition and Security in Central Asia* (London: RoutledgeCurzon, 2003), page 15.

[42] "Deutsche Bank denies it helped prop up 'Turkmenbashi the Great', Bloomberg news, May 10, 2007, available at http://www.bloomberg.com/apps/news?pid=newsarchive&sid=agYviK nuF4bI.

[43] "Turkmen Exiles Demand Deutsche Probe," *Financial Times*, December 23, 2006.

[44] Report by Tom Mayne of Global Witness at the conference "Turkmenistan under Berdymukhammedov: Change or Continuity," The Royal Institute of International Affairs (Chatham House), London, November 8, 2007; Gulnoza Saidazimova, "Turkmenistan: Where is Turkmenbashi's Money?" Radio Free Europe/Radio Liberty, November 19, 2007.

[45] "Mezhdunarodnyi fond Saparmurata Niyazova budet likvidirovan," [The Saparmurat Niyazov International Fund is to be Liquidated] Turkmenistan.ru, June 23, 2007, available at http://turkmenistan.ru.

[46] Report by Tom Mayne of Global Witness at the conference "Turkmenistan under Berdymukhammedov: Change or Continuity," The Royal Institute of International Affairs (Chatham House), London, November 8, 2007; "Germany Must Launch Full Inquiry into Turkmen Funds in German Banks," Global Witness press release, July 3, 2007.

[47] Government Spending to be published in Turkmenistan, ITAR-TASS, August 24, 2007, cited in *Weekly News Brief on Turkmenistan*, August 17–30, 2007, Turkmenistan Project, available at http://www.eurasianet.org/turkmenistan.project/index.php?page=weekly&lang= eng.

[48] "Turkmenistan to Invest US$4 Billion in Raising Living Standards," FBIS Monitoring, November 15, 2007, cited in *Weekly News Brief on Turkmenistan*, November 9–15, 2007, Turkmenistan Project, available at http://www.eurasianet.org/turkmenistan.project/index. php?page=weekly&lang=eng.

[49] Annette Bohr, "Independent Turkmenistan: From Post-Communism to Sultanism," in Sally N. Cummings, *Oil, Transition and Security in Central Asia* (London: RoutledgeCurzon, 2003), page 13; "Turkmenistan: Banker Claims Government Has Own Drug Ring," *Eurasia Daily Monitor*, July 9, 2004, http://jamestown.org/publications_details.php?volume_ id=401&&issue_id=3012; "Pod kryshei MNB" [Under the Protection of the MNB], Gundogar.org, September 4, 2006, available at http://www.gundogar.org.

[50] "Zasedanie kabineta ministrov Turkmenistana" [Session of the Cabinet of Ministers of Turkmenistan], *Neitral'nyi Turkmenistan*, June 23, 2007.

[51] "Turkmeniya na geroinovoi igle" [Turkmenistan on the Heroin Needle], Gundogar.org, July 11, 2007, available at http://www.gundogar.org.

Ukraine

by Oleksandr Sushko and Olena Prystayko

Capital: Kyiv
Population: 47.1 million
GNI/capita: US$6,110

The social data above was taken from the European Bank for Reconstruction and Development's *Transition Report 2007: People in Transition,* and the economic data from the World Bank's *World Development Indicators 2008.*

Nations in Transit Ratings and Averaged Scores

	1999	2001	2002	2003	2004	2005	2006	2007	2008
Electoral Process	3.50	4.00	4.50	4.00	4.25	3.50	3.25	3.00	3.00
Civil Society	4.00	3.75	3.75	3.50	3.75	3.00	2.75	2.75	2.75
Independent Media	5.00	5.25	5.50	5.50	5.50	4.75	3.75	3.75	3.50
Governance*	4.75	4.75	5.00	5.00	5.25	n/a	n/a	n/a	n/a
National Democratic Governance	n/a	n/a	n/a	n/a	n/a	5.00	4.50	4.75	4.75
Local Democratic Governance	n/a	n/a	n/a	n/a	n/a	5.25	5.25	5.25	5.25
Judicial Framework and Independence	4.50	4.50	4.75	4.50	4.75	4.25	4.25	4.50	4.75
Corruption	6.00	6.00	6.00	5.75	5.75	5.75	5.75	5.75	5.75
Democracy Score	4.63	4.71	4.92	4.71	4.88	4.50	4.21	4.25	4.25

* With the 2005 edition, Freedom House introduced separate analysis and ratings for national democratic governance and local democratic governance to provide readers with more detailed and nuanced analysis of these two important subjects.

NOTE: The ratings reflect the consensus of Freedom House, its academic advisers, and the author(s) of this report. The opinions expressed in this report are those of the author(s). The ratings are based on a scale of 1 to 7, with 1 representing the highest level of democratic progress and 7 the lowest. The Democracy Score is an average of ratings for the categories tracked in a given year.

EXECUTIVE SUMMARY

Political, economic, and social reforms have remained incomplete in Ukraine since late 2004, when the Orange Revolution changed the trajectory of the country's development. The trend toward a pluralistic democracy, human rights, and media freedom is obvious, but the overall quality of these democratic transformations has been challenged by numerous obstacles. Since gaining independence in 1991, Ukraine has witnessed four presidential (1991, 1994, 1999, 2004) and five parliamentary (1994, 1999, 2002, 2006, 2007) elections. The Constitution, adopted in 1996 and amended in 2004, introduced a new model of power in 2006, with stronger roles for the Parliament (Verkhovna Rada) and Cabinet of Ministers (government) and decreasing power for the president. The model introduced a de facto "dual executive" dependent on both the president and a parliamentary majority. This dual structure led to infighting and resultant stasis during 2006, which persisted throughout 2007—Viktor Yushchenko's second year in office as the third president of Ukraine. The Parliament was elected by proportional vote in September 2007 following legislative amendments in June. On December 18, a new government of Ukraine was formed, replacing Victor Yanukovych's (Party of Regions) government, when the newly established Coalition of Democratic Forces—led by Prime Minister Yulia Tymoshenko—obtained a slim majority in the Parliament (the Rada of the sixth convocation), winning 228 out of 450 votes. The pace of governance remained largely stagnant even after the formation of the Coalition of Democratic Forces.

Incomplete reforms introduced after the Orange Revolution resulted in general disillusionment in society, despite relatively steady economic growth. Gross domestic product grew by 6.2 percent in 2007, and nominal monthly wages increased from US$210 in late 2006 to US$325 in December 2007. This growth, however, has been substantially challenged by a high inflation rate—10.5 percent, according to the economic survey Consensus Forecast.[1]

National Democratic Governance. The constitutional model introduced at the beginning of 2006 was challenged in the spring of 2007 by a serious political crisis, ultimately resulting in early parliamentary elections on September 30. The new Constitution introduced a "dual executive" approach, garnering the risk of permanent conflict between the Office of the President and the Cabinet of Ministers. The potential for conflict became evident after Yushchenko's 2004 presidential election rival, Viktor Yanukovych, was appointed prime minister and subsequently formed a government from his Party of Regions, a party vocal in its opposition to the president. In the early parliamentary elections on September 30, the political forces that supported the Orange Revolution in 2004 obtained a slim majority in the new Parliament (228 parliamentarians out of 450). Overall, political actors preoccupied themselves with power struggles and pushed legislative reforms from which they stood to benefit instead of focusing on sustainable policy and reforms in 2007. *Ukraine's rating for national democratic governance remains at 4.75.*

Electoral Process. Early parliamentary elections took place on September 30, 2007. According to reports by major international observation missions, the elections were free and fair. Parliament passed amendments to the electoral law on June 1, 2007. According to the Ukrainian ombudsperson, this prevented nearly one million people living de facto outside of their place of registration from voting. Ukrainians traveling abroad two months prior to the elections also faced restrictive obstacles to voting.[2] *Owing to the overall free and fair parliamentary elections, Ukraine's rating for electoral process remains at 3.00.*

Civil Society. Civil society remains a valuable actor in Ukraine. And despite outdated legislation and dependence on foreign funds, in 2007 it continued to grow very slightly. As of January 2007, the number of officially registered nongovernmental organizations (NGOs) reached 50,706 and involved nearly 20 million members (more than 40 percent of the population). According to Counterpart Creative Center, an organization focused on monitoring and developing the third sector in Ukraine, and Ukrainian experts, only 4,000 functioning NGOs really exist.[3] In January 2007, Kyiv-based NGOs launched a process to elaborate the Civil Society Doctrine—a comprehensive document claiming to identify the third sector's current and long-term priorities, which is slated for translation into legislation in the near future. *Ukraine's rating for civil society remains at 2.75.*

Independent Media. At the national level, media freedom appears secure, but local and regional media sectors still lack restructuring and real independence. Neither censorship nor government pressure was detected or reported in 2007. Nonetheless, the influence of political and economic groups remains strong in the media sphere. Ukraine's media sector continued to grow owing to the appearance of new domestic and foreign investments and the development of the advertising market. Also, new independent, quality media projects emerged in 2007, including nationwide daily newspapers, weeklies, and live political shows on television and radio. However, the process of establishing public television remains blocked. *Owing to the growth of Ukrainian media and the appearance of new independent newspapers, weeklies, and non-biased political programs, Ukraine's rating for independent media improves slightly from 3.75 to 3.50.*

Local Democratic Governance. The year 2007 was marked neither by the prolongation of the reform proposed by Roman Bezsmertny, deputy prime minister on administrative reform in 2005, nor by the initiation of new reforms. The draft legislation on administrative and territorial changes (a draft Law on the Introduction of Changes to the Constitution of Ukraine on Improvement of the System of Local Government) submitted to the Constitutional Court in 2006 was not considered by year's end. The new Cabinet of Ministers created on the basis of the Coalition of National Unity claimed the need to strengthen the role of local self-government but did not propose any alternative reform strategies in this regard. *As discussions on reforms and initiatives regarding local governance were notably frozen through 2007, Ukraine's local democratic governance rating remains at 5.25.*

Judicial Framework and Independence. The primary shortcomings of the Ukrainian judiciary include lack of public respect for court decisions and the judicial system as a whole, insufficient financing of the court system, and an inefficient and nontransparent process of appointing judges. These problems remained untouched during 2007. The dismissal of the prosecutor general in May, along with the Constitutional Court decision revoking the president's right to appoint and dismiss heads and deputy heads of courts, led to imbalances in the overall judicial framework and raised broad public discussion over the need to reform the judicial system. Unfortunately, preoccupation with the election campaign and the subsequent process of creating a coalition drew main political players away from creating real initiatives. *As the independence of the judiciary at all levels entered into a state of uncertainty and remained there while judicial reforms were ignored, Ukraine's rating for judicial framework and independence deteriorated from 4.50 to 4.75.*

Corruption. The year did not feature a significant campaign to fight corruption in Ukraine. The months-long process of preparation for the early parliamentary election and the creation of the coalition put anticorruption measures on the political back burner. The August 2007 adoption of the Decree on Measures Plan on the Implementation of the Concept on a Way to Integrity (Measures Plan) by the Cabinet of Ministers proved the only significant event in this regard. The Measures Plan set a number of concrete benchmarks to be reached by 2010, established the aims of the concept, defined the responsible state bodies, and created an implementation timetable for each of the measures. Despite the adoption of the Measures Plan, corruption remains dominant in Ukrainian society. *Ukraine's rating for corruption remains at 5.75.*

Outlook for 2008. The stability of democratic institutions in Ukraine will remain under threat from a frail parliamentary coalition, the Cabinet of Ministers, and the continuous attempts of political forces and leaders to manipulate rules. Early resignation of the government and the disruption of the coalition seem highly plausible. Furthermore, the project of constitutional reform initiated by the president is unlikely to find a consensus among political elites. Various political forces continue to use constitutional reforms as a means to strengthen their political positions. Furthermore, initiatives in the sphere of local governance were not introduced in 2007 and are not expected to be implemented in 2008. Negative trends in the judiciary may lead to a downward spiral for the judicial framework in 2008 in terms of further imbalances and greater loss of independence. The anticorruption activities and initiatives of 2007 will not solve this widespread problem; if left unaddressed, corruption may actually rise in 2008.

Main Report

National Democratic Governance

1999	2001	2002	2003	2004	2005	2006	2007	2008
n/a	n/a	n/a	n/a	n/a	5.00	4.50	4.75	4.75

A new constitutional model introduced on January 1, 2006, was challenged in the spring of 2007 by a serious political crisis, which ultimately resulted in early parliamentary elections on September 30. This crisis focused on the substantial problems of the existing constitutional model, with its number of institutional gaps, deficits, and lack of an efficient system of checks and balances. Formally, the new model appears closer to those of other Central and Eastern European countries and stipulates a substantially stronger role for the Parliament and government while limiting the president's powers. At the same time, the new model introduced a "dual executive" approach, creating the risk of a permanent conflict between the Office of the President and the Cabinet of Ministers. This became evident after President Viktor Yushchenko's 2004 presidential election rival, Viktor Yanukovych, was appointed prime minister and formed a government based on his party, the Party of Regions, which opposed the president.

In 2007, political actors focused their energies on power struggles and pushed legislative reforms from which they stood to benefit (such as the draft law the Cabinet of Ministers adopted in January that introduced further limits to the president's power), instead of advocating for sustainable policy and reforms. Furthermore, at the outset of 2007, continuous attempts by the ruling coalition (Party of Regions, Socialist Party of Ukraine, and Communist Party of Ukraine) to strengthen its position within the Parliament by recruiting "hesitating" members of Parliament (MPs) from the opposition (Bloc of Yulia Tymoshenko [BYT] and Our Ukraine Bloc) also disrupted political processes. The coalition gained a victory in March when the Party of Industrialists and Entrepreneurs, led by Anatoly Kinakh, left Our Ukraine Bloc and joined the ruling coalition. Kinakh later became the economy minister. At the same time, in a move considered an indication of "political corruption" by the opposition, a group of BYT MPs also joined the coalition. Founders renamed the group the Coalition of National Unity.

Leaders of the coalition declared their aim to gain a constitutional majority, or 300 votes, by summer. The president responded by issuing a decree on April 2, 2007, announcing the dissolution of the Parliament (Verkhovna Rada) and scheduling pre-term elections for May 27, 2007. This launched the "active phase" of the political crisis as Yushchenko's opponents immediately challenged the legitimacy of his decree. Furthermore, accusations of corruption disabled the Constitutional Court, the independent arbiter assessing presidential decrees dissolving the Parliament. The duties of the Constitutional Court were suspended by the president.

The next two months were marked with permanent debates, negotiations, and ambivalent decisions that led to a "compromise" that dissolved the Parliament. The final presidential decree on this issue set September 30 as the date for early parliamentary elections. These events demonstrated that major political actors did not follow constitutional norms, but rather toyed with legislative gaps and manipulated the law.

In April 2007, the Parliamentary Assembly of the Council of Europe assessed the political crisis in Ukraine. The report attributed Ukraine's political instability to "the systematic failure by the successive Ukrainian governments to establish coherent policies backed by substantial legal, administrative, and economic reforms." It further noted that "the political reforms that would...enable law-based institutions to guarantee democratic rights and freedoms and promote political competition have not been completed to date."[4]

Throughout the crisis, the Cabinet of Ministers led by Viktor Yanukovych continued its work, but permanent disputes with the president's secretariat proved that the system of checks and balances did not work efficiently.

One of the evident indications of the national governance deficit was the crisis within the state procurement system. Access to tenders was greatly restricted by procedures introduced in 2005–2006, which blocked a large number of tenders at national and local levels.[5] As the World Bank reported earlier, "Granting a private, non-governmental organization (the Tender Chamber of Ukraine) the authority to make a binding decision in the area of public procurement is inconsistent with international practice."[6]

On December 27, the president issued a decree establishing the National Constitutional Council (NCC). The president of Ukraine will head the NCC and will be responsible for drafting a new Constitution for Ukraine. Critics of the NCC stress the possibility of using this institution as a tool to push forward the new Constitution via a referendum bypassing the Parliament—an unconstitutional practice that meets neither the requirements of the existing Constitution nor generally accepted democratic practices.

The military and security sectors also suffered from domestic political battles. Formally, the military and security services are under the auspices of the president, who nominates the defense minister and security service chief (who must also be approved by the Parliament). However, transparency and accountability improved within the Ministry of Defense, under the leadership of reformist Anatoly Grytsenko, from February 2005 to December 2007. To create a balance with Grytsenko, Viktor Yanukovych's government introduced the position of deputy prime minister, responsible for military and security services. The MP from the Party of Regions, former defense minister Oleksandr Kuzmuk, received the position, which was later abolished under Yulia Tymoshenko's government.

In 2007, Ukraine first witnessed a direct conflict between the security units under presidential oversight (State Department of the Guard Service) and those under the oversight of the Cabinet of Ministers (special unit of the Ministry of the

Interior). In May, at the peak of the political crisis, these units clashed at the Office of the Prosecutor General in an attempt to take control of the building. As a result, both units were withdrawn from the Office of the Prosecutor General.

While the current government has proven more transparent and democratic than those prior to 2004, stable and mature institutions ensuring the rule of law and the irreversibility of democratic changes are still lacking.

The political forces that supported the Orange Revolution in 2004 gained a small victory in the early parliamentary elections of September 30, winning a slim majority in the new Parliament (228 MPs out of 450). The election, however, did not solve the political crisis as such but provided the potential for consensus on further constitutional and legal transformations, if the majority coalition can be sustained.

Electoral Process

1999	2001	2002	2003	2004	2005	2006	2007	2008
3.50	4.00	4.50	4.00	4.25	3.50	3.25	3.00	3.00

The pre-term parliamentary elections took place on September 30, 2007. Despite grave doubts over a posssible return to abuse of "administrative resources" to strengthen the electoral positions of their respective political parties, both the presidential administration and the Cabinet of Ministers resisted the temptation, and international organizations declared the September 30 election open and competitive.[7] The election was assessed as in line with Organization for Security and Cooperation in Europe (OSCE) and Council of Europe guidelines, as well as other international standards for democratic elections and national legislation.

The International Election Observation Mission (IEOM)[8] released an official statement on the election process, recognizing both its positive and its negative aspects. The IEOM considered the following as positive outcomes: Only a few isolated incidents interrupted the calm election atmosphere, at which a large number of domestic and international observers were present; the Central Election Commission (CEC) efficiently oversaw the technical aspects of the elections; the District Election Commissions made all preparations in an open manner; local and administrative courts worked to adjudicate cases in a transparent and timely manner; all parties and blocs could convey their messages to the electorate through broad and diverse media coverage, including state media outlets. The IEOM noted a number of shortcomings in the electoral process, including low-quality voter lists; legal provisions allowing political parties or blocs to reorganize or eliminate registered candidates; and delays in Constitutional Court rulings on election-related complaints. The IEOM further expressed concern over measures that excluded voters traveling outside Ukraine for a two-month period prior to the election, the removal of absentee voting, and campaigning by state and local officials who were not candidates—all in violation of the law.[9] Also noted was the lack of transparency in media ownership, the absence of a public broadcaster and independent media regulatory body, and hidden political advertising.

Ukrainian voters chose from 20 political parties and electoral blocs registered in a generally inclusive process and a free and transparent atmosphere. Major parties and blocs enjoyed equal media access. According to the Committee of Voters of Ukraine, extremely poor-quality voter lists proved the greatest problem but infringed on the rights of all political parties, in all regions of Ukraine, and did not give priority to any one group.[10]

On June 1, 2007, Parliament passed amendments to the electoral legislation. These amendments did not improve election procedures but rather introduced restrictions preventing nearly one million people living de facto outside of their place of official residence (according to a statement by the Ukrainian ombudsperson, Nina Karpachova)[11] from voting. Also, people traveling abroad within a two-month period (beginning August 1, 2007) prior to the elections were prohibited from voting.

Ukrainian electoral legislation is usually subject to change prior to elections, making these procedures dependent on the political situation and the interests of parliamentary parties. In general, significant governmental interference was absent from the 2007 elections, although individual cases of abuse of office while campaigning were detected.

The 2007 elections were held according to a proportional voting system. Despite prior experience with the shortcomings of closed party lists, legislators did nothing to change this aspect of the system, nor did they address the lack of transparency in their formation. This resulted generally in parliamentarians lacking close ties to business people, the party, and its ideology.

Five political forces passed the 3 percent threshold to gain seats in the Parliament. These were the Party of Regions, BYT, Our Ukraine Bloc, Communist Party of Ukraine, and Lytvyn's Bloc (see Table 1).[12]

Table 1.
Political Parties Gaining Seats

	Party/Bloc	% Votes	Number of Votes	Number of Seats*
1	Party of Regions	34.37	8,013,895	175
2	Bloc of Yulia Tymoshenko (BYT)	30.71	7,162,193	156
3	Bloc "Our Ukraine—People's Self-Defense"	14.15	3,301,282	72
4	Communist Party of Ukraine	5.39	1,257,291	27
5	Lytvyn's Bloc	3.96	924,538	20

The election proved that regional differences still exist in Ukraine. For example, the Party of Regions won 72–73 percent of the vote in the Donetsk and Lugansk oblasts in the east of Ukraine and only 3 percent in Ternopil and the Ivano-Frankivsk oblasts in the west. The BYT received about 53 percent of the vote in the Kyiv region (central Ukraine), 58 percent in the Volyn oblast in the west, and only 4 percent in Donetsk in the east. At the same time, election results marked the softening of some regional discrepancies: The Party of Regions (considered an east-south party) improved its gains in most central and western regions, and the BYT, with its traditional western and central electorate, performed better in the eastern (especially Kharkiv and Dnipropetrovsk) oblasts than in 2006.

In Mariupol (Donetsk oblast, district 48), the Socialist Party of Ukraine (SPU)—led by Oleksandr Moroz, Speaker of the former Parliament who led his party in a "non-orange" political camp in 2006—won with just over 50 percent of the votes, putting the SPU ahead of the Party of Regions. However, in most Donetsk oblast districts, the SPU did not reach the 3 percent threshold. SPU's unusual victory can be attributed to the strong position of Volodymyr Boyko, an SPU member and industrial magnate from Mariupol. Yet this victory did not help the party cross the 3 percent threshold. Furthermore, the SPU lost nearly all of its traditional central Ukrainian electorate owing to its jump from the "orange" (Yushchenko) to the "white blue" (Yanukovych) camp in 2006.

Civil Society

1999	2001	2002	2003	2004	2005	2006	2007	2008
4.00	3.75	3.75	3.50	3.75	3.00	2.75	2.75	2.75

Civil society plays a valuable role and remains an important actor in Ukraine. Its development, however, suffers from outdated legislation and dependence on foreign funds. As of January 2007, more than 40 percent of the population, or 19,909,038 Ukrainians, were involved in the 50,706 officially registered nongovernmental organizations (NGOs) in Ukraine. However, according to the Counterpart Creative Center (CCC) and Ukrainian experts, only 4,000 NGOs are active.[13] These NGOs vary greatly in their focus and structure, from large trade unions to small think tanks and organizations based on ethnic, cultural, youth, professional, and human rights issues. Yet civil society remains somewhat heterogeneous, with the most influential groups based in the capital (Kyiv), a few regional centers boasting strong NGO networks, and weak structures at the local level.

Some NGOs initiated and continued projects aimed at consolidating third sector activity, such as the Civic Assembly held in Kyiv in July 2007 or the Civic League Ukraine-NATO. Kyiv-based NGOs also launched a process to elaborate the Civil Society Doctrine (a comprehensive document claiming to identify the third sector's current and long-term priorities) and to work with the Cabinet of Ministers to incorporate this document into future legislation. Large initiatives, or NGO coalitions, often try to establish a permanent connection with top political bodies and officials, but only a few examples of sustainable cooperation at a high level emerged in 2007. NGO experts can engage in a structured dialogue with authorities through public councils held at ministries and parliamentary committees. Yet public councils are not attended by high officials, with the exception of the public councils at the Ministry of Defense and the Ministry of Foreign Affairs, and ministries and parliamentary committees do not meet regularly. Nonetheless, 99 percent of active NGOs polled by the CCC claimed to have had some contact with governmental bodies (including central, regional, and local authorities); 47 percent of these NGOS said they had regular communication—at least once a week—with various authorities.[14]

Authorities do not interfere in NGO activity by levying permanent taxes or by creating additional barriers and obstacles to their registration and functioning. During 2007, NGOs did not express concern over unreasonable checks or attacks from governmental bodies—as was the case until 2004.

International donors continued to provide financial support for the majority of Ukraine's NGOs in 2007. At the same time, the role of national businesses in NGO sustainability has increased: During 2002–2006, more than 50 percent of NGOs received funds from local businessmen and companies.[15] However, a new regulation on public tenders introduced by the Tender Chamber of Ukraine (formally an oversight NGO) has restricted NGO access to public funds through a non-transparent and expensive application scheme. As a result, very few NGOs have succeeded in receiving funds from state or local budgets.

Few NGOs have well-trained, professional staff able to ensure efficient management and fund-raising. Only 61 percent of the organizations polled by the CCC have a permanent staff (full- or part-time). Furthermore, the lack of volunteerism in Ukraine also poses limits to the proper development and functioning of civil society.

Parliament again failed to provide essential improvements to outdated NGO legislation; NGO activity remains regulated by the Law on Citizens Associations, adopted in 1992. The restrictive legal definition of not-for-profit activity offers no clear legal differentiation between profit and income. This prevents NGOs from more active fund-raising among local businesses and poses obstacles to accessing public funds. As a recent study from Razumkov Centre (Ukrainian Center for Economic and Political Studies) described: "Different legislative acts refer to those organizations as 'nonprofit,' 'non-commercial,' 'non-business,' leaving space for variance of such definitions and vague interpretation."[16] In particular, the civil code of Ukrainian NGOs falls within the definition of "non-business partnerships." The business code uses the terms *non-state, nonprofit,* and *charity* interchangeably, without defining such organizations in detail. The Law on Taxation of Company Profit uses the term *nonprofit institutions and organizations.*[17]

The state fully respects the right to form and join trade unions, but in practice most trade unions are either old-fashioned, inefficient bureaucratic organizations or controlled by the enterprise's owners (in private industry). Only a few trade unions in Ukraine function efficiently. "Old" trade unions attempt to stifle the efforts of newly emerging unions that stress their interest and clear intent in representing their members.

Extremist and intolerant nongovernmental institutions and organizations represent a small but active part of the third sector. Most of these groups demonstrate a lack of respect for the Ukrainian state and nation. In 2007, authorities in separate regions registered cases of vandalized national symbols and monuments. The most notable case occurred in October when representatives of the Russia-based Euro-Asian Youth Union (and their Ukrainian branch) damaged national symbols on Hoverla, the tallest mountain in Ukraine. Following the incident, Russian leaders of the Euro-Asian Youth Union were denied the right to visit Ukraine.

The rapidly growing media sector appears quite receptive to civil society groups as independent and reliable sources of information and commentary. The presence of NGO experts in both electronic and print media is generally visible, but a large number of NGOs still lack training in media outreach. More than 25 percent of Ukrainian NGOs maintain Web sites, and growing consistently at 15–20 percent per year.

The education system remains mostly free from political influence and propaganda; however, political forces previously "rented" or paid students, especially in big cities, to attend political rallies. This kind of activity has led to the public perception of student activism as a sort of commercial deal.

Independent Media

1999	2001	2002	2003	2004	2005	2006	2007	2008
5.00	5.25	5.50	5.50	5.50	4.75	3.75	3.75	3.50

In the latest Reporters Without Borders Worldwide Press Freedom Index, Ukraine improved its ranking from 105th to 92nd place out of 169 nations; Ukraine stands substantially ahead of Belarus (151), Russia (144), and Turkey (101) but lags behind Georgia (66), Serbia (67), and Armenia (67).[18] Citizens enjoy wide-ranging pluralism in both electronic and print media. However, media freedom in Ukraine at local and regional levels still lacks necessary restructuring and real independence. The government does not censor the private media sector, but regional and local state administrations, acting as owners of numerous newspapers and television channels funded by local and regional budgets, can and do influence editorial policy. The Kyiv municipal media present one clear example of local bureaucratic control. Kyiv city head Leonid Chernovetsky established total control over the editorial policy of the local television company TRK Kyiv, as well as the newspapers *Khreshchatyk* and *Vechirniy Kyiv,* which provided biased information in favor of local leadership.

In most cases, nationwide television channels provide balanced news coverage; representatives of ruling, as well as opposition, parties have equal access to the media. Yet leading financial and industrial groups own most of the nationwide media, which presents grounds for certain biases and subjective preferences. Informal payments from special interest groups also influence the appearance of certain subjects on television. During the election campaign, these groups especially supported widespread, biased reporting and promoted self-censorship. This type of paid information coverage was the most alarming media trend visible in 2007. In November 2007, using the slogan "We are not for sale," the Independent Media Trade Union announced a campaign against coverage ordered by political and financial interest groups. In an open statement, journalists declared, "Prepaid TV subjects and programs are no longer rare cases. They are becoming an industry that competes with normal news, analysis, and discussions."[19]

While the advertising market continues to grow and provide new financial opportunities for the independent media sector, the process of establishing a public television foundation remains blocked. Some new independent, quality media projects emerged over the course of the year, including new nationwide daily newspapers, weeklies, and live political television and radio programs.

The most successful initiative in the sphere of print media in 2007 was the establishment of a new nationwide daily newspaper, *Gazeta 24,* funded by a Ukrainian business. The owners and management declared it their aim to reach the high standards of a European daily. Owing to its professional and nonbiased journalism, the newspaper acquired a positive reputation. In October, however, the newspaper's management, led by well-known journalist Vitaly Portnikov, resigned, accusing the paper's owners of partisan pressure (owner Volodymyr Kosterin heads the Green Party of Ukraine). At the end of 2007, the future of this newspaper remained uncertain.

In 2007, Ukraine's media sector also grew in terms of both domestic and international investments. Foreign media enterprises have invested in the Ukrainian media market, mostly supporting entertainment, or "yellow" media, such as the newspaper *Blick,* owned by the Swiss holding company Ringier AG. At the same time, Ukrainian financial-industrial groups strengthened their position within the media market. The Industrial Union of Donbass created a full-fledged print media consortium including *Kyiv Weekly, Kommentarii,* the weekly magazine *Delovaya Stolitca,* and other media.

Consolidation of the television market has led to conflicts between management and journalists; the most vocal of such conflicts took place in January 2007, when the majority of journalists working at Inter TV, a channel owned by businessman Valery Khoroshkovsky, abruptly quit.

The majority of Ukrainians enjoy free access to the Internet. Furthermore, the government makes no real attempt to control access to, or the content of, the Internet. Concerns over government Internet control in 2007 proved alarmist and were unconfirmed by any real actions.

Local Democratic Governance

1999	2001	2002	2003	2004	2005	2006	2007	2008
n/a	n/a	n/a	n/a	n/a	5.25	5.25	5.25	5.25

Local governance in Ukraine has a four-level, administrative, territorial structure: the Autonomous Republic of Crimea, oblasts (24), and cities with oblast status (Kyiv and Sevastopol) compose the upper layer; *raions* (oblast districts) and cities with *raion* status form the second; the rest of the cities are third; and villages and townships fourth. Furthermore, each *raion* is divided into a number of local councils (village or small-town councils).

No actions were taken in 2007 to ensure the meaningful participation of citizens in local government decision making. Thus, public participation remains mostly formal. In addition, regional and local authorities remain less transparent in comparison with the central government.

The lack of financial and economic independence for territorial communities presents a problem owing to the ineffective structure of local budgets, which still largely resemble centralized budgets.

Local governance is represented by a dual system of authorities: state administration and a self-governance council. The president appoints the heads of the executive in oblasts and *raions*. Citizens elect top city officials and heads of local councils. The Constitution does not outline precise divisions among bodies at different levels, including administrative bodies such as urban communities, village councils, and township councils.

Following the constitutional reform, the duality of Ukraine's regional self-governance became more evident. On the one hand, regional and local councils, elected by a proportional vote, tried to push through politicized decisions beyond their competences. On the other hand, the Cabinet of Ministers attempted to gain the key role of appointing the heads of administration for oblasts and *raions* by invoking a constitutional provision that states the president may appoint and dismiss these officials only with the approval of the Cabinet of Ministers. This situation, however, simply reflected the ongoing confrontations that occurred in 2007 between the president and the Cabinet of Ministers at the local level.

The duality of authority at the local level also lies in the conflict between the locally elected self-governance authorities and local administrations appointed by the central government. The existing legal framework limits the authority of local self-governance. At the same time, mechanisms guaranteeing that self-governance decisions will coincide with legislation remain weak. Meanwhile, the Cabinet of Ministers claimed the need to strengthen the role of local self-government[20] but did not propose any alternative reform strategies.

Administrative and territorial reforms initiated in Ukraine in 2005 have not been implemented, and new reforms were not introduced in 2007. The Constitutional Court has yet to consider the only draft law on administrative and territorial changes (a draft Law on the Introduction of Changes to the Constitution of Ukraine on Improvement of the System of Local Government)[21] submitted in 2006. Yet by freezing the discussion on the territorial and administrative rebuilding of Ukraine, representatives of different political forces were able to say that in the midterm, Ukraine missed its opportunity to make essential and necessary reforms in this sphere.[22]

On January 12, 2007, instead of solving the problems resulting from the closed party list, proportional system, the Parliament adopted the Law on Amendment of Some Laws of Ukraine Concerning the Status of Members of the Verkhovna Rada of the Autonomous Republic of Crimea and Local Councils. This law introduced instructions for local council members and reinforced their dependence on political parties and blocs from whose election lists they gained their seats. The new law gave the political party or bloc the discretion to terminate the powers of the council members. Although the introduction of this norm was strongly criticized by the Venice Commission,[23] the upper level of Parliament persisted in moving it forward. At year's end, 12 draft laws awaited parliamentary approval—among them, the Law on Instruction for Parliamentary Deputies.[24]

Judicial Framework and Independence

1999	2001	2002	2003	2004	2005	2006	2007	2008
4.50	4.50	4.75	4.50	4.75	4.25	4.25	4.50	4.75

The 2006 Constitution of Ukraine did not change the provisions of the 1996 Constitution in regard to fundamental political, civil, and human rights—including freedom of expression, freedom of conscience and religion, freedom of association, and business and property rights. Furthermore, the major international instruments protecting human rights at global (UN) and European levels have been ratified by Ukraine.

The main shortcomings of the Ukrainian judiciary, including lack of public respect for court decisions and the judicial system as a whole, insufficient financing of the court system, and an inefficient and non-transparent process for appointing judges, remained untouched during 2007. The principle of equality before the law was not reinforced during the year. Different judges can still read and apply Ukrainian law differently, in the same courts, depending on the case. Furthermore, 2007 saw the clear insubordination of the Council of Judges.

Although in 2006 the Constitutional Court obtained a long expected quorum, 2007 proved a destructive year for the institution. Preparations for the early parliamentary elections were extremely problematic. On April 26, 2007, with his second decree on the dismissal of the Parliament of Ukraine, the president abolished his first decree regarding the dissolution of Parliament and the call for early elections, dated April 2, 2007. The second decree set June 24, 2007 as the date for early parliamentary elections. On April 27, the Constitutional Court of Ukraine registered 160 members of Parliament in compliance with the decree of the Constitution of Ukraine. This started a long process wherein key political players discredited Constitutional Court judges in order to block the Court from making a decision on holding parliamentary elections. The partial acknowledgment of corruption charges against some judges further discredited the Court by raising wide-sweeping suspicion of corruption in Court decisions.

Blocking the Constitutional Court's decision over the parliamentary elections paved the way for early parliamentary elections on September 30 but did not resolve the dispute over the compliance with constitutional norms and the right of the president to introduce such actions. The final decision to hold elections on September 30 was made through an agreement between the president, prime minister, and Speaker of the Parliament on May 27, 2007. As a result, the judicial system of Ukraine was discredited and its lingering problems were brought to light before the Ukrainian public. This situation clearly showed the intent of key political players to use the judiciary as an outlet for internal political disputes and substantially and negatively impacted the public's perception of judicial power.

On May 16, 2007, the President of Ukraine lost the right to appoint or dismiss heads and deputy heads of courts as the result of a decision of the Constitutional Court. With this decision, the Court also directed the Parliament to adopt corresponding legislation to implement the decision. This led to a struggle between the Parliament and Council of Judges over distinguishing the body to appoint judges to administrative positions. Parliament, instead of elaborating and adopting the law according to the Constitutional Court's decision, adopted a decree on May 30 establishing a temporary procedure allowing the High Council of Justice of Ukraine to appoint judges to administrative positions. The following day, the Council of Judges of Ukraine issued a decision giving the right to make such appointments to the Council of Judges. From May 31 through June 1 (just one day), the Council of Judges of Ukraine appointed more than 100 judges to the positions of heads and deputy heads of courts of general jurisdiction. On June 1, Parliament abolished the decision of the Council of Judges with a decree giving the right of appointment back to the High Council of Justice of Ukraine. This decree was reinforced with the Parliament decree dated June 27, 2007. However, the issue of the appointment of judges clearly demonstrated the intention of political players to influence the judiciary through administrative instruments. As a result of Parliament's absence since midyear, the conflict over the appointment of judges to administrative positions remained unresolved at the end of 2007.

The Constitutional Court was not the only institution involved in a fight with the president, the Cabinet of Ministers, and the Parliament. The dismissal of the prosecutor general, Svyatoslav Piskun, with the presidential decree of May 24, 2007, led to a fight before the Office of the Prosecutor General and clearly underlined the immaturity of political forces and key state players. The conflicts between the Constitutional Court and Office of the Prosecutor General led to an imbalance in the overall judicial framework and raised broad public discussion over the need to reform the judicial system of Ukraine. Unfortunately, preoccupied with the election campaign and the subsequent process of creating a coalition, key political players did not transform talks into real initiatives. Therefore, not only was the opportunity for judicial reform lost in 2007, but the status of the judiciary at all levels entered a state of uncertainty.

Corruption

1999	2001	2002	2003	2004	2005	2006	2007	2008
6.00	6.00	6.00	5.75	5.75	5.75	5.75	5.75	5.75

As was the case in 2006, the year 2007 did not feature a significant campaign to fight corruption in Ukraine. The months-long process of preparation for the early parliamentary elections and subsequent creation of the coalition put anticorruption measures on the political back burner. Consequently, corruption rates stayed at the same level as in the previous year.

Corruption remains an intractable feature of Ukrainian society. In a mid-year survey conducted by the Sociological Service of Razumkov Centre, 23 percent of Ukrainian citizens noted everyday corruption as among the most pressing issues facing society, while 47 percent pointed to corruption at higher political levels. Everyday corruption rated eighth in the list of Ukraine's socioeconomic problems, with corruption among higher politicians rated second on this list.[25]

According to the 2007 national survey on corruption, the vast majority of Ukrainians (77 percent) believe that corruption levels have remained the same or have increased since 2004.[26] Government corruption (90.5 percent) takes fourth place among the most critical problem areas facing Ukrainians. The high cost of living (94.6 percent), crime (92.9 percent), and the high cost and low quality of health care (91.6 percent) are other critical areas.

The year 2007, however, did see some legislative initiatives in the fight against corruption. On August 15, the Cabinet of Ministers of Ukraine adopted the Measures Plan on the Implementation of the Concept on a Way to Integrity (the Measures Plan), by decree, until 2010.[27] The Measures Plan established a number of concrete measures to reach the aims of the concept, defined the state bodies responsible for its realization, and outlined the implementation timetable for each of the measures. Furthermore, the central executive bodies of Ukraine are obliged to provide a report on the implementation of their corresponding parts of the Measures Plan to the Ministry of the Interior by January 20 of each forthcoming year.

Parliament adopted the Law on Ratification of the UN Convention Against Corruption, the Law on Ratification of the Council of Europe Criminal Law Convention on Corruption, and the Law on Ratification of Additional Protocol to the Council of Europe Criminal Law Convention on Corruption, submitted by the president in 2006. Parliament also adopted at its first reading the Law on

Responsibility of Legal Entities for Corrupt Offenses, which envisages assigning responsibility for prosecuting cases of bribery to both central and local authorities; the Law on Principles of Prevention and Countering Corruption; and the Law on Amendment of Some Legislative Acts of Ukraine Concerning Responsibility for Corrupt Offenses. Corresponding draft laws were submitted by the president in 2006, but Parliament used alternative drafts from the representative of the ruling coalition, MP Mykola Dgyga.

In April 2007, Parliament rejected the draft Law on State Committee of Ukraine on Countering Corruption,[28] prepared by the representatives of different factions. At the same time, the Group of States Against Corruption (GRECO), which Ukraine joined in January 2006, made its first evaluation report on Ukraine. GRECO recommended establishing "a body, distinct from the law enforcement functions, with the responsibility of overseeing the implementation of the national anticorruption strategies."[29] It also stated that the level of corruption in Ukraine threatens the principles of democracy in the country.

Initiatives concerning the division of state power and business were notably absent during 2007. Job placement procedures in central and local government bodies still lack transparency and public accountability. For job seekers, professional qualifications were not prioritized over personal or party loyalty. While no examples of authorities limiting media investigations into corruption and bribery arose in 2007, at the same time, nontransparent decision making at local and higher political levels remained a significant problem and made investigations difficult. Furthermore, no changes were made to grant civil councils, which hold sessions and consultations with authorities from state bodies, much control over policy development and implementation.

What have become known as "corporate raids" remained a growing problem for Ukraine businesses. Together with corporate raiders in the conventional sense, raid groups in Ukraine obtain the property rights of an enterprise by manipulation of the law and the courts, or through the assistance of a state body or law enforcement structure. The existing political and business environment in the state facilitates to a "corporate raids" business culture. Raids became possible, especially, due to an inefficient and corrupt judicial system, high corruption levels, the shortcomings of the legal system (such as lack of protect ion for business assets), and the weakness of state authorities. According to the Ukrainian Union of Industrialists and Entrepreneurs (the Party of Industrialists and Entrepreneurs is one of many parts of the Union), at the beginning of 2007, around 50 "corporate raid" groups were active in Ukraine. Their activity led to nearly 3,000 seized enterprises. These attacks severely impact both domestic and foreign investments in the economy. The problem is understood by politicians of all main political parties and representatives of authority. At the same time, preventing such practices will prove quite difficult, while the fight for political and economic power and access to the country's resources continues.

Although 2007 witnessed some legislative initiatives to fight corruption, this intractable feature remains dominant in Ukrainian society. It has become increasingly clear that anticorruption measures should go beyond legal or administrative means to include a comprehensive approach and should run parallel with serious efforts to raise economic and social standards for the Ukrainian people.

▌ AUTHORS: OLEKSANDR SUSHKO AND OLENA PRYSTAYKO

Oleksandr Sushko is research director of the Institute for Euro-Atlantic Cooperation (Kyiv). Olena Prystayko is an associate professor at the National Academy of Public Administration under the President of Ukraine.

1   2007 Eastern Europe Consensus Forecasts, Consensus Economics, http://www.consensus economics.com.

2   Interfax-Ukraine, Ombudsperson's Appeal on Securing Constitutional Rights of the Citizens at 30th of September Parliamentary Elections, 2007, http://www.interfax.com.ua/ua/press-releases/70154/28.09.

3   Yevhen Zakharov's report on the Civic Assembly, July 24, 2007, http://gromada.lviv.ua/articles/2007/07/24/355.html.

4   "Functioning of Democratic Institutions in Ukraine," Parliamentary Assembly of the Council of Europe Resolution 1549 (2007), http://assembly.coe.int/main.asp?Link=/documents/adoptedtext/ta07/eres1549.htm.

5   Andriy Marusov, "Games with Public Procurement," *Dzerkalo Tyzhnya* 6:685, February 16–22, 2008, http://www.mw.ua/1000/1550/62085.

6   World Bank, "Procurement System in Ukraine Is Likely to Be Weakened by a New Law," March 13, 2006, http://web.worldbank.org/WBSITE/EXTERNAL/COUNTRIES/ECAE XT/UKRAINEEXTN/0,,contentMDK:20850138~menuPK:50003484~pagePK:2865066 ~piPK:2865079~theSitePK:328533,00.html.

7   PACE elections observation, "Ukraine's Elections Are Open and Competitive, but Amendments to the Law Are of Some Concern," Parliamentary Assembly of the Council of Europe (PACE), October 1, 2007, http://assembly.coe.int.

8   The International Election Observation Mission to the September 30, 2007 pre-term parliamentary elections in Ukraine was a joint undertaking of the OSCE/Office for Democratic Institutions and Human Rights, the OSCE Parliamentary Assembly, the Parliamentary Assembly of the Council of Europe, the European Parliament, and the NATO Parliamentary Assembly.

9   International Election Observation Mission, Ukraine—Pre-term Parliamentary Elections, September 30, 2007, Statement of Preliminary Findings and Conclusions, http://www1.osce.org/documents/odihr/2007/10/26823_en.pdf.

10   "The CVU Evaluated Voting Process at Early Parliamentary Elections," Committee of Voters of Ukraine, September 30, 2007, http://www.cvu.org.ua/doc.php?lang=eng&mid=docs&id =1492.

11 Ombudsperson's Appeal on Securing Constitutional Rights of the Citizens at 30th of September Parliamentary Elections, Interfax-Ukraine, 2007, http://www.interfax.com.ua/ua/press-releases/70154/ 28.09.

12 Central Electoral Commission of Ukraine Web site, http://www.cvk.gov.ua/vnd2007/w6p001.html.

13 Yevhen Zakharov's report on the Civic Assembly, July 24, 2007, http://gromada.lviv.ua/articles/2007/07/24/355.html.

14 Counterpart Creative Center, Standing and Dynamics of Ukrainian NGOs in 2002–2006, http://www.ccc.kiev.ua/data/ZVIT_ua.pdf.

15 Ibid.

16 Razumkov Centre for Economic and Political Studies, *National Security & Defense* 6 (2007): 25.

17 Ibid.

18 Worldwide Press Freedom Index, Reporters Without Borders, accessed online, http://www.rsf.org/article.php3?id_article=24025.

19 "Ukrainian Journalists Announced Fighting Against Made to Order Publications," Ukrainian National Information Agency, June 11, 2007, http://www.unian.net/ukr/news/news-220422.html.

20 Agreement on Creation of the Anticrisis Coalition, July 7, 2006, , http://zakon1.rada.gov.ua/cgi-bin/laws/main.cgi?nreg=n0005001-06.

21 A draft Law on the Introduction of Changes to the Constitution of Ukraine (on Improvement of the System of Local Government) Registration Number in the Former Parliament: 3207-1. Registration number in the Parliament of the V convocation – 0900, http://zakon1.rada.gov.ua/signal/f0397a0g.doc.

22 For more details, see Yulia Mostovaya and Serhii Rakhmanin, "How Do We Build Up Ukraine, or What Should Be Done with the Administrative-Territorial Reform?," *Dzerkalo Tyzhnya* 31:660, August 24–31, 2007.

23 See, for example, Opinion on the Amendments to the Constitution of Ukraine, adopted on August 12, 2004, Opinion no. 339/2005, Venice Commission, Strasbourg, June 13, 2005.

24 "Agreement on the Creation of the Coalition of Democratic Forces," October 17, 2007, http://razom.org.ua/docs/ugoda20071019.doc.

25 The poll of 10,956 respondents from all regions of Ukraine was made by the Sociological Service of Razumkov Centre on May 31–June 18, 2007.

26 *Corruption in Ukraine, 2007,* Baseline National Survey for the MCC Threshold Country Program, May 10, 2007.

27 Measures Plan on Implementation of the President's Concept on a Way to Integrity for the Period Till 2010, Decree of the Cabinet of Ministers of Ukraine #657:15, August 2007.

28 On Declining the Draft Law on State Committee of Ukraine on Countering Corruption, Decree of the Verkhovna Rada of Ukraine #907:V, April 6, 2007.

29 *Joint First and Second Evaluation Rounds: Evaluation Report on Ukraine,* GRECO, Strasbourg, March 19–23, 2007, p. 47.

30 Evgenij Kritskij, "Raids for Raiders?," *Dzerkalo Tyzhnya* 32:661, September 1–8, 2007.

Uzbekistan

by Bruce Pannier

Capital: Tashkent
Population: 26.0 million
GNI/capita: US$2,190

The social data above was taken from the European Bank for Reconstruction and Development's *Transition Report 2007: People in Transition*, and the economic data from the World Bank's *World Development Indicators 2008*.

Nations in Transit Ratings and Averaged Scores

	1999	2001	2002	2003	2004	2005	2006	2007	2008
Electoral Process	6.50	6.75	6.75	6.75	6.75	6.75	6.75	6.75	7.00
Civil Society	6.50	6.50	6.75	6.50	6.50	6.50	7.00	7.00	7.00
Independent Media	6.50	6.75	6.75	6.75	6.75	6.75	7.00	7.00	7.00
Governance*	6.25	6.00	6.00	6.25	6.25	n/a	n/a	n/a	n/a
National Democratic Governance	n/a	n/a	n/a	n/a	n/a	6.50	7.00	7.00	7.00
Local Democratic Governance	n/a	n/a	n/a	n/a	n/a	6.25	6.75	6.75	6.75
Judicial Framework and Independence	6.50	6.50	6.50	6.50	6.50	6.25	6.75	6.75	6.75
Corruption	6.00	6.00	6.00	6.00	6.00	6.00	6.50	6.50	6.50
Democracy Score	6.38	6.42	6.46	6.46	6.46	6.43	6.82	6.82	6.86

With the 2005 edition, Freedom House introduced separate analysis and ratings for national democratic governance and local democratic governance to provide readers with more detailed and nuanced analysis of these two important subjects.

NOTE: The ratings reflect the consensus of Freedom House, its academic advisers, and the author(s) of this report. The opinions expressed in this report are those of the author(s). The ratings are based on a scale of 1 to 7, with 1 representing the highest level of democratic progress and 7 the lowest. The Democracy Score is an average of ratings for the categories tracked in a given year.

EXECUTIVE SUMMARY

Uzbekistan gained its independence in 1991, and since that time, a government led by President Islam Karimov has maintained strict control over the country. The judicial system has rendered verdicts in step with the government's internal policies, and state media have touted government success while remaining silent on shortages of basic foods and civil unrest. At times, the government has eased control over independent media and political organizations in the country, only to rein in these groups when their criticism increased. The repression became much worse, despite vigorous criticism and heightened attention from international rights organizations and Western nations following the 2005 violence in Andijan, during which Uzbek government troops opened fire on an assembled crowd. This event marked a watershed for the Uzbek government's policies, and since then the Uzbek government has worked with renewed energy to stamp out any perceived opposition or threat to stability. Political and social groups, foreign-based nongovernmental organizations (NGOs), rights defenders, foreign media, and religious communities have all faced legal actions; organizations were closed, and activists were jailed by order. Uzbek authorities also tightened control over local groups, especially the political opposition, rights activists, journalists, and members of various religious communities.

Repressive conditions continued in 2007: Harassment of independent journalists, rights defenders, and members of religious groups (particularly non-mainstream Islamic and non–Russian Orthodox communities) as well as further closures of foreign-based NGOs occurred throughout the year in Uzbekistan. The government denied involvement in the October killing of 26-year-old Alisher Saipov, an independent journalist critical of President Karimov's regime, despite assertions from opposition groups to the contrary. Also in October, the European Union (EU) lifted the visa ban established after the events in Andijan, "with a view to encouraging the Uzbek authorities to take positive steps to improve the human rights situation,"[1] just prior to the release of a 90-page report on the continued use of torture in Uzbekistan.[2]

With political and economic support from Russia and China, and once the government had purged Western organizations from Uzbek territory, the regime's hold on society remained seemingly unchallenged in 2007. Thus, it did not come as a surprise when Uzbek authorities ignored constitutional restrictions and allowed President Karimov to win an unconstitutional third term in the presidential elections held in December.

National Democratic Governance. President Islam Karimov has exerted unchallenged control over Uzbekistan since the country gained its independence in 1991. Members of the five registered political parties, all of them loyal to the president, compose the two-chamber Parliament. Uzbekistan has a strongly centralized government, with nearly all decisions made in the capital. During 2007, no efforts were made to reform the political system or to allow citizens greater participation. *The executive branch of Uzbekistan's government continues to dominate all aspects of society and proved again in 2007 its absolute intolerance of criticism and dissent. Thus, the national democratic governance rating remains at 7.00.*

Electoral Process. In December 2007, Uzbekistan held a presidential election that saw incumbent Islam Karimov win an unconstitutional third term in office without any official attempt to explain the legal basis for this violation. President Karimov's term officially expired on January 22, 2007, yet he remained in office based on a constitutional amendment. State media remained silent regarding the elections until mid-September, when officials announced that elections would take place on December 23, 2007. Six state-approved candidates were forwarded, including the first female and independent candidates, but only four were registered by the November 16 deadline. The Central Election Commission ignored several rights activists and members of the unregistered opposition who announced their intention to enter the presidential race. *While Uzbek authorities, particularly electoral officials, made token gestures of recognizing the mechanics of a democratic election (candidate access to voters and media), all opposition representatives were, in effect, barred and a genuine competition did not take place. Uzbekistan's rating for electoral process for 2007 worsens from 6.75 to 7.00.*

Civil Society. Voicing criticism or publicly disagreeing with government policies remained difficult if not impossible for civil society organizations in Uzbekistan. However, a protest against rising prices of basic goods reported in Uzbekistan's section of the Ferghana Valley did result in government intervention to lower prices. This was an exception resulting from declining social conditions in one area. Other attempts at smaller political protests were quickly broken up. Members of the Birlik movement tried unsuccessfully to register a civic initiative group to forward a presidential candidate. *In 2007,the Uzbek government again harassed and detained rights activists and members of religious communities and ordered the closures of more foreign-based NGOs. As a result, Uzbekistan's rating for civil society remains at 7.00.*

Independent Media. Uzbekistan has never proven fertile ground for independent media. Independent journalists who remained in Uzbekistan faced the usual difficulties in 2007, but reports of their harassment declined, reflecting the authorities' success at silencing critical voices inside the country. The murder of Alisher Saipov, a journalist critical of the regime and its policies, raised the suspicions of many who saw the Uzbek government as the only party interested in the correspondent's death, though it happened in neighboring Kyrgyzstan. The Uzbek government blocked the appearance of these and other news stories on several Internet Websites. *Continued harassment of independent journalists, blocked opposition Web sites, and the government's suspected involvement in the killing of an independent journalist in* *neighboring Kyrgyzstan have assured that Uzbekistan's rating for independent media remains at 7.00.*

Local Democratic Governance. Uzbekistan has a strongly centralized government, and provincial, regional, district, city, and town officials are chosen for their ability to carry out Tashkent's orders. There is no opportunity for citizens to elect their local officials. The right to petition official decisions is provided by law, but few citizens believe they can receive justice in such disputes. *In 2007, nothing was done to address key problems of local democratic governance. Accordingly, Uzbekistan's rating for local democratic governance remains at 6.75.*

Judicial Framework and Independence. The judiciary continued to serve as an arm of the executive branch of government in 2007. Uzbek courts jailed independent journalists, rights activists, and members of minority religious groups and ordered the closures of foreign-based NGOs. Acts of clemency coincided with key foreign policy events for the Uzbek government and thus appeared as token gestures to curry favor. No effort was made at reforming the judicial system or giving it more independence. *The Uzbek court system continued its practice of placing formal legal pronouncements on the decisions of the executive branch by ordering the closures of foreign-based NGOs and fining and incarcerating rights activists, independent journalists, and members of religious communities. With no deviation from this well-established proclivity, Uzbekistan's rating for judicial framework and independence remains at 6.75.*

Corruption. The problem of corruption was not seriously addressed in 2007, though three former provincial governors were dismissed and charged with abuse of office. In other reported cases, however, officials engaged in illegal activities with relative impunity. An international organization tracking corruption worldwide ranked Uzbekistan as one of the most corrupt countries on the planet. *Former and current officials stood trial for abuse of office, though in some cases the punishment seemed lenient for the crime. Uzbekistan's rating for corruption remains at 6.50.*

Outlook for 2008. Concerns have been growing over the future of Uzbekistan after President Karimov, who turns 70 in 2008. Yet little evidence suggests the Uzbek regime will ease its control over society during the coming year, especially after the election of President Karimov to an unconstitutional third term in office. Karimov appears convinced that support from Moscow and Beijing will shield his government from any actions that might come from Western countries. Furthermore, the EU decision to lift sanctions against Uzbekistan, as well as renewed contacts with high-level U.S. officials, will probably be interpreted by Tashkent as proof that Uzbek authorities need only outlast criticism and sanctions for Western nations to eventually seek warm ties again. Thus, there is little hope that Western governments could exert any effective pressure on Karimov's regime to implement democratic reforms or show a greater respect for human rights.

MAIN REPORT

National Democratic Governance

1999	2001	2002	2003	2004	2005	2006	2007	2008
n/a	n/a	n/a	n/a	n/a	6.50	7.00	7.00	7.00

In his speech to the nation on August 31, 2007, the eve of Independence Day, Uzbekistan's president, Islam Karimov, remarked: "The key strategic tasks of this stage are to further promote democracy and to liberalize all aspects of political and economic life, to advance the state and public life, to strengthen the independent judicial system, to protect human rights and liberties, to encourage political and economic activeness, and to build the fundamentals of civic society."[3] Such a strategy would mark a drastic change in the way the Uzbek government has ruled the country. President Karimov has dominated Uzbekistan's politics since the country gained independence. The executive branch exerts control over not only the legislative and judiciary, but nearly every aspect of running the country. Though the Constitution provides guarantees for all basic rights, the law of the land is in fact whatever President Karimov wishes.

The economy is centrally planned, perhaps in part because of the president's background as a Soviet-era trained economist, with quotas established for key sectors—particularly agriculture, where many farmers must sell a percentage of their harvests to the government at low state rates. Furthermore, there are no checks on the Uzbek government, making it difficult to know how decisions are made, how much revenue the country takes in, or how that money is spent.

In 2007, Uzbek government agencies cited economic statistics claiming the country's gross domestic product growth was more than 9.5 percent in the second and third quarters of the year, compared with the same period in 2006.[4] These statistics could not be verified independently. The government also claimed an increase in foreign investment; according to state media, in March foreign investment grew 20 percent compared with the same period in 2006. In July, Uzbekistan's Ministry of Economics and the State Statistics Committee announced that Uzbekistan had attracted US$416 million in foreign investment (a figure that owes much to the Uzbek government's friendship with Russia and China) in the first half of the year—more than twice the amount during the same period in 2006.[5]

Since the violence in Andijan in May 2005, in which the Uzbek government sent in troops who opened fire on an assembled crowd, Uzbek authorities have attempted to build relations with China and Russia while working with renewed energy to stamp out any perceived opposition or threat to stability. Many foreign-funded organizations, including media and humanitarian aid groups, were forced to close. Uzbek authorities also tightened control over local groups, especially the political opposition, rights activists, journalists, and members of various religious communities. Political and social groups, foreign-based nongovernmental organizations (NGOs), rights defenders, foreign media, and religious communities have all faced legal actions, forcing organizations to close and jailing activists by order.

Western nations and international rights organizations vigorously criticized Uzbek authorities for the heavy-handed action in Andijan. In response, in July 2005, the Uzbek government demanded that U.S. forces using a military base in southern Uzbekistan for operations in Afghanistan leave Uzbek territory. Four months later, in November, the European Union (EU) imposed sanctions on Uzbekistan, including an embargo on arms exports to the country and an EU-wide ban forbidding member countries from issuing visas to "those individuals directly responsible for the indiscriminate and disproportionate use of force in Andijan."[6]

In 2007, while Uzbekistan's relations with both Russia and China were strong and cushioning Karimov's regime against Western criticism, Karimov showed some signs of improving relations with the West. Yet despite meeting with EU representatives and U.S. government officials—including Central Command chief General William Fallon—the Uzbek government remained cautious in its dealings. In May, when the EU voted to extend the sanctions, the Uzbek Foreign Ministry responded with a statement calling the EU decision "unfounded and biased" and an "instrument of systematic pressure on Uzbekistan dressed up in human rights rhetoric."[7]However, in October, without the Uzbek government making much effort to demonstrate progress in respect to human rights, the EU lifted the sanctions "with a view to encouraging the Uzbek authorities to take positive steps to improve the human rights situation."[8]

Government stability centers on President Karimov, who has constructed a formidable security force and on occasion pursued enemies of the state into neighboring countries. Usually, civil disobedience is quickly and publicly punished with coverage on state media to set an example of the penalty for opposing the government. Yet in 2007, despite the efforts of security forces, protests against rising prices of basic goods in Uzbekistan's section of the Ferghana Valley did result in government intervention to lower prices. In a telling sign of the security problems, President Karimov himself visited the area in late June. Reports indicated that security measures for Karimov's visit to the provinces included cutting off phones in the region and blocking mobile phone calls, as well as shutting down streets in Namangan.

Banned Islamic groups continue to oppose President Karimov and his government. Several, including Hizb ut-Tahrir and the Islamic Movement of Uzbekistan (IMU), call for the overthrow of the Karimov government and the establishment of an Islamic state. Hizb ut-Tahrir seeks this through nonviolent means, while the IMU has already used violence. Neither is currently in a position to topple the regime, but terrorist attacks in February 1999 and March–April 2004 and small IMU-armed incursions into Uzbekistan in 1999 and 2000 demonstrate that these and other groups do pose at least a security threat in Uzbekistan.

Reported arrests of members of banned Islamic groups decreased in Uzbekistan in 2007, but the number of those arrested in neighboring Kazakhstan, Kyrgyzstan, and Tajikistan increased during the year. In most cases, those arrested had links to Uzbekistan. In September, the German government announced that three men detained on suspicion of planning terrorist attacks in Germany were linked to the Islamic Jihad Union, a group that in March–April 2004 claimed responsibility for terrorist attacks in Bukhara and Tashkent and, according to German investigators, maintains contacts in Uzbekistan.

History has shown that in the wake of terrorist attacks, the Uzbek government's response was quick and severe and, according to statements from international rights organizations, excessive. The government has sponsored at least two documentary films on militants and terrorists; the most recent portrayed the Uzbek government's view of the Andijan violence.[9] Some groups and analysts have warned that the government's heavy hand in dealing with such groups encourages disillusioned youth to join such movements. The government has cast an increasingly wide net over society as these acts of violence occurred, with each incident eliciting an increasingly severe response. Islamic communities have been under surveillance for years, and in September, during Ramadan, authorities limited prayer hours and specified when children could attend mosque. The authorities put a new focus on Christian groups in 2007, with the exception of the Russian Orthodox community.

In late August, the International Crisis Group released a report titled *Uzbekistan: Stagnation and Uncertainty*, which included this assessment: "Two years after the Andijan massacre, the country remains a serious risk to itself and the region." The report also notes: "The political scene is full of uncertainty. The apparent public apathy reflects not support for the regime but rather pervasive fear and a sense of hopelessness."[10] Additionally, the magazine *Foreign Policy* and the Fund for Peace published their third annual Failed States Index Score in June 2007. The survey rates 177 countries "in order of their vulnerability to violent internal conflict and societal deterioration." Uzbekistan ranked 22nd, making it the most vulnerable country in Central Asia.[11]

Electoral Process

1999	2001	2002	2003	2004	2005	2006	2007	2008
6.50	6.75	6.75	6.75	6.75	6.75	6.75	6.75	7.00

Five registered political parties exist in Uzbekistan, all of which are pro-presidential. With the exception of the Erk (Freedom) Democratic Party, which was registered for a brief period after the 1991 independence, opposition political groups have never been allowed to enter elections. Furthermore, Parliament has adopted a law introduced by President Karimov that purportedly strengthens the role of political parties but seems only to give them a louder voice for agreeing with the president.

Having served as first secretary since 1989, Islam Karimov became president of the newly independent Uzbekistan in 1991. In 1995, a referendum extended his first term in office. In 2000, presidential elections were held, and Karimov's sole opponent, Abdulhafiz Jalolov, emerged from the voting booth and announced that he himself had voted for the incumbent. Karimov was therefore elected to his second, and constitutionally last, term in office. A national referendum in 2002, however, changed the Constitution and again extended the president's term in office an extra two years.

Karimov's presidency was due to expire on January 22, 2007, the seventh anniversary of his inauguration—a date ignored by Uzbekistan's state media. Yet even in early 2007, signs suggested that improvements to presidential election procedures were not likely.

Opposition groups and rights activists posted open letters and appeals for international help in pressuring the Uzbek government to speak about the planned 2007 elections. According to the Constitution, elections must be announced 90 days before the opening of the polls. However, a report leaked on September 18 revealed that the Central Election Commission (CEC) had named December 23 as the election date, based on a constitutional amendment from the 2002 referendum.

When campaigning officially started on September 21, there were no declared candidates. According to CEC chairman Mirza-Ulughbek Abdusalomov, campaigning begins with the process of preparing documents and collecting the signatures of 5 percent of eligible voters—814,870 individuals.[12] Furthermore, according to the CEC, the candidate's registration process would finish only in mid-November.

None of the country's five registered, pro-presidential political parties held congresses to nominate candidates until November, though by early October the parties' elites had already named their candidates. The party with the largest parliamentary faction—the Liberal Democrat Party—nominated President Karimov as its candidate, despite the fact that Karimov was constitutionally bound to step down after two terms in office. Two other parties—the People's Democratic Party of Uzbekistan and Adolat Social-Democratic Party—nominated their own candidates, unlike in previous elections when all five parties backed Karimov. Candidates from Fidokorlar and Milli Tiklanish were later denied registration because they failed to collect the requisite number of eligible voters' signatures.

True opposition groups such as the Birlik Popular Movement, Erk Democratic Party, or Ozod Dehkonlar Partiyasi (Free Peasants Party) had their registration denied. One civic initiative group backed by the government managed to nominate a candidate, Akmal Saidov, but other such groups without government backing were rejected. Others who declared their intention to run, like Suhbat Abdullayev,[13] Akbar Aliyev,[14] and rights activists Abdullo Tojiboy Ogli, Akhtam Shoymardonov, and Jahonghir Shosalimov, were simply ignored and excluded.

Karimov easily won the election. None of his opponents received even half a million votes.[15] Western election monitors have never deemed any of Uzbekistan's previous elections free or fair. In 2007, the Organization for Security and Cooperation in Europe (OSCE) sent a "limited election observation mission" that did not "conduct any systematic and comprehensive observation of election-day proceedings" because of "the apparent limited nature of the electoral competition."[16]

Observers from the Commonwealth of Independent States, however, and those from the Shanghai Cooperation Organization (a monitoring team of three people) said the election was well organized, free, fair, and transparent.

Civil Society

1999	2001	2002	2003	2004	2005	2006	2007	2008
6.50	6.50	6.75	6.50	6.50	6.50	7.00	7.00	7.00

Uzbekistan's Constitution provides for freedom of assembly and freedom to form social organizations. It also provides for freedom of religion. According to Uzbekistan's Religious Affairs Committee, a total of 2,222 religious organizations are registered in Uzbekistan (2,042 Islamic, 164 Christian, 8 Jewish, 6 Baha'i communities, 1 Krishna community, and 1 Buddhist temple).[17] In 2007, although there was a drop in the number of people reportedly arrested for being members of banned religious organizations, Uzbek authorities did not demonstrate improved respect for the rights of religious groups, including small Christian communities.

The Norway-based group, Forum 18, chronicled the case of Protestant pastor Dmitri Shestakov, convicted in March of inciting inter-religious hatred, leading an illegal religious organization, and possessing illegal extremist recordings. He received a four-year sentence of internal exile and was subsequently imprisoned in his home in Andijan province. By late March, Forum 18 reported that Shestakov was prevented from kneeling while praying and that his copy of the New Testament was taken away from him and he was offered a Koran to read instead. Two months later, Forum 18 reported Shestakov's transfer to a labor camp in central Navoi. The camp was reportedly "much harsher" than the prison in Andijan, and Shestakov remained much farther from family and friends in eastern Uzbekistan.[18]

Forum 18 reported in September that the Uzbek National Security Service (NSS) had stepped up surveillance of religious communities in recent years. The human rights organization said surveillance included "hidden microphones in places of worship, the presence of NSS agents during worship, and the recruitment of spies within communities."[19] The Muslim community also came under special scrutiny, and reports indicated that during the fasting month of Ramadan, authorities banned children from attending night prayers and placed adults on a ten P.M. curfew.

Transitions Online published an article by Felix Corey of Forum 18 in late September in which Corley wrote that Uzbek state television aired a two-part program (November 30–December 1, 2006) on Christian groups called "Hypocrites."[20] The program reportedly accused some Christian groups of luring people in with the promise of money, and "soon the targeted people become complete zombies." In October, the Russian news agency Interfax reported that the Tashkent Office of the Prosecutor accused the local Evangelical community, registered in Uzbekistan since 1992, of using psychotropic drugs. Other Christian groups, including Jehovah's Witnesses and members of the Pentecostal, Grace Presbyterian, and Baptist churches, faced legal problems, and some members were jailed for illegal religious activities.

Overall, the number of reported arrests of members of banned Islamic groups in Uzbekistan declined in 2007. There were, however, several reported arrests of Hizb ut-Tahrir members and "Wahhabis,"a term the Uzbek government uses to denote anti-government Muslims rather than the Islamic sect from Saudi Arabia. The decreased number of arrests in Uzbekistan has accompanied an increase in the number of members from such groups detained in neighboring Kazakhstan, Kyrgyzstan, and Tajikistan.

Also in 2007, the Uzbek government continued its crackdown against foreign-based NGOs through the assistance of the legal system. In February, the Justice Ministry stated that "dozens" of foreign-based NGOs failed to submit reports on their activities and financial sources, as required by Uzbek law. Quite often the Justice Ministry included other charges to discredit foreign-based organizations. In late February, the Justice Ministry claimed that not only did the U.S.-based NGO Population Services International[21] fail to submit required legal paperwork, but the group also supported the "interests of homosexuals" in Uzbekistan. The ministry said, "PSI is especially famous for its projects universally asserting interests of persons with unorthodox sexual orientation," adding that homosexuality is punishable by up to three years in prison in Uzbekistan.[22]

The Uzbek state Website (press-uz.info) reported in January that the U.S.-based NGO Counterpart International, closed down in Uzbekistan in 2006, was providing radioactive rice to areas in Kyrgyzstan's Jalal-Abad province. That charge was rejected shortly afterward by the Kyrgyz NGO Center for Supporting Civil Society, which took the opportunity to thank Counterpart International for its help.

In mid-April, Human Rights Watch said the Uzbek government had halted the rights organization's activities in Uzbekistan. On April 13, the Uzbek Justice Ministry notified the director of the Human Rights Watch office in Tashkent that her work accreditation had been denied, as she had "exceeded her authority" and "worked outside the office charter."[23] The accreditation was reportedly taken away two weeks before the EU met to consider extending sanctions against Uzbekistan.

A few rights defenders continue their activities and reports from Uzbekistan, among them the Initiative Group of Independent Human Rights Defenders of Uzbekistan, the Rights Defenders Alliance of Uzbekistan, and Ezgulik (Goodness).

Throughout 2007, the case of rights activist Gulbahor Turayeva was closely followed within and outside of Uzbekistan. Turayeva was detained on the Uzbek-Kyrgyz border in January when a search of her belongings revealed books that prosecutors claimed called for the overthrow of Uzbekistan's constitutional government. In late April, Turayeva was found guilty of encroachment on the constitutional regime, slander, and proliferation of materials posing a threat to society. She received a six-year jail sentence. On May 10, Human Rights Watch released a statement announcing Turayeva had received an additional prison sentence during a second trial on May 2–7. However, the sentence against Turayeva was overturned in June after she reportedly criticized several independent journalists in court who had fled the country after the May 2005 violence in Andijan. Rights defenders, including some Turayeva mentioned, attributed the alleged statement to the authorities' pressure on her while she was detained.

Yelena Urlayeva and her colleague Abdulla Tojiboy-Ogli, of the Rights Defenders Alliance of Uzbekistan, were placed under house arrest in early February. Urlayeva was arrested, along with two others, on February 12 for trying to stage a protest against Turkmenistan's presidential election outside Turkmenistan's embassy. On November 6, the independent uznews.net reported that Urlayeva had been denied permission to fly to Ireland for an international rights activist conference.

On February 21, police broke up an attempted demonstration outside the Senate building in Tashkent. Rights activists planned to protest the detention of independent journalists and rights defenders Umida Niyazova and Mutabar Tojibayeva. That same day, Akrom Khoja Mukhitdinov and activists from the Human Rights Alliance of Uzbekistan held a protest outside the Foreign Ministry building, calling for the resignation of the foreign minister, Vladimir Norov. Mukhitdinov received a sentence of 10 days' administrative detention for organizing the demonstration.

At the end of 2007, poet and rights activist Yusuf Jumayev protested in Bukhara, demanding the resignation of President Karimov and calling for his son's release from jail. His son, Mashrab, had been arrested at the end of November for involvement in a fight. On December 10, Yusuf Jumayev staged a "picket on wheels" around Bukhara with banners calling for Mashrab's release. Later that day, police arrived at Jumayev's home, reportedly killing the family dogs before arresting Jumayev. On the day of his arrest, the Website press-uz.info posted an article claiming Mashrab had stabbed a man in the back because Mashrab was having an affair with the man's girlfriend. The article asked Yusuf Jumayev how "he could raise a son who would stab people in the back?" The article also said that "the Jumayevs apparently think that 'if we defend the people's rights, then we can do anything we want.'"[24]

At the beginning of November, the organization Human Rights Watch released a 90-page report about the continued use of torture in Uzbekistan. By the end of that month, Uzbek rights activists reported two separate incidents in which men convicted for religious activity—Fitrat Salohiddinov and Tohir Nurmuhammedov —were tortured to death while in prison. In an April 19 statement, Holly Cartner, Europe and Central Asia director of Human Rights Watch, urged the EU (preparing to review sanctions against Uzbekistan in May) to make respect for human rights an integral part of a new EU strategy toward Uzbekistan. Cartner mentioned the plight of many of Uzbekistan's rights defenders now jailed or kept under house arrest and surveillance, saying, "These prisoners of conscience are paying the price of the EU's feeble human rights policy."[25]

Independent Media

1999	2001	2002	2003	2004	2005	2006	2007	2008
6.50	6.75	6.75	6.75	6.75	6.75	7.00	7.00	7.00

Uzbekistan's Constitution states, "The mass media shall be free and act in accordance with the law. It shall bear responsibility for trustworthiness of information in the prescribed manner. Censorship is impermissible." Yet Reporters Without Borders ranked Uzbekistan near the bottom of its list, 160th out of 169 countries, in its annual Worldwide Press Freedom Index in October—a move that perhaps more accurately reflects the state of media freedom in Uzbekistan.

At the beginning of 2007, a 32-year-old woman with a small child was investigated for attempting to overthrow the constitutional government. Umida Niyazova traveled to Kyrgyzstan in May 2005 to speak with people in Andijan. Upon her return to Uzbekistan in late December 2006, Niyazova was detained, while authorities confiscated her research and her computer. She was released but taken into custody again at the end of January 2007 under charges of illegal border crossing, smuggling subversive literature, and distributing materials that threaten national security. International rights organizations issued dozens of statements and appeals leading up to and following Niyazova's trial. OSCE Representative on Freedom of the Media Miklós Haraszti also publicly called for her release. Nonetheless, on May 1 she was convicted and sentenced to seven years' imprisonment. A Tashkent appellate court suspended Niyazova's sentence one week later, just prior to an EU meeting to consider maintaining the November 2005 sanctions.

In August, Reporters Without Borders issued a statement concerning the declining health of independent journalist Jamshid Karimov (President Karimov's nephew). In 2006, Jamshid was arrested and placed in a psychiatric hospital. The August 2007 statement revealed that Jamshid had smuggled a note to friends describing his failing health and asserting that he had been given psychotropic drugs. That same month, Reporters Without Borders issued a press release on the eve of Uzbekistan's independence celebrations to condemn "the severity of governmental repression of independent news media and human rights activists, especially when they try to point out the lack of democracy and freedoms, combat discrimination or expose corruption or torture."[26] Reporters Without Borders cited the cases of Said Abdurakhimov of uznews.net and Aleksei Volosevitch of ferghana.ru, who were detained and interrogated by the military on July 23 "for unclear reasons." The release from the Paris-based organization also claimed that "Deutsche Welle correspondent Nataliya Bushuyeva would almost certainly have been imprisoned if she had not fled the country after being accused of working without a license and tax fraud in March." Bushuyeva and three other Deutsche Welle journalists[27] were accused of failure to pay taxes and working without accreditation.

The absolutely dire situation of independent media in Uzbekistan was demonstrated on October 24, when Alisher Saipov, a 26-year-old Voice of America journalist and father of a three-month-old daughter, was gunned down as he left work in Osh, Kyrgyzstan. Saipov reported critically on the crackdowns on dissent and the use of torture in Uzbekistan. Two days before his murder, Saipov reportedly told friends he thought Uzbek security agents were following him. Friends, colleagues, and opposition figures such as Erk Democratic Party leader Muhammed Solih directly accused Uzbek authorities of the killing. Websites such as centrasia.ru, ferghana.ru, and others carried a number of articles asserting similar accusations against the authorities.

The Uzbek government denied any involvement in Saipov's murder, but two days after the tragedy occurred, state-controlled Web providers reportedly blocked Websites carrying articles on the slain journalist. The Website ferghana.ru reported that several Russian-language Internet publications became inaccessible in Uzbekistan after they published articles speculating on the possible reasons for Saipov's murder. Uzbek authorities had also blocked Russian Websites earlier in the year, including the Russian-language religious news Website portal-credo.ru, newsru.com, rian.ru (RIA Novosti), lenta.ru, gazeta.ru, and trud.ru.[28]

According to amendments to Uzbekistan's media legislation that came into effect in January 2007, Websites fall under the category of media outlets—meaning they come under legislation requiring all local and foreign media to register with the authorities and must provide the names of their founder, chief editor, and staff members. Furthermore, Websites must provide authorities with copies of each publication.

Print media also came under attack. In late July, authorities ordered the closure of the independent weekly *Odam Orasida* (*Among the People*). The Islam-oriented weekly reported on issues such as infant mortality, homosexuality, and prostitution from a Muslim point of view. *Odam Orasida* began publishing in February, but by July, at the time of its closure, its circulation had reportedly reached 24,000 in Tashkent. Editor Khairullo Khamidov told the Associated Press that authorities claimed they had breached media legislation, but did not elaborate on these breaches.

Local Democratic Governance

1999	2001	2002	2003	2004	2005	2006	2007	2008
n/a	n/a	n/a	n/a	n/a	6.25	6.75	6.75	6.75

Citizens of Uzbekistan do not choose their provincial, regional, district, or city officials. Instead, local authorities are chosen according to their perceived ability to remain loyal to the regime while carrying out tasks from Tashkent. As a result, local officials must balance the wants and needs of constituents with the possible personal repercussions for making special requests from the central government. Furthermore, while citizens have the right to petition for change or register complaints, most citizens assume they will face punishment for their suggestions or complaints.

Officials receive sets of tasks or goals to be met for their area. Once officials achieve these, they have completed their duty. This system leads to reporting false figures when target figures cannot be met and, in cases of surplus, the opportunity for officials to enrich themselves.

This system of local governance lacks personal initiative, as demonstrated during the Andijan violence of May 2005. Officials in Andijan initially allowed the demonstration, as orders did not come from Tashkent to prohibit it. When the violence broke out, the same Andijan officials proved too slow in reacting, and some were taken hostage during the disorder.

Family and clan play a significant role in local governance. Families tend to be large in rural areas, which constitute most of the country. A local official is likely to have dozens of blood relatives and relations by marriage living within a 50-kilometer radius. Such relatives usually profit from this situation, and it is not uncommon that local leading businesspeople are somehow related to local officials. In a number of areas, particularly in western Uzbekistan, communications with Tashkent are poor, which, when combined with nepotism, creates a favorable environment for corruption.

Rights defenders have complained about corrupt local officials in open letters posted on opposition Websites, but officials rarely look into such stories. For example, the governor of Jizzakh province served as the source of complaints posted on opposition Websites for several years, yet his dismissal and detention came only in 2007.

Saidullo Begaliyev, governor of Andijan province in May 2005, went on trial in January 2007 for abuse of office. Some held him partially responsible for the Andijan incident, suggesting he upset the arrangements his predecessor had with local businessmen when he took office in 2004. The businessmen whose trial sparked the original Andijan protest allegedly had agreements with Begaliyev's predecessor, but not with Begaliyev.[29] That predecessor, Kobiljon Obilov, also went on trial in 2007. The Web site uznews.net reported on his conviction for helping to organize the Andijan unrest. He received a one-year suspended sentence in a closed trial in late January.

A new law passed in 2007 gives political parties more influence in the selection of regional and local officials as well as in the naming of a prime minister. The new law refers to elections of provincial governors chosen by the president and approved by the five parties, but does not provide citizens with the ability to elect their local officials.[30]

Judicial Framework and Independence

1999	2001	2002	2003	2004	2005	2006	2007	2008
6.50	6.50	6.50	6.50	6.50	6.25	6.75	6.75	6.75

Despite the separation of branches of government enshrined in Uzbekistan's Constitution, the judiciary does not function independently but is an extension of the executive branch in Uzbekistan. Prosecutors and courts give formal, legal backing to the government's internal policies. The government selects judges, but the criteria these judges must meet to receive their positions remain unclear.

One judge, Zokir Isayev, who presided over the trials of alleged organizers of the Andijan violence, fled to Kazakhstan at the end of October, asking for political asylum. Should Judge Isayev ever decide to speak to the media, he may provide details regarding the inner workings of Uzbekistan's court system. He has already accused unnamed government officials of using the president's name to "destroy anyone who is in their way."[31]

Trends in Uzbekistan's judiciary are clearly visible. Defendants must overcome a number of obstacles to meet with lawyers. Those facing charges of supporting banned religious groups or conspiring to overthrow the government are assumed and treated as guilty prior to their trial. Owing to closures of foreign-based NGOs, a decreasing number of observers are able to attend the trials of independent journalists, rights activists, and members of religious groups—when those trials are open to the public.

Local and international rights groups have chronicled the cases of numerous defendants who claimed their confessions were made under torture. Uzbek courts regularly ignore these claims, but the UN's special rapporteurs on torture have consistently confirmed these statements of coerced confessions. Uzbek rights activist Elena Urlayeva sent an open letter in March to the UN Committee Against Torture, asserting that the systematic beating of prisoners continues in police detention centers.

During 2007, Uzbek courts convicted independent journalist Umida Niyazova, rights activist Gulbahor Turayeva, Isroil Kholdarov of the opposition Erk Democratic Party, Birlik member Mukhamadali Karabayev, and Pentecostal pastor Dmitri Shestakov and sentenced them to several years in jail. In March, Rustam Muminov, extradited from Russia amid great controversy in 2006, was found guilty of being a Hizb ut-Tahrir member and sentenced to five years and six months in jail. Courts gave lesser sentences to Jehovah's Witnesses Irfon Hamidov and Dilafruz Arziyeva (both received two years in a labor camp), members of God's Love Pentecostal Church Hudoer Pardaev and Igor Kim (10 days detention in a holding cell), and Akrom Khoja Mukhitdinov from the Human Rights Alliance of Uzbekistan (10 days detention in a holding cell). However, in October, the Tashkent Economic Court annulled the 1999 purchase of a former cinema used as a house of worship by the Grace Presbyterian Church.

Corruption

1999	2001	2002	2003	2004	2005	2006	2007	2008
6.00	6.00	6.00	6.00	6.00	6.00	6.50	6.50	6.50

The levels of corruption in Uzbekistan remain difficult to gauge owing to the secrecy of the government—for example, beyond a few individuals, no one knows the key governmental officials. The information available suggests that a great deal of state corruption persists. Many lower-level representatives, such as police officers and border guards, are likely to take, or demand, bribes as opportunities present themselves.

Occasionally, local officials are dismissed and taken to court on embezzlement charges. In January, the independent Website uzmetronom.com reported that Interior Ministry spokesman Alisher Sharipov and Aziz Ernazarov, head of the Interior Ministry's newspaper (*On Duty*) and magazine (*Defense*), faced charges of abuse of office. Both had served for several years as the voice of Uzbekistan's Interior Ministry, explaining arrests and imprisonments and denying accusations of beatings or other mistreatment of prisoners. In 2007, Uzbek courts convicted other former officials, including Andijan governor Kobiljon Obidov, who was given a one-year suspended sentence for abuse of office. The punishment for fallen officials, however, appears light compared with what is given the rest of society under similar circumstances. Reports have also surfaced about the construction of a new special prison for incarcerated bureaucrats in Tashkent's Yunus-Abad district.

Transparency International's Corruption Perceptions Index (CPI) for 2007 revealed Uzbekistan as the most corrupt country in Central Asia and ranked 175th out of 180 countries globally. According to the CPI the state of perceived corruption in Uzbekistan had worsened from its score of 2.1 in 2006 to a score of 1.7 in 2007—a significant drop on the 0–10 scale (where 10 is the best possible score, indicting perceived as least corrupt).

In October, Surat Irkamov, chairman of the Initiative Group of Independent Human Rights Defenders of Uzbekistan, posted an open letter on the Website centrasia.ru claiming that the local administrative head, prosecutor's office, and district judges of Tashkent's Yunus-Abad district were using the law to seize people's apartments.[32] Later in October, another article was posted on centrasia.ru reporting that Jizzakh governor Ubaidulla Yamonkulov was brought handcuffed to Tashkent by helicopter, facing charges of embezzlement of millions of dollars during his six years in office. Reports also indicated that Yamonkulov terrorized his constituents for several years.[33]

▮ AUTHOR: BRUCE PANNIER

Bruce Pannier has been covering events in Central Asia for Radio Free Europe/Radio Liberty since 1997. Since 1990, he has been a frequent visitor to the region.

1   "Council Conclusions on Uzbekistan (16/10/2007)," 2824th External Relations Council meeting, Luxembourg, October 15–16, 2007, http://www.delukr.ec.europa.eu/page44676. html.

2   Human Rights Watch, *Nowhere to Turn; Torture and Ill-Treatment in Uzbekistan,* November 6, 2007.

3   "Karimov Hopes to See Strong Civil Society," Interfax, August 31, 2007, http:// 64.233.183.104/search?q=cache:0BJDFbx3ON0J:goliath.ecnext.com/coms2/summary_ 0199-6908975_ITM+%22The+key+strategic+tasks+of+this+stage%22&hl=en&ct=clnk&c d=1.

4   Prime Minister Sharif Mirziyayev on July 18 said gross domestic product (GDP) growth in the first half of 2007 was 9.7 percent, compared with 2006. On October 18, the government reported GDP growth for January–September was 9.8 percent, compared with the same period in 2006.

5   "Foreign Investment in Uzbekistan Up 2.2 Times," Interfax news agency, July 26, 2007.

6   "Press Release: 2678th Council Meeting, General Affairs and External Relations, External Relations Council Conclusions (Provisional), Luxembourg," Summary: EU External Relations Council Conclusions, Luxembourg: October 3, 2005, http://www.europa-eu-un.org/articles/en/article_5086_en.htm.

7   "Uzbekistan Rebuffs EU Sanctions," Agence France-Presse, May 17, 2007, as appeared in *Turkish Daily News,* http://www.turkishdailynews.com.tr/article.php?enewsid=73353.

8   "Council Conclusions on Uzbekistan (16/10/2007)," 2824th External Relations Council meeting, Luxembourg, October 15–16, 2007, http://www.delukr.ec.europa.eu/page44676. html.

9   The other was a 1999 film about the February 1999 bombings in Tashkent that showed victims and their relatives and interviews with the alleged perpetrators.

10   "Uzbekistan: Stagnation and Uncertainty", International Crisis Group, Asia Briefing No. 67, August 22, 2007, http://www.crisisgroup.org/home/index.cfm?id=5027.

11   Tajikistan was at position 39, Kyrgyzstan at position 41, Turkmenistan at position 43, and Kazakhstan at position 103.

12   Abdusalomov also noted there were 16,297,400 registered voters in Uzbekistan.

13   Suhbat Abdullayev, a medical doctor from the western Kworezm province, told Radio Free Europe/Radio Liberty's Uzbek Service in a September interview that officials "summoned me to the regional national-security committee and told me so openly [that I should run]." Gulnoza Saidazimova, "Uzbekistan: Field of Presidential Hopefuls Wider, Not Deeper," Radio Free Europe/Radio Liberty, September 29, 2007, http://rferl.com/featuresarticle/ 2007/09/a05355ba-bbb7-44ad-8ef3-240ca340967c.html.

14   Akbar Aliyev described himself in a September interview with Radio Free Europe/Radio Liberty's Uzbek Service as a "scientist, poet, sociologist, philosopher, historian, and specialist in literature" and said he had been unemployed since 1997. Aliyev said the authorities had no role in his decision to seek the presidency. Gulnoza Saidazimova, "Uzbekistan: Field of Presidential Hopefuls Wider, Not Deeper," Radio Free Europe/Radio Liberty, September 29, 2007, http://rferl.com/featuresarticle/2007/09/a05355ba-bbb7-44ad-8ef3-240ca340967c. html.

15   According to the final tally given by Uzbekistan's Central Election Commission on December 28, Karimov took 88.1 percent of the vote—Asliddin Rustamov of the People's Democratic Party of Uzbekistan received 3.17 percent, Diloram Tashmukhamedova of Adolat Social-Democratic Party 2.94 percent, and Akmal Saidov, who was nominated by a civic group, 2.85 percent.

16 OSCE/Office for Democratic Institutions and Human Rights—Elections, "Election Observation Mission: Presidential Election in Uzbekistan," December 12, 2007, http://www.osce.org/odihr-elections/item_12_28715.html.

17 "Underground Sect Members Fined," Interfax news agency report, July 16, 2007.

18 Felix Corley, "Uzbekistan, Imprisoned Pastor Transferred to Harsher Camp," Forum 18 News, June 12, 2007.

19 ———, "Uzbekistan: Spies and Videotape," Forum 18 News, September 5, 2007.

20 ———, "Christians: The Soul Snatchers," *Transitions Online,* September 27, 2007.

21 Population Services International Web page says the organization "harnesses the vitality of the private sector to address the health problems of low-income and vulnerable populations in more than 60 developing countries, including offering programs in malaria, reproductive health, child survival and HIV." Available at http://www.psi.org.

22 "NGO Shutdowns and Uzbek Rapprochement with West," registan.net, February 28, 2007, http://www.registan.net/index.php/2007/02/28/ngo-shutdowns-uzbek-rapprochement-with-the-west.

23 "Crackdown on Human Rights Before EU Meeting," Human Rights Watch, Human Rights News, April 16, 2007, http://www.hrw.org/english/docs/2007/04/16/uzbeki15703.htm.

24 Rafik Komolov, "Pravozashitnik nauchil syna bit' nojom v spinu" [The Rights Defender Taught His Son How to Knife Someone In The Back], press-uz.info, December 12, 2007.

25 "EU: Put Rights at Heart of Central Asia Strategy," Human Rights Watch, Human Rights News, April 19, 2007, http://hrw.org/english/docs/2007/04/18/uzbeki15731.htm.

26 "National Holiday Reminder About Severe Repression of Media," press release, Reporters Without Borders, August 31, 2007.

27 The other three were Yuri Chernogayev, Saiera Ruzykulova, and Obid Shabanov.

28 "Internet." *Kommersant Vlast* 22, No. 11 (June 2007): 56.

29 "Andijan Massacre Linked to Local Power Struggle Source," eurasianet.org, September 29, 2005, http://www.eurasianet.org/departments/insight/articles/eav092905.shtml.

30 Article 6 of the new Law on Political Parties states, "The candidatures for the post of khokim of a province and the city of Tashkent are introduced by the President of the Republic of Uzbekistan for approval by the regional and Tashkent municipal Kengash [council] of people's deputies after holding consultations with each of the party groups represented in the relevant Kengashs of people's deputies."

31 "Former Judge Flees Uzbekistan, Seeks Political Asylum," Radio Free Europe/Radio Liberty Uzbek Service report, October 26, 2007. http://www.rferl.org/features/features_Article.aspx?m=10&y=2007&id=942BE4AF-DD34-4FC0-A2F8-172C6FDD3964.

32 Open Letter of Surat Ikramov, "In Tashkent There Is An Organized Criminal Group of Employees of the City Administration, Prosecutor's Office and Judges Working to Appropriate the Homes of Citizens," October 7, 2007, http://www.centrasia.ru/newsA.php?st=1191744180.

33 "Uzbek Farmer Abuse Claims," Institute for War and Peace Reporting, September 23, 2004; press release from the Ezgulik Human Rights Society of Uzbekistan, September 10, 2004, http://www.centrasia.ru/newsA.php?st=1094798880.

About Freedom House

Freedom House is an independent private organization supporting the expansion of freedom throughout the world.

Freedom is possible only in democratic political systems in which governments are accountable to their own people, the rule of law prevails, and freedoms of expression, association and belief are guaranteed. Working directly with courageous men and women around the world to support nonviolent civic initiatives in societies where freedom is threatened, Freedom House functions as a catalyst for change through its unique mix of analysis, advocacy and action.

- **Analysis.** Freedom House's rigorous research methodology has earned the organization a reputation as the leading source of information on the state of freedom around the globe. Since 1972, Freedom House has published *Freedom in the World*, an annual survey of political rights and civil liberties experienced in every country of the world. The survey is complemented by an annual review of press freedom, an analysis of transitions in the post-communist world, and other publications.

- **Advocacy.** Freedom House seeks to encourage American policymakers, as well as other governments and international institutions, to adopt policies that advance human rights and democracy around the world. Freedom House has been instrumental in the founding of the worldwide Community of Democracies; has actively campaigned for a reformed Human Rights Council at the United Nations; and presses the Millennium Challenge Corporation to adhere to high standards of eligibility for recipient countries.

- **Action.** Through exchanges, grants, and technical assistance, Freedom House provides training and support to human rights defenders, civil society organizations and members of the media in order to strengthen indigenous reform efforts in countries around the globe.

Founded in 1941 by Eleanor Roosevelt, Wendell Willkie and other Americans concerned with mounting threats to peace and democracy, Freedom House has long been a vigorous proponent of democratic values and a steadfast opponent of dictatorships of the far left and the far right. The organization's diverse Board of Trustees is composed of a bipartisan mix of business and labor leaders, former senior government officials, scholars and journalists who agree that the promotion of democracy and human rights abroad is vital to America's interests abroad.

1301 Connecticut Avenue, NW, Washington, D.C. 20036 USA
(+1) 202 296-5101
120 Wall Street, New York, NY 10005 USA
(+1) 212 514-8040
www.freedomhouse.org

About Freedom House Europe

Freedom House Europe is a Hungarian nonprofit organization that strengthens democracy and supports human rights in Southeast Europe, the Newly Independent States, and the greater European neighborhood. Freedom House Europe's identity is at once global and local. As an integral part of the worldwide Freedom House family, Freedom House Europe contributes its unique experience as a catalyst for democratic change in the heart of Europe.

Established in 1995 as the European hub of the organization, Freedom House Europe supports nonviolent civic initiatives in societies where political rights and civil liberties are denied or under threat. The office also helps to consolidate democratic transitions in countries where recent democratic breakthroughs have taken place. Freedom House Europe combines analysis, advocacy, and action to advance and safeguard freedom, democracy, and human rights.

■ **Analysis.** Freedom House has long been recognized as the definitive source of information on the state of freedom and democracy around the globe. Freedom House Europe is the editorial office for *Nations in Transit*, a Freedom House flagship publication providing comprehensive assessment of governance issues for 29 countries from Central Europe to Eurasia.

■ **Advocacy.** Freedom House Europe helps to focus the attention of European leaders and the general public on core issues of freedom, democracy, and human rights. By advocating for and monitoring democratic reforms, it encourages policymakers to adopt strategies that support democratic change and respect for human rights, rule of law, and civil liberties.

■ **Action.** Providing training, technical guidance, and material support to democracy and human rights advocates, Freedom House Europe assists the advance of indigenous reform efforts. Freedom House Europe builds genuine partnerships throughout the region to facilitate transfers of experience on national, regional, and international levels.

Falk Miksa u. 30. 4/2, 1055 Budapest, Hungary

(+36) 1 354-1230

www.freedomhouse.hu